D1326700
X2000000014947

OXFORD *Illustrated* SCIENCE ENCYCLOPEDIA

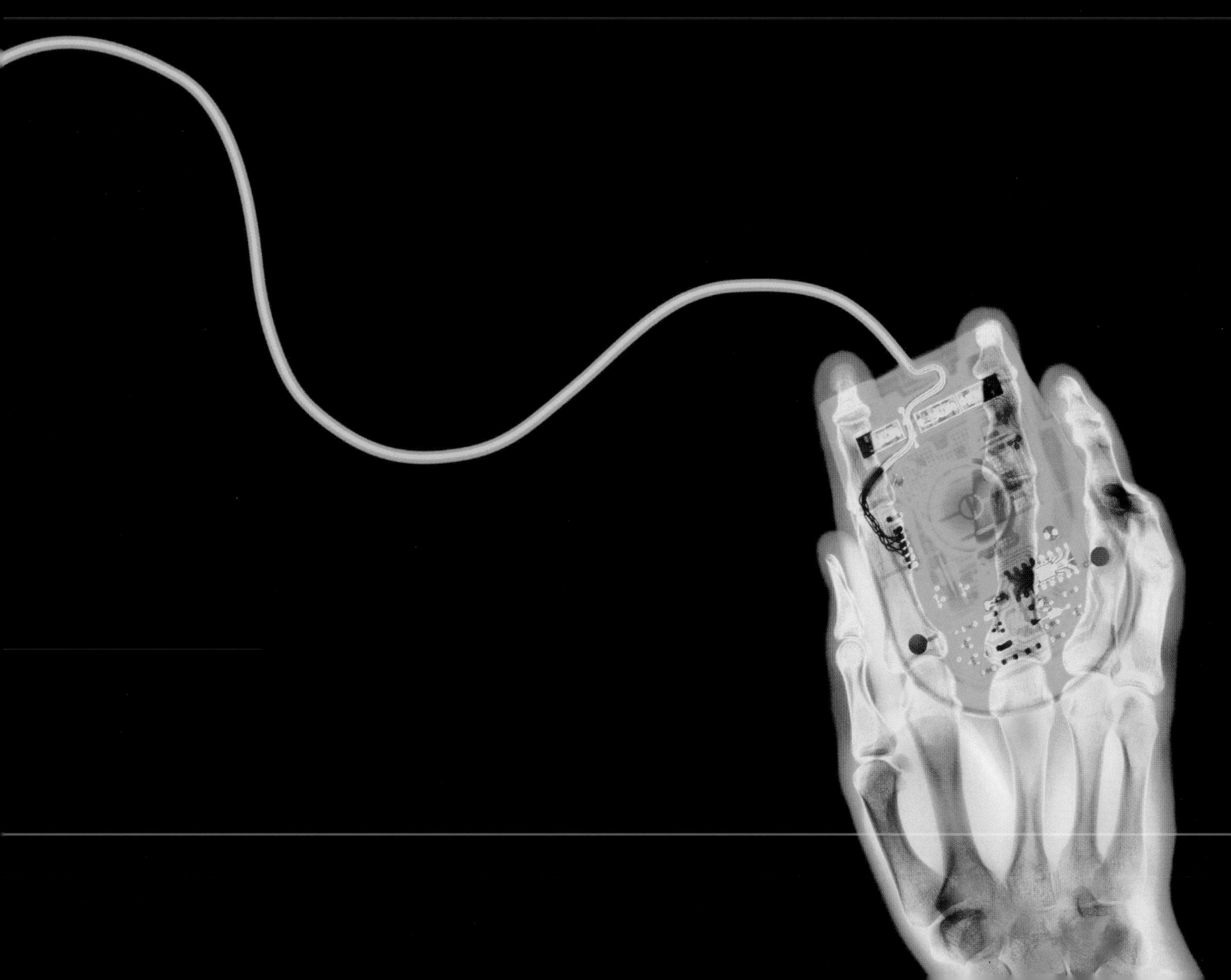

OXFORD *Illustrated* SCIENCE ENCYCLOPEDIA

Consultant editor: Professor Richard Dawkins
General editor: Robin Kerrod

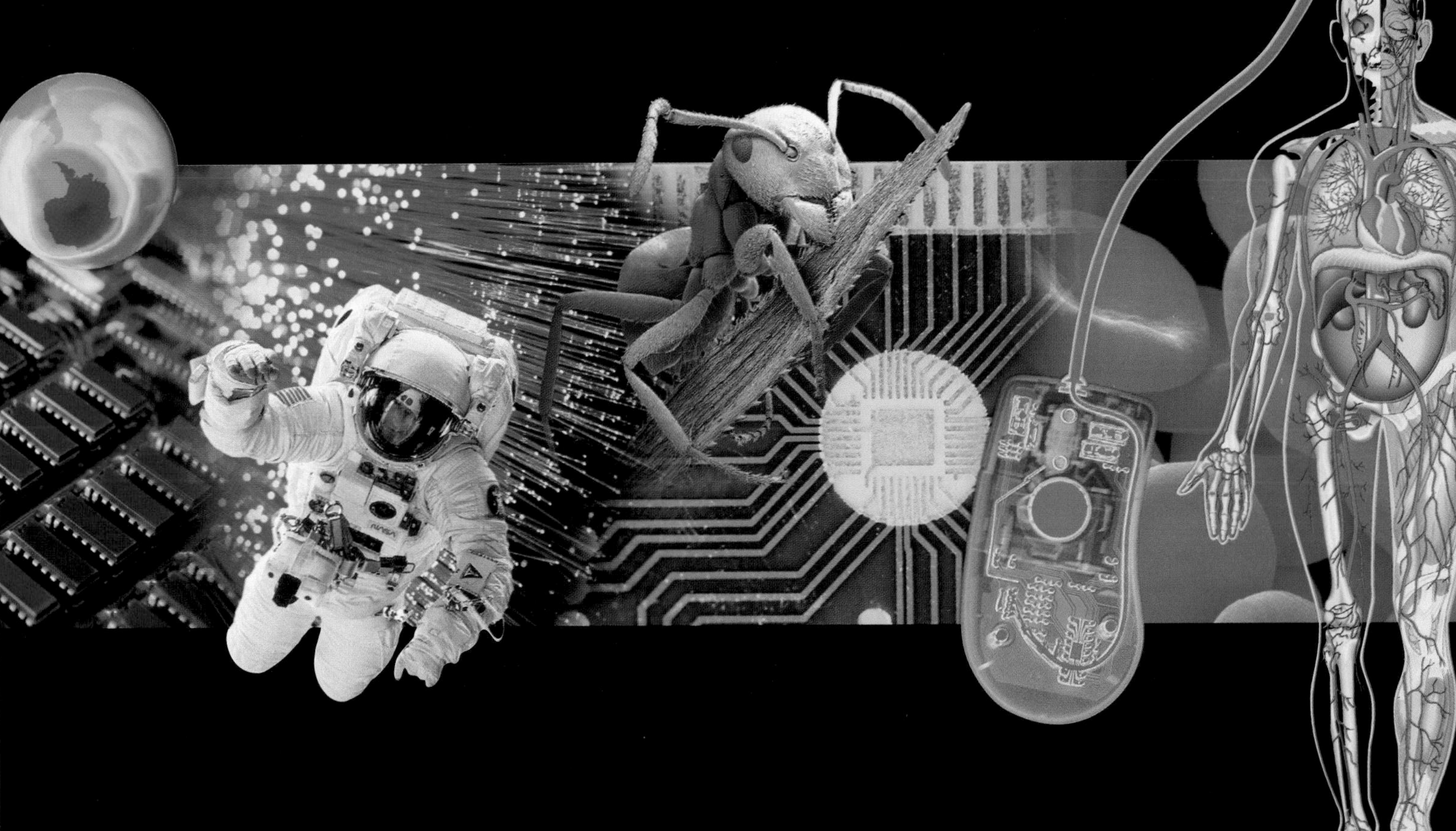

OXFORD
UNIVERSITY PRESS

OXFORD
UNIVERSITY PRESS

Great Clarendon Street, Oxford OX2 6DP

Oxford University Press is a department of the University of Oxford. It furthers the University's objective of excellence in research, scholarship, and education by publishing worldwide in

Oxford New York

Auckland Bangkok Buenos Aires Cape Town Chennai Dar es Salaam Delhi Hong Kong Istanbul Karachi Kolkata Kuala Lumpur Madrid Melbourne Mexico City Mumbai Nairobi São Paulo Shanghai Taipei Tokyo Toronto

Oxford is a registered trade mark of Oxford University Press in the UK and in certain other countries

Copyright © Oxford University Press 2001

Database right Oxford University Press (maker)

First published 2001
Reprinted (with updates) in 2003

All rights reserved. No part of this publication may be reproduced, stored in a retrieval system, or transmitted, in any form or by any means, without the prior permission in writing of Oxford University Press, or as expressly permitted by law, or under terms agreed with the appropriate reprographics rights organization. Enquiries concerning reproduction outside the scope of the above should be sent to the Rights Department, Oxford University Press, at the address above

You must not circulate this book in any other binding or cover and you must impose this same condition on any acquirer.

British Library Cataloguing in Publication Data available

ISBN 0 19 910711 4

1 3 5 7 9 10 8 6 4 2

Designed and typeset by Full Steam Ahead
Printed in Singapore

Third-party website addresses listed on the Oxford Illustrated Science Encyclopedia website are provided by Oxford University Press in good faith and for information only. Oxford University Press disclaims any responsibility for the material contained therein.

WOLVERHAMPTON PUBLIC LIBRARIES
14947
TR 3/04
£19.99 P
980187

CONTENTS

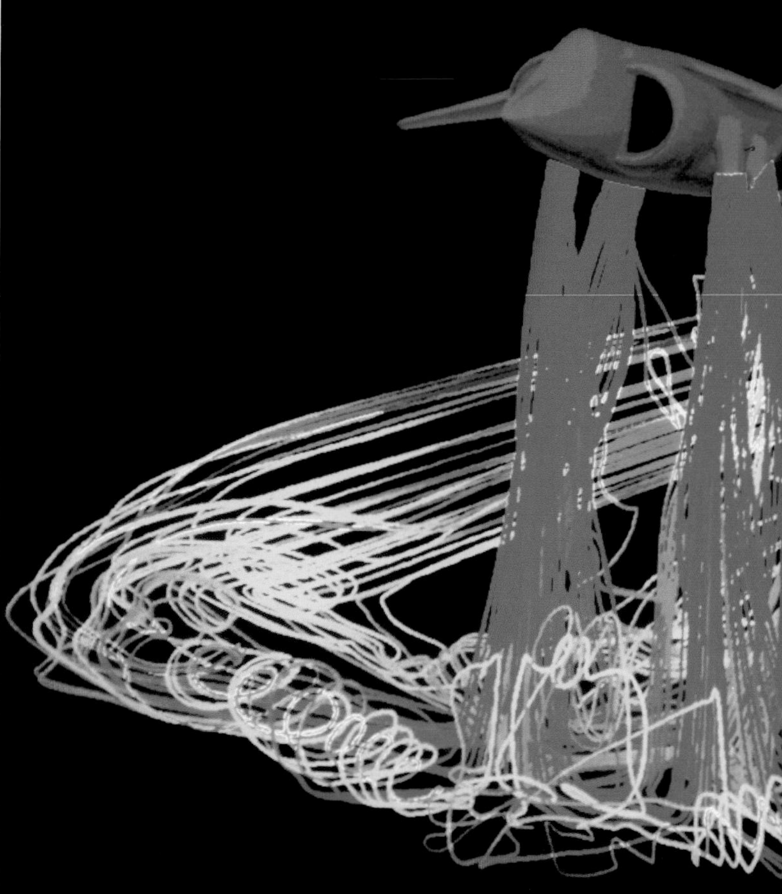

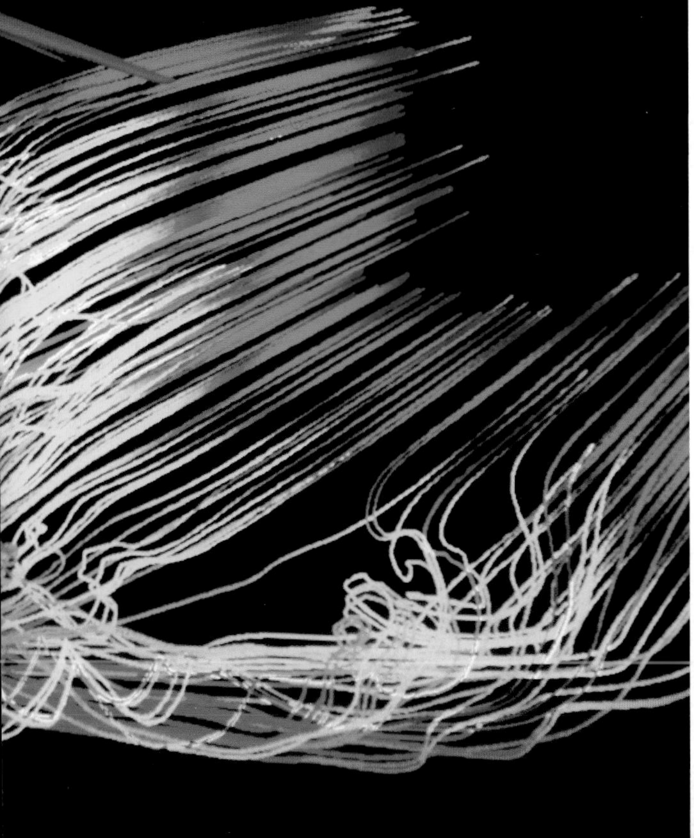

CONTRIBUTORS

Consultant editor
Professor Richard Dawkins
Charles Simonyi Professor of the Public Understanding of Science, Oxford University, UK

General editor
Robin Kerrod
Royal Astronomical Society

Authors
Jonathan Allday
Head of Science, King's School, Canterbury
Neil Ardley
David Bradley
Freelance science writer
Margaret Carruthers
Formerly Geologist and Educator, American Museum of Natural History, New York, USA
Ian Crofton
Dr David Glover
Robin Kerrod
Paul Marks
Technology Editor, New Scientist *magazine*
Dr Jacqueline Mitton
Royal Astronomical Society
Barbara Taylor
Freelance science and nature writer
Dr Brenda Walpole

General consultant
Stephen Pople
Former Head of Physics, author of Science to 14 *and co-author of the* Oxford Children's Book of Science

Consultants
Dr Peter Atkins
Professor of Chemistry, Oxford University and Fellow of Lincoln College, Oxford
Michael Chinery
John O. E. Clark
Mick Hamer
Consultant, New Scientist *magazine*
Dr Stuart Milligan
School of Biomedical Sciences, King's College London, UK
Dr Jacqueline Mitton
Royal Astronomical Society
Dr N. W. Rogers
Department of Earth Sciences, The Open University, UK
Michael Scott
Frank Tapson
Dr Irene G. Turner
Department of Materials Science and Engineering, University of Bath

Managing editor
Ben Dupré

Editor
Andrew Solway

Assistant editors
Lara Dennis
Joanna Harris
Rebecca Heddle
Susan Mushin
Michelle Nobbs
Clare Oliver
Alison Ritchie
Richard Spilsbury
Elizabeth Tatham

Indexing
Ann Barrett

Art editors
Jo Samways
Hilary Wright

Photographic research
Caroline Wood

Finding your way around

The *Oxford Illustrated Science Encyclopedia* has many useful features to help you find the information you need quickly and easily. This guide will help you to get the most out of your book.

When you want to find out about a particular topic, the first step is to see whether there is a main **article** on it. The headwords are in A–Z order, from Acids and alkalis to X-rays.

If the topic doesn't have its own article, the next step is to look at the **footers** at the bottom of the page. The footers include a great many additional topics and tell you where to go to find out about them.

You can also look the topic up in the alphabetical **index** at the back of the book. This tells you which page or pages to go to find out the information you are looking for.

Online support

The *Oxford Illustrated Science Encyclopedia* has its own website, which you can find at www.oup.com/science-encyclopedia. Here you will find hundreds of recommended websites, which give access to a mass of scientific resources online, including illustrations, animations, experiments and activities. There is also an interactive quiz, and many pictures from the book that you can download for use in your project work.

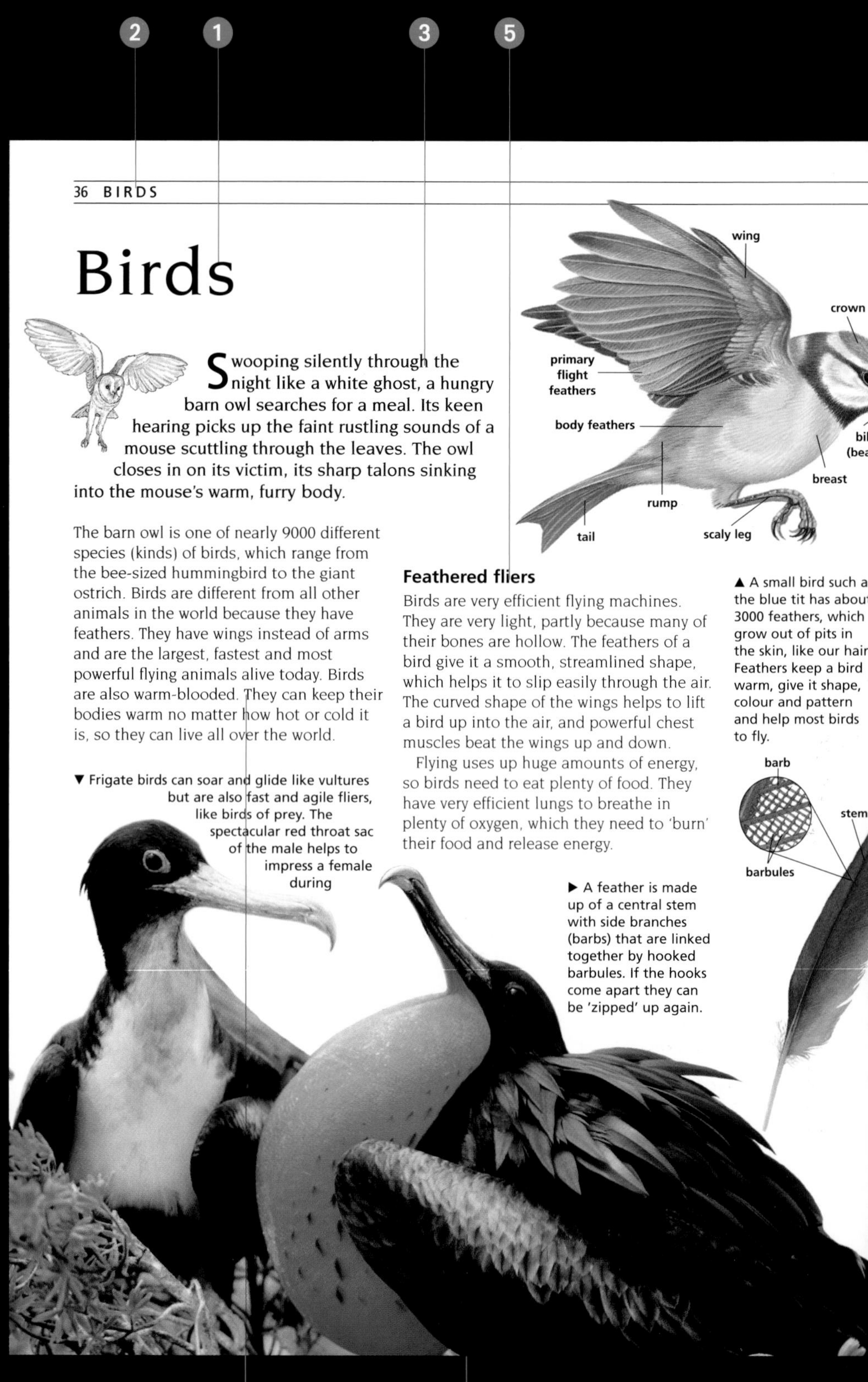

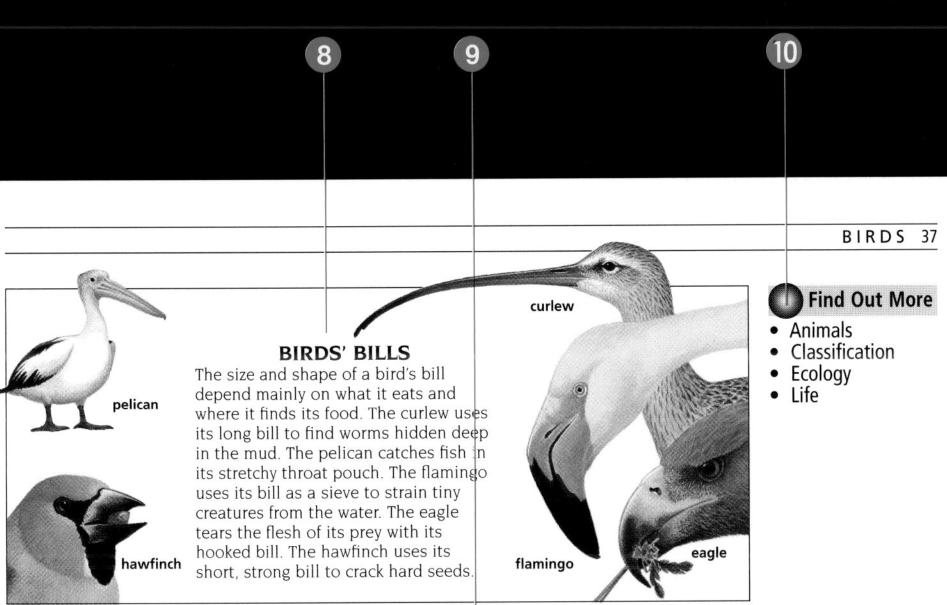

BIRDS' BILLS
The size and shape of a bird's bill depend mainly on what it eats and where it finds its food. The curlew uses its long bill to find worms hidden deep in the mud. The pelican catches fish in its stretchy throat pouch. The flamingo uses its bill as a sieve to strain tiny creatures from the water. The eagle tears the flesh of its prey with its hooked bill. The hawfinch uses its short, strong bill to crack hard seeds.

Find Out More
- Animals
- Classification
- Ecology
- Life

Bird food
Different kinds of bird eat different kinds of food. Some birds are vegetarians, eating fruit, seeds, nuts or leaves. Others eat insects and worms. Many are meat-eaters, catching fish, amphibians, birds and small mammals. The most efficient hunters are the birds of prey, like the eagle and falcon.

Did all the dinosaurs really die out 65 million years ago? Perhaps they didn't. Some scientists think that birds – including the birds in your garden – may be the direct descendants of the dinosaurs.

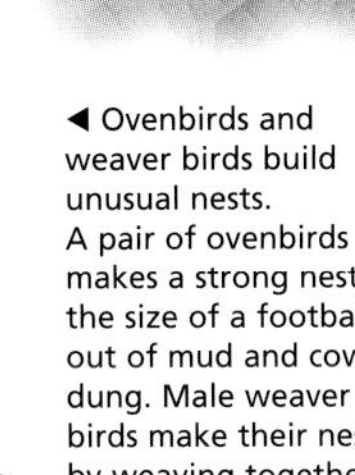
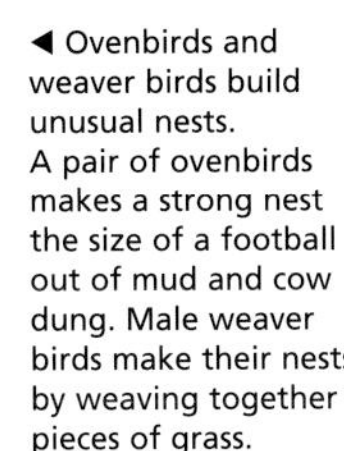

◀ Ovenbirds and weaver birds build unusual nests. A pair of ovenbirds makes a strong nest the size of a football out of mud and cow dung. Male weaver birds make their nests by weaving together pieces of grass.

▶ Penguins, such as these emperors, have stiff, strong wings, which they use like flippers to swim very fast underwater. Their wings are no use for flying. Other birds that do not fly include ostriches, emus, and kiwis.

Courtship and mating
Male birds are usually more colourful than females and sing or perform daring acrobatics to persuade females to mate with them. After mating, birds lay eggs. They would be too heavy to fly if they carried their young around inside them.

Many baby birds are naked when they hatch from the eggs. They stay safe and warm inside a nest while they grow their feathers. Other birds, such as ducks and geese, hatch out with fluffy feathers. They can run around soon after hatching and feed themselves.

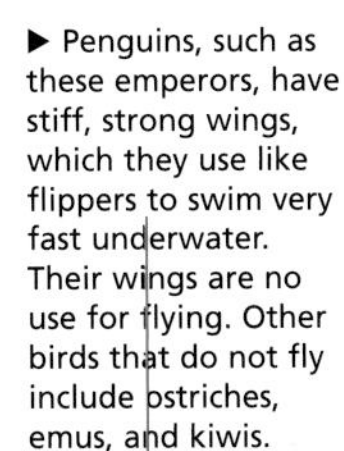

Birth *see* Human reproduction • **Black holes** *see* Galaxies • **Blood** *see* Heart and blood • **Body** *see* Humans

8 9 10 7 11

1. **Headwords** are arranged alphabetically, to make topics easy to find.
2. A **running head** on every page makes it easy to find articles that run over several pages.
3. The **opening paragraph** gives a lively and friendly introduction to the topic.
4. The **main text** gives a detailed account of the topic.
5. Clear **section headings** tell you what each part of the article is about.
6. Detailed, annotated **illustrations** – photographs, drawings, diagrams, maps and graphs – highlight important issues and explain key aspects of the topic.
7. **Captions** both describe the photographs and illustrations and give extra information.
8. **Feature boxes** cover a particular aspect of the topic in greater depth.
9. **Fact flashes** highlight amazing and extraordinary facts.
10. The **Find Out More** panel points you to other articles related to the topic.
11. The **footers** give short cuts to topics that do not have their own article but are covered elsewhere in the encyclopedia.

Acids and alkalis

If you taste something sour, like lemon juice, vinegar or milk that's gone off, your tongue is detecting the acid in these liquids. Your body can detect acids in other ways too – when you get stung by an ant or a nettle, it is the acid in their stings that makes it hurt.

▲ Like ant bites, bee stings contain formic acid. People used to treat bee stings by rubbing them with bicarbonate of soda. This is an alkali, and neutralizes the sting.

Lemon juice and vinegar are weak acids. Strong acids are much too dangerous to taste or touch. They are corrosive, which means that they can eat into skin, wood, cloth and other materials.

The chemical opposite of an acid is an alkali. Many alkalis, such as bleach and oven-cleaner, can be just as corrosive as strong acids.

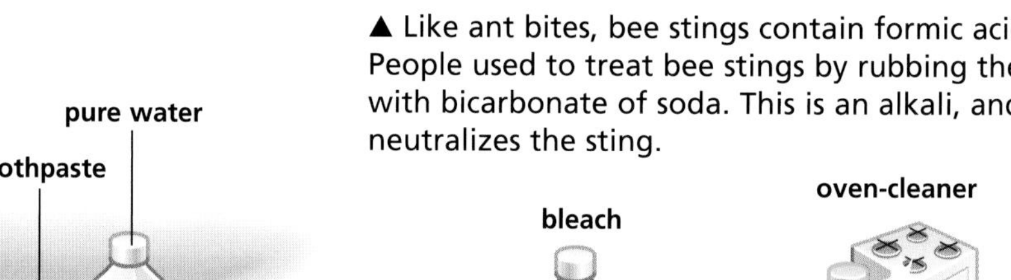

▲ Scientists use the pH scale to measure how acid or alkali something is. Neutral substances, such as pure water, have a pH of 7.

◀ Cola drinks contain phosphoric acid to give them flavour. But the acid combines with the sugar in the drink to rot your teeth.

Properties

Acids form a big group of chemicals that all behave in similar ways. Acids all contain hydrogen, and when they react with metals such as iron and zinc, they give off hydrogen gas. When acids touch a special paper, called litmus paper, they turn it red.

Alkalis are part of a group of chemicals called bases: alkalis are bases that dissolve in water. Many alkalis have a bitter taste and feel soapy. But do not try to taste or touch an alkali – you will be badly burned. Alkalis all contain hydroxide (hydrogen joined to oxygen), and turn litmus paper blue.

Scientists measure the strength of acids and alkalis on a scale of numbers called the pH scale. The scale ranges from 14 (the strongest alkalis) to 0 (the strongest acids).

Acoustics *see* Sound • **Adhesives** *see* Glues and adhesives

Mixing acids and alkalis

When an acid meets an alkali, both are changed – they are neutralized. What happens is that the hydrogen from the acid joins the hydroxide from the alkali to make water (a molecule of water has two hydrogen atoms and one oxygen atom). The parts of the acid and alkali left behind make a salt. For example, when hydrochloric acid reacts with sodium hydroxide (an alkali), the result is water and sodium chloride – common table salt.

Uses

Lots of acids occur in nature, and are found inside your body. For example, your stomach produces hydrochloric acid to help digest your food. DNA, the complicated chemical that stores your genetic code, is deoxyribonucleic acid.

Strong acids, especially sulphuric acid, are used in factories to make fertilizers, explosives, plastics, synthetic fabrics, paints, dyes, medicines, detergents, and many other chemicals.

Weak alkalis such as milk of magnesia are good for indigestion caused by too much acid in the stomach. They work by neutralizing the acid.

▶ This portrait by the Dutch artist Rembrandt is an etching. Etching is a way of printing pictures that uses acid. The artist draws lines with a steel needle on a copper plate covered in acid-resistant material. The plate then goes into a bath of acid, which bites into the copper where the artist has drawn the lines. The coating is then removed, and the plate is ready to make prints.

Strong alkalis such as sodium hydroxide (caustic soda) feel slippery to touch, because when they react with oils on your skin they form a kind of human soap – don't try this, it will burn your skin. Because sodium hydroxide solution dissolves fats, it is used to clear blocked drains and in oven cleaners.

In industry, alkalis are used in the manufacture of soap, glass, paper and textiles, and in the refining of crude oil.

Find Out More

- Chemicals
- Genetics
- Reactions
- Salts

◀ This 'volcano' works using a neutralization reaction. The vinegar (acid) and baking powder (bicarbonate of soda – an alkali) react together to form a neutral chemical (a salt), water and the gas carbon dioxide. It is the gas that makes the 'volcano' erupt.

Air

You are surrounded by gases. You can't see them, and you can't smell them. But you can feel them gently move in and out of your body as you breathe, or brush against your skin when a breeze blows.

The mixture of gases that surrounds us is called air. Air surrounds the whole Earth in a thick layer called the atmosphere. Air is mostly made up of nitrogen (78%) and oxygen (21%), but there are also smaller quantities of other gases, including carbon dioxide.

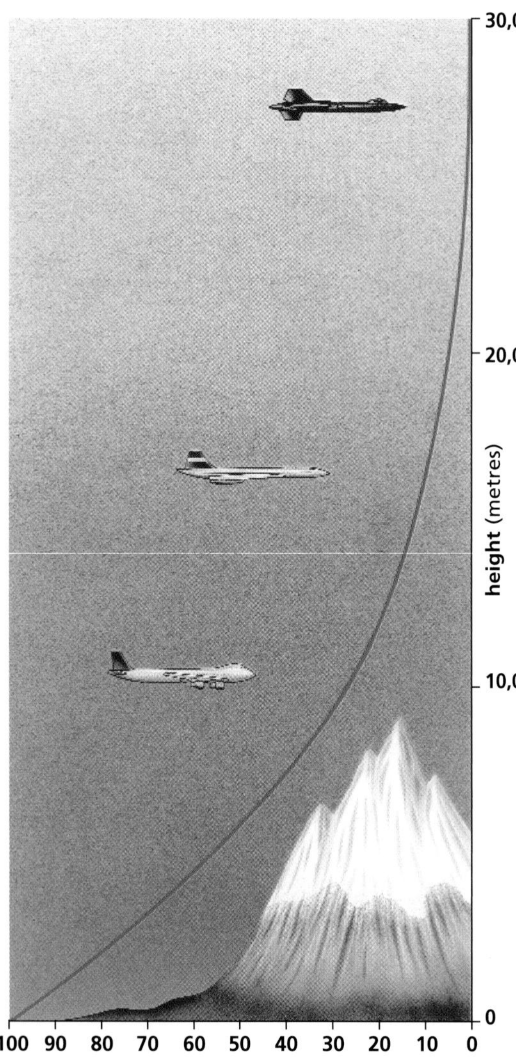

◀ At sea level, the weight of air is about 1 kg for every square centimetre (100,000 pascals). As you go higher in the atmosphere, the pressure falls rapidly.

The importance of air

For humans and other animals, the most important gas in air is oxygen. We need to breathe in oxygen to make our bodies work – without it we would die. We breathe out another gas, carbon dioxide.

Plants need carbon dioxide. They use the power of the Sun to combine carbon dioxide with water to make their own food. As they do so, they give out oxygen.

The proteins that are an essential part of our bodies are chemicals containing nitrogen. Factories can turn the nitrogen in the air into fertilizers, which help crops to grow. Unfortunately, factories and cars also release other gases into the air, which cause pollution.

▲ If the air inside a balloon is heated, it becomes less dense (thinner) than the surrounding air and rises, lifting the balloon with it.

Air pressure

The atmosphere extends upwards for many hundreds of kilometres. Although the air gets very thin high up, there is still a lot of air pressing on us. At sea level, there is a force of about 1 kilogram pressing on every square centimetre of your body. You don't feel this pressure because your body fluids are at pressure too, and push back with the same force.

Find Out More

- Atmosphere
- Carbon
- Lungs and breathing
- Nitrogen
- Oxygen
- Pollution

Aircraft

Just after dawn on 21 March 1999, a silvery balloon as tall as a skyscraper landed in the sand of the Egyptian desert. *Breitling Orbiter 3* had set off from a snowy village in Switzerland 19 days earlier. Its crew, Bertrand Piccard (Switzerland) and Brian Jones (Britain), had become the first people to fly around the world by balloon.

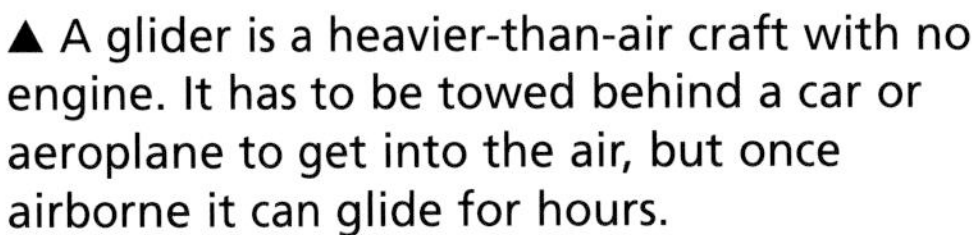

▲ A glider is a heavier-than-air craft with no engine. It has to be towed behind a car or aeroplane to get into the air, but once airborne it can glide for hours.

The first aircraft to lift a human into the skies was a balloon. But it is heavier-than-air craft such as aeroplanes and helicopters that dominate our skies today. Almost every minute of every day, airliners carrying up to 400 people take off from or land at our main airports.

Lighter than air

Balloons fly because they are light: they float in air in the same way that boats float in water. There are two main types – hot-air balloons and gas balloons. Hot-air balloons are filled with air heated by a burner. Because the hot air is lighter (less dense) than the surrounding cold air, the balloon floats upwards. Gas balloons are filled with a light gas, usually helium.

▼ *Breitling Orbiter 3* on its way to becoming the first balloon to fly non-stop around the world. Unlike most balloons, the *Breitling Orbiter* used a combination of helium gas and hot air. Climbing as high as 11,755 metres above the Earth's surface, the crew travelled in a sealed capsule with its own air supply.

Airships are elongated balloons, fitted with engines. In the early 20th century, huge airships pioneered long-distance air travel. Today, small airships are used for such things as aerial photography.

Heavier than air

How can something as big and as heavy as a 400-tonne airliner leave the ground and stay in the air? The answer lies in the wings. A wing has a special shaped cross-section, called an aerofoil. When air flows across the wing, it tends to lift upwards. It is this lifting force that supports the plane in the air. Like birds, planes need a tail as well as wings. The tail helps to keep the plane steady. It has a vertical tail fin and horizontal tailplanes.

Building aircraft

Most aircraft are made out of lightweight materials, particularly aluminium alloys. These are nearly as strong as steel but much lighter. For key parts of the aircraft, especially those that get hot, titanium or stainless steel may be used. These metals stay strong even at high temperatures.

The main structure of a plane (the airframe) is made up of a framework of ribs and spars. On top is a thin shell of aluminium sheets. In parts where extra strength is required, such as the wings, the airframe may be made out of a single piece of metal.

The jet set

An aeroplane's engines provide the power, or thrust, to move it along. Until the 1950s, most planes were powered by piston engines, which turned large propellers. But most planes now have jet engines.

A jet engine burns fuel to produce a jet of high-speed gases. As the jet shoots backwards, it moves the plane forwards. In the turbofan engines used in airliners, the jet of gases also turns a large fan, which pushes large amounts of cooler air out backwards, too. Turboprops are engines which use the jet of gas to spin a propeller.

▲ The eurofighter is one of the world's most advanced fighter planes. It is powered by twin jet engines, and has a sharply pointed nose and delta (triangular) wings for supersonic flight. The body and wings are made not from metal, but from plastics reinforced with carbon fibre.

Keeping in shape

All planes have the same basic parts – wings, fuselage (body), engines and tail – but they vary widely in design. The greatest differences between aircraft lie in the shape of their wings. Slow planes have long wings that stick out from the fuselage almost at right-angles. But higher-speed planes have wings that are swept back at an angle.

The overall shape of a plane is streamlined, so that it slips through the air easily. Aircraft designers test models of their craft in wind tunnels. This gives them a good idea of how the real planes will behave flying through the air.

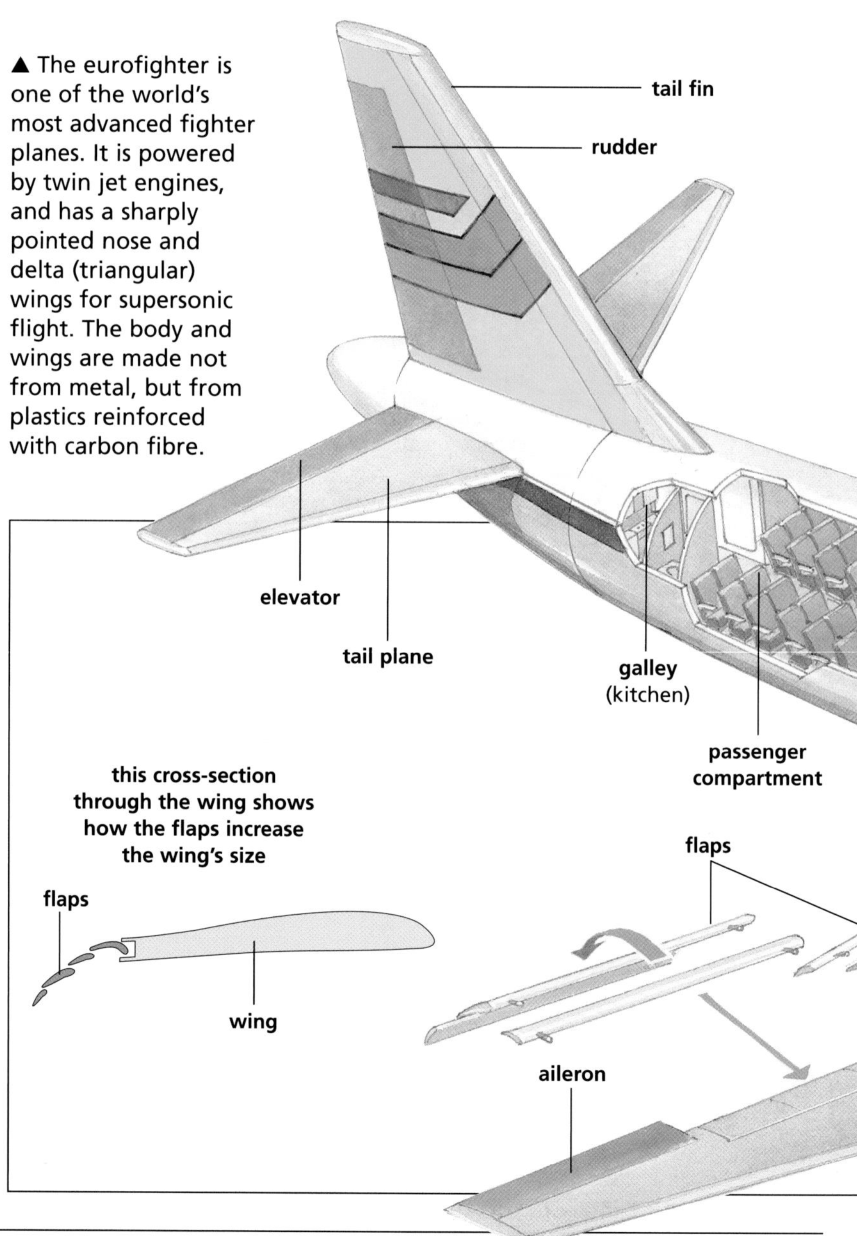

Vertical take-off

Most aeroplanes need a long runway for taking off and landing. The plane has to be moving quite fast before the wings produce enough lift to get it off the ground. But a few aircraft can take off and land vertically. The Harrier jump-jet is a VTOL (vertical take-off and landing) aeroplane. But the most widely used VTOL craft is the helicopter.

Like an aeroplane, a helicopter is supported in the air by wings. These wings are the blades of the rotor, which spins round on top of the helicopter's body. The rotor blades have the same aerofoil shape as ordinary wings. But instead of the aircraft moving forwards to create lift, the rotor spins round.

▶ A US coastguard helicopter carrying out a rescue on the coast of north California. The rotation of the helicopter's rotor tends to make the body of the helicopter spin. To stop this happening, there is a small rotor at the tail, facing sideways.

Find Out More

- Flight and flow
- Jet engines
- Transport

By 2006, the Airbus A380 (the 'Super-Jumbo') could be flying. Measuring about 79 metres long and about the same across the wings, the A380 will carry more than 600 passengers. Fully loaded, it will weigh nearly 600 tonnes.

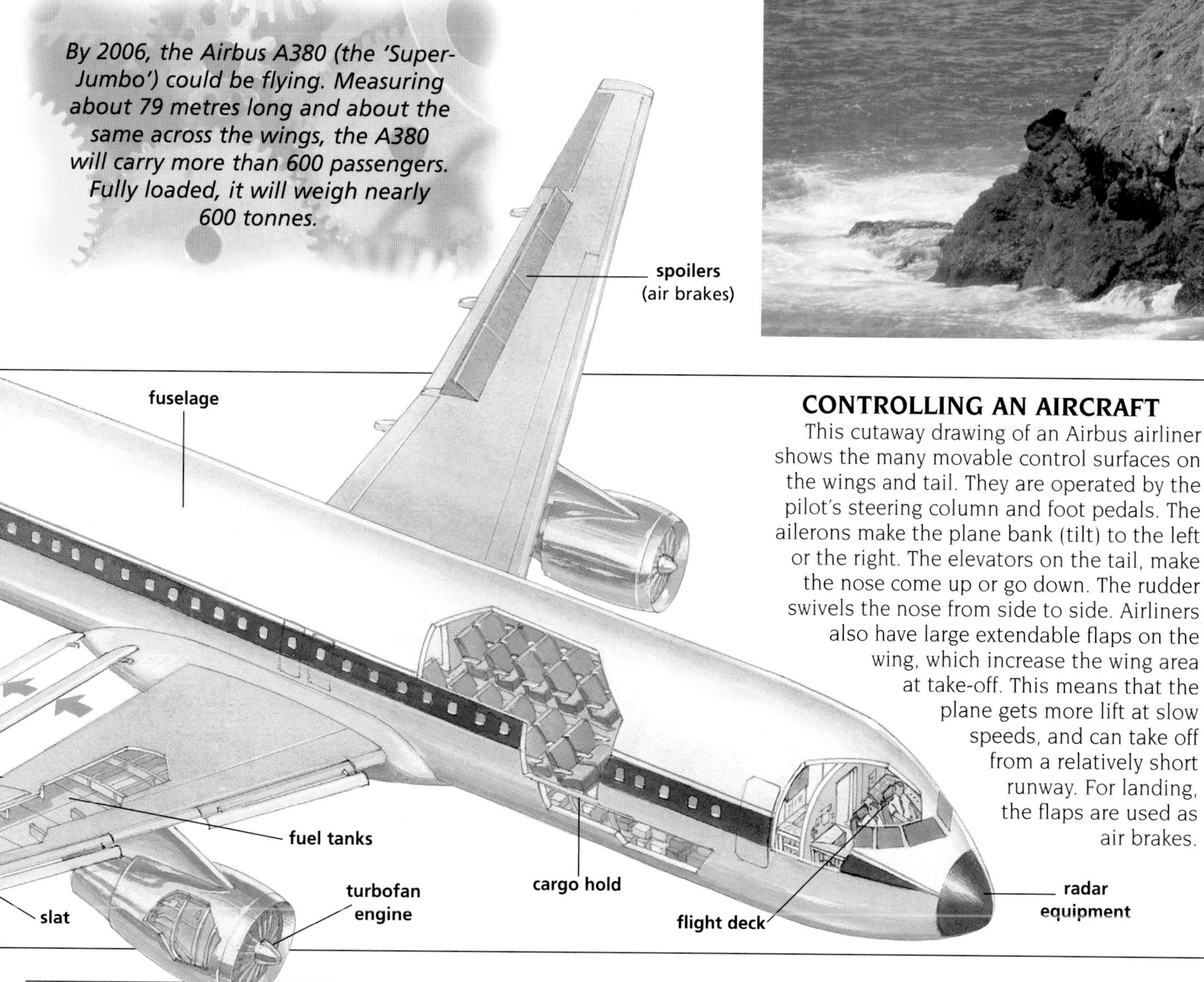

CONTROLLING AN AIRCRAFT

This cutaway drawing of an Airbus airliner shows the many movable control surfaces on the wings and tail. They are operated by the pilot's steering column and foot pedals. The ailerons make the plane bank (tilt) to the left or the right. The elevators on the tail, make the nose come up or go down. The rudder swivels the nose from side to side. Airliners also have large extendable flaps on the wing, which increase the wing area at take-off. This means that the plane gets more lift at slow speeds, and can take off from a relatively short runway. For landing, the flaps are used as air brakes.

Alcohol *see* Diet • **Algae** *see* Classification

Aliens

Story writers have dreamed up an incredible variety of fearsome creatures inhabiting other worlds in space. So far, though, scientists have found no evidence for life of any kind beyond the Earth.

Earth seems to be a special place for life. There is plenty of liquid water, and living things can get the energy they need from the warm sunlight, or from the heat inside the Earth.

We are now sure that none of the other planets in the Solar System have large plants or animals. Mars, the planet most like the Earth, is one place that might have microscopic life. In the past, Mars was warmer and wetter than it is now. If life started and died out, spacecraft or human explorers might one day find fossils on Mars.

Find Out More

- Life
- Mars
- Planets

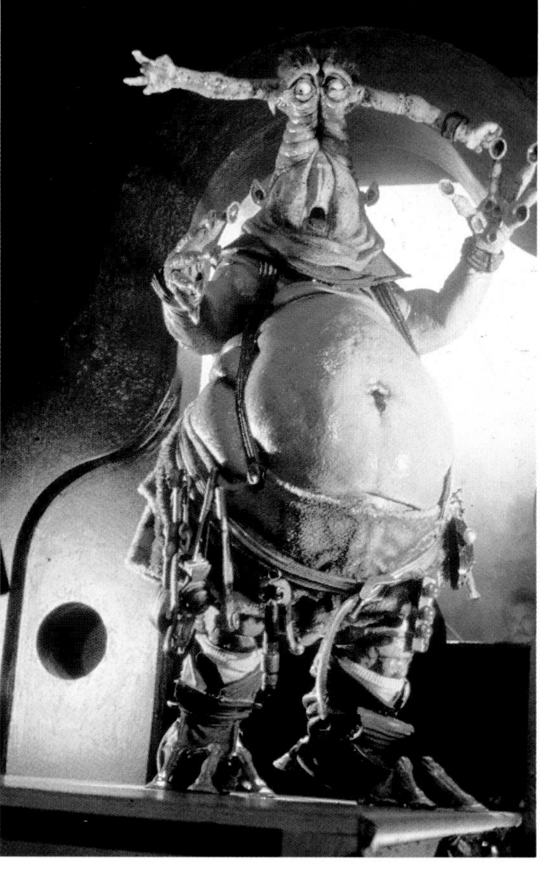

▶ Writers and artists have imagined all kinds of strange alien life, but no one knows whether creatures like this could exist somewhere in the Universe.

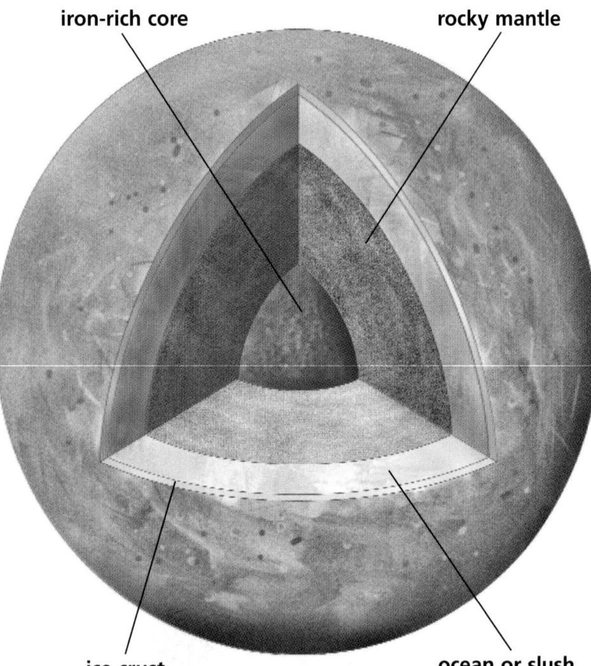

◀ Jupiter's moon Europa could possibly have life. There is probably liquid water under its icy crust. The ice melts because it is stirred around by Jupiter's strong gravity. If there is water, there might be life.

Hunting for extraterrestrials

The Universe is so large, that many people think there must be life of some kind on other planets somewhere. But intelligent life could be very special. We humans might be unique.

Astronomers hope in the future to build telescopes in space to look for telltale signs of life in the atmospheres of planets around nearby stars. Meanwhile, there are projects using large radio telescopes to search for unnatural radio signals from space. Alien radio astronomers up to about 50 light years away could pick up radio signals generated by humans on Earth.

Some people claim that aliens have already visited Earth, but no evidence has yet convinced scientists. There are a whole variety of natural and human explanations for sightings of Unidentified Flying Objects (UFOs).

▶ Millions of people around the world have used their home computers to help in the search for aliens. They sift through huge amounts of data from radio telescopes, looking for artificial signals. The project is called SETI@home. 'SETI' stands for 'Search for Extraterrestrial Intelligence'.

Alloys

Copper and tin have many useful properties – for example, they do not easily corrode, or rust. The trouble is that they are quite soft and weak. But the metal you get when you mix them together is hard and strong, and still doesn't rust. It is one of our most useful metal mixtures, or alloys, and it is called bronze.

Like copper and tin, most metals are quite soft and weak in their pure state. But they become much harder and stronger when they are mixed with other metals to form alloys. Most metals used today are alloys, from the coins in our pockets and the cutlery we eat with, to the airframes and engines of aircraft.

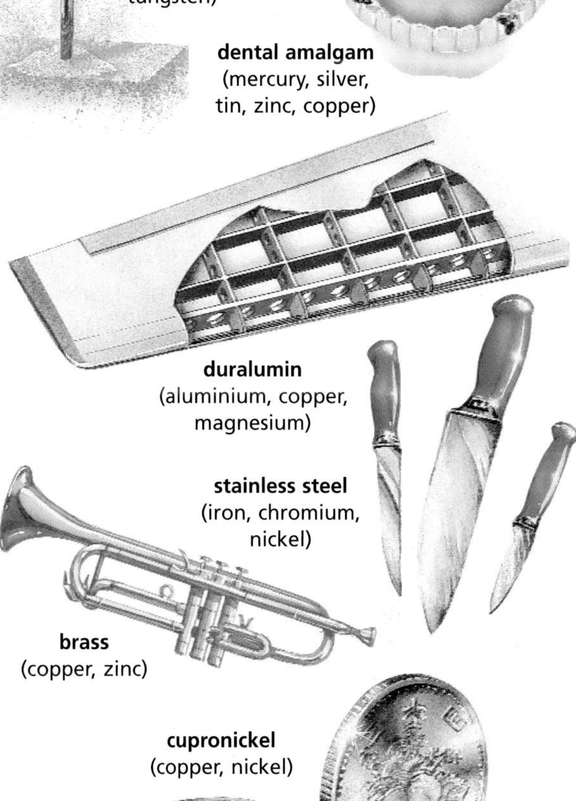

▶ Some common alloys, with typical uses.

Find Out More

- Aluminium
- Copper
- Iron and steel
- Metals and non-metals

The right recipe

Alloys have been used for thousands of years. Today, metallurgists, the scientists who work with metals, can produce alloys with a wide range of different properties. They do so by carefully selecting the alloying ingredients – choosing the right 'recipe'.

Our most common metal, steel, is an alloy. It is a mixture of iron, a little carbon, and traces of other metals. It is the carbon that makes it so strong.

One drawback with ordinary steel is that it corrodes, or rusts. To stop it rusting, metallurgists add chromium and nickel to it. These metals do not rust and make the steel rust-resistant too. The alloy formed is stainless steel.

Some of the most advanced alloys are found inside jet engines. They have to remain strong at temperatures up to 1000 °C. Some of these so-called superalloys may contain 10 or more different metals, including titanium and tungsten, which melt only at high temperatures.

The value of alloys was discovered in very ancient times. Bronze was made before 3000 BC, and brass (copper and zinc) has been used for nearly as long. Pewter is an ancient alloy made from tin and lead, first used over 2000 years ago. Modern pewter uses other metals instead of lead. This makes it safe to use for plates and mugs.

▶ Bronze is hard and does not rust. People have used this alloy for thousands of years to make things like sculptures.

Memory metals are alloys of titanium and nickel that can 'remember' their shape. If an object made of memory metal becomes twisted, it will return to its original shape if it is gently heated.

Aluminium

Without aluminium, aircraft would probably still be built of wood, wire and fabric. And we would probably not be living in a space age. But thanks to aluminium we can build planes and spacecraft that are both lightweight and strong.

After iron, aluminium is the second-most important metal to us. Over 20 million tonnes of aluminium are produced each year. Its lightness is the main reason why aluminium is so useful. It is less than half as heavy as iron. Unlike iron, it does not corrode, or rust.

Pure aluminium is soft and weak. It is used as thin foil – for cooking, for example. But it becomes much more useful when traces of other metals (such as copper) are mixed with it to form alloys.

▶ Aluminium is used to make bodies for aircraft and other vehicles like cars and coaches.

Find Out More

- Alloys
- Metals and non-metals
- Resources

Light conductors

Aluminium alloys have many uses. The alloys from which aircraft and spacecraft are made are as strong as steel but very light. Some are used to make cookware for the home. They heat up readily because aluminium is a good conductor of heat, allowing heat to travel through it easily. The metal is also a good conductor of electricity, which is why it is used for the transmission lines that carry electricity from power stations to our homes.

Making the metal

There is more aluminium in the Earth's crust than any other metal (8 per cent). It is found combined with other elements in many minerals in clays and rocks. But it can only easily be extracted from an ore called bauxite, which contains the mineral alumina, or aluminium oxide. Australia has the largest bauxite deposits.

Aluminium metal is obtained from alumina by electrolysis – passing electricity through it. The process was discovered independently in 1886 by Charles Hall in the USA and Paul Héroult in France.

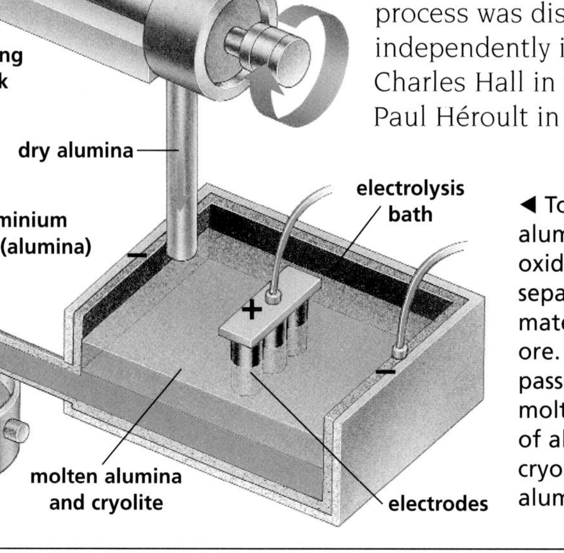

◀ To make aluminium, alumina (aluminium oxide) is first separated from other material in the bauxite ore. Electricity is then passed through a molten (liquid) mixture of alumina and cryolite (another aluminium mineral).

Amphibians

The male midwife toad hops around for about four weeks with a string of yellow eggs twisted around his back legs. Every so often, he dips the eggs in a pool or a puddle to stop them drying out. When the eggs are ready to hatch, he takes them to a pool and the tadpoles swim away.

▲ The bright colours of the fire salamander warn predators of its poisonous skin. The poison is even powerful enough to kill small mammals.

Like many other amphibians, midwife toads are caring parents. Amphibians were the first vertebrates (animals with backbones) to live on land, and the first to have true legs, tongues, ears and voice boxes. Most amphibians live a 'double life', partly on the land and partly in the water.

Three groups

There are three main groups of amphibians. Salamanders and newts feed on slow-moving animals such as snails, slugs and worms. Most are small and secretive, but giant salamanders grow up to 1.6 metres long, The second group, frogs and toads, are also meat-eaters. They have large, wide mouths to swallow the food that they catch on their long, sticky tongues. The third group, called caecilians, look more like worms than amphibians. They wriggle through the damp soils of tropical forests.

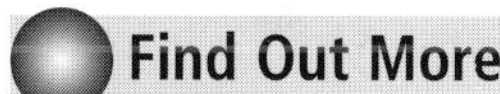

Find Out More

- Animals
- Classification

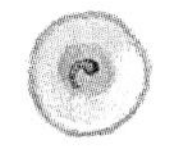

1 day old frog's soft eggs are protected by a jelly-like covering

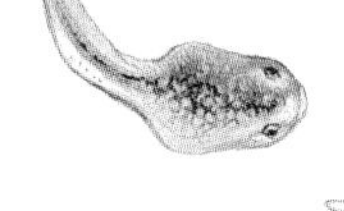

10 days eggs hatch into tadpoles with a tail but no legs. They breathe through gills

7–13 weeks as tadpole grows, it loses its gills and develops lungs and legs

▶ A frog has three stages in its life cycle – egg, tadpole and adult frog.

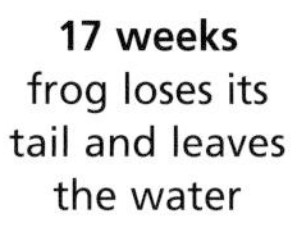

17 weeks frog loses its tail and leaves the water

▲ Caecilians use their heads like garden trowels to dig in the mud for worms, termites and lizards. Adults have a small tentacle on the head to detect chemicals.

Amphibian features

Amphibians do not usually have scales, and their skin is thin, loose-fitting and moist. They usually live in damp places. A few give birth to live young, but most mate and lay their eggs in the water. The eggs hatch into tadpoles, which look very different from the adults. The tadpoles go through a series of changes, called metamorphosis, before becoming adults.

Amplifiers *see* Sound recording • **Anaesthetics** *see* Surgery • **Analogue** *see* Sound recording

Animal behaviour

A young chimpanzee watches closely as its mother breaks off a strong, bendy plant stem and pulls off the leaves. Then she pushes the stem inside a termite mound and pulls out a juicy termite snack. It will take the young chimp many years to learn how to do this properly.

▲ In a wolf pack, each wolf knows its place. High-ranking (dominant) wolves stand tall, with their tail and ears up. Low-ranking or submissive wolves lie on their back to show that they will not fight.

Almost anything an animal does is a form of behaviour. Chimpanzees digging for termites, cranes leaping into the air in a courtship dance, lion cubs playing, wasps building a nest – all these are examples of animal behaviour. Many of the most interesting types of behaviour happen within a species as individuals defend a territory, find a mate, help each other to hunt, drive enemies away or raise young.

Learned or in-built?

A young chimp can learn how to 'fish' for termites because it has inherited the ability and intelligence to carry out this type of behaviour from its mother. There are two main types of behaviour – instinctive or innate behaviour, which is handed on from generation to generation; and learned behaviour, which an animal learns during its lifetime. An animal's behaviour is often a complex mixture of instinctive and learned behaviour.

Animals are born with the ability to behave in certain fixed or automatic ways. Some animals rely almost entirely on this automatic behaviour. Insect behaviour is largely automatic, for instance, and spiders do not have to learn how to spin a web. Fixed or instinctive behaviour is controlled by an animal's genes. If the environment changes, those animals that are best suited to the new conditions are more likely to survive to reproduce, and so pass on their genes to the next generation. Learned behaviour, on the other hand, is not passed on from one generation to the next.

TERMITE MOUNDS

Millions of termites live together in a termite mound – a tall tower built from soil glued together with saliva and droppings. If people built on the same scale as termites, their towers would be over a kilometre high. Different types of termite live in the mound, each with their own special job to do.

▶ Male bighorn sheep fight to decide which are the strongest and most dominant individuals. Their fights are head-butting contests, which involve tremendous clashes of horns.

Find Out More

- Animals
- Genetics
- Seasons

Communication

The way an animal behaves is influenced by the way it interacts or communicates with other members of its own species. Although animals cannot talk, they can send each other messages using sounds, scents or body language, such as facial expressions. Female fireflies even use patterns of flashing lights to attract a mate.

KONRAD LORENZ

Konrad Lorenz (1903–1989) was one of the first scientists to study animal behaviour. He noticed that there is a period of intense learning during the first few hours of an animal's life, called imprinting, in which it learns to recognize its parents and its species. Some young geese treated Lorenz as their 'mother' because he was the first large object they saw when they hatched.

Surviving the seasons

Different patterns of behaviour may help animals to survive seasonal changes in the weather. Many birds and some mammals, fishes and insects migrate – they make long journeys to avoid bad weather and poor food supplies, or to find a safer place to give birth to their young.

Other animals survive very cold weather or very dry weather by going into a deep sleep. Surviving cold conditions like this is called hibernation. Sleeping through hot, dry conditions is called aestivation.

▶ Monarch butterflies migrate from Canada to Mexico for the winter, a journey of some 4000 kilometres. Among the Mexican pine trees, the butterflies hibernate in enormous clusters so that the trees seem to be dripping with butterflies.

Animals

Even though it is small enough to fit into a jam jar, the blue-ringed octopus is one of the world's deadliest animals. Its poison glands are as large as its brain and one octopus contains enough poison to kill 10 people. The octopus normally uses its poison to catch the crabs it feeds on.

All animals have to eat plants or other animals instead of making their own food, and this is the main difference between animals and plants. The variety of ways in which animals catch their food is an important reason for the huge diversity in their shapes and sizes. Most animals need a gut in which to digest their food.

Animal characteristics

Animals need to be able to move around to find their food. Most use muscles that pull on some sort of rigid framework, usually an internal or external skeleton. They also have nerves to control their movement and senses to detect what is happening around them. Most animals have some form of 'brain' to control their nerves and senses, which is usually located in a head.

Keeping warm

The body temperature of most animals varies with that of their surroundings. This is called being a 'cold-blooded' animal (although their blood can be warm or cold depending on the temperature around them). Cold-blooded animals are more common in warmer places.

Only two groups of animals, birds and mammals, can control their body temperature. This is called being warm-blooded and it means that the animal's body stays at the same high temperature, no matter how hot or cold it is around them. Warm-blooded animals can live in both warm and cold places. However, keeping their bodies warm all the time uses a lot of energy, so they must eat more often than cold-blooded animals.

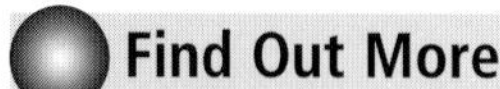

- Classification
- Ecology
- Invertebrates
- Plants
- Sex and reproduction

▲ Anemones are animals, although they look rather like flowering plants and they do not usually move around. Instead they use their petal-like tentacles to catch food, such as tiny fishes, which they stun with stinging cells on their tentacles.

▼ A cheetah chasing a Thomson's gazelle. Cheetahs are the world's fastest land animals over short distances, and so they are excellent hunters. They can accelerate from 0 to 90 km/h in just three seconds and run at nearly 100 km/h. But they have to rest after about 20 seconds because they get too hot and run out of oxygen.

Invertebrates
About 33 different groups, including sponges, jellyfishes, worms, snails, insects and starfishes. Many live in water but some, such as insects, live on land. They are all cold-blooded.

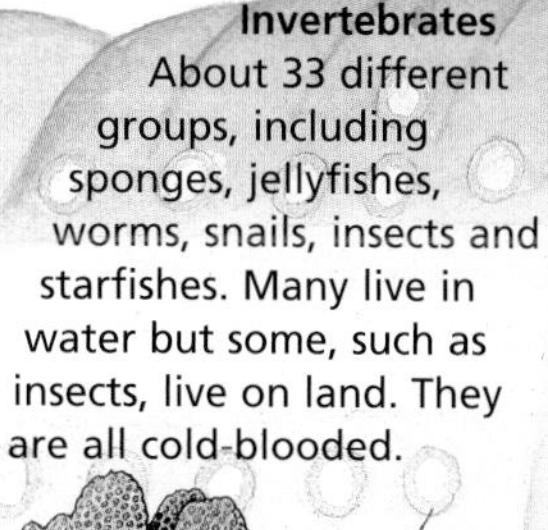

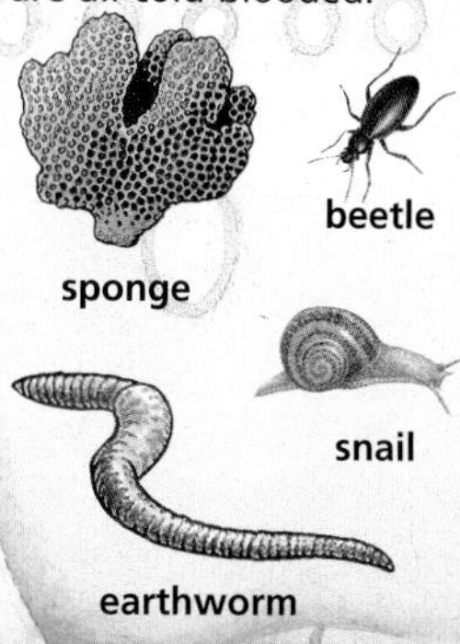

Fishes
Two main groups – fishes with a bony skeleton (most fishes) and fishes with a skeleton made of cartilage, such as sharks and rays. They live in water, have a scaly skin and are cold-blooded.

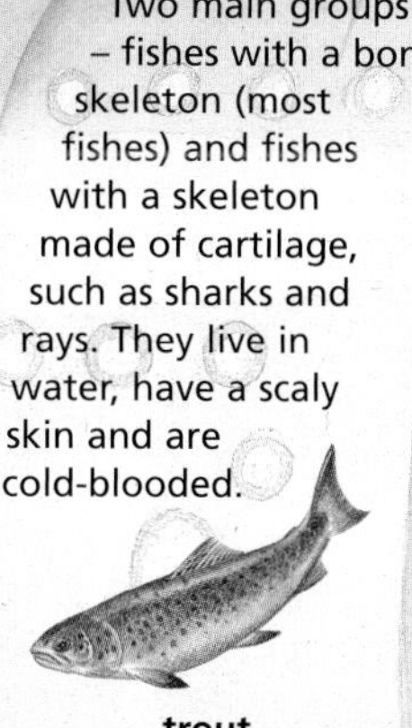

Amphibians
Three main groups – salamanders and newts, frogs and toads, and blindworms (caecilians). They live partly in water and partly on land, have a smooth, moist skin and are cold-blooded.

Reptiles
Three main groups – turtles and tortoises, snakes and lizards, and crocodiles and alligators. Many live in warm places on land but some, such as turtles, live in water. They have scales and are cold-blooded.

Birds
28–30 different groups, from sparrows and parrots to eagles and penguins. They live all over the world, have feathers and are warm-blooded.

Mammals
21 different groups, from mice and bats to giraffes and bears. They live all over the world, have fur and are warm-blooded.

▲ Animals can be divided into six major groups. About 1.5 million different species of animals have been identified so far, and over 1 million of these are insects. The five groups of vertebrates include only about 50,000 known species.

Animal skeletons

Animals are sometimes divided into two groups, vertebrates and invertebrates. A vertebrate is an animal with a backbone, which is a column of segments or vertebrae supporting the central nerve cord. Its body is supported by a bony skeleton. Most of the bigger, more complicated and more familiar animals – including fishes, reptiles, birds and mammals – are vertebrates.

An invertebrate is an animal without a backbone or any bones. Over 90 per cent of all animals are invertebrates, including insects, snails and worms. The bodies of invertebrates may be supported by a hard shell or an outer skeleton, called an exoskeleton. But a jellyfish is supported only by the water around it, while worms are supported by the pressure of fluid-filled spaces inside their bodies.

The external skeleton of an invertebrate animal such as a scorpion is made of a hard, lightweight substance called chitin. An external skeleton cannot grow. It has to be shed, or moulted, to allow the animal to grow.

◀ Skeletons are especially important for animals that live on land.

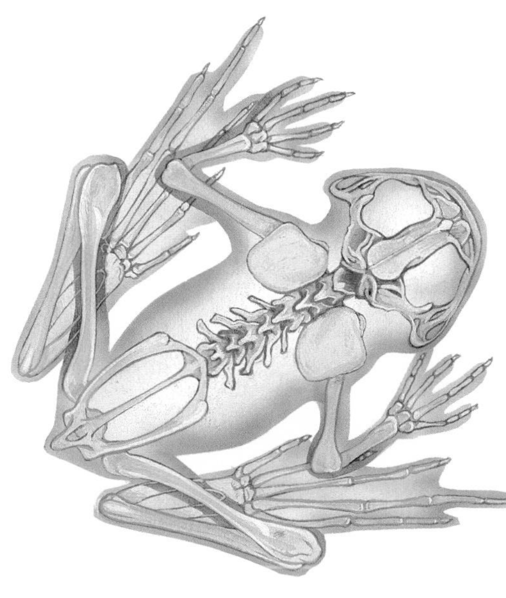

The internal skeleton of a vertebrate such as a frog supports its body and protects its soft internal organs, such as its heart. Muscles attached to the bones of the skeleton enable the animal to move. As the frog grows, its skeleton grows too.

Arthropods *see* Insects, Invertebrates • **Artificial intelligence** *see* Robots and artificial intelligence

Asteroids

Millions of asteroids orbit the Sun in the asteroid belt between Mars and Jupiter. Though there are so many, all these small rocky chunks together would only make one seventh of our Moon.

The asteroids (sometimes called minor planets) are made of rock, metal or a mixture of both. They are small pieces left over from when the planets were forming 4600 million years ago. The first asteroid to be discovered was Ceres. It was found by the Italian astronomer Guiseppe Piazzi in 1801, while he was searching for planets between Jupiter and Mars. At 975 kilometres across, Ceres is the largest asteroid. The smallest ones are no bigger than boulders.

The largest asteroids are ball-shaped. Most have odd, elongated shapes. Spacecraft have returned detailed pictures of several asteroids. All of them are pitted with craters where smaller rocks have crashed into them.

▶ Twelve views of the asteroid Eros. In February 2000 a spacecraft called *NEAR Shoemaker* went into orbit around Eros. Eros is 33 kilometres long and 13 kilometres wide.

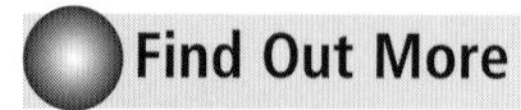

- Planets
- Solar System
- Space astronomy

Unusual orbits

A few asteroids are in orbits outside the main asteroid belt. In 1994, a 10-metre-wide rock passed the Earth only 105,000 kilometres away – less than one third the distance to the Moon. Chiron is one of several distant asteroids with orbits between Jupiter and Uranus. Two clusters of asteroids, called the Trojans, orbit the Sun at exactly the same distance as Jupiter.

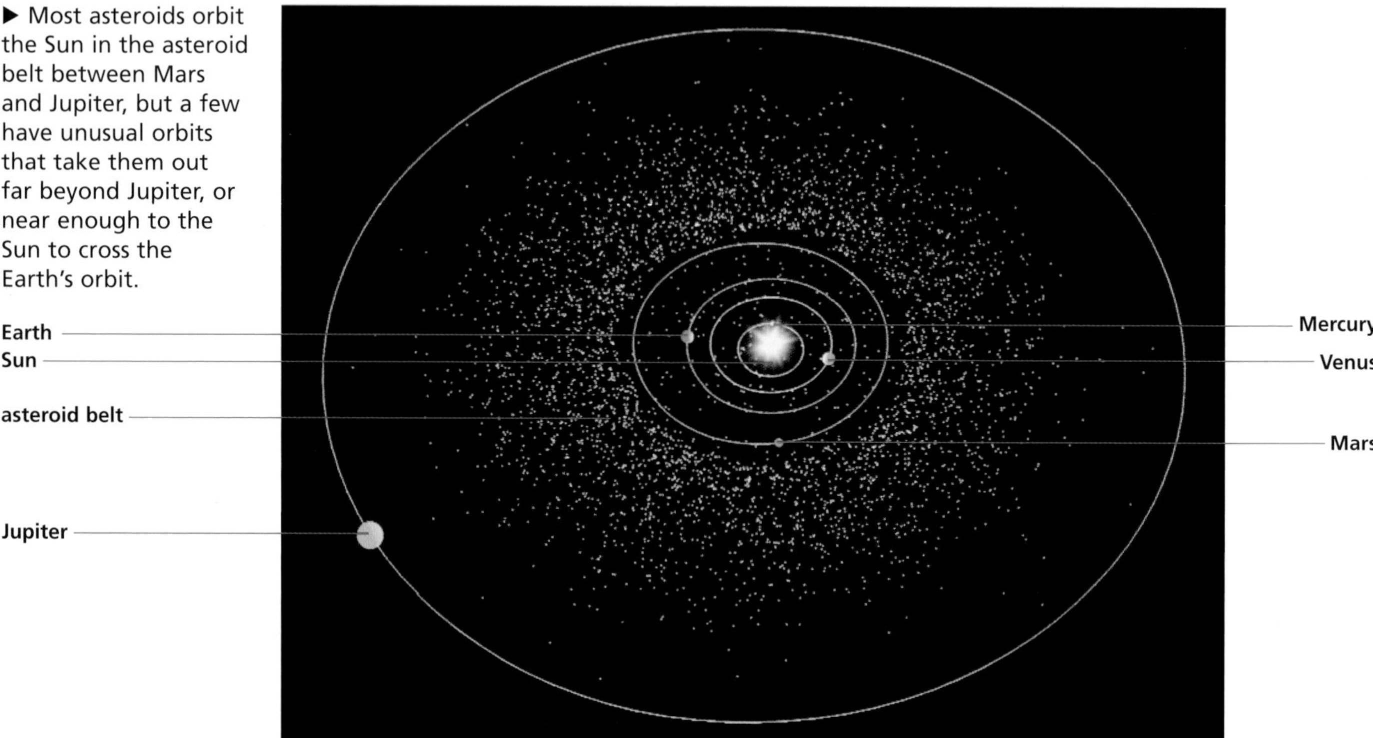

▶ Most asteroids orbit the Sun in the asteroid belt between Mars and Jupiter, but a few have unusual orbits that take them out far beyond Jupiter, or near enough to the Sun to cross the Earth's orbit.

Astrologers *see* Constellations

Astronauts

If you were an astronaut up in space, you would find life very strange. You wouldn't be able to walk, because in space you can't keep your feet on the floor. You couldn't pour yourself a drink, because drinks don't pour in space. And you would have to sleep strapped in your bed to avoid floating away.

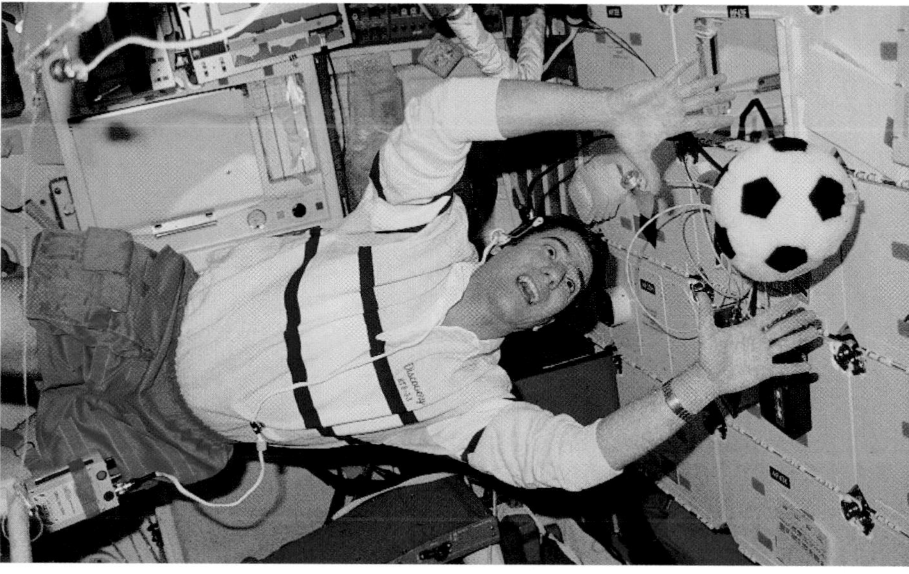

▲ An astronaut 'goalkeeper' appears to dive to catch a ball. But he's just kidding. Both he and the ball are floating motionless in space.

Astronauts are people who travel in space. The Russians call them cosmonauts. The Russian cosmonaut Yuri Gagarin became the first space traveller in 1961. Since then hundreds of astronauts and cosmonauts have flown into space – men and women, young and old, from many countries.

Find Out More

- Astronauts
- Satellites
- Space astronomy
- Space shuttles
- Space stations

Getting ready

Imagine you are an astronaut about to set out on a space mission. Before you set out, you have to train hard, rehearsing the work you will carry out in orbit. You spend a lot of time in simulators. These are machines that behave in the same way as your spacecraft without leaving the ground. You go over and over the details of your trip with mission control, the centre that controls missions from the ground.

▶ Astronauts train for space walks (EVA) in a large water tank. This gives them the same sense of weightlessness that they will have when floating in space.

Into orbit

When it is time for the launch, you strap yourself into your seat, facing away from the ground. As the launch rockets fire, you feel yourself flattened against the seat. Your body feels much heavier than usual. This is because of the forces set up as the rocket accelerates. They are called g-forces, the g standing for gravity.

Floating free

Once the rockets stop firing and you are circling the Earth in orbit, your body no longer feels heavy. If you unstrap yourself, you float gently out of your seat. It appears that your body has no weight at all! We call this peculiar state zero-g, or weightlessness.

Weightlessness affects everything you do in orbit. It's best not to eat crumbly foods, because the crumbs will float away and get into everything. You have to drink liquids through a straw because there is no gravity to make them pour. Even the lavatory you use in space has to be flushed with air, rather than water.

Russian cosmonaut Valery Polyakov holds the record for the longest stay in space. He spent over 437 days in orbit in the Mir space station, between January 1994 and March 1995.

Space medicine

Weightlessness not only affects the way you behave in orbit, it also upsets your body. It affects the balance organs in your ears, and this could make you feel travel sick for a while. Your face will get fatter, but your waist will get slimmer and you will grow a few centimetres taller.

If you stay in space for a long time, the effects of weightlessness are more serious. Because your muscles no longer have to battle against gravity, they get flabby and start to waste away. To keep them in good shape you will need to exercise regularly. You might jog on a treadmill, or ride on a bicycle machine. Because the effects of long stays in space can be serious, astronauts take part in medical experiments to see how weightlessness affects their bodies.

Walking in space

While you are in orbit, you might have to go on a spacewalk. The correct term for a spacewalk is extravehicular activity, or EVA.

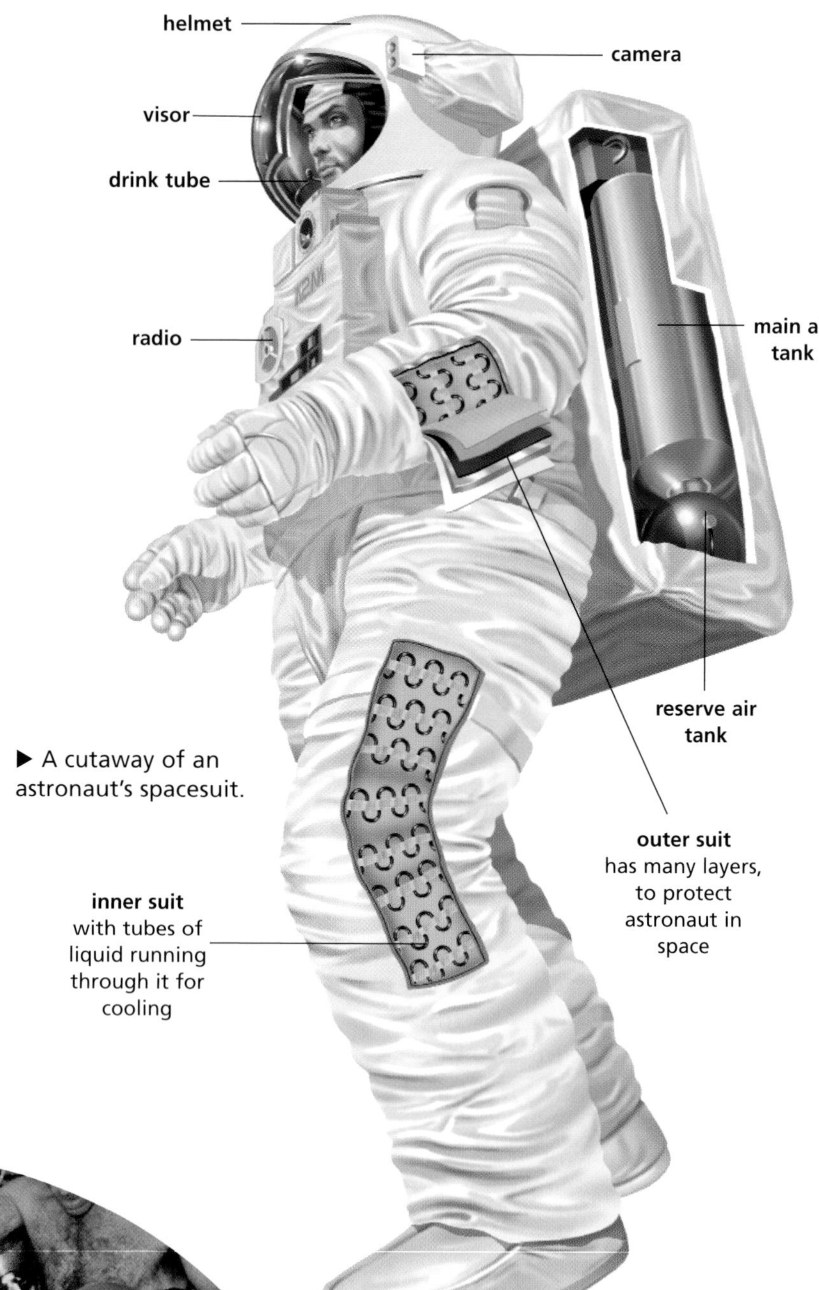

▶ A cutaway of an astronaut's spacesuit.

To go outside the spacecraft you will need a spacesuit. This gives you air to breathe and protects you from the heat, cold and dangerous radiation of space. You may also have a backpack with small jets on it to help you move about.

◀ An astronaut takes part in a medical experiment to check on her breathing and circulation. Such experiments are vital for the long-term future of human beings in space.

Astronomy

On a clear moonless night, far from city lights, the starry sky is an awe-inspiring sight. You can see about 4000 stars when the sky is really dark. Astronomy is about far more than 'stars'. It is the science that aims to discover the secrets of the Universe.

Find Out More

- Solar System
- Space astronomy
- Stars
- Telescopes

The Sun and all these stars belong to the huge star family we call the Milky Way Galaxy. Beyond our own galaxy, there are billions more in the Universe.

Some nights you might spot one or more of the bright planets, such as Venus or Jupiter. Like our own planet Earth, they belong to the Sun's family, called the Solar System. The planets are much nearer than the stars. They gradually move against the background of stars, which stays the same.

◀ An observatory at the Canada-France-Hawaii telescope on top of the Mauna Kea volcano, Hawaii. The dome-shaped building houses a large telescope. Its roof slides open and turns around. This picture was taken over a period of several hours. The trails of light in the sky are made by the stars. The stars slowly move round in the sky (like the Sun does during the day), because the Earth spins once a day.

▲ The Lovell Telescope at Jodrell Bank in England is 76 metres across. It is one of the largest radio astronomy dishes in the world and can be pointed anywhere in the sky.

Telescopes for astronomy

Spacecraft have been sent to explore the Moon and planets. However, most astronomy is done at observatories, with the help of telescopes and the electronic instruments that go on them.

The most familiar astronomical telescopes are optical ones, which pick up light from far-off objects. Astronomers also use special telescopes to detect invisible radiation from space, such as X-rays, infrared and radio waves.

They use the information they get from light and other kinds of radiation to find out how hot stars are, what gas clouds between stars are made of, and how fast the galaxies are moving away from us. They also find out many other facts about the Universe.

Large telescopes detect fainter objects and distinguish finer detail than smaller ones. The largest telescopes for optical and infrared astronomy have mirrors 8 or 10 metres across. The best places for these great observatories are remote mountain-tops where the air is clear and dry. Radio telescopes can pick up signals even through cloud, so they can be built almost anywhere. Some have large single dishes. Others use many smaller dishes that work together.

Astronomy as a hobby

You don't have to be a professional scientist to do astronomy. You don't even need a telescope to start discovering the night sky. The first step is to learn some of the constellations. Next you can planet-spot and watch for meteors.

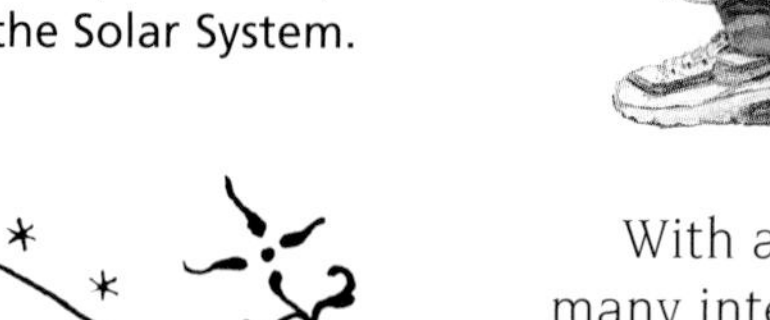

▶ You can discover lots of things about the night sky with the naked eye, or with the help of a small pair of binoculars.

▼ Copernicus's plan of the Solar System.

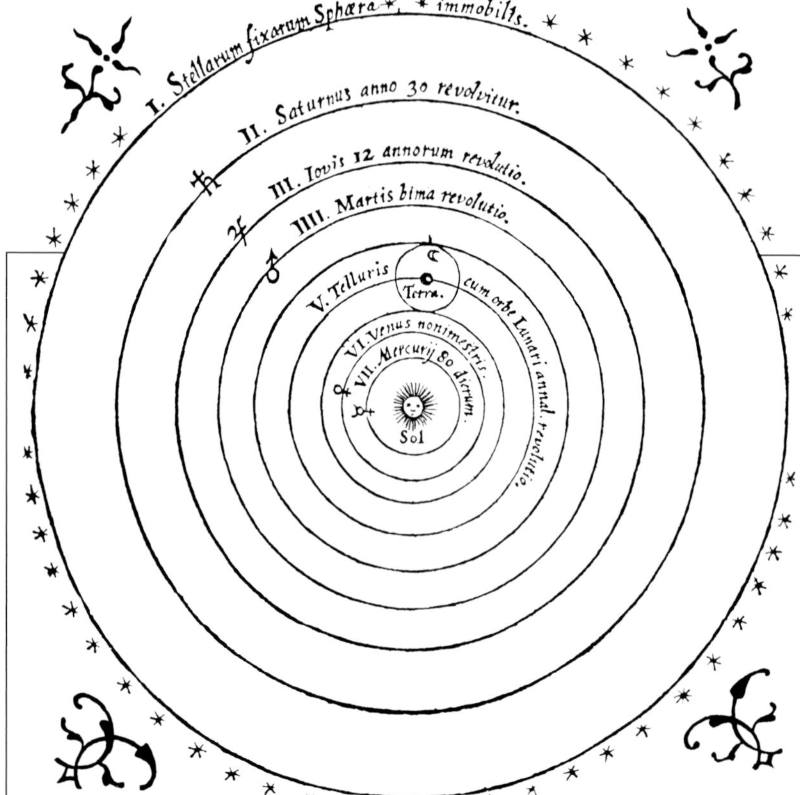

With a small telescope you can find many interesting sights, such as the rings around Saturn, but an ordinary pair of binoculars is a good start. They will show you the craters on the Moon, and clusters of stars in the Milky Way.

NICOLAUS COPERNICUS

Nicolaus Copernicus (1473–1543) was born in Poland. He was a student for many years, and was especially interested in astronomy. At that time most people believed that the Sun, the Moon and the planets all travelled around the Earth. Copernicus realized it is easier to explain the Solar System if the Sun is at the centre with the Earth and other planets orbiting around it.

Atmosphere

Seen from space, the Earth's atmosphere is a thin blue layer of air. Without it, the Earth would be a very different place. The atmosphere traps heat from the Sun, keeping it from escaping into space. Winds in the atmosphere carry vital rain from place to place. And two of the gases in the air, oxygen and carbon dioxide, are essential for life.

An atmosphere is a blanket of gas that surrounds a planet. Earth's atmosphere is over 1000 kilometres deep, but most of it is in the 30 kilometres closest to Earth.

Atmospheric pressure

Although it may not feel like it, air pushes on us from all sides. The weight of the air pushing on us is known as *atmospheric pressure*, or air pressure. As you rise in the atmosphere, there is less and less air pressing down from above, so atmospheric pressure decreases.

You can also think of air pressure as the amount of air in a certain volume of space. This idea is very important to mountain climbers and pilots. At the top of Mount Everest, at 8848 metres above sea level, a lungful of air contains less than a third as many oxygen molecules as it does at sea level. Where jets fly, 14 kilometres high, the atmospheric pressure is only 15 per cent of what it is on the ground. If we didn't pressurize airline cabins by pumping air into them, passengers would suffocate.

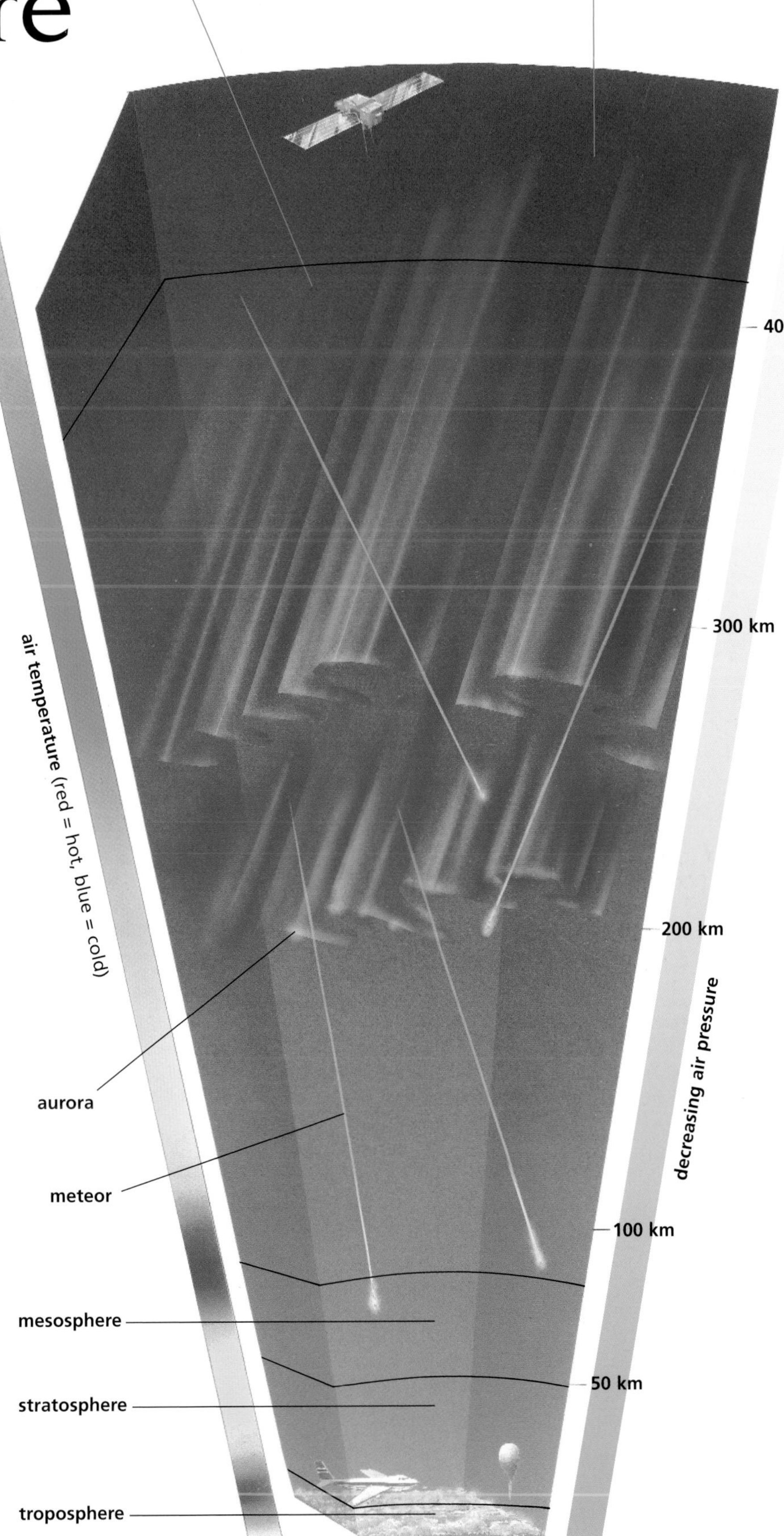

▶ Without an atmosphere, the Earth would be a very different planet. The atmosphere moves heat and water from place to place on Earth. It also acts like a blanket, keeping heat from escaping out into space. Oxygen and carbon dioxide gases in the atmosphere 'feed' plants and animals. Ozone gas in the upper atmosphere absorbs harmful ultraviolet light.

Find Out More
- Air
- Earth
- Pressure
- Sun
- Venus

▶ View of Earth at sunset. You can see how thin the atmosphere layer is in this picture.

From the ground up

From the ground up, the atmosphere changes. In the lower atmosphere (called the *troposphere*), the air gets colder as you go higher. This is because we actually get warmth from the Earth's surface, not directly from the Sun. The Sun heats the surface, which then radiates the heat back out and warms the air.

It is also much easier to get sunburned high in the atmosphere because there are fewer air molecules to absorb and scatter the Sun's rays.

Other atmospheres

Every planet has a slightly different atmosphere. The atmosphere on Mars is mainly carbon dioxide, while that of Uranus is hydrogen and helium. Larger planets have thicker atmospheres because they have a stronger gravitational pull. Gases have a hard time escaping the gravity of a large planet like Jupiter. By contrast, the Moon is so small and its gravity is so low that it has almost no atmosphere at all.

◀ Even though Venus is about the same size as Earth, Venus's atmosphere is 90 times thicker than ours. It traps heat so well that the temperature of Venus's surface is about 430 °C.

LIFE CHANGED OUR ATMOSPHERE

When Earth's atmosphere first formed over 4 billion years ago, it contained very little oxygen. No one is exactly sure what the first living things were like, but eventually they evolved into tiny simple plants. Like plants today, they made food for themselves using sunlight, water and carbon dioxide. One of the products of this food-making process was oxygen. As these organisms grew and multiplied, they changed the atmosphere, reducing the amount of carbon dioxide and increasing the amount of oxygen, eventually making it possible for oxygen-breathing animals to evolve.

Earth's atmosphere today is made mostly of nitrogen and oxygen. It also contains small amounts of other gases such as water vapour, argon, carbon dioxide and ozone. Animals need oxygen to breathe, while plants make their food from carbon dioxide.

Human beings have changed the atmosphere in only a few hundred years. For instance, through pollution we have added extra carbon dioxide which has caused global warming.

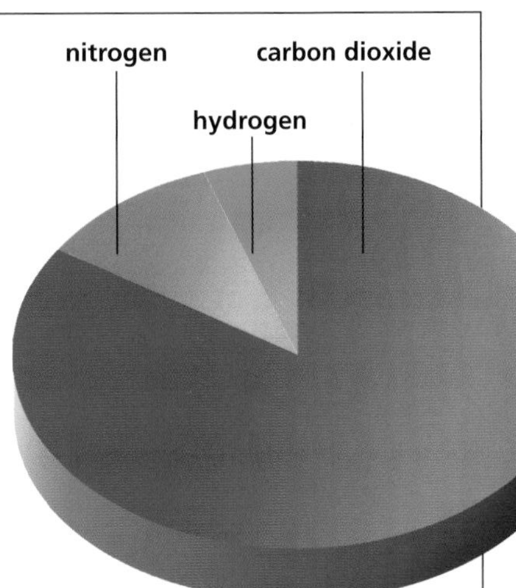

▲ Composition of Earth's early atmosphere.

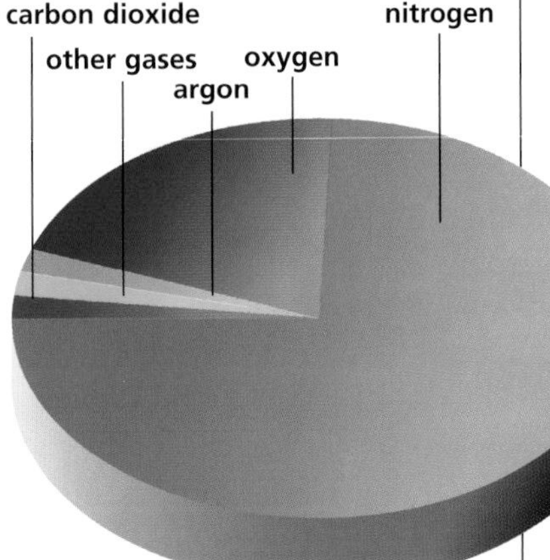

▲ Earth's atmosphere today.

Atoms and molecules

Everything is made of atoms – from this book to your body, from trees and rocks to air and water and the planets and stars. Atoms are very tiny particles of matter – much too small to see with the naked eye. In a single drop of water, there are more than a thousand million million million atoms.

Matter is made up of different kinds of substances called elements. Oxygen, gold, iron, sulphur, carbon and hydrogen are all examples of elements. About 90 different elements occur naturally. Each element is made up of a single type of atom, and each one behaves differently.

Often atoms are joined together in larger particles called molecules. Molecules do not behave in the same way as the separate atoms. For example, the molecules of water are each made of two hydrogen atoms and one oxygen atom. Water is very different from either oxygen or hydrogen. Hydrogen is a very light gas that burns easily. Oxygen is a gas in the air we breathe. We cannot breathe water, or burn it! A substance such as water that is made up of the same kind of molecules is called a chemical compound.

▶ Very powerful microscopes can actually 'see' atoms. In this picture, the red, yellow and brown lumps are atoms of gold.

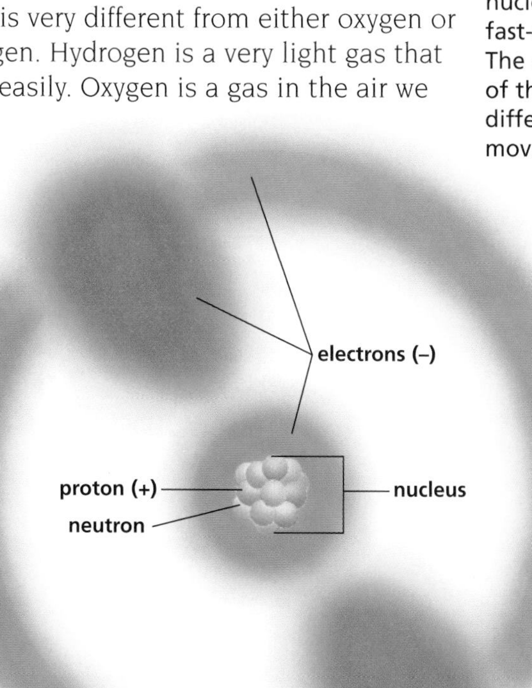

▼ An atom of carbon. At the centre is the nucleus, made up of protons and neutrons. Surrounding the nucleus are clouds of fast-moving electrons. The different colours of the clouds indicate different types of movement.

The story of the atom

The ancient Greeks first came up with the idea of atoms. They suggested that all matter was made up of tiny particles which could not be split into any smaller pieces. In about 1803 the English scientist John Dalton described the atom as the smallest amount of an element that still behaves like that element. He realized that atoms of different elements have different weights (masses). He also showed that atoms of different elements combine together in various ways to make different chemical compounds.

Smaller and smaller

Until 1897, scientists thought there could be nothing smaller than an atom. In that year the British scientist J.J. Thomson discovered the electron. The electron has a negative electrical charge, and is much smaller than an atom. In 1911 Ernest

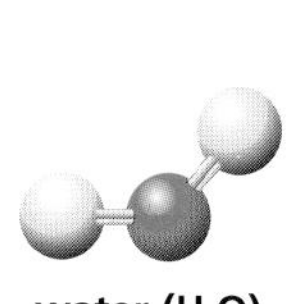

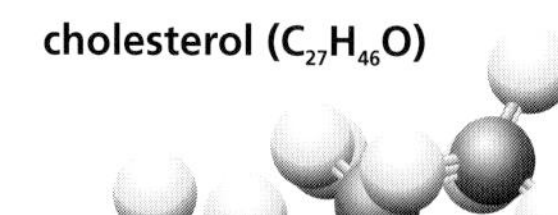

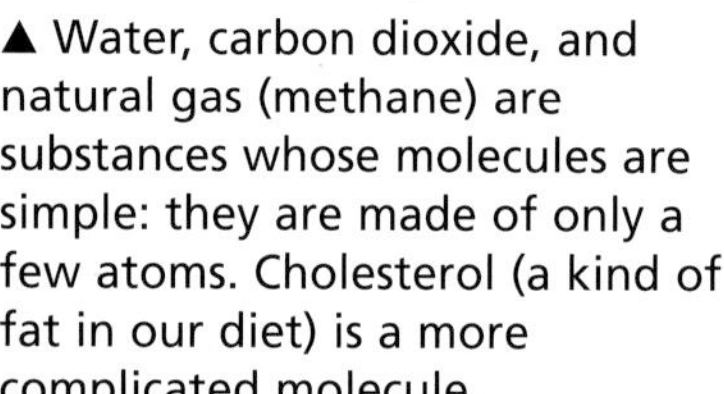

▲ Water, carbon dioxide, and natural gas (methane) are substances whose molecules are simple: they are made of only a few atoms. Cholesterol (a kind of fat in our diet) is a more complicated molecule.

Rutherford, a New Zealander living in Britain, carried out experiments with atomic particles. He concluded that atoms were mostly empty space, with a small blob of matter at the centre. He called this the nucleus. The nucleus has a positive charge, balancing the negative charge of the electrons. Rutherford thought of the electrons as flying around the nucleus like planets orbiting the Sun.

Today, scientists think of electrons as more like clouds of negative electrical charge around the nucleus. We also know that the nucleus is made up of smaller particles called protons and neutrons. Protons have a positive electrical charge, and in an atom there are the same number of protons as electrons. Opposite electrical charges attract each other, and this attraction keeps the atom together. Scientists now think that protons and neutrons are themselves made of still smaller particles, called quarks. They have also found all kinds of other particles that are smaller than atoms.

If an atom was the size of a sports stadium, then the nucleus would be the size of a housefly sitting on the grass at the centre.

Isotopes

Atoms of a particular element all have the same number of protons and the same number of electrons. But there may be different numbers of neutrons in different atoms, giving them different masses (weights). These different

◀ Ernest Rutherford (right) in 1908, with the equipment he later used to discover the atomic nucleus. The other man is Hans Geiger (1882–1945), who invented the Geiger counter used to measure radioactivity.

▶ Scientists use enormous machines called particle accelerators to discover and find out about subatomic particles (particles smaller than atoms). This is part of the 'Main Ring' accelerator in the USA. The circular tunnel housing it is over 6 km long.

▶ By far the commonest isotope of the element carbon is carbon-12. Carbon has two other isotopes, carbon-13 and carbon-14, but these are much rarer in natural carbon.

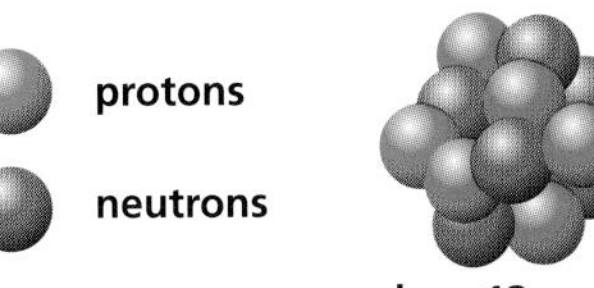

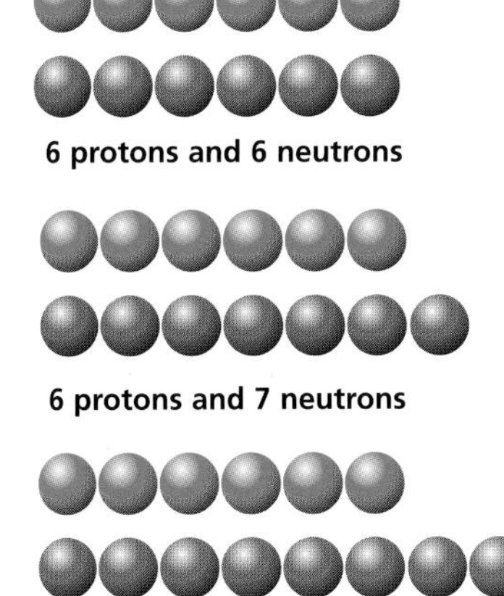

carbon-12 nucleus — 6 protons and 6 neutrons

carbon-13 nucleus — 6 protons and 7 neutrons

carbon-14 nucleus — 6 protons and 8 neutrons

▼ Scientists have found many ways to detect subatomic particles. This computer simulation shows the kinds of tracks made by various particles. For example, the yellow lines are the paths of particles called muons.

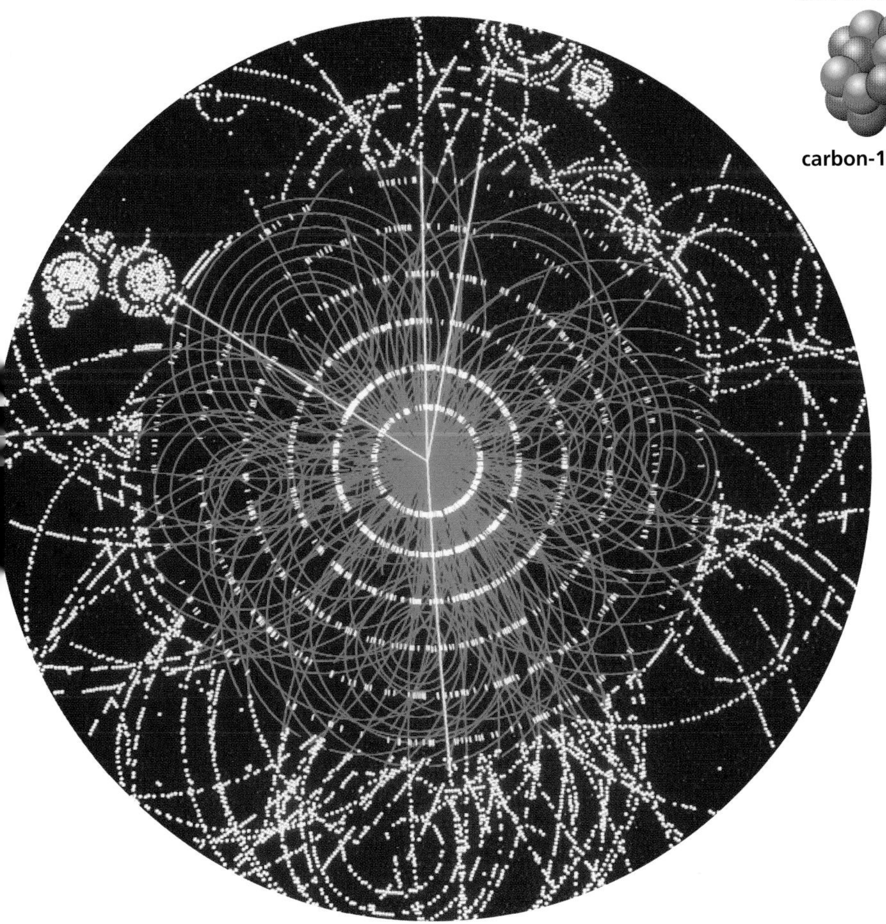

versions of the element are called isotopes. To identify different isotopes scientists write the total number of protons and neutrons in the isotope after the name of the element. For example, carbon-14 is an isotope of carbon with 6 protons and 8 neutrons in each atom.

Different isotopes of the same element behave in the same way in chemical reactions, but they may have different physical properties. For example, carbon-14 is radioactive, but carbon-12 is not. However, both isotopes can combine with oxygen chemically to make the compound carbon dioxide. Most elements found in nature are a mixture of different isotopes.

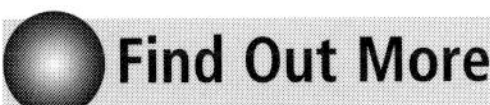

Find Out More

- Elements and compounds
- Matter
- Nuclear energy
- Periodic tables
- Radioactivity

Ions

In an atom, the positive electrical charges of the protons are balanced by the negative electrical charges of the electrons. The atom is therefore electrically neutral. However, if you add or take away one or more electrons from an atom, it becomes either negatively or positively charged. Such charged particles are called ions.

If you combine sodium and chlorine atoms, you can make a chemical called sodium chloride – common salt. When salt is made, the sodium atoms each give an electron to a chlorine atom. When this happens, the atoms become ions. The sodium ion has a positive charge and the chloride ion has a negative charge. The ions are attracted to each other, because opposite electrical charges attract. This is known as ionic bonding.

▼ Ions with opposite charges (+ and –) are attracted to each other.

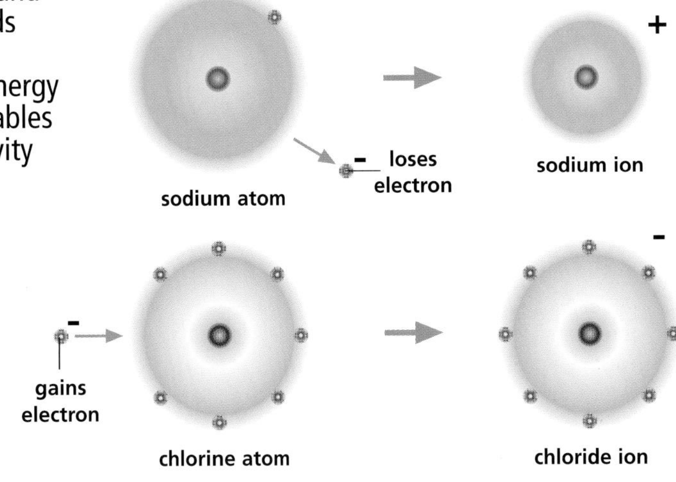

Bacteria and viruses

Your body is carrying over 100,000 billion hitchhikers. They are bacteria, the most abundant life forms on Earth. The bacteria that live on you are just a tiny fraction of the millions of different kinds of bacteria that exist.

Bacteria can only be seen with a very powerful microscope. A typical bacterial cell is about 1000 times smaller than an animal cell. Viruses are even smaller, and are not made up of cells. These tiny packages of genetic material are not true living things because they cannot grow and reproduce on their own. They come to life inside living cells, and some of them cause diseases such as the common cold, measles and Aids. They have to invade other cells in order to make copies of themselves.

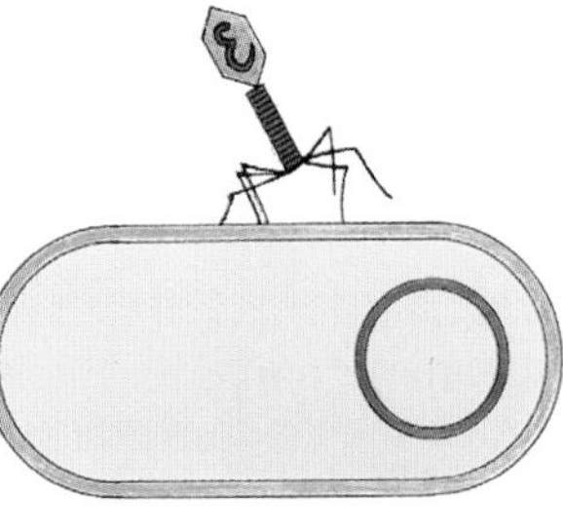

1. Virus lands on cell wall of bacterium.

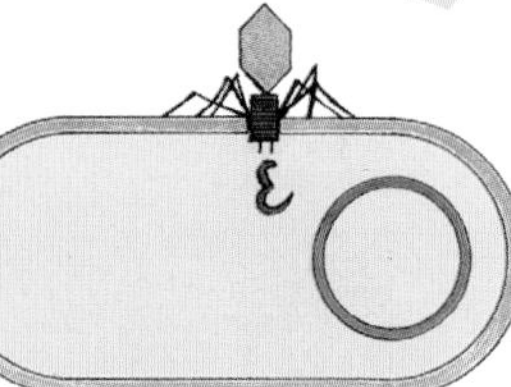

2. Tail of virus injects genetic material into bacterium.

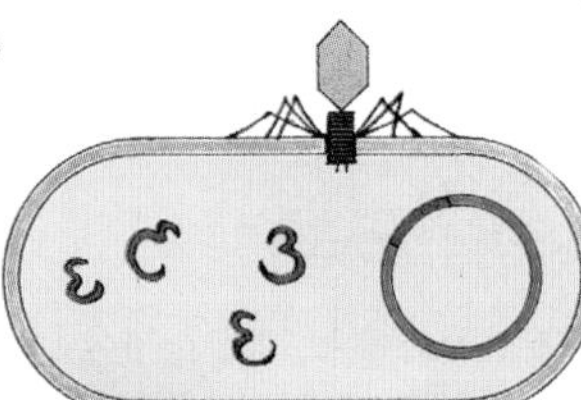

3. Bacterium makes copies of virus's genetic material and protein coating.

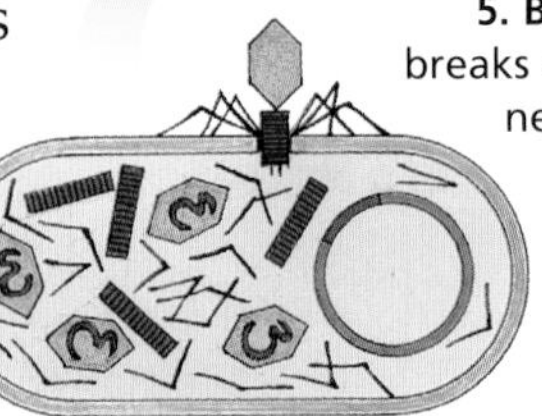

4. Parts of new viruses come together.

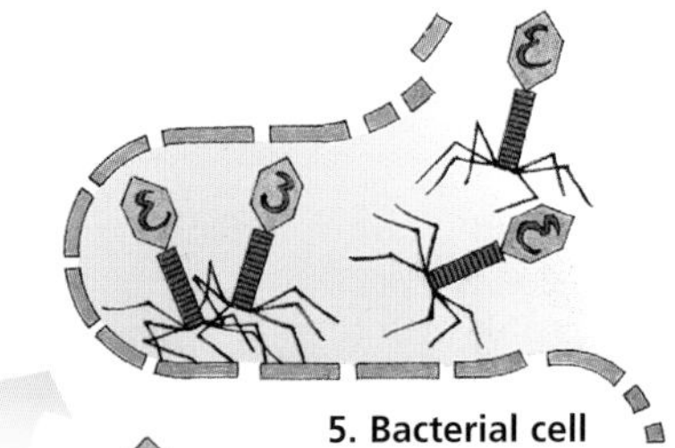

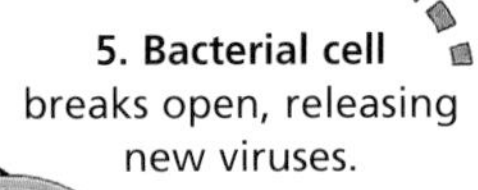

5. Bacterial cell breaks open, releasing new viruses.

▲ Viruses called bacteriophages invade the cells of bacteria. They 'hijack' the cell's chemical processes, so that, instead of working normally, the cell makes copies of the virus.

Inside bacteria

Most bacteria consist of just one microscopic cell, without a control centre, or nucleus. Instead, bacteria have just a single loop of genetic instructions, or DNA.

Most bacteria have rigid cell walls with a slimy outer covering. The cell walls are usually covered with tiny hairs. There are also larger strands called flagella, which help the bacteria to move.

Helpful and harmful bacteria

Most bacteria are harmless or even useful – sometimes extremely so. People use bacteria to make yoghurt and cheese, and some bacteria are used to 'grow' proteins such as insulin, which is used to treat diabetes. Bacteria play a vital role in breaking down natural wastes. But other bacteria, sometimes called germs, cause diseases such as cholera, tetanus and typhoid.

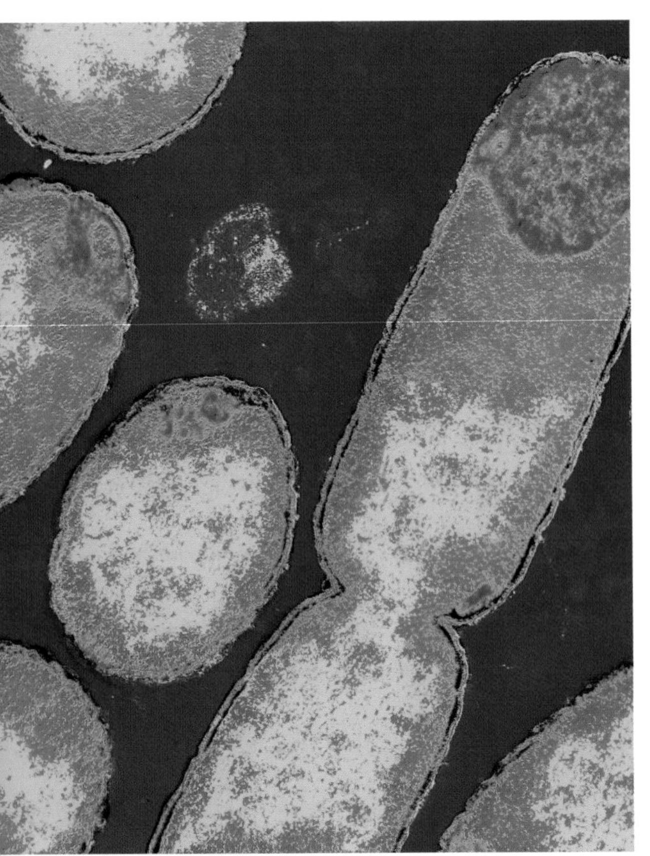

◀ Dividing *Bacillus* bacterium. A bacterium can divide into two once every 30 minutes, producing (in theory) 8 million new bacteria in a day. Fortunately, the numbers of bacteria are limited by the available food and space.

In theory, one bacterium could produce nearly 5000 billion billion offspring in 24 hours.

Find Out More

- Cells
- Diseases
- Drugs
- Genetics

Batteries and cells

There's a car accident, and someone who saw the crash uses their mobile phone to call an ambulance. Minutes later, the injured are being rushed to hospital. The time saved by using a mobile phone could help to save their lives.

Portable gadgets like mobile phones and portable TVs can be extremely useful. But to be portable, they have to get their power from batteries. A battery is a clever collection of chemicals that can react together to make electricity.

Find Out More

- Circuits
- Electricity
- Hydrogen
- Renewable resources

Electrical chemistry

How does a battery release electrons? It does so through a carefully chosen pair of chemical reactions. A battery can have one or more parts, called cells. Each cell has two pieces of metal (the electrodes) dipped in a chemical called an electrolyte.

▼ Solar power. Out in space, satellites cannot be serviced or refuelled. Many of them rely on huge solar panels to generate the electricity they need to work.

BATTERY VARIETY

Different types of battery use different chemicals to produce electricity. A car has a powerful, rechargeable lead-acid battery (a). The electrodes are made of lead compounds, while the electrolyte is an acid. A personal stereo uses an alkaline battery (b). In this the electrodes are powders, mixed with an electrolyte to make a paste.

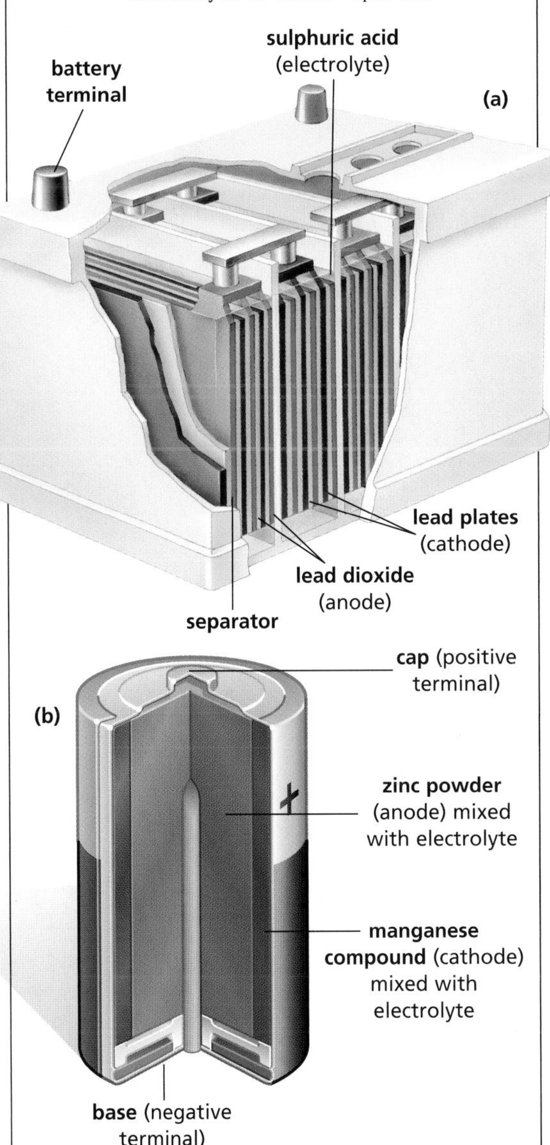

When a battery is connected up, chemical reactions takes place between the electrodes and the electrolyte. At one electrode (the negative terminal or anode), there is a chemical reaction that produces electrons. These electrons can then flow as electricity. At the other electrode (the positive terminal or cathode), another chemical reaction uses up electrons.

Bauxite *see* Aluminium • **Beaufort scale** *see* Winds • **Bell, Alexander Graham** *see* Telephones

Dissolving away

The chemical reactions that happen at the anode and the cathode of a battery affect the materials that they are made of. The anode slowly dissolves away, while the cathode becomes encrusted with chemicals. In some kinds of battery this process cannot be reversed, and the anode eventually wears out. This is what happens when a battery goes flat. But in a rechargeable battery, the chemical reactions that make the battery work can be reversed by connecting the battery up to an electricity supply and running it in reverse. This is what happens when you use a charger to recharge a battery.

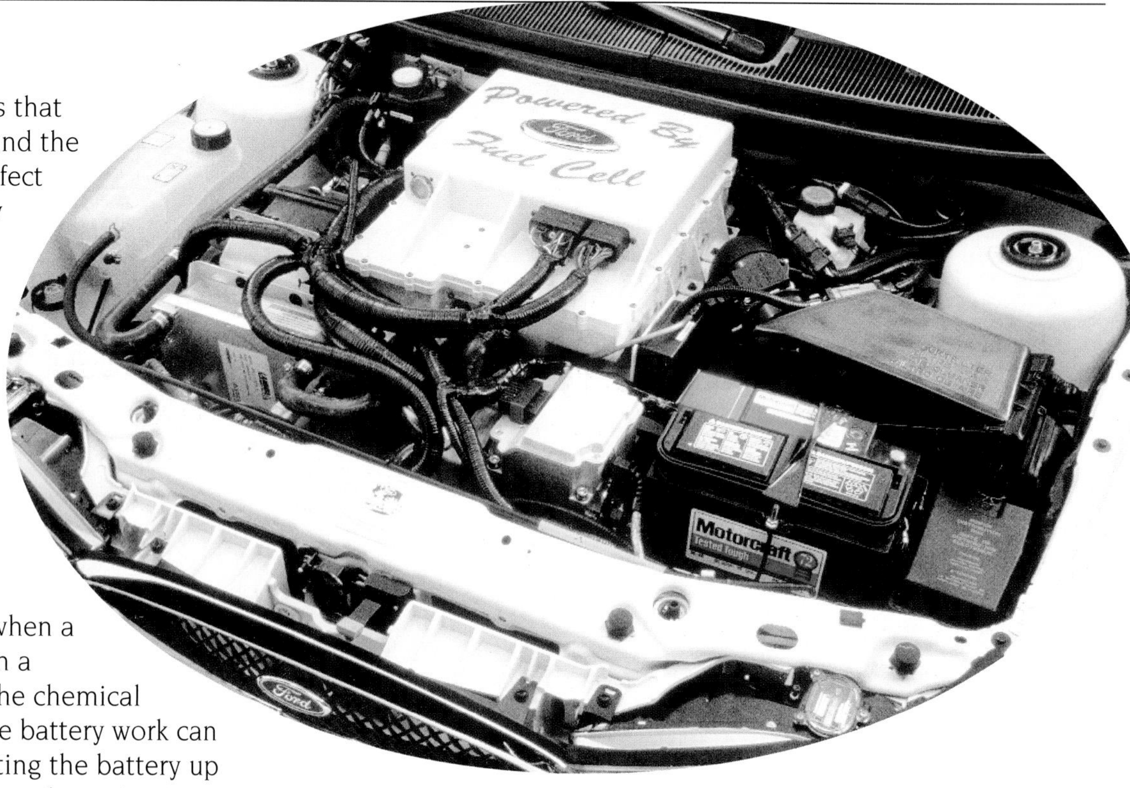

▲ The electric motor that drives this experimental car is powered by a fuel cell instead of a battery.

Solar cells and fuel cells

Batteries are not the only portable sources of electric power – solar cells and fuel cells can also make electricity.

A solar cell makes electricity using sunlight. Inside the cell are special materials that release electrons when they are bathed in light. Solar cells are used for example in space probes and satellites. At present they are not very efficient – they can only turn about 15 per cent of the light that falls on them into electrical energy. But scientists hope to make better solar cells in the future.

Fuel cells make electricity using hydrogen as a fuel. A chemical reaction in the fuel cell turns the hydrogen into water, at the same time producing electrons that can flow in a circuit. But hydrogen is difficult and dangerous to store, so engineers are now trying to make fuel cells safe. Fuel cells are more powerful than batteries, and scientists hope that they can soon be used to power cars. Tiny fuel cells may also be used to power personal stereos and tiny 'wearable' computers.

GALVANI AND VOLTA

In 1791 an Italian anatomist called Luigi Galvani (1737–1798) was probing a dead frog's nerves with tools made of different metals. He noticed that when he did this, the frog's leg muscles twitched. Alessandro Volta (1745–1827) at the University of Pavia heard about Galvani's discovery. Volta worked out that the twitching was caused by electricity. The metal instruments were acting like electrodes in a battery, while the fluids in the frog's body were the electrolyte.

Alessandro Volta

This discovery inspired Volta to developed the voltaic pile, in 1799. The pile was a battery with a number of cells, each with one electrode of zinc and one of silver, with a layer of card soaked in salt water between them. This was the world's first-ever battery.

Volta's pile

Luigi Galvani

Benz, Karl *see* Cars and trucks • **Bessemer, Henry** *see* Iron and steel

Bicycles and motorcycles

With a strong, light frame, chunky tyres, good suspension and up to 24 gears, a mountain bike is designed for off-road use. It lets you go where you want – along muddy tracks, down rocky slopes, through streams and over potholes.

▲ Motorbikes are used for fun as well as for transport. These jumping motorbikes are competing in a moto-cross race.

Mountain bikes are specially built for rough riding. The frames are built more strongly than road bike frames, they have better brakes, and extra-low gears for getting up really steep slopes. But they are heavier than road bikes, and the chunky tyres make them harder work on smooth roads.

Bicycle basics

All bicycles work in much the same way. They have a strong, light frame and spoked wheels, fitted with air-filled tyres. They are driven by a chain, which connects the pedals with the rear wheel.

Bicycle frames are most commonly made from steel, or an alloy (mixture) of steel and a lighter metal. But expensive bikes have super-light frames made of aluminium, titanium, or plastic reinforced with carbon fibre.

Most bicycles have several gears. The commonest kind are called derailleur gears. They have different-sized gear wheels attached to the pedals and on the rear wheel. A mechanism shifts the chain from one gear wheel to another.

Under power

Motorcycles are a cross between a bicycle and a motor car. Like a bicycle, they are steered by the front wheel, and most have the rear wheel driven by a chain. Like a car, they have a petrol engine, a clutch and a gearbox. Some motorbikes have a shaft instead of a chain connecting the engine to the rear wheel.

Motorcycles have similar kinds of brakes to a car. They work by hydraulic (liquid) pressure. Applying the brakes forces tough pads to grip a disc mounted on the wheel.

Find Out More

- Cars and trucks
- Petrol and diesel engines

▼ Bicycle technology has improved enormously in recent years. New frame materials, brake designs, and front and rear suspension are just some of the changes that have been introduced.

one-click levers quickly move the gear mechanism from one gear wheel to the next

lightweight wheels are made of aluminium alloy or carbon fibre. They may have a few large spokes, or even be solid

cantilever brakes pivot as the lever is pulled, to press the brake blocks against the wheel

new frame designs are possible using materials such as carbon-fibre plastics

suspension at front and rear smooths the ride over rough ground

Big bang *see* Universe • **Binary** *see* Computers

Birds

Swooping silently through the night like a white ghost, a hungry barn owl searches for a meal. Its keen hearing picks up the faint rustling sounds of a mouse scuttling through the leaves. The owl closes in on its victim, its sharp talons sinking into the mouse's warm, furry body.

wing
crown
primary flight feathers
body feathers
bill (beak)
breast
rump
tail
scaly leg

▲ A small bird such as the blue tit has about 3000 feathers, which grow out of pits in the skin, like our hairs. Feathers keep a bird warm, give it shape, colour and pattern and help most birds to fly.

The barn owl is one of nearly 9000 different species (kinds) of birds, which range from the bee-sized hummingbird to the giant ostrich. Birds are different from all other animals in the world because they have feathers. They have wings instead of arms and are the largest, fastest and most powerful flying animals alive today. Birds are also warm-blooded. They can keep their bodies warm no matter how hot or cold it is, so they can live all over the world.

Feathered fliers

Birds are very efficient flying machines. They are very light, partly because many of their bones are hollow. The feathers of a bird give it a smooth, streamlined shape, which helps it to slip easily through the air. The curved shape of the wings helps to lift a bird up into the air, and powerful chest muscles beat the wings up and down.

Flying uses up huge amounts of energy, so birds need to eat plenty of food. They have very efficient lungs to breathe in plenty of oxygen, which they need to 'burn' their food and release energy.

barb
stem
barbules

► A feather is made up of a central stem with side branches (barbs) that are linked together by hooked barbules. If the hooks come apart they can be 'zipped' up again.

▼ Frigate birds can soar and glide like vultures but are also fast and agile fliers, like birds of prey. The spectacular red throat sac of the male helps to impress a female during courtship.

BIRDS' BILLS

The size and shape of a bird's bill depend mainly on what it eats and where it finds its food. The curlew uses its long bill to find worms hidden deep in the mud. The pelican catches fish in its stretchy throat pouch. The flamingo uses its bill as a sieve to strain tiny creatures from the water. The eagle tears the flesh of its prey with its hooked bill. The hawfinch uses its short, strong bill to crack hard seeds.

Find Out More

- Animals
- Classification
- Ecology
- Life

Bird food

Different kinds of bird eat different kinds of food. Some birds are vegetarians, eating fruit, seeds, nuts or leaves. Others eat insects and worms. Many are meat-eaters, catching fish, amphibians, birds and small mammals. The most efficient hunters are the birds of prey, like the eagle and falcon.

Did all the dinosaurs really die out 65 million years ago? Perhaps they didn't. Some scientists think that birds – including the birds in your garden – may be the direct descendants of the dinosaurs.

◀ Ovenbirds and weaver birds build unusual nests. A pair of ovenbirds makes a strong nest the size of a football out of mud and cow dung. Male weaver birds make their nests by weaving together pieces of grass.

Courtship and mating

Male birds are usually more colourful than females and sing or perform daring acrobatics to persuade females to mate with them. After mating, birds lay eggs. They would be too heavy to fly if they carried their young around inside them.

Many baby birds are naked when they hatch from the eggs. They stay safe and warm inside a nest while they grow their feathers. Other birds, such as ducks and geese, hatch out with fluffy feathers. They can run around soon after hatching and feed themselves.

▶ Penguins, such as these emperors, have stiff, strong wings, which they use like flippers to swim very fast underwater. Their wings are no use for flying. Other birds that do not fly include ostriches, emus, and kiwis.

Birth *see* Human reproduction • **Black holes** *see* Galaxies • **Blood** *see* Heart and blood • **Body** *see* Humans

Bones and muscles

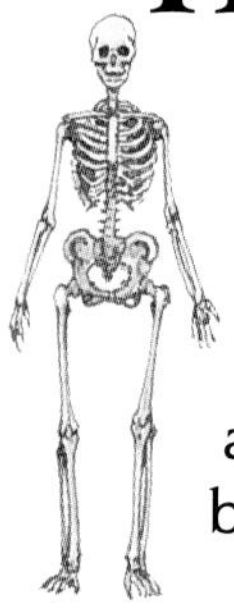

The longest bone in your body is your thigh bone (femur). Your smallest bone is in your ear. It is about the size of a grain of rice.

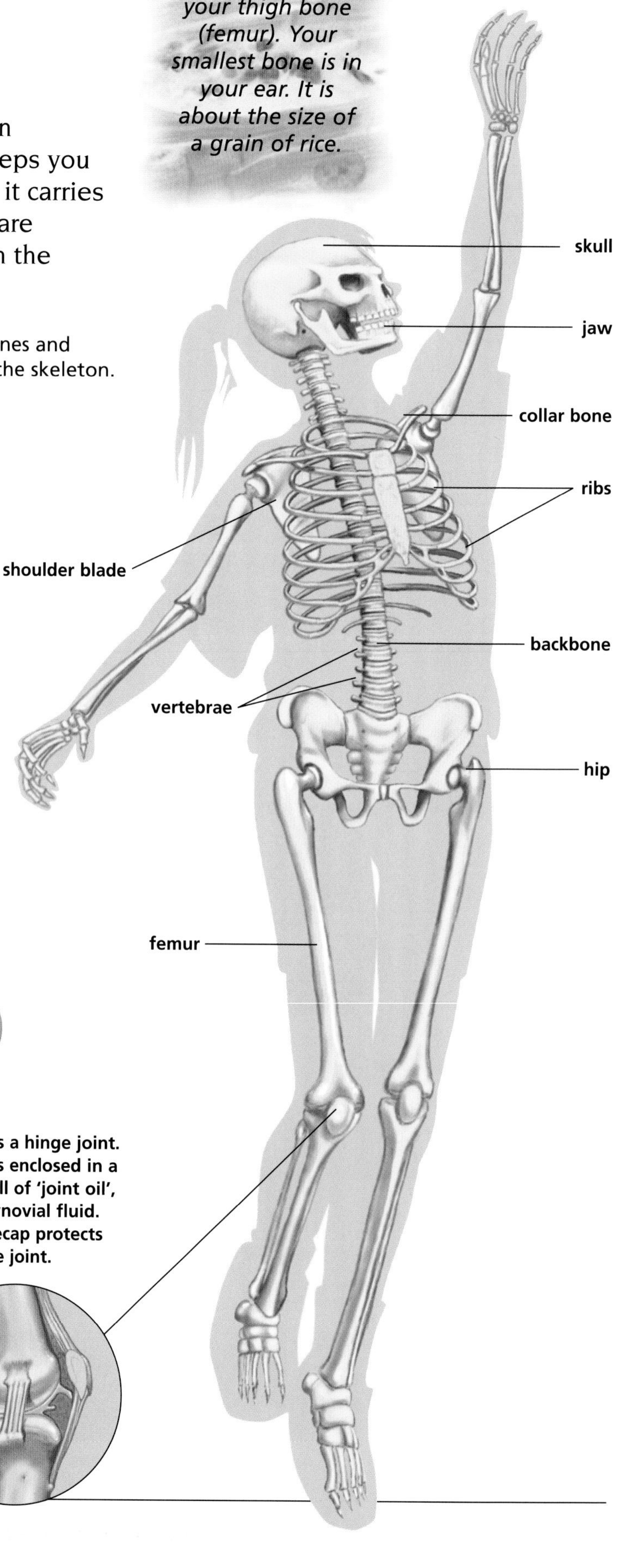

Your skeleton is a scaffolding of more than 200 living bones. It supports you and keeps you upright. The skeleton may seem fragile, but it carries the whole weight of the body. Your muscles are attached to this bony scaffolding. They pull on the bones to make you move.

The word skeleton comes from a Greek word meaning dried up, but bones are not dry or brittle. Bones are alive. They grow as we do, repair themselves if they are broken and become stronger as we exercise. A living bone has layers of hard calcium phosphate on the outside, and a honeycomb of hard bone and living cells within. This makes it strong and light.

▶ The bones and joints of the skeleton.

skull
jaw
collar bone
ribs
shoulder blade
backbone
vertebrae
hip
femur

Bony protection

Most organs of the body are soft and delicate. Our bones protect these soft organs from injury. The skull bones, for example, fit tightly together to form a tough case for the brain. The ribs form a rigid cage around the lungs and heart, and the hip bones enclose the bladder and intestines.

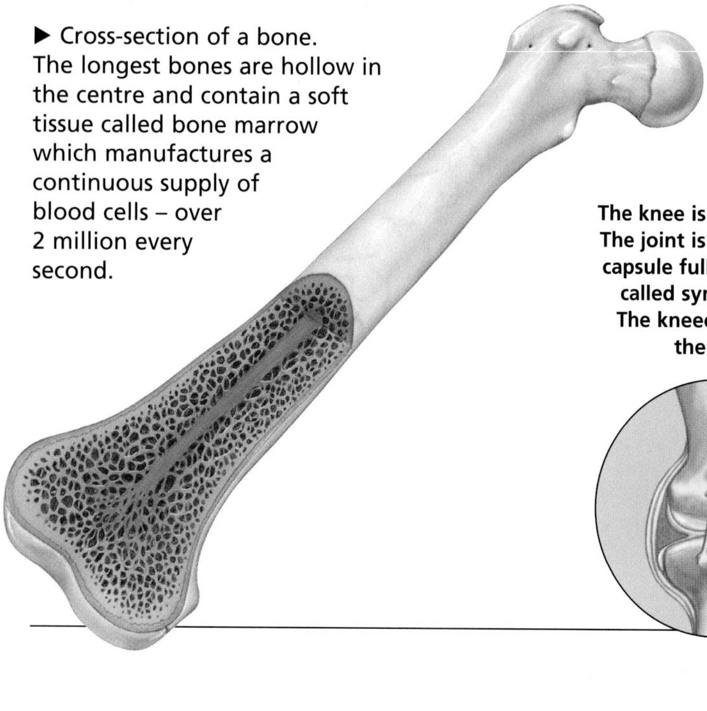

▶ Cross-section of a bone. The longest bones are hollow in the centre and contain a soft tissue called bone marrow which manufactures a continuous supply of blood cells – over 2 million every second.

The knee is a hinge joint. The joint is enclosed in a capsule full of 'joint oil', called synovial fluid. The kneecap protects the joint.

Find Out More
- Brain and nerves
- Ears
- Heart and blood

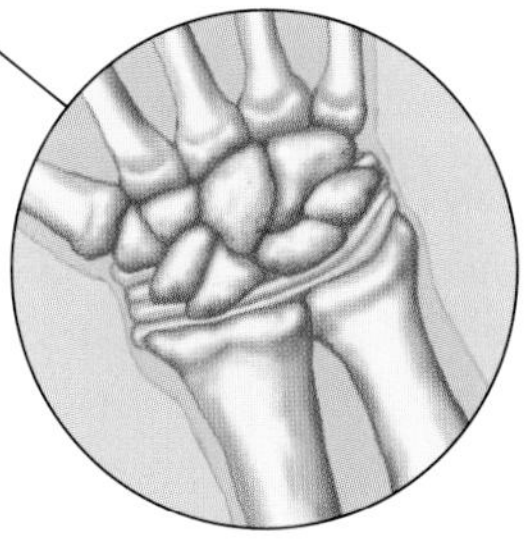

The wrist contains many small bones so we can move it in several directions.

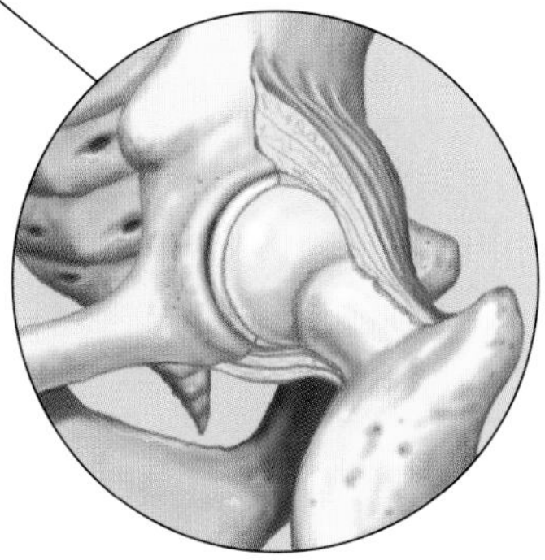

The hip joint is a ball-and-socket joint. It is very strong and stable and is surrounded by muscles.

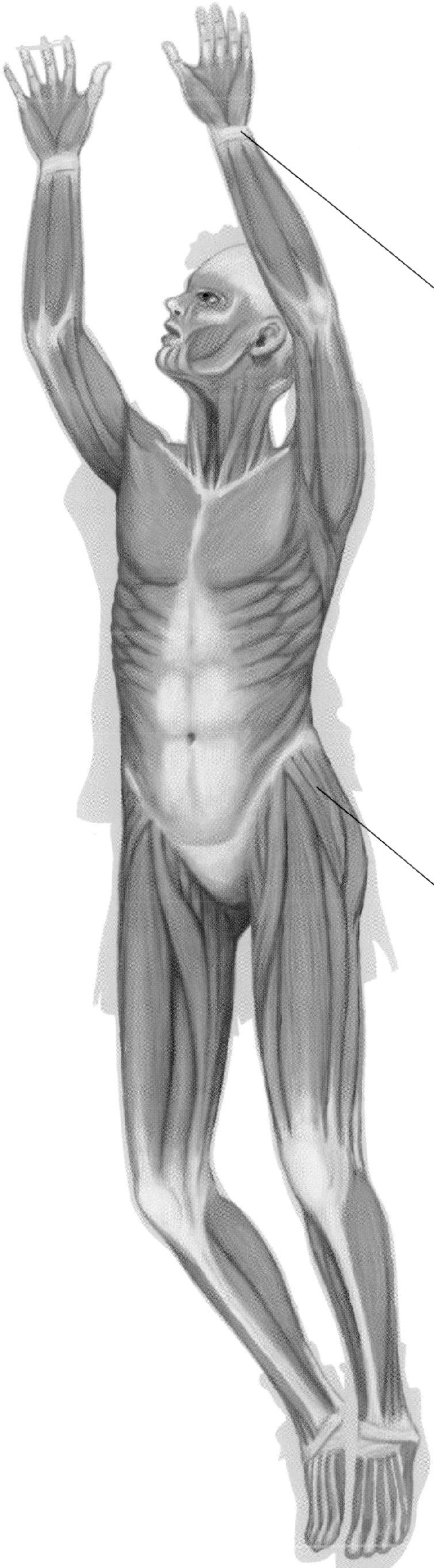

◀ Some of the outer muscles of the body.

Joints

Bones join each other at joints. We have different types of joint for moving in different ways. Hinge joints at the knee and elbow allow our limbs to bend like the hinge on a door. Ball-and-socket joints at the shoulder and hip allow movement in almost any direction. Each individual joint in the spine allows only a little movement, but together the 20 or so joints in our back allow us to twist and bend with ease.

Muscles and movement

Muscles account for about 40 per cent of the body's weight. We have about 600 muscles that we can control at will. These are our skeletal muscles. But we have other muscles that work automatically, such as the heart muscles, muscles in the digestive system and muscles involved in breathing.

Muscles are usually attached to two bones across a joint. Within every muscle are thousands of long, thin muscle fibres, collected together in bundles. Nerve connections from the brain run through the bundles of muscle fibres. The fibres contract (shorten) when they get a signal from the nerves to do so.

▼ Muscles can only move us by contracting. Contraction is a pulling force. Because an individual muscle can only pull, muscles usually work in pairs. One muscle contracts to move a joint in one direction. Its partner contracts to move the joint back again. In the upper arm, the biceps muscle contracts to bend the arm, while the triceps contracts to straighten it.

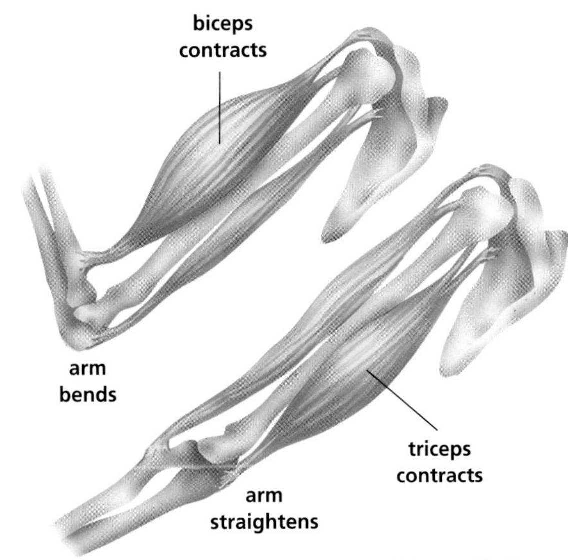

Botany *see* Plants • **Boyle, Robert** *see* Gases

Brain and nerves

▶ Nerves connect from the brain to every part of your body. Most nerves run down the spinal cord, then branch to every part of the body.

Every second, hundreds of tiny pulses of electricity shoot through your body along living wires called nerves. The electrical pulses are messengers, carrying information about the outside world to your brain, and instructions from your brain to the rest of your body.

Your brain and nerves together make up the nervous system. The 'main road' of this nervous system is the spinal cord, which runs from the brain down the inside of the spine. Nerves branch off from the spinal cord to every part of your body. Some carry messages to the brain from your internal organs and your senses. The brain sorts the information it receives and sends out messages via other nerves to control everything from your blood pressure to the way you move.

Nerve cells

Nerve cells, or neurons, can transmit electrical messages at high speed. Each neuron has several 'inputs', called dendrites, along which messages travel into the main cell. Leading out from the cell is a single 'output', the axon. This connects to another nerve, or to a muscle or other cell. Neurons do not touch one another. Messages cross the gap, or synapse, between one neuron and the next with the help of a chemical.

Outside the brain, neurons connect to each other in simple pathways. But within the brain itself, the neurons are interconnected in an amazingly complex network. Only some of these billions upon billions of interconnections are ever used. But new pathways are always opening up as we have new experiences, learn new things, and lay down new memories.

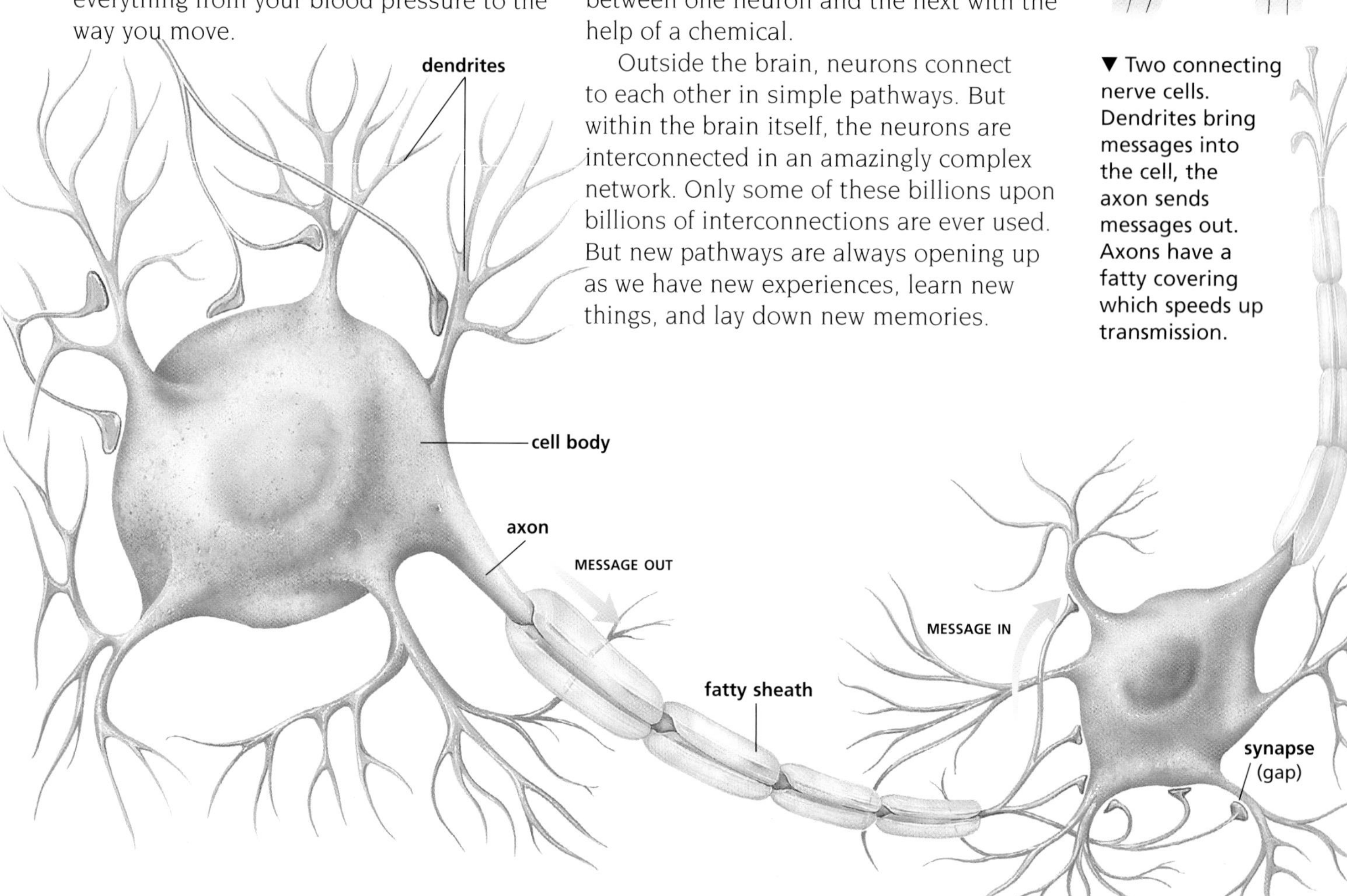

▼ Two connecting nerve cells. Dendrites bring messages into the cell, the axon sends messages out. Axons have a fatty covering which speeds up transmission.

▶ The different parts of the brain.

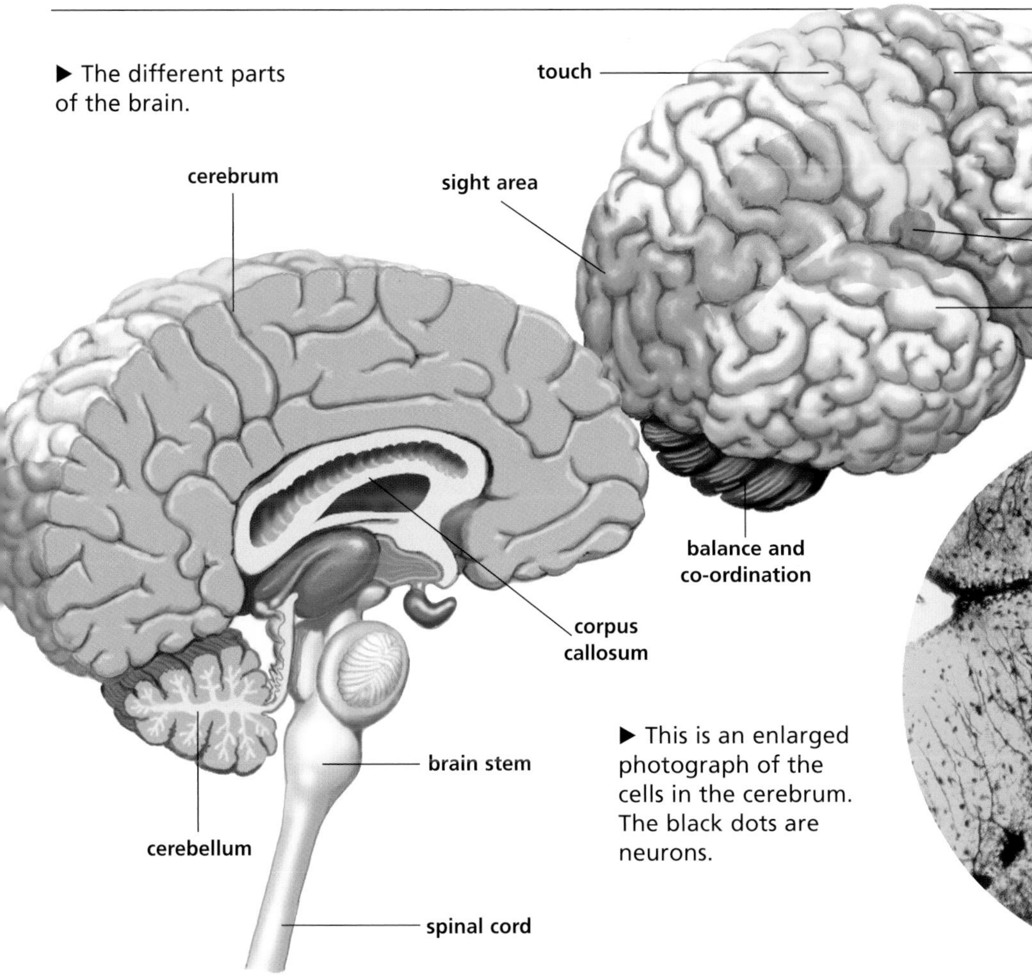

touch
motor area
cerebrum
sight area
speech centre
taste
hearing centre
balance and co-ordination
corpus callosum
brain stem
cerebellum
spinal cord

▶ This is an enlarged photograph of the cells in the cerebrum. The black dots are neurons.

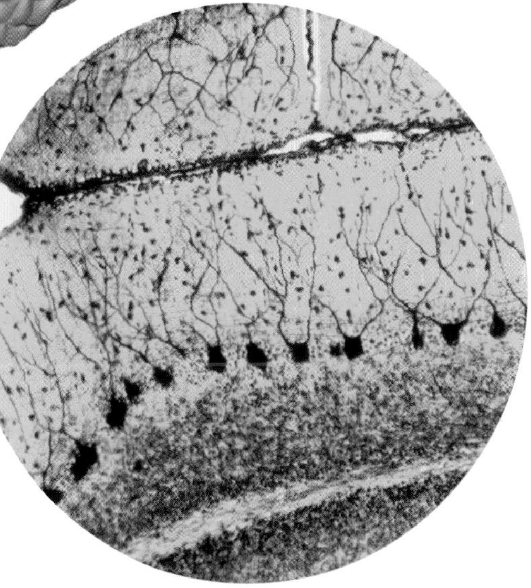

Automatic pilot

There are three important areas of the brain, each one responsible for different kinds of action. Close to the spinal cord is the brain stem. This controls automatic activities such as breathing and digestion. At the back of the brain is the cerebellum. This co-ordinates movement, conscious control and balance, allowing you to move smoothly.

The largest and most complicated part of the brain is the cerebrum. It controls your conscious actions, speech and all your senses. It also does all your thinking, and is the centre of memory and learning.

The cerebrum has two halves (cerebral hemispheres), linked by bundles of nerve fibres. Sensations from one side of the body connect to the opposite side of the brain, and movements of one side of the body are controlled by the other side of the brain. The right side is most important in artistic, creative tasks, while the left is responsible for understanding, reading and thinking.

The brain contains 100 billion neurons and there are as many again in the rest of the body.

Find Out More

- Bones and muscles
- Digestion
- Human senses
- Lungs and breathing
- Mind

INSTANT ACTIONS

Sometimes we do not have time to think – in an emergency we must act right away. For example, if you tread on a sharp stone with bare feet, you immediately pull your foot away. An action like this is called a reflex.

A simple reflex is controlled by the nerves of the spinal cord without involving the brain. Messages pass from pain receptors in the foot along a neuron to the spinal cord. Here, the messages trigger off an immediate return signal activating the muscles of the leg.

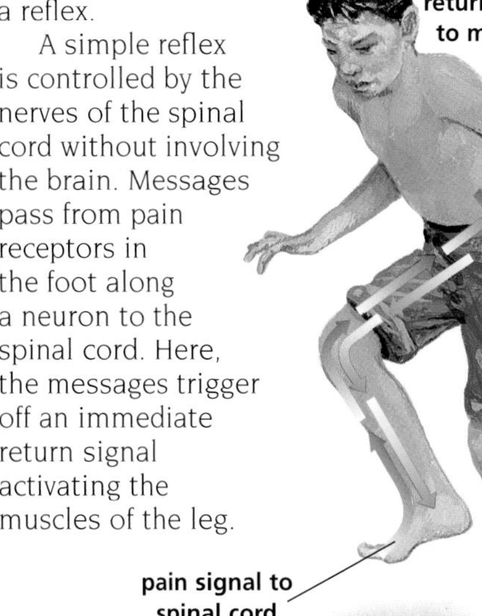

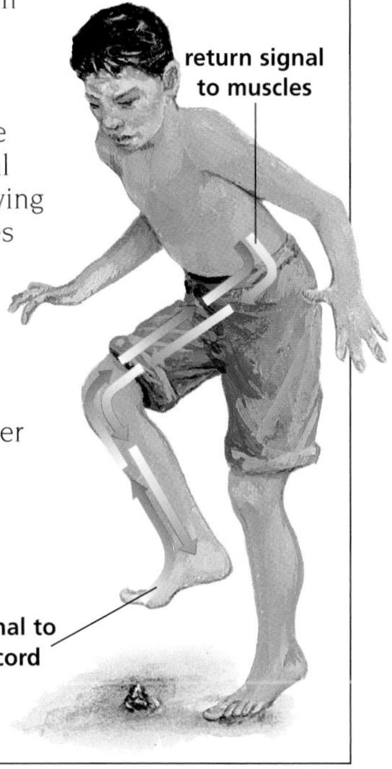

Bridges

When the bridge across the Great Belt in Denmark was finished early in 1998, it had the world's longest span – 1624 metres. But before it was officially opened in June, it had lost the record to the Akashi-Kaikyo bridge in Japan, which had a span of 1990 metres.

Both the Great Belt and the Akashi-Kaikyo bridges are suspension bridges. They are spectacular structures, in which the road deck hangs from a pair of steel cables. These cables pass over tall towers and are attached to anchor points at each end.

Like all big bridges, the Akashi-Kaikyo bridge is designed not only to take the weight of heavy traffic, but also to allow for the stresses created by wind. Designers worked out these stresses by testing scale models of the bridge in wind tunnels. They also gave the bridge added strength to help it resist earthquakes.

▶ Different kinds of bridges can span different widths. Suspension bridges can be built with the longest spans. Cable-stayed bridges are now widely built.

Beams and arches

There are many other kinds of bridge. The simplest and oldest kind is the beam bridge, which is made out of a beam supported at each end. Beams tend to sag in the middle, so simple beam bridges cannot cross a very wide gap.

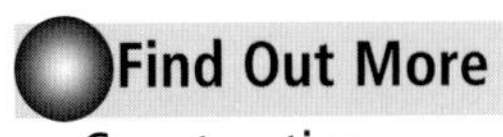

- Construction
- Flight and flow

A long beam bridge can be built if the beam is supported by piers (columns). Even longer spans can be built by using cables to stiffen the deck. This produces what is called a cable-stayed bridge, in which cables lead from the deck to a tall central tower.

Arch bridges can be used for wide spans too, because the weight of the bridge is carried down to the foundations by the arch shape.

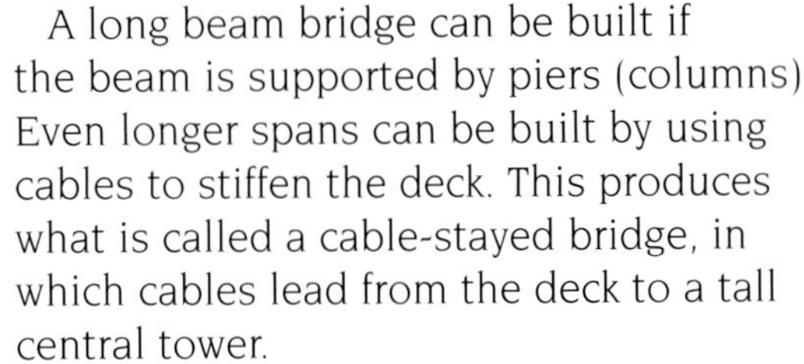

◀ The steel-arch Sydney Harbour Bridge (1932) has a central span of 503 metres. The deck carries eight traffic lanes and a railway.

Buildings

In the year 2000, the city of Kuala Lumpur in Malaysia boasted the world's tallest building – the Petronas Towers, which are 452 metres high. But work had already started on buildings that would be even taller. One was 7 South Dearborn in Chicago, USA. When it is completed in 2004, 7 South Dearborn will soar to 472 metres and become in its turn the world's tallest building, but probably not for long.

Very tall buildings like the Petronas Towers are called skyscrapers. The world's first skyscraper, the 10-storey Home Insurance Co. Building, was built in Chicago in 1885.

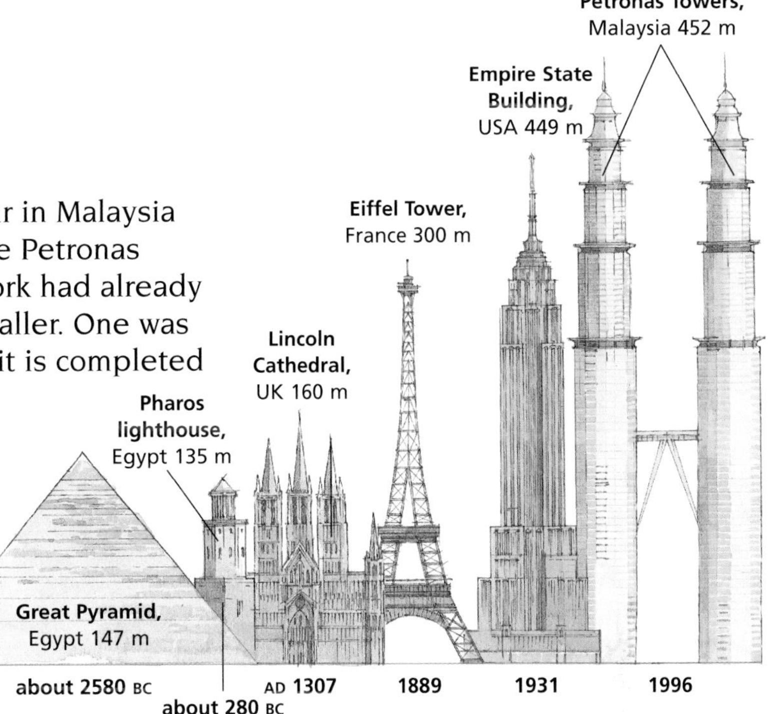

▲ Milestones in building construction over the ages, beginning with Egypt's Great Pyramid, completed in about 2580 BC. Like the Pharos lighthouse and Lincoln Cathedral, it was built of stone, unlike modern structures, which are built of steel and concrete.

Strong to the core

Skyscrapers and most large modern buildings are built with a skeleton of steel girders. Steel is immensely strong, and this is what makes it possible for buildings to soar to such dizzy heights. Many have a central core of reinforced concrete. The floors are built out from the core to an outer steel skeleton.

In these structures, the frame carries all the weight. This means that the walls can be built of thin and lightweight materials. The favourite material for walls is glass, which is fixed in an aluminium or stainless-steel frame. The glass is often covered with a very thin film of gold. This filters out sunlight, and prevents the building heating up like a greenhouse.

Building high

Some tall buildings are built to show off the wealth and importance of a company or city. Others are built for the very good reason that land in cities is scarce and expensive. It is cheaper to expand upwards rather than sideways.

Back home

When you build skyscrapers and tower blocks, the walls are built last. But the walls

▼ Immensely strong steel girders form the framework of this skyscraper, which towers above other city buildings.

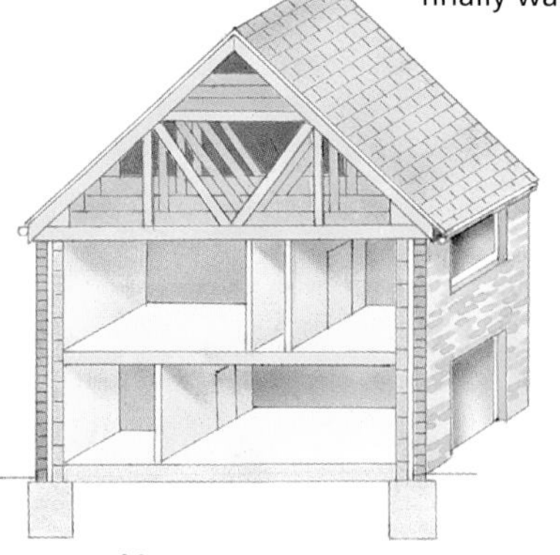

skin construction
skin (outer walls) built first to support floors and roof

frame construction
steel frame is built first, then floors and finally walls

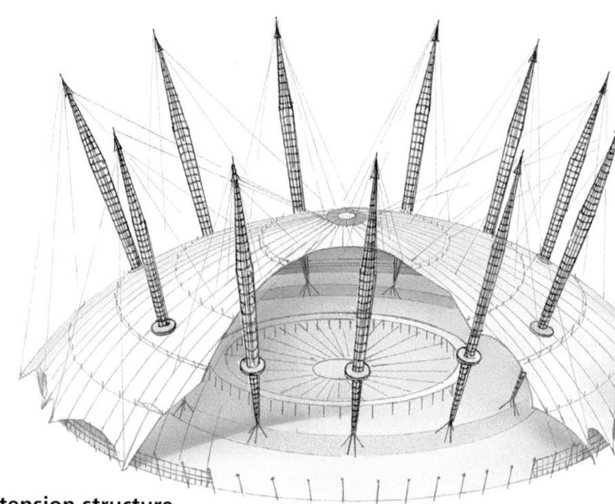

tension structure
steel masts and cables provide support for fabric roof

▲ Three quite different methods of building. Ordinary houses are built with outer supporting walls. Tower blocks and skyscrapers have a metal frame to support their weight. Tension structures are an exciting new way of building. They have tent-like roofs supported by cables.

of an ordinary house are built first because they carry all the weight of the building.

Bricks have been a common material for walling for thousands of years. Early bricks were made of mud and dried in the sun. Modern bricks are made of a clay mixture, and baked in a high-temperature kiln (oven). They are bonded together with a cement mortar.

Many buildings are built with timber frames. Such buildings may be built up of standard sections, which are made elsewhere and then just put together on site. This prefabricated (ready-built) method greatly speeds up construction.

Tension structures

Some of the most exciting buildings being built today are known as tension structures. They include the Hajj airport terminal in Saudi Arabia and London's Millennium Dome. They have tent-like roofs, supported by steel cables in tension. The roofing material is a strong and long-lasting plastic composite.

Domes are a common method of covering large areas, such as sports stadiums. Usually they are supported around the edge. The Pontiac Silverdome Stadium in Detroit, however, has a dome that has no visible means of support, either from below or above. Its fibreglass roof is supported by air pressure. Spectators enter the building through an airlock.

BUILDING WITH MUD

People who lived in what is now Palestine were building mud-brick houses 8000 years ago. And mud bricks, often called adobe, are still used today in countries with a hot, dry climate. They are made from mud and chopped straw, which helps strengthen them. Another traditional mud-building method, called wattle and daub, is used to fill in the spaces in timber-framed buildings. Mud (daub) is applied to a lattice of wooden sticks (wattle).

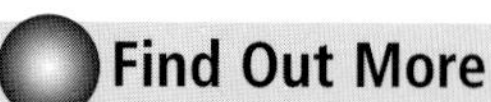

Find Out More

- Ceramics
- Construction

Calcium

What do sea shells, eggshells, milk, bones and teeth have in common? They all contain lots of calcium. Calcium is one of the commonest metals on Earth. It is found in many rocks – especially chalk, limestone and marble – in the form of calcium carbonate (a compound of calcium, carbon and oxygen).

Calcium belongs to a group of metallic elements that also includes beryllium, magnesium, strontium, barium and radium, which is radioactive.

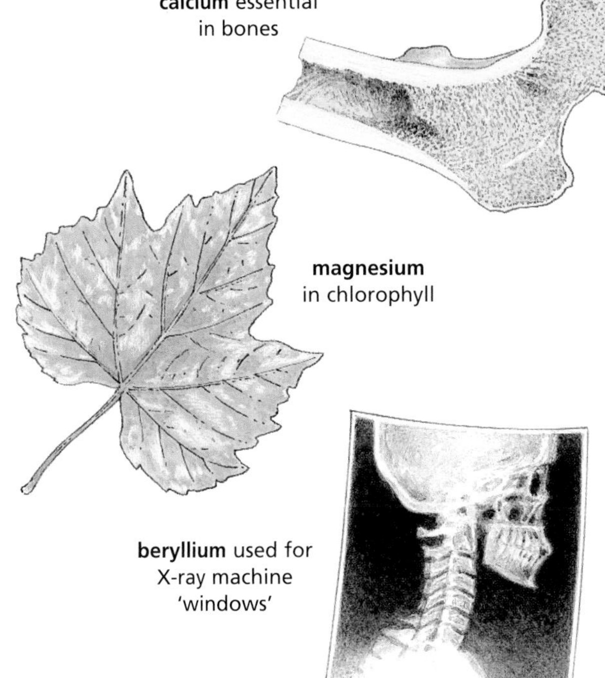

▶ Some important functions of the calcium family of elements.

Properties and uses

These metals appear in the same column in the periodic table of the elements. They behave similarly to soft metals such as sodium, but are less reactive, harder and have higher melting points.

The least reactive member of the group is beryllium. It is used in alloys (mixtures of metals) to make cutting tools where it is important to avoid sparks. Minerals containing beryllium don't show up on X-rays, and are used for the 'windows' of X-ray machines.

Magnesium is also used in alloys because it is strong and light. It is present in small quantities in living things. Most important of all, it is found in the chemical on which nearly all life on Earth depends – chlorophyll. Chlorophyll is a green pigment that can trap energy from sunlight. It is an important part of the process of photosynthesis, in which plants use the Sun's energy to make food from carbon dioxide and water.

Calcium is more reactive than beryllium or magnesium. When it reacts with air, a crust forms on its surface, stopping further reaction. Calcium is important in our diet, because it makes our bones strong. Calcium compounds have many uses, for example in the manufacture of cement, glass, fertilizers and explosives.

Find Out More
- Bones and muscles
- Metals and non-metals
- Periodic table
- Rocks
- X-rays

◀ These chalk cliffs are made from calcium carbonate. The chalk formed 80 million years ago as the shells of tiny sea creatures built up at the bottom of an ancient sea.

When you see a white flash in a firework display, that is magnesium burning. Red colours are produced by strontium compounds.

Calendars *see* Time • **Calories** *see* Diet

Cameras

Cameras are not just used for taking holiday snaps. They can reveal a world that we would not normally see. High-speed cameras can freeze very fast motion so we can see what is happening. They can even photograph a bullet in flight!

▶ The shutter of a high-speed camera had to open and close very quickly to 'freeze' the motion of this bullet as it cut through a playing card.

Cameras use a lens to make a small, upside-down picture on a film (or on an electronic plate, if it is a digital camera). The film is made from special chemicals that react to light. It 'remembers' the picture as a pattern of chemicals that have been changed by the light. Later the film can be developed using other chemicals to make the picture visible.

When you take a photograph, a metal blind called the shutter slides to one side. This lets light fall on the film. The shutter closes again after a short time. To get to the film, the light has to pass through an adjustable hole called the iris. If you are taking a photograph in dim light, the iris needs to be wide open to let as much light as possible fall on the film.

The right exposure

A picture will only come out correctly if the right amount of light is used. This can be done either by using a lot of light (big iris opening) for a very short time, or not much light (small iris opening) for longer. The combination of light and time is called the exposure.

Simple cameras used to have two or three exposure settings. These were labelled as bright, slightly cloudy or overcast. Most cameras today have light-sensitive circuits that set the exposure automatically.

Stay sharp

The picture formed by the lens will only be sharp if the lens is the right distance from the film. When the object you are taking a picture of is close, the lens needs to be moved away from the film. When the object is distant, the lens needs to be moved

▼ Just the right amount of light needs to fall on a film to get a good photograph. Too little light will make the photo very dark and murky (left). Too much light will make the photograph too bright and wash out the colours (right).

closer to the film. Changing the position of the lens like this is called focusing. Many cameras today can focus themselves. A tiny computer in the camera looks at how fuzzy the picture is. The computer controls a motor that moves the lens back and forth until the picture is sharp.

Find Out More

- Eyes
- Light
- Mirrors and lenses
- Movies
- Photography

▼ Press photographers at the Wimbledon tennis tournament. Professional photographers today use very sophisticated camera equipment.

Movie cameras

Movie cameras work rather like ordinary cameras, except that they take lots of pictures one after another (usually 24 every second). When the film is developed, each picture shows a 'frozen' image at one moment. Projected onto a screen at the right speed, the rapid series of still pictures gives the illusion of motion.

Digital cameras

In a digital camera, the lens forms the picture on a light-sensitive electronic plate. This changes the information about colour and light levels into a pattern of electric charge. The information is then digitized (turned into numbers) by microchips and stored on a memory card or, sometimes, on a disk similar to that in a computer. Often, there is a small screen to show you each picture taken, so that you can decide whether to keep it or not. Later, the camera or its removable card can be plugged into a printer or a PC (personal computer). With a PC, you can alter the images before printing the photos.

THE SLR CAMERA

Single-lens reflex (SLR) cameras are often used by professionals and other keen photographers.

There is a mirror behind the lens that reflects light to the viewfinder. The photographer can then see exactly what is coming through the lens. An electronic circuit measures the light coming through the lens to set the exposure.

The mirror prevents the light from reaching the shutter, so just before the picture is taken it flips up out of the way, so that light falls on the film when the shutter opens.

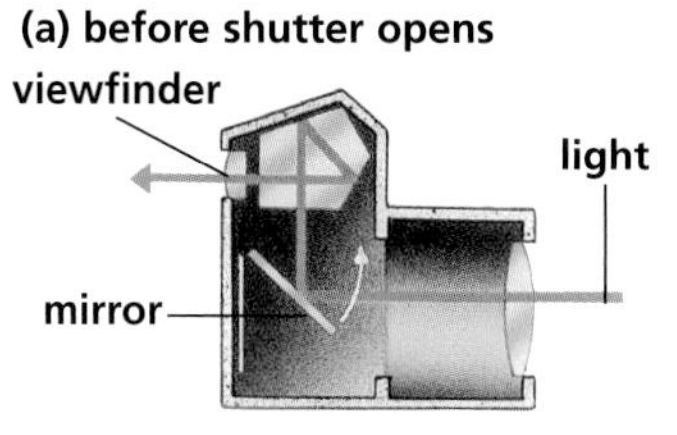

(a) before shutter opens

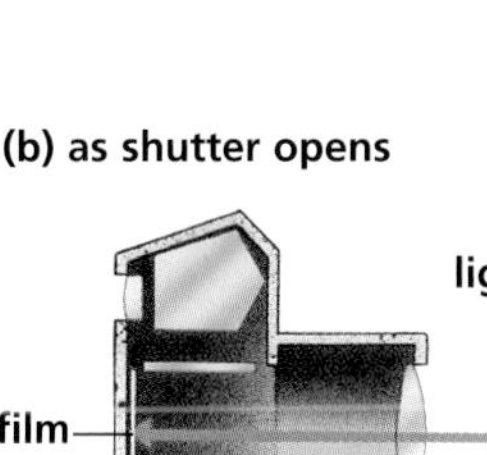

(b) as shutter opens

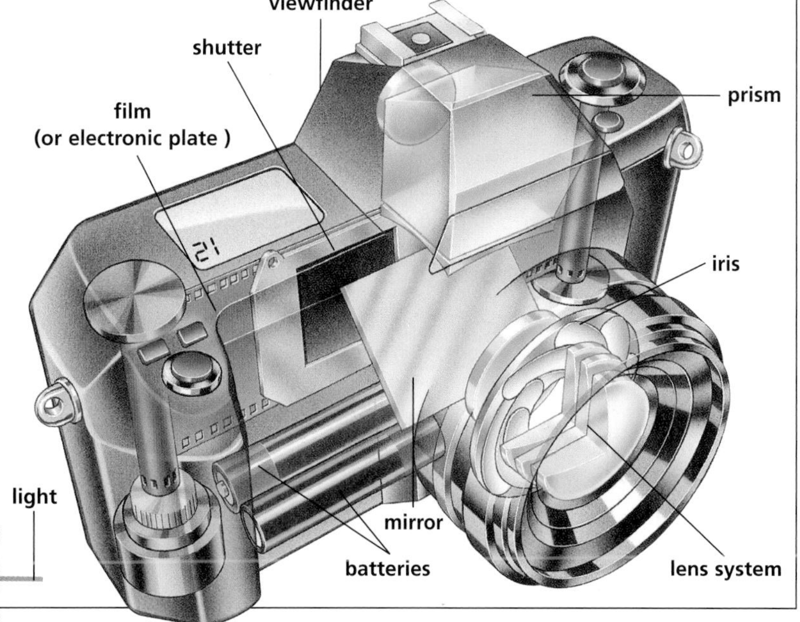

Cancers

Cells in our bodies are always dividing, as new cells replace old ones. But sometimes the process goes wrong, and a cancer cell is formed. Cancer cells divide rapidly and form growths called tumours. They can spread to take over a whole organ and stop it working properly. If cells break away from the tumour, they can travel to other parts of the body and start new tumours.

We do not know why some people get cancer while others don't, but faulty genes are certainly the cause of some cancers. Others are caused by chemicals in the environment, or by germs.

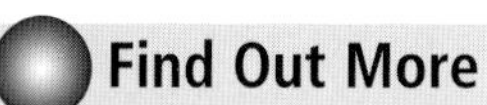
Find Out More
- Cells
- Diseases
- Health
- Immune system
- Medicine

Different cancers

Cancer is not a single disease – different cancers can affect almost any part of the body. The most common types affect the digestive system and lungs. In women, cancers of the breasts and cervix (the neck of the womb) are also common.

Smoking is the cause of almost all cases of lung cancer. Tobacco smoke contains chemicals called carcinogens, which irritate the delicate linings of the lungs. The more cigarettes a person smokes, the greater their risk of suffering from lung cancer. Fortunately, the risk of getting cancer is reduced when someone stops smoking.

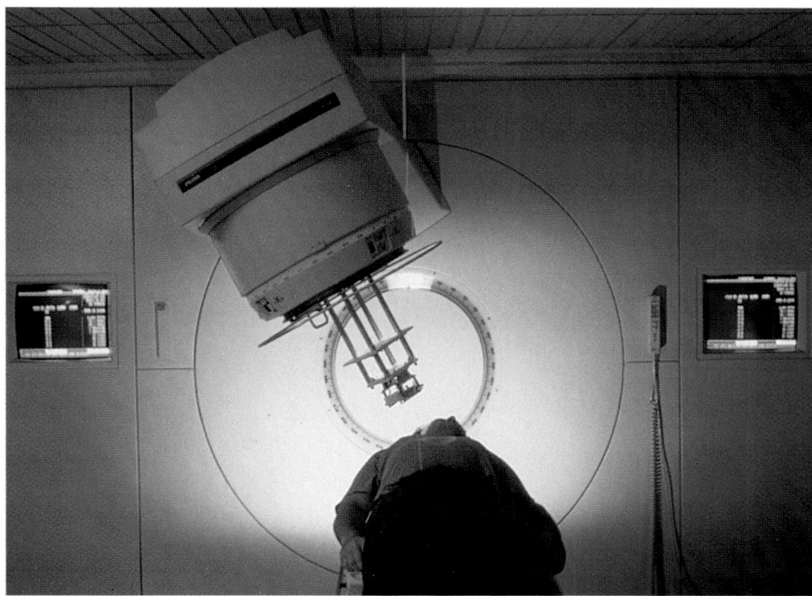

▼ Radiotherapy is a type of cancer treatment which uses radiation to kill cancer cells. A narrow beam of radiation is focused directly at a tumour so that the healthy cells nearby are not damaged.

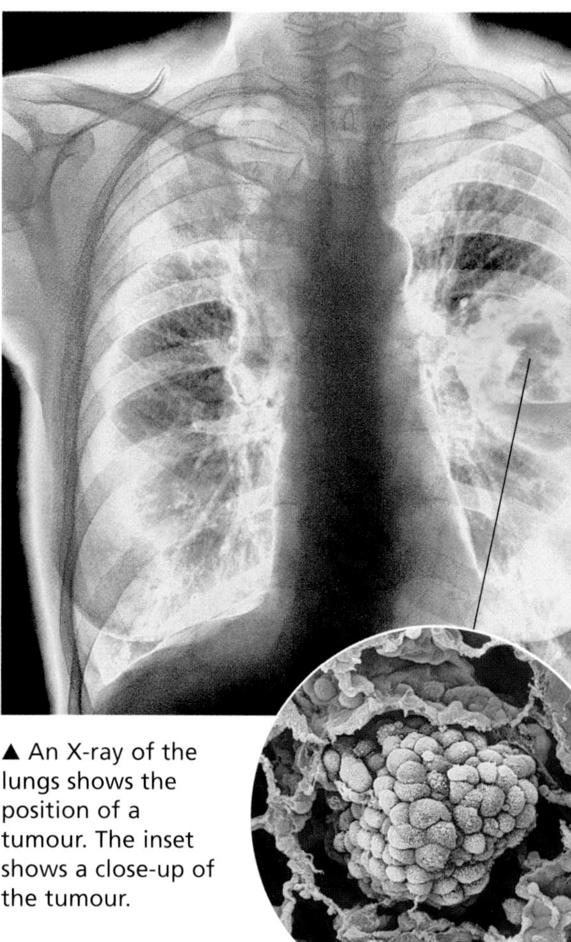

▲ An X-ray of the lungs shows the position of a tumour. The inset shows a close-up of the tumour.

Cancers of the skin are also quite common. Many types of radiation, especially ultra-violet rays from the Sun, can damage skin cells and cause cancer.

Cancer treatment

Most cancers can be treated successfully if they are caught early enough. Some treatments involve surgery to remove the tumour. This is often followed by a course of strong drugs (chemotherapy). Many of these drugs have unpleasant side-effects because they kill healthy cells as well as cancer cells.

In the most up-to-date treatments, drugs are delivered directly to the cancer cells using 'magic bullets'. These are special antibodies which only attach themselves to cancer cells.

Carbohydrates *see* Diet

Carbon

What links a clear, sparkling diamond and the dirty black soot inside a chimney? Amazingly, although they look so different, they are both made of pure carbon. Perhaps even more amazingly, all known forms of life – from microscopic bacteria to human beings – are mainly made up of substances containing carbon. Carbon is the element of life.

▶ Animals, such as the wolf shown here, use oxygen in their bodies, and produce carbon dioxide as a waste product. The air that animals breathe out is rich in carbon dioxide. (You can't actually see the carbon dioxide: what you see here is the moisture in the wolf's breath.)

Pure carbon exists in several different forms, including diamond, soot and graphite (the material used for the 'lead' in your pencil). Carbon also combines with many other elements, making millions of different chemical compounds.

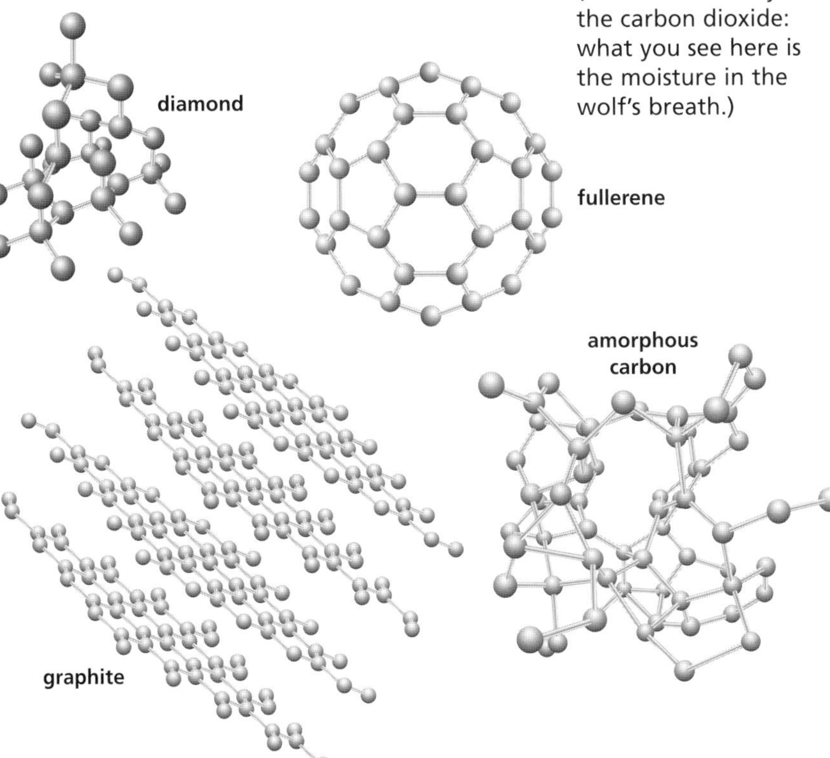

▲ Pure carbon takes different forms because of the different ways that carbon atoms fit together. Fullerenes come in various shapes and sizes. In the 'buckyball', there are 60 atoms fitted together in 20 hexagons and 12 pentagons. Soot is an example of amorphous carbon, in which the atoms do not make a regular shape.

Find Out More

- Atoms and molecules
- Coal
- Crystals
- Iron and steel

Forms and uses of pure carbon

Different forms of the same element are called allotropes. Carbon has several allotropes. Diamond is a crystalline form of carbon. It is the hardest material known. This hardness makes it excellent for cutting tools as well as for jewellery.

Another allotrope, graphite, has a different crystalline structure. It is grey or black, and is soft and flaky. It feels greasy when you touch it, and is used as a lubricant (a substance that helps machines run smoothly). It is also used for pencil leads and as a pigment (colouring) in inks used for printing. It also conducts electricity and is used, for example, in batteries. It has a very high melting point, and so containers made of graphite are used to hold molten metals.

The carbon you find in soot, charcoal and burnt toast is amorphous ('shapeless') carbon – the carbon atoms do not form a regular shape. Specially treated charcoal is used in gas masks and for absorbing unpleasant smells.

Coal is mostly carbon, and is built out of rings and chains of carbon atoms. Coke – which is made from coal – has an even higher amount of carbon. The carbon from coke is added to iron to make steel, which is a much stronger metal. The fullerenes are the most recently discovered allotrope of carbon. The atoms in fullerenes form molecules with shapes like soccer and rugby balls as well as tubes.

Carbon compounds

A carbon atom can have up to four other atoms joined to it at a time. Carbon atoms can join up with other carbon atoms to make rings and chains. They can also join with almost every other element – from hydrogen to tungsten – to make a huge number of different compounds.

One of the simplest and most important compounds of carbon is carbon dioxide. This gas is formed when your body takes energy from food – the carbon in the food combines with the oxygen you breathe in from the air. You then breathe out carbon dioxide. Carbon dioxide from the atmosphere is essential to plants, which use it to make their own food.

When carbon combines with hydrogen, it forms a group of materials called hydrocarbons. Crude oil and natural gas are made mostly from hydrocarbons. When they are burnt, carbon dioxide is released into the atmosphere.

When carbon combines with oxygen and hydrogen it forms carbohydrates – foods like sugar and starch. Plants make carbohydrates from carbon dioxide and water, and we get carbohydrates from plants.

When carbon combines with nitrogen as well as oxygen and hydrogen, it can make very complicated chemicals called proteins. Proteins are among the most important substances that make up living things.

The compounds of carbon that contain hydrogen, or carbon and hydrogen and any other element, are called organic compounds. This is because chemists once thought they were formed only by living things. However, chemists can now make millions of different organic compounds in the laboratory.

▲ Carbon fibre is made by heating textile fibres. The carbon fibres are only a few thousandths of a millimetre across. They can be squashed together to make tough, flexible materials. These are used for making many things, from tennis rackets to the racing yacht shown here.

THE CARBON CYCLE

In the natural world, carbon is used again and again in a process called the carbon cycle. Plants take in carbon dioxide from the air to make their own food. Carbon is transferred to animals when they eat the plants, or eat other animals that eat plants. Animals release carbon back into the air in the form of carbon dioxide when they breathe out. When animals and plants die they decompose (rot). Over millions of years the remains of plants and animals can form fossil fuels. When we burn fossil fuels as a source of energy, carbon is returned to the air in the form of carbon dioxide.

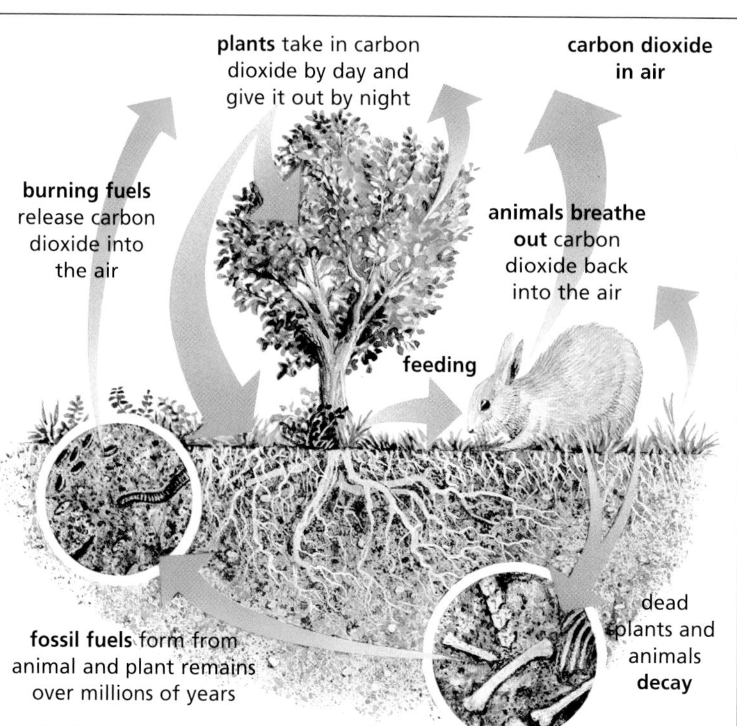

Carnivores *see* Classification

Cars and trucks

A hundred years ago, the streets of most cities were filled with the clattering of hooves, the creak of wooden wheels, and the smells of manure. But within 50 years, carts pulled by animals had been replaced by the 'horseless carriage' – the car.

▲ A Formula 1 racing car is fitted with aerofoils, or wings, front and back. As they move through the air, they produce a downwards force that makes the car hold the road better.

Today, hundreds of millions of motor vehicles run on the world's roads, and up to 50 million new ones are made each year. Most of these vehicles are cars. The rest are commercial vehicles such as trucks and buses. In richer countries especially, the car plays an important part in people's lives. It influences where they live and work, and what they do in their leisure time.

Health warning

Cars are not all good news – they can be dangerous. Tens of thousands of people around the world are killed each year in car accidents. Cars also emit (give off) carbon dioxide gas and other fumes that pollute the air. Some of these fumes are bad for people's health. Others are part of the cause of the greenhouse effect, which is gradually warming our climate.

The outer shell

The body of most vehicles is made from steel sheets, welded together. Cars usually have an all-in-one body shell. Design engineers test model vehicles in wind tunnels, to make the shape as streamlined as possible.

Rather than an all-in-one body, most commercial vehicles have a strong frame, or chassis, separate from the body.

The engine

Two main kinds of engine are used in motor vehicles – petrol and diesel engines. Cars most commonly have petrol engines, while most commercial vehicles have diesel engines. Motor manufacturers normally fit devices called catalytic converters to reduce the harmful fumes these engines emit. They are also testing

Find Out More

- Electric motors
- Global warming
- Petrol and diesel engines
- Pollution
- Renewable energy

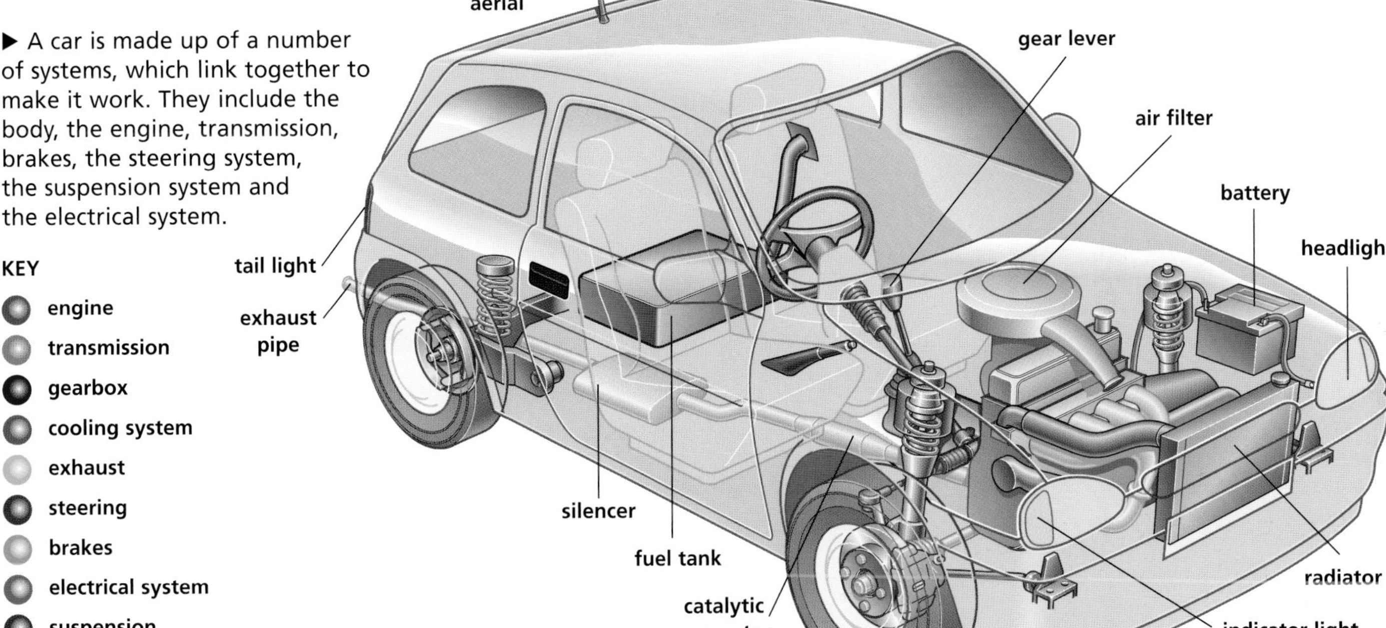

▶ A car is made up of a number of systems, which link together to make it work. They include the body, the engine, transmission, brakes, the steering system, the suspension system and the electrical system.

engines that run on liquefied petroleum gas (LPG) and electric cars powered by new batteries called fuel cells. These cause less pollution.

The transmission

The transmission system transmits power from the engine to the wheels. The major parts are the clutch and the gearbox.

If you want to ride a bicycle up a steep hill, you need a low gear. In a high gear, your legs just aren't strong enough to turn the pedals. Cars and trucks need gears for similar reasons. Some vehicles have a manual gearbox, while others change gear automatically.

The clutch smoothly disconnects and reconnects the engine with the rest of the transmission as a driver changes gear. Without the clutch, the gearbox would be damaged by gear-changes.

In some cars and most trucks, the transmission drives the rear wheels. But most modern cars have an engine at the front driving the front wheels. Some vehicles have four-wheel drive, with the engine driving both pairs of wheels.

▲ Manufacturers carry out crash tests to make sure that cars are as safe as possible in an accident. Modern car bodies have 'crumple zones' at the front and back, designed to absorb some of the impact of a crash.

The brakes

Brakes are designed to slow down a vehicle quickly and safely. Heavy trucks and buses have powerful air brakes, which work using compressed air. Cars have hydraulic brakes, which work by liquid pressure. When the driver presses the brake pedal, pipes full of brake fluid (liquid) carry the pressure to the wheels. At each wheel, the liquid pushes on a piston, which presses the brake pads against a disc or drum on the wheel.

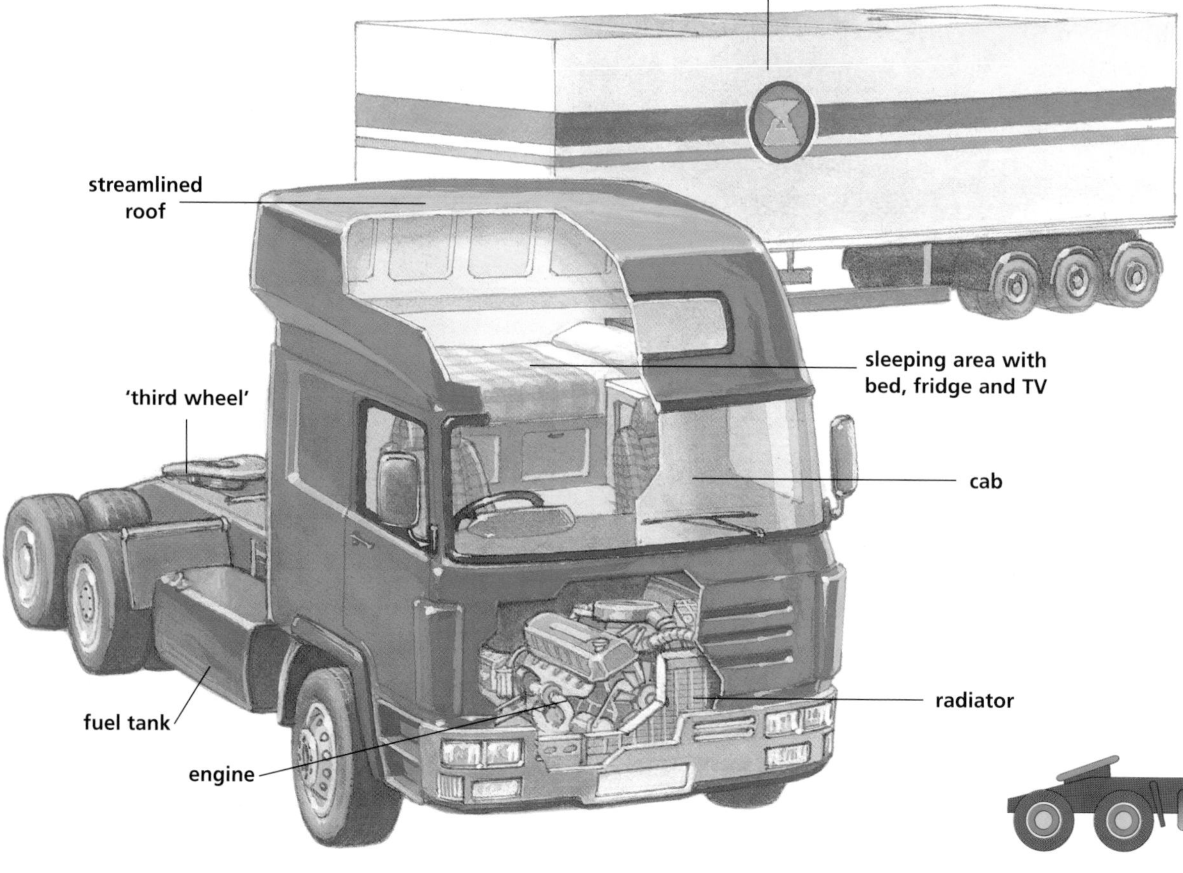

trailer
streamlined roof
'third wheel'
sleeping area with bed, fridge and TV
cab
radiator
fuel tank
engine
cab tips forward to allow access to engine

◀ Small trucks have a rigid, one-piece chassis. Different bodies can be built on the same chassis to produce quite different kinds of vehicle. Longer trucks are usually articulated – they hinge where the cab and the body join. This makes it easier for the truck to get round corners.

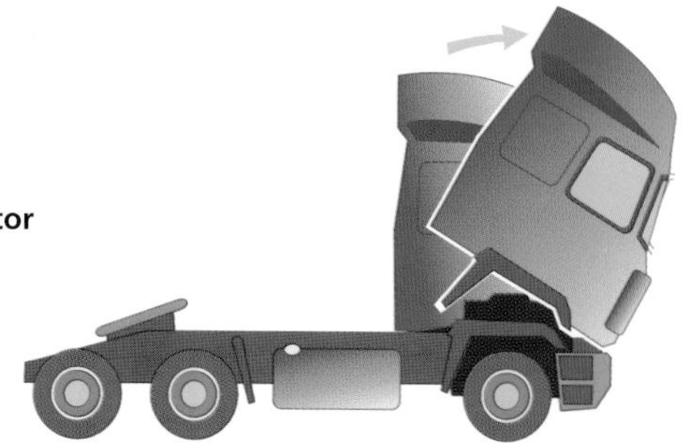

Casting *see* Metalworking • **Catalysts** *see* Reactions, chemical

Caves

In a limestone cave, deep in a mountainside, thousands of icicle-shaped stalactites hang from the ceiling, and tall, pointed stalagmites jut up from the floor. Water drips slowly down the wall, trickling over paintings made by prehistoric people. A caver looking for new passageways disturbs thousands of bats asleep on the ceiling. The underground river that runs through the cave is slowly eating through the rock, making the cave bigger every day.

Caves are natural underground rooms and passageways. Some are small, but others have huge chambers the size of cathedrals, and passages that extend for many kilometres.

Different kinds of cave

There are several kinds of cave. Sea caves form where waves pound a cliff and slowly carve a hole in the weak rocks. Ice caves are caverns in glaciers, carved out by rivers. Lava tube caves form near volcanoes. As a river of lava flows, its surface cools and turns solid, but the lava inside stays warm and keeps flowing. Eventually the liquid lava drains away, leaving an empty cave.

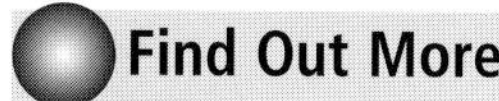

Find Out More
- Coasts
- Ice caps and glaciers
- Minerals
- Rocks
- Volcanoes

▲ These 200-metre limestone pinnacles near Guilin, China, are all that is left of a thick bed of limestone. Over millions of years, water has dissolved away the rest of the rock. There are small passages and caves within the pinnacles.

Limestone caves

The most common kinds of cave are limestone caves. Limestone is a rock made of the mineral calcite, which is a calcium compound. Caves form when slightly acidic water seeps through cracks in the rock and dissolves it away. Similar caves can form in other rocks – such as marble, gypsum and dolomite – that dissolve in acidic water.

▼ How a limestone cave forms. Acidic rainwater seeps through cracks in the limestone and slowly dissolves away the rock.

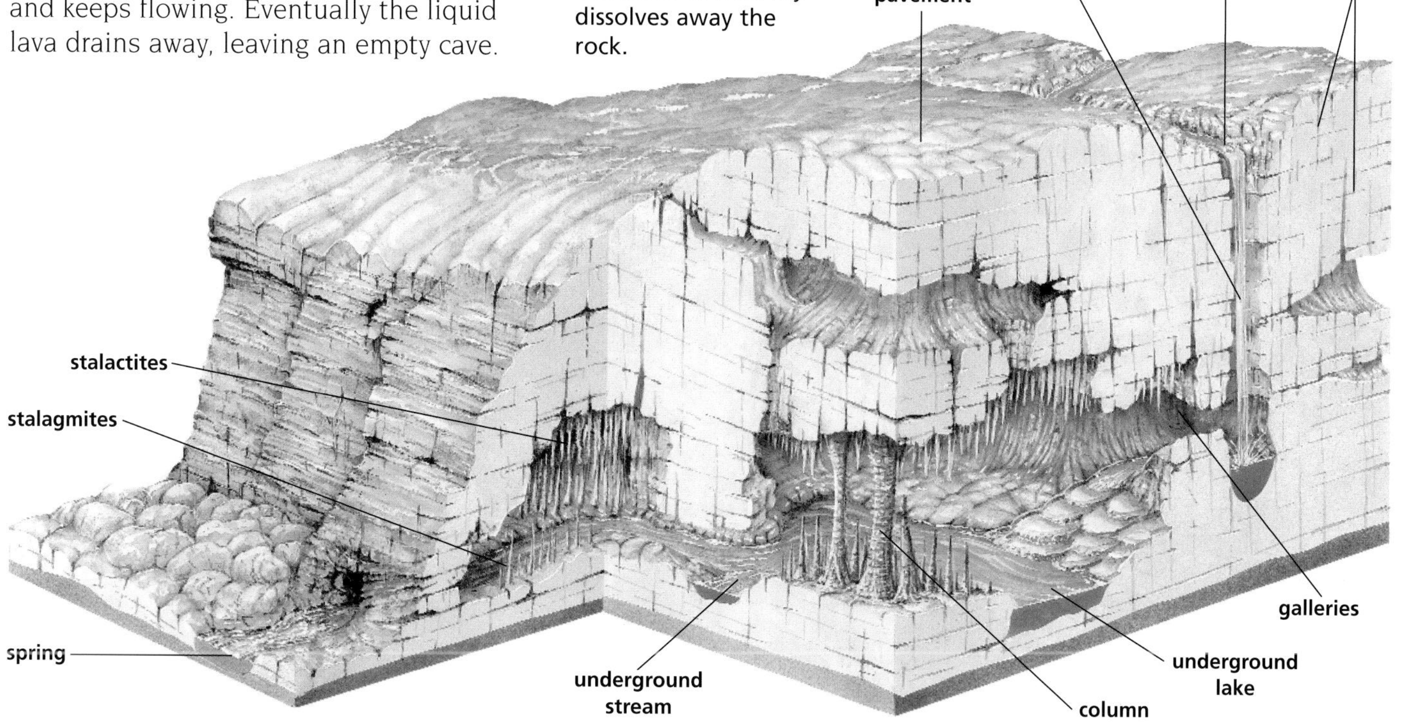

Cells

What do you have in common with a tree, a worm and a crocodile? The answer is cells. Trees, worms, crocodiles, humans and all living things are made up of the same tiny building blocks, called cells. Some very simple living things are made of just one cell, but a tiny worm has about 1000 cells and an adult human being has about 10 million million cells.

Cells are usually far too small to see without a microscope, but they are remarkably complicated. They are like tiny chemical factories. Substances constantly stream in and out of cells. Chemical reactions happen in a carefully controlled way, and energy is released from food to fuel all of life's activities.

Most cells are microscopic, but the egg cell of an ostrich is 15–20 cm long, and some giraffe nerve cells reach more than 4 m long.

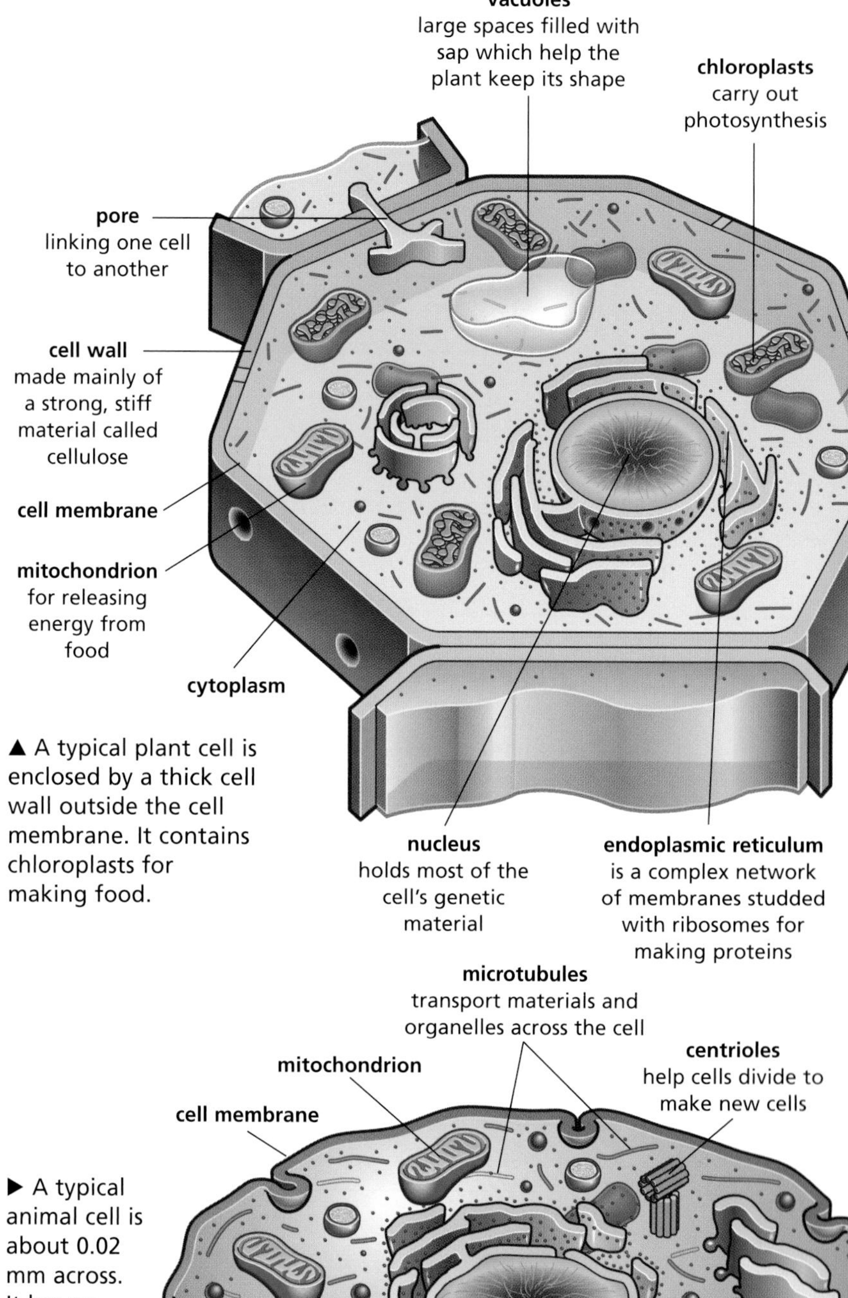

▲ A typical plant cell is enclosed by a thick cell wall outside the cell membrane. It contains chloroplasts for making food.

▶ A typical animal cell is about 0.02 mm across. It has no chloroplasts or vacuoles and is surrounded by a thin cell membrane. This makes it soft and flexible, whereas a plant cell is firm and rigid.

ROBERT HOOKE

The first person to draw the cells he saw under a microscope was the English scientist Robert Hooke (1635–1703). He built his own light microscope and drew pictures of the honeycomb of cells in cork in 1665. He even called them cells, although the importance of his work was not recognized for another 100 years. Hooke's studies of microscopic fossils led him to become one of the first people to put forward a theory of evolution.

Inside a cell

A cell is a bag full of jelly-like fluid called cytoplasm. Most cells have different structures, called organelles, within the cytoplasm.

The different organelles carry out different tasks, such as releasing energy from food, which is called respiration. Respiration takes place in sausage-shaped organelles called mitochondria. The cell is usually controlled by a nucleus, which contains the chemical instructions, or DNA, needed to make it work.

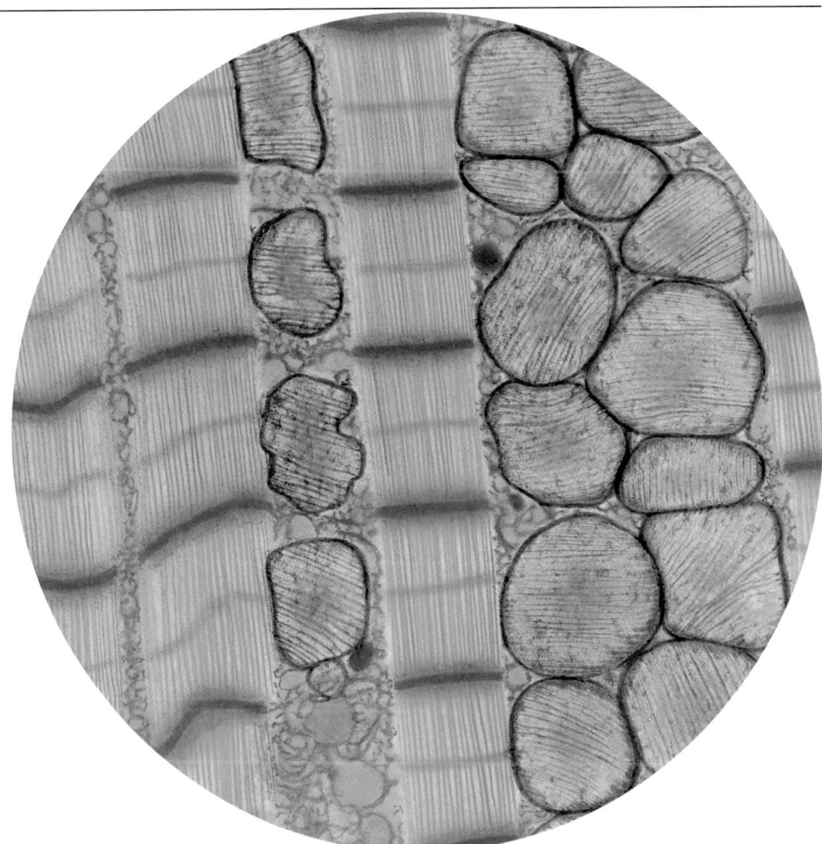

▶ A microscope picture of heart muscle. Muscle cells use a lot of energy, so the long, thin muscle cells are tightly packed with mitochondria, which are the cells' power stations.

Cell boundaries

To stay alive, all cells have to create a stable set of conditions inside that are different from those outside. To do this, they seal themselves off from their surroundings by means of a thin 'bag', or membrane. A cell membrane is so thin that a pile of 10,000 cell membranes, one on top of the other, would equal the thickness of this page. Cell membranes control the substances that pass in and out of the cells as well as detecting and responding to chemical signals from their environment and other cells.

Each organelle inside a cell is also surrounded by a membrane so that the different activities of a cell are separated and do not interfere with one another. The nucleus, mitocondria and chloroplasts have double membranes. The membranes inside a cell provide a large surface area on which chemical reactions can occur.

Simple cells

Bacteria have much smaller, simpler cells than other forms of life. Although they have rigid cell walls and membranes, they have no nucleus and no mitochondria. They have just a single loop of DNA, called the nucleoid, as well as food granules and ribosomes, which produce proteins.

Working together

In living things made of large numbers of cells, there are many different types of cell. A rabbit has more than 250 different cells; you have about 200. Groups of cells of the same type are packed together to form tissues, such as nerve tissue. In a complex plant or animal, separate tissues are joined together to form organs, such as leaves, flowers, lungs or eyes.

Find Out More

- Bacteria and viruses
- Bones and muscles
- Brain and nerves
- Genetics
- Microscopes

▼ A nerve cell, like these brain cells, has a special membrane that passes electrical signals along its length. The signals pass from one nerve cell to another across tiny gaps called synapses.

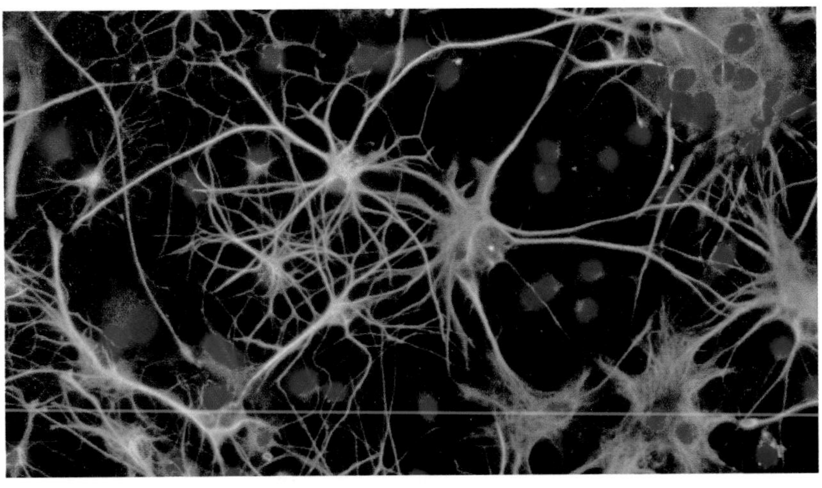

Celsius *see* Temperature

Ceramics

When the space shuttle returns to Earth, it uses the atmosphere to slow it down. Friction of the air against the fast-moving craft produces great heat, which makes the tiles covering the shuttle glow red-hot. But the astronauts inside are safe because the tiles stop the heat from reaching them.

The space shuttle tiles are products we call ceramics. Many ceramics are made by baking earthy materials such as sand and clay at high temperatures. Pottery is the most common ceramic product, and has been around for many thousands of years. So have those other common ceramic materials – bricks and tiles.

Preparing pottery

All pottery is made from clay. Different kinds of pottery are made from different kinds of clay and are fired (baked) at different temperatures. Firing takes place in ovens called kilns.

The ordinary kind of pottery, such as the crockery we use everyday, is known as earthenware. It is fired at about 1000 °C.

▶ An ancient Greek black-figure vase showing women running. In this kind of vase, the figures were painted in black. Details were added to the black figures by scraping away the paint to reveal the red clay beneath.

▼ A potter shapes wet clay with his hands as it spins round on a rotating wheel.

rotating kiln
lumps of cement (clinker)
gypsum
ball mill (grinder)

CEMENT AND CONCRETE

Concrete is the most widely used material in engineering construction. Hundreds of thousands of tonnes of it are used every day throughout the world. It is made by adding water to a mixture of cement, sand and gravel or stones, to form a pasty mass. When the mass sets, it forms a material that is very hard – concrete.

Cement is a ceramic product, made by fiercely heating earthy materials like limestone and clay. This is usually done in a long, rotating kiln in which temperatures may reach 1500 °C (see left).

Concrete is strong under compression – when it is squeezed. But it is weak under tension – when it is stretched. To prevent this weakness, construction engineers cast steel rods into the concrete. The result is called reinforced concrete.

By itself it is dull in appearance and porous, which means that it lets water through. To make it look better and make it watertight, it has to be glazed, which involves giving it a glassy coating.

The finest-quality pottery is porcelain. This is made from only the purest white clays, such as kaolin, also called china clay. It is fired at temperatures up to about 1400 °C. At these temperatures, the clay vitrifies, or becomes glass-like. This makes it watertight. Bone china is an imitation porcelain made using clay mixed with bone ash.

Brickmaking

The first bricks were shaped blocks of mud that were dried in the sun. Houses are still built of mud bricks, called adobe, in some sunny countries.

Ordinary house bricks are now made of a mixture of clay, shale and iron ore. The mixture is first crushed fine and then kneaded with water into a doughy mass. This is forced through an opening to form a long ribbon, rather like toothpaste being squeezed out of a tube. Rotating wires cut the ribbon into individual bricks. The bricks then pass through a tunnel-like kiln, which slowly heats them, then cools them again.

Remarkable refractories

Special bricks are made to line the inside of industrial furnaces, like those used to make iron and steel. They are made from naturally occurring minerals such as silica (sand), dolomite and alumina, which melt only at high temperatures.

▶ A technologist removes a sample of cermet from a furnace. This cermet (ceramic metal) is made by heating and mixing together the ceramic material boron carbide and aluminium. It is lighter than aluminium and stronger than steel.

Materials that resist high temperatures are known as refractories. They include the space shuttle tiles already mentioned, which are made out of silica fibres. Some of the best refractory materials contain tungsten, the metal with the highest melting-point (3410°C). They include tungsten carbide, which is used to make cutting tools that remain sharp even when they get red-hot. Tungsten and titanium carbides are mixed with ceramics to form cermets, which are used in the high-temperature parts of jet and rocket engines.

Find Out More

- Construction
- Iron and steel
- Jet engines
- Rockets
- Space shuttles

The wheel was first used for making pottery around 3500 BC, probably before it was used to make the first vehicles.

Cereals *see* Farming • **CFCs** (chlorofluorocarbons) *see* Global warming • **Charcoal** *see* Wood and timber

Chemical analysis

If you have a glass of salty water and a glass of sugary water, how do you tell which is which? The easiest way is to taste them. Your tongue is actually a very clever chemical laboratory. But if you don't know what a liquid is, it is best not to taste it. It might be poisonous!

Finding out what things are made of is called chemical analysis. Scientists have developed a whole range of tests to help them do this.

Chemical analysis is used to test for all kinds of things. Chemists test drinking water to see if it has been polluted with dangerous chemicals. In hospitals, biochemists test samples of blood, saliva and urine from patients. They are looking for chemicals that show someone has a particular illness. Forensic chemists help the police, for example, by checking for poison in the body of a murder victim.

▼ You can spot different metals in chemical compounds by seeing what colour flames they produce. Here are the flames produced by sodium (on the left), strontium (middle) and boric acid (which contains the metal boron).

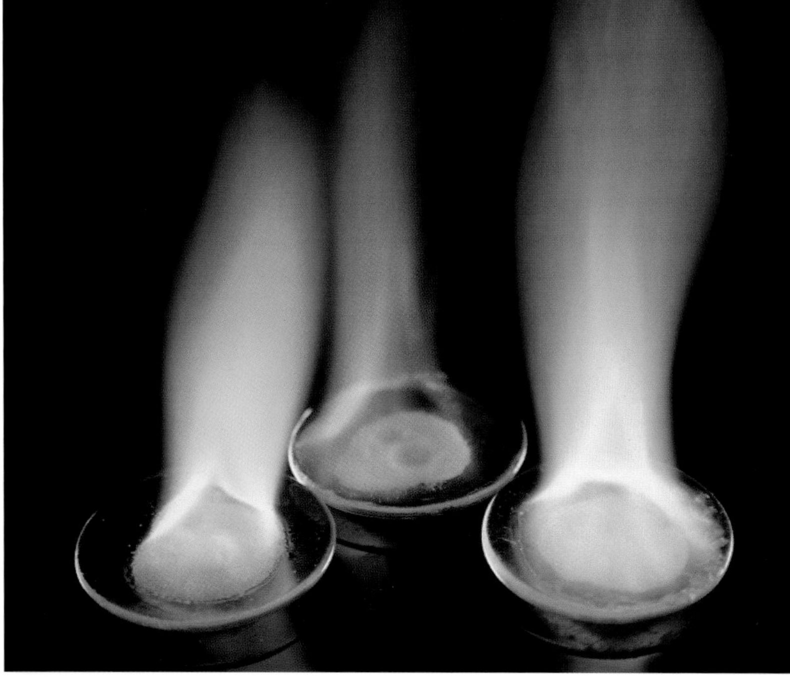

Flame and fire

One of the simplest chemical tests is to check for the presence of a metal in a sample. All you need to do is burn a tiny amount of the sample and look at the colour of the flame. Different metals burn with different colours. For example, calcium has an orange-red flame, while potassium burns lilac.

▲ Scientists testing the chemicals in a hot spring in Yellowstone National Park, USA.

Burning is also used to analyse organic compounds (chemicals containing carbon). The method involves burning a sample of the compound until it breaks down into its individual elements (basic substances). Scientists can then measure how much there is of each of the common elements in organic compounds – carbon, hydrogen, oxygen and nitrogen.

Changing colours

Chemists use various substances to check for the presence of particular chemicals. These substances, called indicators, change colour if the chemical is present. Iodine in solution has a purplish colour, but if you put a drop onto something containing starch, the solution will turn black. Another important indicator is special paper called litmus paper. It turns red if touched by an acid, and blue if touched by an alkali (the chemical opposite of an acid).

Another technique using colour is called chromatography. A simple experiment using chromatography shows what's in the coloured coatings of some sweets. Dissolve the coating of the sweet in a little bit of water. Then put a drop of the solution onto blotting paper. You will see that there are actually different colours, each one spreading out from the drop at a different speed. You are left with a series of coloured rings, one for each of the chemicals in the coating of the sweet.

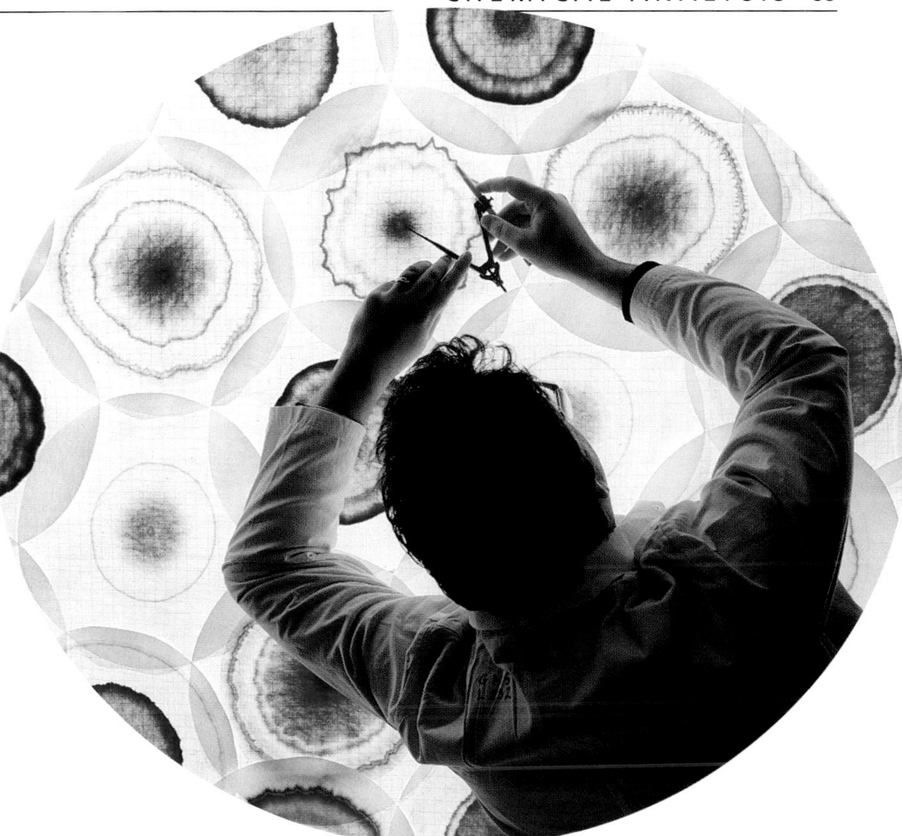

▲ Chromatography is used in laboratories to separate and analyse some substances. Here a scientist measures the results for different industrial dyes.

Using spectra

White light is actually made up of different colours, called the spectrum. If you shine white light through a thin slice of material, the light will be broken up into different colours in a particular way. Scientists can use this to spot particular substances or elements. This technique is called spectroscopy. Other forms of radiation, including infrared, ultraviolet and X-rays, can also be used this way.

Mass spectrometry is one of the most powerful ways of analysing many kinds of chemical. In this technique, a substance is broken up into charged fragments, and electric and magnetic fields are used to measure the mass (weight) of each fragment. Different compounds have their own characteristic mass spectrum, which can be used to identify them.

DNA FINGERPRINTING

DNA is the genetic material in the cells of all living things. Each individual has a virtually unique set of DNA (only clones or identical twins have the same DNA). DNA fingerprinting is a way of identifying the differences between people's DNA. It is used to identify criminals and to find out how closely people are related. It is also used to study breeding in wild animals.

The technique works by breaking up the long DNA molecule into fragments. Certain 'core' fragments are then tagged with radioactivity and separated using a technique called electrophoresis. The result is a pattern of bands that is different for each individual. Similarities between patterns can show how closely related individuals are.

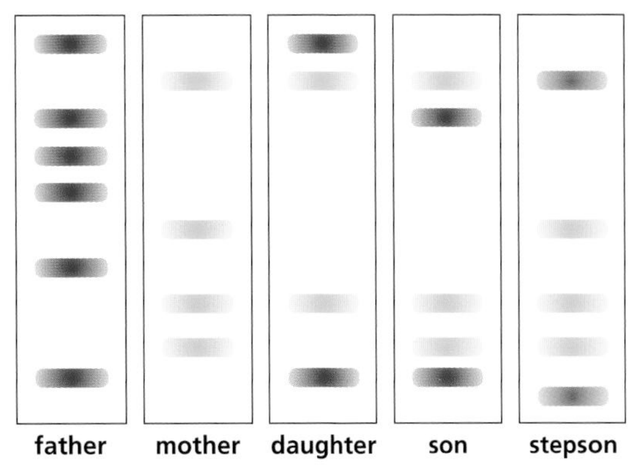

The patterns shown here are for a family (the colours have been added to help the explanation). Two of the children have a mixture of the mother's and the father's DNA fingerprints. The third child has a different father (red).

Find Out More

- Acids and alkalis
- Elements and compounds
- Magnetism and electromagnetism
- Reactions
- Spectrum

Chemicals

Salt is a very useful substance. In the home, we use it to make our food taste better. In industry, it is a valuable raw material. From salt, a wide range of chemicals is produced, including sodium carbonate (used in making glass) and caustic soda (used in making soap).

The chemical industry makes millions of tonnes of sodium carbonate and caustic soda every year. They are produced in such large quantities that they are known as heavy chemicals. Other heavy chemicals include sulphuric and nitric acids, ammonia and benzene.

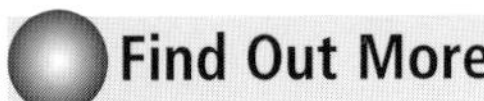

- Oil products
- Plastics
- Polymers
- Reactions, chemical

▼ Froth flotation tanks like this are used to concentrate silver and zinc ores. Froth flotation is a process that separates the minerals from earthy impurities. The ore is ground to a fine powder and mixed with water and chemicals to make a froth liquid. The mineral particles cling to the froth bubbles at the surface, while waste earthy material sinks to the bottom.

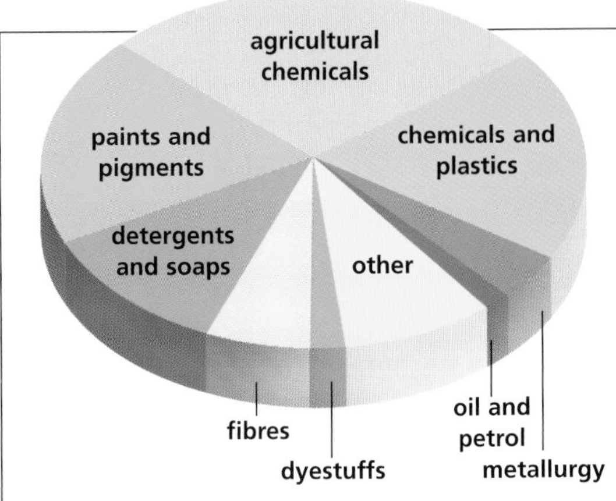

▲ The main uses of sulphuric acid.

SULPHURIC ACID

The world produces almost twice as much sulphuric acid as any other chemical. It is so important in manufacturing that it is often called the 'lifeblood of industry'.

Sulphuric acid is made from sulphur by the contact process. The sulphur (S) is first burned in air (containing oxygen, O_2) in a furnace, which produces sulphur dioxide (SO_2) gas. The gas then passes with more air into a converter containing a catalyst, such as platinum.

In contact with the catalyst, the sulphur dioxide combines with more oxygen from the air to form sulphur trioxide (SO_3). Sulphur trioxide can then be combined with water (H_2O) to form sulphuric acid (H_2SO_4).

Benzene is what is known as an organic chemical (organic chemicals are ones with carbon in them). The other heavy chemicals are classed as inorganic. Most inorganic chemicals are produced from minerals (chemicals extracted from rocks). Organic chemicals are mainly produced from crude oil, or petroleum, which is a mixture of hydrocarbons (compounds made from hydrogen and carbon). The different hydrocarbons provide chemical starting points for a huge variety of products.

Chemical operations

The chemical industry uses all kinds of processes, or reactions, to make chemicals. A common one is oxidation, which means adding oxygen to a substance. Oxidation is involved in the manufacture of sulphuric acid, for example. Hydrogenation is another common reaction, which means adding hydrogen. It is used in making margarine and other spreads.

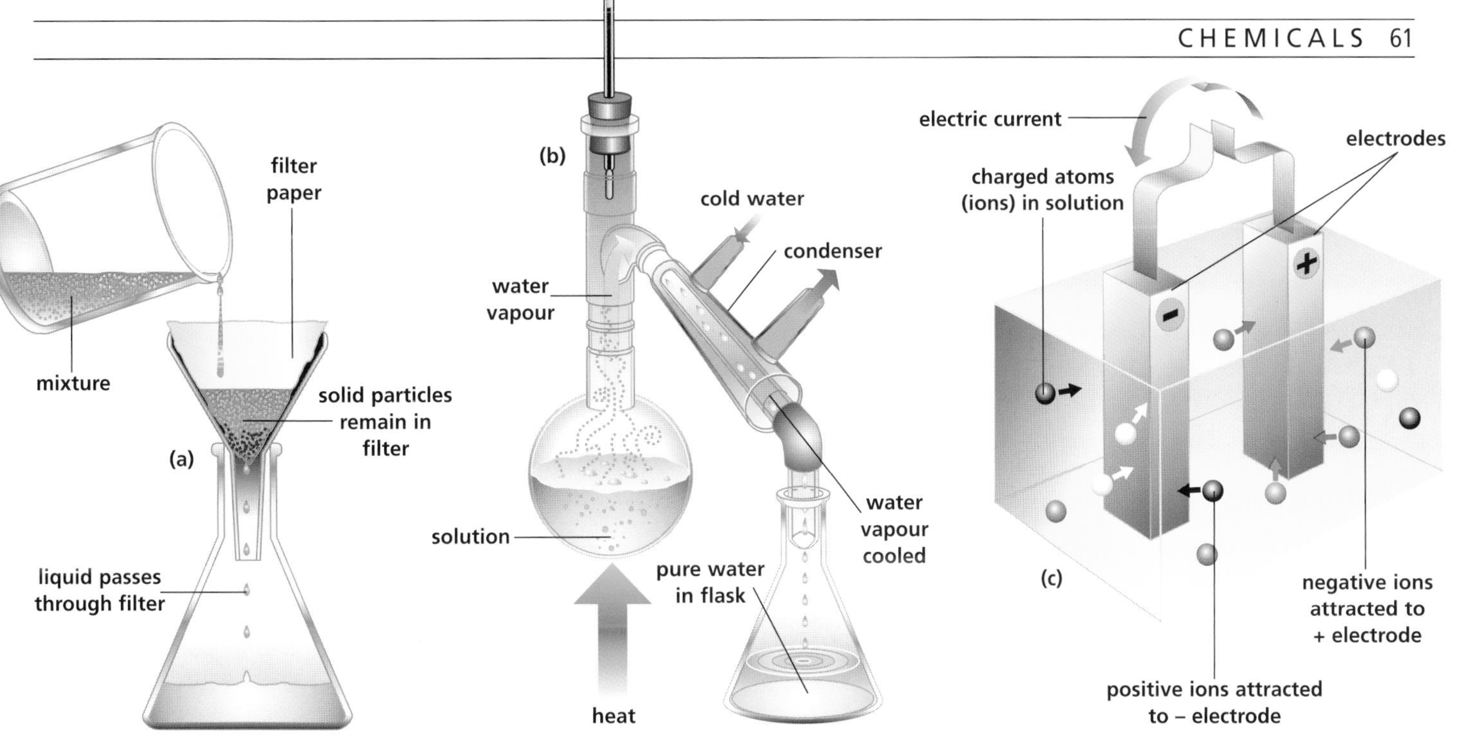

▲ Common processes used in chemical plants include mixing, dissolving, filtering (a) and distilling (b shows distilling water). Electrolysis (c) is a process in which electricity is used to separate chemicals.

Polymerization is the reaction by which plastics are produced. It involves the linking together of small molecules (monomers) to form large ones (polymers). Cracking is an operation in which the opposite happens – large molecules are broken down into smaller ones. It is an important reaction in refining petroleum.

▼ A chemical engineer inspects a small pilot plant to find out how a large chemical plant might work.

Many reactions have to take place at high temperatures or high pressures: the common plastic polyethylene is produced at pressures of up to 2000 times normal atmospheric pressure. Other reactions will not take place properly unless a catalyst is present. A catalyst is a substance that can make a reaction go faster, but is not itself changed in the process.

Chemical engineering

The people who design the chemical plants (factories) in which the reactions are carried out are called chemical engineers. They have to take a chemical process that works in the laboratory and make it work on a large scale.

Chemical engineers have to design the vessels (containers) in which reactions take place. They must also design the equipment that ensures that the chemicals involved are in the right state and in the right place at the right time. This includes pumps, heaters, pipes, valves, and so on.

When designing a new chemical plant, the engineers first build a small-scale one, called a pilot plant. If this works, they can go ahead with the full-size one.

Chemistry *see* Science • **Childbirth** *see* Human reproduction

Chlorine

On a misty wet evening, a car's headlights shine brightly through the dusk. The gases that allow the headlights to shine so brightly are part of a group called the halogens. Another halogen is used to keep swimming pools clean, and is half of common table salt.

▲ Chlorine is put in swimming pools to kill germs. Chlorine can react with sweat and urine in the water to make chemicals that sting your eyes – so many swimmers wear goggles.

Chlorine combines with sodium to make salt (sodium chloride). It is one of the halogens, a group of highly reactive non-metals that are all poisonous in their pure forms. They react with metals to make various kinds of salts ('halogen' means 'salt-making'). The other halogens are fluorine, bromine, iodine and astatine.

Properties and uses

The halogen light bulbs used in car headlamps have a halogen gas, usually iodine or bromine, surrounding the light filament. Halogen bulbs are brighter and last much longer than ordinary light bulbs.

Fluorine forms very corrosive acids, such as hydrofluoric acid, which can be used to etch (make patterns in) glass. Small amounts of fluoride compounds in toothpaste and drinking water help to prevent tooth decay.

Chlorine reacts with lots of other elements to make some very useful compounds such as PVC, a plastic used for pipes and waterproof fabrics. Compounds of chlorine, fluorine and carbon – the chlorofluorocarbons (CFCs) – were once widely used in aerosols. Then it was found that CFCs damaged the ozone layer, which protects us from the sun's harmful ultraviolet rays.

Iodine is a purplish black crystalline solid. At room temperature it sublimes (turns straight into a gas). It is found in small amounts in sea water, and in larger amounts in some seaweeds. The thyroid gland in your neck needs a tiny amount of iodine. It uses the iodine to make chemicals that keep your cells working properly. Iodine and its compounds are also used in medicine and photography.

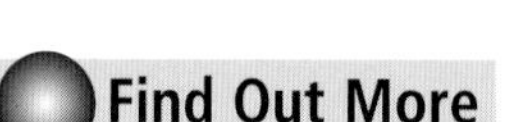

Find Out More

- Atmosphere
- Lights and lamps
- Periodic table
- Plastics
- Salts

◀ Chlorine and bromine were used in gas attacks in World War I (1914–1918). Soldiers had to wear gas masks to protect themselves.

In parts of the world where there is no iodine in the drinking water, some people used to suffer from goitre – a hugely swollen thryoid gland in the neck. Nowadays, small amounts of iodine compounds are added to table salt to prevent this.

Chlorophyll *see* Dyes • **Chromatography** *see* Chemical analysis

Circuits

Have you ever wondered how flicking a switch on the wall can cause a light bulb to glow on the other side of the room, as if by magic? When you press the switch, a lever brings two pieces of metal together inside the switch. This opens a pathway for electric current to travel along – like lowering the drawbridge for people to enter a castle. Electricity gushes into the light bulb, making it burn brightly.

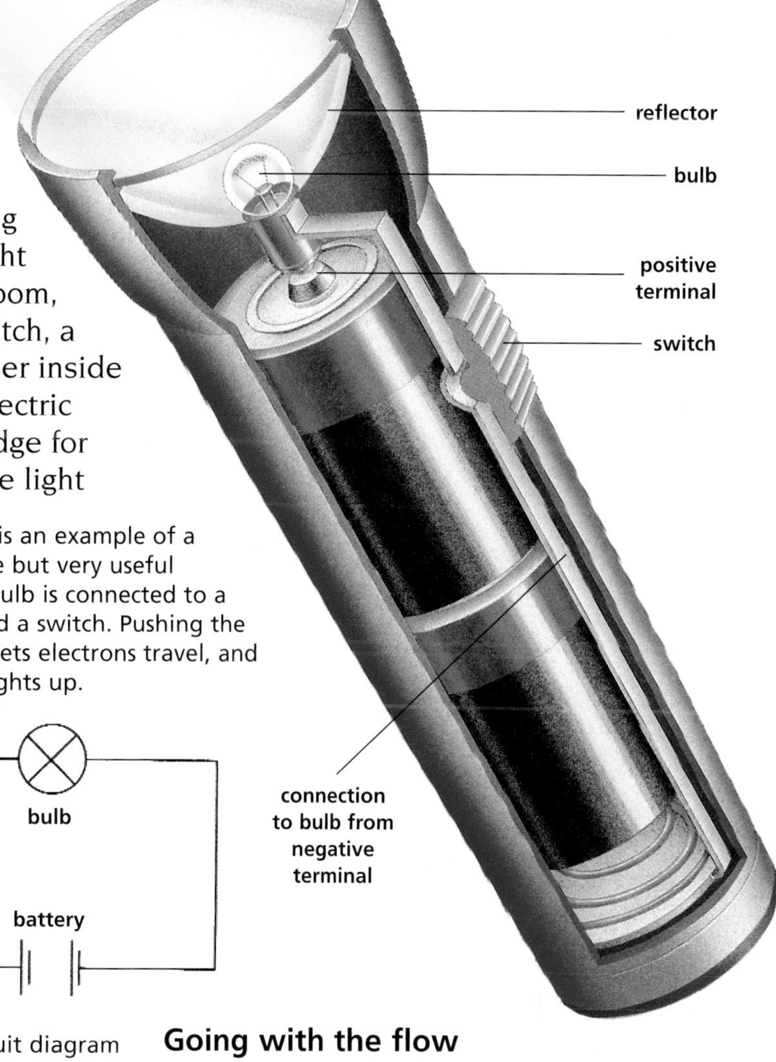

▶ A torch is an example of a very simple but very useful circuit. A bulb is connected to a battery and a switch. Pushing the switch on lets electrons travel, and the bulb lights up.

The path that the electric current flows along is called a circuit. A torch, for example, contains a simple circuit that has three components parts – a battery, a light bulb and a switch. These are joined together in a loop by strips of metal, which conduct electricity.

All electrical equipment and gadgets depend on circuits, which may have different components connected in different ways, depending on the job the piece of equipment does. Whether you are adding numbers on a calculator, watching TV or heating food in a microwave oven, an electric circuit is doing the work for you.

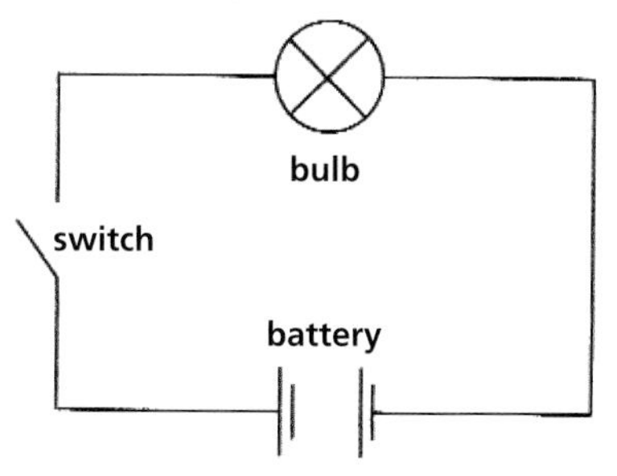

▲ This circuit diagram shows the torch circuit very simply, using symbols for the bulb, the battery and the switch.

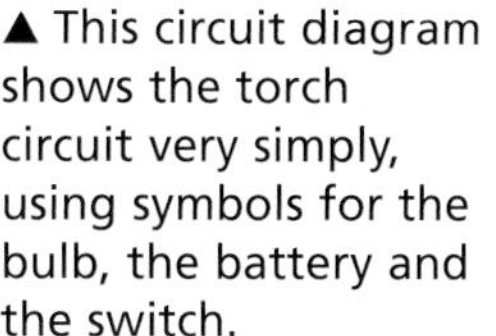

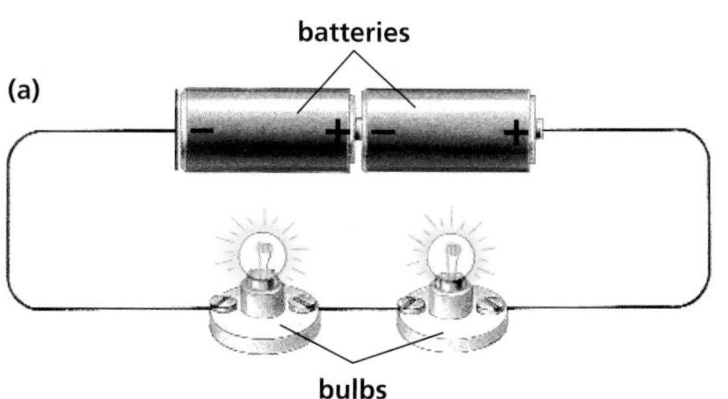

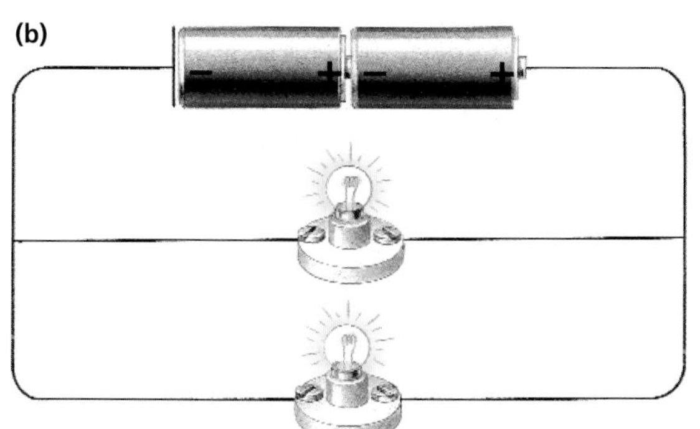

◀ Two identical light bulbs connected in series (a) and in parallel (b). The bulbs in series glow more dimly because the current is reduced. Also, if one bulb breaks in the series circuit, the other goes out because the circuit is broken. In parallel, each bulb has its own circuit, so if one bulb blows, the other keeps working.

Going with the flow

All circuits need a supply of electricity. The supply will set electrons (tiny particles found in atoms) moving around the circuit.

Electrons carry an electric charge, so as they move they produce a flow of electricity called a current. Current is measured in amperes, or 'amps'(A). If there is a break in the circuit, the current will stop flowing. Electricity does not flow through a circuit by itself. It needs a 'push', or energy, to keep it moving. We call this energy the voltage of the circuit. Voltage is measured in volts (V).

The power used by a device is a measure of how fast it uses energy. Power is measured in watts (W). A bar of an electric fire uses about 1000 W.

Electric power can come either from a battery or from a mains socket. A battery produces direct current (DC): this means that the current flows one way around the circuit. Mains electricity is alternating current (AC). Alternating current flows first one way round the circuit, then the other, changing direction many times per second.

Resistance

Some electrical components reduce – or resist – the flow of current through a circuit. We say that they have a resistance. When a current flows through a light bulb, for example, the atoms in the bulb's filament – the coiled wire inside the bulb – resist the flow. This causes the atoms to get hot, making the filament glow. Resistance was discovered by Georg Ohm in 1826, and is measured in ohms.

Components called resistors are put into circuits to help control the flow of current through the circuit.

When there is a current of 1 ampere in a circuit, more than a million, million, million electrons flow through it every second.

OHM'S LAW

The German scientist Georg Ohm (1787–1854) is best remembered for working out Ohm's Law. He discovered that the voltage across a conductor – such as a strip of metal or a wire – and the current flowing through it, always vary in the same proportion. So if you double the voltage, you double the current. This is incredibly useful, because it lets you predict the current you will get for a particular voltage.

Series and parallel

If several bulbs (or other components) are powered by the same battery, they can be connected in series (in line) or in parallel. In parallel, each bulb is directly connected to the battery, so each gets the full voltage and glows brightly. If one bulb breaks, the others keep working. In series, the bulbs get less current and glow dimly. If one breaks, the others go out.

Find Out More

- Batteries and cells
- Electricity
- Electricity supply
- Lights and lamps
- Power stations

▼ Machines like TVs and radios have very complicated circuits with lots of parts. Instead of connecting all the parts with wires, the components are fastened to a circuit board, which has tiny silver tracks connecting them in the right order.

Classification

Gorillas, chimpanzees and orang-utans are closely related to humans. Our blood is so similar that we could get a transfusion from a chimpanzee. We suffer from the same diseases. Even the brain cases of humans and gorillas are the same size at birth. So we are put together with them in the same group, called hominoids.

HOW A TIGER IS CLASSIFIED

GROUP	SUBDIVISION	MEANING
Kingdom	Animalia (animals)	
Phylum	Chordata	Nerve cord down back
Sub-phylum	Vertebrata (vertebrates)	Having a backbone
Class	Mammalia (mammals)	Animal with fur or hair, feeds on mother's milk
Order	Carnivora (carnivores)	Meat-eating
Family	Felidae	Cats
Genus	*Panthera*	Big cats
Species	*Panthera tigris*	Tiger

▲ The scientific naming system was thought up by the Swedish naturalist Linnaeus in the 18th century. A tiger's two-part Latin name labels it as a tiger (*tigris*) that belongs to the big cat group (*Panthera*).

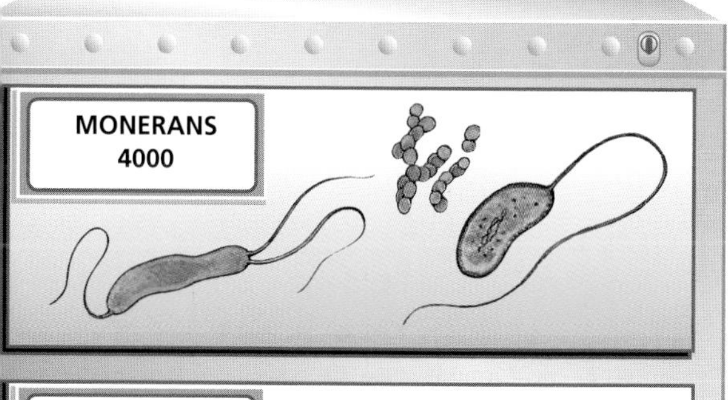

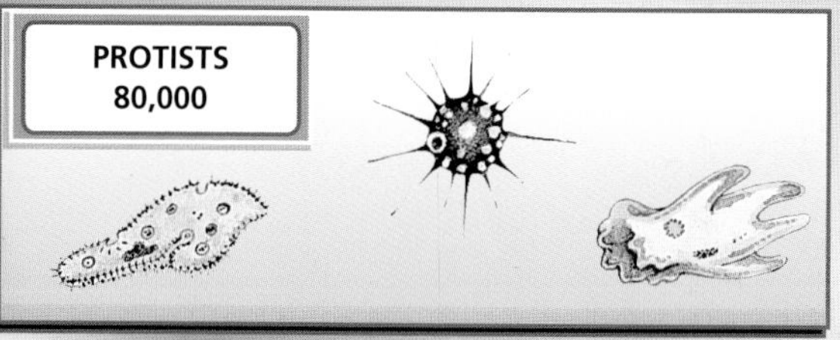

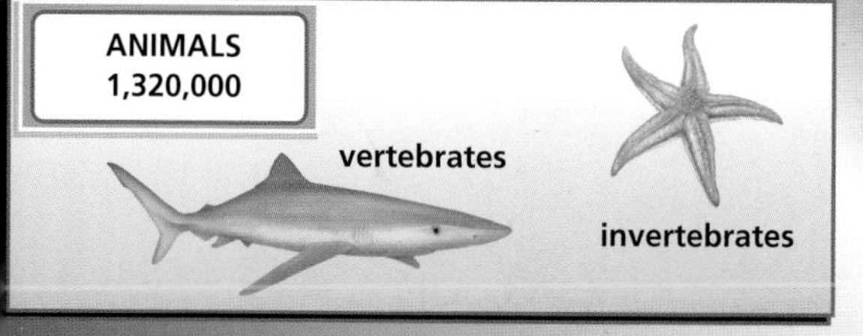

◀ Today, the living world is usually classified into five kingdoms – animals, plants, fungi, monerans (such as bacteria) and protists (such as algae and diatoms). The number beneath the name of each kingdom indicates the approximate number of species (kinds of creature) in each group. These are just the ones we know about – there are many millions more waiting to be discovered.

Find Out More

- Animals
- Bacteria and viruses
- Fungi
- Genetics
- Invertebrates
- Plants

Classification is like a filing system. It is a way of organizing and making sense of the millions of kinds of living thing with which we share this planet. It is also often used as a way of understanding evolution.

Classification is about putting living things into groups that share certain features. The animal kingdom contains millions of different kinds, or species, of living thing. The smallest groups contain just one species.

A species is a collection of similar living things. In those living things that have males and females, members of a species can breed together.

Common features

Scientists once classified living things mainly by their shape and appearance and the way they develop. Now they can also compare the DNA (the chemical that makes up the genes) that parents pass on to their offspring. Living things that look the same (such as barnacles and limpets) may have very different DNA, which shows that they are not closely related.

Cliffs *see* Coasts

Climate

Six thousand years ago, the Sahara was a lush grassland watered by the summer rains. Crocodiles and hippos lived in the rivers and lakes while giraffes, elephants and cattle grazed on the savannah. Slowly the climate changed and the Sahara dried out. It is now the largest desert on Earth.

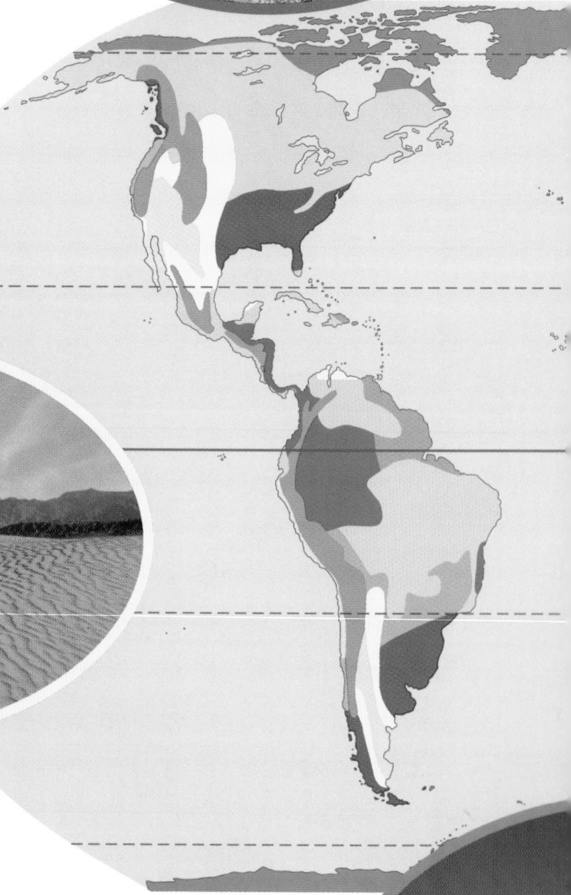

Climate is the average weather of a particular place over many years. Although the weather can change from day to day, and even during a single day, climate stays the same for many years.

Climate zones

Different parts of the world have different climates. Land is grouped into particular climate zones according to its average temperature, how much rain and snow fall, and how much the weather changes from season to season. Since plants depend so much on temperature, sunshine, and rainfall, each climate also tends to have its own typical vegetation.

What makes climate

The main reason that some places are warmer than others is because different places on Earth receive different amounts of the Sun's energy. The tropics are warm because the Sun shines almost directly overhead all year long. The Arctic and Antarctic are cold because they receive less sunlight over the year.

Water absorbs and gives out the Sun's energy more slowly than the land, so places near the coast have more even climates than places in the middle of a continent. Climates are also affected by ocean currents. Some currents bring warm water, and warm, rainy weather. Others bring cold water, and cool, dry weather.

tropical: warm and humid

- rain all year
- monsoon (short dry season, long wet season)
- dry winters

hot desert: dry

- no reliable rain
- a little rain

temperate

- no dry season
- dry winters

Find Out More

- Atmosphere
- Deserts
- Global warming
- Seasons
- Weather

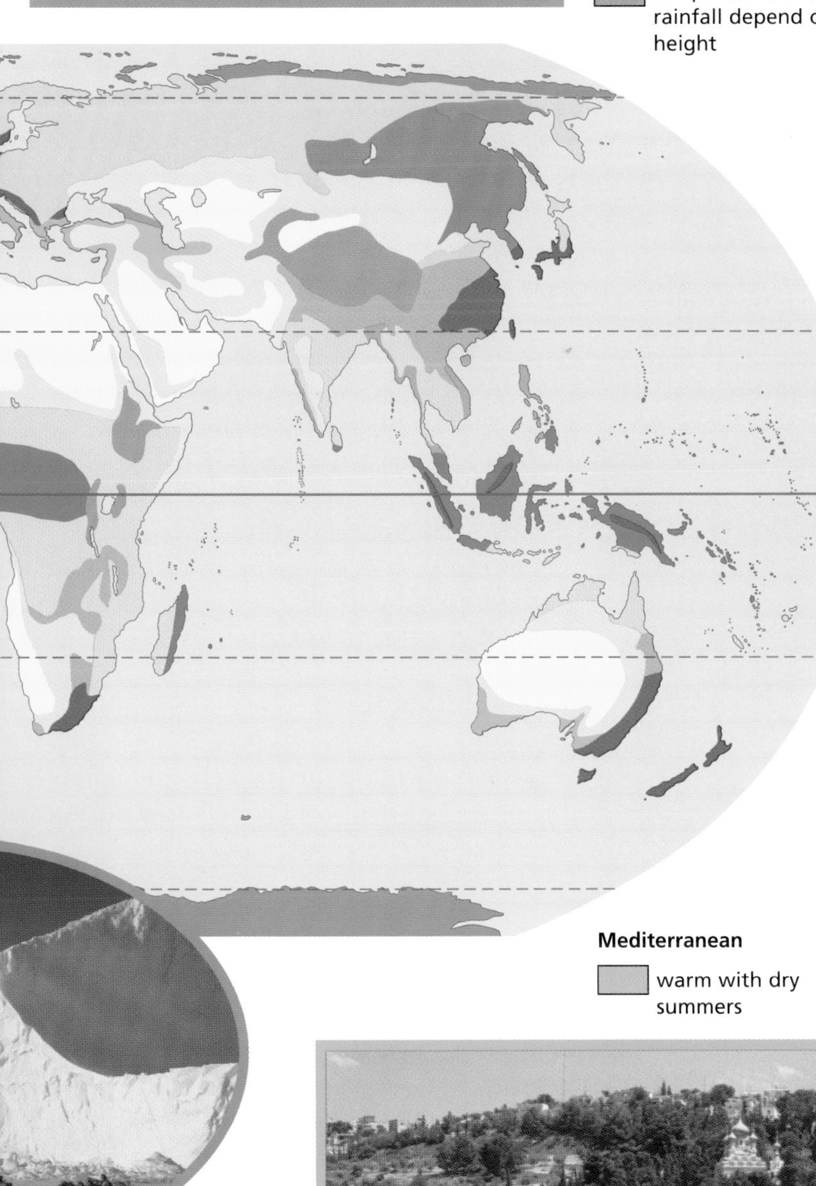

CONSTRUCTING PAST CLIMATES

We can learn about climates far in the past by looking at things like rocks, ice and trees. For instance, salt forms in hot, dry climates, so a layer of salt in a rock formation is evidence that the climate was hot and dry when the rocks were formed. A layer of boulders and gravel left by a glacier is evidence of a cold climate.

Every season, trees add a new ring of growth to their trunks. The thickness of the ring depends on the climate and how good the growing conditions were.

In the section of part of a tree shown below, the thinner rings may have formed when the climate was cooler or drier than when the thick rings formed.

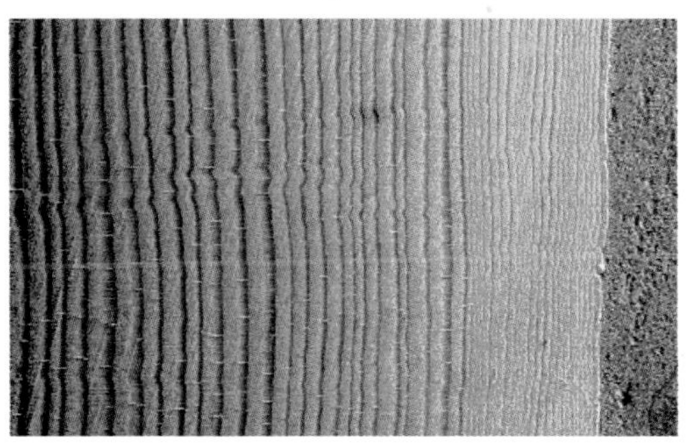

◀ This map shows the world's major climate zones. Within each zone there are smaller differences. For instance, mountains are generally cooler than low areas, and cities are always warmer than the countryside.

Winds affect the climate, too. Winds can bring warm air to cold places, for example, or moist air to dry places.

Climate change

Although climate often stays the same over many years, it does slowly change. Over thousands of years, continents move, ocean currents change and wind patterns change.

Climate also changes when the atmosphere changes. Some scientists think that the Earth was so warm 50 million years ago because the atmosphere contained more greenhouse gases (such as carbon dioxide), which trapped more heat.

Powerful volcanic eruptions can cool climates for a few years. In 1815, Tambora volcano erupted, sending clouds of ash and gas into the atmosphere. The clouds reduced the amount of sunlight reaching the Earth, and the climate was cooler.

Clouds

The view of Earth from space is always changing. Swirling white patterns move over the surface, hiding then revealing the lands and oceans beneath. These patterns are clouds.

▶ This photograph, taken on a space shuttle flight, shows clouds in the Earth's atmosphere.

Clouds are made of water droplets, ice crystals, particles of dust, and air.

How clouds form

The lower part of Earth's atmosphere is full of water vapour. We can't see the water in the air because water vapour is a gas. Clouds form when some of this water vapour condenses (becomes liquid) and forms tiny water droplets. If the air is cold enough, the water will form ice crystals instead of droplets.

Dust is a very important ingredient in clouds. In the air there are salt particles from the oceans, ash particles from volcanoes, tiny bits of rock and soil blown off the continents, and soot particles from factories. The particles attract water molecules and give them a place to gather into droplets. Without dust, it would be difficult for clouds to form.

▼ Different kinds of clouds have different shapes and form at different heights in the atmosphere.

KEY
1 cirrus
2 cirrocumulus
3 altocumulus
4 altostratus
5 cumulonimbus
6 stratus
7 cumulus

Why clouds form

The main reason clouds form is because the air cools down. Warm air can hold more water vapour than cold air. When the air cools, some of the water vapour condenses and makes clouds.

Exactly how cold the air has to be before a cloud forms depends on how much water there is in the air. The less water vapour there is in the air, the colder the air has to be to form a cloud. This is why, on a dry day, the clouds are high in the sky, where it's coldest.

Find Out More
- Atmosphere
- Floating and sinking
- Gases
- Rain and snow
- Water

Clutch *see* Cars and trucks

Coal

A century ago, many cities were full of grimy, dark, black buildings. They were coated with soot – black powder from the smoke from coal fires. Nowadays, cities are much cleaner as smoke no longer fills the air. But coal remains an important fuel.

Coal is a hard, black substance made of carbon. It catches fire and burns fiercely when strongly heated. It is found in deposits underground and at the surface of the ground. Coal formed over millions of years from the remains of trees and plants.

Peat is coal at an early stage of its formation. It is brown and softer than coal, and is found at the surface, not deep underground.

Find Out More

- Fuels
- Industry and manufacturing
- Mining
- Steam engines

Mining coal

If the deposits of coal are at or near the surface of the ground, the coal is dug out in vast pits called opencast mines. Huge excavating machines strip off any soil covering the coal, and dig out the coal beneath.

▲ This massive excavator cuts coal from a huge opencast mine.

Coal often lies in seams or layers deep underground. At underground mines, shafts go down to the seams. Miners take lifts down to the seams, and then dig tunnels through the seams as they remove the coal. They use cutting machines to dig out the coal. Conveyor belts take the coal back to the shafts, where lifts raise it to the surface buildings.

North America

Europe

Former Soviet Union

Africa and Middle East

Asia Pacific

South and Central America

▲ This map shows the world's known reserves of coal. Europe (including the former Soviet Union) has about a third of the world's coal, while North America and Asia each have about a quarter. These reserves should last for several hundred years.

Key to map

coal reserves

Industrial power

Coal brought the people of the 17th and early 18th centuries comfort at home, the means to travel widely, and lots of useful goods and products. It powered steam locomotives on railways, and ocean-going passenger ships. Factories burned coal to power steam engines and to produce heat for manufacturing products. People used coal and peat to heat their homes, burning them in open fires that could also heat running water for warm baths.

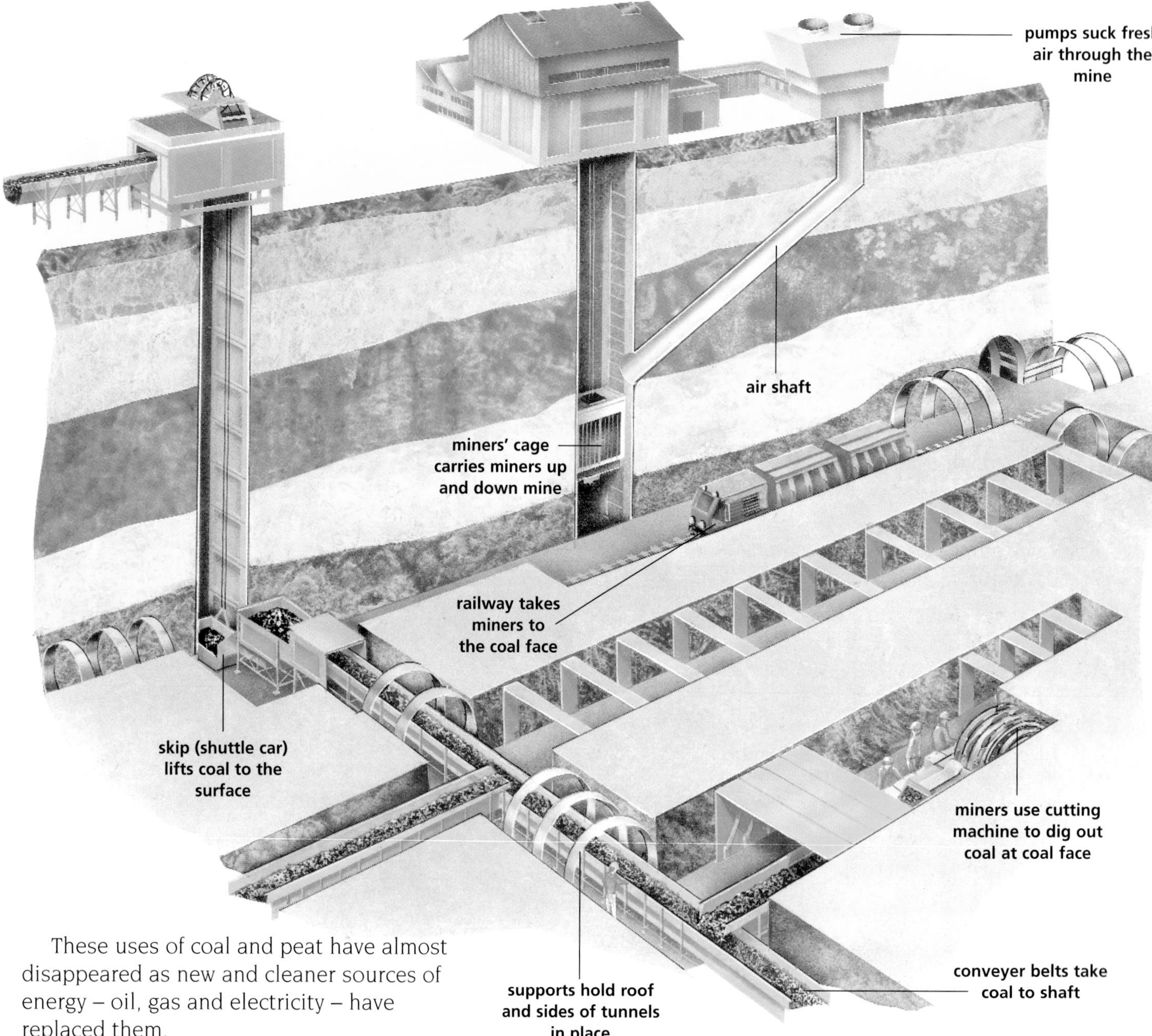

▲ An underground coal mine is a maze of tunnels. Some lead from the main shaft to the seams or layers of coal. Other tunnels are formed as the miners cut away the coal deposits. The tunnels may be many kilometres long: in coastal areas, they may extend out under the seabed.

These uses of coal and peat have almost disappeared as new and cleaner sources of energy – oil, gas and electricity – have replaced them.

Useful products

Peat is now used mainly for growing garden plants, but coal is still an important source of power. Many power stations burn coal to raise steam to drive electricity generators. Factories making products such as cement burn coal to provide the heat for the manufacturing process.

Coal also provides useful products for industry. Heating coal without air produces coke, which is used to make steel. Bitumen for surfacing roads comes from coal, and coal also contains chemicals used to make dyes, drugs and plastics.

Did you know that you can use coal products to wash yourself? Coal is not only used as a fuel. Coal is also a source of chemicals that can be processed to make soap and dyes, as well as medicines, pesticides and other products.

Coasts

Some coasts are sandy, with soft, wide beaches. Some are muddy deltas at the mouth of a river. Other coasts are lined with boulders and pebbles. Some are straight and some are jagged, with hundreds of bays and inlets. In some places the land slopes gradually towards the ocean for hundreds of kilometres, and in others it drops off suddenly into the sea with a steep cliff.

A coast is where the land meets the sea. Coasts are constantly changing.

Find Out More

- Erosion
- Ice caps and glaciers
- Oceans
- Rivers and lakes

Building and destroying coasts

A map of a shoreline today might look very different from a map made a hundred years ago. This is because coastlines change over time.

Rivers bring sediments to the sea, and their deltas grow. The ocean erodes rocks from one part of the coast and then moves them to another. Cliffs retreat inland as waves hammer away at the rocks. Over millions of years, a hilly coast with cliffs and boulders can evolve into a wide, gently sloping sandy plain.

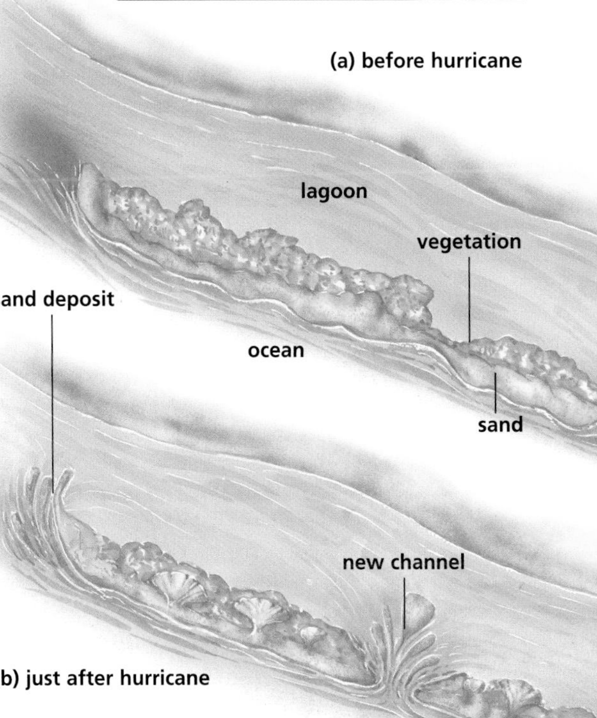

▲ Barrier islands are strips of loose sand that protect the mainland from the ocean. They change shape all the time as they are easily moved by wind and water. A hurricane can change a barrier island in less than a day.

Sinking and rising

Some coasts are actually sinking into the sea or rising up out of it. In the last ice age glaciers covered northern Britain, pushing down the land under their weight. Since the ice melted around 10,000 years ago this land has been rising up, slowly tilting the south coast of Britain into the sea.

The coasts of California, Japan and the Mediterranean have recently been pushed up out of the ocean during powerful earthquakes. Coasts also change as sea levels rise and fall.

▼ The shape of a coastline depends on things like how strong the waves and currents are, how much sand and mud is being carried by the ocean water, how the rocks along the coast respond to being battered by the waves, and how the landscape was shaped in the past.

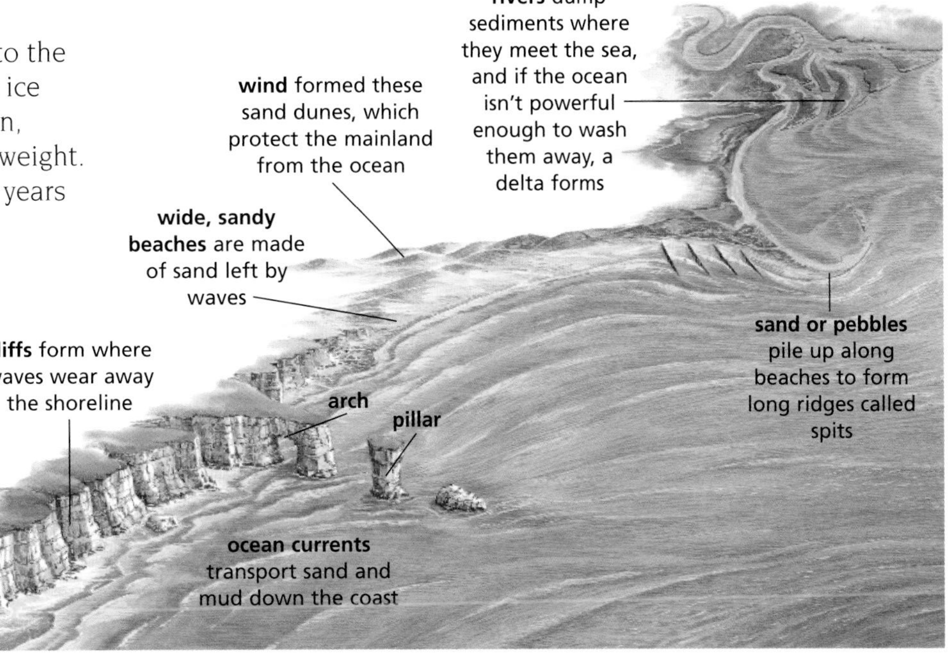

Colour

Caught in the light, a soap bubble shimmers with a beautiful and complex pattern of colours. This is an example of the gift evolution has given us – a marvellous colour-sensitive eye.

All colours come from light. White light is really a mixture of different colours. There are several ways to separate these colours so that we can see them. The surface of a bubble does this, and so do drops of rainwater, which hang in the air and make a rainbow.

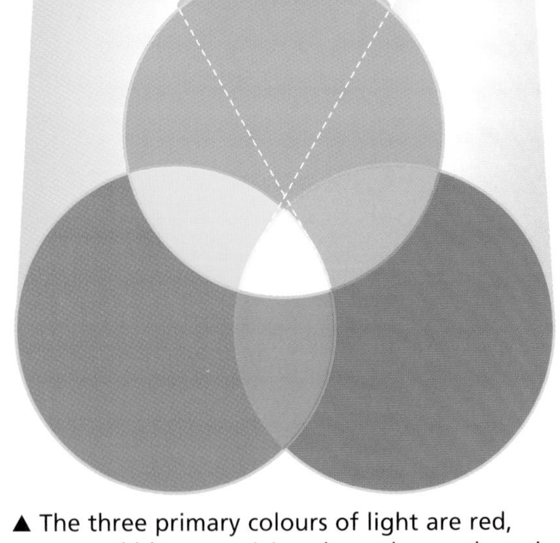

▲ The three primary colours of light are red, green and blue. By mixing these three colours in different combinations, it is possible to make any other colour.

▼ If a disc is painted with the three primary colours and then spun very fast, we see the disc as white.

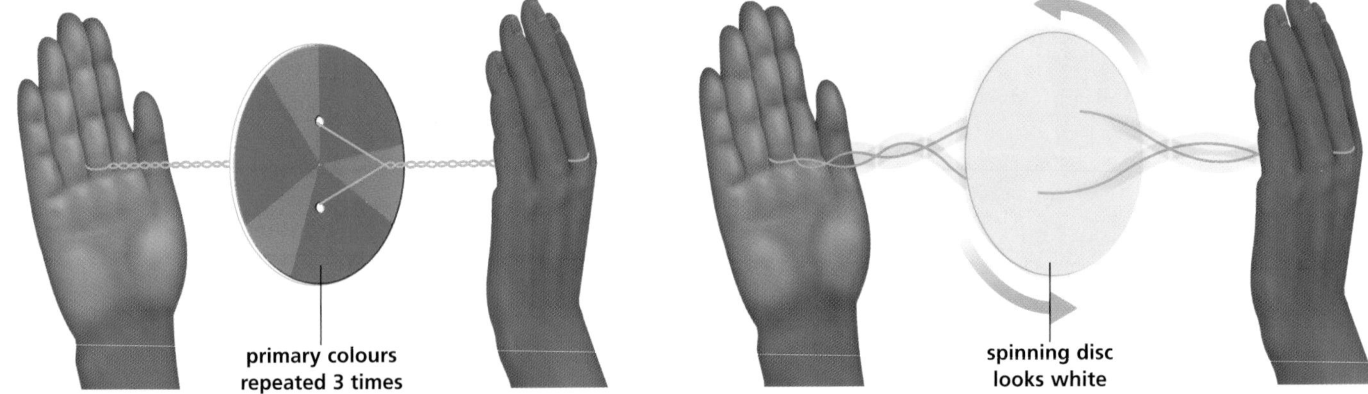

The colours of light

The pattern of colours in a rainbow is the same as that made by a prism (red to violet) and is called a spectrum. Light travels in the form of waves. The different colours of the spectrum have different wavelengths. If you think of light as being like ripples on the surface of a pond, the wavelength is the distance between the wave peaks. The wavelength of visible light is very small: between 1350 and 2500 light waves would fit in a millimetre, depending on the colour of the light.

Some objects, such as lamps, produce their own light. If they are producing all of the colours, they look white. If they only

◀ A rainbow over Victoria Falls in Zimbabwe. Rainbows are made when sunlight is split into a spectrum of colours by tiny water droplets in the air.

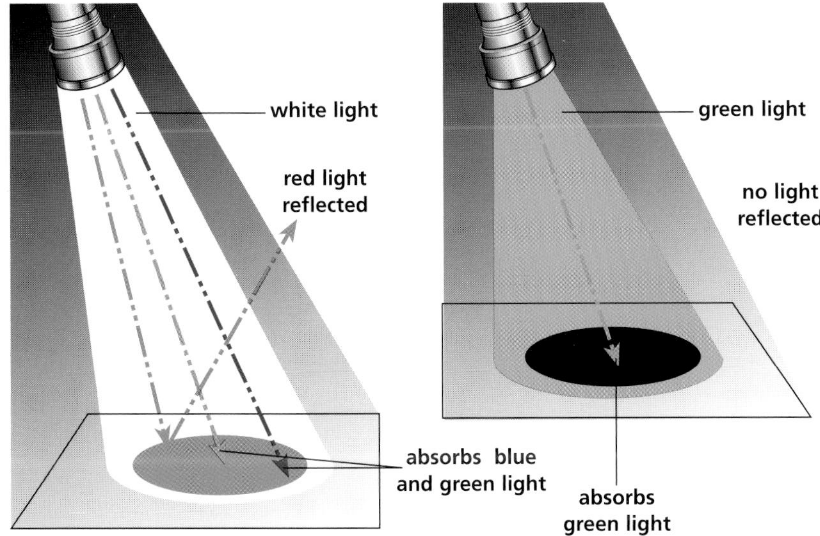

▲ The spot in this picture absorbs blue and green light, but reflects red. In white light the spot looks red, but in green light, no light is reflected, and it looks black.

produce some of the colours, they will be a colour of the spectrum. Yellow street lamps are yellow simply because they are only making yellow light.

The colours of things

Most of the objects we see reflect light to our eyes. An object that reflects all of the colours equally well (such as a snowman) will look white. A tarmac road looks black because it is hardly reflecting any light at all. Other colours are produced if the object is reflecting some of the light hitting it and absorbing the rest. For example, a red car reflects red light, and absorbs the other colours of the spectrum.

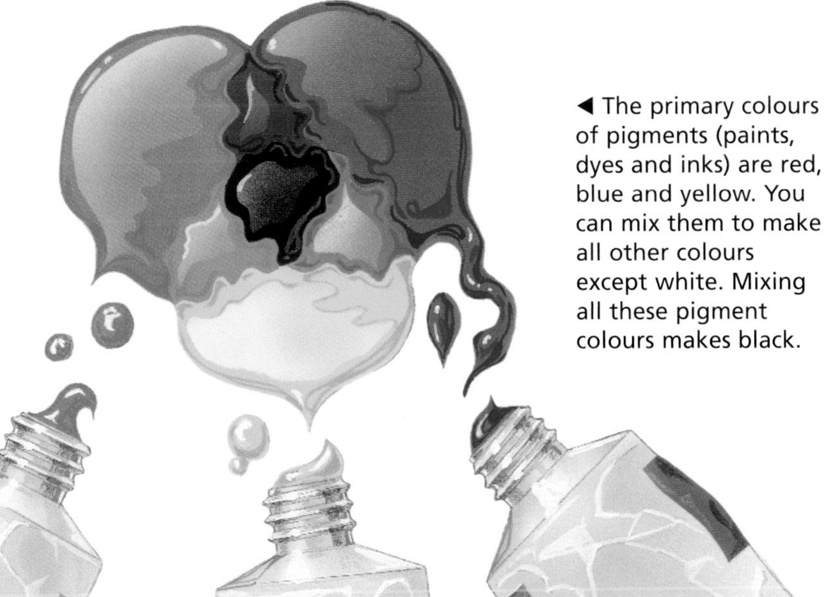

◀ The primary colours of pigments (paints, dyes and inks) are red, blue and yellow. You can mix them to make all other colours except white. Mixing all these pigment colours makes black.

Find Out More

- Cameras
- Electromagnetic spectrum
- Eyes
- Light
- Paints
- Photography
- Spectrum

COLOUR VISION

Surprisingly, the eye contains only three types of colour-sensitive cell. These cells (called cones) are at the back of the eye (the retina). The cones respond to red, green and blue light. The brain makes out all the other colours by combining the signals from these cells. Yellow light stimulates the red and green cells, but not the blue cells. The brain has learnt to recognize this combined signal as being due to yellow light.

Some of the colours that we see are not part of the spectrum at all. For example, there is no wavelength of light for the colour brown. Such colours are invented by the brain using some combination of signals from the eye.

We can use the way the brain recognizes colours to fool it into seeing colours that are not really there. A colour TV picture is made up of tiny red, green and blue strips close together. We see a whole variety of colours because these strips are made to shine at different brightnesses. A yellow shirt is shown on the screen by making the red and green strips shine much more brightly than the blue ones. This produces exactly the same signal to the brain as yellow light. In this way the eye is 'tricked' into seeing a yellow shirt.

▼ You can see any colour on your TV screen, but if you look at the screen closely enough, you will see that the picture is made up of tiny strips of just three colours: red, green and blue.

Combustion *see* Oxygen, Reactions, chemical

Comets

Not many sights in the night sky are as awesome as a bright comet. Often arriving without warning, a comet can inspire fear and wonder.

Though comets look spectacular, they contain very little material. The Earth has passed through the tail of a comet without any noticeable effect. Only the comet's nucleus is solid, made of a mixture of ice and dust. Photos of the nucleus of Halley's Comet taken by the spacecraft *Giotto* showed that it is only about 10 kilometres long.

Thousands of millions of comet nuclei swarm around the Solar System far beyond Neptune and Pluto. A few find their way to the inner Solar System. They generally sweep around the Sun then travel back out into space, not to return for thousands of years. But some are pulled off course by massive Jupiter's strong gravity. This changes their orbits. They stay nearer the Sun and are seen regularly every few years.

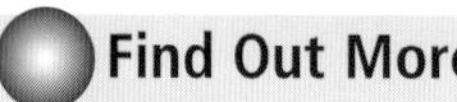

- Jupiter
- Meteors and meteorites
- Solar System

▼ Halley's Comet follows a long elliptical orbit around the Sun. It takes about 76 years to complete one orbit. The last time it came near the Sun and the Earth was in 1986. Several spacecraft were sent to study it.

▲ Comet Hale-Bopp was an unusually bright comet seen by many people in 1997. Its dust tail is bright and curved. The fainter blue tail is gas. Radiation from the Sun makes it glow.

Parts of a comet

When a comet is warmed by the Sun, a large cloud of gas and dust, called the coma, comes off the central nucleus. The coma can be a million kilometres across. Sunlight and gas streaming from the Sun push the dust and gas away from the comet in two separate tails. The tails can grow to be hundreds of millions of kilometres long. The dust tail shines with reflected sunlight.

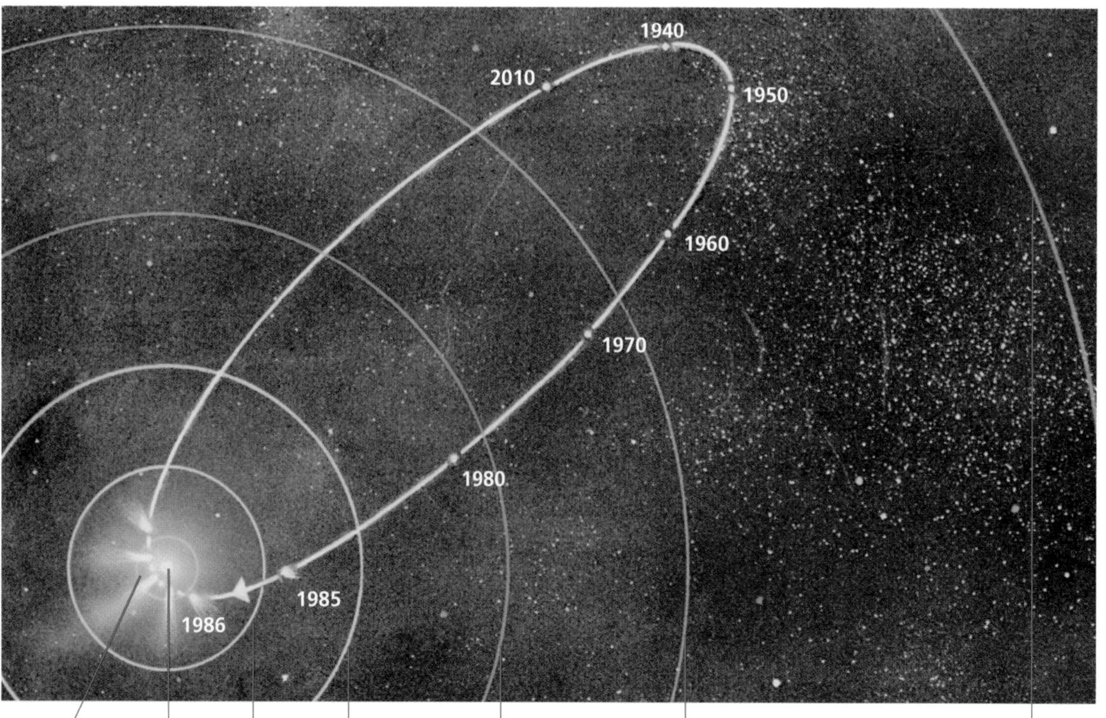

▼ Edmond Halley (1656–1742) was the first person to calculate the path of a comet and predict when it would be seen again. Halley's Comet was named in his honour even though he did not discover it. Historical records show that Halley's Comet has been observed for more than 2000 years.

Communications

'That's one small step for a man, one giant leap for mankind', said the US astronaut Neil Armstrong in 1969, as he took his first steps on the Moon. Radio signals beamed Armstrong's words and TV pictures live to Earth, and they were broadcast around the world.

The Moon landing broadcasts were a triumph of modern communications. But today, people can communicate in many more ways than in 1969, using mobile phones, faxes, emails and satellite links.

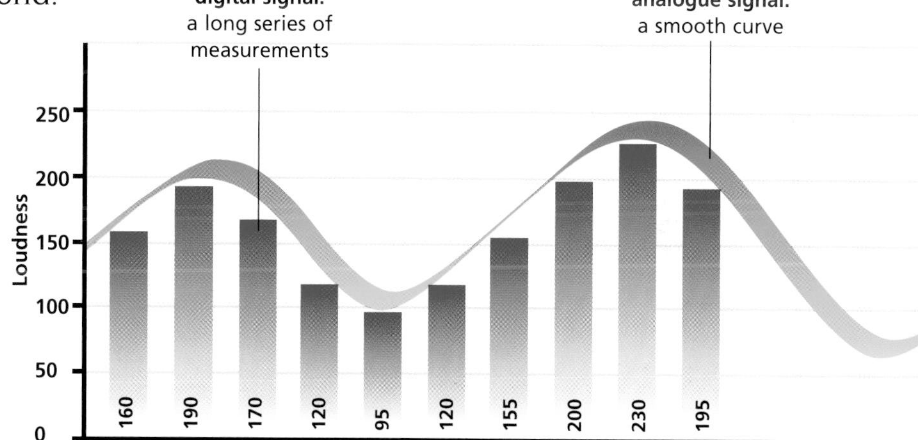

▶ A sound or a picture can be recorded as an analogue signal – an electrical copy of the sound or image. This signal changes smoothly. But modern communications are mostly digital. In a digital signal, the sound or picture is 'sampled' (measured) at regular intervals. The string of measurements is the digital signal.

Reaching out

However different they are, all communication systems have one thing in common. They turn a message – made up of spoken words, music, text or pictures – into something that can be sent (transmitted) in some way. This is called a 'signal'. At the receiving end, the signal is turned back into the message.

One of the first long-distance communication systems, invented in 1790, was the semaphore tower. Semaphore towers had two long wooden arms that could be moved to different positions. Each position of the arms stood for a different letter or number. Using semaphore, messages could be sent between distant hilltops many kilometres apart. But semaphore was very slow.

Going electric

Communications speeded up after the discovery in 1821 that an electric current flowing in a wire can make a compass needle turn. This led to the invention of the telegraph, which could send messages both further and faster than semaphore.

◀ Digital phone calls can be transmitted as flashes of light, through cables made of optical fibre. Today, most telephone networks use fibre, as they can carry more calls.

▶ A type of semaphore signalling was used by sailors for many years to communicate between ships. The sailors signalled using two flags, one in either hand.

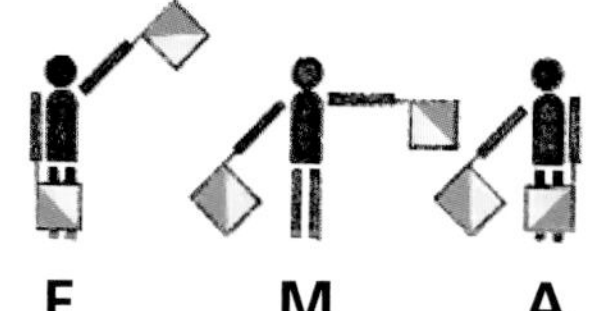

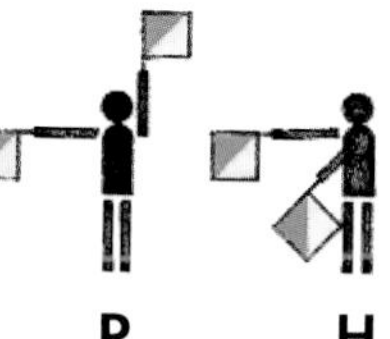

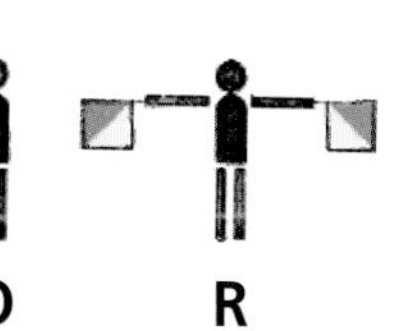

Telegraphs sent different electric currents down the wires. At the receiver, these made needles point to different letters or numbers.

The telegraph became faster with the invention of a springy switch called a telegraph key, which could send messages in Morse code. This coded letters and numbers as mixtures of short 'dots' or longer 'dashes' of electric current.

Sounds and waves

The invention of the telephone in 1876 made it possible for people to actually speak to each other, rather than sending messages by code. As with the telegraph, the messages were sent as electrical signals along wires.

Radio waves can also carry communications. Television, radio, telephone and Internet signals can all be sent this way. Radio waves travel in straight lines. This means that over long distances radio signals do not follow the curved surface of the Earth. Satellites circling in space can be used to send such signals around the world. The satellite receives a signal – such as a TV sports broadcast – then re-transmits it to another part of the Earth that could not be reached otherwise.

▼ Some mobile phone masts are made to look like trees so that they blend into the environment.

Calls on the move

Mobile phones transmit messages using radio-type waves called microwaves. Special masts with aerials that can send and receive mobile phone transmissions are dotted all over the country. A call from a mobile usually goes to the nearest of these masts. If the receiving phone is a mobile too, the signals travel through the telephone network to the mast nearest to the receiving phone. This mast then transmits the call via microwaves.

Modern mobiles and television networks send very clear digital signals. These turn a normal, or analogue signal, into a stream of numbers.

SAMUEL MORSE'S CODE

The US inventor Samuel Morse (1791–1872) became interested in the telegraph in the 1830s. He eventually developed the system of dots and dashes that became known as Morse code. He demonstrated the code for the first time in 1844.

Although Morse code was punched into paper tape at the telegraph receiver, operators found they could decode it much quicker by simply listening to the noise made by the tape punch.

▶ The alphabet and numbers 1 to 10 in Morse code.

A •—	B —•••	C —•—•	D —••
E •	F ••—•	G ——•	H ••••
I ••	J •———	K —•—	L •—••
M ——	N —•	O ———	P •——•
Q ——•—	R •—•	S •••	T —
U ••—	V •••—	W •——	X —••—
Y —•——	Z ——••	1 •————	2 ••———
3 •••——	4 ••••—	5 •••••	6 —••••
7 ——•••	8 ———••	9 ————•	10 —————

Find Out More

- Faxes and modems
- Fibre optics
- Internet
- Radio
- Satellites
- Telephones
- Television

Compact discs

The ancient library at Alexandria, in Egypt, contained 500,000 scrolls, filling many rooms. Nowadays we can put the same amount of information on a few hundred CDs, which would fit on a couple of library shelves.

Compact discs (CDs) can store a great deal of information. Often this information is music. A CD-ROM is a compact disc that stores text (words), pictures, sound, computer games or computer software. The 'ROM' stands for 'Read Only Memory'.

The information is held on the disc as a series of bumps on its shiny surface. The bumps follow a spiral track, starting near the middle of the disc and ending at the edge.

The disc is read by shining a laser beam onto it. As the beam sweeps over the bumps, it reflects as a series of flashes which are picked up by a light-sensitive circuit and turned into electrical signals.

Turning sound into bumps

Sound is vibrations in the air. When a CD is recorded, the sound is 'written down' as a series of numbers, each recording the size of the sound vibration at a particular moment. With complex music, the vibrations change quickly, so the sound has to be written down thousands of times per second. On the CD the sound values are coded as binary numbers – numbers written using only 1s and 0s. Each bump is a 1, no bump is a 0.

▲ An electron microscope photo of the surface of a CD. The bumps are just 5 millionths of a metre across and about twice as long. The whole spiral track is over 8 kilometres long!

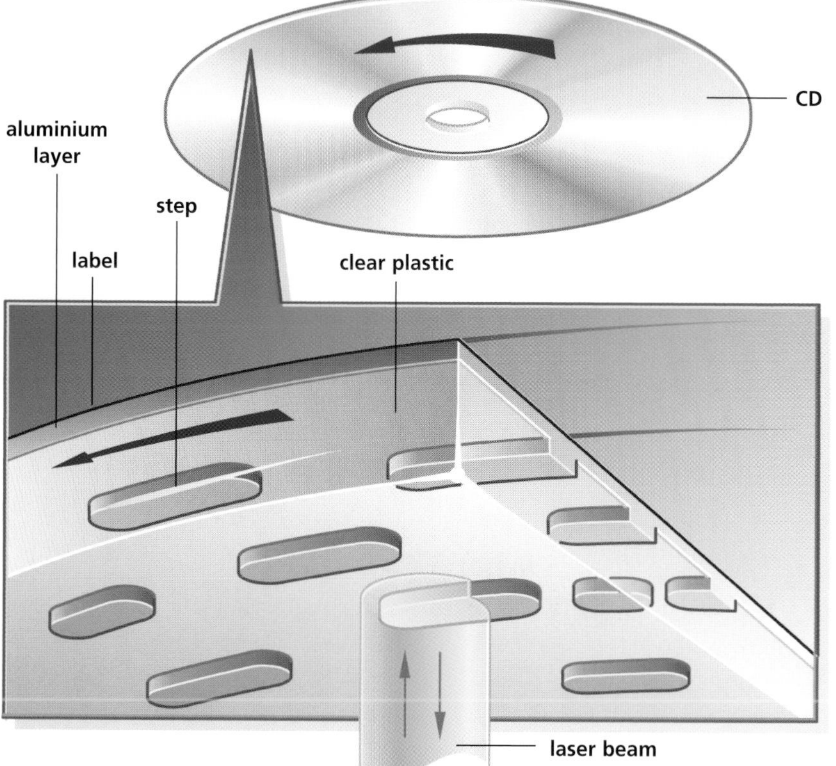

◀ How a CD player works. The laser reads the spiral track by sweeping across the disc as it spins. A detector picks up the changes in the reflected beam when the laser hits a bump.

Other types of disc

Digital videodiscs (DVDs) hold even more information than CDs. They use smaller bumps and have two reflective layers. Recordable CDs (CD-Rs) do not have bumps. They use patches of colour on the disc to change the reflected laser light.

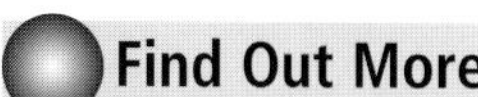

Find Out More

- Computers
- Lasers and holograms
- Sound recording
- Video equipment

Compasses *see* Magnetism and electromagnetism • **Composites** *see* Plastics • **Computer games** *see* Software

Computer graphics

© Disney Enterprises, Inc

Animated movies like *Toy Story* and *A Bug's Life* were made entirely on computers. To make computer graphics appear to move naturally, a computer has to make about 24 pictures for every second of the movie. And each picture is made up of millions of coloured dots called pixels. This needs a lot of computing power.

It took about 35 years after the invention of computers for the technology to become good enough to make computer movies. But movies are only one of many areas where computers are being used to design things.

▶ A CAD drawing of a future NASA space shuttle that might use a magnetic track to speed its take off.

© Disney Enterprises, Inc

◀ The characters Woody and Buzz Lightyear from the *Toy Story* movies were created on computer. Extremely fast, powerful supercomputers are needed to create a full-length animated film.

Planes, trains and cars

If you travel in a car, train, bus or plane, the vehicle has almost certainly been designed on a computer. The same goes for bridges, buildings and even clothes.

There are many advantages to designing things on a computer. The main one is that you can try many different designs until you have one that is just right. And the computer can make sure that you use the least amount of material to make, say, a new style of jacket. So you save money.

What a CAD

Designing things with the help of computers is called Computer Aided Design (CAD). This takes advantage of the fact that it is easy to save pictures of things in a computer's memory.

Find Out More

- Astronomy
- Bridges
- Computers
- Software

Using a CAD system, drawings are made on the computer screen using a special pen that you press on a rectangular pad called a graphics tablet. This uses the pressure of the pen tip on the pad to draw on the computer screen. A mouse could also be used. But if you already have a hand-drawn picture of a car, you can use an image scanner to capture it on the computer.

The pixels (dots) that make up the drawing are saved as a number of digital 'bits' in the computer's memory and displayed on the computer's screen. The software then lets you do things like show the design from a different angle, or colour it differently.

Designs drawn with a CAD system can be printed out as plans for making something, or they can be used to control the machines that are used to make the parts. With a technique called rapid prototyping, it is even possible to print out a solid, three-dimensional model of the object in rubber, wax, plastic, metal or a material similar to plywood.

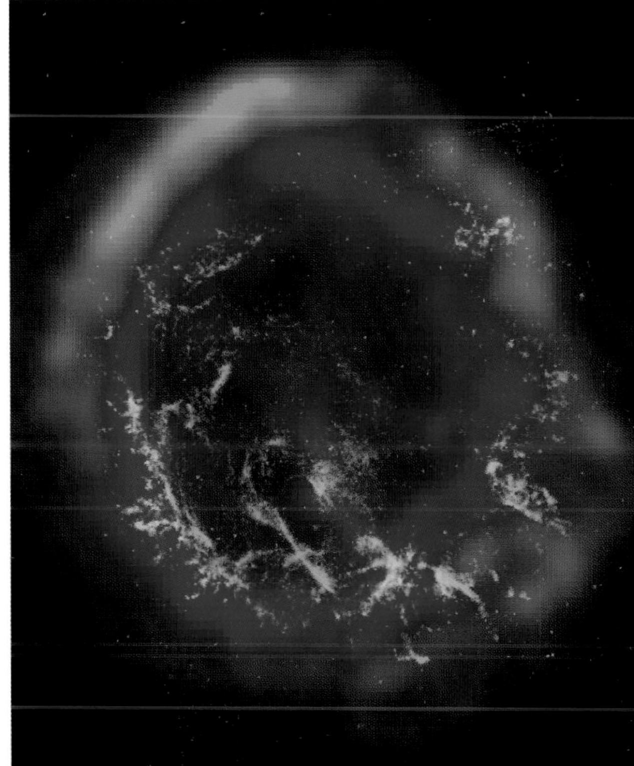

▶ Astronomers can use computers to put together information from different types of telescope into a single picture. In this picture of the remains of an exploded star, the blue parts came from an X-ray telescope, the green from an optical telescope and the red from a radio telescope.

▼ Engineers usually work out their designs in three dimensions, then produce plans on paper. But using rapid prototyping, they can now make solid models of objects from computerized plans. The printer works by building up the object in thousands of thin layers.

Applying physics

But drawing is only part of the design. Computers also let you check, for example, how a bridge design will stand up to high winds or very low temperature. This is called simulation. Computer simulations save money, as engineers don't have to build the design to see how it behaves. If the simulation shows problems, they can be corrected before anything is built.

Simulation using computer graphics is also useful for teaching. Airline pilots 'fly' a computerized flight simulator before they fly a real plane.

Computer images also help scientists to understand things. Molecules are too small to see, but models of them can be drawn on computers and studied to see how they might be useful. And radio telescope images of space can be cleaned up so that far-off galaxies can be seen more clearly.

Computers

Thud! You feel the wheels of your aircraft touch down on the runway – but you're surprised that you've landed already. Outside, the fog's so thick you thought you were still up in the clouds. So how did the pilots manage to land the aircraft without seeing the runway? Well, they had a computer to help them.

Computers are very good at storing and handling information (data). The Internet provides a vast store of data that we can all tap into from a computer at home.

Computers are also very good at controlling all kinds of machines, from dishwashers to the space shuttle. In industry, computers are at the heart of control systems that run everything from car assembly lines to oil refineries.

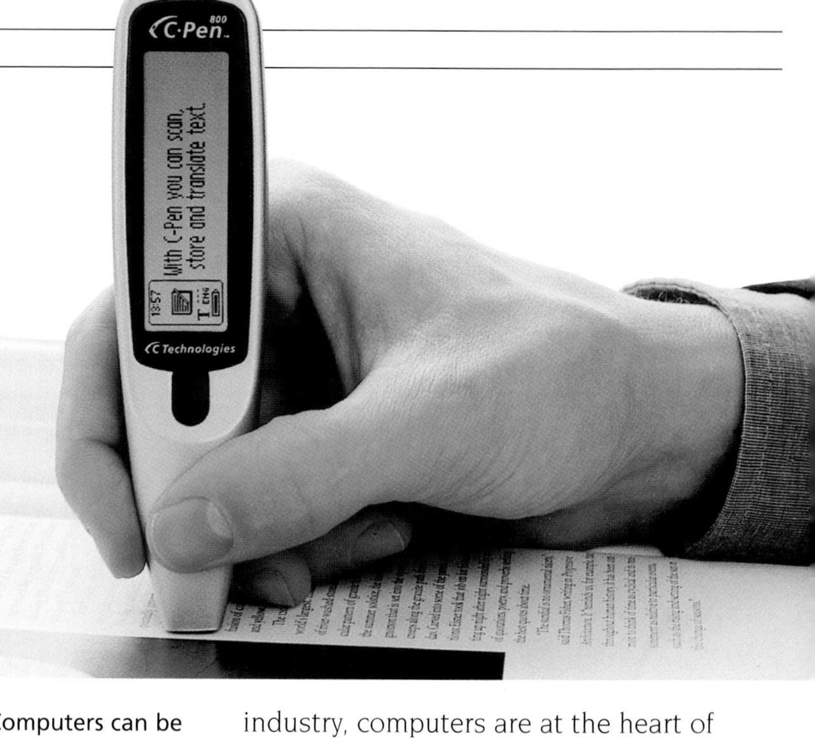

▲ Computers can be built into many gadgets. This electronic 'pen' can scan text into its memory and then translate it into many different languages.

Find Out More

- Computer graphics and design
- Electronics
- Hardware
- Internet
- Microchips
- Software

How computers work

But what exactly is a computer? It is an electronic machine that works under the control of a list of instructions called a program. The computer takes in data, which is called an input. It processes the data in a central processing unit (CPU). The CPU contains one or more microchips, or microprocessors. A microprocessor is basically a calculator that performs a few simple types of sums very quickly.

The result of all the processing is called the

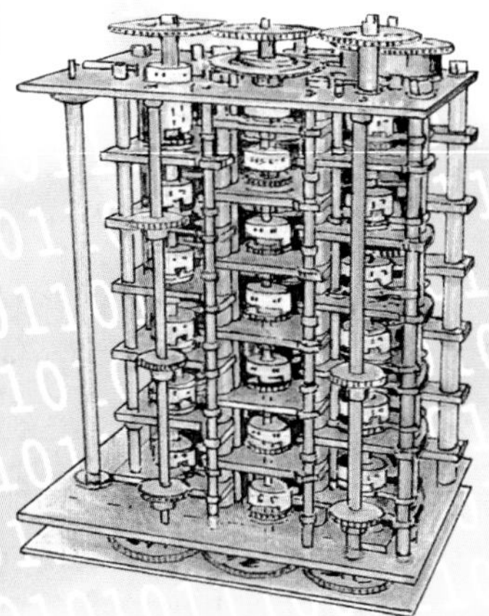

1830s
British mathematician Charles Babbage (1791–1871) designs a machine to calculate numbers correctly. Although it was not built, his Difference Engine contained ideas used in computers today.

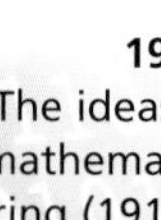

1890s
American Hermann Hollerith (1860–1929) develops a machine that uses punched cards to calculate the results of the 1890 US census. In 1896 Hollerith sets up the company that later becomes IBM.

1940s
The ideas of British mathematician Alan Turing (1912–1954) lead to the development of computers like the Colossus, which helps crack German secret codes in World War II.

1951
Univac-1 (above), the world's first commercial computer, is designed by John Mauchly (1907–1980) and J. Presper Eckert (1919–1995). Mauchly and Eckert built ENIAC, the first electronic computer, in 1946.

▲ A timeline of some of the important events in the history of computing.

computer's output. The computer is called the hardware, while the program is the software.

Only two numbers

Most computers are digital computers. This means they handle all their data in the form of binary numbers. The two numbers in binary are simply 0 and 1 (the decimal system we count in runs from 0 to 9). Binary is easy for a computer to deal with. The microprocessor contains millions of tiny electronic switches equivalent to miniature transistors, which can be turned on or off. 'On' can represent the 1 in a binary number, and 'Off' can represent the 0. Using these simple numbers, the microprocessor is able to do sums at lightning speed.

It's not just calculations that a computer uses binary numbers for. Words, pictures and sounds are all created, changed and stored digitally using binary numbers. In a word processing program each letter and number is coded for by a particular binary number. Pictures are broken up into tiny dots (pixels), and the brightness and colour of each pixel is coded as a binary number. Sounds can also be coded in this way.

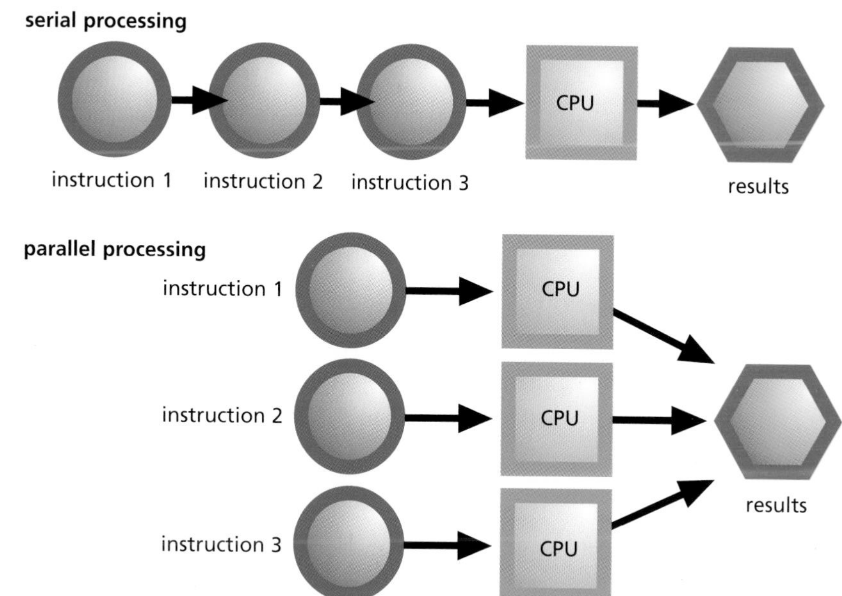

▲ Serial processing – working on one piece of data at a time – is slow but cheap, while parallel processing is fast but expensive.

Call an architect

The way computers process data can be chosen to best match the task in hand. In a serial processor, a microprocessor carries out the first part of the task it has to do, then the next part, then the next, and so on. In a parallel processor, software divides up a task and splits it between many microprocessors, which all work on it at the same time.

Parallel processing is very fast, but also very expensive. Some parallel processors are so fast that they are called supercomputers.

1968
'Mainframe' computers beginning to be used in large businesses.

1976
The first supercomputer, the Cray-1, is built. Modern supercomputers are used for weather forecasting, complex maths and physics problems, and animation in modern films.

1981
IBM produce the IBM PC, with software written by American Bill Gates (born 1955). The machine is a success for IBM, and for Gates's company Microsoft.

1998
A team of researchers at IBM build a very simple quantum computer. Quantum computers work using single atoms or even electrons. They have the potential to be enormously more powerful than ordinary computers.

Supercomputers are used for very special projects like weather forecasting or making computer models of the surface of the Sun. They might be used to predict hurricanes – which could save lives, if they help raise the alarm in time. Supercomputers are needed for such jobs because so many things happen at once in weather systems that only a very powerful computer can hope to keep track of them.

Total recall

The computer's software is stored in a memory of some kind. A computer has two kinds of memory, stored on microchips. The software that controls how the computer's various pieces of hardware operate is stored in a memory that cannot be interfered with. This is called the Read-Only Memory, or ROM.

Before the computer starts up a program, the software will be sitting on a disk. When the computer software is running, this software will be copied into another memory, called the Random Access Memory, or RAM.

In operation

The operating system (OS) is a piece of software that controls how the user works the computer. Some systems use a lot of 'windows' and small pictures called icons, which represent different programs. You point to them, then click using a hand-held device called a mouse. Other operating systems, like those in early PCs, have a rather boring screen in which you enter commands, such as 'run word processor,' using a keyboard.

Future ideas

The microchips in today's computers are made up of thousands of tiny transistors, made from silicon. But future machines could use even smaller parts, capable of even greater speeds. Some scientists want to use single chemical molecules (groups of atoms) as computer on/off switches. Meanwhile, others think that single atoms, or even parts of atoms, could be used to make 'quantum' computers.

▲ Tiny notebook computers like this one can link to the Internet over mobile phone networks.

▼ In older aircraft, the pilot controlled the plane using mechanical links from the cockpit controls to the plane's engine, flaps and rudder. But in airliners like this Airbus A340, computers can control the aircraft by sending electrical signals to the engine, flaps and rudder.

Concorde *see* Flight and flow • **Concrete** see Ceramics • **Condensation** *see* Matter

Conductors and insulators

The ring of an electric fire glows red-hot when electricity is passing through it. But if the ring were made of wood instead of metal, it would not let electricity pass through – and it wouldn't get hot! That's because some materials let electricity pass through them, but some don't.

Materials that let electricity pass through them are called conductors. Materials that are good conductors of electricity are usually good conductors of heat, too. Things that block the flow of electricity or heat are called insulators. Both kinds of material have many uses.

free electron

metal atom

▲ Electricity can flow through a metal, such as copper, because the metal contains electrons that are free to move.

Electrical conductors and insulators

Electrical conductors are usually metal, or at least mainly metal. Silver and copper are two of the best conductors. Silver is the best conductor of all, but it is expensive, so copper is usually used for electrical wiring. Carbon is the only non-metal that is a good conductor.

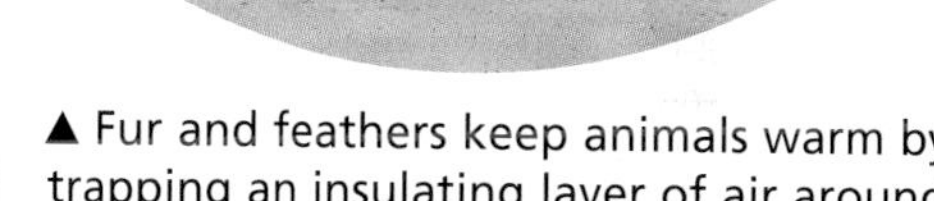

▲ Fur and feathers keep animals warm by trapping an insulating layer of air around the animal's body.

All materials are made of very tiny particles called atoms, and atoms themselves are made up of even tinier parts called protons, neutrons and electrons. Metals are good conductors because some of their electrons are not tied to a particular atom, but are free to move. The electrons can be made to move by a battery or by mains electricity – this flow of electrons is an electric current.

Materials such as concrete, wood, rubber and plastic are good electrical insulators. Air is a good insulator too. Unlike conductors, insulating materials hold on tightly to their electrons. Because the electrons aren't free to move, no electricity can flow.

Electric fires get hot because even metals are not perfect conductors. As electrons flow through the bars of the electric fire, they bump into neighbouring metal atoms, causing them to vibrate and give out heat energy.

◀ This Japanese train is powered by mains electricity. Thick metal cables carry the high-voltage electricity above the track. The train connects to the cables through a sliding contact called a pantograph.

Heat conductors and insulators

Metals are good conductors of heat as well as of electricity. Saucepans are made of metal, because this allows heat to reach the food more easily. Good-quality saucepans often have a copper base, because copper is a better heat conductor than most other metals.

Heat insulators are materials that do not allow heat to flow easily through them. Saucepans often have handles made of insulating materials such as plastic or wood. This stops the handle from getting too hot while the pan is on the heat.

Air is a good heat insulator. Some of the best insulating materials, such as the feathers or hollow fibres in a duvet, have tiny pockets of air trapped within the material.

Aerogel, nicknamed 'frozen smoke', is a super-light , very strong material that is an amazing heat insulator. If you heat one side of a thin sheet of aerogel with a blow-torch, you can still comfortably touch the other side.

▶ These ceramic (pottery) insulators are placed between high-power electricity cables and the pylons that support them. They stop electricity from flowing into the pylon itself.

Find Out More

- Circuits
- Electricity
- Magnetism and electromagnetism
- Microchips
- Trains

Semiconductors and superconductors

Electrically, some materials are between conductors and insulators. Materials like this are called semiconductors. Silicon is the best known. Semiconductors can be treated with chemicals to change how well they conduct electricity. For example, a single crystal of silicon can be treated so that lots of microscopic circuits are formed on it. The result is a microchip.

Other materials called superconductors have an even more remarkable property. At very low temperatures, these materials hardly resist electron flow at all: hardly any energy is needed to send an electric current through them. Superconductors are also strongly diamagnetic: this means that they strongly repel magnets.

▼ The small disc in this picture is a magnet. It is repelled so strongly by the superconductor below it that it floats in mid-air.

Superconductors are used in very fast computers. They are also used in special trains called maglevs. These use the repelling force between superconductors and magnets to lift the whole train up so that it hovers above the track.

Because superconductors have to be kept at such low temperatures, they are not yet very widely used. But scientists are working to create new superconductors that do not need to be cooled so much.

Conifers *see* Plants, Forests, Wood and timber

Conservation

By 1980, less than 100 golden lion tamarins survived in the wild. Much of their Brazilian forest home had been cut down, to provide timber and to make way for farms, mines, towns and cities. Tamarins born in zoos have been put back into the wild to try and save the species from extinction.

▲ Tigers, gorillas, giant pandas and thousands of other animal species are in danger of dying out, mainly because their homes in the wild are being destroyed.

Breeding rare animals and plants in captivity is one way to stop them disappearing for ever. But in the long term, they need wild places in which to live if they are to survive. Preserving the habitats of wild animals is therefore vitally important. This is often difficult when there are so many people in the world who need places to live and land to farm. But plants and animals are a vital part of our world. Living things help to control the balance of gases, heat and moisture in the atmosphere and the flow of nutrients through the soil. By protecting the Earth's wildlife, we are protecting our own future and the whole planet as well.

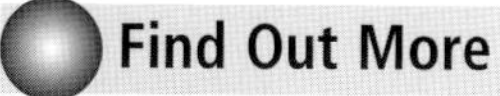

Find Out More

- Animals
- Ecology
- Pollution
- Recycling

▼ Sea birds that get covered in oil from leaking tankers can sometimes be cleaned up. But we still do not know enough about how the oil from tanker accidents affects the ocean ecosystem.

Big help

There is a lot that governments and countries can do to conserve plants and animals. They can ban the hunting and collection of rare species. They can stop people selling rare animals or their body parts, such as their horns and skins. They can set up nature reserves to protect vital habitats, and preserve rare species in zoos, botanical gardens and seed banks. And they can pass laws to reduce pollution, which is a major threat to wildlife.

Small help

On a smaller scale, each one of us can make a difference. Scientists help by finding out more about how plants and animals live. The more we know about the natural world, the more we can do to protect it. All of us can help to raise money for conservation work and protest against things that harm living things or their environment. We can recycle waste, reduce pollution from our homes or cars, help to clean up the local environment and encourage wildlife.

Conservation of energy *see* Energy

Constellations

Look up at the starry sky and you will soon notice how the bright stars make shapes. There are lines, squares, crosses and a letter 'W' and a cross. Seeing patterns in the stars and giving them names goes back thousands of years.

The patterns in the stars are called constellations. Through history, different civilizations have had their own constellations. People making new star maps have made changes to the constellations and invented new ones. In 1930, astronomers finally agreed how to divide the whole sky into 88 areas, which are now the official constellations. Forty-eight of them date back to the 2nd century AD.

The constellations you can see depend on your latitude on the Earth. If you live in the northern hemisphere, there are constellations you will never see unless you travel to the southern hemisphere – and the other way round. Most of the southern constellations were named by travellers in the 16th and 17th centuries.

Many of the brighter stars also have traditional names of their own. They are usually Latin or Arabic words.

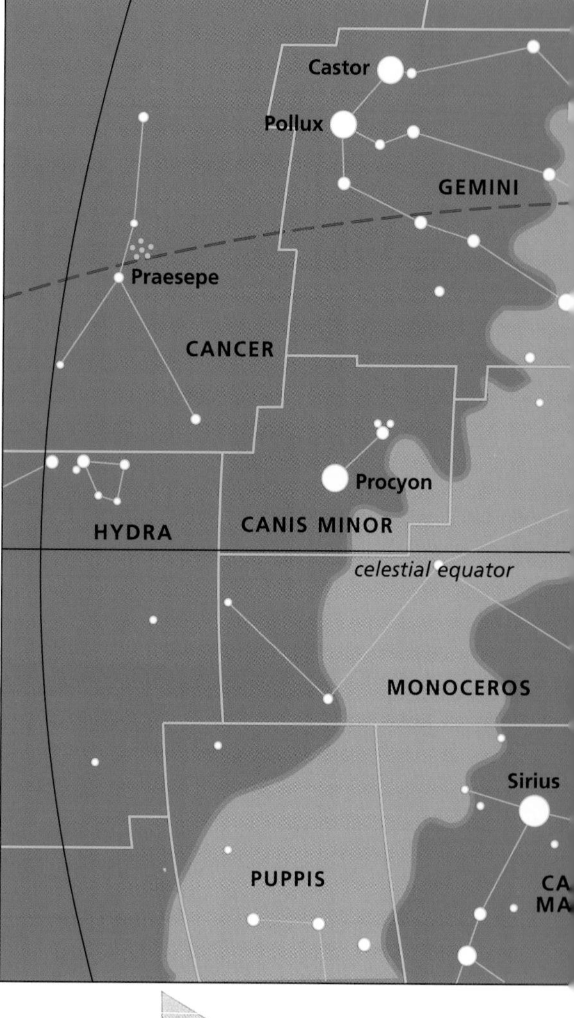

▶ This star map shows some constellations visible (names in capitals) and some of the brightest stars between December and March in the northern hemisphere. The yellow lines are the official boundaries between the constellations and the light band is the Milky Way. The dotted line shows the ecliptic.

Find Out More

- Astronomy
- Light
- Stars

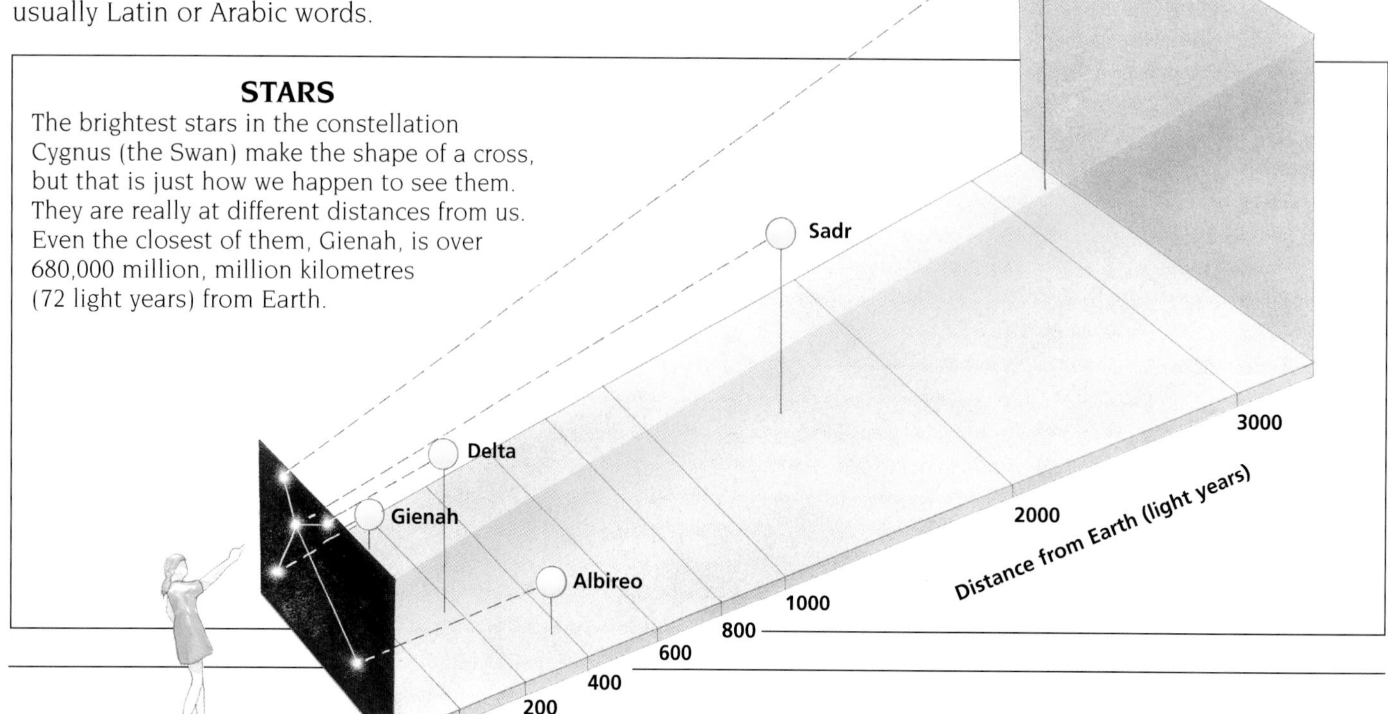

STARS

The brightest stars in the constellation Cygnus (the Swan) make the shape of a cross, but that is just how we happen to see them. They are really at different distances from us. Even the closest of them, Gienah, is over 680,000 million, million kilometres (72 light years) from Earth.

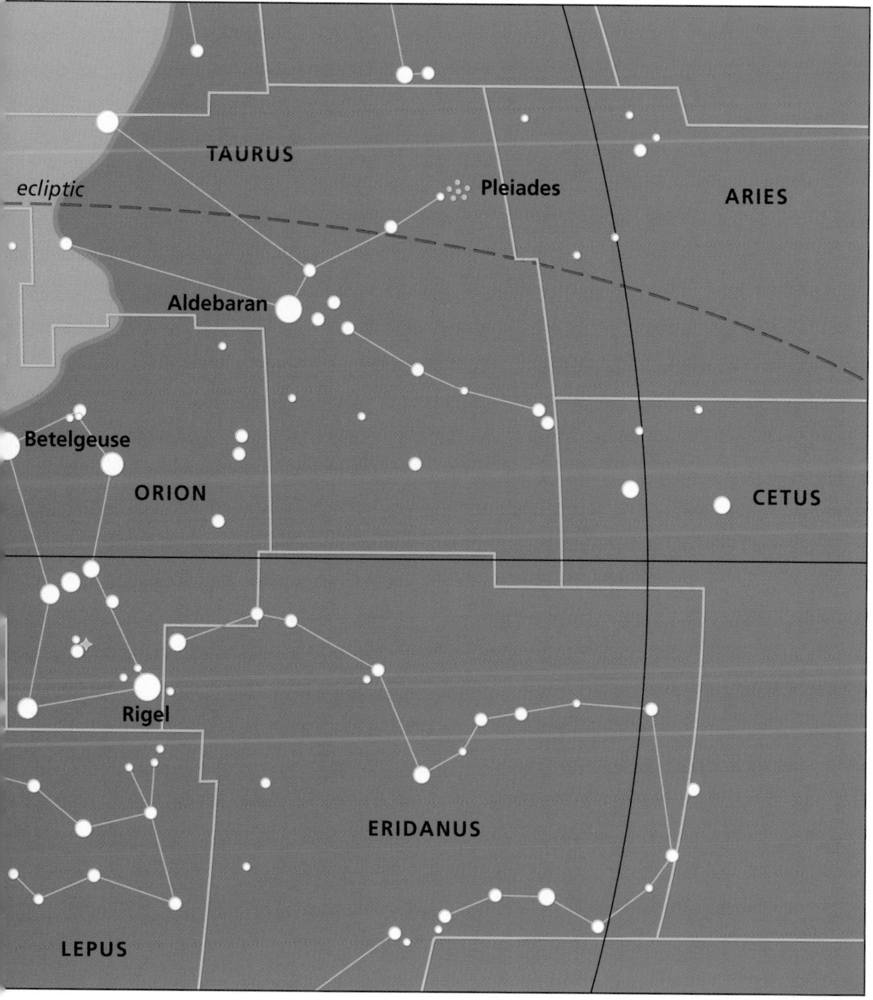

The Sun and the zodiac

If the stars were visible during the day, we would see that the Sun gradually moves through the constellations. Over a year, it covers a complete circle, called the ecliptic. The planets are always near to the ecliptic too.

The ecliptic goes through the 12 constellations traditionally called the zodiac: Aries, Taurus, Gemini, Cancer, Leo, Virgo, Libra, Scorpius, Sagittarius, Capricornus, Aquarius and Pisces. Astrologers divide the zodiac band into 12 equal parts, called 'signs', with the same names, but these do not coincide with the astronomical constellations.

The stars are so far away that their distances are often given in light years instead of kilometres. A light year is the distance light travels in one year. The speed of light is nearly 300,000 kilometres per second. In a year light travels 9461 million million kilometres.

▼ The constellations of the zodiac and how the Sun moves around the ecliptic through the year.

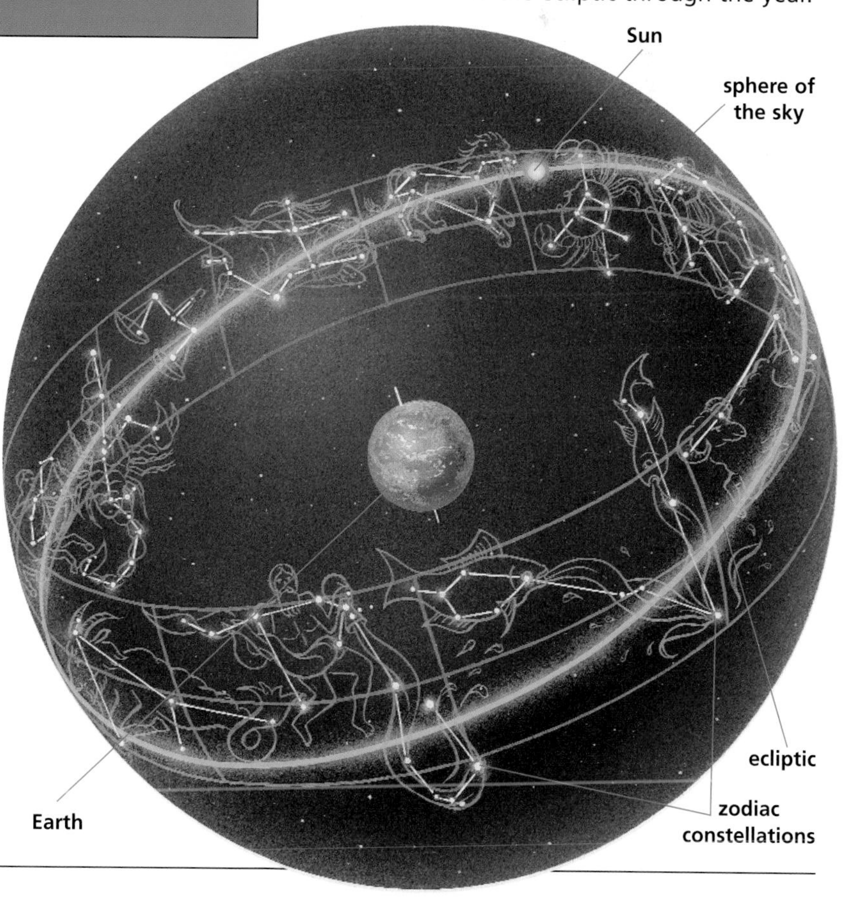

The sphere of the sky

The stars in a constellation look as though they are close together, but in actual fact they are scattered through space at different distances from us. It is simply that we cannot tell that just by looking up at the sky.

At any particular time, half of the stars visible in space are hidden below our horizon. But we see a sequence of different constellations through the night, because the Earth is turning.

The whole sky seems to revolve about its North and South Poles. In the same way that the Sun rises and sets each day, stars also rise in the east and set in the west. Some constellations near the poles never set, though. They circle around the sky without ever sinking below the horizon.

The constellations visible when it is dark also change gradually through the seasons. This happens because the stars rise 4 minutes earlier every day.

Construction

For thousands of years humans have been changing the face of the Earth to make their lives easier. They have built houses and skyscrapers, temples, churches and mosques. They have made roads and railways to improve communications, and bridges and tunnels to get over or under obstacles. And they have constructed dams to store water or to generate electricity.

The branch of engineering that deals with the construction of massive structures such as skyscrapers, dams and bridges is called civil engineering.

▶ Civil engineers use giant excavators like this dragline to remove soil from construction sites.

▼ Engineers surveying a construction site. They are levelling, or measuring heights. The engineer on the left is using an electronic theodolite and range-finder to measure the distance and angle to a calibrated staff held by the other engineer.

Once a site has been surveyed, the engineers have to come up with a design for the structure on the site. They also need to choose materials that give their structure the necessary strength. And they prepare detailed engineering drawings of the whole structure and its separate parts, showing how they will fit together.

Site work

For all kinds of construction work, civil engineers have to begin in a similar way. For example, they have to measure (survey) the land accurately so that construction can start in the right place. Surveyors use instruments like theodolites, levels and range-finders.

Theodolites measure angles accurately, using a small telescope that swivels round on a tripod. Levels help surveyors measure the height of the ground. Range-finders measure distances: modern ones work by reflecting laser beams.

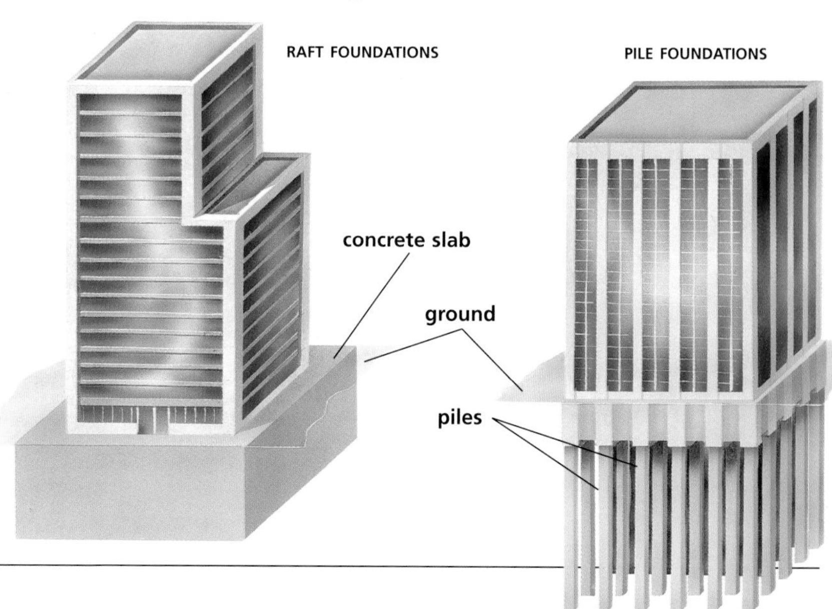

Shifting the muck

When plans have been finalized, work can begin on site. The first task is usually earth-moving (often called muck-shifting). To shift the earth, they use all kinds of machines, including bulldozers, excavators and scrapers.

A bulldozer has a tough, curved blade in front, which can strip off a layer of soil or uproot tree stumps or rocks. It runs on caterpillar tracks so that it can travel better over rough ground. Excavators usually have digging buckets on hydraulic-powered arms, but some are draglines – machines like cranes, that scoop up soil in a large bucket.

Scrapers scoop up soil in a huge bowl with a cutting blade at the bottom. They are used particularly in road-building.

Firm foundations

After the site has been cleared, construction can begin. The first stage is to build a strong supporting base for the structure – the foundations. The bigger the structure, the more massive its foundations will need to be to carry its weight and stop it sinking into the ground.

The best foundations of all are solid rock. There is solid rock just below the surface in New York City, which makes it easy to build skyscrapers there. In most places, however, rock lies too far underground to reach. Then other kinds of foundations must be used.

◀ Pouring concrete for dam foundations. Concrete is a cheap material for construction and sets as hard as rock. It is strong under compression (squeezing), but weak under tension (stretching). To make it stronger, it is reinforced (strengthened) with steel rods, which are strong under tension.

Rafts and piles

The type and size of the foundations chosen depends on the properties of the soil. As a result of soil tests, engineers may use a raft foundation. This is a huge slab of concrete, which spreads the weight of a structure over a large area. Or they may use pile foundations. Piles are long columns sunk deep into the ground to where there is firm soil.

Sometimes, particularly in bridge construction, foundations have to be built in water. A temporary dam may be built around the site and the water pumped out while the foundations are built. Or, a prefabricated (ready-built) unit called a caisson may be sunk to form the foundations.

Find Out More

- Bridges
- Buildings
- Dams
- Roads
- Tunnels and pipelines

▼ Four common kinds of foundations, used to provide a firm support for structures. Large buildings may have raft or pile foundations. Houses use concrete 'footings' and blocks. Ready-built concrete caissons are often used to support bridge piers.

HOUSE FOUNDATIONS

bricks

ground

damp-proof membrane

concrete blocks

cavity

concrete footings

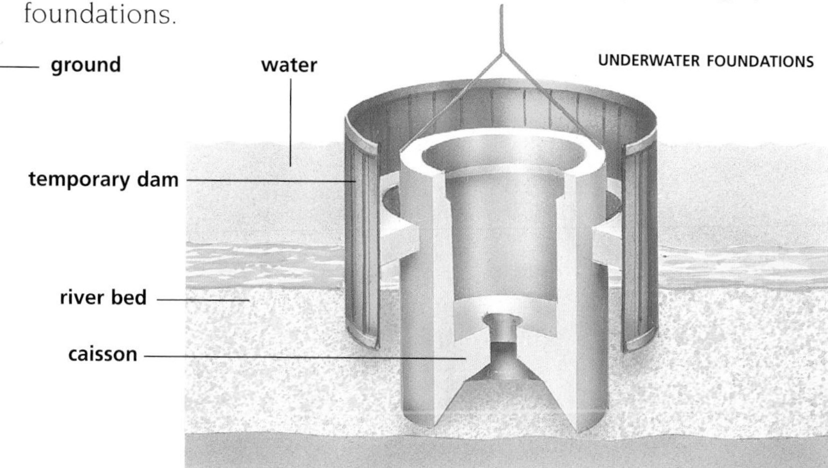

Continents and plates

When the dinosaurs first roamed the land 230 million years ago, there was only one huge continent on Earth. This supercontinent is known as Pangaea, which means 'all land'. About 200 million years ago, Pangaea started to break apart into the continents we know today.

Continents are the dry, high land that most people live on. If the entire crust of the Earth were all the same – the same rock, the same thickness, the same age – everything would be underwater. The reason continents are high and dry and ocean floors are low and underwater is because they are made of different rocks.

Floating rock

Continental crust is very thick and the rocks are relatively light. The ocean crust, however, is thinner and denser. The continents float high on the mantle, while the ocean crust sinks low in the same way that a tall, light, empty ship floats higher on the sea than a short, heavy one.

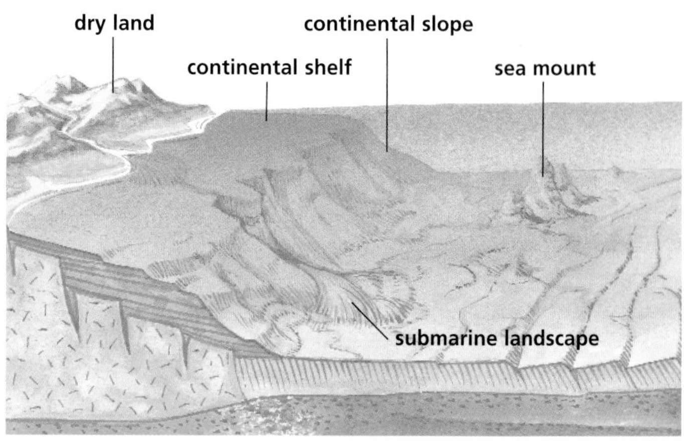

▲ This diagram shows the edge of a continent. Continents seem smaller than they actually are because the edge of the continent (the continental shelf) is covered by shallow seas.

ALFRED WEGENER

In 1912, a German scientist called Alfred Wegener (1880–1930) suggested that the continents drift around on Earth's surface.

Wegener had many reasons for believing this was true. He had noticed that if you took away the Atlantic Ocean, South America and Africa would fit neatly together. On an island in the Arctic, he had found rocks that could only have formed near the Equator. The Equator couldn't move, so the island must have moved. Wegener also noticed that there were fossils of the same extinct animals and plants on different continents. Surely these creatures didn't swim across the oceans? It made more sense if all the continents had been together at one time and then split apart.

◀ These folded rocks in Hamersley Gorge, Western Australia, are some of the oldest on Earth. They are part of an ancient section of a continent (a craton) that is more than $3\frac{1}{2}$ billion years old.

Find Out More

- Earth
- Earthquakes
- Floating and sinking
- Mountains
- Oceans
- Volcanoes

EARTH'S PLATES

Earth's surface is broken into about a dozen plates. Some plates are made of continental and ocean crust, and others are just ocean crust. At the edges of the plates are faults where the rocks are broken and the plates move against each another. Earthquakes occur along the plate boundaries all the time. Since it's not always easy to see the faults that separate the plates, geologists use earthquakes to find the boundaries instead.

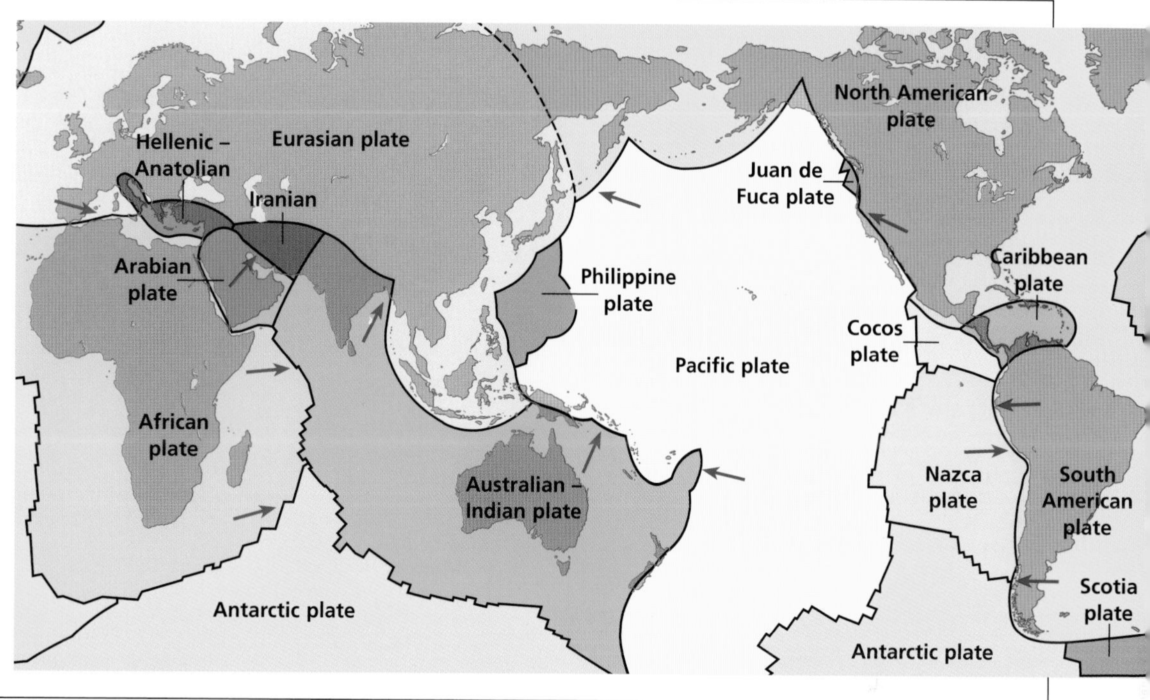

colliding plates

PANGAEA

▲ Triassic period

▼ late Cretaceous period

shape of today's continents

ATLANTIC OCEAN

In a few places, the ocean crust is so thick that it does rise out of the sea. It forms ocean islands like Hawaii and Iceland. Even though they are dry land, the islands are not continents.

Continental rocks

The continents are made of rocks of all ages and all kinds – igneous, sedimentary and metamorphic. Continents probably began forming soon after the Earth formed 4.5 billion years ago. But because rocks wear down and get buried and melted, it is unlikely that any of the first rocks still survive. The oldest rock we know of is a 4 billion-year-old metamorphic rock from Canada.

▼ last Ice Age

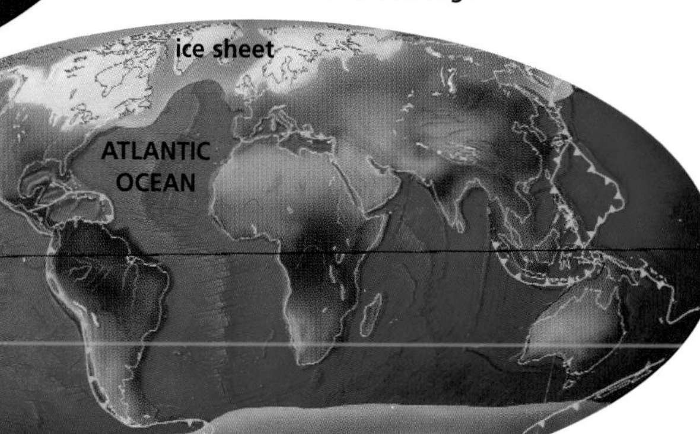

▲▶ These maps show how the face of the Earth has changed in the last 240 million years. The continents formed Pangaea in the late Triassic period, 237 million years ago. By the late Cretaceous, about 94 million years ago, the Atlantic Ocean had begun to open as Pangaea split up. By the end of the last Ice Age (about 18,000 years ago) the continents were almost in their present positions.

Plates

When people talk about 'continental drift' today, what they usually mean is 'plate tectonics'. Alfred Wegener was right that the continents move around on the Earth's surface, but it is not only the continents that move. The sea floor moves too.

The Earth's surface is like a jigsaw puzzle, broken into many pieces. Geologists call these jigsaw pieces *plates* and they are made up of both continents and ocean floors. The plates move around like icebergs packed together on a frozen lake. They ram into each other, grate past each other, ride on top of one another, and try to move away from each other.

Plates don't stay the same forever. They grow and shrink. Sometimes they rip into two or three new plates. At other times they collide with another plate to form a new, bigger plate.

The theory of plate tectonics

The word *tectonics* refers to the forces that create large features such as mountains, volcanoes and continents on the Earth's surface. For instance, *bulldozer tectonics* would be the theory that huge bulldozers push everything into place. *Plate tectonics* is the theory geologists prefer. It says that huge slabs of crust and mantle move around on the Earth's surface, causing earthquakes, making volcanoes erupt, and creating continents, ocean floors, tall mountains and deep valleys.

How plates move

No one is exactly sure what makes the plates move. Most geologists think that they are carried around by currents in the mantle below.

Even though the mantle is solid rock, it can flow. It flows because it is hotter in some places and cooler in others. In the same way that hot air rises and cold air sinks, hot rocks rise and cold rocks sink. The rocks near the Earth's core are so hot that they rise up towards the surface. At the same time, the cool rocks near the crust sink. The mantle flows very slowly, just several centimetres every year.

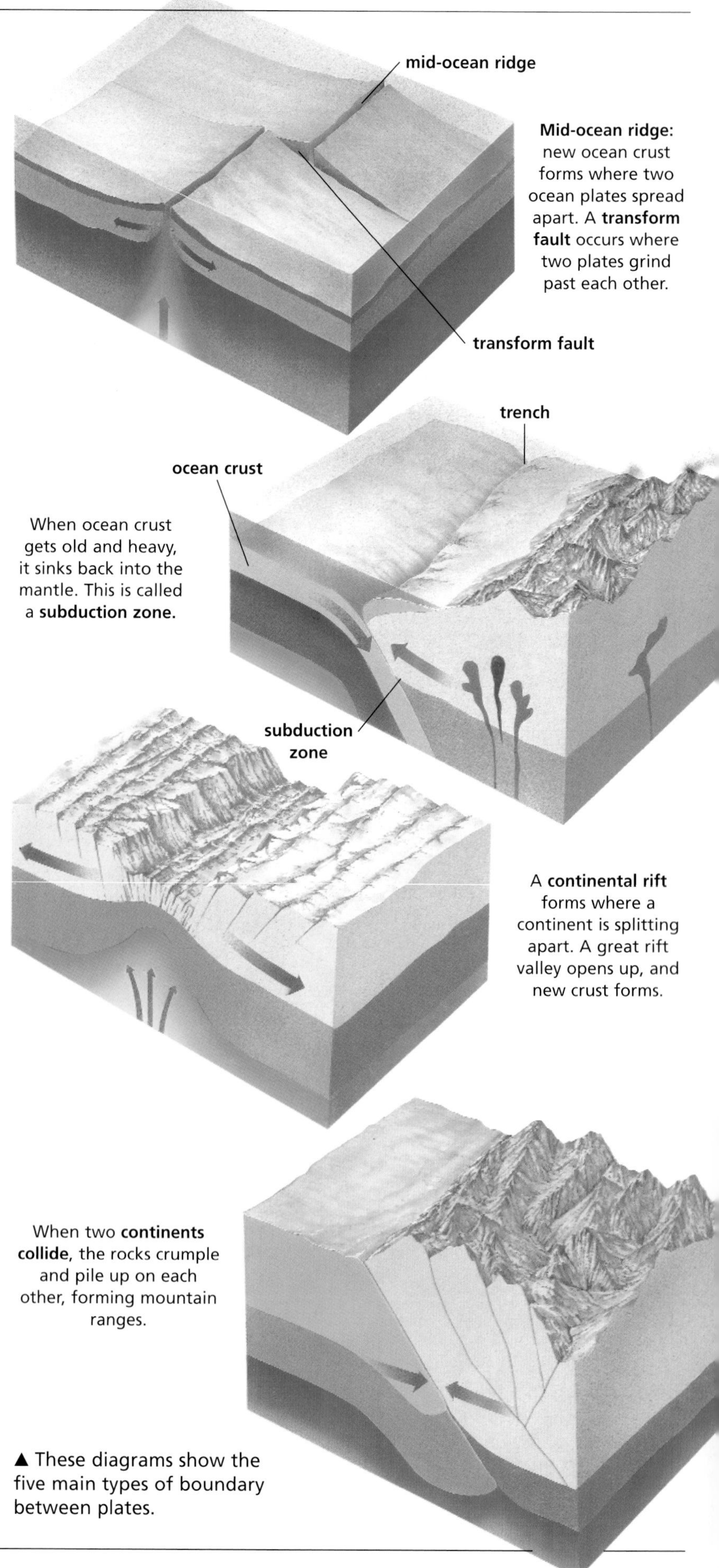

▲ These diagrams show the five main types of boundary between plates.

Cooking *see* Reactions, chemical • **Copernicus** *see* Astronomy

Copper

Nearly 10 million tonnes of copper are produced worldwide every year. About half of it is used by the electrical industry because copper conducts, or passes on, electricity better than any other metal except silver. And silver is too expensive to use for electrical wiring.

Millions of kilometres of copper wires carry electricity into and around homes throughout the world. Copper is easy to make into wires because it is one of the most ductile of metals. This means that it can be pulled, or drawn out, into long lengths without breaking.

Copper is not only used by itself, but also in alloys, or mixtures with other metals. Common alloys are bronze, brass and cupronickel. Copper and its alloys are very useful to us because they can resist corrosion, or rusting. This means that they last a long time.

▼ Bingham Canyon copper mine in the USA is the largest opencast mine in the world. It is nearly a kilometre deep and 20 kilometres wide. The mine is the richest source of copper in the world, but mining operations have caused a great deal of damage to the environment.

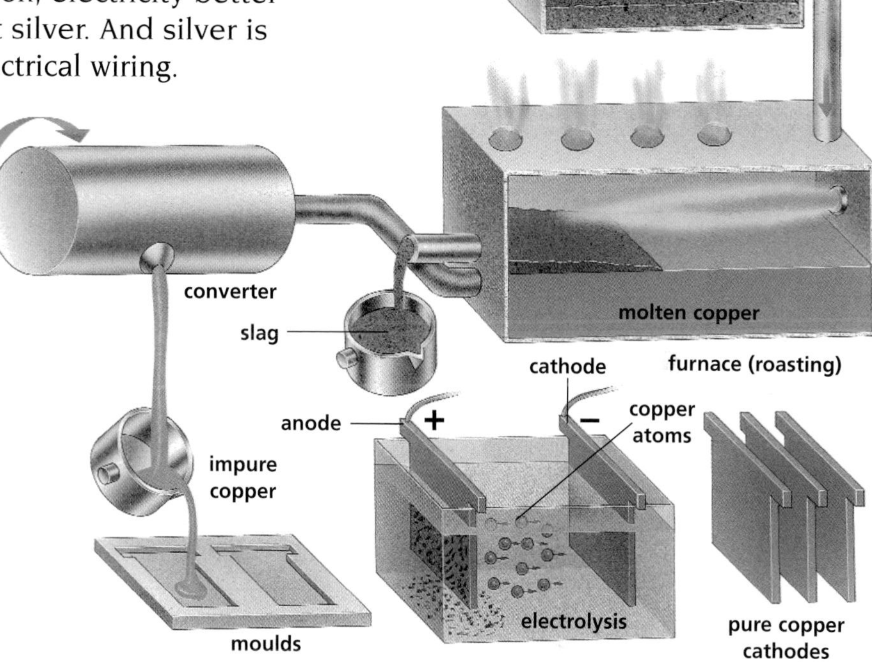

▲ To extract copper from copper ore, the ore is crushed and then fed to flotation tanks. These concentrate the copper minerals. The minerals are roasted in furnaces, where impurities burn off or form a slag. The nearly pure metal is finally refined by electrolysis. Electricity causes pure metal to be deposited on the cathode, or negative electrode, of the electrolysis cell.

Going native

Copper was one of the first metals people used, at least 10,000 years ago. This is because copper is one of the few metals that can be found in metal form in the ground. We call this kind of metal 'native metal'.

But native copper is rare, and most copper is produced from copper ores found in rocks. There are huge deposits of copper ores in the Andes Mountains of South America, the Rocky Mountains of North America, and in Congo and Zambia, sometimes called the copper belt, in central Africa.

Find Out More

- Alloys
- Conductors and insulators
- Electricity
- Metals and non-metals
- Resources

Corona *see* Sun • **Cotton** *see* Farming, Textiles

Crystals

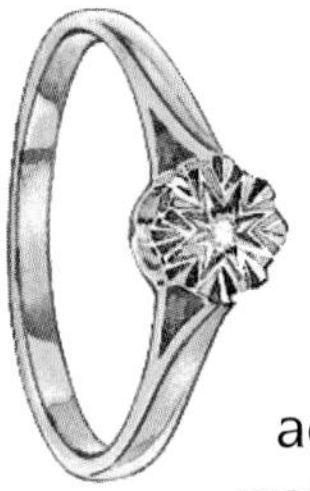

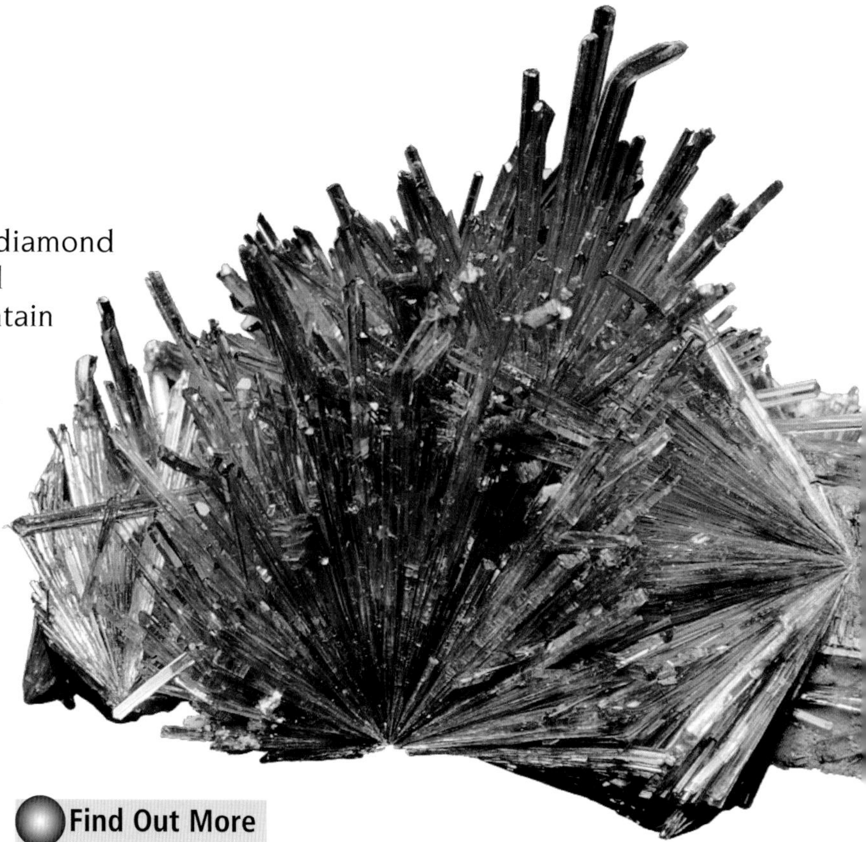

What do digital watches, diamond rings and gold ingots all have in common? They all contain crystals. A tiny piece of quartz acts as the timekeeper for digital watches, diamond is the crystal form of carbon, and all metals, except mercury, are crystalline.

All matter is made up of tiny particles (atoms or molecules). A crystal is a solid in which the particles form a regular, repeated pattern. The particles have exactly the same arrangement over and over again throughout the material. This gives a pure crystal a regular shape.

▲ These natural crystals of iron phosphate were found in Bolivia, South America.

Shapes, sizes and colours

In many crystals – such as diamonds and quartz – the crystals are big and can be seen clearly. If you look at table salt through a magnifying glass, you can also see the crystalline shape. But in metals the crystals are so tiny that they can only be seen through a powerful microscope.

Crystals of table salt are shaped like tiny cubes. Other crystals form different geometrical shapes, such as pyramids, hexagons and prisms.

Lots of pure crystals, such as salt and sugar crystals, are white or transparent because all the light that hits them bounces off or travels through them. Other crystals are coloured because they contain impurities. For example, both rubies and sapphires are made mostly of a material called alumina, but rubies are red because they contain tiny amounts of chromium, whereas sapphires are usually blue and contain tiny amounts of iron.

Find Out More

- Atoms and molecules
- Carbon
- Metals and non-metals
- Solids

▼ Fluorite is a common mineral (a material found in rocks). Fluorite crystals have the 14-sided shape shown here (c). But the atoms in fluorite are arranged in a repeating pattern (the unit cell) that is cube-shaped (a, b).

(c) crystal shape

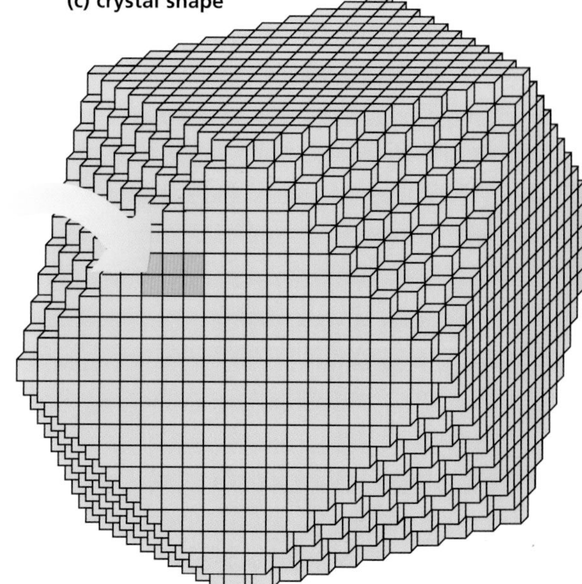

(a) unit cell

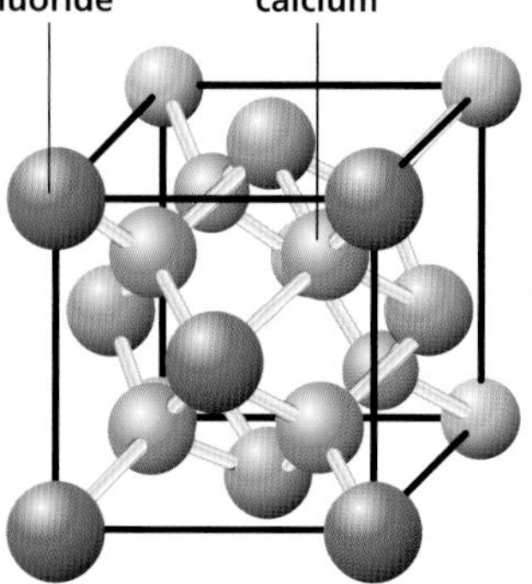

(b) 12-unit cell

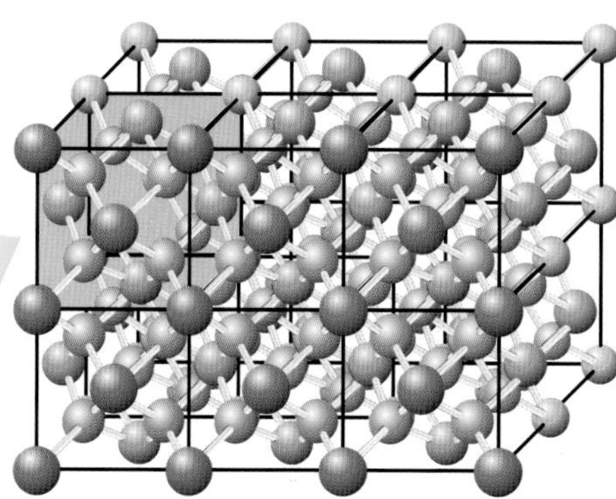

Dams

The year is 2010. After more than 15 years' work, the Three Gorges dam on the River Yangtze in China is finished. At last the mighty Yangtze – whose floods killed 300,000 people in the 20th century – has been tamed.

Engineers build dams to stop flooding, store water and improve navigation. The water stored behind a dam is called a reservoir. This water is often used as a source of power. It is fed through water turbines that spin generators to produce electricity. This is hydroelectric power.

◀ The Hoover Dam on the Colorado River, USA. Completed in 1936, it is a huge concrete-arch dam, 221 metres high. The enormous reservoir behind the dam is called Lake Mead.

Sheer weight

Dams are the biggest of all man-made structures. The Three Gorges dam, for example, will be massive – about 2 kilometres long and 175 metres high and containing 30 million cubic metres of concrete.

Three Gorges is a type of dam known as a gravity dam. Its huge weight keeps it in place and holds back the water behind it. Even larger gravity dams are built using soil, rock and clay. They are called earth-fill or embankment dams. The biggest, such as the Syncrude Tailings dam in Alberta, Canada, contain more than 500 million cubic metres of earth-fill.

Some dams have a different design. They are made of concrete, but it is their shape not their weight that gives them strength. They have a curved, arch shape, with the outward curve facing upstream. The curving concrete carries the water pressure to firm foundations at the sides and base.

Affecting the environment

Dams bring a lot of benefits, but they can also bring problems to communities and the environment. The reservoir created by the Three Gorges dam will submerge more than 150 towns, and make up to 1,500,000 people homeless. Dams also reduce the flow of water down a river, which can have environmental effects.

▶ The embankment dam is made up of earth and rock. It has a clay core to make it watertight. The concrete gravity dam has a triangular cross-section. The arch dam is slender, but its shape makes it strong. The columns of the buttress dam give it extra strength.

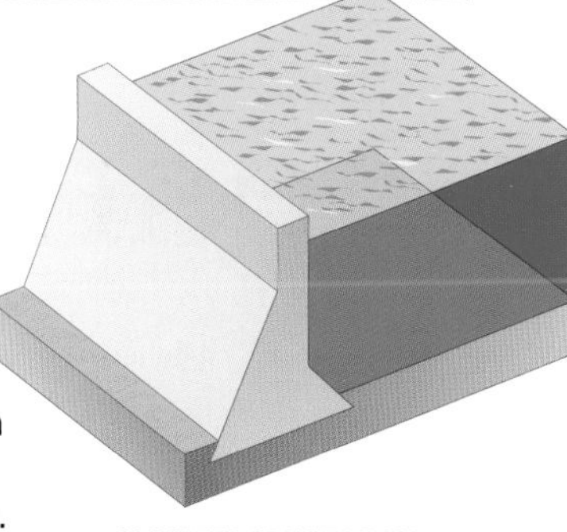

CONCRETE GRAVITY DAM

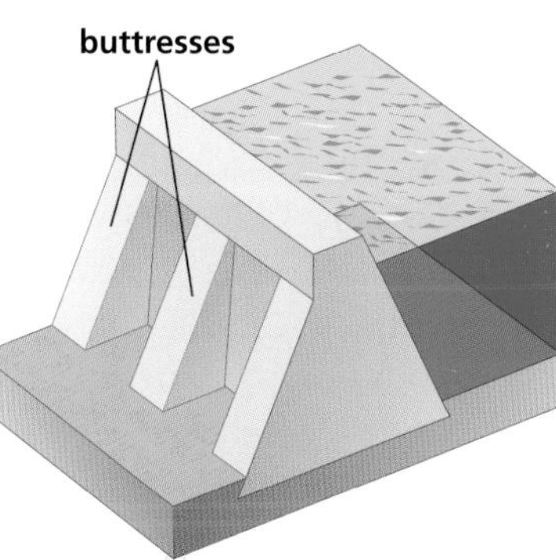

BUTTRESS DAM

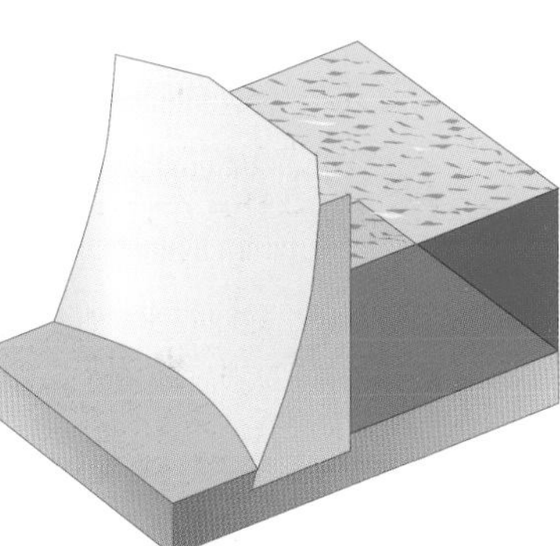

CONCRETE ARCH DAM

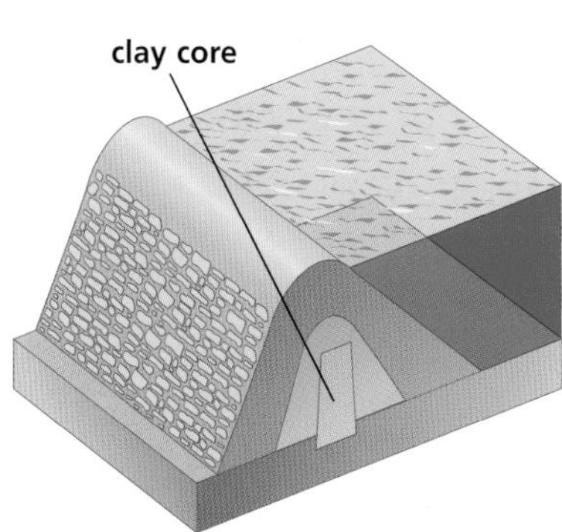

EMBANKMENT DAM

Find Out More

- Construction
- Power stations
- Water power

Darwin, Charles *see* Evolution • **Databases** *see* Software • **Density** *see* Matter

Desert life

The oversize ears of the African fennec fox can be up to 15 centimetres long. They give off heat rather like a radiator, and so help keep the fox cool. The fox's big ears are also useful for picking up the sounds of its prey when it hunts at night.

Keeping cool and finding food and water are two of the main problems for desert animals. Smaller animals often escape the heat of the day by hiding away beneath rocks or in burrows and coming out in the cool of the night. Most desert animals survive with very little water. Some, such as the kangaroo rat, do not drink at all but get all the moisture they need from their food. Camels store fat in their humps. They can break down this fat to provide them with energy and water.

Find Out More

- Animal behaviour
- Climate
- Deserts

Desert plants

Desert plants have deep or wide-spreading roots to soak up as much water as possible. Some, such as cacti or pebble plants, store water in swollen stems or leaves. Some plants spend most of their lives as seeds, buried in the desert soil. When it rains, they quickly flower and produce seeds. When the ground dries out again they die, leaving their seeds behind.

Shifting sands

Sand is difficult to move across because it shifts and slips under an animal's weight. Camels have wide, cushion-like feet to spread out their weight and stop them sinking. The big hairy paws of the sand cat work in the same way. Sidewinder snakes loop diagonally across the surface of the sand, hardly touching it at all. Lizards called sandfish 'swim' beneath the sand by wriggling their bodies from side to side.

▲To escape the heat of the day, elf owls shelter and nest inside holes in giant cacti. They are the smallest owls in the world.

▼ The dromedary, or Arabian, camel can go for several weeks without water. It can also close its nostrils to keep out drifting sand.

◀ Reptiles such as the frilled lizard are fairly common in deserts because they have waterproof skins and can go for long periods without food.

Deserts

The Rub'al Khali desert of Saudi Arabia is the largest sand sea on Earth. Giant sand dunes shaped like stars, crescents and fishhooks grow up to 150 metres high. It only rains about 15 centimetres each year and some years it doesn't rain at all. There are not enough plants to hold down the sand or block the winds, so the dunes are continuously changing shape as they drift over the hard rock below.

▲ Sand dunes in the Sahara Desert. Sand dunes can move up to 30 m in a year. Although we usually think of deserts as sandy, less than a third of the Sahara is covered with sand.

A desert is a place where very little rain or snow falls. The rain that does fall evaporates quickly in the dry air. Some deserts are hot and some are cold. Some are sandy and some are rocky. The one thing they all have in common is that they are dry.

No rain

There are several reasons why rainfall is low in some parts of the world. Rain comes from clouds, and most of the water in clouds comes from water that evaporated from the oceans. Deserts like the Gobi in the middle of Asia are dry because they are so far from the oceans. By the time the air gets to the Gobi Desert, it has lost most of its moisture.

The desert in Argentina is dry because it is on the 'rain shadow' side of the Andes Mountains. When moist air from the Pacific Ocean reaches the mountains, it rises up. As it rises it cools, and all the moisture falls as rain on the ocean side of the mountains.

The largest deserts, like the Sahara, the Rub'al Khali and the Great Australian, are in the subtropics, just north and south of the tropical region around the Equator. The subtropics are so dry because the air comes from the tropics, where it has already lost most of its water.

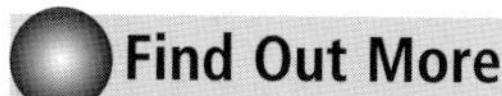

Find Out More

- Climate
- Desert life
- Rain and snow
- Winds

The driest deserts on Earth are the cold, dry valleys of Antarctica.

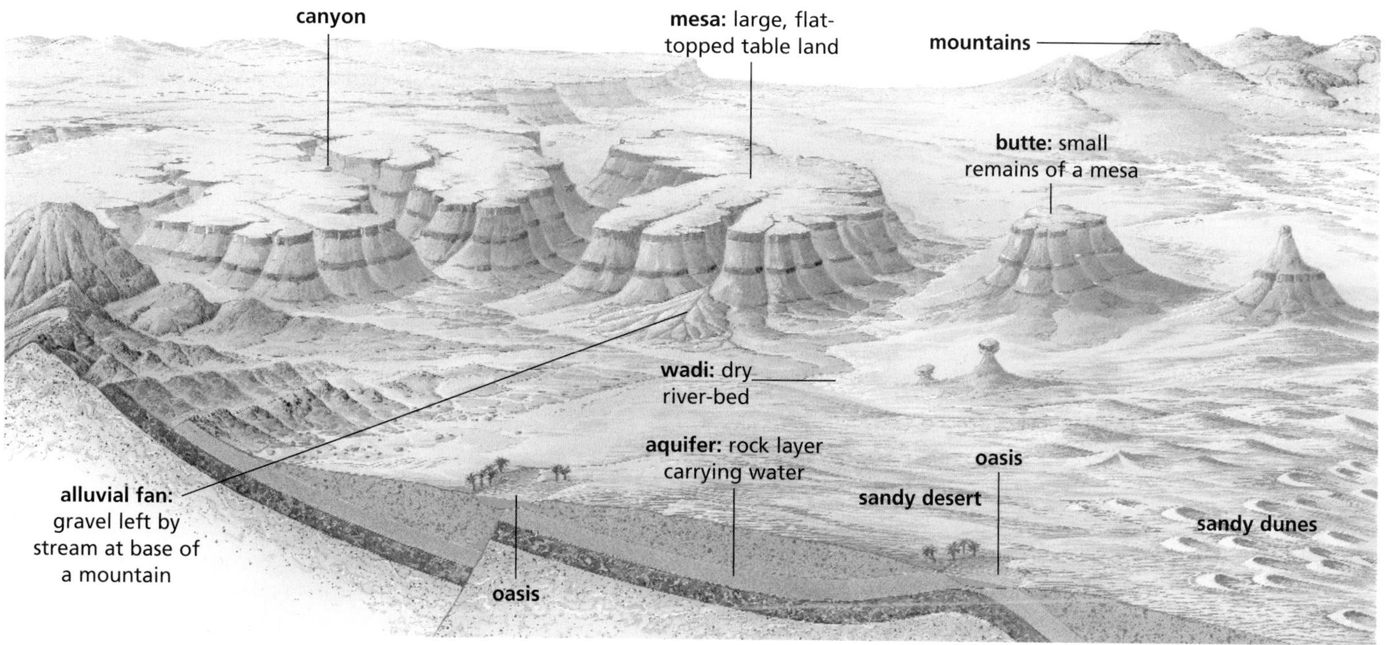

▼ A desert landscape, similar to one you might see in the American South-west.

Detergents

At the bird sanctuary, a team of workers has brought in a flock of sea birds. They have been covered in oil leaking from a wrecked ship. The team sets to work cleaning the birds with detergent. This breaks up the oil into droplets, which are then washed away with water. The birds look bedraggled, but they will survive.

Detergents are powerful cleaning agents that will get rid of oil on sea birds, as well as grease and dirt on dishes, clothes, and so on. Detergents are synthetic products made from petroleum chemicals. Before people had detergents, the main cleaning agent was soap. Today we use soap mainly for cleaning ourselves.

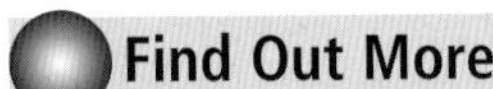

Find Out More
- Acids and alkalis
- Oil products
- Textiles

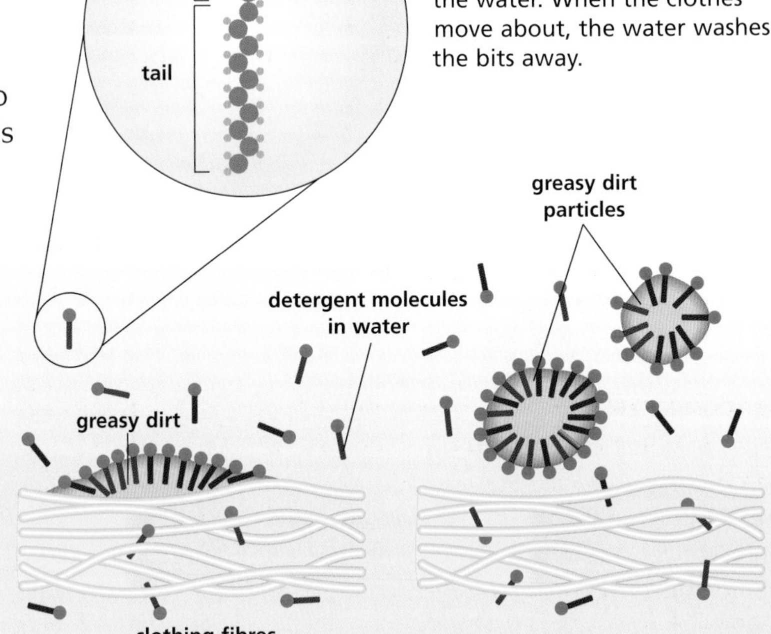

▼ Soaps and detergents are made up of a similar type of molecule (basic unit). These molecules have a head and a tail. The head 'likes' water, while the tail 'likes' grease and dirt. When soap or detergent is used to wash clothes, the tail ends of the molecules attach themselves to the bits of dirt. Soon the bits are surrounded, leaving only the heads in contact with the water. When the clothes move about, the water washes the bits away.

▼ Following an oil spill off the South African coast, teams of workers clean penguins by scrubbing them with detergent.

Soap has been made for thousands of years. It is produced by heating fat or oil with a substance that is an alkali, like caustic soda. In the past, animal fats were used, but now soaps are made using vegetable oils such as palm oil. Another product we get from making soap is glycerine, which can be used to make plastics and explosives.

Beating the scum

The problem with soap is that it sometimes forms a messy scum. Detergents do not. They also have a more efficient cleaning action than soap. Different detergents are made for different purposes. Washing-up liquid, laundry detergents for washing clothes, and shampoos all contain different ingredients. Laundry detergents, for example, can contain brighteners to make fabrics look extra bright, and enzymes, which can dissolve stains such as sweat and blood.

Diet

Some people say, 'you are what you eat'. And it's true – our bodies are made from the food we eat. Food contains all the nutrients – the raw materials – our bodies need to build everything from muscles and bones to the brain and the heart. Food also provides energy, to keep us alive.

There are three main kinds of nutrient in food – carbohydrates, proteins and fats. We also need small amounts of other nutrients called vitamins and minerals.

Food for energy and growing

Carbohydrates should make up the bulk of what we eat. They are sugary and starchy foods that give us energy for everything we do. The more active we are, the more energy-giving food we need.

There is protein in many foods, including meat, fish, cheese and beans. Protein is essential for growth and repair of the body. Children who are growing need more protein than adults who have reached their full size.

Fats provide energy and help to insulate the body. Our bodies use fat as an energy store, and every cell needs a little fat to build its structure. But too much fat in the diet can be bad for us. It can clog up blood vessels and make it harder for the heart to pump blood round the body.

To stay healthy and fit, we need to eat a variety of foods with the right mixture of carbohydrates, fats and proteins. This is what we call a balanced diet.

fatty foods simple sugars and 'junk food' keep to a minimum – or an occasional treat

protein foods eat a little of these foods with meals

fruit and vegetables eat at every meal and include as snacks

carbohydrate-rich foods eat at every meal and include as snacks

▲ This food pyramid can be used as a guide to healthy eating.

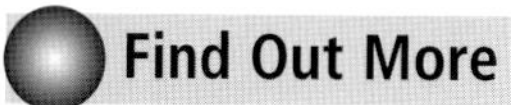
Find Out More

- Digestion
- Energy
- Farming
- Growth and development

Vitamins and minerals

We need small amounts of vitamins and minerals in our diet each day. They help to keep our bodies working properly and help to protect us from illness. Fruits and vegetables are rich in vitamins such as vitamin C, which is found in oranges, and vitamin A, found in carrots. Milk contains minerals such as calcium, which we need for healthy bones, while meat is rich in the iron we need to make blood cells.

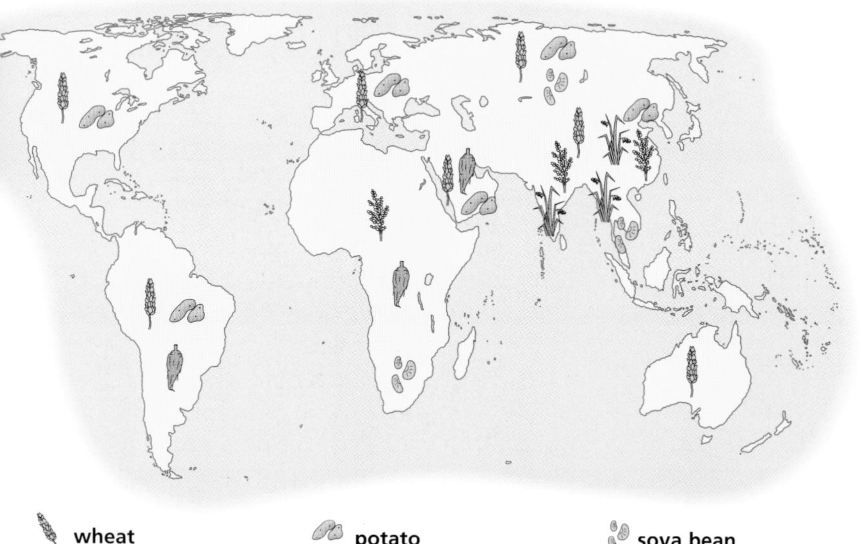

◀ Staple foods are rich in starch for energy. Wheat, barley, rye and potatoes are part of the staple diet in cooler parts of the world. Millet, rice sorghum, soya and cassava are staples in Africa and Asia.

Digestion

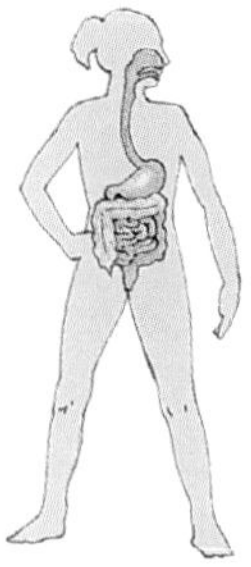

Take a bite, chew and swallow, and you are starting your food on a 9-metre journey through your digestive system. The journey may take more than a day. In that time, your body will take the goodness you need from the food, and get rid of the waste.

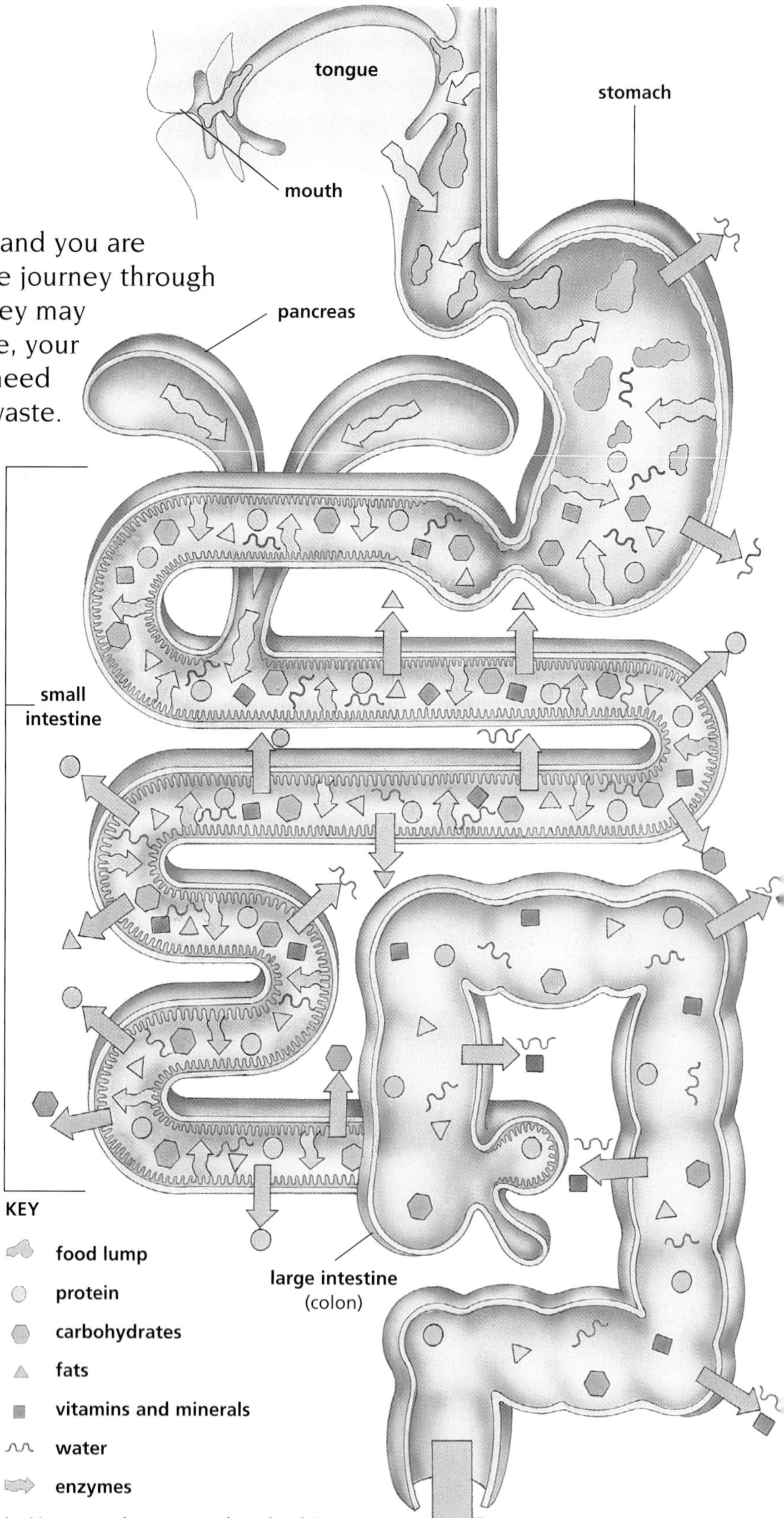

Food helps the body to work, grow and repair itself. It contains the nutrients we need for good health. But before food is of any use, it has to be digested, or broken down into smaller parts. These can then be absorbed into the blood and used anywhere in the body.

The digestive system is a long, winding tube running right through the body. We put food into it at one end (the mouth), and waste material leaves through an opening called the anus at the other end.

Journey to the stomach

Digestion begins in the mouth as teeth tear and grind our food into tiny pieces. As we chew, the pieces mix with a watery liquid called saliva, which makes them slippery

PERISTALSIS

Muscles along the digestive system contract in a sequence called peristalsis to squeeze food along.

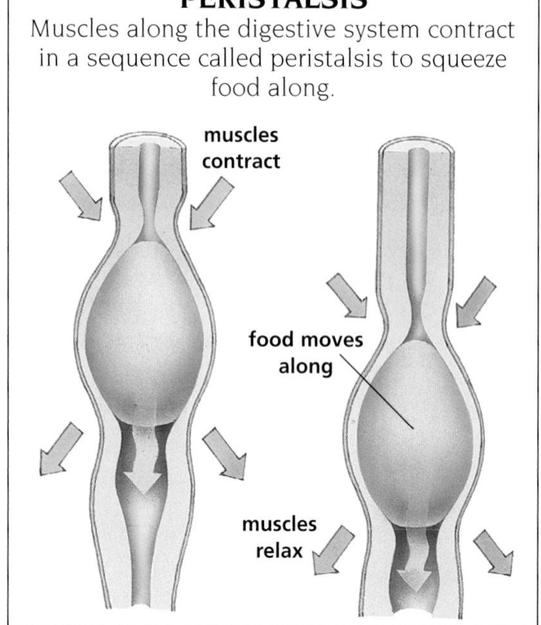

tongue
mouth
stomach
pancreas
small intestine
large intestine (colon)
waste (leaving anus)

KEY
food lump
protein
carbohydrates
fats
vitamins and minerals
water
enzymes

▶ How nutrients are absorbed into the blood. Most foods contain large molecules of carbohydrate, protein and fat, as well as vitamins and minerals, which all have to be digested with the help of enzymes as they pass along the digestive system.

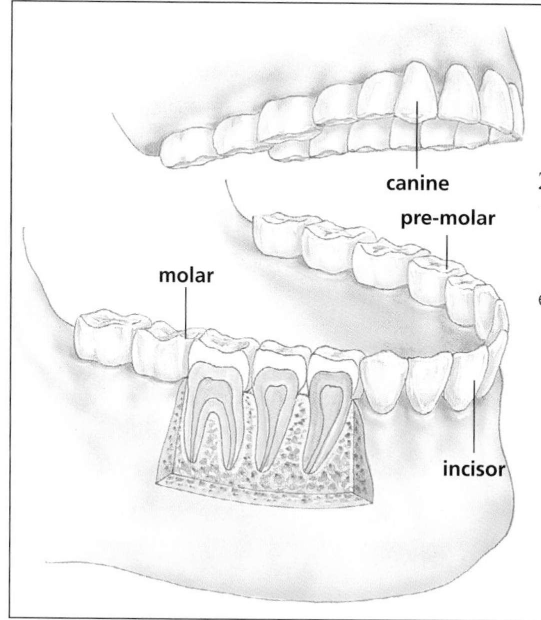

TEETH

A full set of adult teeth is 32. There are eight flat incisors at the front for cutting up food, four pointed canine teeth at the side for tearing, and 20 flat-topped pre-molars and molars at the back of the mouth, for grinding and crushing food.

Every tooth is covered by tough white enamel, which protects the softer bone-like dentine beneath. Enamel is the hardest substance in the body and resists almost everything, except the acid produced by certain bacteria. These bacteria feed on bits of sugary food left on the teeth.

Brushing teeth helps to get rid of food particles and bacteria. Fluoride toothpaste actually strengthens the enamel, too.

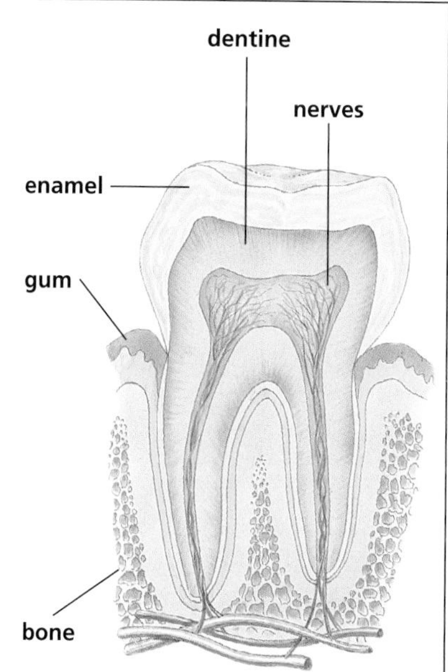

and easier to swallow. As we swallow, muscles squeeze little balls of food down the food pipe (the oesophagus) to the stomach, where they will stay for about three hours. The stomach turns the food over and over, and mixes it with digestive juices that pour from the stomach walls. Strong acid in these juices kills any bacteria you may have eaten. Eventually, all the food turns into a soupy liquid.

Little by little, the liquid trickles out of the stomach into the small intestine. Here, glands in the pancreas add more digestive juices, which complete the digestion process.

Find Out More

- Bacteria and viruses
- Diet
- Heart and blood

▼ This is an enlarged photograph of villi. These tiny folds in the lining of the small intestine give a huge area for absorbing food.

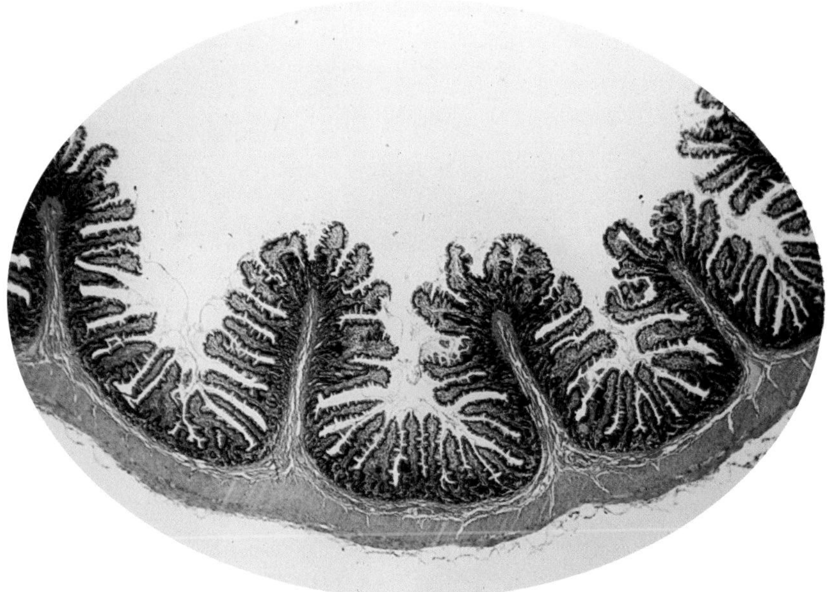

The cells which line the digestive system are rapidly worn away by the food which flows past them. Cells have to be replaced every 2–3 days.

Absorbing activities

Once food has been digested, the nutrients from it can be absorbed into the blood. This happens in a long section of the intestine called the the ileum. Uncoiled, the ileum is 5–6 metres long, more than three times the height of a person. Its thin, creased lining is made of millions of tiny folds called villi. Villi increase the total area available for absorbing food to around 10 square metres, about the area of a small room. Each of the villi contains tiny blood vessels called capillaries, which collect nutrients and carry them quickly away.

Waste disposal

Not everything we eat can be digested. Undigested food passes from the ileum into the large intestine, or colon. Here, the body reabsorbs most of the liquid that was added to the food during the digestive process. The soft lumps of waste (the faeces) pass into the rectum, where they are stored. Eventually they leave the body through the anus.

Digital *see* Communications, Sound recording • **Dinosaurs** *see* Life

Diseases

Every time you sneeze, millions of water droplets and germs shoot into the air at the speed of a racing car. People around you breathe the germs in. This is one of the ways in which coughs and colds spread rapidly from person to person.

▲ Although we cannot see them, millions of bacteria and viruses fly out every time we sneeze. Flu, pneumonia and tuberculosis can all be spread in this way.

Infections of the nose, throat and chest are among the most common of all diseases. But other diseases, such as heart disease and cancer, are not caught from other people. They are usually caused by the way we live, the genes we have inherited from our parents, by what we eat, or by chemicals in the environment.

Infectious diseases

The germs, or bacteria and viruses, that can make us ill reach our bodies in many different ways. They can enter through the air we breathe, from dirty water or food, or from contact with animals or insects that carry diseases.

We pick up infections such as chickenpox several days before they begin to affect us. This time is called the incubation period, when viruses are multiplying inside us. Then the itching spots, which are symptoms of the disease, appear. They are the body's reaction to the chickenpox viruses. Gradually, our immune system kills the viruses, and we recover.

Sometimes, so many people are affected by the same infection at once that an epidemic develops. Influenza, or flu, epidemics occur every few years, as new strains of influenza virus emerge.

Today, epidemics can spread from country to country very quickly, as air passengers take infections with them on their travels round the world. SARS (Severe Acute Respiratory Syndrome) is a new and deadly pneumonia-like disease that has spread in this way. It causes severe breathing difficulties and, in some countries, has killed more than one in 10 of those who have caught it. When a dangerous disease like SARS first emerges, it is vital to stop it spreading while drugs are being developed to fight it. This is done by isolating people who have the disease and those they have been in contact with.

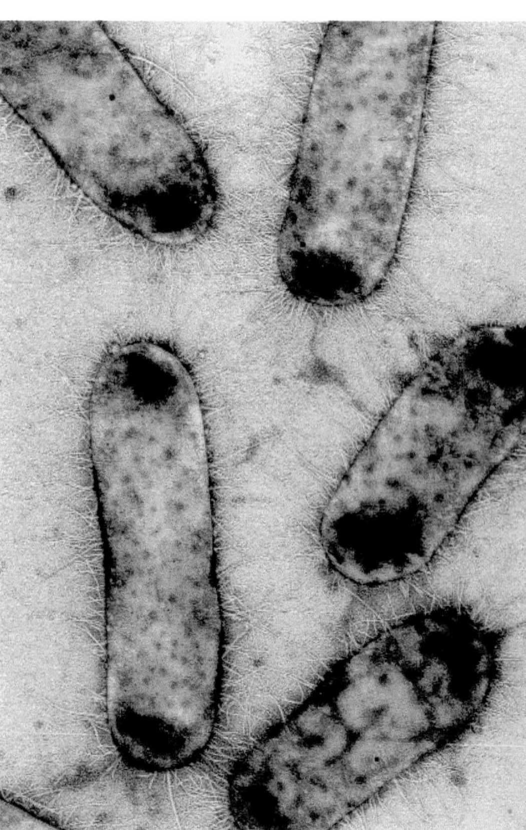

◀ These bacteria are called *E. coli*: they occur naturally in our digestive systems. Some strains of *E. coli* can cause vomiting and diarrhoea if they are eaten with food.

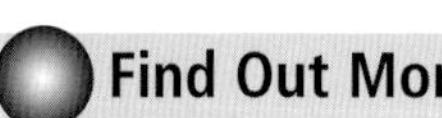

Find Out More

- Bacteria and viruses
- Cancers
- Health
- Immune system
- Medicine

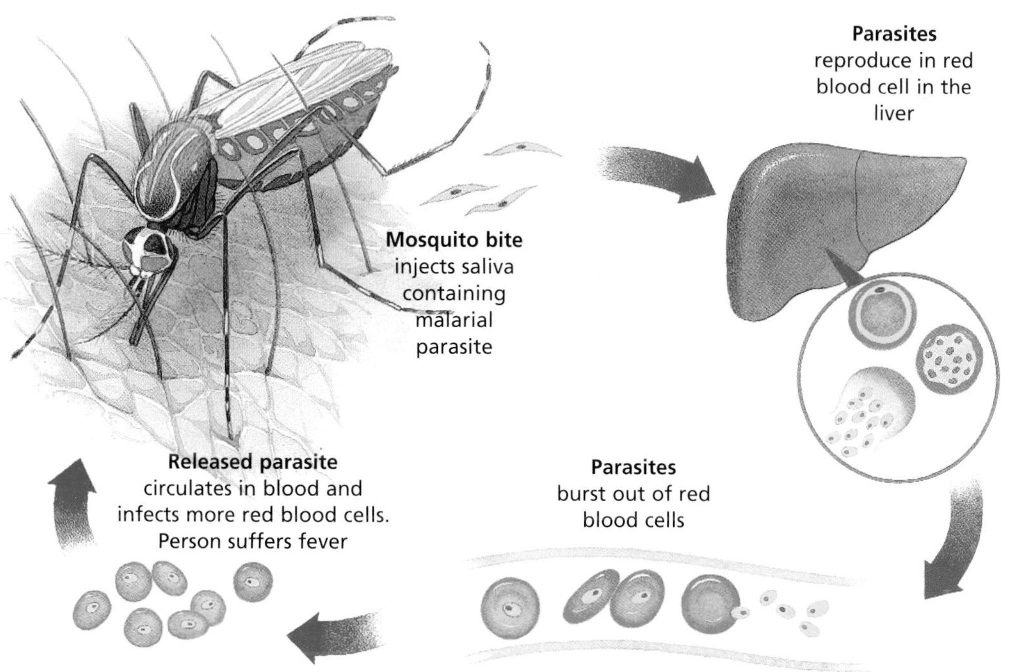

◀ The lifecycle of a malarial parasite. When a mosquito bites a human, it injects saliva containing the parasite. The parasites reproduce inside red blood cells, then burst out into the blood. The new parasites infect more red blood cells, and the person suffers from fever.

Some people are thought to have caught CJD (Creutzfeldt-Jakob Disease) from eating beef from cows infected with 'mad cow disease', or BSE (Bovine Spongiform Encephalopathy).

Viruses

Viruses can only reproduce inside other living cells. They cause many diseases, from cold sores to rabies. Each of these viruses affects different cells in the body. Human immuno-deficiency (HIV) viruses affect the white blood cells that help us fight infections. People who carry the virus become less able to fight off minor infections. If the damage to their immune systems becomes very severe, it may result in Aids (Acquired Immune Deficiency Syndrome).

Parasites

Malaria is a disease that kills more than 3 million people every year. It is not caused by bacteria or viruses, but by a tiny parasite that lives in the blood. The parasites are transferred from person to person by mosquitoes.

LOUIS PASTEUR

Louis Pasteur (1822–1895), a French chemist, was the first person to realize that diseases are caused by germs. In 1881 he successfully found a vaccine for anthrax, a fatal disease of animals. The Pasteur Institute in Paris was founded in 1888 to investigate rabies. It is now one of the world's most famous centres of medical and biological research.

Many other parasites can live on or in our body. They come in many different shapes and sizes. Some of the largest are tapeworms, which live and feed in our intestine. Our most common parasites are tiny mites which feed on dead skin cells under our nails and even in our eyelashes.

▼ Victims of the plague being taken for burial in the 14th century. Almost a third of Europe's population died of plague in the 1300s. Bacteria carried from person to person by rat fleas are the cause of plague.

DNA *see* Genetics • **Drag** *see* Flight and flow • **Dreams** *see* Mind

Drugs

When the native peoples who live in the Amazon jungle get a fever, they chew the bark of the cinchona tree. The fever is brought on by malaria. Cinchona bark contains a drug, quinine, that fights the disease.

Malaria is one of the most widespread diseases in the world, affecting as many as 500 million people. Quinine is still one of the main drugs used to treat it. But nowadays quinine is a synthetic product, manufactured from chemicals.

Most drugs, also called pharmaceuticals, are now synthetic. But quite a few natural drugs are still used. One long-used plant drug, digitalis, is extracted from foxglove. It is used to treat heart conditions.

Another natural drug is morphine, extracted from the seeds of the opium poppy. It is a powerful painkiller. Heroin comes from the same plant. Both morphine and heroin are highly addictive, or habit-forming. The use of heroin is one of the major causes of drug addiction.

▲ This enlarged picture shows the effect of an antibiotic on bacteria. The bacterium on the right has not yet been damaged, but that on the left has been attacked and destroyed.

PENICILLIN PIONEERS

Alexander Fleming (1881–1955) discovered penicillin in 1928 while working at St Mary's Hospital, London. But it was not produced in a pure form until 1940, when it was shown to have amazing antibiotic properties. This latter work was carried out at Oxford by a team led by Ernst Chain (1906–1979) and Howard Florey (1898–1968). The three pioneering scientists shared the 1945 Nobel prize for medicine.

Ernst Chain

Howard Florey

◀ Certain drugs are illegal and people try to smuggle them from country to country in their luggage. Police use specially trained dogs to sniff out these hidden drugs.

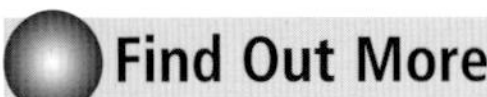

Find Out More

- Bacteria and viruses
- Diseases
- Medicine

Beating bacteria

Tiny, microscopic organisms called bacteria are the cause of most dangerous diseases, including blood poisoning, cholera, typhoid and tuberculosis. Bacterial infection can be treated by synthetic drugs such as the sulphonamides, but these days it is usually treated by antibiotics.

Antibiotics are substances produced naturally by certain moulds and bacteria. Penicillin was the original antibiotic and is still the most widely used. Others include streptomycin, terramycin and tetracycline. Each of these antibiotics is suited to treating certain diseases.

The use of antibiotics over the years has dramatically reduced the death rate from disease. But antibiotics have been used so much that some bacteria are becoming resistant to them – which means that the antibiotic cannot destroy the bacteria. So scientists are always looking for new antibiotics.

Viruses and vaccines

Antibiotics cannot cure all diseases. In particular, they cannot treat diseases caused by viruses, such as influenza, measles, mumps, hepatitis and polio.

But doctors can prevent some virus diseases by vaccination. This involves injecting a vaccine into the patient's body. A vaccine is made up of a dead or weakened form of the same virus. The body produces antibodies to fight the invading virus. Later, if the body is exposed to the real virus, the antibodies are already there to attack it before it multiplies.

The English doctor Edward Jenner pioneered vaccination to treat smallpox in 1796. A worldwide mass vaccination programme 200 years later wiped the disease from the face of the Earth.

Designer drugs

Some synthetic drugs, such as quinine, are exact copies of natural substances.

▲ This chemist is using a virtual reality program to look at the action of a drug molecule.

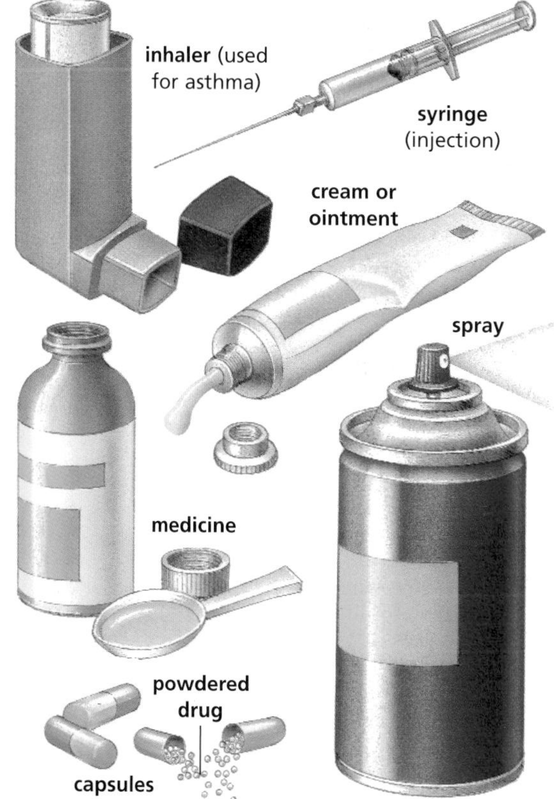

▶ Different ways of administering (giving) drugs.

COMMON TYPES OF DRUG	
Type	**Effects**
Anaesthetic	Prevents patients feeling pain; local anaesthetic acts locally; general anaesthetic creates unconsciousness
Analgesic	Prevents or reduces pain
Antibiotic	Kills the bacteria that cause disease
Antihistamine	Relieves symptoms of asthma, hay fever and other allergies
Hormone	Used to overcome a hormone deficiency in the body
Narcotic	Helps prevents pain by deadening the whole nervous system
Sedative	Helps induce sleep
Tranquillizer	Helps calm a person
Vaccine	Helps the body fight a virus disease by triggering its natural defences in advance

Increasingly, though, new drugs are being created to target diseases. Biochemists, who design drugs, can test a drug using a process called molecular modelling. This involves drawing models of the molecules (basic units) that make up the drug and the disease, on a very powerful computer. They then see how the different molecules behave together. This tells them whether or not the drug will be able to fight the disease.

Dunes *see* Deserts

Dyes and pigments

Buddhist priests the world over wear bright-orange robes, which get their colour from the dye saffron. This dye is obtained from the stigmas (pollen-collecting organs) of crocus flowers. The stigmas of over 150,000 blooms are needed to make just 1 kilogram of saffron dye.

Saffron is one of several natural dyes that have been used to colour fabrics since ancient times. Other plant dyes include madder (red) and indigo (blue), which come from the madder and indigo plants. Natural dyes can also come from animals. Cochineal red, for example, is a dye extracted from insects.

Most dyes used today, however, are synthetic. They are usually made from chemicals obtained from crude oil. Aniline, for instance, is a compound from oil that is the starting point for making many dyes.

The molecules that make up most dyes, whether natural or synthetic, contain rings of carbon atoms. These carbon rings are important in giving a dye its colour.

▶ Newly dyed cloth hangs out to dry in the streets of Marrakesh, Morocco.

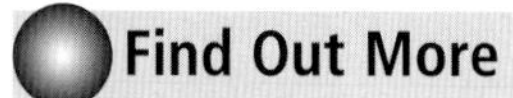

Find Out More

- Carbon
- Colour
- Oil products
- Paints

Fast colours

In general, synthetic dyes have more brilliant colours than natural dyes. They bond well with fabric fibres so that they do not readily wash out. Also, they are colour-fast, which means they do not fade easily.

Natural dyes do not bond well with natural fibres such as cotton. These fibres first have to be treated with a substance called a mordant. The mordant clings to the fibres and then bonds with the dye.

Pigments

Dyes are colouring substances that dissolve in water. Pigments are colouring substances that do not dissolve in water or other solvents (dissolving liquids). They are used to colour materials such as inks, paints and cosmetics. Traditional pigments include coloured earths such as ochre, and metal compounds such as iron and titanium oxides. Most pigments are now synthetic.

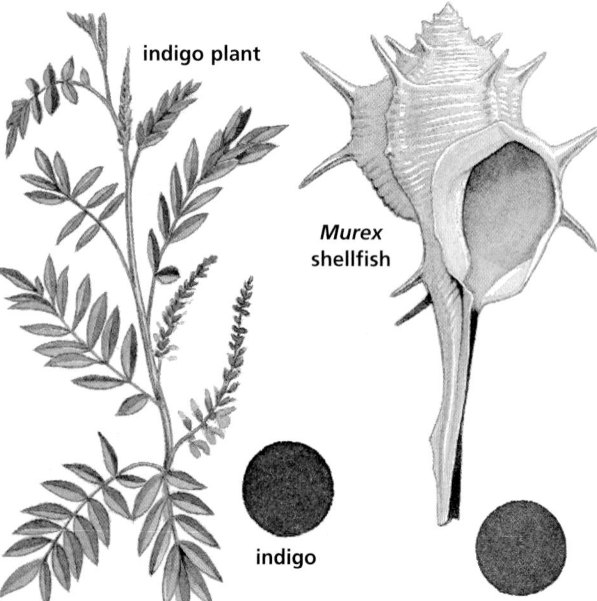

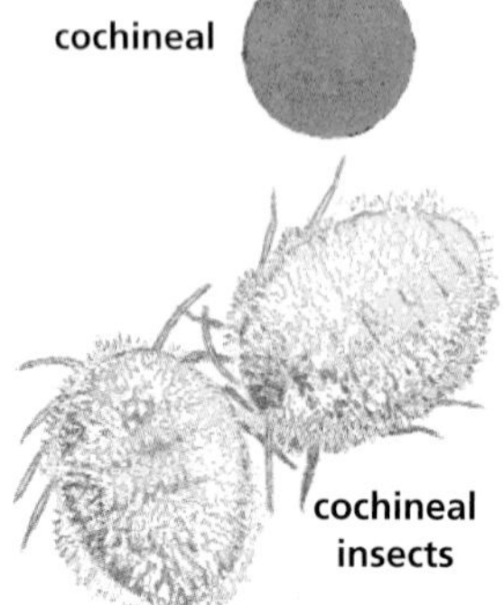

▼ Traditional dyes come from a wide variety of sources. The blue dye indigo is made from a plant; a purple dye used by the Romans came from a shellfish. Cochineal is a red dye made from cochineal insects.

WILLIAM PERKIN

The English chemist William Perkin (1838–1907) discovered the first synthetic dye, mauvein, in 1856, and set up a factory to produce it. He made it from aniline, a chemical now extracted from oil.

Ears

A rabbit's ears turn and twitch as it feeds, listening for the tiniest sounds. Suddenly it hears something, too quiet for human ears, and scuttles away to its burrow.

Hearing is very important in the natural world. Any organ that senses sounds has to be able first to collect sounds, which are vibrations in the air. It then has to amplify them (make them stronger). Finally, it must turn the amplified vibrations into electrical nerve signals, which go to the brain.

▲ A bat's ears are a vital part of its 'radar', or echolocation system.

Find Out More

- Human senses
- Radar and sonar
- Senses
- Sound

The human ear

In a human, the funnel-shaped outer ear collects sounds and guides them to a thin membrane called the eardrum, making it vibrate. These vibrations pass through a set of tiny bones called the ossicles, which amplify the sounds, to another membrane (the oval window).

On the other side of the oval window is the cochlea, part of the inner ear. This snail-shaped container is filled with liquid. The vibrations of the oval window move the liquid, which in turn moves tiny hairs in the walls of the cochlea. The hairs are rooted in sensitive cells, which send electrical signals to the brain.

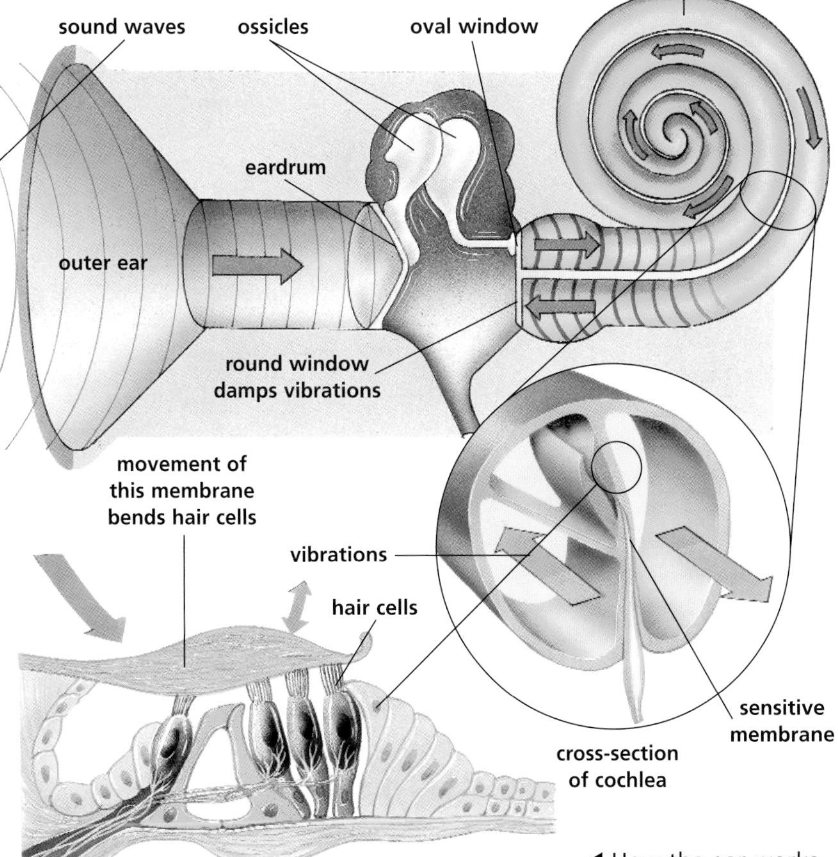

◀ How the ear works.

Other ears

Mammals such as rabbits and fennec foxes have huge ears in relation to their size. Large ears are very sensitive: they pick up sounds too quiet for humans to hear.

Bats are mammals that mostly hunt in the dark. Bats use sound like radar. They make bursts of short, high-pitched sounds (too high for humans to hear), then wait to hear the echoes coming back. The pattern of echoes tells them about their surroundings.

Many insects hear with a small membrane on their legs or on the side of the body. Fishes have a type of hearing in their 'lateral line' organs, which detect vibrations in the water.

Earth

The third planet from the Sun is the largest rocky planet. It has craters like Mercury, volcanoes like Venus and polar caps like Mars. But unlike any other planet, the Earth has oceans and millions of different kinds of living things.

The Earth is the Solar System's water world. Viewed from space, Earth is a beautiful blue planet. The blue is the Earth's oceans. About 70 per cent of the surface is submerged under oceans that are 4 kilometres deep on average. Frozen water covers about 10 per cent of the Earth, mostly at the North and South Poles. White clouds swirling in the atmosphere are droplets formed from the water vapour in the air.

No other planet in the Solar System has just the right range of temperature and a thick enough atmosphere for water to be liquid on the surface. And it is the water that makes the Earth a home for life.

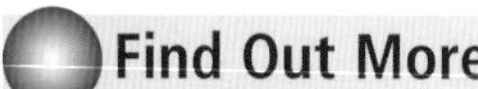

Find Out More

- Atmosphere
- Continents and plates
- Oceans
- Planets
- Rocks
- Seasons
- Solar System

Moving through space

The Earth is constantly moving through space, orbiting the Sun at an average distance of about 150 million kilometres. The complete journey takes a year – just over 365 days. As it orbits, the Earth spins on its own axis, once each day. On the side of the Earth facing the Sun it is day, on the side in shadow it is night. The Earth is tilted on its axis – for half the year the North Pole leans towards the Sun, for the other half the South Pole is closer. This tilt gives the Earth its seasons.

EARTH DATA
Diameter at equator: 12,756 km
Average distance from Sun: 150 million km
Time taken to spin on axis: 24 hours (relative to Sun)
Density (water = 1): 5.5
Time taken to orbit the Sun: 1 year
Moons: 1

▲ At night, the lights on Earth from human habitation can be seen from way out in space.

◀ Earth from space, showing clouds cover the continent of South America. This view was taken from space by the *Galileo* spacecraft when it was about 2.5 million kilometres away.

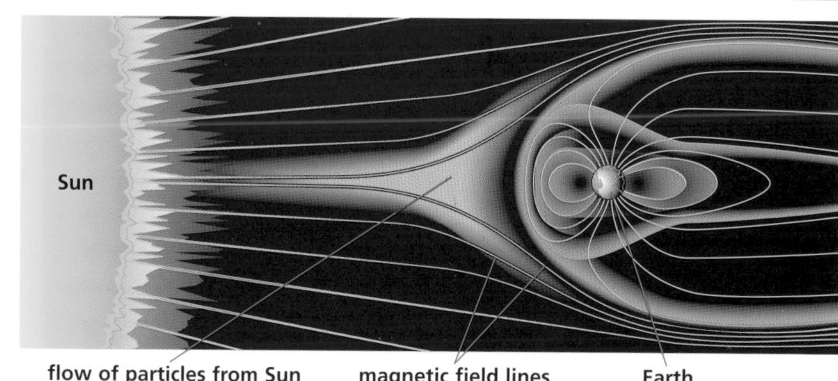

MAGNETIC EARTH

A large core of molten iron inside the Earth makes the whole planet strongly magnetic. Magnetic compasses point north because of this magnetism. It also influences the flow of gases from the Sun. Particles streaming from the Sun are deflected by the magnetism, like water round the bow of a ship. Auroras (northern or southern lights) are one of the results of the magnetism.

The life zone

If the Earth were much nearer the Sun or much farther away, it would be too hot or too cold for water and life. As it is, with the help of the atmosphere to keep warmth in and even out the climate, the Earth is just right. The atmosphere is important. Earth's only satellite, the Moon, is at the same distance from the Sun as the Earth but it is too small to have enough gravity for an atmosphere. Without one, the Moon is dry, dead and inhospitable.

Today the Earth's atmosphere is 78 per cent nitrogen, 21 per cent oxygen, and 1 per cent water vapour, with tiny amounts of other gases. Humans and most other animals depend on oxygen to breathe, but long ago there was no oxygen in the atmosphere.

Born from dust

Just over four and a half billion years ago, our Solar System was just a cloud of dust and gas floating among the stars. Then the cloud began to collapse, and the dust and gas spiralled inward.

Most of the dust and gas fell into the centre and became the Sun. But some of the dust particles that were spinning around the Sun began to stick to each other and to form large chunks of rock. These chunks joined together and grew until they became rocky planets. One of these planets was the Earth.

When it first formed, the Earth was much hotter than it is now. The atmosphere was made up of nitrogen, water vapour and carbon dioxide belched out by volcanoes.

▲ The coloured glow of an aurora. These lights in the atmosphere are most often seen in the far north and far south. The photo shows a northern aurora.

The cooling Earth

The early Earth was so hot that the surface was an ocean of liquid rock. Light parts floated to the surface, where they cooled and hardened into the crust. The heavier parts sank to the centre and formed the Earth's core. A middle layer, the mantle, formed between the light crust and the dense core.

Because the Earth was so hot, there were many more volcanoes. Gases erupted from the volcanoes and formed the Earth's atmosphere. One of the gases was water vapour. As the Earth started to cool, the water vapour became rain, which fell to the ground and formed the oceans. Life began in the oceans about 4 billion years ago. Over millions of years, early sea life and the first plants reduced the amount of carbon dioxide in the air and produced great amounts of oxygen.

The changing Earth

Everything we see on Earth today is the result of billions of years of changes by heat, water, air, gravity and life. And the Earth is still changing today. Water breaks rocks and moves them from place to place. The continents slowly move over the surface of the Earth, coming together and ripping apart. And living things change the Earth's surface.

Billions of years ago, when rocks were regularly crashing onto the surface of both the Earth and the Moon, both had many craters. Little has changed on the Moon, but the Earth has altered so much that only faint outlines of about 100 craters can be identified today.

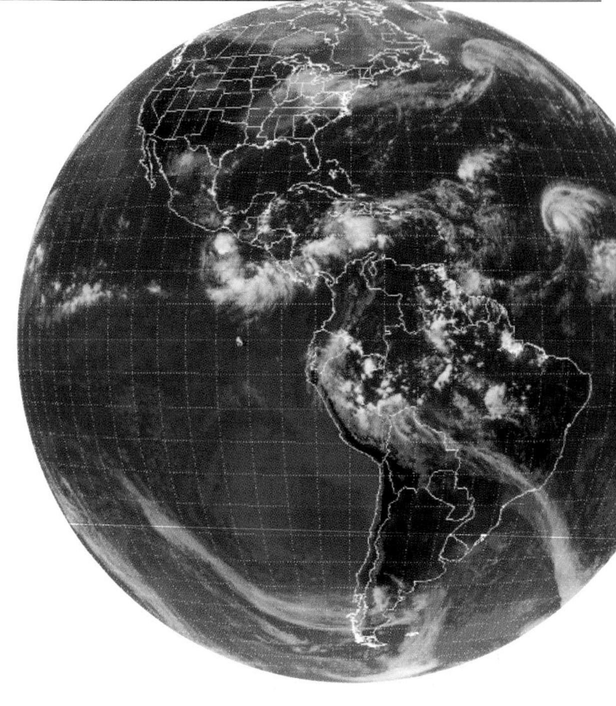

▲ This image of the Earth was taken on 25 September 2000 by a weather satellite. The satellite 'hovers' above one point on the Earth's surface, and scans it every half hour. It is an infrared image. Infrared is a type of light that human eyes can't see. Meteorologists use the images to track weather systems, but anyone who has access to the world wide web can view the images as soon as they are received.

Rocks from space probably had a great influence on the way life developed on Earth. Many scientists now think that the impact of a large meteorite 65 million years ago led to many kinds of animal dying out, including the dinosaurs.

Exploring the Earth's insides

It is impossible to drill all the way through the Earth and actually see what's inside, so we have to explore it in other ways. When rocks on the Earth's surface erode (wear

▼ Scientists think that the Earth, Sun and other planets formed around 4560 million years ago from a cloud of dust and gas.

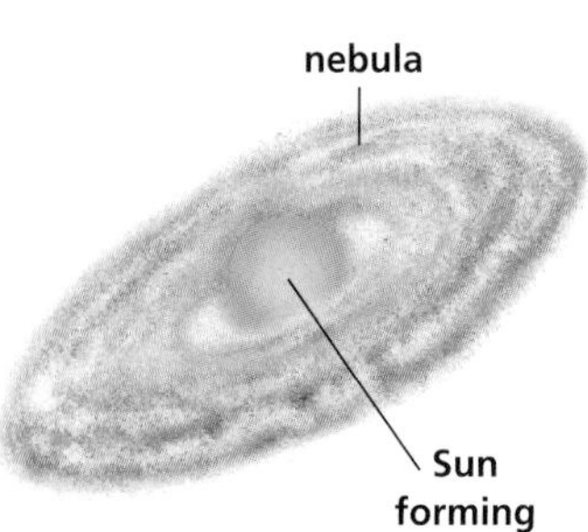

1. The Solar System began as a rotating cloud of gas and dust (a nebula).

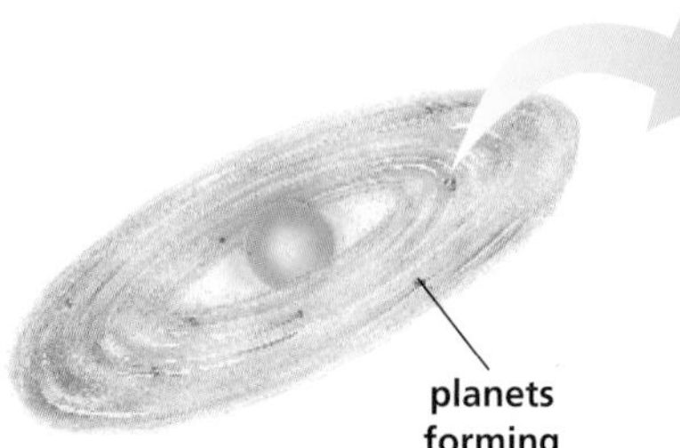

2. Most of the gas and dust formed the Sun. Around the Sun the planets formed, one of which was Earth.

3. At first, **the Earth was so hot** that its surface was almost all molten.

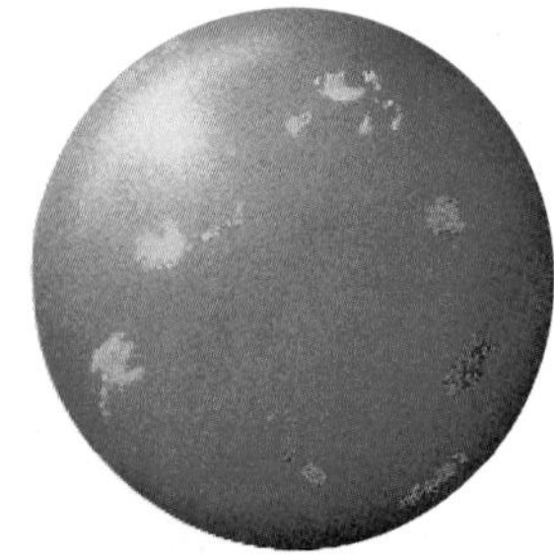

4. Over time, **the Earth cooled.** A crust of hard rock formed, and water vapour condensed from the air to form oceans.

away), other rocks from deep in the crust are exposed on the surface, and we can study them. Volcanoes sometimes bring up rocks from even deeper down.

Earthquakes also give us clues about the Earth's insides. Earthquakes send out waves of energy that bounce off different layers inside the Earth. By carefully studying these waves, geologists can estimate how deep each layer is, and what each one is made of.

If you were actually able to travel through the Earth, you would notice that the deeper you go, the hotter the rocks get. No one is sure exactly how hot Earth's centre is, but it is probably about 4500 °C.

You would also notice that the rocks get denser as you go down. The deeper rocks are made of heavier materials, and they are squashed tightly by the weight of all the rocks above.

▲ This is what Earth would look like without oceans hiding the seafloor. As on the land, there are high mountain ranges, deep valleys, and flat plains on the ocean floor.

INSIDE THE EARTH

The Earth isn't the same all the way through. It is made of five different layers – the atmosphere, crust, mantle, outer core, and inner core.

ocean crust

atmosphere

continental crust

40 to 70 km

2900 km

5140 km

The mantle, like the crust, is made of solid rock, but it is much hotter and the rocks are denser. Even though the mantle is solid, it flows very slowly – just a few centimetres every year.

The outer core is made of hot, dense, liquid iron. Geologists think that the iron liquid moves around slowly inside the core and creates the Earth's magnetic field. (The magnetic field is what makes a compass needle point towards the North Pole.)

The inner core is made mostly of iron. But even though the inner core is even hotter than the outer core, it is under so much pressure from the weight of the rocks above that it is solid, not liquid.

The crust is the rocky shell of the Earth, which we live on and the oceans rest on. There are two kinds of crust. The crust below the oceans is made of volcanic rocks, covered in a layer of mud. The crust that makes up the continents is thicker than the ocean crust, and is made of all kinds of rock.

The atmosphere is the layer of gas between the Earth's surface and outer space. The atmosphere is primarily made of nitrogen and oxygen.

Earthquakes

In the early morning of 17 August 1999, rocks began to break deep beneath the small city of Izmit, Turkey. As they broke, they moved past each other. Izmit and the surrounding area shook. By the end of the earthquake, there was a tear in the ground more than 100 kilometres long, and the rocks had moved 3 metres.

The earthquake at Izmit destroyed hundreds of buildings and killed 18,000 people. It also created a tsunami, a huge sea wave that drowned part of the Turkish coastline. Earthquakes happen when rocks break and then move along large cracks, called faults, in the Earth's crust.

Breaking rocks

The surface of the Earth is made of many large pieces, or *plates*, that are moving very slowly. Most earthquakes occur at the edges of these plates, where they grate against one another. In some places, the rocks are moving all the time, so small tremors happen almost every day. In other places, the rocks try to move past one another, but they get stuck. The stress builds up for many years until finally the rock snaps and a powerful earthquake jolts the land.

▶ Aerial view of the San Andreas fault in California, the site of many earthquakes. The city of San Francisco lies directly on the fault, and suffered major earthquakes in 1906, 1989 and 1994.

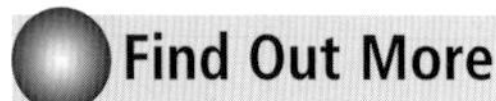

Find Out More

- Continents and plates
- Energy
- Rocks
- Waves and vibrations

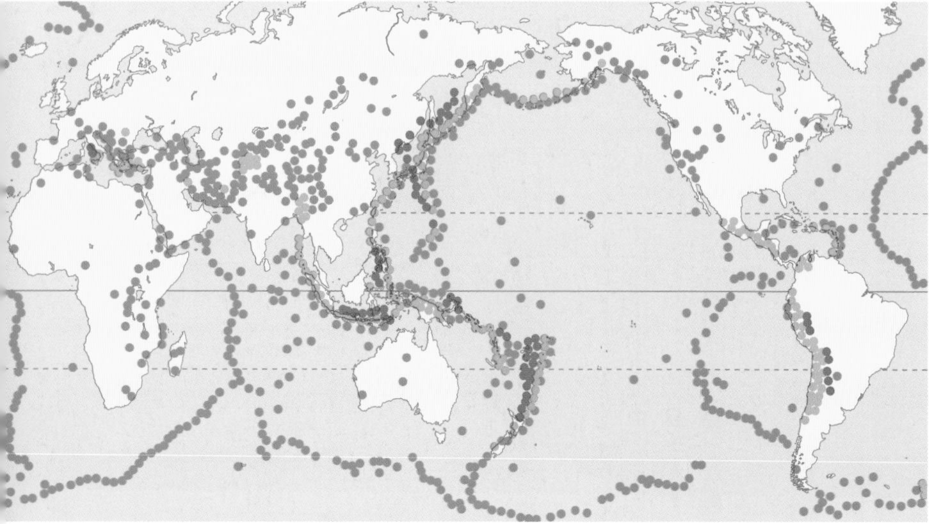

Key
earthquake depths:
- less than 70 km
- 70 to 300 km
- 300 to 700 km

▼ A seismogram of the Izmit earthquake. Seismograms are recordings of how the ground shakes. Even though earthquakes only destroy things in the small area near where the rocks move, seismic waves pass all the way through and around the Earth. This seismogram was recorded in Urumquin in West China, thousands of kilometres away from Izmit.

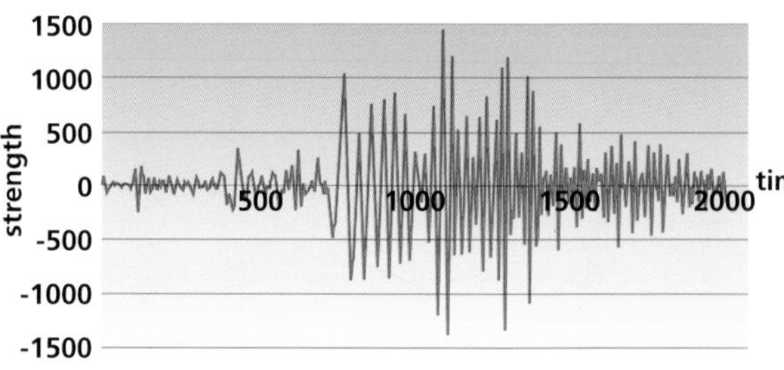

Seismic waves

When rocks break, they release energy into the other rocks nearby. The energy is called *seismic energy* and it travels through the Earth as *seismic waves*. Seismic waves travel through rock in almost the same way that ocean waves travel through water. Some travel through the inside of the Earth and others travel around the Earth on the surface. Some move the rocks up and down and some move them from side to side. Some squeeze and stretch the rock. Seismic waves are what shake the ground and the buildings during an earthquake.

◀ A map of strong earthquakes that occurred between 1977 and 1992 shows that earthquakes are concentrated in particular areas. They also occur at different depths. Deep earthquakes occur near ocean trenches, where the ocean crust dives into the mantle below it.

Echoes *see* Radar and sonar • **Echolocation** *see* Sound

Eclipses

Only a narrow crescent of Sun is visible and the sky is darkening rapidly. Suddenly, the last bead of sunlight disappears behind the Moon. A thin ring of pink fire and a halo of pearly light surround the dark disc of the Moon. A total eclipse of the Sun has reached its climax.

When the Moon passes between the Earth and the Sun, it can just cover the Sun's dazzling yellow disc. Then the faint outer part of the Sun, called the corona, becomes visible. We can see this awe-inspiring sight because of an amazing coincidence: the Moon and the Sun appear nearly the same size. In reality, the Sun is 400 times larger than the Moon, but it is also 400 times farther away.

Totality is the time while the Sun's yellow disc is completely covered. It can last several minutes. This can only be seen where the Moon's deepest shadow sweeps across the Earth's surface. Over a larger region there is a partial eclipse, which means that the Sun is partly covered by the Moon. During a partial eclipse the sky does not get dark and the corona is not visible. There can be partial solar eclipses when nowhere has totality.

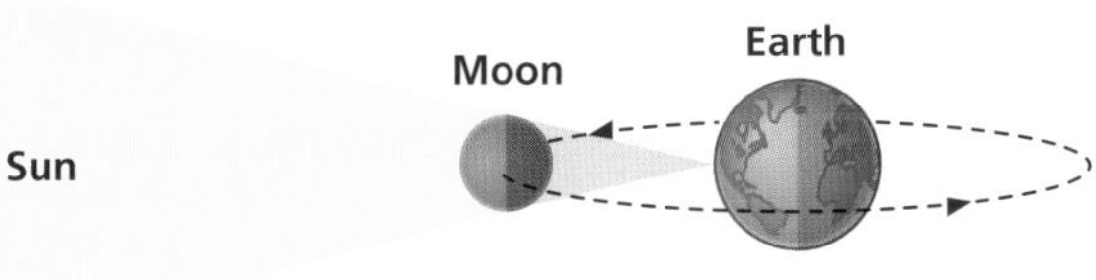

SOLAR ECLIPSE

▲ Totality during an eclipse of the Sun. Solar eclipses happen at New Moon when the Moon passes between the Earth and the Sun. The Sun's corona is visible as long as the bright disc of the Sun is covered by the Moon.

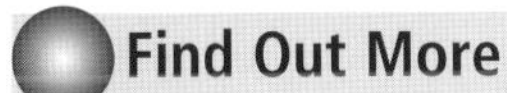

Find Out More

- Earth
- Moon
- Sun

▼ Lunar eclipses take place at Full Moon, when the Moon moves into the Earth's shadow. The Moon looks orange during a total lunar eclipse.

Lunar eclipses

The Moon sometimes passes into the Earth's shadow. Nearly all sunlight to the Moon is cut off and there is a lunar eclipse. The Moon does not vanish from sight, though. It usually looks a dim orange-brown colour. It is lit by sunlight spilt into the Earth's shadow by the atmosphere. Lunar eclipses are visible from all places on the Earth where the Moon is up and can last as long as 2.5 hours.

Ecology

Darting across a city street at night, a red fox narrowly misses being run over by a car. Yet it survives to search through the city's waste bins for scraps of left-over food. Foxes have adapted well to urban life. But many animals have been driven out of their homes by the spread of towns and cities.

◀ Grass, voles and kestrels make up a simple, three-link food chain. The grass is called a producer, because it produces its own food using the Sun's energy. The vole and the kestrel are consumers because they eat ready-made food.

Understanding how foxes survive in cities is part of the science of ecology. Ecologists (scientists who study ecology) explore the ways that living things depend on each other for survival. They try to discover the many complicated links between plants, animals and their environment.

Feeding links

One of the ways in which plants and animals are linked together is through their food. Plants make their own food, using energy from sunlight and water from the soil. Animals cannot make their own food – they have to eat plants, or other animals that have already eaten plants. The path that the food follows, through a plant to two or more animals, is called a food chain.

Most animals eat several kinds of food, so they are part of a complicated web of food connections, rather than a simple chain. A food chain usually contains less than six kinds, or species, of animal, but a food web may contain hundreds or thousands.

Living connections

Ecologists recognize that all living things live in particular 'zones' of life. The largest zones are called 'biomes' – these include forests, deserts and grasslands. Each biome is divided into different ecosystems. For example, an oak wood and a pine wood are different ecosystems in a forest biome. Each group, or community, of animals and plants lives in a particular habitat within that ecosystem: perhaps on the forest floor, or high in the canopy of branches.

The individual way of life of a plant or animal is called its 'niche'. A wood ant occupies a niche on the forest floor, while a bird's niche is up in the canopy of branches.

Find Out More

- Animals
- Climate
- Evolution
- Plants
- Pollution

Colonies of ants sometimes make a safe home inside the swollen stems or leaves of special 'ant-plants'. The ants' rubbish provides the plants with extra nutrients.

▶ On the African grasslands, oxpeckers search the skin of large grazing animals, such as this impala, for ticks and bloodsucking flies to eat. Both the oxpecker and the grazing animals gain from their partnership.

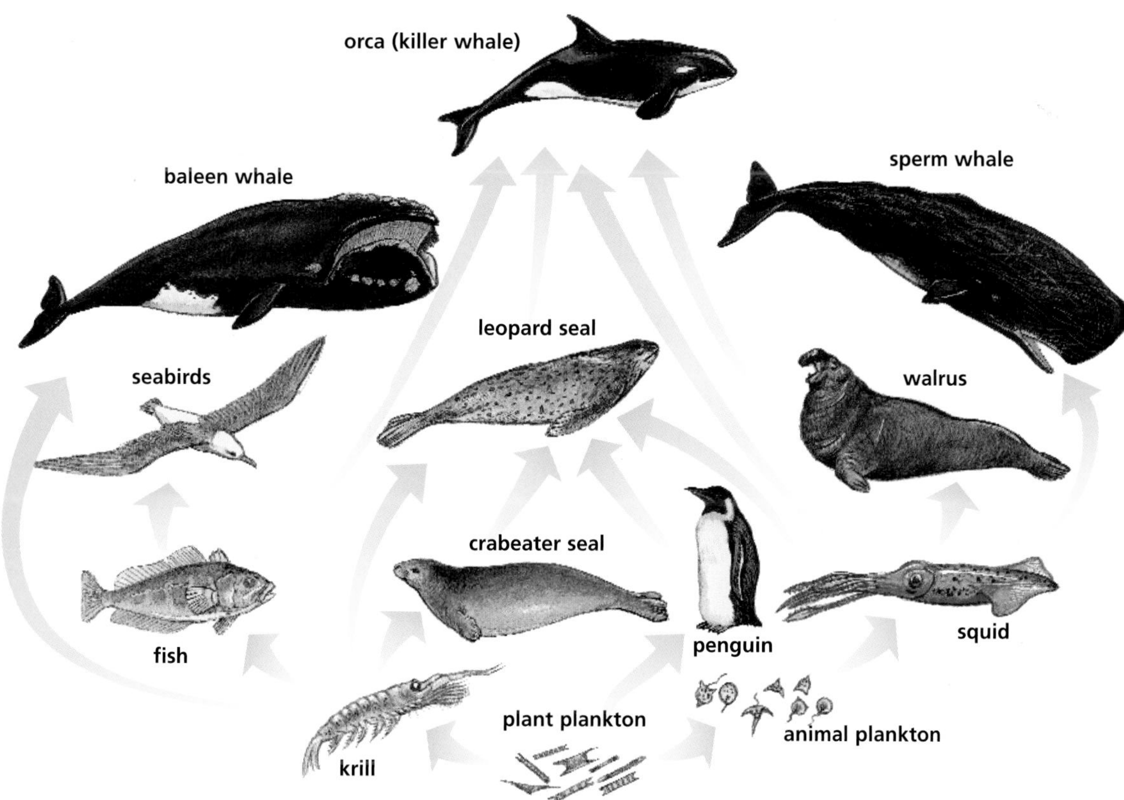

◀ This is a simplified food web for an ecosystem in a polar ocean. The producers are plankton, which are like the 'grass' of the sea. A change in just one of the plants or animals in the web will affect all the others.

Wood ants feed on leaf-eating insects. In woodlands where there are no wood ants, the trees lose far more of their leaves to leaf-eating insects than in woodlands where there are wood-ant colonies. So the ants help the woodland trees to thrive. This is one example of the way plants and animals living side by side affect each other in many different ways – not just through food.

Upsetting the balance

There are 6 billion people living on the Earth and the way we live has upset the natural balance of life. We have destroyed or polluted the habitats of many plants and animals and driven some to extinction.

We have changed the climate of the whole world. Understanding ecology can help us to solve the problems we have caused, and to avoid creating new ones.

▼ A map showing the world's biomes. Each biome has a characteristic type of vegetation and wildlife. They are shaped mainly by climate, because this determines where different types of plants can grow.

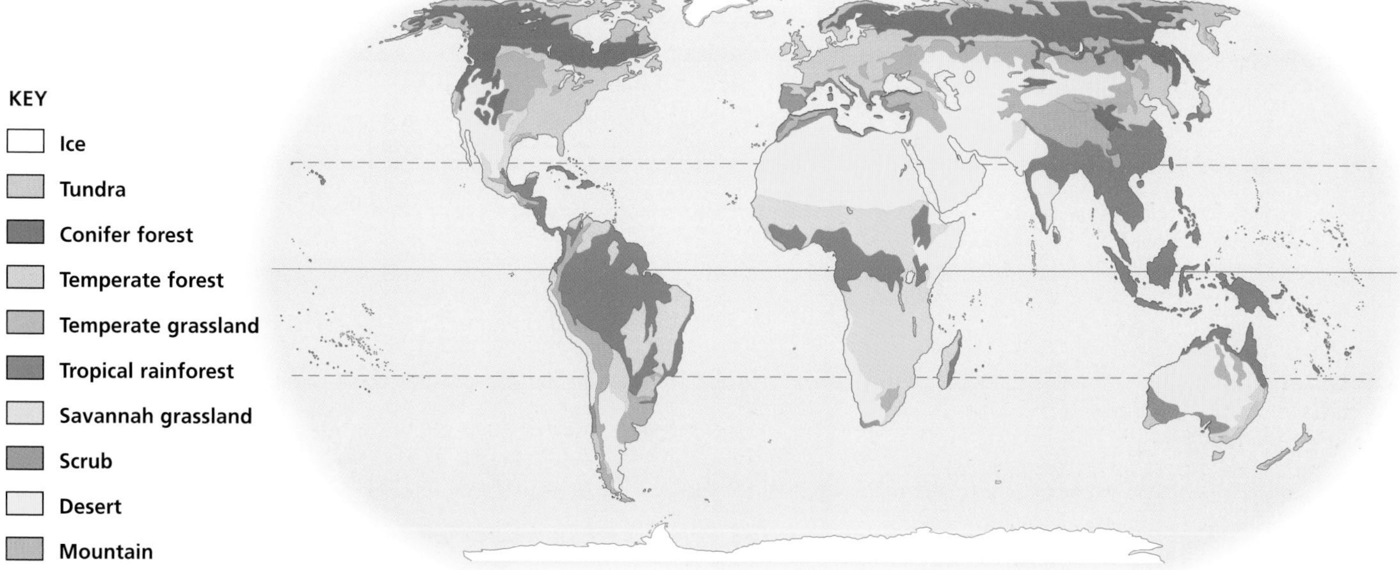

Eggs *see* Birds, Insects, Reptiles, Sex and reproduction • **Einstein**, Albert *see* Relativity

Electricity

Blasting out of the sky like a jagged laser beam, a bolt of lightning strikes a tree, scorching it to a blackened crisp. The power of a lightning strike is spectacular and dangerous. What is this strange, violent energy that comes from the sky?

The answer is that lightning is a form of electricity. During a thunderstorm, clouds can store up electricity. When enough electricity has built up, it zaps between the clouds and the ground in the form of a lightning strike.

Electric power

Lightning is one way in which electricity occurs in nature. But it's man-made electricity that powers much of today's world. Without it, we would have no commonplace gadgets such as personal stereos, computers, televisions, toasters, programmable dishwashers and mobile phones. So what exactly is this stuff called electricity that we all depend on so much?

Charging about

All substances are made of tiny particles called atoms. In the middle of each atom there is a core called a nucleus. Around this nucleus is a cloud of very light particles called electrons. Electricity results from the behaviour of the electrons, which possess a strange property called electric charge.

No-one knows exactly what electric charge is, but we know there are two kinds: positive and negative. Electrons have a

FRANKLIN'S EXPERIMENT

In 1752, the American statesman and inventor Ben Franklin (1706–1790) undertook a very risky experiment. He flew a kite with a salty thread (which electricity could flow through) near thunderclouds. He managed to get electric current to leak down the thread to charge a Leyden jar – a very early form of battery. This proved that lightning was another form of electricity. Others who tried to copy Franklin's experiment were not so lucky – at least two were struck by lightning and killed.

▼ Lightning over a city. Metal rods called lightning conductors, mounted high on buildings, have been used for hundreds of years to help lightning strikes leak harmlessly to earth.

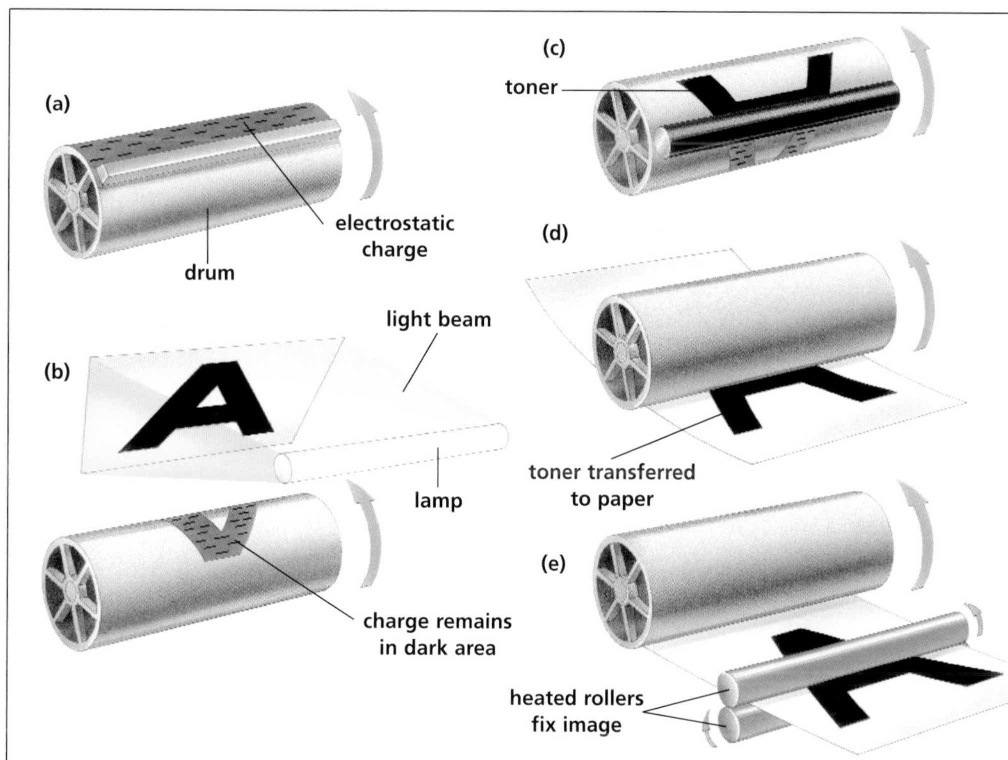

USING STATIC TO MAKE COPIES

Static electricity plays an important part in the photocopying process. First, a drum inside the photocopier is charged with static electricity (a). Then light is shone on the image being copied. The light reflects onto the drum, and in the bright areas it makes the drum lose charge (b). There is now a pattern of charge on the drum, a copy of the pattern of light and dark on the original image. An ink powder called toner is now spread on the drum, but it only sticks to the charged areas (c). This toner pattern is then transferred from the drum to a piece of paper (d) and fixed by two heated rollers (e).

negative charge. They are attracted towards positive charges (the nucleus of an atom is positively charged) and forced away from, or repelled, by other negative charges.

Atoms have a balance of electric charge, because the positive charges in the nucleus balance out the negative charges of the electrons. But some substances can accept extra electrons, while others lose electrons quite easily. So objects can become electrically charged. This is known as static electricity. Charge cannot build up on materials such as metals because they let electrons flow through them. We call a flow of electric charge 'current electricity'.

Passing on the charge

If you have ever received a small electric shock after walking across a thick carpet and grasping a metal door handle, you will have experienced the effects of static electricity. Static electricity will also make a balloon stick to the wall after you have rubbed it on your hair.

In static electricity, electrons create a stationary charge. For example, when you rub the balloon on your hair, loosely held electrons in your hair are rubbed off on to the balloon. The object that loses the

Find Out More

- Batteries and cells
- Circuits
- Conductors and insulators
- Electricity supply
- Magnetism and electromagnetism

▶ The charge on a balloon can make your hair stand on end.

electrons (your hair) builds up a positive charge, while the object that gains the electrons (the balloon) builds up a negative charge. The balloon will then stick to the wall because its negative charges are attracted to positive charges in the wall. Similarly, when you walk across a fluffy carpet, loose electrons in the carpet hop on to your body, charging you up. You don't feel this until you grab a metal door handle. Then the electron charge is released into the metal through your hand, and you feel a small shock. You may also hear a crackle, as this electricity makes a spark as it jumps to the metal.

▶ Doctors use the electrical signals made by the brain to find out whether people have certain illnesses.

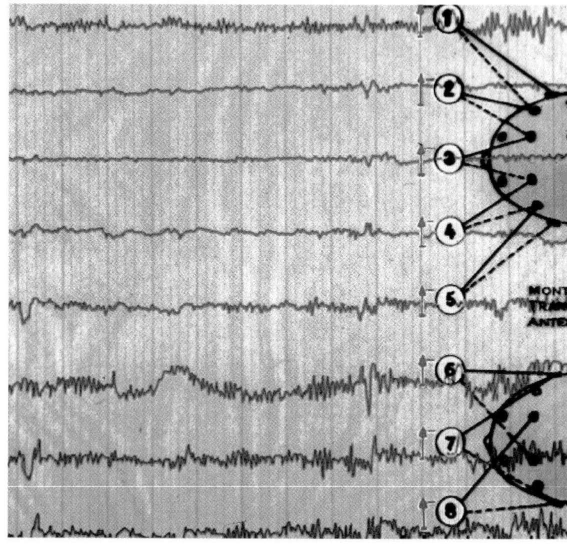

Interestingly, lightning involves both static and current electricity. During a storm, electrons build up inside the lower surface of clouds to make a static electric charge. When the attraction between the negatively charged cloud and the positively charged ground (or even another cloud) is great enough, electrons flow through the air in a searing current that makes the air glow. This is what we call lightning.

Electricity and magnetism

Electricity is very closely related to magnetism. That's because both depend on the way electrons behave. A material can be magnetic if many of its electrons spin in the same direction. When an electric current moves through a wire, it also creates a magnetic field around it. And moving a wire through a magnetic field can produce an electric current in the wire. Both these effects are used in many of the electric machines that we use every day.

Current affairs

In current electricity, electrons are made to flow through a material such as a metal wire. A battery, or another power supply such as mains electricity, pushes electrons through the wires. This flow of electrons creates an electric current. As electric current passes through metal wires, it can power a light bulb, turn a motor or do many other useful jobs.

▲ The high electric current that flows through an electric arc-welder creates a high-temperature 'spark' that is hot enough to melt metal. It can be used to cut through pieces of metal or to join them together.

Our bodies are full of electricity. The 10 billion nerve cells in your brain work by sending messages in the form of bursts of electricity (impulses) to each other. Reading this page will have set off hundreds of impulses as your nerves sent messages from your eyes to your brain.

Electricity supply

Stretching all over the country, thousands and thousands of kilometres of cables carry electricity to factories, offices and homes. These cables are carried by tall pylons (towers) or buried underground. They join many power stations in a vast network, called a national grid.

Power stations produce electricity at a voltage (electrical pressure) of about 20,000 volts. It is alternating current (AC), which means that the current changes direction many times per second.

But it is not economic to transmit (send) electricity over long distances at 20,000 volts. Too much power would be lost. If the electricity is transmitted at a much higher voltage, the power losses are much lower.

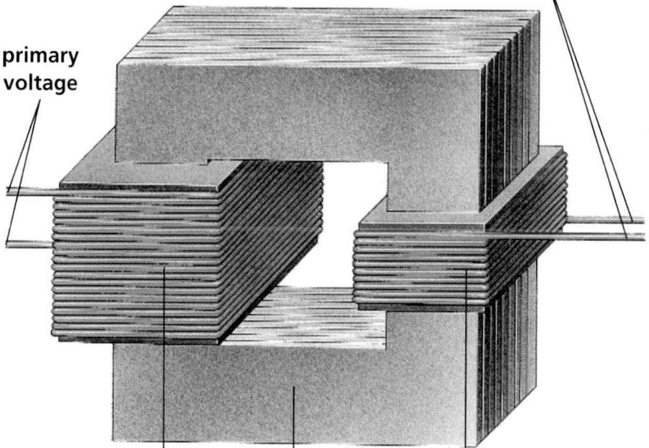

▶ A simple transformer. A voltage applied to the primary coil produces a voltage in the secondary coil. If the secondary coil is smaller than the primary coil, the transformer reduces the voltage (step-down). If the secondary coil is bigger, the voltage is stepped up.

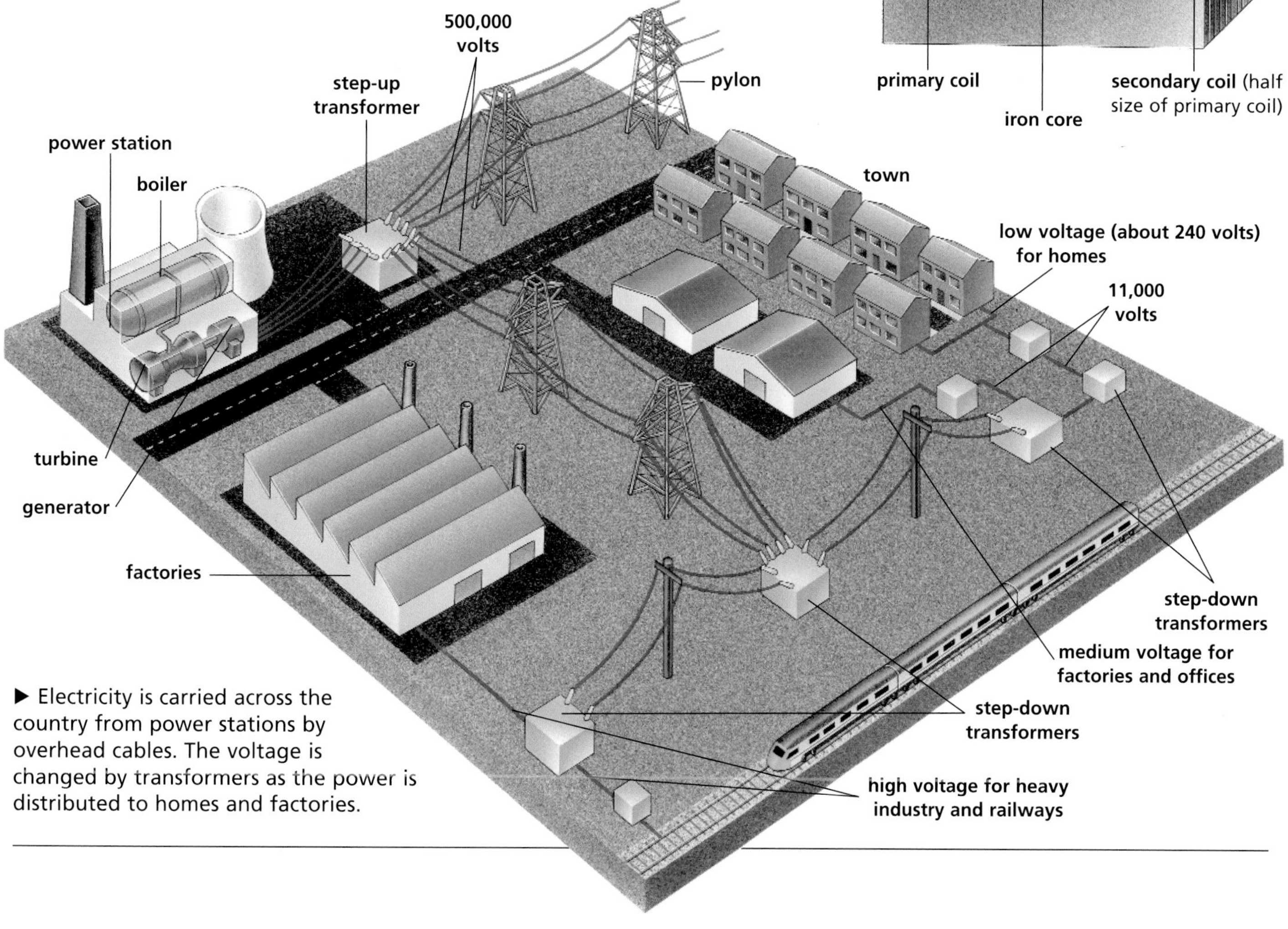

All change!

The kind of electricity produced by power stations is called alternating current (AC). AC does not travel through the cables in one direction only, but changes direction many times a second. It is easy to change the voltage of AC electricity, using a device called a transformer. At the power station a 'step-up' transformer boosts the generated voltage to as much as 500,000 volts. The power travels along high-voltage cables (which lose much less power) to where it is needed.

▶ Electricity is carried across the country from power stations by overhead cables. The voltage is changed by transformers as the power is distributed to homes and factories.

Of course, we don't want electricity coming into our homes at 500,000 volts! Other transformers are used to 'step down' the voltage to more useful levels: several thousand volts for factories, and about 240 volts for homes. This process normally happens at local substations.

Electricity in the home

We call the electricity that comes into our homes 'mains electricity'. It travels to where it is needed along circuits. There are separate circuits for different things. One may carry heavy current to drive an electric cooker. Another will power the sockets we use to plug in things like dishwashers and TVs. A third circuit powers the lights.

Occasionally a broken machine might use more electricity than is safe, and could catch fire. To prevent this, plugs are fitted with fuses. These are thin pieces of wire that melt when too much current flows through them, so breaking the circuit.

A circuit-breaker is another safety device that we have in our homes. This cuts off the electricity automatically if the amount of current flowing in a circuit gets too high.

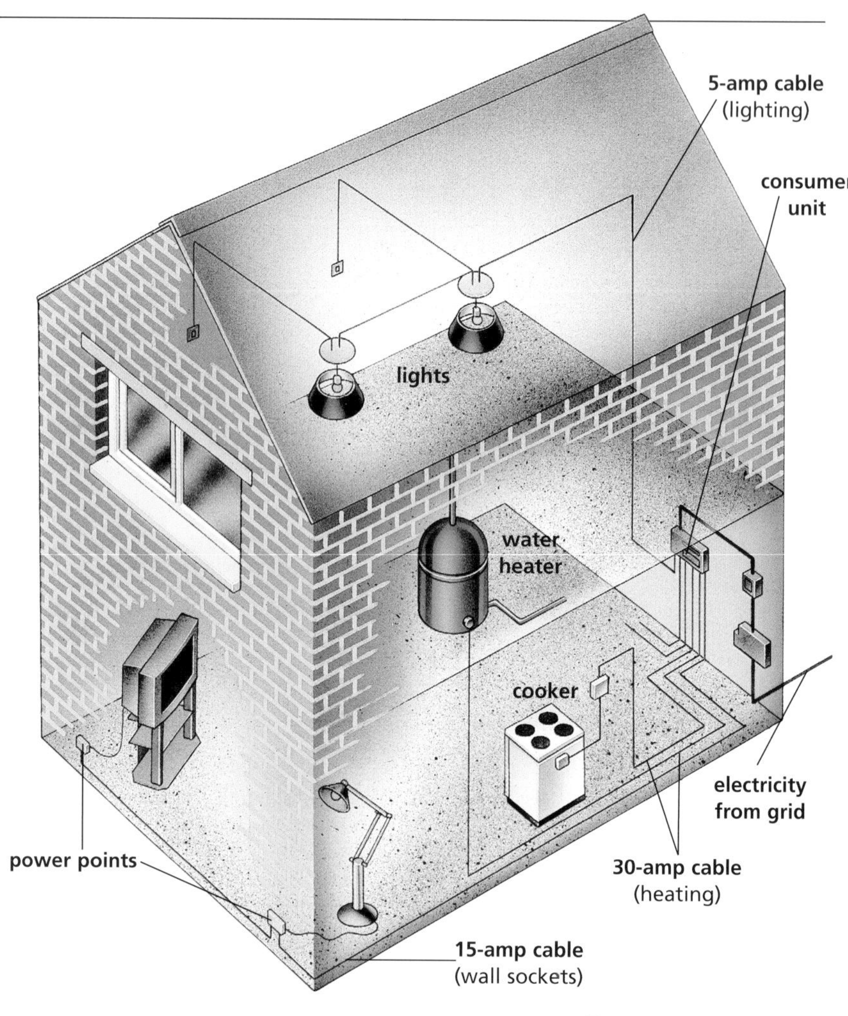

▲ The wiring in a house. In many houses, the main cable branches out to several circuits at the consumer unit. The power points are usually all connected to the same cable, called a ring main.

Find Out More

- Circuits
- Electricity
- Power stations
- Generators

▼ The pylon in the background (left) brings high-voltage electricity to the transformers (centre) in this electricity substation.

Powerful plug-ins

Companies that supply electricity keep a constant check on how much electricity people are using. Sometimes, more electricity is being used in an area than is available. The electricity company will then connect to other power stations in the grid and use some of their electricity.

Electricity supply is now a big international business. This means that different countries can share electricity if they have some to spare. At peak times, for instance, when everybody is using electricity, Britain can use power from France.

Electric motors

Electric motors power most of the machines we use in our homes, and most machines in industry, from drills and printing presses to trains and milk floats. In fact it probably won't be long before electric motors, using a new type of battery called a fuel cell, are powering the latest cars.

Electric motors work in the opposite way to electricity generators. They convert electricity into energy to make things move, whereas generators use movement to make electricity. The English physicist Michael Faraday made the world's first electric motor in 1822. He showed that electric current could be used to move a wire in a magnetic field.

How motors work

An electric motor is built in much the same way as a generator. It has a set of wire coils, wound round a block called an armature, and mounted on a shaft, or rotor. Magnets or electromagnets around the armature create a magnetic field.

When electric current is fed into the wires of the coils, the shaft of the motor rotates. The rotating shaft can then be used to drive machines.

Electric motors may be driven by direct (one-way) current or alternating (two-way) current. Direct current machines need a switching device called a commutator to keep the rotor spinning in the same direction.

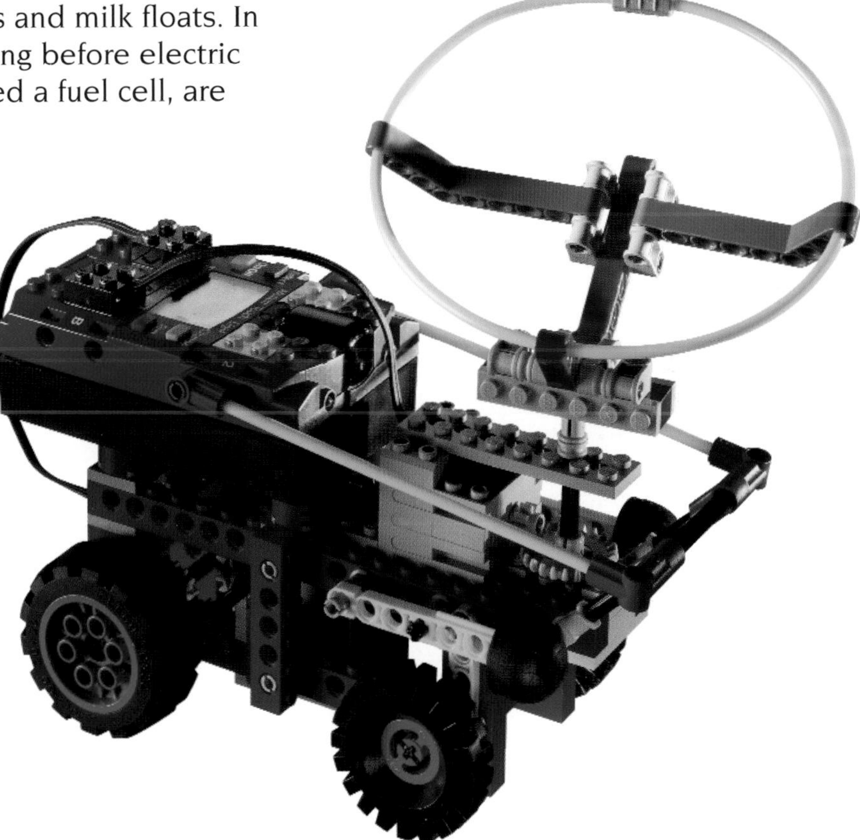

▲ Many toys today have electric motors in them. The motor in this vehicle drives the wheels and also turns the radar aerial.

A SIMPLE MOTOR

This diagram of a simple direct-current (DC) motor shows a motor with just one turn of the wire coil. When current passes through the coil, it creates a magnetic field around the wire. This magnetic field interacts with the field between the poles of the permanent magnet. The coil turns until its own poles are next to the opposite poles of the magnet, because opposite magnetic poles attract each other. At this point, the commutator, which connects the coil to the battery, reverses the direction of the current flowing through the coil. The magnetic field around the coil is reversed, forcing the coil to make another half-turn.

Find Out More

- Electricity
- Generators
- Magnetism and electromagnetism

Electrodes *see* Batteries and cells • **Electrolysis** *see* Aluminium, Chemicals

Electromagnetic spectrum

Imagine it's a sunny day and you're listening to the radio. The ultraviolet rays from the Sun are giving you a tan, and you are very warm, so you are giving off infrared rays. Radio waves, ultraviolet and infrared rays are just some of the invisible waves that belong to the electromagnetic spectrum (range).

Colours are part of this spectrum, too. Since we can see them, we say they are part of the visible spectrum. Blue and red are at opposite ends of the visible spectrum.

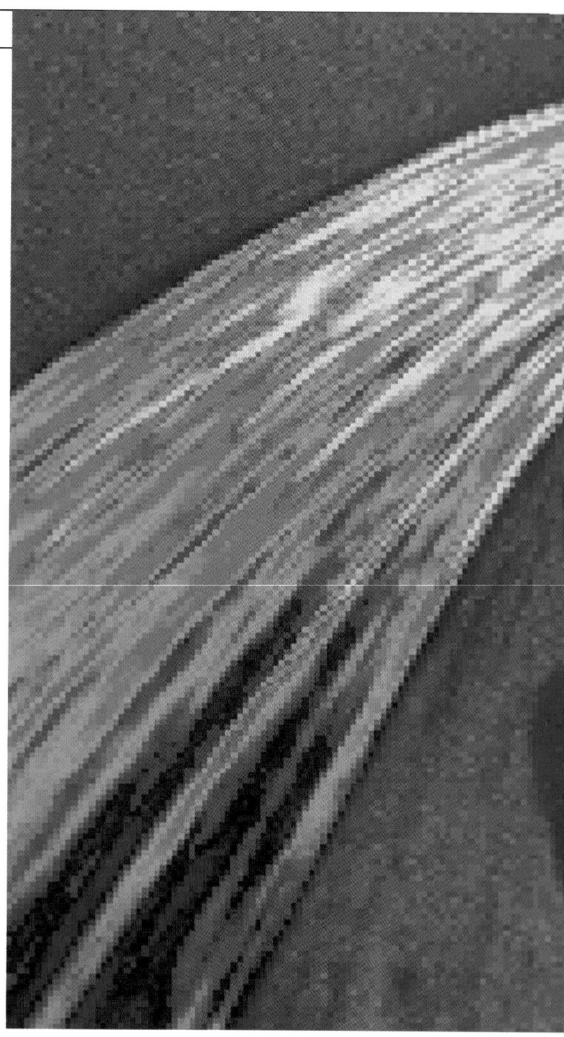

▶ A photograph of a shower taken by a camera which detects infrared (heat) radiation. The different temperatures are shown in the picture as different colours, ranging from red (hot) to blue (cold).

Waves of light

Light travels as a series of very tiny waves, rather like ripples spreading out over a lake. The waves are tiny electrical and magnetic disturbances. That is why they are sometimes called electromagnetic waves.

All waves have their own wavelength and frequency. The wavelength is the

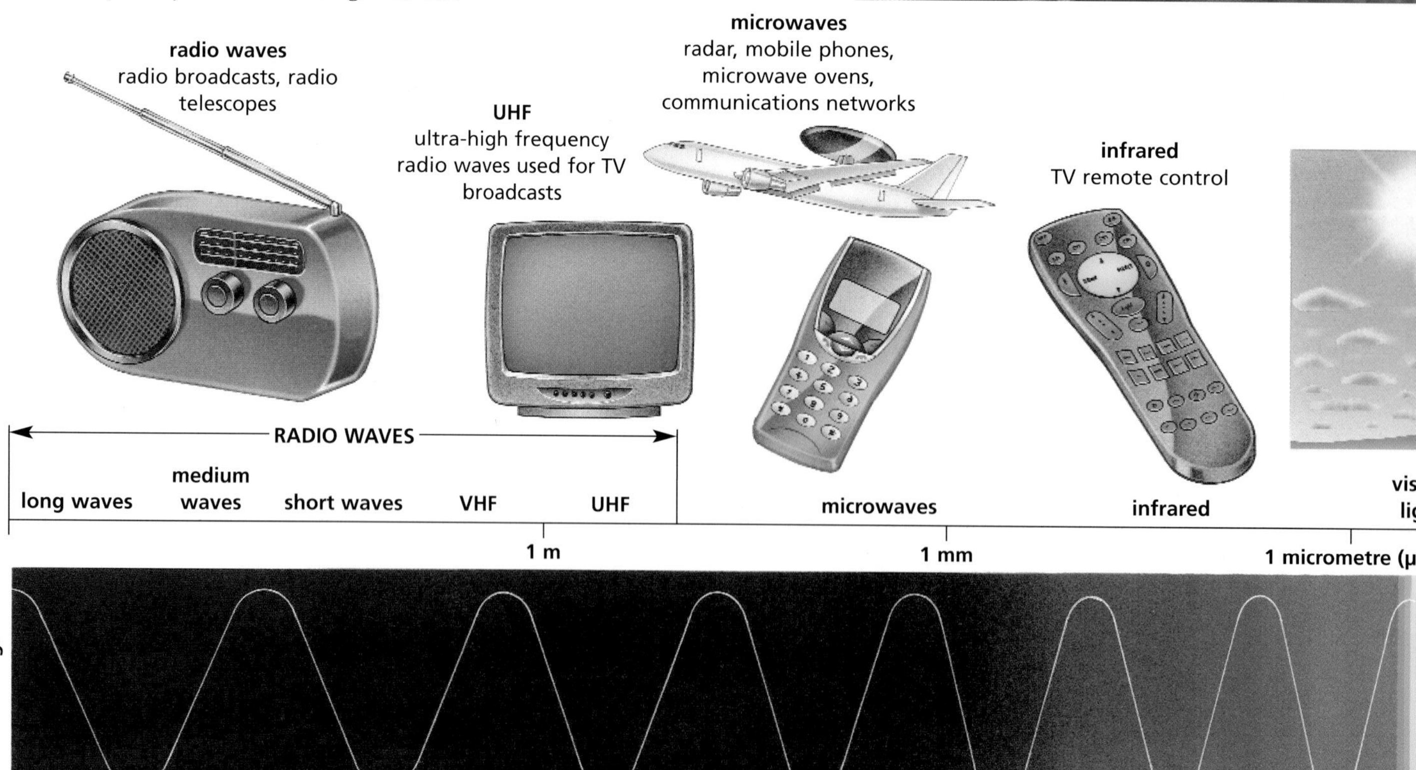

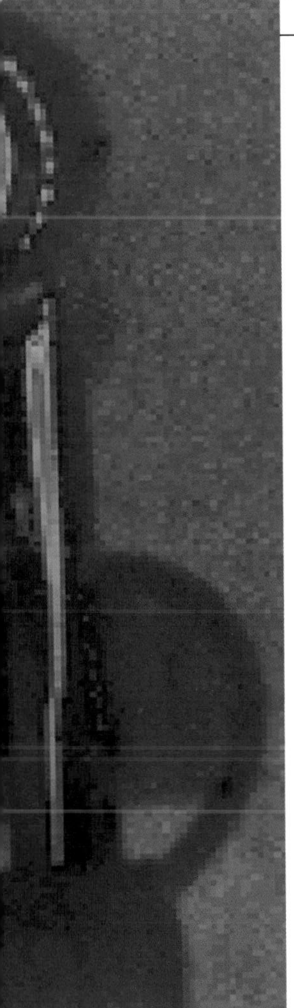

distance between peaks on the wave – for visible light, this is very small. The frequency is how many times the wave vibrates (shakes) each second.

'White' light is really a mixture of all the colours in the rainbow. Each colour has its own wavelength, blue having the shortest wavelength and red the longest. But light is only a small part of the full range of electromagnetic waves. There are similar, invisible waves, some with wavelengths much longer than red light, others with shorter wavelengths than blue light. The complete range is known as the electromagnetic spectrum. Like light, all these kinds of wave can travel through the vacuum of space, and they move at the speed of light (300,000 km/s).

Radio waves

There are radio waves everywhere. We use them to send messages to each other and to broadcast music and television programmes. This is possible because we have found a way to alter radio waves, so that their pattern carries all the information needed for radios, TVs and telephones to recreate sounds and pictures. Each programme or channel has a specific frequency that the radio or TV can tune to.

Radio waves also come from the Sun and outer space. Astronomers use special radio receivers (called radio telescopes) to listen to them. The radio signals tell them about fantastic things going on in deep space, such as fast-spinning pulsars and dying galaxies.

Not just for cooking

Microwaves are a broad band of electromagnetic waves with a shorter wavelength than radio waves. Mobile phones use microwaves to send words and information to a receiver. Recently, people have become quite worried about this. It is possible that the waves from these phones are harmful to the brain.

Radar uses microwaves, too. A radar aerial sends out pulses of microwaves in all directions and then sweeps round to pick up any reflections coming back. Ships use radar to detect other craft at sea.

Microwave ovens use microwaves to heat food. The wavelength is carefully chosen so that it is easily absorbed by water molecules. The energy transferred in this way warms the water up. Most food has a lot of water in it, so this is an effective way to cook it.

Heat waves

Anything that is warm produces infrared (IR) waves – including you. The hotter a thing is, the more IR it produces. Night-vision goggles and cameras work by detecting the IR given out by people and animals and displaying it as visible light.

Some electronic components (parts) in machines produce IR. These are used in TV remote controls to beam IR signals to the television. Many computers have IR transmitters and receivers which they use to send information to other computers.

visible light, ultraviolet (UV)
oth from Sun, but most UV blocked by atmosphere

X-rays
medical X-rays, baggage checking, X-ray telescopes

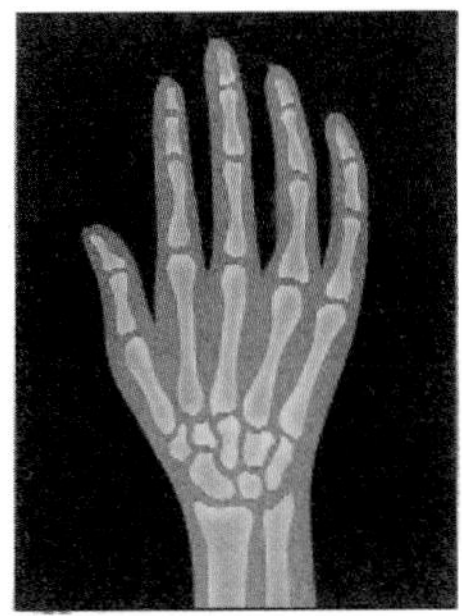

gamma rays
given off by radioactive materials, cosmic rays from space

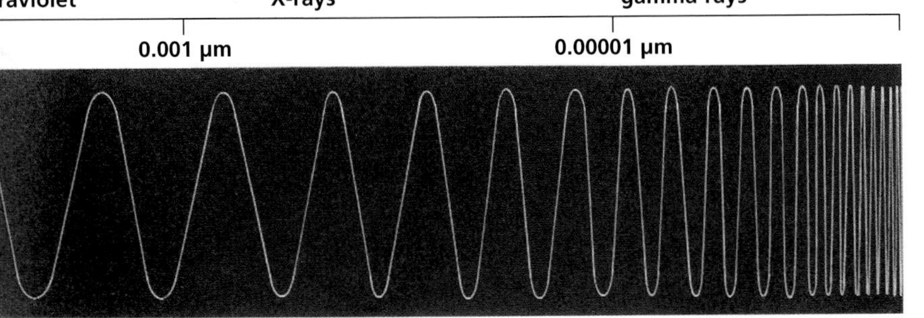

SHORTER WAVES, HIGHER ENERGY

◀ The full electromagnetic spectrum. All the waves in this spectrum travel at the same speed – the speed of light. They all carry energy, but the amount of energy increases as the wavelength gets shorter.

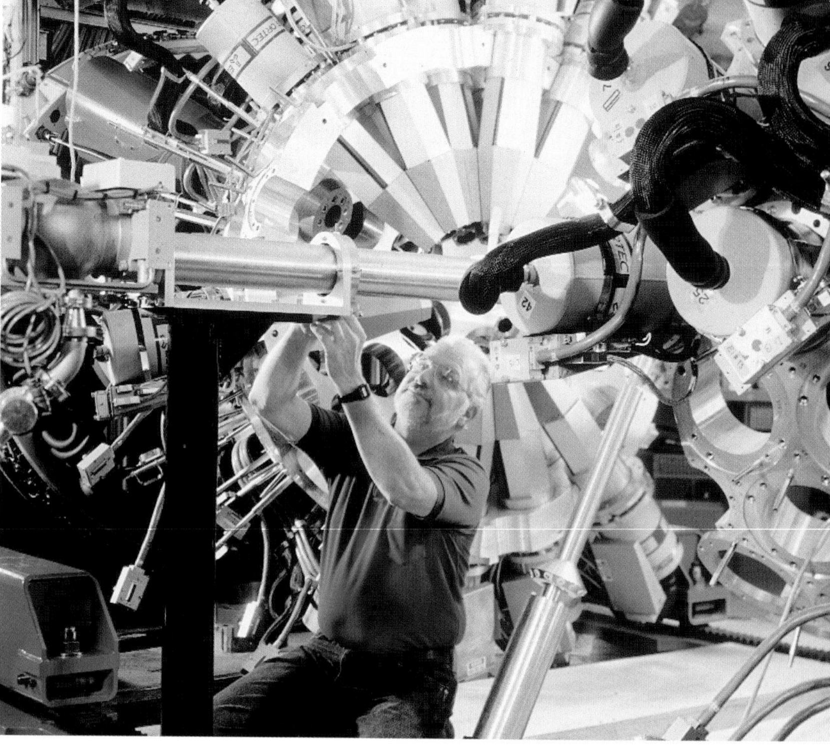

▲ A research scientist working on the Gammasphere, a sensitive instrument for detecting gamma radiation. The Gammasphere has been used to study collisions between the centres (nuclei) of certain heavy atoms, which briefly join to form a very large nucleus and then break up, releasing gamma radiation.

Waves we can see

Visible light includes a very small range of wavelengths compared to the whole spectrum, but it is important because it is the only range of waves that we can see. When white light passes through a prism (a triangular piece of glass), the different colours in it are bent by different amounts because they have different wavelengths.

Burning waves

Ultraviolet (UV) waves can be harmful. Too much exposure to them can cause sunburn, blindness and skin cancer. The Sun produces a lot of UV. This would wipe out life on Earth if it all reached the planet's surface. Fortunately, we are protected by a layer of gas in the atmosphere (ozone), which absorbs most of the UV. Scientists are becoming concerned that some of the gases that industry produces are removing ozone from the atmosphere. As this could be very dangerous, people are working to cut down on the emission of these gases.

Some ultraviolet still gets through, so it is important to protect yourself in bright sunlight or at high altitudes, where the atmosphere is thin. Sun creams and sunglasses help to block UV. We all need some exposure to ultraviolet, though. Without it, our bodies would not be able to make vitamin D, which is important for keeping us healthy.

Amazing rays

X-rays have a shorter wavelength and more energy than ultraviolet rays. They have many uses. Doctors and dentists use X-rays to make shadow pictures of the body so they can see broken bones or damaged teeth.

At airports, X-rays are used to check passengers' luggage. The X-rays pass straight through clothes but are stopped by metal objects, such as guns. X-rays also allow manufacturers to see inside a product, such as a television, and check that it has been put together correctly – without taking the whole machine apart.

Danger rays

Gamma rays come from radioactive materials. They can be very harmful and they can pass through nearly all materials quite easily.

Gamma rays are used to kill cancers, but they have to be carefully controlled to prevent damage to healthy tissues.

Satellites have detected bursts of gamma rays striking the Earth from outer space. No one knows what causes them, but they are too weak to harm us.

Find Out More

- Astronomy
- Communications
- Electricity
- Light
- Radar and sonar
- Radio
- Satellites
- Waves and vibrations
- X-rays

JAMES CLERK MAXWELL

The Scot James Clerk Maxwell (1831–1879) was one of the greatest physicists that has ever lived. He made huge contributions to many areas of physics, but he will be most remembered for his work on the theory of electromagnetism. This built on the ideas of earlier pioneers such as Michael Faraday and led to the idea that light was an electromagnetic wave. Later, the German Heinrich Hertz used Maxwell's theory in his discovery of radio waves.

Electronics

Mobile phones, pocket computers and many other devices have been made possible by the incredible advances in electronics since the mid-20th century. Of all the devices invented since then, none has matched the impact of the transistor.

The transistor is at the heart of electronics. This is the branch of electrical engineering involving small-scale devices. Where electrical engineers tend to look at heavy currents in large devices, electronics engineers are concerned with light currents in small devices.

More from less

One of the most important jobs an electronic circuit does is to make a small signal into a bigger one. This is called amplification. When you turn up the volume on your hi-fi, you are amplifying the electrical signal that produces the sound.

Early amplifiers used big, fragile devices called valves to amplify signals. The development of the transistor, a small 'sandwich' made of semiconducting material, was an important step in electronics. Transistors provided amplification from a very low-powered device the size of a peanut.

The first transistor radios appeared in 1955. Soon transistors were being used in

THE FIRST TRANSISTOR

In 1947, three scientists working at the Bell Telephone Laboratories in New Jersey, USA, made an important breakthrough in electronics. John Bardeen (1908–1991), Walter Brattain (1902–1987) and William Shockley (1910–1989) used a semiconductor called germanium to make the world's first transistor. The three scientists shared the Nobel Prize for Physics in 1956.

The invention of the transistor, shown below resting on a fingertip, made it possible to build much smaller and more reliable electronic circuits.

▼ A transistor on a fingertip.

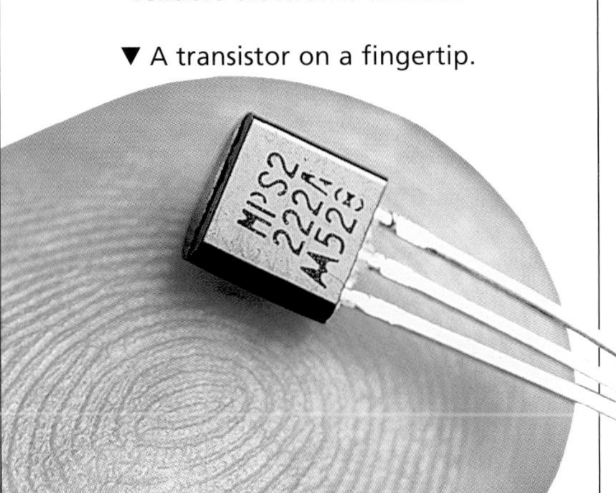

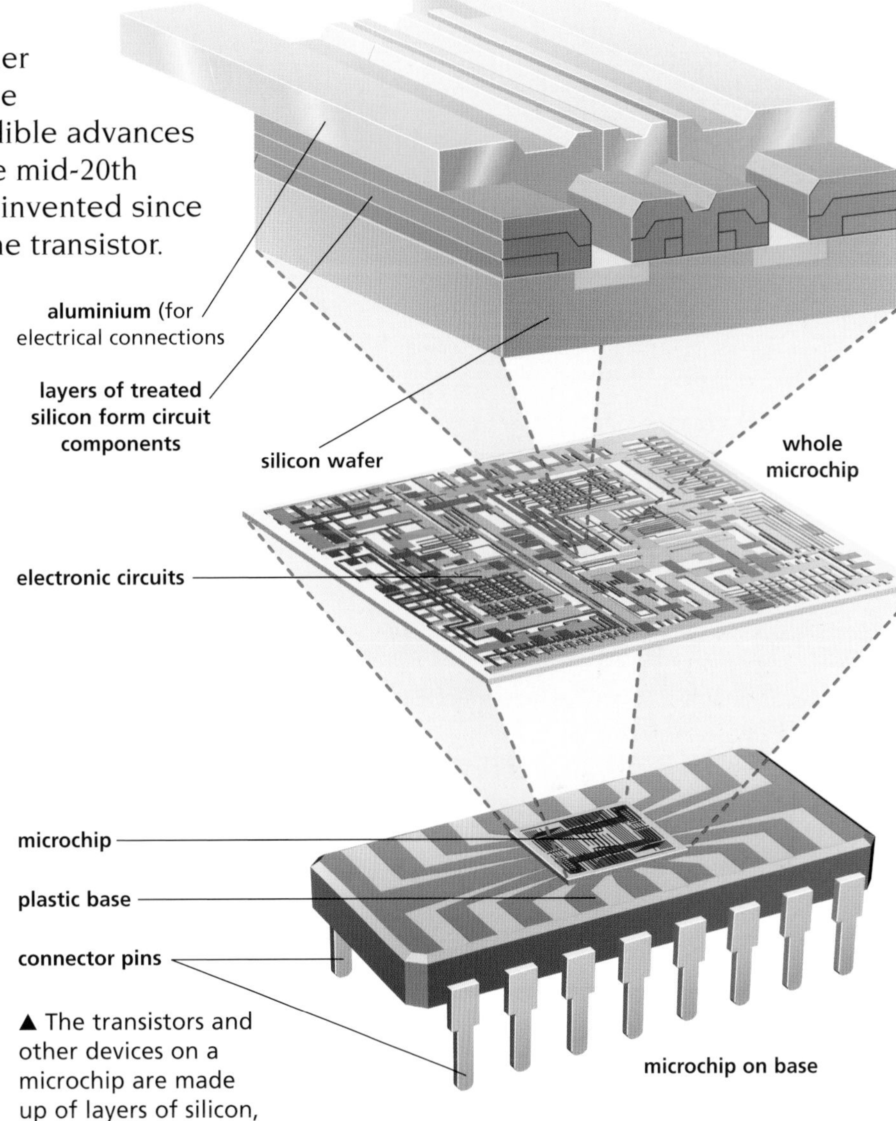

▲ The transistors and other devices on a microchip are made up of layers of silicon, treated in different ways to have different electrical properties. A final layer of aluminium 'tracks' connects the devices together. The complete microchip is fastened to a plastic base, which has connector pins.

all sorts of gadgets, such as TVs and hi-fis. Transistors also helped to make equipment in spacecraft much lighter.

In the 1970s integrated circuits (microchips), containing many transistors and other parts on one tiny chip of silicon, began to replace individual transistors. Now there are millions of transistors in the microchip circuits used in computers.

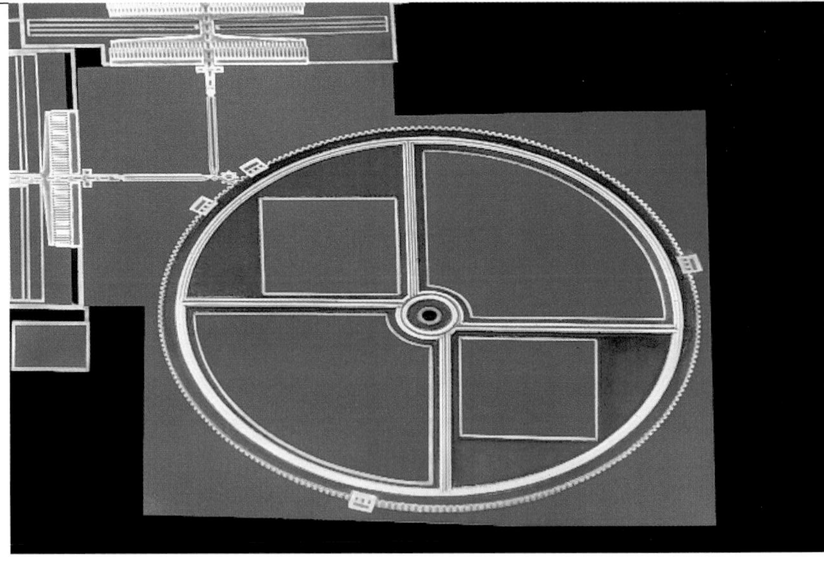

▲ Future electronic devices may include minute motors like this one, etched on to a wafer of silicon. Two 'microengines' at top left (green and yellow) turn a tiny gear (centre), which is smaller in diameter than a human hair.

Capacitors and diodes

Capacitors and diodes are two other devices used in electronic circuits.

A diode conducts electricity easily in one direction, but resists the flow of electricity in the other. It is an important part of many circuits.

A capacitor stores electric charge between two conducting plates. It takes a certain amount of time for a capacitor to charge up. So capacitors are important components for making timers.

Capacitors can also be used in filtering circuits. These get rid of signals you don't want. When you turn up the bass and turn down the treble on your hi-fi, you are using filtering circuits.

television

radio

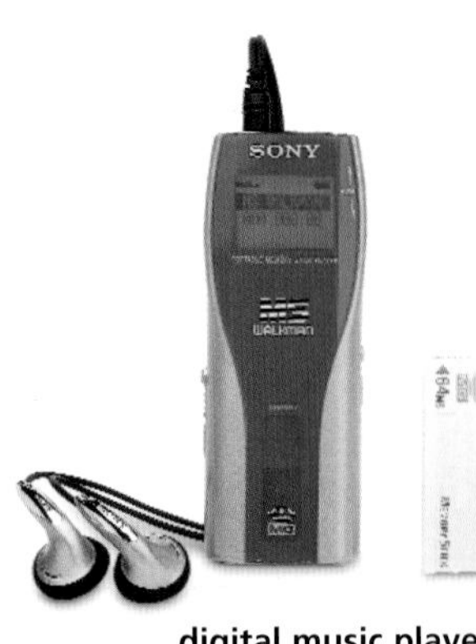

digital music player

▲ Radios, TVs, personal stereos and many other devices we use every day rely on electronics to work.

LOGIC GATES

As well as working as amplifiers, transistors can be used to switch signals on and off. This makes them particularly useful for circuits called logic gates, which are central to computers. An OR logic gate, for example (a), has two inputs. An electrical pulse can pass through the 'gate' if there is a signal from either or both inputs. A NOT gate (b) lets a pulse through if there is no input, but doesn't let it through if there is an input. These and other logic gates can be combined to make circuits that can work out simple sums. A computer's central processor has thousands of such circuits.

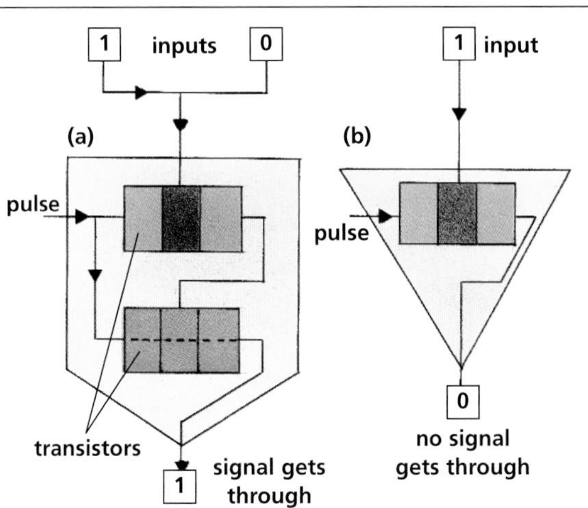

Find Out More

- Circuits
- Conductors and insulators
- Electricity
- Microchips

Electron microscopes *see* Microscopes • **Electrons** *see* Atoms and molecules, Electricity

Elements and compounds

In the ancient world people believed that all things were made from mixtures of four basic substances – earth, water, air and fire. We know now that this is not true. All things are made of basic substances, which are called elements. About 90 different elements are found in nature. But earth, water, air and fire are not among them.

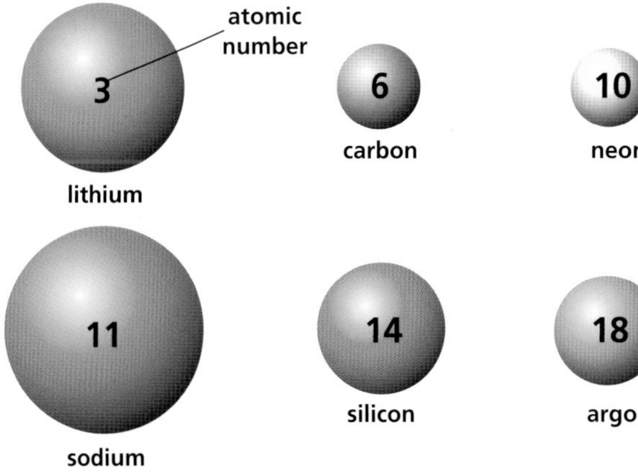

▲ The atoms in an element are all the same, but the atoms of different elements are different sizes. Heavier atoms (ones having more protons and electrons) are not always bigger than lighter ones. The elements shown here are in order of increasing atomic number (number of protons).

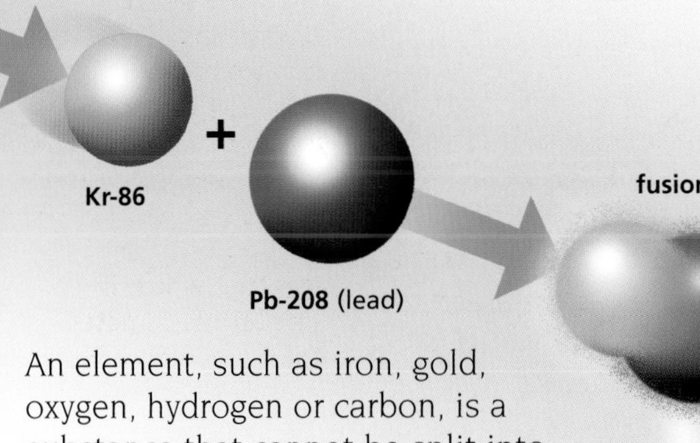

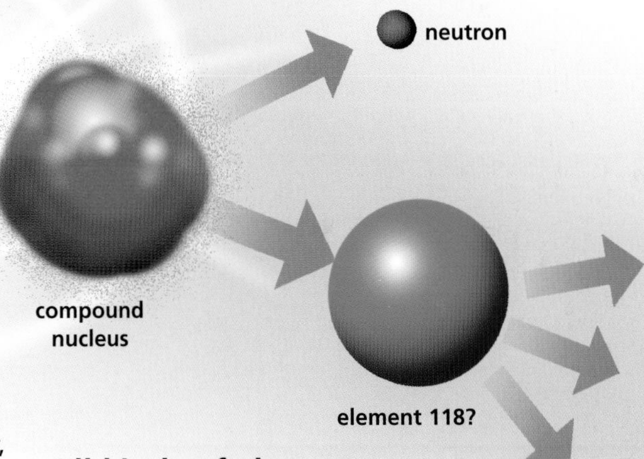

◀ Recently, scientists tried to make a new element – ununoctium, or element 118. They did this by bombarding lead atoms with krypton atoms, but the new atoms they claimed to have produced broke up almost immediately.

An element, such as iron, gold, oxygen, hydrogen or carbon, is a substance that cannot be split into simpler substances. Each element is made up of tiny identical particles called atoms. Each element has a unique size of atom that behaves in a particular way.

Atoms of different elements can combine together to form larger particles called molecules. Chemical compounds are substances made of molecules that contain atoms of different elements. For example, a molecule of methane (natural gas) is made from an atom of carbon and four atoms of hydrogen.

▼ Most elements exist in nature as parts of mixtures or compounds. However, gold is often found in its pure form.

All kinds of elements

Although only about 90 elements exist naturally, scientists have made around 25 new elements in nuclear reactors and scientific laboratories. Many of these 'artificial' elements are very unstable and only exist for fractions of a second.

At room temperature most elements are solids, but a number are gases (for example, oxygen, hydrogen, nitrogen, helium and neon). Only two are liquids – mercury and bromine. Most elements are metals – only 19 are non-metals (for example, carbon, sulphur and iodine). A further 5 are metalloids – elements such as silicon that are half-way between metals and non-metals.

Email *see* Internet

Quite a number of the heavier elements are radioactive (they give off radiation). Some elements, such as gold, rarely combine with others to make chemical compounds. Others, such as fluorine, are highly reactive.

Some elements exist in different forms, called allotropes. For instance, diamonds and graphite are allotropes of carbon.

Millions of compounds

While there are fewer than 120 elements, scientists have found or made more than 26 million different compounds – most of them in the last 70 years or so.

Some compounds are very simple. Water consists of molecules containing two hydrogen atoms and one oxygen atom. Scientists write this as H_2O. Other compounds are more complicated. For example, the common drug aspirin contains 21 atoms, and is written by scientists as $CH_3COOC_6H_4COOH$ (C stands for a carbon atom, H for a hydrogen atom and O for an oxygen atom). The molecules of some compounds – like the enzymes in your stomach that help you digest your food – each contain thousands of atoms.

Compounds do not behave in the same way as the elements they are made of. You can sprinkle a little sodium chloride (table salt) on your food without coming to any harm. However, pure sodium would burn a hole in your tongue, and pure chlorine is a gas that would poison you.

The way a compound behaves also depends on how many atoms of a particular element are in each of its molecules. For example, you breathe in the small amounts of carbon dioxide (CO_2) in the atmosphere all the time. In contrast, carbon monoxide (CO) is a highly poisonous gas.

▶ The Greek philosopher Aristotle (384–322 BC) first suggested that everything was made of four basic substances or elements: earth (*terra*), water (*aqua*), air (*aeris*) and fire (*ignis*). This belief lasted for 2000 years. It became mixed up with all kinds of mystical and magical ideas – as you can see in this early 17th-century engraving featuring the astrological signs of the zodiac.

Find Out More

- Atoms and molecules
- Matter
- Periodic table
- Reactions, chemical

CHEMICAL BONDS

The molecules in chemical compounds are held together by bonds between the atoms.

In some kinds of compound, bonds are made when one atom gives at least one electron to another atom. This is called an ionic bond. In example (a), sodium gives an electron to chlorine to form sodium chloride (salt).

In other kinds of compound the atoms share at least one pair of electrons, one from each atom. This is called a covalent bond. Water (b) is a covalent compound, in which oxygen shares electrons with two hydrogen atoms.

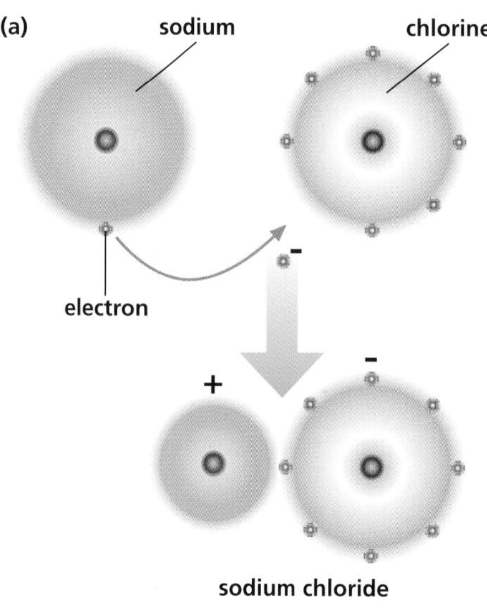

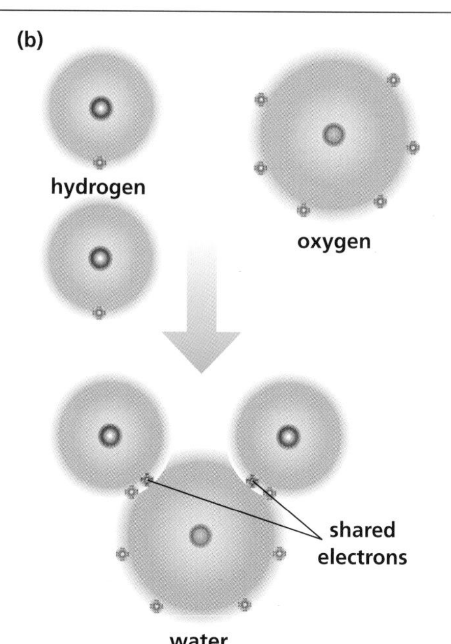

Energy

Do you have days when you want to run, jump, shout, sing and be very active? If you do, people will say that you are 'bursting with energy', and they would be right. You need energy to do these things, and all the other actions that you carry out every day.

Every action of any kind needs energy to make it happen – not just here on Earth but throughout the entire Universe. Energy makes your body work so that you can see, hear, think, speak, move and do all kinds of things. Energy keeps all living things – including us – alive. This energy comes from the Sun's heat and from food.

But non-living things use energy too. All machines need a supply of energy to work, and they stop when their energy supply gives out or is turned off. Machines get energy from fuels, such as petrol, or from a supply of power such as electricity or running water.

FROM CORNFLAKES TO CONSERVATION

Many foods have their energy value printed on the packet. It is in kilojoules (kJ), or thousands of joules. A joule is a unit that scientists use to measure energy. It is named after the British scientist James Prescott Joule (1818–1889). He discovered the principle of conservation of energy in the 1840s, which says that energy cannot be destroyed, but changes its form.

What is energy?

Energy makes things happen, and it takes several different forms. The energy in movement is just one of them. Other forms of energy include light and sound, which you use to see and hear things, and heat, which keeps you warm.

Your body has a large amount of stored energy, which keeps it working. Non-living things may contain stored energy too. A battery is a store of electricity, which is yet another form of energy.

◀ Petrol stores a lot of energy. As it burns in this dragster's engine, the petrol's chemical energy changes to heat energy. This heat energy changes to kinetic (movement) energy as the engine drives the car along.

Find Out More

- Fuels
- Pollution
- Renewable resources
- Water power
- Waves and vibrations

▼ Most of our energy comes through space from the Sun in the form of heat and light. After arriving on Earth, the energy may change its form several times as it is used. Every set of changes ends with the production of heat or light.

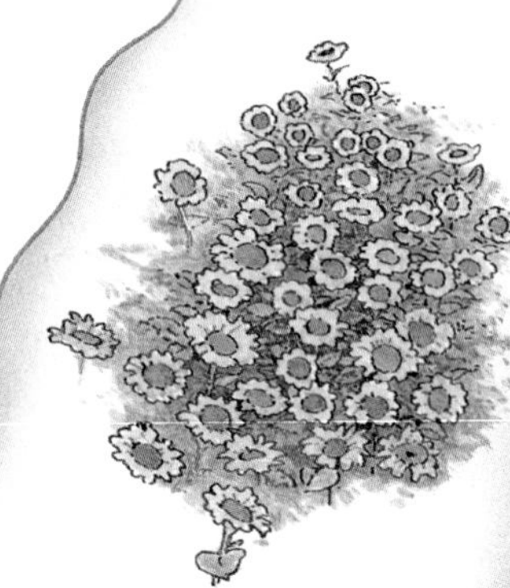

Plants use light energy from the Sun to grow. The light energy becomes chemical energy and is stored inside the plant.

All animals (including us) get their food from plants – or from eating other animals that have eaten plants.

The Sun powers the world's weather systems – even when it is not a sunny day! Heat energy makes winds blow and water evaporate into the air to form rain clouds.

Wind turbines harness the power of the wind and turn their kinetic energy into electricity that will power machines.

Rigs drill for oil on the seabed. Oil is an important source of fuel. It is formed from the remains of living things.

Fuels such as oil and coal are burned in power stations. The chemical energy inside the fuels is turned into electrical energy.

The chemical energy in food allows people and animals to move and play. Their bodies change the chemical energy into kinetic (movement) energy.

Electrical energy powers machines, such as high-speed trains. It changes into kinetic energy as the motor turns and drives the train along the track.

Using energy

Energy is needed for an action of any kind to happen. This energy has to come from somewhere. You get energy from food and drink. An electrical machine, such as a radio, gets a supply of electrical energy (electricity) from a power point or a battery.

Although every action needs some energy to happen, it does not use up the energy. Energy cannot be destroyed. Instead, it changes form as the action happens. For example, when you throw a ball, the muscles in your arm take some of your stored energy, which has come from food, and change it into energy of movement. A computer takes electrical energy from a power point and changes it into light energy as a picture appears on the screen.

You need about 10,000 kilojoules of energy every day to keep your body working. Most of this energy comes from your food, and it is about the same amount of energy as there is in a 500-gram box of cereal.

The source of our energy

Our main supplies of energy are food to make our bodies work and fuels to drive our machines. We eat plants, or meat and fish which come from animals that ate plants. So all the energy in our food comes from plants. Our main fuels are coal, oil and gas. All these fuels are the remains of animals and plants that lived millions of years ago. So the energy in fuel comes from plants, too.

But plants are not the original source of this energy. They are just energy stores. The energy that they store comes from the Sun. As plants grow, they turn the Sun's light and heat into stored energy. In fact, the source of almost all the energy on Earth is the rays of heat and light that stream through space from the Sun.

▼ Strip lights use less energy than most light bulbs, which get warm and change much of the electricity they use into heat energy instead of light.

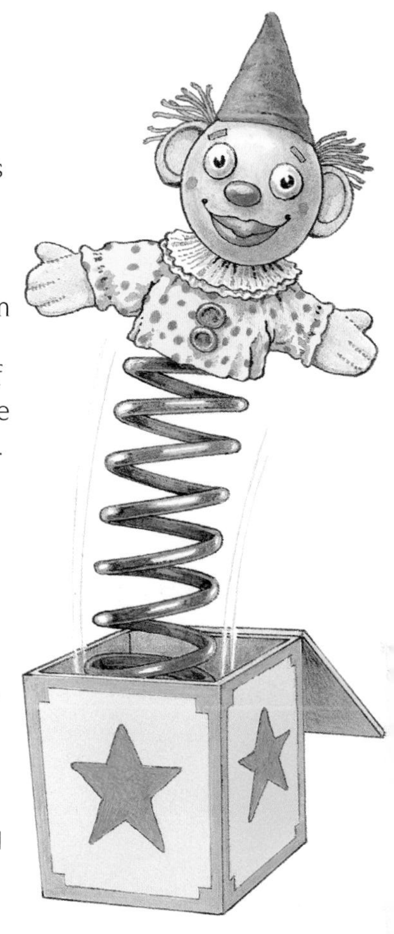

▶ When a jack-in-the-box jumps out at you, it changes energy stored in its spring into energy of movement. The stored energy is also called potential energy.

Engines and turbines

jet of gas, steam or water

rotating shaft

turbine blades

Have you ever had a machine in your mouth? You probably have – when you were at the dentist's. Inside a dentist's drill is a tiny turbine whizzing round thousands of times a second. It is powered by a stream of air.

Engines, turbines and motors drive most machines and make parts move. Engines burn fuel, while turbines require moving air, steam or water.

Find Out More

- Electric motors
- Jet engines
- Petrol and diesel engines
- Rockets
- Steam engines

Heat engines

Most engines use heat. They burn fuel, such as petrol, in air they suck in. The hot gases produced expand rapidly, and make the parts of the engine move. Petrol and diesel engines in road vehicles and trains, and jet engines in aircraft, work in this way. All these engines are called internal-combustion engines as they burn fuel inside the engine.

In steam engines, hot steam drives the moving parts. Fuel is burned in boilers outside the engine to produce the steam, so these engines are called external-combustion engines.

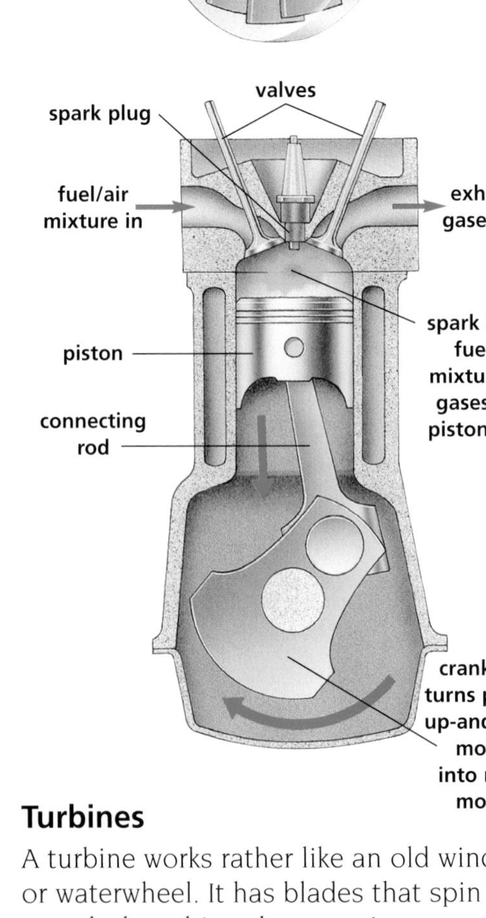

▶ A turbine (top) produces circular or rotary motion directly. A piston engine (bottom) produces up-and-down motion, which is changed into rotary motion by the crankshaft.

Turbines

A turbine works rather like an old windmill or waterwheel. It has blades that spin round when driven by a moving gas or liquid. Wind turbines use moving air, and water turbines in hydroelectric power stations are driven by moving water. Steam turbines in other power stations are driven by heated steam.

◀ The jet engine of an aircraft is a gas turbine. The blades of the turbine can be seen in the centre of the picture.

Enzymes *see* Detergents, Reactions, chemical • **Equator** *see* Maps

Erosion

In northern Venezuela in December 1999, nearly a metre of rain fell in just three days. The rain soaked into the El Avila Mountains until the rocks and soil were so wet that parts of the mountain began to slide down towards the sea. Tonnes of mud, rocks, and boulders the size of houses came roaring down the valleys, cutting through the mountainside, burying villages, and creating new landforms at the base of the mountains.

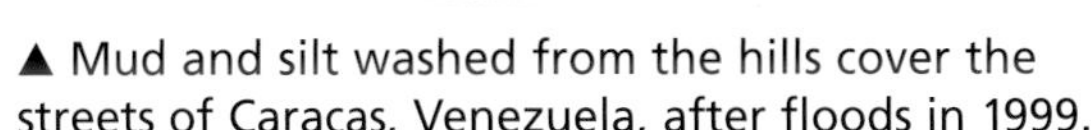

▲ Mud and silt washed from the hills cover the streets of Caracas, Venezuela, after floods in 1999.

The El Avila landslide is a dramatic example of *erosion*. Erosion is when rocks fall apart and then move from one place to another. Landslides can move tonnes of rock in just seconds. The strong waves and winds in hurricanes can erode a beach overnight. But most erosion happens slowly, over thousands or millions of years.

Weakening the rocks

Before erosion can take place, rocks have to be weakened. Rocks are constantly falling apart. When rocks are exposed to air and water, the minerals in them start to change or break up. For example, iron minerals get rusty, while hard feldspars turn into soft clay, and salt dissolves completely. This process is called *weathering*. Weathering turns solid rock into soft soil.

Weathering happens more quickly in warm, wet areas than in cold, dry regions. Some rocks weather much more easily than others. Salt, for instance, quickly dissolves away in water. Granite, however, takes much longer to weather away.

Find Out More

- Caves
- Coasts
- Ice caps and glaciers
- Mars
- Rivers and lakes

What causes weathering?

Air and water cause most weathering. Sometimes they change the chemicals in the rocks, and sometimes they just break apart the rock physically. When water freezes, it expands. If it seeps into a crack in a rock and then freezes, it can pry the rock apart. Wind can pick up small rock particles and hurl them at other rocks. Many rocks in deserts get sand-blasted in this way by the wind.

Living things can also weather rocks. For example, plants growing in cracks slowly pry the rocks apart with their roots. People also cause weathering by walking and driving on rocks. People also pollute the atmosphere, causing acid rain, which eats away at rocks.

▼ Uluru, also called Ayer's Rock, is a monolith ('single rock') that rises 350 m above the Australian desert. It is made of a hard rock. At one time, the whole of the desert was at the same level. But weathering and erosion gradually wore away the softer rock around Uluru, leaving it rising above the plain.

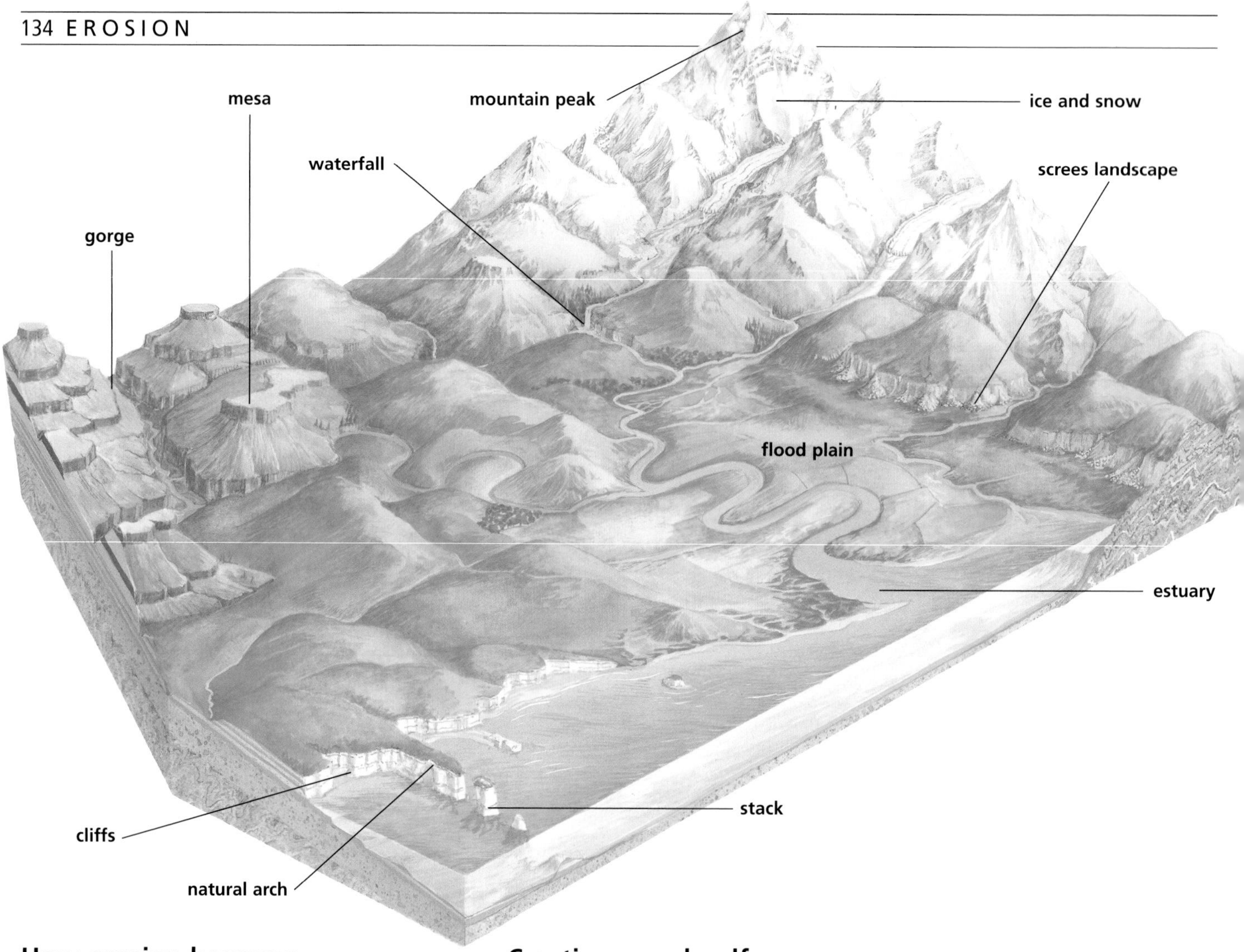

mesa
mountain peak
ice and snow
waterfall
screes landscape
gorge
flood plain
estuary
stack
cliffs
natural arch

How erosion happens

Once rocks have weathered, it is much easier for them to erode.

Many things can cause erosion, but water is the most powerful force. Rain washes soil into rivers. Rivers scour the land, breaking rocks and then taking them downstream towards the ocean. Glaciers (rivers of ice) grind up the rocks beneath and beside them, and then dump ground-up rock at the end of the glacier.

Wind is important because it creates waves that pound the seashore, breaking down cliffs and moving sand from one place to another. Earthquakes can speed up erosion by breaking and crushing rocks. More importantly, they can trigger huge landslides, and cause tsunamis – giant waves that erode coasts.

All of these forces are helped along by gravity. If a rock is weathered enough, and the slopes are steep enough, gravity alone will be enough to cause erosion.

Creating new landforms

Weathering and erosion shape the Earth's landscape. Running water cuts river valleys and etches out caves. Waves shape the shoreline. Glaciers carve mountains into sharp peaks. Every piece of rock that gets eroded from one place, gets deposited in another. Erosion is one of nature's ways of rearranging the landscape.

▲ This diagram shows a few of the many landforms on Earth that have been shaped by erosion – the forces of water, wind and gravity.

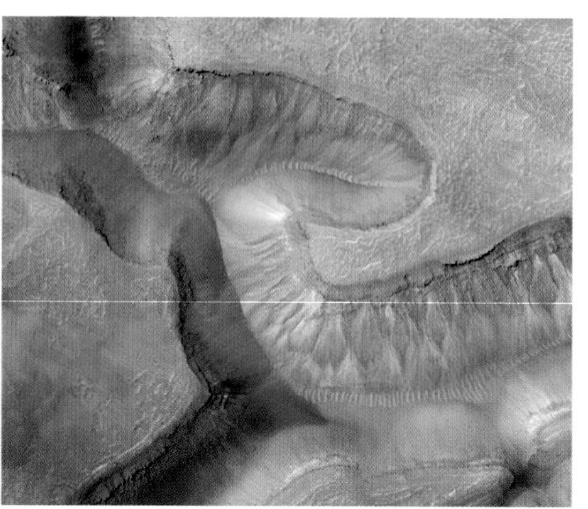

◀ The canyon in this photo of Mars looks as if it was carved by running water. There is no water on the surface of Mars today. Landforms like these show that there was probably water eroding Mars's surface millions of years ago.

Escape velocity *see* Orbits • **Evaporation** *see* Liquids

Evolution

It is hard to believe that dogs such as wolfhounds and dachshunds are related. Yet people have developed over 100 breeds of dog from just one dog – the wolf – simply by choosing which dogs to breed together. This has been possible because of the huge amount of doggy variation that is hidden inside wolves.

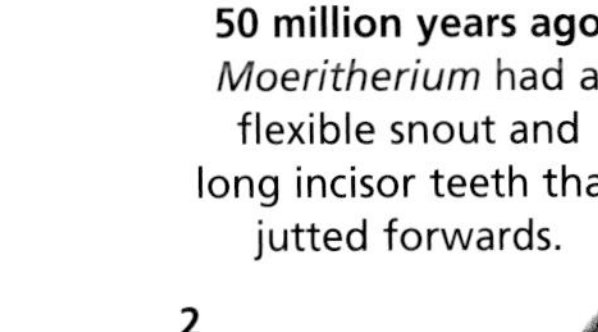

1
50 million years ago
Moeritherium had a flexible snout and long incisor teeth that jutted forwards.

2
35 million years ago
Phiomia was larger than *Moeritherium* and had a short trunk, a long lower jaw and four short tusks.

3
20 million years ago
Platybelodon was bigger than *Phiomia*, with a longer trunk and wide, spade-like teeth to scoop up plants.

3a
Deinotherium had large tusks which curved backwards. It was almost as big as modern elephants but became extinct about 2 million years ago.

▲ The first elephants were pig-sized animals with small tusks and no trunk. Over tens of millions of years, elephants evolved, finding better ways to survive, and to get their food. They changed into larger species, with long trunks, huge tusks and grinding teeth.

If just one type of animal has so much hidden variation, think how much more there must be in the many millions of living things on the planet. Why are there so many different kinds of animal and plant, and why are they so good at what they do – flying, swimming, producing flowers, and so on? One of the main reasons is evolution. Variety is the raw material of evolution – the development of different forms of life over long periods of time.

4
Present day
Modern African elephants usually have two long tusks, a very long trunk and a large body.

Natural selection

In the middle of the 19th century, Charles Darwin and Alfred Russel Wallace suggested that evolution happened because nature selected which variations would survive. As the environment changes over time, those individuals with variations that make them best suited to the environment are more likely to survive and reproduce, while other individuals die out. So as the environment changes, the individuals change too. This idea is called natural selection or 'the survival of the fittest'.

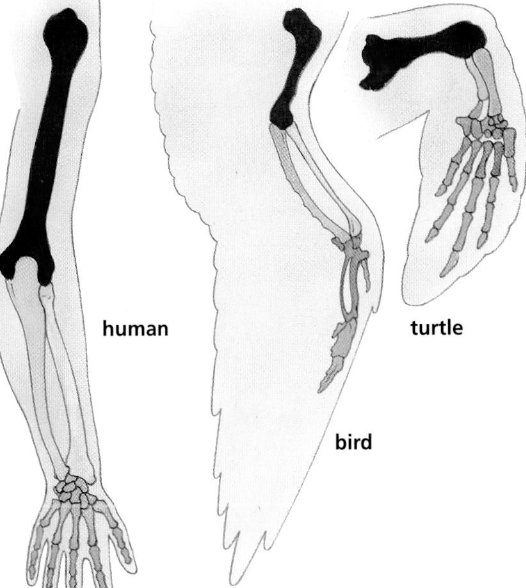

▶ Animals with backbones all have the same limb bones, which suggests that they evolved from the same ancestor. This illustration shows how the same set of bones has evolved to support flippers in turtles, wings in birds and arms in humans.

DARWIN'S FINCHES

Charles Darwin found some of the most important evidence for his theory of evolution when he visited the Galapagos Islands in 1835. He suggested that the many different kinds, or species, of finch on the islands had all evolved from one species that somehow managed to reach the islands from mainland South America, some 1000 kilometres away. Over a long period of time, this one finch ancestor then evolved into 13 different species to take advantage of the different types of food and living space available on these isolated islands.

New life for old

Since life first appeared on Earth, millions of living things have died out (become extinct). They have been killed off by competition from other life forms, rapid changes in climate or changes caused by the drifting of continents about the globe. So the millions of different living things on Earth today are only a tiny fraction of all the living things that have ever existed.

Some extinctions happened gradually, but others were more sudden, and affected large numbers of living things. One of these mass extinctions took place about 65 million years ago, and wiped out the dinosaurs. It may have been caused by a large volcano exploding, or a meteorite hitting the Earth and throwing up clouds of dust that blocked out the Sun.

Evidence for evolution

Evidence for evolution comes partly from preserved remains of plants and animals that lived in the past, called fossils. These can be dated and some show the path that evolution has taken, for instance how amphibians evolved from fishes or how birds evolved from reptiles. A few fossils record a sequence of changes over time, as with elephants or horses. There are many gaps in the fossil record however, since only one per cent of all life has been preserved as fossils.

Plants and animals alive today also provide evidence for evolution. Comparing the genes of both living and fossil creatures has helped scientists to work out which species have similar genes and so may be related to each other.

▲ Animals that look similar, such as modern dolphins and extinct ichthyosaurs, are not always related to each other. They may look the same because they have independently evolved to suit the same environment and way of life. This is called convergent evolution.

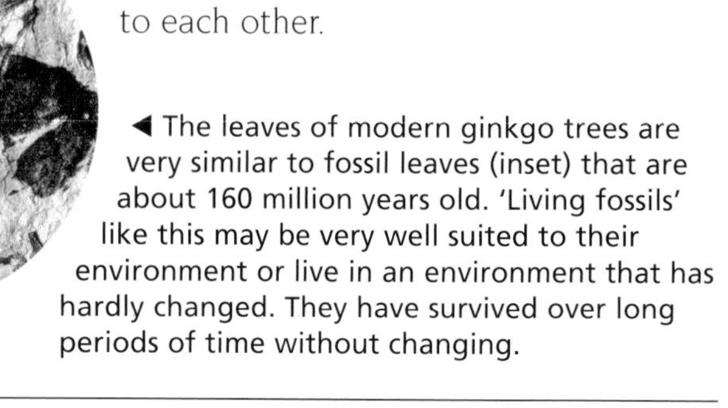

◀ The leaves of modern ginkgo trees are very similar to fossil leaves (inset) that are about 160 million years old. 'Living fossils' like this may be very well suited to their environment or live in an environment that has hardly changed. They have survived over long periods of time without changing.

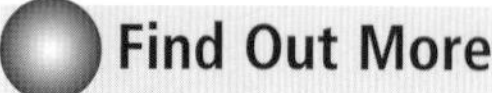

Find Out More

- Animals
- Continents and plates
- Fossils
- Genetics
- Life
- Plants

Explosives

ALFRED NOBEL

The Swedish chemist Alfred Nobel (1833–1896) invented dynamite in 1867. Feeling guilty that his invention caused so much death and destruction, he set up a fund to award the annual Nobel prizes, one of which was to be a peace prize.

'Whoosh!' goes the firework rocket as it shoots high into the sky. The coloured stars it releases explode with bangs like pistol shots. The substance that propels the rockets and makes the bangs is gunpowder, an explosive the Chinese first made over 1000 years ago.

Gunpowder got its name because it was once used to fire bullets from guns. It is a mixture of chemicals – carbon (in the form of charcoal), sulphur and potassium nitrate. When ignited (set alight), these substances burn rapidly and produce large amounts of gases. These gases expand suddenly, in a violent explosion. The explosion creates shock waves, which we hear as a bang.

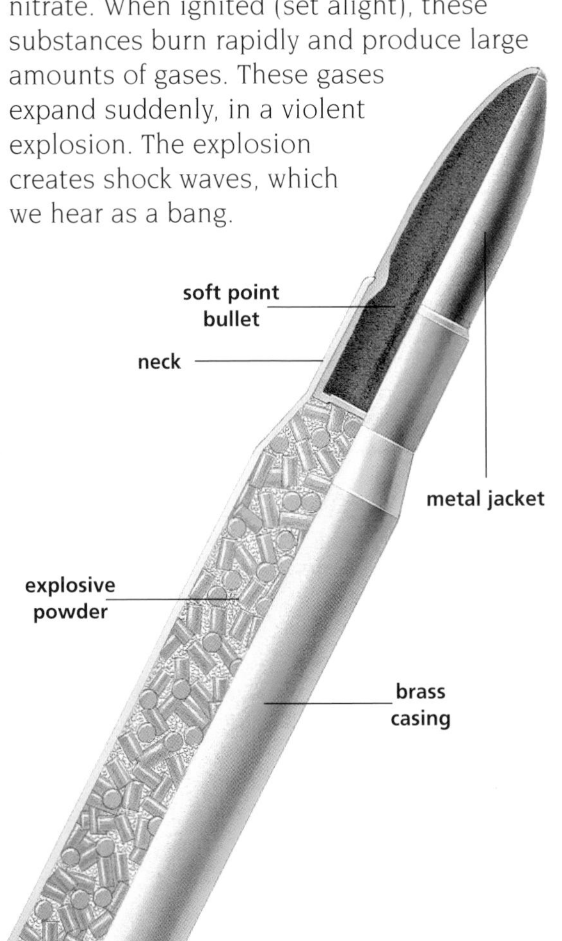

◀ The ammunition used in rifles is called a cartridge. When the rifle's firing pin strikes a detonator in the base of the cartridge, it ignites a low-explosive powder. This fires a metal bullet from the gun.

▲ High explosives blast open a hillside in Arizona, USA, to make way for copper miners.

Find Out More

- Mining
- Nitrogen
- Tunnels and pipelines
- Weapons
- Wood and timber

All explosives work in this way. Some, called high explosives, burn many thousands of times faster than gunpowder. They are used in mining and tunnelling to blast rocks apart, and in weapons such as shells and bombs.

The nitrogen connection

Almost all explosives contain nitrogen. The nitrogen compound ammonia is the starting point for several explosives.

Two of the most powerful high explosives are nitroglycerine and TNT (trinitrotoluene). Nitroglycerine is an oily liquid that is very dangerous to handle, because it explodes easily. In dynamite, nitroglycerine is mixed with an earthy material to make it safer to use.

All explosives need something to set them off. Low explosives can be set off by a burning fuse or by a sharp blow. High explosives have to be set off by a detonator.

Exposure *see* Photography • **Extinction** *see* Evolution • **Extrusion** *see* Metalworking, Plastics

Eyes

We get 80 per cent of our information about the world around us through a small pair of sense organs – our eyes. For animals such as birds of prey, sight is even more important. Nearly all animals have eyes of some sort. Even plants and very simple creatures have ways of sensing light.

The eyes are our organs of sight, just as our ears are our organs of hearing. The eye is a means of turning light into electrical signals. The brain takes these signals and uses them to make the colourful, moving world we see about us.

The parts of the eye

At the front of the eye is a clear, curved cornea, which bends light as it passes into the eyeball. It is covered by a thin membrane called the conjunctiva. A lens inside the eye bends the light further. Together the lens and cornea focus light onto a sheet of light-sensitive cells at the back of the eye called the retina. When these cells are stimulated by light, they send electrical signals to the brain. The image that the eye makes on the retina is actually upside down, but our brain turns the image the right way up.

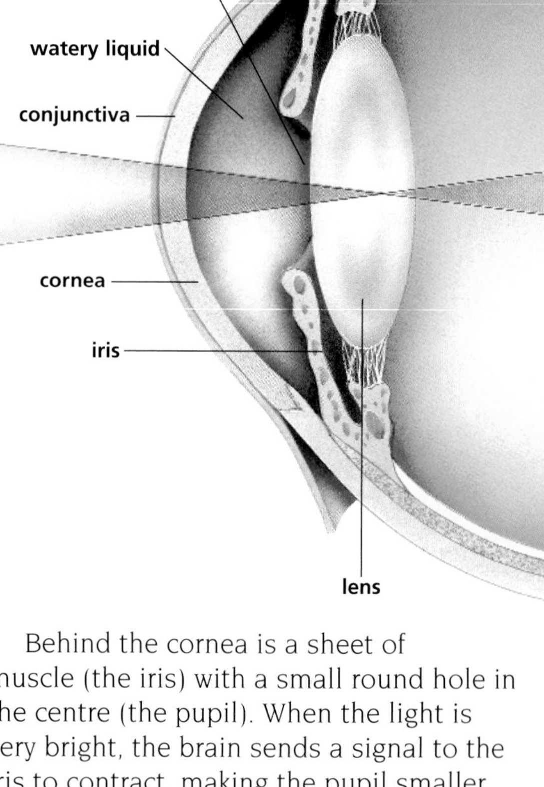

▶ The parts of the human eye.

Find Out More

- Colour
- Human senses
- Light
- Mirrors and lenses
- Senses

Behind the cornea is a sheet of muscle (the iris) with a small round hole in the centre (the pupil). When the light is very bright, the brain sends a signal to the iris to contract, making the pupil smaller. This cuts down the amount of light entering the eye. Without this, we would be dazzled on a bright sunny day. If it is dark, then the iris relaxes, opening the pupil to let in as much light as possible.

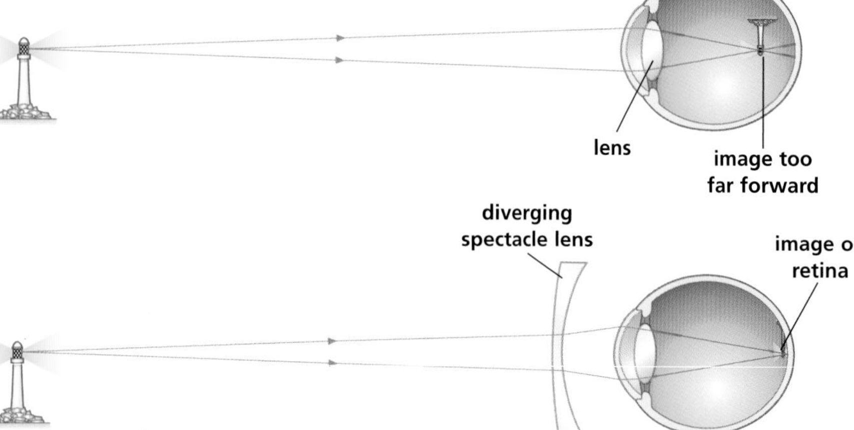

▲ In a short-sighted eye (top), the light is brought to a focus before it reaches the retina. To correct this, a diverging (concave) lens is worn in front of the eye.

lens

converging spectacle lens

▲ In a long-sighted eye (top), the light strikes the reti before it can be brought to a focus. To correct this, a converging (convex) lens is worn in front of the eye.

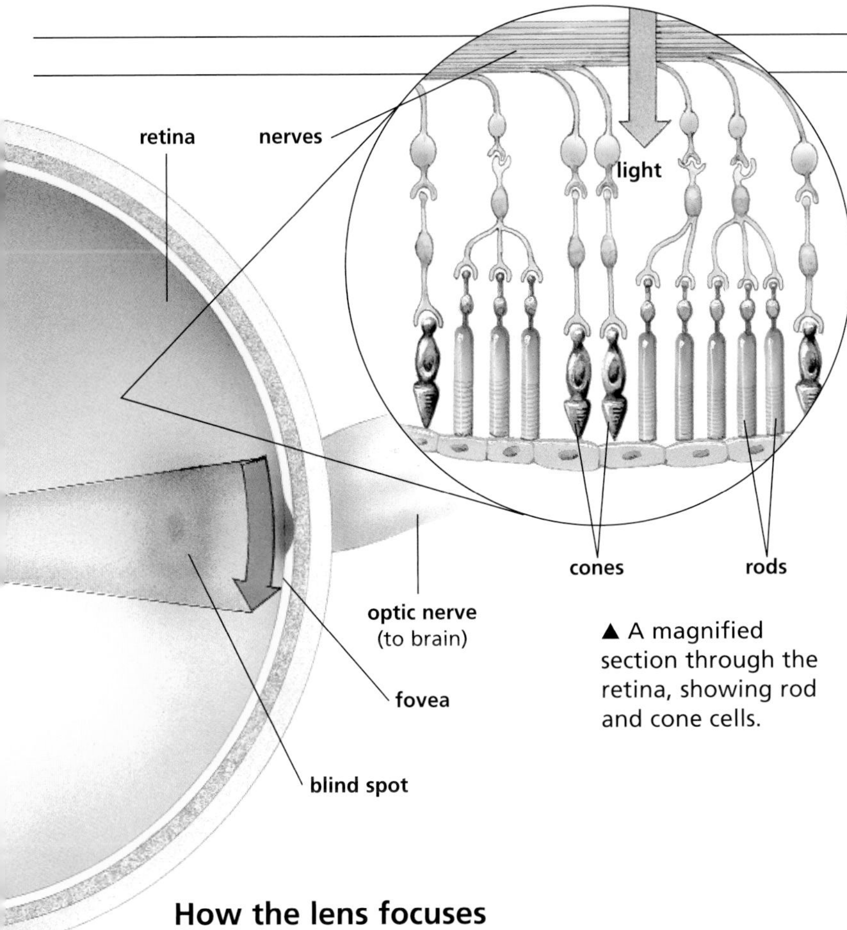

▲ A magnified section through the retina, showing rod and cone cells.

The retina

The retina contains cone-shaped cells that can detect colours. There are also rod-shaped cells that can see in dim light. Rods are not sensitive to colour. This is why things look rather grey at night.

In the centre of the retina is a small yellow area (the fovea) where each cell has its own connection to the brain. In other parts of the retina, many cells have to share a connection. The fovea lets us see in detail, but this only happens at the centre of the image. (Notice that you can make out only a few words on this page at a time). To make up for this, the brain continually moves the eyes back and forth to scan the whole image.

How the lens focuses

The picture on the retina must be sharp if we are going to see clearly. Light is partly focused by the curved cornea, but it cannot focus objects that are close and distant things at the same time. To cope with this problem, the eye has a lens that can change shape. Muscles attached to the lens (the ciliary muscles) can contract to make the lens thin, for looking at distant objects. When the ciliary muscles relax, the lens becomes more curved, for close focus.

Other eyes

The structure of an animal's eye is often a good clue to how it lives. Owls, cats and other creatures that are mostly active at night have very large pupils so that they can gather in as much light as possible. Dolphins have 7000 times more rods in their eyes than humans do, which helps them to see in the dim light underwater.

▶ You can prove that your eyes have a blind spot using this picture. Cover your right eye, and focus on the blue dot with your left one. Keep concentrating on the blue dot, and move the page towards you until the red cross disappears. It has vanished because the image of it is focused on your blind spot.

+ ●

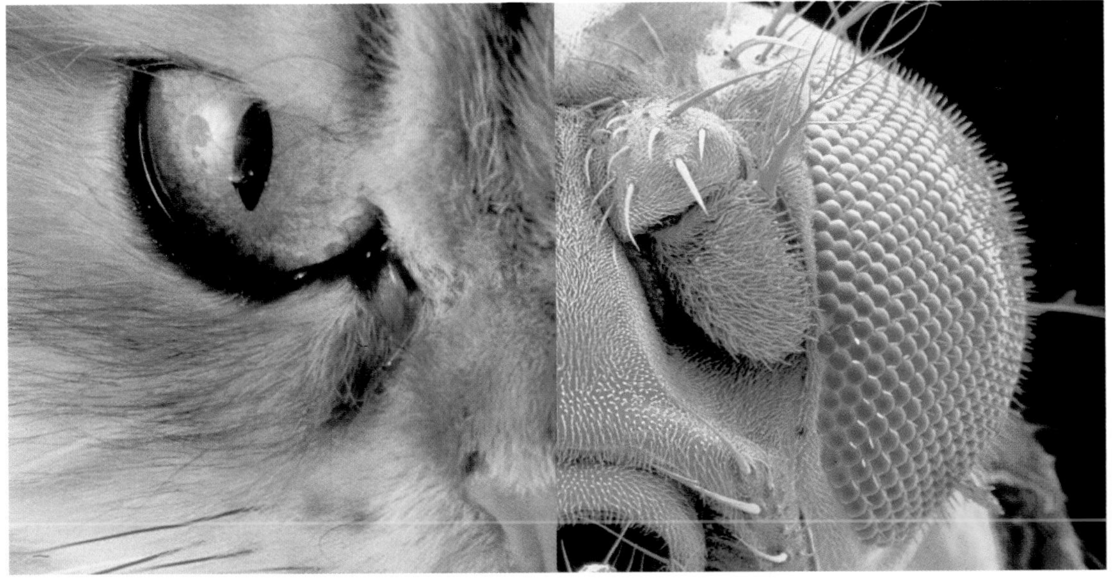

◀ A cat's eye and a fly's compound eye. A cat's pupil is a slit because it is a night hunter. At night, a slit can open much wider than a round pupil, so the cat's eye can take in as much light as possible. A fly's compound eye has 4000 individual tubes, with a lens at one end and light-sensitive cells at the other. The fly's brain puts together the tiny images from each tube to get an image of the world.

Faraday, Michael *see* Magnetism and electromagnetism

Farming

In the vast prairie wheat fields of North America, it is harvest time. A convoy of combine harvesters is advancing through the golden grain, cutting swathes 10 metres wide. By the end of the day each one will have harvested 200 tonnes of wheat.

Today, the world is producing more food than ever before. Yet in countries such as the USA and UK only 2 per cent of working people farm the land. In these countries farming has become an efficient industry. Farmers make use of the latest research into growing crops and raising animals. And they use machines such as tractors, ploughs and combine harvesters to do much of the work.

People in some countries, however, still farm in traditional ways. One common method is shifting cultivation. Farmers clear land by cutting down and burning the vegetation. Then they plant their crops. After a few years, the soil becomes too poor to grow crops, and the farmers move on, leaving the land to recover.

▲ A water buffalo pulls a plough in a waterlogged rice paddy field in South-east Asia. Modern machinery would be of no use in such conditions.

Cultivating crops

Farmers grow all kinds of crops, including cereals, vegetables, fruit and nuts, sugar, oil, tea and cotton. Different crops grow best in different climates.

Cereals, such as wheat, rice and maize (corn), are by far the most important crops. They provide the staple (basic) food for most people.

Improved crop varieties are being introduced all the time. These may produce a bigger crop or give greater resistance to disease. Scientists produce new varieties by careful breeding.

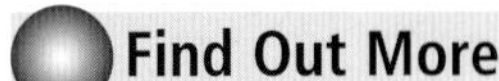

Find Out More

- Fertilizers
- Genetics
- Pesticides
- Pollution

▶ Combine harvesters cut cereal crops such as wheat and barley. The machine separates the grain from the stalks, then binds the cut stalks (straw) into bales.

Many farmers use chemicals to increase crop production. They add fertilizers to the soil, and spray their crops with pesticides and herbicides. Pesticides kill insects that attack the crops, and herbicides kill weeds. The problem with these chemicals is that they can harm other wildlife. Organic farmers avoid using such chemicals, and produce their crops using only natural fertilizers and pest control methods.

GM crops

Scientists can use genetic engineering techniques to alter the genes of plants. The crops are called GM (genetically modified) crops, and they can be made resistant to weedkillers, pests, diseases or drought. Many people are worried that altered genes from GM crops may get into other plants and change them. However, there is no evidence that food made from GM crops is less safe than other food.

Raising livestock

Raising cattle is one of the main kinds of livestock farming. Beef cattle are raised for their meat, and dairy cattle for their milk. A Friesian cow can produce as much as 6000 litres of milk a year. Sheep, pigs and chickens are also important livestock.

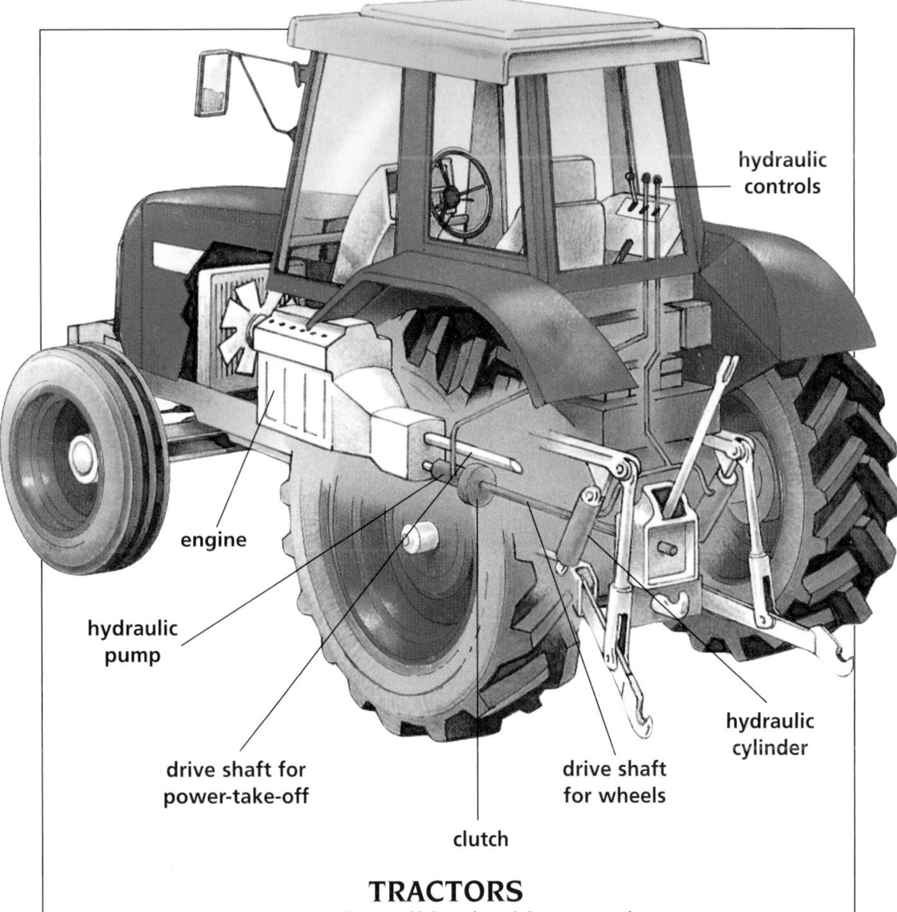

TRACTORS

A tractor can be used to drive all kinds of farm machinery, using power taken from the engine. The engine also powers a hydraulic (liquid pressure) system for lifting and lowering machinery. This cutaway drawing shows how the engine provides turning power (orange) and hydraulic power (green) to the back of the tractor.

Outdoors and indoors

Most livestock are raised outdoors, in fenced fields or on the open range. Farmers in North America and Australia have the biggest open-range farms, or ranches, where they raise beef cattle and sheep in vast numbers.

Some livestock are raised by what are called factory farming methods. They are kept indoors under controlled conditions. Pigs and chickens are often farmed in this way. Factory farming produces meat and eggs cheaply, but many people think that it is cruel.

	CROPS				LIVESTOCK			
	rice	sugar	coffee	cotton	cattle	sheep	pigs	goats
top producing countries	China India	India Cuba	Brazil Colombia	China USA	India	Australia	China	China (meat) India (milk)
world production	520 million tonnes	120 million tonnes	5 million tonnes	20 million tonnes	1200 million	1100 million	800 million	450 million

Fats *see* Diet • **Faults** *see* Continents and plates, Earthquakes

Faxes and modems

Did you know that you can squeeze pictures down your telephone line? A fax machine lets you do just that. And phone lines can carry other information besides voices and pictures.

0 0 1 1 1 0 0 0 0 0 0 0 0 0 0 1 1 1 0 0

light sensors

sending fax

Light sensors change blacks and whites of image into electrical 0s and 1s.

▶ Sending and receiving a simple image via a fax. Telephone lines were designed originally only to carry voice signals, and this means that the speed at which a fax can work is limited.

Phone lines are useful for sending documents to people by fax. But if you have a modem and internet connection, you can also use a phone line for surfing the web and keeping in touch by email.

Fax is short for facsimile, which means 'identical copy'. Fax machines turn an image or document into information that can be sent down a phone line. Modems can also send information down a phone line – in this case, computer data. A computer with a modem can send faxes, too.

Sending and getting faxes

Once a fax machine gets through to the machine it is sending to, light sensors inside it scan across the page in a series of thin lines. Scanning turns the pattern of light and dark on each line of the original into electrical signals, which are sent through the telephone system to the receiving fax machine. This machine takes the signals one line at a time. It sends them to a line of tiny heating elements. Where the original document was dark, the heating element is turned on. Where it was light, the element is turned off. Heat-sensitive paper moves past the heating elements, and where the elements are on, the paper turns black. Gradually, the pattern of light and dark on the original document is drawn at the receiving fax.

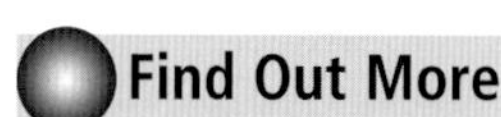

- Communications
- Computers
- Internet
- Telephones

◀ Missed the post? Birthday wishes are just one kind of message that can be sent anywhere in the world over the Internet. The picture and text are stored on computer as digital information. A modem converts this information into packets of electrical signals that can be sent down the phone line.

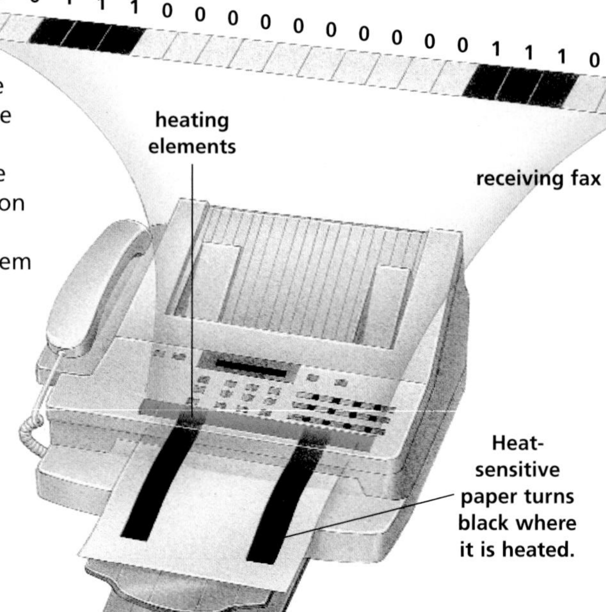

Feathers *see* Birds • **Ferns** *see* Plants • **Fertilization** *see* Sex and reproduction, Human reproduction

Fertilizers

In farming country, autumn can be a smelly time of year because many farmers pump sewage sludge onto their land. This sludge contains nitrogen compounds, which get washed into the soil and will help the next crop of plants to grow well.

▶ Manure is scattered over a field by a mechanical spreader.

Sewage sludge is one of several materials farmers spread on their land to help make the soil more productive, or more fertile. It is a fertilizer.

As plants grow, they take in certain essential elements from the soil. Fertilizers are designed to put back these elements so that future crops can also grow well. The most important elements are nitrogen, phosphorus and potassium.

Nitrogen fertilizers

Sewage sludge is just one way of replacing nitrogen. Farmyard manure is another. But most fertilizers are synthetic, produced from chemicals. These fertilizers include ammonia, and two chemicals made from ammonia – ammonium nitrate and urea. Ammonia production is a big part of the chemical industry.

Some plants make their own fertilizer. They are the legumes, and include crops such as beans and clover. Sometimes farmers grow these crops and then plough them into the soil as fertilizer. This process is called green manuring.

Find Out More

- Chemicals
- Farming
- Waste disposal

From rocks and bones

The chemical industry makes huge quantities of fertilizer that contains phosphorus. Called superphosphate, it is manufactured by treating phosphate rock with sulphuric acid.

Bone-meal is a phosphorus fertilizer used widely by gardeners. It is made from animal bones, which consist mainly of calcium phosphate. The phosphorus is released from the bone-meal slowly.

Potassium fertilizers come mainly from mineral deposits. Often they are mixed with nitrogen and phosphorus compounds to form a compound fertilizer.

▼ The effects of growing plants with different amounts of nitrogen fertilizer ('N' on the labels). The plant on the left has added sulphur (S) but no fertilizer.

Fibre optics

The journey starts at the touch of a button. Into the tunnel they dive, bouncing one way then the other. They crash against the walls, but keep moving at the fastest possible speed. A hundred kilometres later, the light waves emerge from the tiny glass wire.

▶ The inner and outer cores of an optical fibre are designed so that nearly all of the light bounces back when it tries to escape. The light can travel up to 100 km without getting much dimmer.

Optical fibres are thin strands made from glass or plastic. They are usually about one-eighth of a millimetre in diameter. These amazing fibres play a vital role in science, medicine and communications.

Fibre optics in medicine

Doctors use endoscopes, which have optical fibres to carry light into the body and bring a picture back. They can be used to see inside a person's stomach to find ulcers and other problems. It is not very comfortable having a tube pushed down your throat, but better than being cut open.

For keyhole surgery (operations performed through a small hole), surgeons use endoscopes fitted with little tools. A small hole is cut in the skin and the endoscope is pushed in. The optical fibres allow the surgeons to see what they are doing.

Getting the message

Optical fibres are also used in communications. They carry TV and radio signals, telephone messages and other information. A device sends the information as pulses of infrared light. Fibres can carry far more information than electrical wires.

cladding

core

light bounces off surface of core

- Communications
- Light
- Surgery

◀ A single optical cable contains hundreds of optical fibres. These fibres are conducting white light.

Fibres

The little worm has been gorging itself on mulberry leaves for five weeks. Now it is starting to spin its cocoon. Two streams of liquid coming from its spinning glands harden into fine threads of one of the most prized fibres – silk.

Silk is just one of several natural fibres we use to make fabrics, or textiles. Equally important are synthetic fibres such as rayon – made by processing natural materials – and nylon, which is made from chemicals.

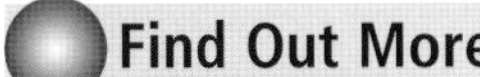

- Industry and manufacturing
- Plastics
- Textiles

Natural fibres

Silk is one of two main fibres we get from animals. The wool from sheep is the other. Goats, camels and llamas also produce useful fibres.

Cotton is by far the most important plant fibre. Cotton plants produce fibres in the seed pod, or boll. Linen is another plant fibre, made from the flax plant.

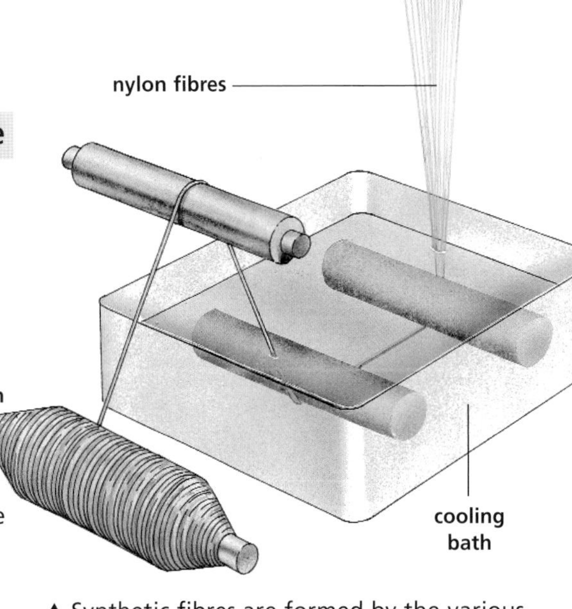

▲ Synthetic fibres are formed by the various 'spinning' processes. Nylon is made by melt-spinning. Molten (liquid) plastic is forced through the holes of a spinneret and then cooled to form fibres. Bundles of fibres are gathered to form a strong yarn.

▼ Both natural and synthetic fibres can be woven on a loom to make cloth. On this industrial loom, the warp (lengthways) fibres are clearly visible.

Rayon and synthetics

Rayon is made either from cotton or from wood pulp. Both of these materials contain cellulose fibres. The most common type of rayon, viscose, is made by dissolving the cellulose with chemicals. The solution is then pumped through tiny holes in a device called a spinneret, then solidified into thin fibres of pure cellulose.

Synthetic fibres are mostly plastics, made from petroleum chemicals. Examples include nylon, polyester and acrylic fibres. Synthetic fibres have some advantages over natural fibres. They are usually much stronger, resist insect attack and do not rot. Also they do not absorb water, which means that they dry quickly.

Films *see* Movies

Fire

Humans first learnt how to tame fire about a million and a half years ago. They used it to warm themselves, to cook food and to frighten off wild animals. Later, our ancestors discovered how to use fire for baking clay and making metals.

OLD IDEAS

In the ancient world, people believed that all things were made of four basic elements: fire, air, water, and earth. Later, scientists thought flammable (burnable) materials must contain a mysterious substance called 'phlogiston', which escaped when the material was burned, leaving ash behind. Just over 200 years ago, the French chemist Antoine Lavoisier showed that combustion is actually a chemical reaction between a fuel and a newly discovered gas – oxygen.

Fire is a collection of very fast chemical reactions. These reactions – called combustion – give out lots of energy in the form of heat, light and sound.

When a substance burns, it is reacting fiercely with oxygen in the air. Combustion is a kind of oxidation reaction. During the reaction, each molecule (tiny particle) of the substance is torn apart to combine with oxygen, releasing the energy that held the molecule together.

Burning fuels

Fire is the quickest and simplest way to release energy from fuels. Energy is stored in fuels as chemical energy. The energy released can cook food, power cars and generate electricity.

◀ In every flame, complex chemical reactions are taking place. Air currents cause a candle flame to be teardrop-shaped. They also carry soot to the flame's tip, making it yellow.

The commonest fuels are hydrocarbons – materials such as coal, gas and oil, which contain compounds of carbon and hydrogen. When you burn hydrocarbon fuels, carbon dioxide and water are released as waste. If there is not enough oxygen, however, the fire will release other products, such as carbon monoxide and particles of partly burnt fuel (smoke), which pollute the atmosphere.

◀ In nature, fires are usually started when lightning strikes dry vegetation. Some kinds of forests and grasslands actually need regular fires to flourish.

Find Out More

- Fuels
- Humans
- Oil and gas
- Oxygen
- Reactions

Firearms *see* Weapons • **Fireworks** *see* Calcium, Reactions

Fishes

The sailfish can swim at 110 kilometres an hour for short distances – as fast as a cheetah can sprint on land. It is probably the fastest fish in the sea. The sailfish's long, tapering, streamlined body and its powerful tail fin help it to swim fast.

◀ Like the first fishes that crawled out of the water onto the land, mudskippers can breathe in air as well as in water, and crawl over the mud using their stiff, fleshy fins like crutches.

Fishes were the first animals with backbones to live on the Earth. They have existed for nearly 400 million years, and there are more than 25,000 different kinds, or species, today.

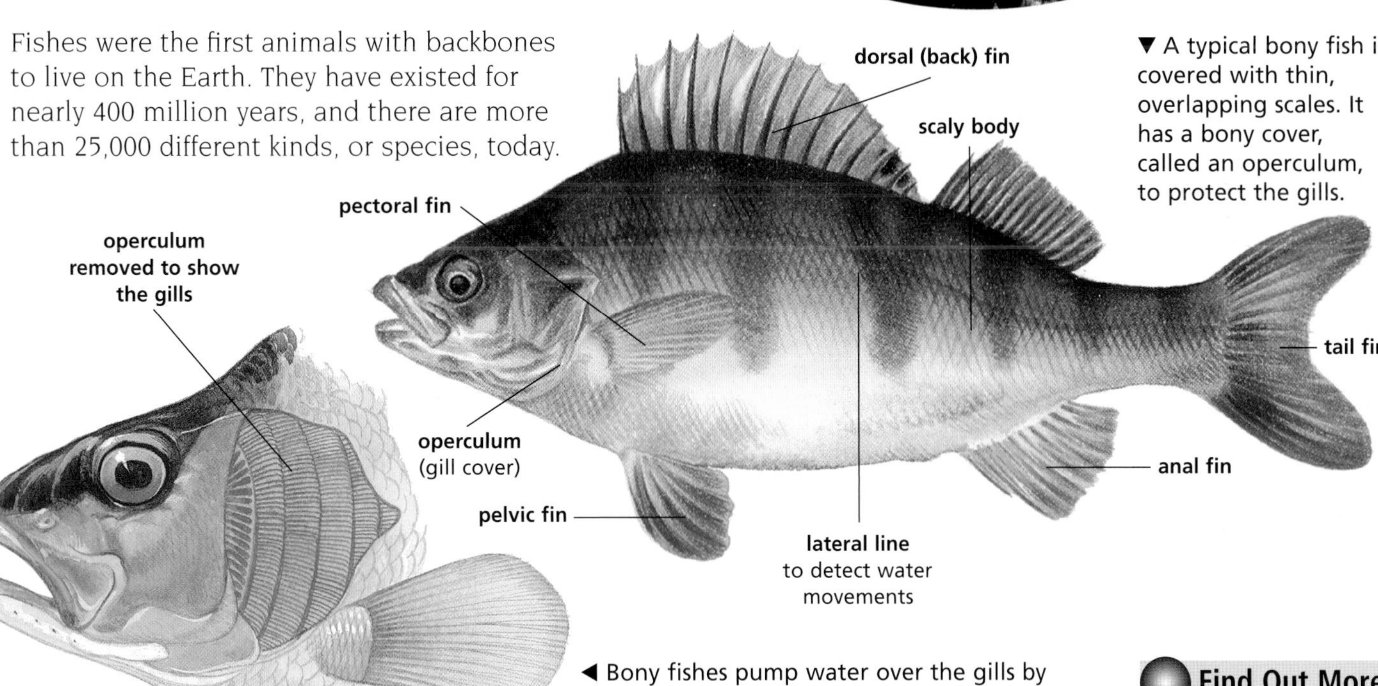

▼ A typical bony fish is covered with thin, overlapping scales. It has a bony cover, called an operculum, to protect the gills.

◀ Bony fishes pump water over the gills by opening and closing the mouth and the gill cover. The gills have a large surface area to absorb oxygen from the water.

Scales and gills

The body of a fish is supported by its backbone and protected by a coat of hard, often slippery, scales. Most fishes have gills to take in oxygen from the water. They are cold-blooded, which means that their body temperature changes with the temperature of their surroundings.

Cartilaginous fishes, such as sharks and rays, have skeletons made of tough gristle, or cartilage. They do not have a swim bladder. Hagfishes and lampreys are unusual fish groups. They have no jaws, no scales and no proper gills. Their skeleton is made of cartilage.

Kinds of fish

More than 95 per cent of fishes today are bony fishes. They have jaws, a skeleton made of bone, and a bag of gas called a swim bladder inside their bodies that helps them float and sink.

Fish life cycles

Most fishes lay lots of very small eggs although a few, such as many sharks, give birth to live young. Some eggs float in the sea, while others stick to plants and rocks. Most fishes do not take care of their young.

Find Out More

- Animals
- Classification
- Life
- Ocean life
- Sex and reproduction

Flight and flow

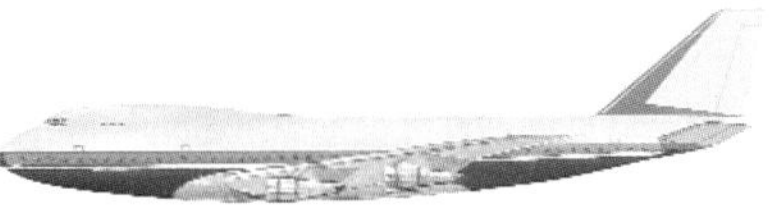

A jumbo jet is like 100 cars all in the air at once – it transports about the same number of people and weighs about the same too. How does such a heavy machine stay up? It all depends on how the air flows around it.

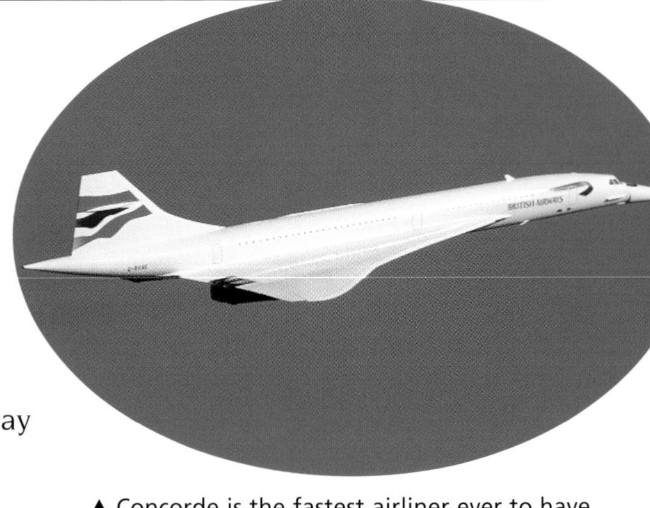

▲ Concorde is the fastest airliner ever to have flown. It flies at twice the speed of sound (about 2000 kilometres per hour), more than twice as fast as other airliners.

Aircraft of all kinds and flying animals such as birds or butterflies can fly because they have wings. As the wing cuts through the air, air flowing around it creates a force called lift which pushes the wing upwards. It supports the wing (and everything attached to it) in the air.

Helicopters have wings too. As the whirling blades of the helicopter's rotor cut through the air, they work like moving wings to create lift.

▼ Aircraft wings give an arched cross-section called an aerofoil. Air moving over the aerofoil produces lift: the faster the aircraft moves, the greater the lift.

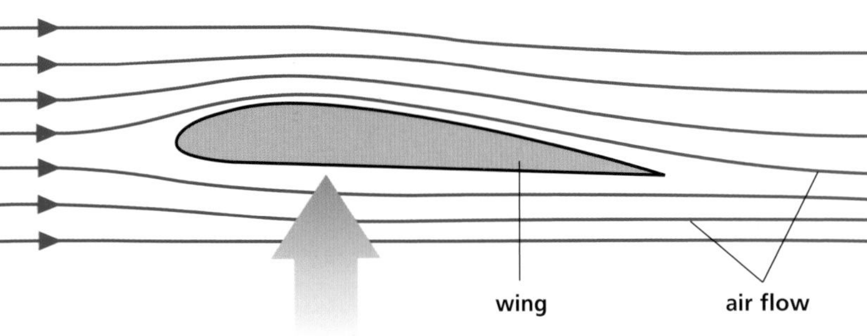

How wings work

When you fly a kite, the wind hits its underside and pushes the kite upwards. A wing works partly like a kite. It slopes at an angle so that its underside hits the air. Air is pushed out of its way and the air forces the wing upwards.

Wings also get lift from the way the air flows over them. The top of the wing is curved, so the air moves rapidly up and over. When air moves faster, its pressure drops. The air under the wing has a higher pressure because it moves more slowly, and this higher pressure also forces the wing upwards.

▼ A glider has no engine, so it is towed along the ground to get up enough speed to take off. Once in the air, it flies at a slight downward angle to keep up enough speed for the wings to generate lift. To regain height, the pilot may fly to a rising air current and circle in it.

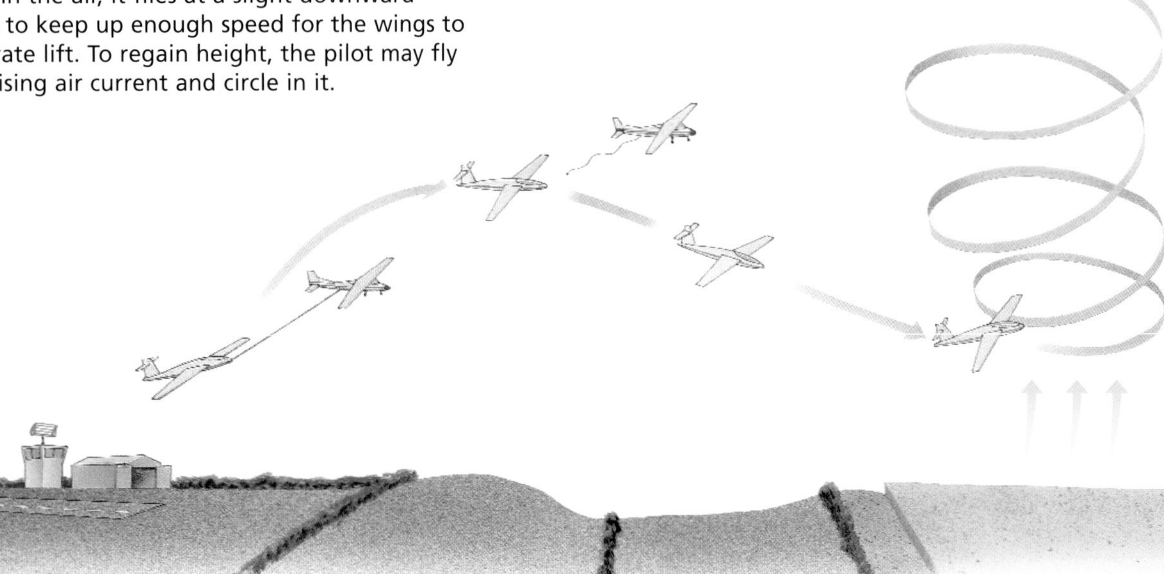

▲ A bird flaps its wings to generate lift, the upward force that holds it in the air, and to propel itself forwards. Once the bird is moving, it may hold its wings out straight and soar, getting lift from the way the air flows around its wings.

Up into the air ... and down again

To take off in the first place, aircraft speed along a runway until they are going so fast that the lift overcomes their weight and they fly. Birds can flap their wings to produce lift to take off from the ground, or simply open their wings and jump off a perch. Helicopters whirl their rotors until the blades generate enough lift, and then they go straight up.

When an aircraft, helicopter or bird is flying level, its lift equals its weight. Slowing, or altering the rotors, decreases the lift, and it begins to descend and may land.

Find Out More

- Aircraft
- Birds
- Forces
- Friction
- Pressure

Flow and friction

When anything moves through air, the air parts and flows around it. The air rubs against the moving object's surface, producing a force called friction that slows its speed. The same thing happens when an object moves through water. Reducing friction helps to gain speed, and saves fuel.

One way to achieve this is by a streamlined design. Streamlined shapes are narrow and dart-like. A pointed nose or bow makes it easier to cut through the air or water. A smooth surface or skin allows the air or water to rub as little as possible. Streamlining is important for aircraft, cars and ships, and for animals such as fish and birds.

As an airliner takes off and lands, flaps come out from the back of the wings. These flaps are like extra wings. They enable the wings to generate more lift at slow speeds.

◀ The design of an aircraft, such as this jet fighter, can be checked out in a wind tunnel. Air is blown over a model at high speed. The designer studies how the air flows around the model plane, to see how the real aircraft will behave when it flies through the air.

Floating and sinking

Push an empty plastic bottle with a cap into a bowl of water. Push hard, as the water pushes back strongly. Let go, and the bottle springs back up and floats. It is this force in water that makes things float.

As the bottle enters the water, it pushes aside or displaces water. The weight of this displaced water pushes back on the bottle, forcing it upwards. This upward force overcomes the weight of the bottle and the bottle rises until it floats.

All things that float, such as pieces of wood or hollow objects, get enough upward force from the displaced water to equal their weight.

▶ Even non-swimmers cannot sink in the Dead Sea. The water there is so salty that it gives more upward force than fresh water or ordinary seawater.

To sink, or not to sink

If the weight of an object is always more than the upward force of the displaced water, then it sinks. This is why heavy stones and bricks sink.

◀ The ancient Greek scientist Archimedes once got into a full bath and made it overflow. He realized that immersing an object provided a simple way of measuring its volume. Archimedes' discovery led him to explain why things float.

Solid pieces of metal sink too, but not hollow metal objects such as ships and boats. Submarines and submersibles vary their weight to float, dive and return to the surface.

Find Out More
- Forces
- Ships and submarines

SUBMARINES

Submarines are ocean-going vessels that can travel on the surface or underwater. Submersibles are smaller vessels, some of which are remote-controlled. Both submarines and submersibles have ballast tanks which can be filled with air or water. To dive underwater, the tanks are filled with water to make the vessel heavier. To return to the surface, water is blown out of the ballast tanks by compressed air. This makes the vessel lighter, and it rises again.

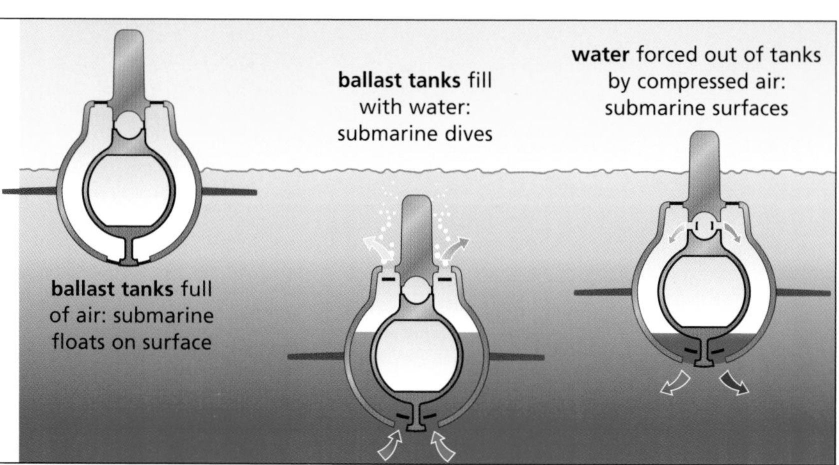

Floods *see* Rivers and lakes, Rain and snow • **Flowers** *see* Plants • **Food** *see* Diet, Energy • **Food chains** *see* Ecology

Forces

What lifts a plane from the ground and sends it zooming through the air? An engine moves the plane forwards, and more forces operate under the wings, holding the plane up. Forces are at work everywhere all the time. Many are powerful enough to crush you, others so weak that you cannot feel them.

A force is a push or a pull. You exert a force when you kick a ball or open a book. When anything begins to move, a force starts it off. Forces also make moving things speed up, slow down, stop or change direction. You use a pulling force to stop a lively dog on a lead.

But forces do not disappear when things are not moving. All the parts of a building – the floors, walls and beams – push or pull on each other. These forces exactly balance. If they didn't, a part of the building would begin to move and the whole structure might collapse.

▶ Strong internal forces between the particles inside a pole-vaulter's pole give it elasticity and stop it from breaking. Instead, the pole bends, then springs back to thrust the vaulter into the air.

FORCES

All the forces that make things move or hold things together are composed of a few basic forces. Electrostatic force, magnetic force and the force of gravity are three of these basic forces.

Rubbing a balloon makes it stick to a wall with **electrostatic force.**

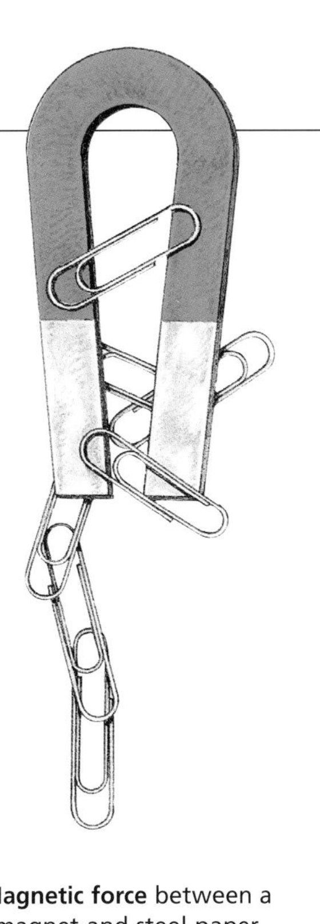

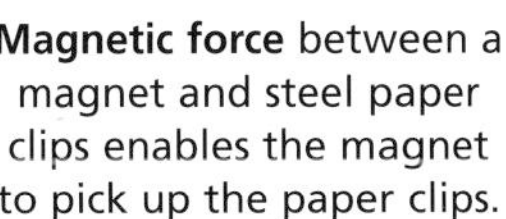

Magnetic force between a magnet and steel paper clips enables the magnet to pick up the paper clips.

Gravity is the force that makes things fall to the ground when you drop them.

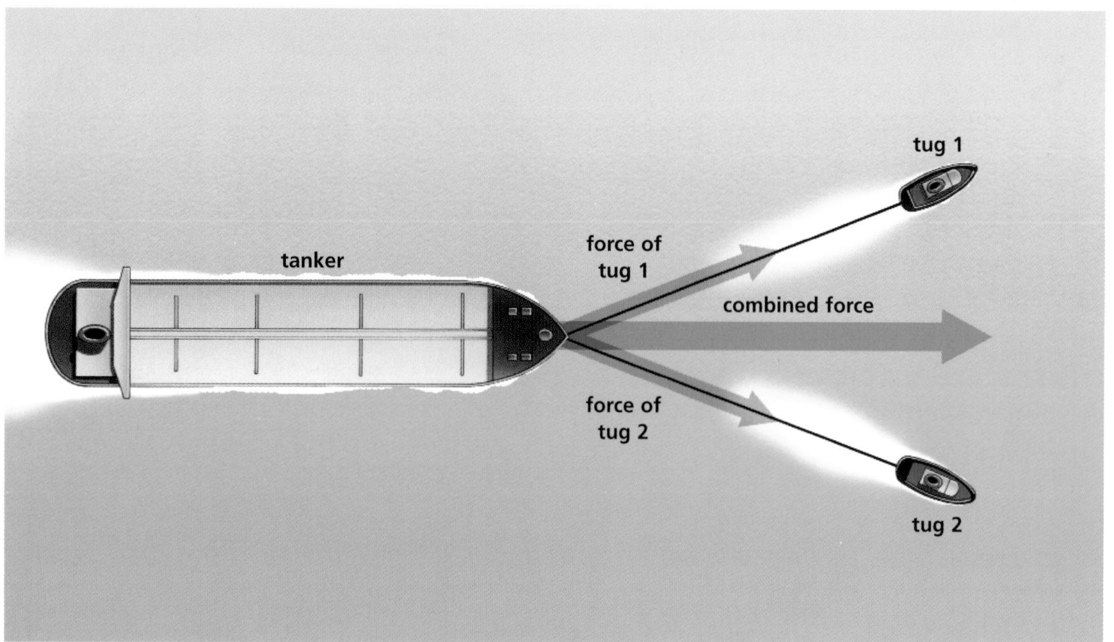

◀ If several forces act on an object, they combine to create one overall force. Here, the forces from the two tugs combine to produce a force that pulls the tanker forwards.

Sources of forces

In people and animals, muscles produce the force to move arms, legs and other body parts. Machines have motors or engines to produce force. Magnets attract other magnets, exerting force that is put to use in electric motors. Springs drive machines such as wind-up clocks or toy mice. When you wind them up, the spring inside stretches and then it contracts to produce a force. This makes the clock hands move round or the mouse shoot across the floor.

Another force – gravity – is present everywhere in the Universe. It makes things fall or roll down slopes. Gravity also makes everything press down on the ground with a force, and this force is their weight.

Adapting or breaking

What happens when forces try to move fixed objects? The objects adapt by changing shape. They may get smaller or bigger, bend, twist or even snap! When you pull a rubber band, you can see it stretch. But many things change shape so little that you cannot see it happening.

▶ On a rollercoaster ride at a theme park the carriages are first raised to a great height, and then released. The force of gravity gives them enough power to complete the ride, even when they loop the loop.

Inside forces

Everything that exists is made up of tiny particles called atoms, or groups of atoms called molecules. Forces between the particles cause them to grip each other and hold things together. These internal forces are strong in hard, tough materials such as steel. But they are weak in liquids and gases, such as air and water. Because the internal forces in liquids and gases are weak, the particles can move about more, and the materials can flow easily.

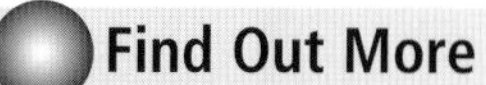

Find Out More

- Bones and muscles
- Gravity
- Magnetism and electromagnetism
- Motion
- Pressure

Ford, Henry *see* Transport

Forests

High in the branches of a rainforest tree, a poison arrow frog is looking for a place to lay her eggs. In the cup-shaped leaves of a plant called a bromeliad, a pool of rainwater has collected. The mother frog lays her eggs there. Soon the tadpoles hatch and begin to grow, in their own private swimming pool.

◀ A dormouse goes into a deep sleep called hibernation to survive the cold winter months. It uses the fat stored in its body to survive.

Find Out More

- Climate
- Plants
- Seasons

Rainforests grow near the Equator, where it is hot and wet all year round. The tree-tops, or canopy, receive year-round rain and sunshine, and the trees are bursting with life. Thousands of different insects, birds and animals live on the leaves, flowers and fruits that the trees provide.

Cooler forests

In other parts of the world, too, forest trees provide food and shelter for the animals and plants that live there. Further away from the Equator, deciduous forests grow in places with warm summers, cool winters and year-round rainfall. Many deciduous trees lose their leaves in winter. In the cool, drier regions across the north of the globe, dark conifer forests grow. The needle-like leaves of the conifers usually stay on the trees all year round.

Surviving the seasons

In both deciduous and coniferous forests life is dominated by the seasons. Spring and summer are times for plants to grow and flower, and for animals to have their young. In the autumn nuts and berries ripen on the trees, and animals feast or store food for the winter. In winter, some birds and mammals migrate, travelling to warmer places to find more food.

At least half of all the animal and plant species in the world live in rainforests.

▼ To get nearer to the light, rainforest plants such as orchids, ferns, mosses and bromeliads perch high on the tree branches.

▼ In the autumn, deciduous forests glow with brilliant red and gold colours as the leaves dry up and fall off the trees. This lets light through to the forest floor and encourages plants to grow, especially in spring.

Fossils

In AD 79, Mount Vesuvius exploded. Poisonous gases poured out of the volcano and suffocated almost everyone in the Roman city of Pompeii. Hot ash buried the city with everyone in it. People and animals burned, leaving imprints of their bodies in the ash. In just hours, thousands of people became fossils preserved in rock.

Fossils are remains of living things, preserved in rocks. There are many kinds of fossil. Some, like mammoth bones or shells in limestone, are actual pieces of things that were once alive. Others, such as leaf imprints or dinosaur tracks are signs of a plant or animal that was once alive.

▶ How a sea creature becomes a fossil.

Find Out More

- Evolution
- Life
- Rocks

Fossilization

Most things don't turn into fossils as quickly as the people in Pompeii. It usually takes thousands or millions of years.

When something dies and its body sits out in the air and rain, it will decompose. Eventually there won't be much sign of it anywhere. But if the body or the tracks are quickly buried by sediments (such as mud or sand) then they can be preserved. As the sediments turn into rock, the fossil is locked in.

Fossils tell a story

Fossils are the only evidence we have for what life was like on Earth in prehistoric times. They tell us what animals and plants were alive and what the environment was like at different times in the Earth's history.

▼ The fossil of an ammonite, nearly 200 million years old. Ammonites were shelled sea creatures that became extinct 65 million years ago, at the same time as the dinosaurs.

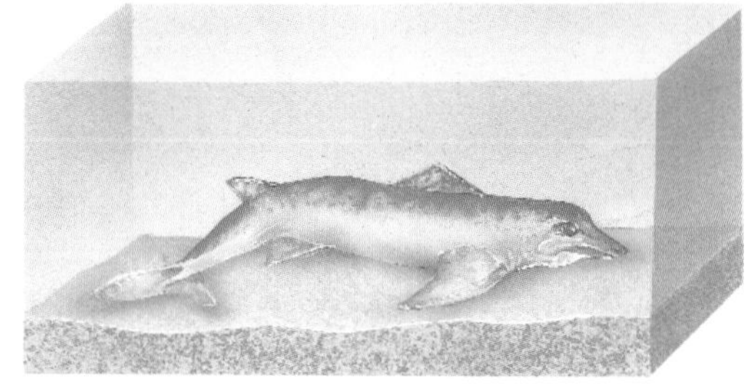

The creature dies and settles to the sea floor.

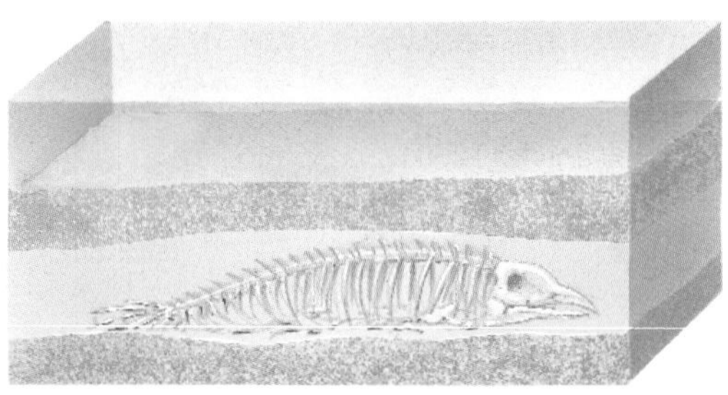

Over time it gets covered by sediments (mud and sand). The flesh rots away, but the **skeleton remains.**

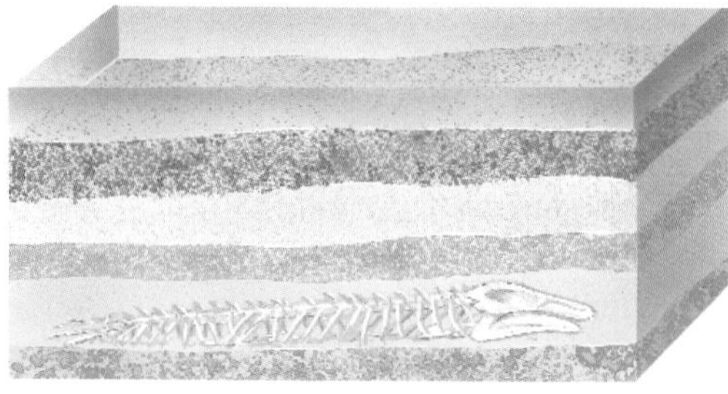

As the sediments pile up, they harden to form **rock.** The skeleton gets squashed and broken.

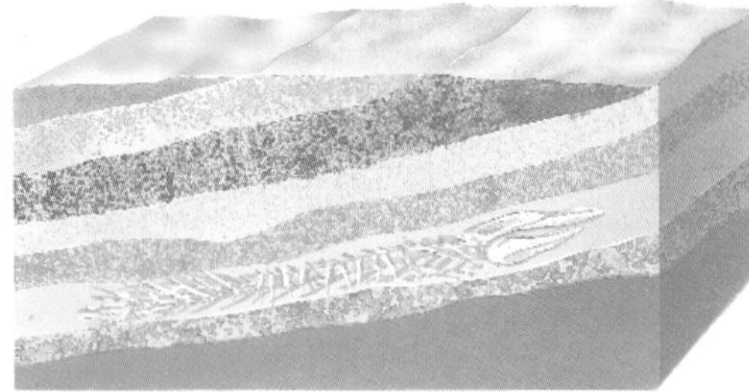

Earth movements lift up the rock layers, and the sea level drops.

The rocks are exposed to the weather and the upper layers are slowly worn away, revealing the **fossilized skeleton.**

Friction

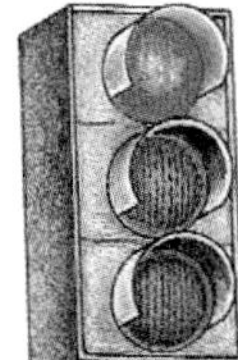

You pedal hard to get a bicycle up to speed. And yet to stop, all you do is grip the brake levers lightly. How can just a gentle pull of the hands so quickly cancel out all the power you put into pedalling? Friction comes to your aid.

As you brake, blocks in the brakes rub against the rim of each wheel. Tiny irregularities in the surfaces of the brake blocks and the rim catch on each other. This produces a strong force, called friction, that acts to slow and stop the wheel rim.

Friction occurs whenever two objects meet, or when an object comes into contact with a liquid such as water, or a gas such as air. If they are moving, then friction slows or stops them. If they are still but try to move, it may prevent movement from starting.

Using friction

Brakes are just one use of friction. It is also needed for a vehicle to move in the first place. Friction enables the wheels to grip the ground so that they do not slide.

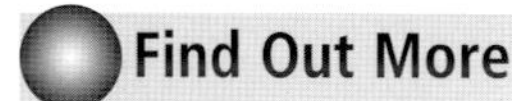

Find Out More

- Flight and flow
- Forces
- Heat
- Motion

▶ Cars have powerful disc brakes. A pair of brake pads close and grip a disc attached to the wheel hub, producing a powerful force of friction between the pads and the disc.

All the many things that are held together by screws or nuts and bolts would fall apart without friction. Friction gives the screw a strong grip on the wood around it, or a nut on the metal bolt.

Reducing friction

Friction is not always useful. In moving parts it produces heat, which could damage machines. Oil or grease is used to make the moving parts slippery. This is called lubrication and it reduces friction and heat. This is why you oil the chain on your bicycle.

Lubrication makes a surface smooth because the oil or grease smoothes out any irregularities in the surface. A smooth surface has little friction. Ice is very smooth, which is why you slip on it.

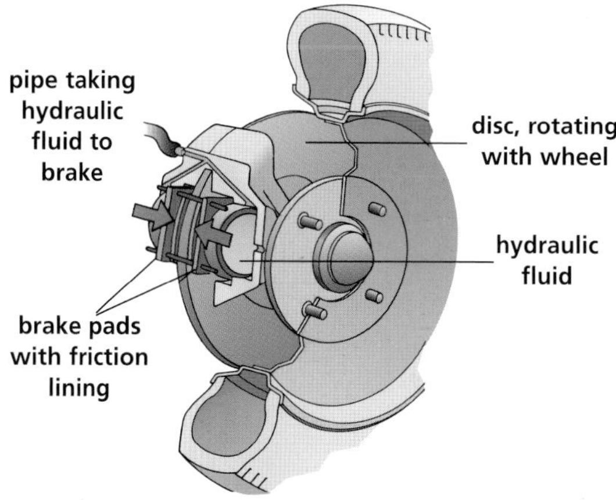

◀ The undersides of skis are very smooth so that there is very little friction between the skis and the snow, enabling the skier to move very fast. However, friction comes into play as the skier tilts the skis to grip the snow and change direction.

Frogs *see* Amphibians • **Frost** *see* Rain and snow • **Fruits** *see* Plants, Diet

Fuels

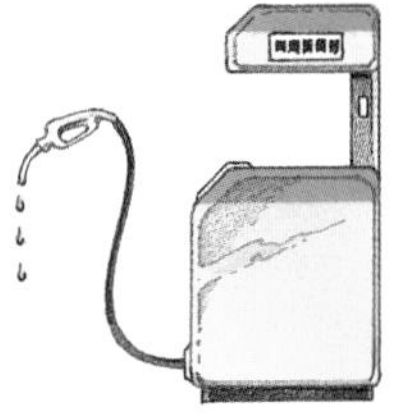

If you could take the energy from just one litre of petrol and use it to power yourself, then you would be able to cycle over 500 kilometres! Petrol is just one of several energy-rich fuels that we use to produce power.

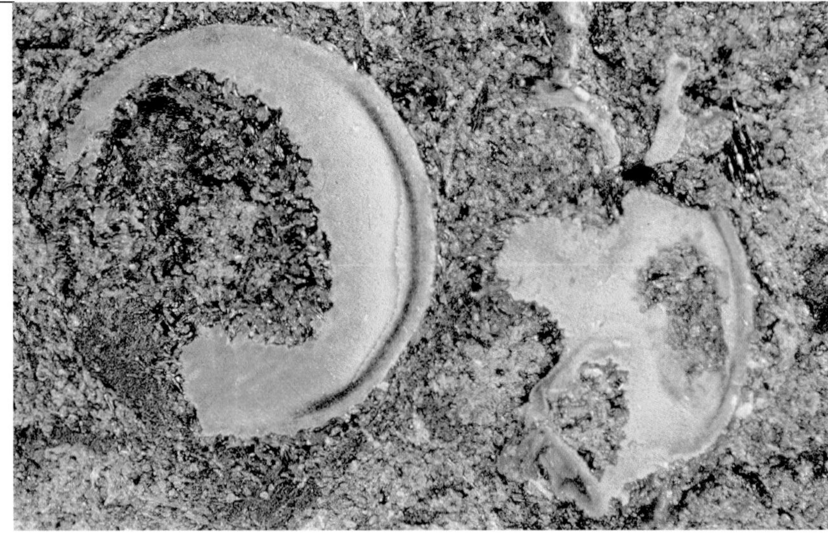

▲ In this slice of coal, the yellow areas are the leaves of some of the plants that formed the coal.

Just about every time you switch on a light, use a heater, cooker or a powered machine, or take a ride in a car, bus, train or plane, you are causing fuel to burn.

We depend on machines like these, so we need an abundant source of energy to power them. Fuels are the most useful energy source we have. They contain a lot of energy that we can release as heat energy simply by burning them. Fuels provide much more energy than other energy sources such as solar power and wind power.

▶ Coal, oil and gas are known as fossil fuels because they are the remains of things that lived millions of years ago. Coal is the remains of ancient forests that grew millions of years ago. Oil and gas are found where there were seas long ago.

Heat is power

Some heaters and cookers burn fuel like gas to make and use heat directly. Cars and most other kinds of transport have engines that burn petrol or other fuel. Even electric trains, lights and other electrical machines use fuel – the electricity that powers them comes mostly from power stations that burn fuel such as coal.

The main fuels are coal, crude oil or petroleum, and natural gas. These are known as fossil fuels. Petrol and diesel for engines come from crude oil.

Another important fuel is nuclear fuel. It produces huge amounts of heat energy, and is used in nuclear power stations to generate electricity.

An energy-hungry world

We burn fuels in huge quantities, but this produces smoke, fumes and waste gases that pollute the air, causing illness and damaging buildings. One product of burning fuels is carbon dioxide, an invisible gas that enters the atmosphere. Rising levels of carbon dioxide are causing global warming, a gradual rise in temperature at the Earth's surface that could bring about serious damage in the future.

The waste from nuclear fuel is very dangerous to health, and storing this waste is also a cause for concern.

3 The liquid oil and gas slowly moved upwards through tiny holes in the rocks above them.

4 Eventually the oil and gas reached a rock layer that they could not pass through, and deposits collected.

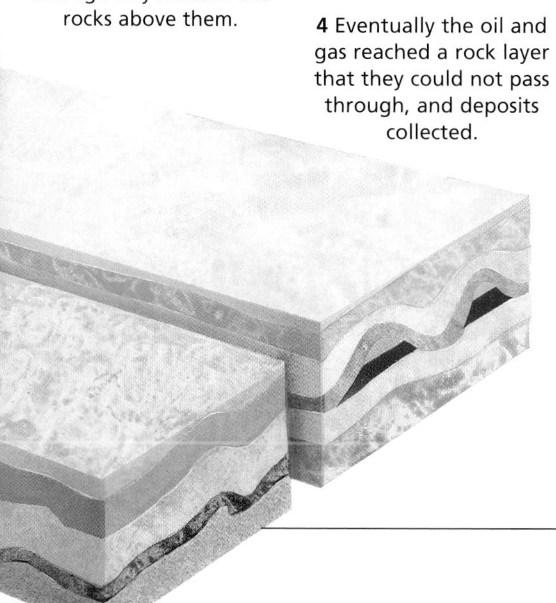

THE FUTURE OF FUEL

Fuels come from deposits underground, which will eventually run out. Although new deposits may be found in the future, it makes sense to try to use up less fuel so that the deposits will last longer.

Using cars with smaller engines, and insulating houses to reduce heat losses, are two good ways of cutting back on fuels. Using less fuel also helps to reduce pollution and global warming.

We can also tackle the problem by finding alternative sources of fuel. Renewable resources include energy from the Sun, which will not run out for another 4500 million years.

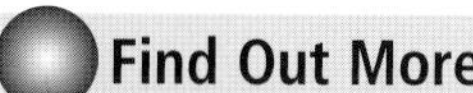

Find Out More

- Energy
- Global warming
- Nuclear energy
- Oil and gas
- Renewable resources

▼ In hot countries, people may collect cow dung and then dry it in the Sun to produce a fuel.

Fungi

The mushrooms we eat and the mould that makes the drug penicillin are different kinds of tiny organisms called fungi. Fungi are found in every kind of environment – some can even live on petrol or plastic. For most of the time, fungi exist as nothing more than microscopic cells or a mass of branching threads. We only notice them when their reproductive structures, mushrooms or toadstools, burst out of the ground.

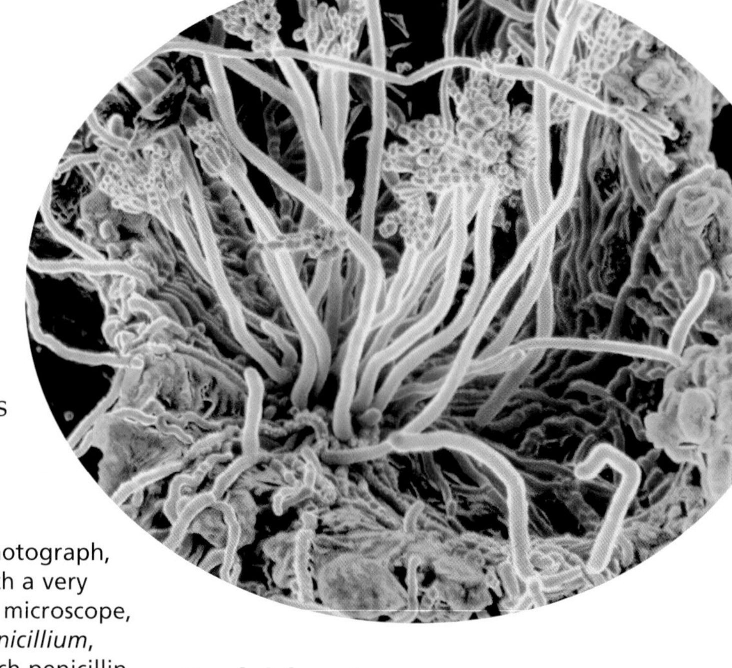

▶ This photograph, taken with a very powerful microscope, shows *Penicillium*, from which penicillin is made, growing on bread.

Fungi are neither plants nor animals – they are classified in their own separate kingdom. The cells of fungi divide in a completely different way from those of other living things. The cell walls of fungi are made of chitin, the material from which insects make their hard outer skeletons. Unlike green plants, fungi cannot use the Sun's energy to make food. Instead they absorb their food from other living things, or the dead remains of living things.

Find Out More

- Cells
- Classification
- Drugs
- Plants

Useful fungi

Fungi play a vital role in the natural world because they break down dead and decaying materials so that they can be recycled. They are a vital ingredient in the formation of soil. They are also useful to people in making bread, wine, beer and drugs such as penicillin. But fungal infections also destroy crops and cause diseases such as athlete's foot or ringworm.

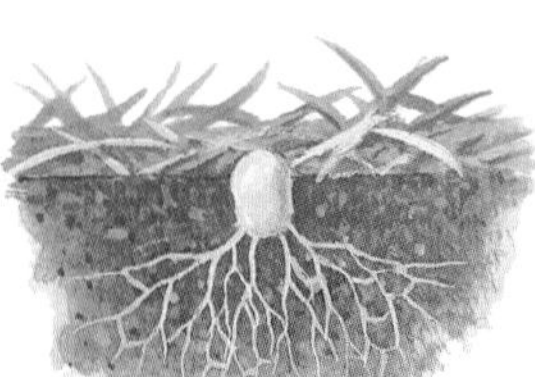

2. Some of the hyphae join together to form a button-shaped fruiting body – the toadstool.

3. This cross-section shows how the red cap expands into an umbrella shape.

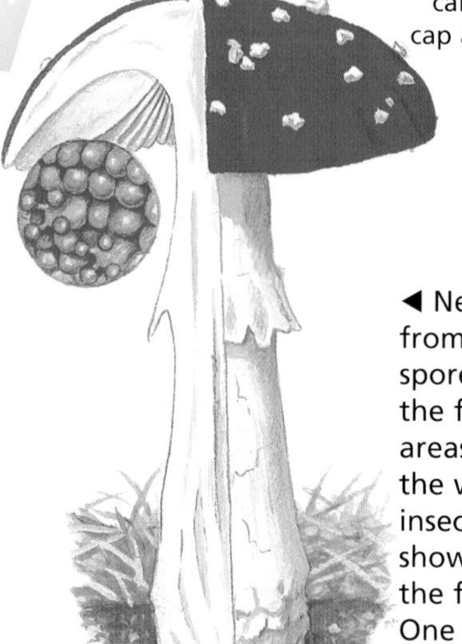

4. Ripe spores drop from vertical flaps called gills under the cap and are blown away by the wind.

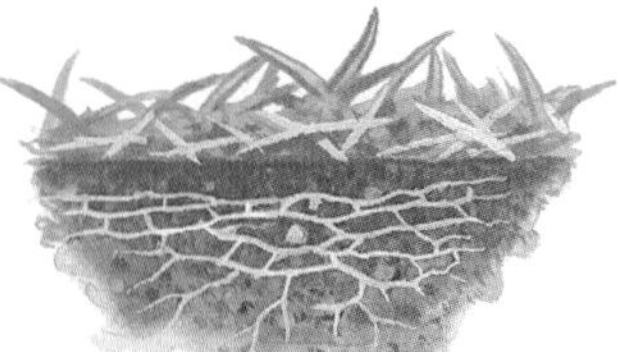

1. A spore germinates to form a network of branching threads called a mycelium. Each thread is called a hypha (plural hyphae).

5. The toadstool quickly decays.

◀ New fungi grow from microscopic spores, which spread the fungus to new areas with the help of the wind, rain or insects. This diagram shows the life cycle of the fly agaric toadstool. One toadstool can produce as many as ten thousand million spores.

Fuse *see* Electricity supply • **Fusion** *see* Nuclear energy

Galaxies

On a dark night you might be able to spot an oval-shaped misty patch in the constellation Andromeda. Telescopes reveal that this smudge of light is a spiral galaxy. The Andromeda Galaxy is the nearest large galaxy to our own – 2.5 million light years away.

There are countless galaxies scattered through the Universe. Galaxies are families of stars. Large galaxies have many billions of stars in them. But hardly any stars exist outside galaxies. The Sun belongs to our own galaxy, the Milky Way.

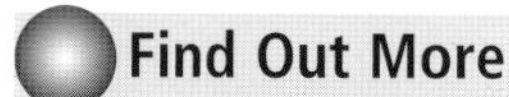

Find Out More

- Constellations
- Electromagnetic spectrum
- Stars
- Universe

Shapes and sizes

Galaxies come in a wide range of sizes. Some dwarf galaxies are only 2000 light years across while the largest giant galaxies extend for more than 500,000 light years.

▲ This image of a spiral galaxy was made by combining several pictures taken by the Hubble Space Telescope. As in most spiral galaxies, the central region contains mostly older, yellow and red stars, while in the outer spiral arms there are younger, blue stars.

About 80 per cent of all galaxies, including both the largest and some of the smallest, are elliptical. They are the shape of a squashed ball. Most of the others are spiral galaxies, with arms that wind outwards from a bulge or bar of stars at the centre. A few fit into neither category so are described as 'irregular'.

Elliptical galaxies contain very little gas and dust. Hardly any new stars are forming in them. Spiral galaxies are disc-shaped with a bulge in the middle. They usually have clouds of dust and gas in the disc where new stars are still being born.

Many galaxies, perhaps all larger ones, have a huge black hole at the centre. Like the black hole that forms when a large star explodes, the one at the centre of a galaxy is so dense, with such strong gravity, that not even light can escape from it. It may have as much mass as thousands or even millions of Suns.

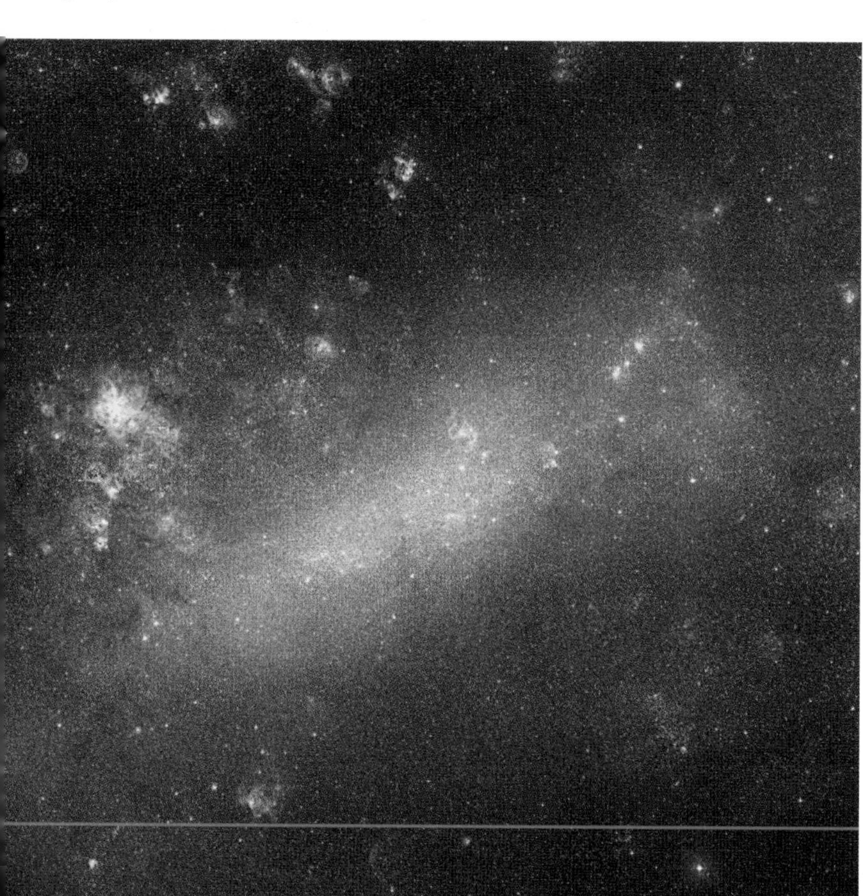

◀ The Large Magellanic Cloud. This small irregular galaxy is a near neighbour, only 170,000 light years away. It is easily visible to the naked eye in the southern constellation Dorado.

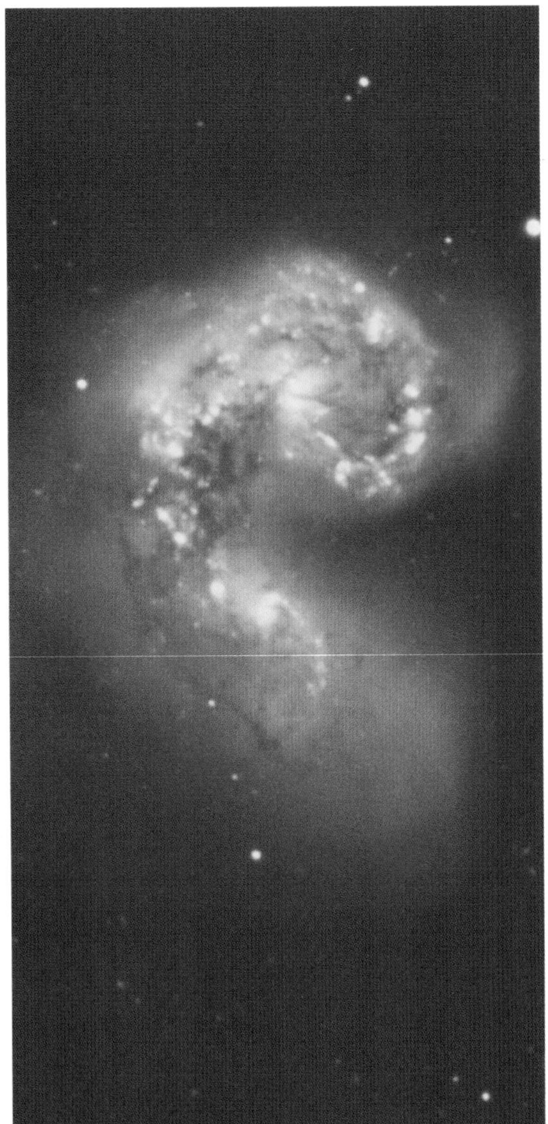

Active galaxies

In a few galaxies, called 'active galaxies', the black hole at the centre is dragging in disintegrated stars and gas from a great swirling disc of material around it. So much material falls in that enormous amounts of energy are given off. The galaxy's central region is just a few light years across, but it can be as bright as 100 ordinary galaxies.

These bright point-like sources of light are visible even when they are billions of light years away and the rest of the galaxy is too faint to be seen. They are called quasars – short for 'quasi-stellar radio sources'. They got their name because the first ones to be discovered appeared to be like stars, but emitted powerful radio waves. The most distant objects visible in the Universe are quasars.

The black hole in an active galaxy fires out two opposing jets of particles travelling at close to the speed of light. Some jets give out light but mostly they are detected by radio telescopes. The jets fan out into huge blobs emitting radio waves.

▼ An artist's idea of how the centre of an active galaxy may look. A disc of hot gas swirls around the black hole at the centre. As it falls into the black hole, immense amounts of energy are given out.

▲ Here, two galaxies are colliding. As a result their shapes have been distorted and the shock blasting through their gas clouds has caused a burst of new stars to form.

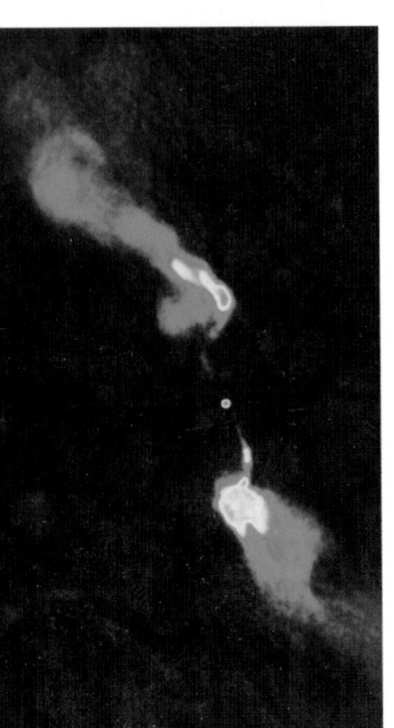

◀ This colour-coded map made by a radio telescope shows two huge lobes of radio-emitting gas on either side of a galaxy called Hydra A. Active galaxies of this kind are called radio galaxies.

Galilei, Galileo *see* Jupiter, Telescopes • **Gamma rays** *see* Electromagnetic spectrum

Gases

You may think of gases as smelly, unpleasant substances, polluting the atmosphere. Some gases are like this, but the atmosphere itself is made of air, which is a mixture of gases. We can't see or smell these gases. Air is mostly nitrogen and oxygen. We need to breathe in oxygen to live.

Liquids turn into gases when they are heated to boiling point. Water boils at 100 °C. But many substances only turn into gases at very high temperatures – you need to heat molten iron to nearly 3000 °C for it to boil. When you cool a gas enough, it turns into a liquid (condenses). You can also turn a gas back into a liquid by applying high pressure (squeezing it hard).

◀ Airships today are filled with helium gas. Helium is lighter than air and so 'floats'. Early airships used hydrogen, a gas that is also lighter than air. However, hydrogen easily catches fire, and this led to some terrible disasters.

Whizzing particles

Like liquids, gases have no fixed shape and flow easily – they are fluids. But unlike liquids, gases will completely fill whatever container they are in. You can squeeze a gas to fit into a smaller container. If you put the same amount of gas into a larger container, it will expand to fill the bigger container completely.

Gases behave like this because the particles they are made of (such as atoms) are moving around very fast. This means the particles can escape the forces trying to hold them together. The particles are constantly banging into each other and against the walls of their container. This puts pressure on the walls of the container.

If you heat a gas, the particles get more energy to move even faster, and the pressure of the gas increases. If you increase the pressure of the gas by squeezing it, then the gas heats up. This is why a bicycle pump warms up when you are using it to squeeze air into your tyres.

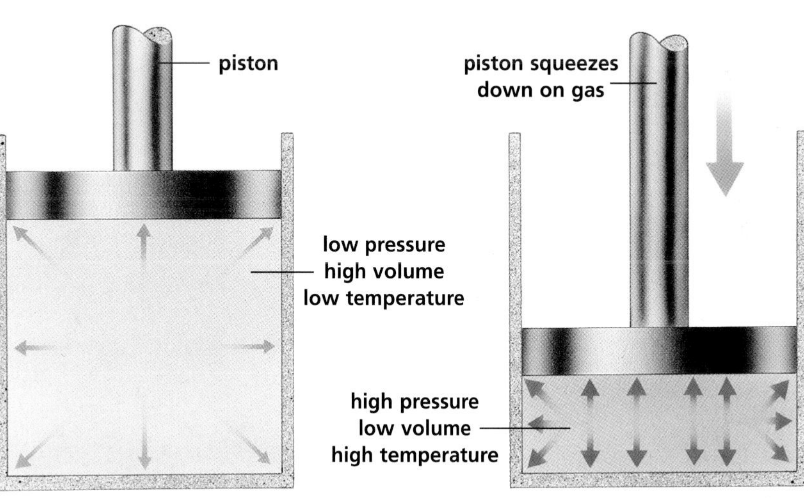

▲ If you squeeze a gas using a piston (like in a bicycle pump), the pressure and temperature increase as the volume of the gas gets smaller.

At room temperature, the particles in air travel at around 1800 kilometres per hour – the same speed as a bullet fired from a rifle.

Find Out More

- Air
- Atoms and molecules
- Hydrogen
- Nitrogen
- Oxygen
- Pressure

Gasoline (petrol) *see* Oil and gas • **Gears** *see* Machines • **Gems** *see* Crystals, Minerals

Generators

What does a rock star playing an electric guitar have in common with a power station? They both use electric generators. When the musician belts out some power chords on the electric guitar, the guitar uses tiny generators to convert vibrations from the strings into electrical energy.

Generators are machines that produce (generate) electricity. They convert mechanical energy – the energy of motion – into electrical energy. The small dynamo that makes electricity for bicycle lights is a generator, driven by one of the bike's wheels. Giant spinning turbines drive the generators in power stations, which make mains electricity for our homes.

The principle behind the generator is called electromagnetic induction. It was discovered by the English scientist Michael Faraday in 1831. He found that he could produce an electrical current in a wire if he moved the wire in a certain direction near a magnet. The same happened when he moved a magnet near a wire – again, in a certain direction only. (The wires had to be part of a closed loop called a circuit, because you don't get a current in a wire that's not connected to anything.)

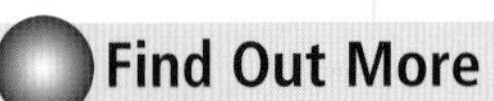

Find Out More

- Circuits
- Electricity
- Electric motors
- Magnetism and electromagnetism
- Power stations

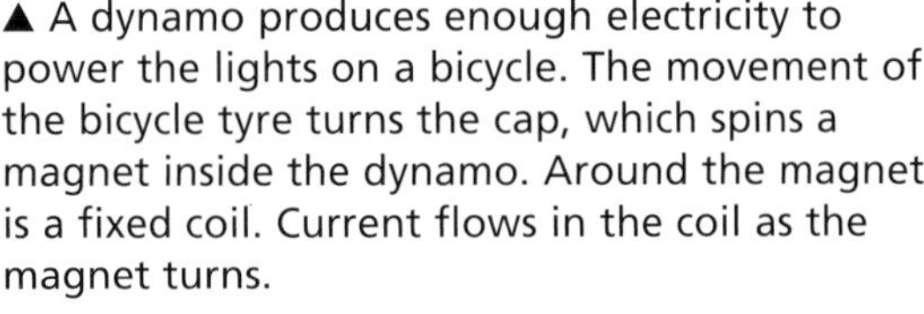

▲ A dynamo produces enough electricity to power the lights on a bicycle. The movement of the bicycle tyre turns the cap, which spins a magnet inside the dynamo. Around the magnet is a fixed coil. Current flows in the coil as the magnet turns.

▼ The outer part of this generator is a large electromagnet. The hole through the centre is where the coil will go.

Building generators

Some generators work by moving coils of wire in a magnetic field. In some generators the coil spins on a shaft surrounded by magnets. As it spins, electricity flows through the coil. However, in a bicycle dynamo, and in the large generators used in power stations, the coil is fixed. Down the centre of it runs a shaft carrying a magnet (in a power station generator, a powerful electromagnet is used). As the magnet spins, electric current is generated in the coils.

Generators normally produce two-way, or alternating current (AC), which is why they are often called alternators. If one-way, or direct current (DC), is needed, generators must be fitted with a switching device to keep the current flowing in only one direction.

Genes *see* Genetics

Genetics

Can you roll your tongue? If you can, the chances are you will find someone else in your family who can do it too. One in four of us are tongue-rollers. It is just one of the thousands of characteristics we may inherit from our parents through our genes.

▲ Identical twins look alike because they have exactly the same set of genes. They are formed from the same fertilized egg, which splits in the mother's womb into two cells, each of which grows into a baby.

Every child is like their parents in some ways, but each of us has our own unique combination of genes. Except for identical twins, no two people have the same genes.

Where are genes?

Your genetic material is found in every cell in your body. Each cell has the same set of about 30,000 genes. These genes add up to a complete set of instructions for building you from scratch – your genome.

Genes are in the nucleus, or control centre, of a cell. They are arranged along long, thin thread-like structures called chromosomes, rather like beads on a necklace. Chromosomes come in pairs, each of which carries genes for the same characteristics.

Different chromosomes

Different animals and plants have different numbers of chromosomes – most snakes have 36, horses have 63, while some ferns have 500 or more.

Humans have a total of 46 chromosomes – 23 pairs – in every cell. The only exceptions are sperm and egg cells, which have 23 unpaired chromosomes. When a sperm fertilizes an egg cell, each parent contributes 23 unpaired chromosomes. So the new baby has its own unique set of 46 chromosomes.

How genes work

Genes are made of a chemical called deoxyribonucleic acid, or DNA. DNA works by telling a cell how to make the proteins that keep the cell alive and growing. Every cell in your body contains at least 10,000 different kinds of protein. Small sections of

CHROMOSOMES

The 23 pairs of human chromosomes. One half of each pair comes from the mother and the other half from the father. Bottom right are the sex chromosomes. This person has an X chromosome and a Y chromosome and so is male. Every egg contains an X-chromosome. Sperm may contain either an X or a Y chromosome. If a sperm carrying an X chromosome joins with the egg, the child will be a girl. If a sperm carrying a Y chromosome joins with the egg, the child will be a boy.

the enormous DNA molecule carry the instructions for making individual proteins. The machinery for making these proteins is on structures called ribosomes, which are outside the nucleus. The DNA itself never leaves the nucleus. Instead, small sections are copied on to another chemical, called messenger RNA. This carries the instructions for making a particular protein to the ribosomes.

Copying genes

Every time a new cell is made, the DNA is copied so that each new cell has its own identical copy of all the genes. The structure of DNA makes the genes easy to copy. A DNA strand separates down the middle and spare chemical building blocks join up with their matching pairs on the separated strands. So one strand of DNA makes two identical new strands.

Problem genes

Genes can change if mistakes are made during the copying process, or if they are damaged by chemicals or radiation. They also change when they are mixed up during sexual reproduction. A permanent change to a piece of DNA is called a mutation. Most mutations are harmful, but a few produce helpful characteristics. Such mutations allow a species to change and evolve over time.

Some combinations of genes can cause disorders and diseases. For example, about 8 per cent of men are colour-blind – they cannot distinguish the colours red and green. It is rare for women to be colour blind, but many women are carriers. This means they can pass the problem genes on to their children.

Genes and environment

The final appearance and behaviour of an individual is determined both by its genes and by outside influences. These influences include things like how much food it eats, what climate it lives in and whether it has suffered disease or injury during its development. But only those characteristics controlled by its genes can be inherited.

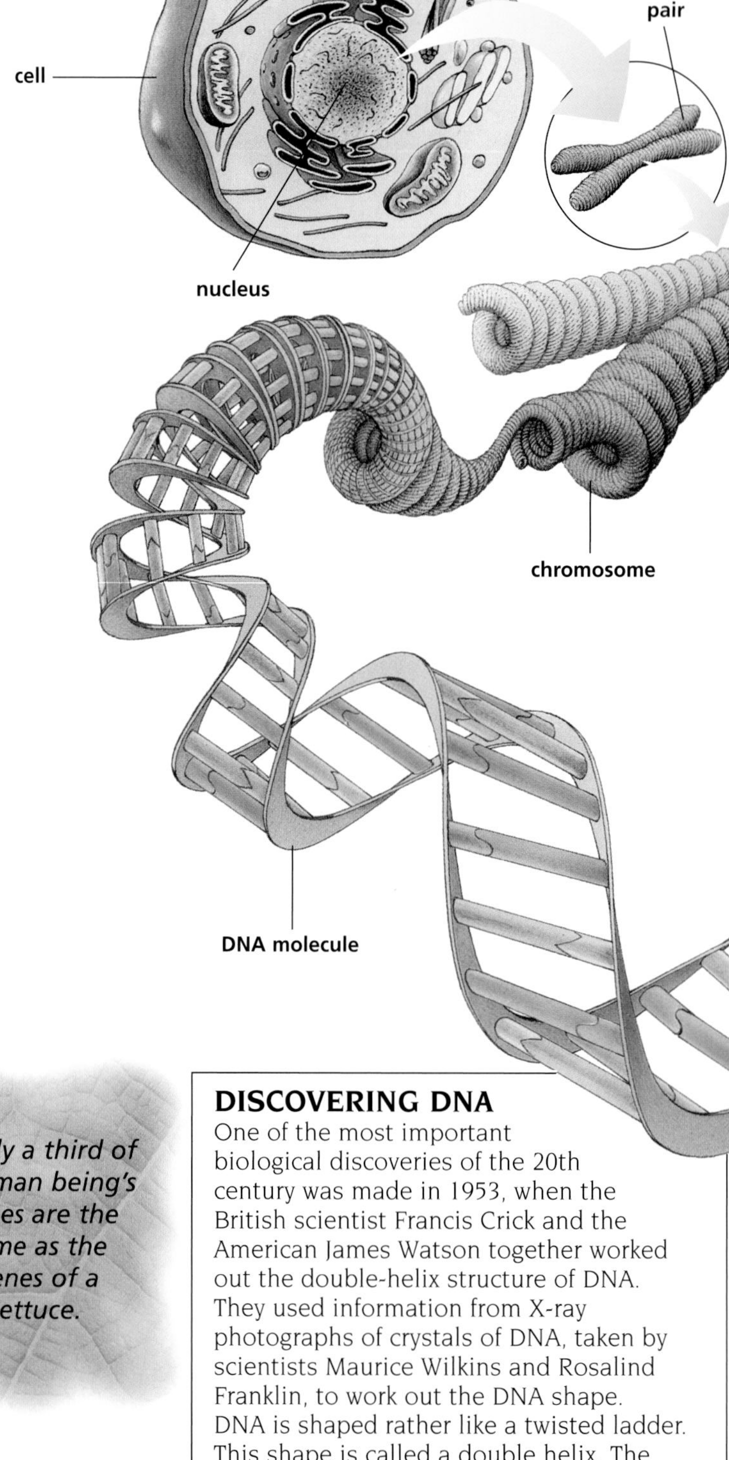

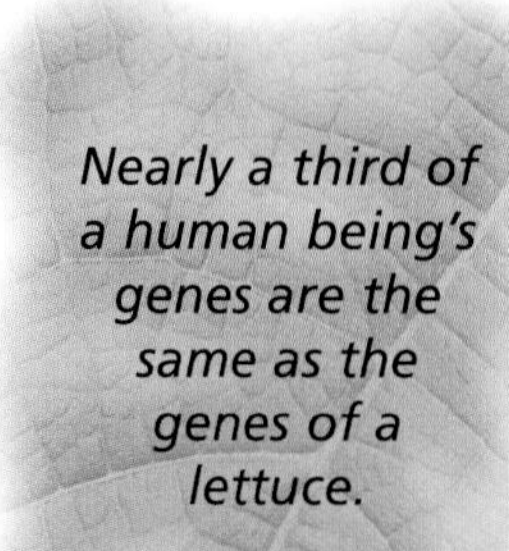

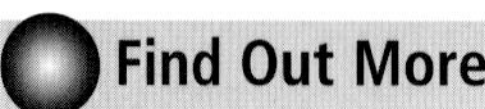

- Cells
- Evolution
- Life
- Sex and reproduction
- X-rays

DISCOVERING DNA

One of the most important biological discoveries of the 20th century was made in 1953, when the British scientist Francis Crick and the American James Watson together worked out the double-helix structure of DNA. They used information from X-ray photographs of crystals of DNA, taken by scientists Maurice Wilkins and Rosalind Franklin, to work out the DNA shape. DNA is shaped rather like a twisted ladder. This shape is called a double helix. The rungs of the ladder are made up of four chemical building blocks, adenine, guanine, thymine and cytosine. Like the letters of an alphabet, these building blocks can be arranged in different ways to make up the 'words' of the genes. So genetic instructions are in the form of a chemical code.

GREGOR MENDEL

A Czech monk called Gregor Mendel made the first important discoveries in genetics. 1865, Mendel was experimenting with pea plants. In one experiment, he bred together plants that had white flowers with ones that had purple flowers. Instead of getting some white and some purple flowers, he found that all the new plants had purple flowers.

To explain this, we have to remember that chromosomes come in pairs, so each plant has two genes for flower colour. What Mendel showed was that the gene for purple flowers

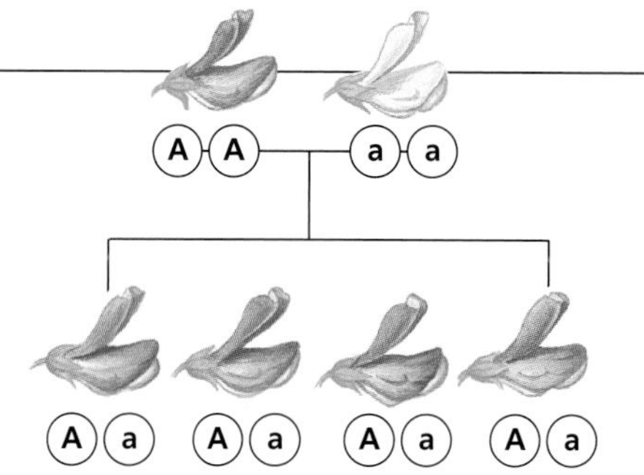

(**A** in the diagram) is dominant over the gene for white flowers (**a**). So if a plant has one purple-flower gene and one white-flower gene, the plant has purple flowers. The white flower gene is called recessive. It only shows if a plant has two white-flower genes.

KEY

adenine always pairs with thymine

thymine

guanine always pairs with cytosine

cytosine

◀ Each chromosome in the nucleus is an enormously long molecule of DNA, coiled and coiled again. This diagram shows how the double-stranded DNA copies itself, by splitting into two single strands and forming a new double strand on each half.

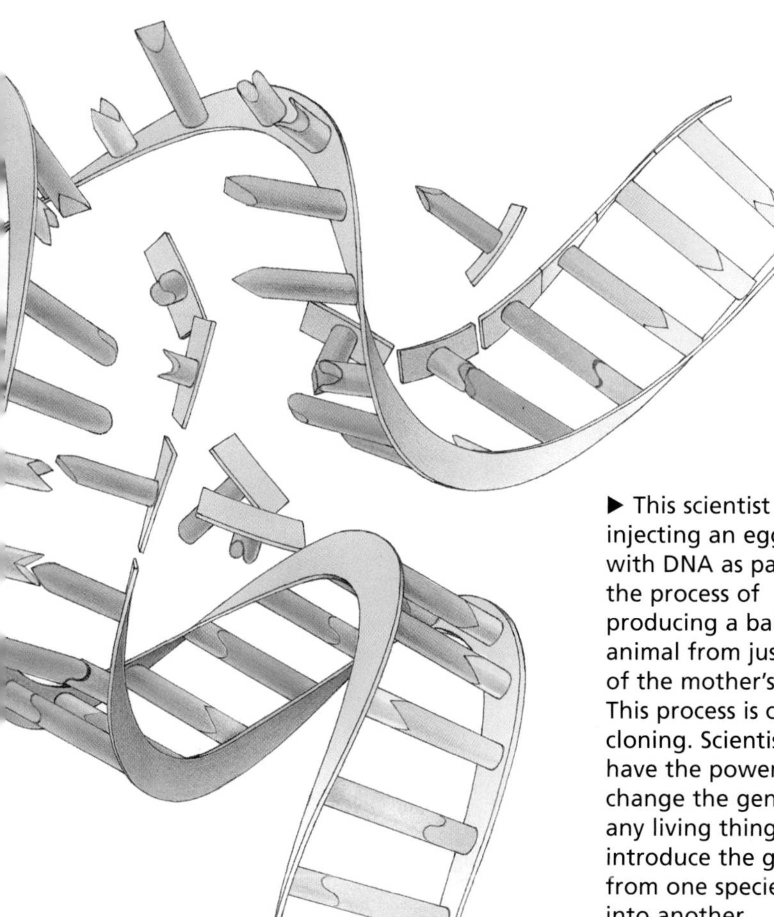

Finding out about our genes

The human genome project is an international research programme that has recently worked out the complete sequence of all the genes on our chromosomes. As yet, scientists do not know what all the different genes do, but finding faulty genes is becoming easier, and new treatments for genetic diseases may result.

Many medicines, such as insulin, are now produced in large amounts thanks to advances in our knowledge of genetics. Genetic engineers insert human genes, such as the gene for insulin, into harmless microbes. As they grow, the microbes produce large quantities of high-quality insulin. Genetic engineers can also insert human genes into larger animals, for example sheep have been genetically modified (changed) so that they produce medicines in their milk.

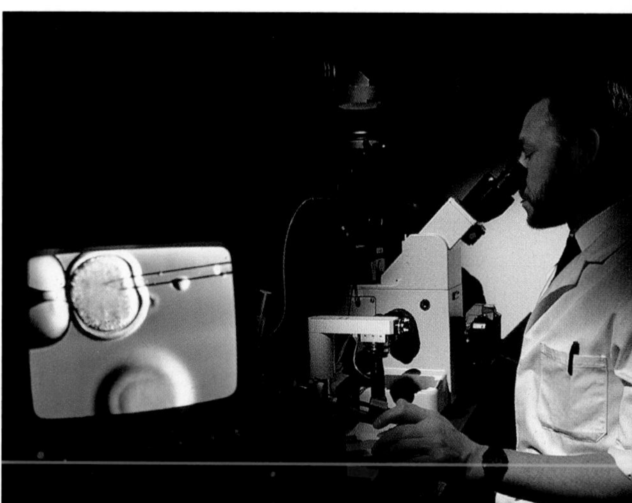

▶ This scientist is injecting an egg cell with DNA as part of the process of producing a baby animal from just one of the mother's cells. This process is called cloning. Scientists also have the power to change the genes in any living thing and introduce the genes from one species into another.

Geological time

Chondrite meteorites are the oldest rocks in the Solar System. They formed over 4½ billion years ago, at the same time as the Sun and the planets.

Imagine that the entire 4.56 billion (4560 million) years of Earth history were squeezed into a single year. The Earth formed on 1 January. The Moon formed a few days later. Life began at the beginning of March, but large plants and animals didn't evolve until November. Dinosaurs lived only from 12 to 26 December. And human-like animals didn't evolve until 31 December at four o'clock in the afternoon.

This X-ray and drawing show a **fossil bacterium** from Australia that is about 3½ billion years old. It is one of the oldest fossils known on Earth.

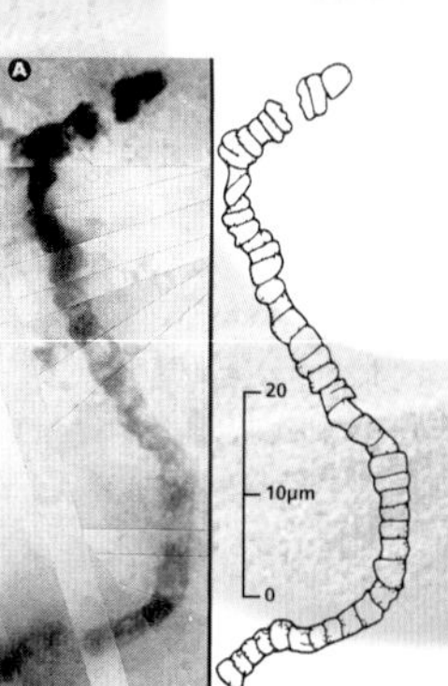

Evidence from rocks suggests that the Moon formed when a **small planet** smashed into the Earth soon after it was formed.

Ever since geologists first began studying the Earth more than 200 years ago, they have been trying to unravel its history. By studying rocks and fossils, geologists can work out what was happening on Earth when the rocks formed. To work out when different events were taking place, they need to put the rocks and fossils in chronological order (oldest to youngest).

▶ This timeline shows how rocks can tell us about the Earth's history.

WHAT HAPPENED FIRST AT THE GRAND CANYON

The Grand Canyon in the western USA is one of the natural wonders of the world. Over millions of years, the Colorado River has cut through over 1500 m of rock, exposing layer after layer laid down over hundreds of millions of years. Using various basic principles (the laws of superposition and cross-cutting relationships, and the evidence of fossils; see main text), geologists can work out the order of events in the formation of the rocks.

Muav limestone

Bright Angel shale

Tapeats sandstone

The Kaibab limestone is the youngest rock formation.

This uneven boundary is called an 'unconformity'. It marks a period of time where rocks were eroding away rather than forming.

The Redwall limestone must have formed after the Muav limestone and everything below it, but before everything above.

Fossils of trilobites in the Bright Angel shale and the Muav limestone show that the rocks must have formed in Cambrian or Devonian times, when trilobites were still alive on the Earth.

The Vishnu schist and gneiss is the oldest formation.

Granite cuts across the schist and gneiss, so it must be younger.

The Colorado River cuts through everything, so it must be youngest of all.

Trilobites were among the most successful early animals. This fossil is about 500 million years old.

Coal is a good fuel. It formed from the remains of forests that grew in the Carboniferous period, about 300 million years ago.

An asteroid or comet hit central America 65 million years ago, making this huge **impact crater.** This event may have caused the extinction of the dinosaurs and other plants and animals.

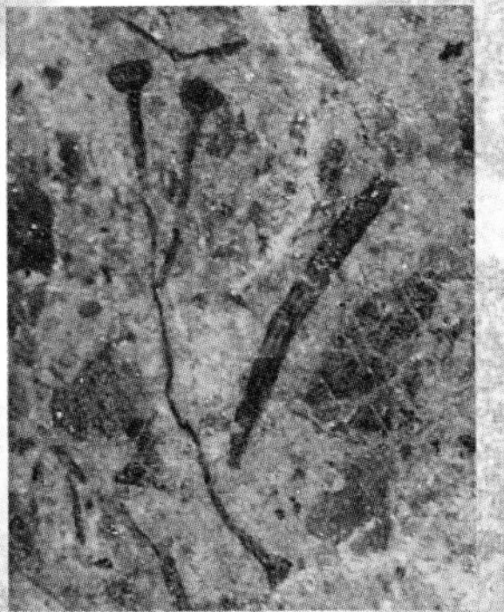

The **first land plant** fossils are about 420 million years old. The best-known of these is Cooksonia (shown).

These **human footprints** were made by our ancestors about 3.6 million years ago, as they walked through some soft volcanic ash in Tanzania.

Reading the rocks

Geologists can work out the sequence of events that created a rock formation by looking closely at rocks out in the field, making maps and studying fossils. There are three important things a geologist takes into account when trying to work out which rocks formed first.

The law of superposition

Sedimentary rocks (rocks formed by tiny fragments settling on the bottom of seas and lakes) and volcanic rocks (rocks made from the lava from volcanoes) form on top of each other. Therefore, the oldest rocks are at the bottom and the youngest are at the top. 'Superpose' means 'lie on top of'.

The law of cross-cutting relationships

Igneous rocks (rocks made from hot liquid rock) can form within cracks running through other rocks. A rock that cuts through or across another rock must be younger than the rock it cuts through.

Fossils

Over time, animals and plants have lived and then become extinct. They have left fossils in the sedimentary rocks that were forming when they died. Using the law of superposition (older fossils lie beneath younger fossils), geologists have been able to put ancient plants and animals in chronological order.

If you know when a particular species (or a group of species) was alive, then you can use its fossils as a time-marker. For instance, if a sedimentary rock has dinosaur bones in it, it must have formed during the Mesozoic era when dinosaurs were alive. Fossils can also help you work out whether a rock in one part of the world formed before, after, or at about the same time as a rock in another part of the world.

Working out how old rocks are relative to each other is called relative dating.

Dating rocks using radioactivity

One way geologists work out the absolute age of a rock in years is by studying the atoms in a mineral grain in the rock. Every mineral is composed of atoms. Some kinds of atoms turn into different atoms over time. For instance, some uranium turns into lead, and some potassium turns into argon. These atoms are 'radioactive' because they give off radiation as they change.

If you know how fast the 'parent' atoms turn into 'daughter' atoms, and you measure how many parent atoms and daughter atoms there are in the mineral grains, you can calculate the age of the rock. This is known as radiometric dating.

Find Out More

- Earth
- Fossils
- Life
- Radioactivity
- Rocks

Geology

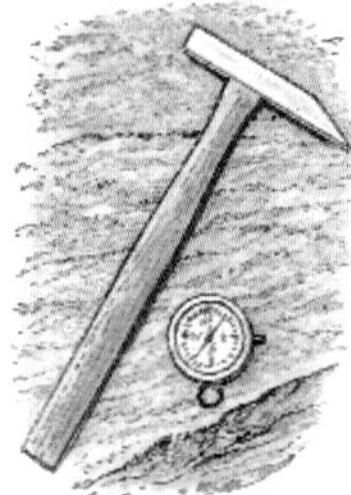

To a geologist, a piece of sandstone is not just a rock. It is part of an ancient beach or desert. Its sand particles were once part of a mountain. The sandstone could be used to build a house or it may hold oil that could be used for energy. It might contain the bones of an extinct animal, or imprints of an ancient plant that could tell us about the Earth's history.

Geology is the study of the Earth – what it is made of, how it formed, how it has changed, and how it is changing today.

Detective work

Geologists use many tools to understand the Earth, but the most important tools are their powers of observation and reasoning. They watch rivers flow, carefully observe rock formations, and analyse minerals under a microscope. After gathering all the evidence, they form theories about how the Earth formed and how it changes over time.

When geologists see limestone full of fossils, they know that the ground they are standing on must have once been a shallow, tropical sea. Limestone forms today in shallow tropical seas, so it must have formed there in the past. Geologists work out how rocks formed millions of years ago by watching them form today.

Different kinds of geologist

Geologists study different parts of the Earth for many different reasons. Some study volcanoes so that they can predict eruptions. Some search for deposits of important minerals like copper and gold. There are geologists who help engineers by making sure the rocks are stable enough to build on, and others who look for water underground. Many geologists study rocks just because they are interested in how the Earth formed.

▶ This geologist is measuring the temperature of a recent lava flow from a volcano.

Find Out More

- Continents and plates
- Minerals
- Mining
- Rocks

▼ James Hutton (1726–1797) inspecting the rocks near his home in Edinburgh, Scotland. Hutton is called the 'father of modern geology'. In his time most people concluded from the Bible that the Earth was only 6000 years old. By watching the forces that destroyed old rocks and created new ones, Hutton reasoned that the Earth must be millions of years old.

Geometry *see* Mathematics • **Germs** *see* Diseases • **Glaciers** *see* Ice caps and glaciers

Glands and hormones

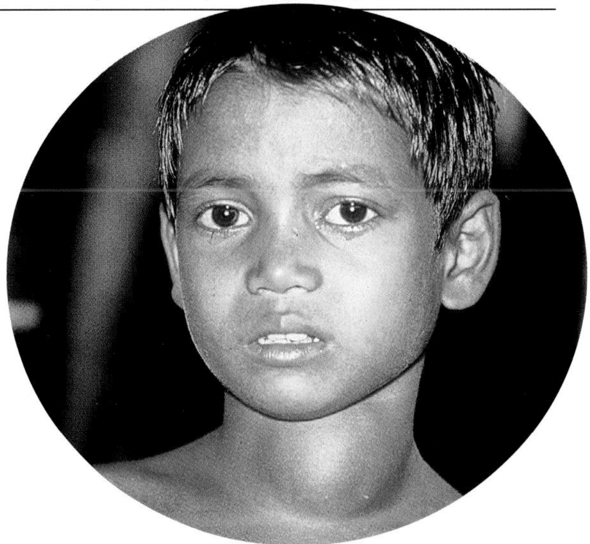

▲ This boy has goitre – a swollen thyroid gland in his neck. It may be caused by a lack of iodine in his diet or because the gland itself is not working properly.

Imagine being woken at night by a strange noise, or being chased by a vicious dog. Your heart starts thumping, you breathe more quickly and you break out in a sweat. All these changes are caused by a chemical messenger called adrenaline, which prepares you to react to danger.

Adrenaline is just one of many chemical messengers that your body produces. We call these messengers hormones. Some, like adrenaline, affect many parts of the body. Others may affect only one organ.

There are thousands of different processes going on in your body at any one moment. Hormones help to control these processes. They make sure that you grow at a steady rate, and that you always have the right amount of sugar in your blood. Hormones also control the changes that happen at puberty, when you become sexually mature, and during pregnancy.

Blood messengers

Hormones are made in glands known as endocrine glands, which pour them straight into the blood. Hormones are not released all the time – they are produced in short bursts. And cells respond to hormones at different speeds. This means that hormones can control anything from slow processes such as growing up to the high-speed reaction to an emergency.

▼ How the hormone insulin works. Insulin is produced in the pancreas. It acts on the liver and muscles to stop the level of glucose in the blood from getting too high.

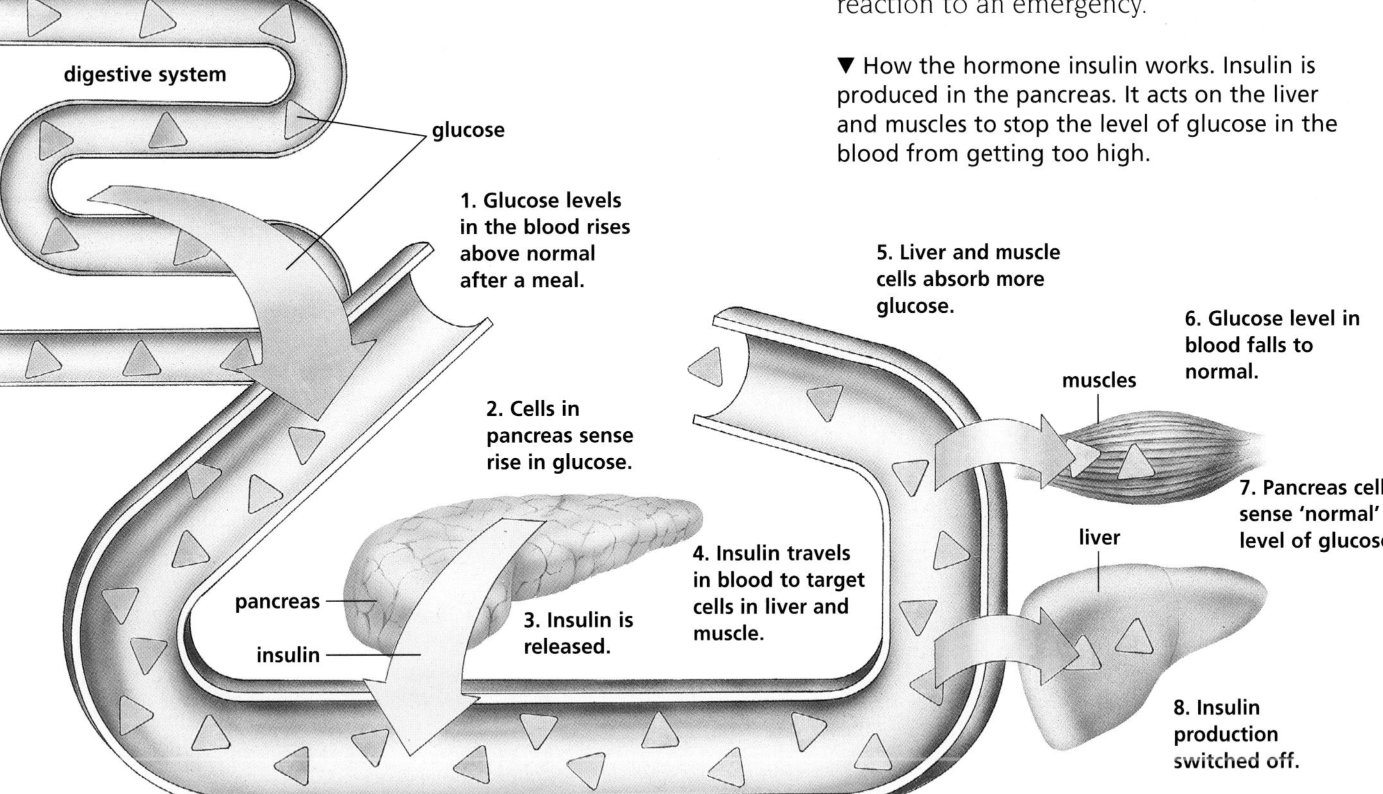

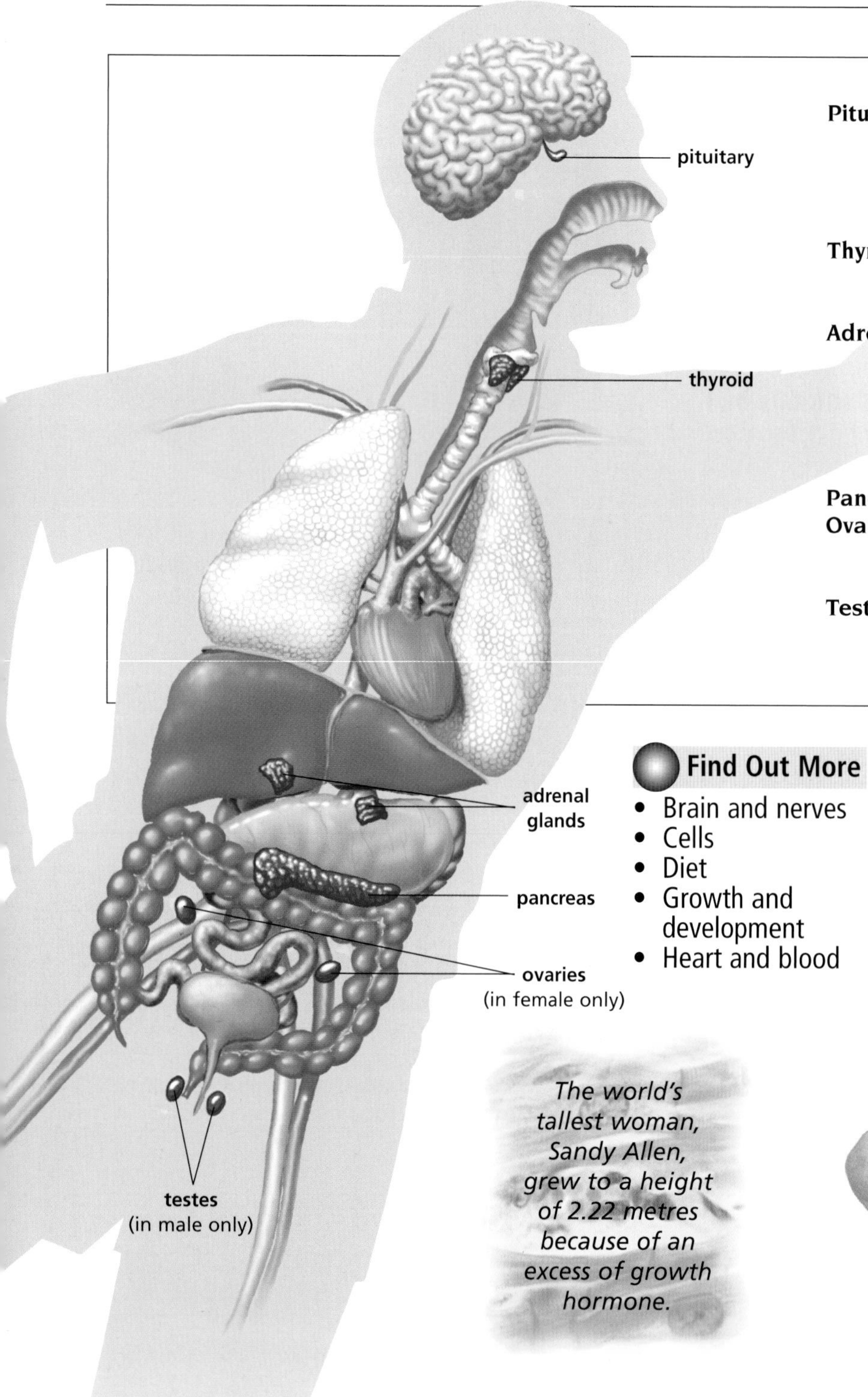

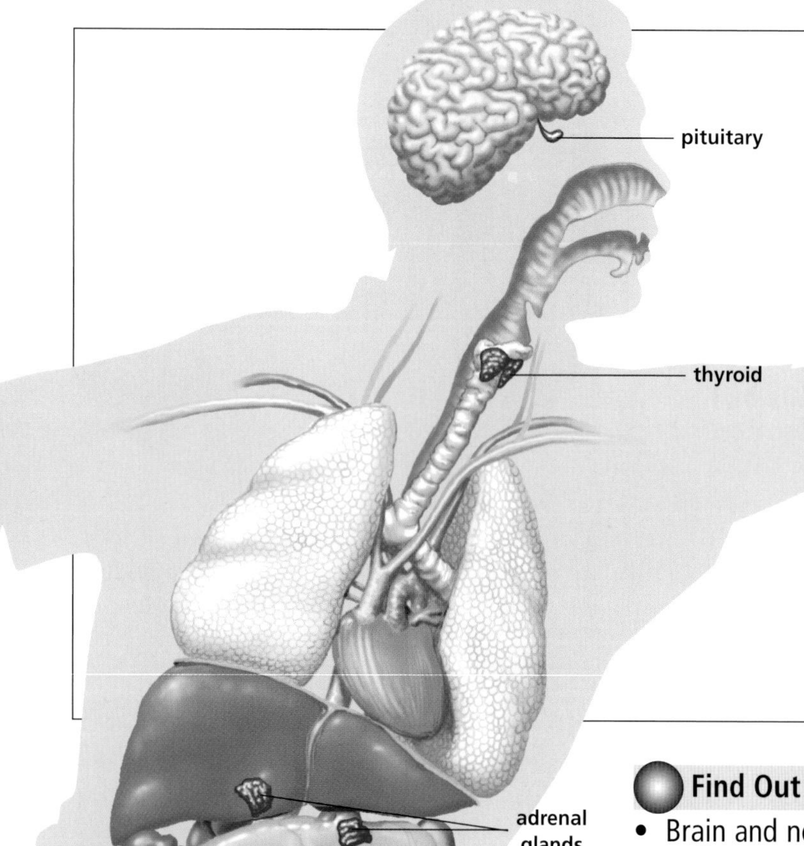

THE BODY'S HORMONES

Pituitary: controls activity of thyroid, adrenal and reproductive glands. Other hormones stimulate the womb to contract during birth, and stimulate milk production after a baby is born.

Thyroid: thyroxine controls the rate at which we grow, and how fast food is converted to energy in our cells.

Adrenal glands: adrenaline speeds up the heart and breathing, causes sweating and diverts blood to the muscles, in response to an emergency. Cortisone helps fight stress and shock. Aldosterone helps regulate water and salt in the blood.

Pancreas: insulin controls the body's use of glucose.

Ovaries: oestrogen and progesterone control female appearance and the release of eggs, and prepare the body for pregnancy.

Testes: testosterone controls the development of male appearance and the production of sperm cells.

Find Out More

- Brain and nerves
- Cells
- Diet
- Growth and development
- Heart and blood

The world's tallest woman, Sandy Allen, grew to a height of 2.22 metres because of an excess of growth hormone.

Hormone control centre

The pituitary gland, attached to the underside of the brain, releases hormones that control the activities of other endocrine glands. It also produces other hormones, for example one that controls the amount of water filtered in the kidneys. The pituitary is attached to the brain by the hypothalamus, which links together the nervous system and the hormonal system.

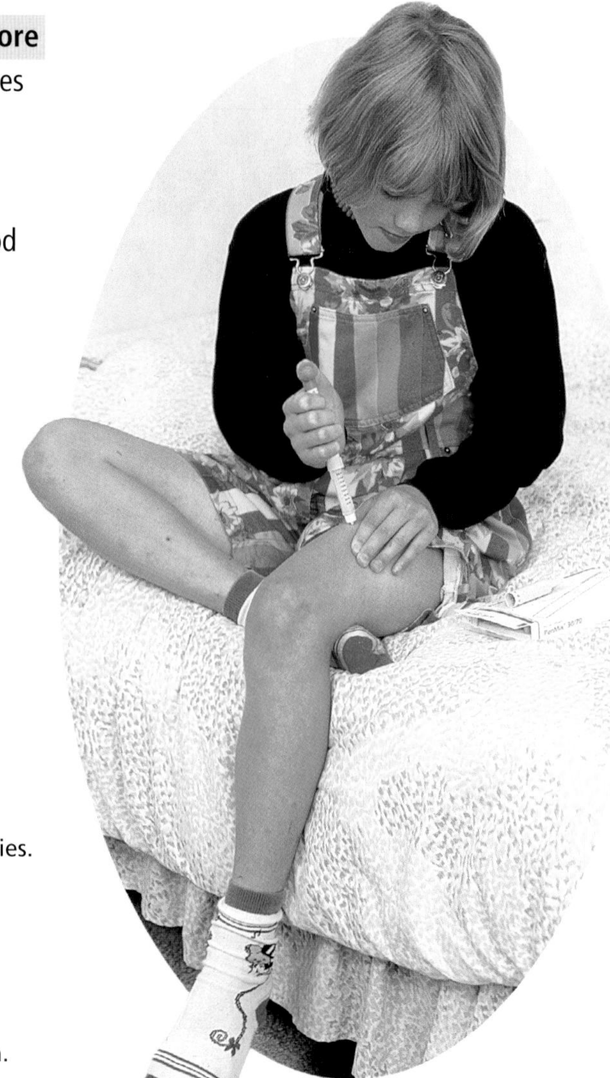

▶ People suffering from the disease diabetes do not produce enough insulin in their bodies. Their blood sugar levels can become dangerously high unless, like this girl, they give themselves regular injections of insulin.

Glass

Take some sand and some limestone, two of the most common materials in the ground. Add some soda ash, and heat the mixture to about 1500 °C, until it becomes a red-hot, molten mass. Let it cool, and the mass becomes transparent. It has turned into glass.

Glass is one of the most remarkable materials there is. Not only is it transparent, but it is also waterproof and does not rot or rust. It is resistant to all common chemicals and is easy to clean. It can easily be shaped into blocks, sheets and fibres. Glass fibres are widely used for reinforcing (strengthening) plastics. In fibre optics, very fine glass fibres are used to carry data and communications, such as telephone calls.

The main ingredient in glass-making is sand, the mineral silica. If this is melted, then cooled, it forms glass. But other ingredients must be added to it to make it melt at a reasonable temperature. The ordinary glass used for bottles and windows is known as soda-lime glass because it is made using soda ash and limestone.

▶ A magnificent stained-glass window in Canterbury cathedral, UK. Coloured glasses are made by including compounds of certain metals (copper, chromium, nickel, cobalt) in the glass-making recipe.

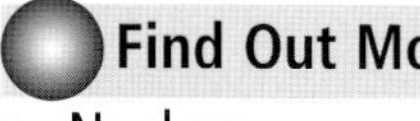

- Nuclear energy
- Plastics

Special glasses

Other ingredients are added to the glass-making recipe to produce glasses with special properties. Adding lead oxide, for example, makes lead, or crystal, glass. This has extra brilliance and, when expertly cut, gleams and sparkles like a diamond. Glass with a very high lead content is made for the nuclear industry, because it blocks harmful radiation.

Ordinary glass expands rapidly when it is heated. When you pour boiling water into a cold glass bottle, for example, the sudden expansion will make it crack and shatter. But when you add boron to the glass-making recipe, you produce a glass that hardly expands at all. This borosilicate glass is used to make heat-resistant cookware and laboratory equipment.

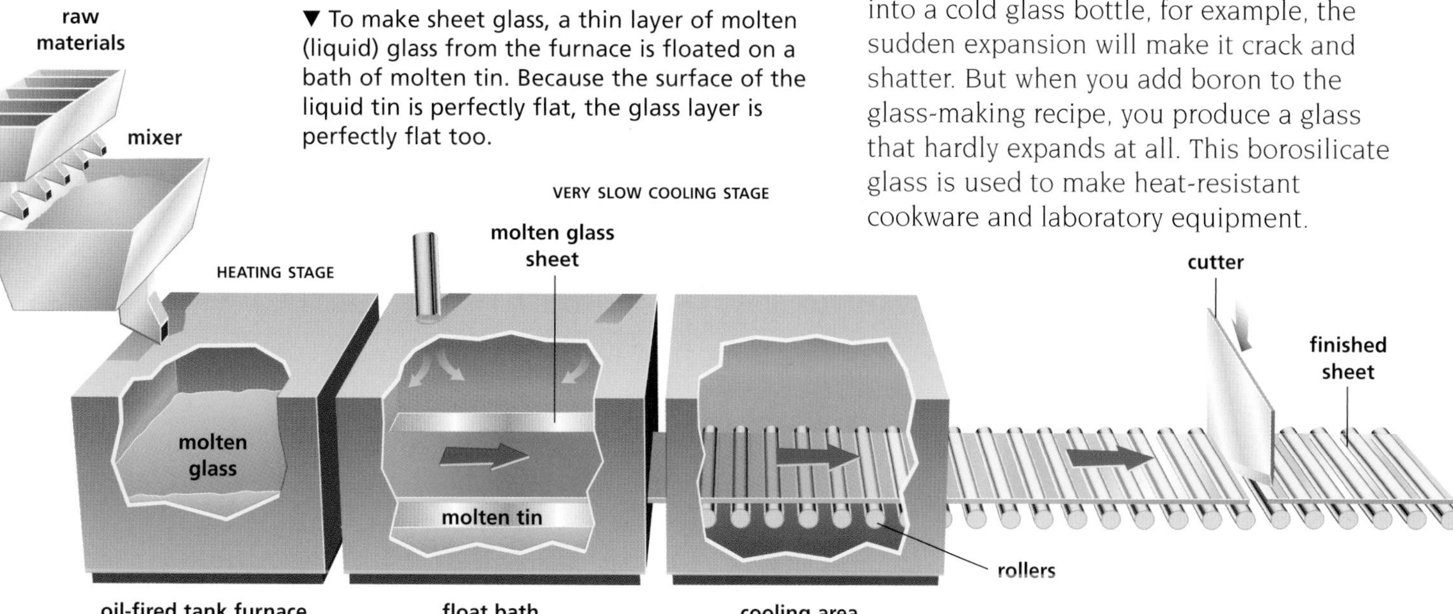

▼ To make sheet glass, a thin layer of molten (liquid) glass from the furnace is floated on a bath of molten tin. Because the surface of the liquid tin is perfectly flat, the glass layer is perfectly flat too.

Gliders *see* Flight and flow

Global warming

Scientists estimate that the Earth's surface is warming up by 1 °C every 40 years. Two and a half degrees in one century might not sound like much, but it is at least 50 times faster than any climate change in the past 10,000 years.

▶ Ice calving (breaking off) from the Childs glacier, Alaska, USA. Global warming is causing glaciers and ice sheets to melt at both the North and South Poles.

Earth's climate changes naturally, but the global warming of the last century can't be explained by natural processes alone. Most global warming is probably caused by our pollution of the environment.

The greenhouse effect

The Earth's surface absorbs sunlight and turns it into heat. Some of this heat escapes into space, but some is absorbed by gases such as carbon dioxide and water vapour in the atmosphere. These gases are known as 'greenhouse gases' because they act like the glass of a greenhouse, letting sunlight in, but not letting heat out.

Without the natural greenhouse effect, the Earth's surface would be too cold for anything to live on. The problem is that people are polluting the atmosphere with extra greenhouse gases. The gases build up in the atmosphere and trap more and more heat.

Effects of global warming

It is impossible to know exactly what will happen if it keeps getting warmer, but global warming will certainly change weather patterns. More ocean water will evaporate and create more rain, causing flooding in coastal areas. More water will evaporate from the land, leaving many places drier. As the climates change, some plants and animals will migrate into new areas, but others will die out.

The results of global warming could be disastrous. But there are many things we can do to slow global warming down, such as using less electricity, recycling rubbish, and walking or cycling instead of driving.

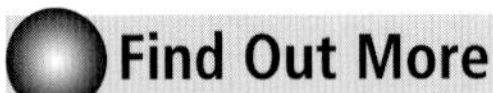

Find Out More

- Atmosphere
- Climate
- Water cycle

Global warming will make sea levels rise, causing coastal areas to flood and contaminating fresh water supplies with salt water. Many islands in the Pacific will be drowned completely.

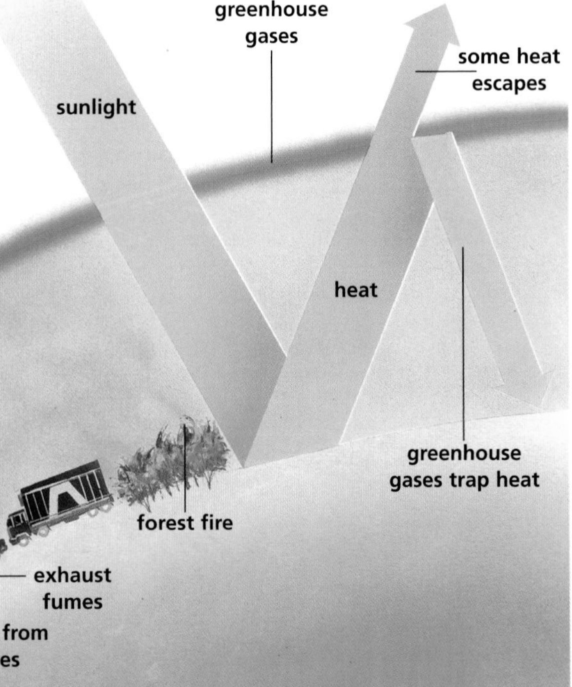

▼ Many different things contribute to the greenhouse effect. As well as burning fuels and releasing chemicals into the air, humans have cut down many forests. Plants absorb carbon dioxide, so the loss of trees increases the levels of this greenhouse gas.

Glues and adhesives

When you lick a stamp, join the parts of a model together, or stick a Post-it note in a book, you are using adhesives. Adhesives are sticky substances that bond surfaces together.

Glues and gums are adhesives made from natural materials. Glues come from animals. They are made by boiling up such things as the bones and skin of cattle, and fish bones. Gums come from the sticky resins made by certain plants.

However, most adhesives used these days are synthetic, and are usually made from petroleum chemicals. These adhesives are plastic materials, or polymers, which set after they have been applied.

Find Out More

- Mixtures and solutions
- Oil products
- Plastics

Making contact

There are hundreds of different kinds of synthetic adhesives. For example, contact adhesives are made from synthetic rubber dissolved in a solvent. You coat each of the surfaces to be joined with adhesive, let them dry for a while, and then press the surfaces together.

Model-makers use an adhesive containing the plastic polystyrene in a solvent. After it has set, it can be softened by warming, which makes it easy to reshape joints. It is called a thermoplastic adhesive, because it softens when heated.

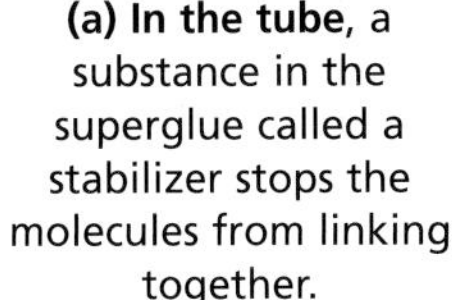

(a) In the tube, a substance in the superglue called a stabilizer stops the molecules from linking together.

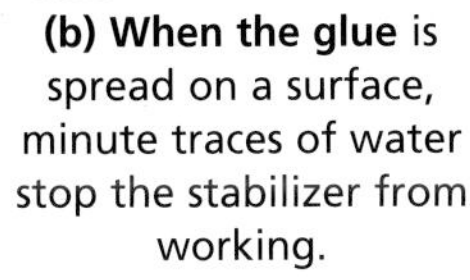

(b) When the glue is spread on a surface, minute traces of water stop the stabilizer from working.

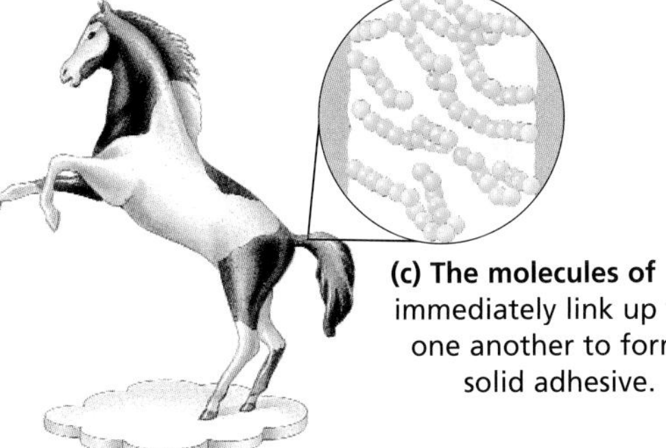

(c) The molecules of resin immediately link up with one another to form a solid adhesive.

▶ How superglue works.

Big sticks

Among the strongest adhesives are the epoxy resins. They have even been used to stick cars to advertising hoardings. Epoxy resins often come in two parts that have to be mixed together. One part is the resin, the other is a hardener. Adding the hardener makes the resin set into a rigid plastic material, or thermoset polymer. This process takes about half an hour. The adhesives called superglues, however, set in seconds. They are made from acrylic resins.

▼ High-tech aircraft like this B-2 Spirit stealth bomber are made from a number of different extra-light materials. Super-strong adhesives are often used to join these materials together.

Gold and silver

◀ This gold necklace, found in a Roman grave, is almost 2000 years old.

In 1939, a horde of treasure was found in the remains of a buried ship at Sutton Hoo in eastern England. It included 41 items made of solid gold, among them a beautiful helmet. When they were washed, they looked as good as they must have done when they were buried 1300 years earlier.

Gold has always been admired for its rich beauty. It remains beautiful because it does not corrode, or rust, in the air or in the ground.

Because gold is so prized, it is called a precious metal. It was once used to make coins, but its main use today is in jewellery. Usually, other metals (such as copper) are added to it to make a harder alloy.

Beat that!

Many metals can be beaten into shape. We say they are malleable. Gold is the most malleable metal of all. It can be beaten into gold leaf so thin that 10,000 sheets stacked together would measure only 1 millimetre thick. Gold is also the most ductile of metals, which means that it can be pulled into very fine wire without breaking.

Silver is another beautiful precious metal that has been used for jewellery since ancient times. But its main use today is in photography, because many silver salts darken when they are exposed to light.

Like gold, silver is ductile and malleable. It is also the best conductor of heat and electricity that we know.

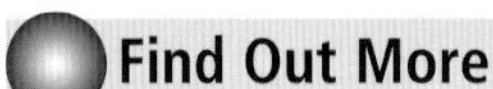

Find Out More

- Metals and non-metals
- Mining
- Photography
- Resources

▶ This piece of rock, which contains native gold, comes from California, USA.

▼ When gold was discovered in Australia in the 19th century, people flocked to the gold-fields from all over the world. This painting shows prospectors hoping to strike it rich.

The platinum group

Some metals are even more precious than gold. Platinum, for example, is rarer, harder and melts at a higher temperature. Its main use in industry is as a catalyst, a substance that helps chemical reactions take place. Platinum is one of a group of heavy metals with similar properties.

Rich deposits

All the precious metals are found native, or in metal form in the ground. Native deposits provide most gold and platinum. But most silver comes from silver ores, such as argentite. The ores are treated with chemicals to produce the metal.

Gorillas *see* Classification, Conservation • **Granite** *see* Rocks • **Graphite** *see* Carbon

Grasslands

For part of their lives, locusts are solitary insects. But then sometimes, if food runs short, billions of them gather in vast swarms and take to the air. The hungry swarms land on grasslands, and eat all the grass. A large swarm of locusts can eat as much food in a day as 10 elephants or 2500 people.

▶ The sharp eyes of the steppe eagle spot prey such as this hamster from high in the air. The eagle swoops in for the kill, using its powerful talons to stun or kill its prey.

Grasslands grow in places where it is too dry for forests but too wet for deserts. There are still some natural grasslands left, such as the savannah in Africa, the prairies in North America, the pampas in South America and the steppes in Asia. But in many areas grasslands have been ploughed up by people and used to grow crops.

Grass and grazers

Grasses are tough plants. Grasslands are home to grazing animals such as antelopes and kangaroos, which chew the grasses almost down to the ground. But most grasses just grow thicker and faster after being eaten. They also grow back well after fires, which are common on grasslands. In dry or cold seasons, grasses die back completely above the ground. Animals may have to migrate long distances to find enough food and water.

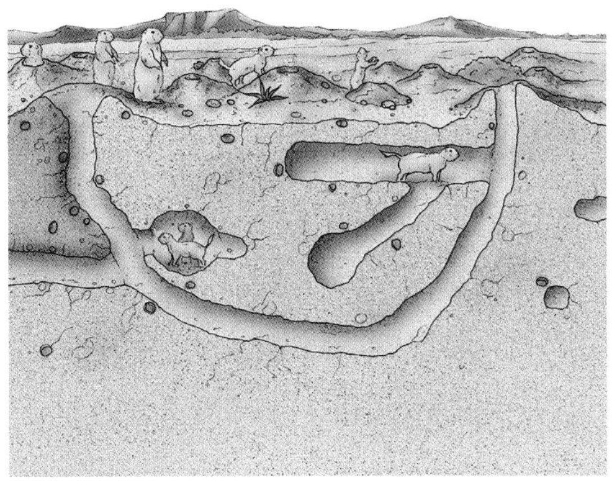

◀ Prairie dogs dig tunnels under the North American prairies to escape predators and shelter from hot or cold weather.

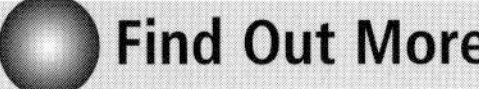

Find Out More

- Birds
- Ecology
- Insects

Insects

Scurrying around among the grass stems are hordes of tiny insects such as beetles, ants, grasshoppers and caterpillars. Because there are so many of them, insects can eat far more than the big grazers. Many of them, especially termites and dung beetles, play an important role in turning animal dung and the remains of dead plants and animals into rich soil.

◀ These cheetahs have just made a kill on the African savannah. Cheetahs – the fastest land animals on Earth – rely on their speed to catch their prey because they can be seen easily on the open grassland.

Gravity

However hard you toss a ball up into the air, it will fall back down. A mysterious force called gravity pulls everything towards the ground. It's mysterious because no one knows why gravity exists – it's one of the great unsolved questions of science.

Gravity pulls whole objects together. If they are free to move, then gravity gets them moving. This is why raindrops, autumn leaves and balls fall towards the ground, the surface of our planet Earth.

Forces and fields

Whenever two objects are near each other, gravity acts between them and tries to pull them together. The strength of the force depends on the mass (the amount of material) in both objects. Because our planet is so massive, there is a strong force of gravity between the Earth and everything that is on or near it.

The Earth's field of gravity extends out into space to the Moon and beyond. Gravity keeps the Moon in its orbit or path around the Earth. In the same way, the Sun's gravity holds the Earth, and all the other planets of the Solar System, in their orbits around the Sun.

Find Out More

- Forces
- Moon
- Orbits
- Solar System
- Universe

FROM AN APPLE TO THE UNIVERSE

As a young man, British scientist Isaac Newton (1642–1727) saw an apple fall from a tree. Of course, he wasn't the first to see this, but he was the first to explain what was happening. He believed that gravity causes an apple to fall, and then had the daring idea that gravity is a force that exists not only on Earth but throughout the whole Universe. Newton went on to prove this to be true in 1687, and scientists now use his ideas to predict the future of the Universe.

▼ The force of gravity acting on a rocket is related to its distance from the centre of the Earth. The pull of gravity falls very quickly as the rocket leaves Earth. At twice the distance from the Earth's centre, gravity is a quarter the strength it is on the Earth's surface.

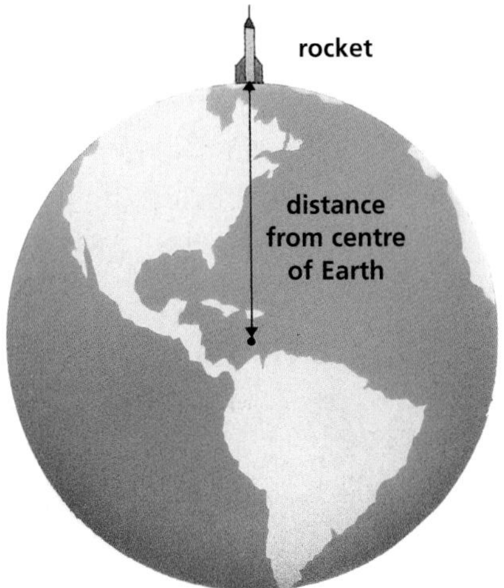

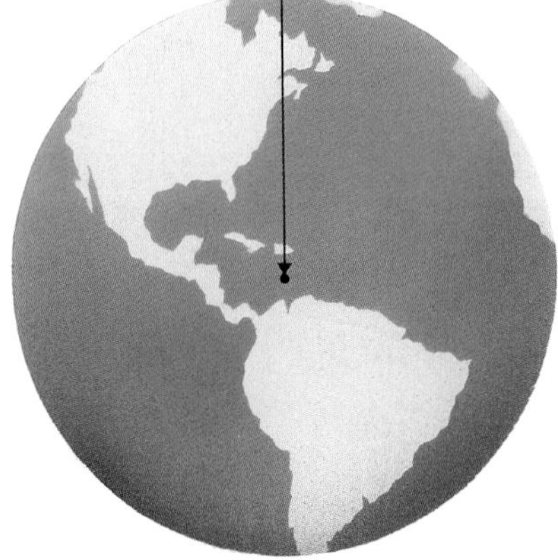

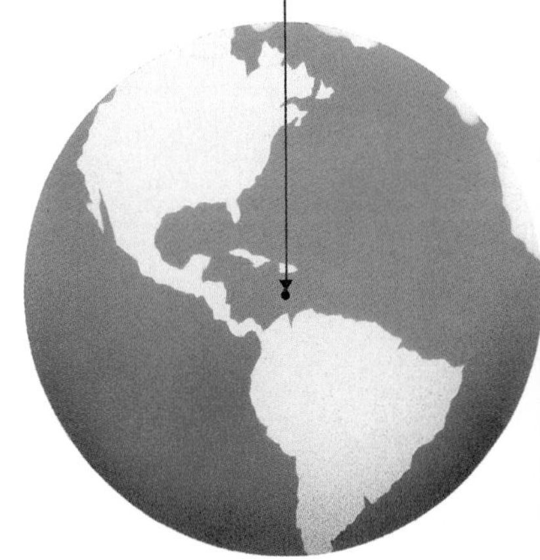

▶ If you drop one ball and throw another forward from the same height, both balls take exacly the same time to reach the ground. This is because both balls fall the same vertical distance.

▼ An astronaut floats in space high above the Earth. In space, an astronaut is weightless and is said to experience 'zero gravity'. However, gravity is not zero in space. It is still acting on the astronaut and causes him or her to move in an orbit around the Earth.

▼ Imagine standing on a tower high enough to be outside the Earth's atmosphere. If you threw a ball from the tower, gravity will pull it to Earth (a). But if you could throw the ball as fast as a rocket (b), the curve of its fall would match the curve of the Earth, and the ball would orbit the Earth.

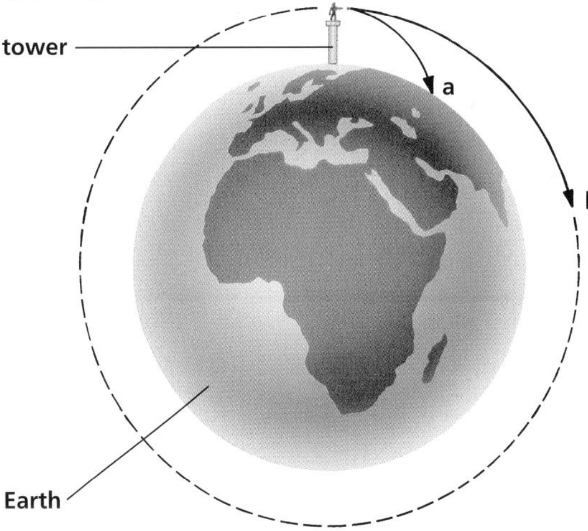

Gaining and losing weight

Gravity gives everything its weight. The force of gravity between you and the Earth pulls you down, and your weight is the amount of force that you exert on the ground – or on a weighing machine.

However, if you were to fly to the Moon, you would weigh only a sixth of your Earth weight. This is because the Moon is much smaller than the Earth, and has only about a sixth of the Earth's gravity.

Gravure *see* Printing • **Greenhouse effect** *see* Global warming

Growth and development

Young babies are almost helpless: they can suck, swallow and grasp, but they must have almost everything done for them. And yet, within one or two years, they will probably be walking and starting to talk. By the age of 5 they will be able to speak fluently, draw and may be starting to read.

▶ We learn to read from about the age of five. Reading gives us another way to learn about the world about us.

As babies grow to become children, and then adults, the shape and proportions of their bodies change. A baby's head makes up a quarter of its body length, but in an adult, the head accounts for only an eighth of the total height. Our bodies and minds develop much more quickly when we are babies than at any other time. Over our first few months of life, our muscles become stronger and we learn to co-ordinate our actions. New, exciting activities such as climbing the stairs, jumping and riding a bike become possible.

Growing and changing

From the age of about 5 years, a child's body grows steadily. Then, from the age of 10 years for girls and a little older for boys, there is a sudden growth spurt.

At this time, known as puberty, the ovaries of a girl start to release the sex hormone oestrogen. Her body shape changes. She grows taller, her breasts develop and hair starts to grow under her arms and between her legs. She also starts to menstruate, as her ovaries start to release one egg each month.

A boy also gains height rapidly at puberty. His testes start to produce the hormone testosterone.

Girls are fully grown by the age of 16 years.

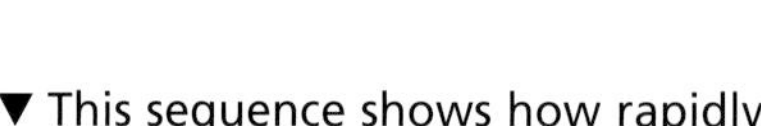

▼ This sequence shows how rapidly boys' and girls' bodies change as they grow up.

baby **toddler** **child** **adolescent** (at puberty) **young adult**

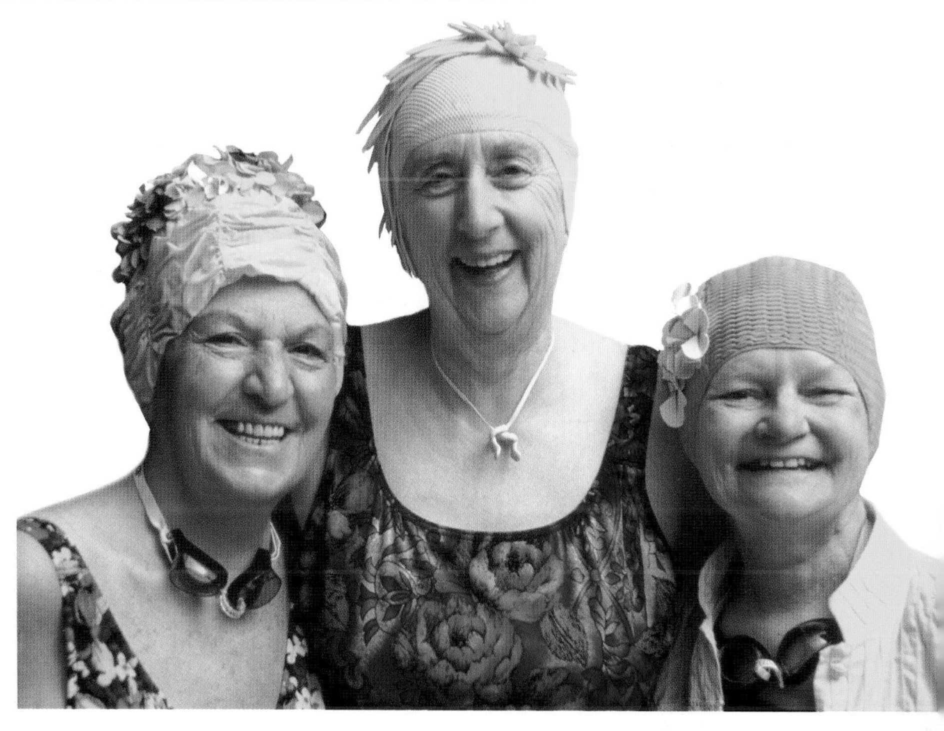

▶ It is important to stay fit and healthy no matter what your age. Swimming is one activity for people of all ages.

He grows hair under his arms, on his face and between his legs, and his voice gets deeper. His penis and testes enlarge and begin to produce sperm.

New skills

As children, we learn to read and write. We also develop important social skills, such as how to co-operate with others and make friends. Learning continues throughout our lives. When we leave school and go to work, we must learn new skills to do our jobs. We must also learn how to organize our time and money. Later we may learn to care for our children and teach them the things we have learned.

Growing older

By the age of about 20, the human body is fully developed. Muscles are in peak condition and so is the brain.

Gradually a person's body starts to age. No one can explain exactly why. Although our cells are renewed throughout our lives, it seems that over time our genetic code becomes less precise and more mistakes creep in. Our skin starts to wrinkle, and our eyesight and hearing become less sensitive. Older people tend to have slower reactions and do not resist disease so well.

Find Out More

- Cells
- Genetics
- Glands and hormones
- Sex and reproduction
- Speech and language

Boys are fully grown by the age of 18 years.

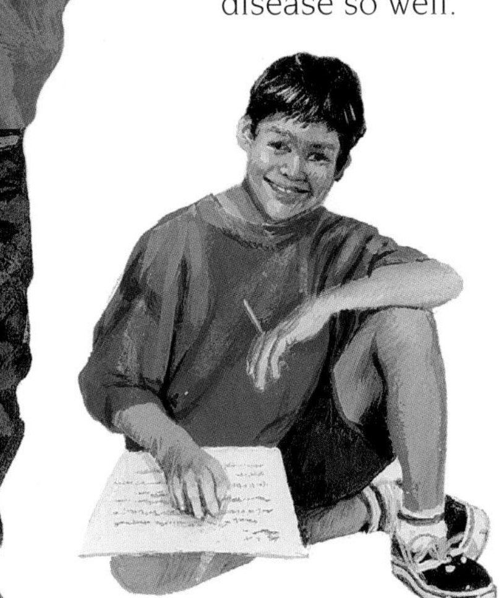

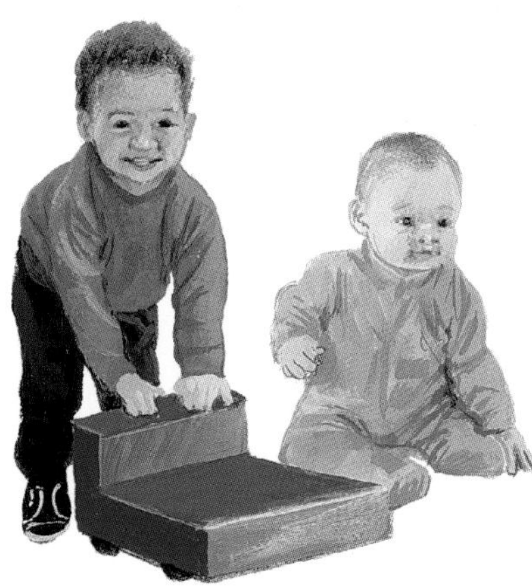

young adult **adolescent** (at puberty) **child** **toddler** **baby**

Guns *see* Weapons • **Gyroscopes** *see* Navigation • **Hair** *see* Skin and hair

Hardware

One day, scientists will be able to make plastic computers that can be rolled up and put in your pocket. These computers will have colour screens made of an amazing bendy plastic that makes light when electric current passes through it.

Plastic computers and screens are still some way off. In the meantime, we must make do with rigid screens.

The computer and screen are part of what is called computer hardware. This contrasts with the software – the programs and instructions that run the computer.

The main computer unit is the box that contains all the electronic circuits that make the computer work, such as the processing and memory units. These are circuit boards carrying microchips and other parts. The main computer unit also has sockets to plug in to other hardware, and a power supply. It also contains one or more disk drives.

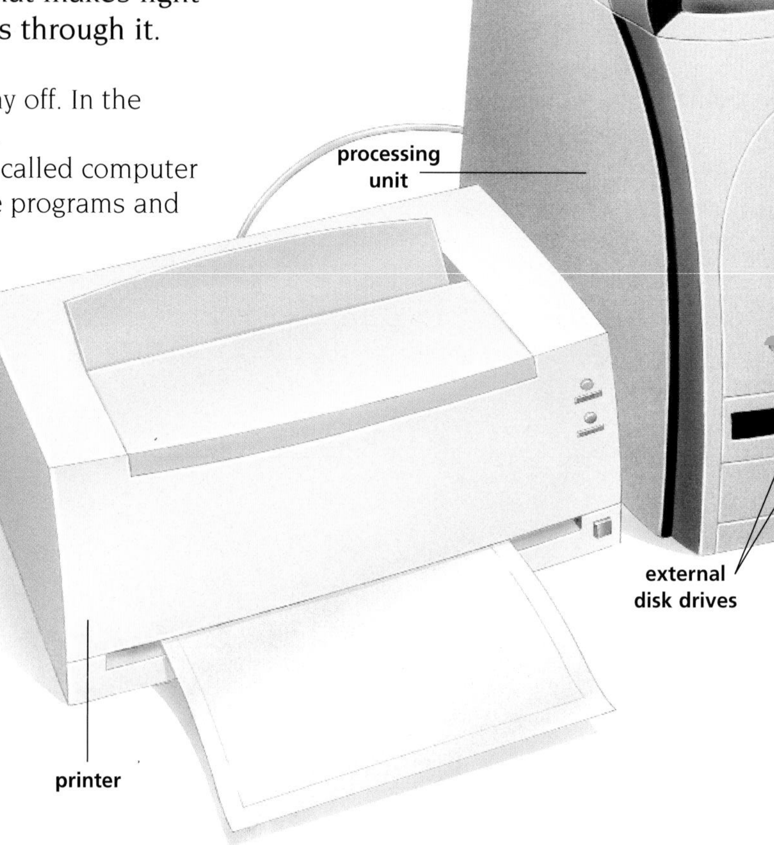

The computer's hard-disk drive is actually a number of disks, one on top of the other. Each one has its own recording and playback head. Using a number of disks makes storing and retrieving data much faster.

Window on a computer's world

The screen (called a monitor or VDU) helps us keep a check on how the computer is working, and displays information and pictures.

The common type of monitor uses a cathode-ray tube (CRT). These tubes are big and take up a lot of desk space.

Some newer computers have flat-screen monitors. They use only a third of the power of a CRT and take up much less space. But they are more difficult and expensive to make. Laptop screens use liquid crystals to form an image. These work in much the same way as the display on a digital watch.

▶ Laptop computers have to squeeze everything into a small space. Instead of using a mouse, you can move your finger on a screen-shaped rubber pad.

Keyed up

Information is typed into a computer using a keyboard. Pressing a key on a keyboard connects two metal contacts. This makes electric current flow, so the computer knows which key has been pressed.

A mouse makes a computer easier to use. Instead of having to type everything, you can point and click anywhere on the screen. A simple mouse has a ball inside it that rolls as you move the mouse around. Rollers around the ball sense the ball's movement, and pass this information to the computer. Some mice now use a laser instead of the ball.

▶ Computer screens based on CRTs are bulky and use a lot of power. Newer flat screens use low power but are very expensive.

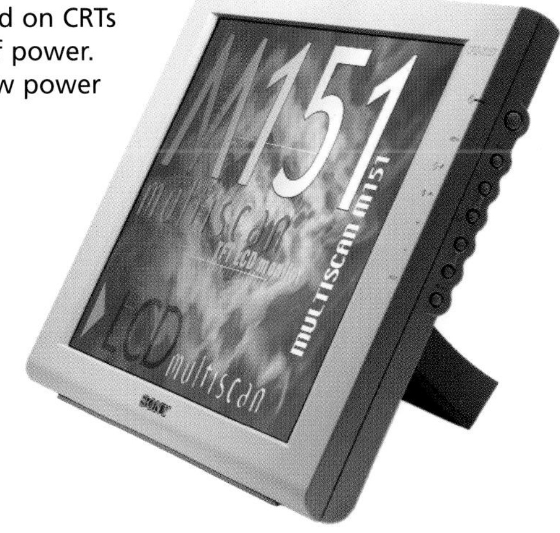

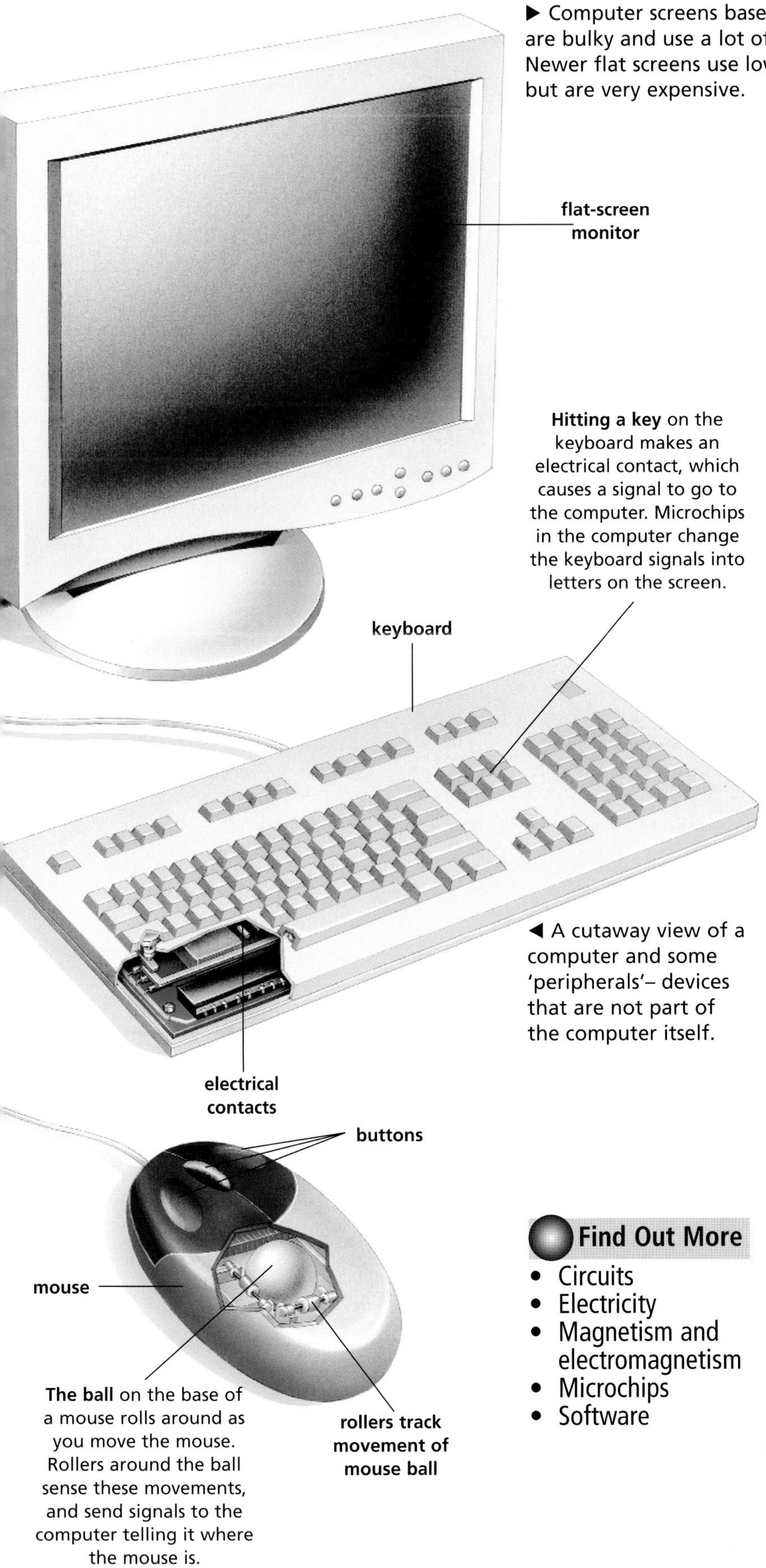
flat-screen monitor
Hitting a key on the keyboard makes an electrical contact, which causes a signal to go to the computer. Microchips in the computer change the keyboard signals into letters on the screen.
keyboard
electrical contacts
buttons
mouse
The ball on the base of a mouse rolls around as you move the mouse. Rollers around the ball sense these movements, and send signals to the computer telling it where the mouse is.
rollers track movement of mouse ball

◀ A cutaway view of a computer and some 'peripherals'– devices that are not part of the computer itself.

If you like computer games, you can plug in a joystick. This not only lets you steer, say, a starship around the screen, but it also has extra buttons that make games more fun.

Going for a spin

Disks are a good way of either storing data or taking it from one computer to another. There are two main types of disk. Magnetic disks, like a computer's hard drive or a floppy disk, store data as patterns of magnetism. Optical disks, like CDs or DVDs, store data (or music) in the form of tiny pits in the shiny surface. Optical disks can store hundreds, or even thousands of times more information than a floppy disk.

Disks store all sorts of things – including pictures. Digital cameras take pictures that are stored in memory chips or on a tiny floppy disk. They can be used directly in computer files. For pictures that already exist on paper, you can use a scanner to copy the image into the computer.

To get copies of documents out of the computer, you need a printer. Printers simply turn the text or pictures on the screen into tiny dots on paper. The dots can be made of ink or, in a laser printer, a powder called toner.

Find Out More

- Circuits
- Electricity
- Magnetism and electromagnetism
- Microchips
- Software

Microchips will soon be able to store as much data as a computer hard drive. So hard disks will one day be replaced by cards containing memory chips.

Harmony (musical) *see* Music • **Harvey, William** *see* Heart and blood

Health

London in the middle of the 19th century was a filthy and unhealthy place. Sewage found its way into rivers and into the drinking water. In 1858 – in what is known as the Great Stink – the River Thames became so smelly that Members of Parliament fell ill. They decided to build an underground sewage system for the city.

▲ Senior marathon runners show how regular exercise keeps the heart and muscles fit and healthy.

By the end of the 19th century people in Britain and other wealthy countries were living much longer, healthier lives. A clean water supply was one of the main reasons why.

In poorer countries clean water is still one of the most pressing health needs. Water contaminated by sewage spreads diseases such as cholera, typhoid, dysentery and river blindness. And across the world more people die each year from malaria than any other disease, and mosquitoes, which carry malaria, breed in stagnant water.

Find Out More
- Diet
- Diseases
- Immune system
- Medicine

▼ These people in West Africa are being given a pill to prevent river blindness. The medicine kills the parasites before they can damage a person's eyes.

Diet and exercise

Conditions in the environment can have a huge impact on your health. But the way you live also makes a big difference. A healthy diet and lots of exercise are vital for good health.

For a balanced diet, you need to eat foods that give you energy, and build up your strength, but vitamins, minerals and fibre are also important. A shortage of vitamin C, for example, reduces the body's ability to fight infection.

Healthy hearts

Many deaths in the developed world are caused by heart attacks. Being overweight can cause high blood pressure and make it harder for the heart to pump. Regular exercise reduces the risks of heart disease.

Prevention is better than cure. Vaccination programmes have succeeded in getting rid of smallpox, reducing deaths from polio and saving thousands of people's lives.

Hearing *see* Ears, Sound, Human senses, Senses

Heart and blood

A city needs a transport system to carry people and goods from place to place. In the same way our bodies need a transport system to carry nutrients and oxygen. The body's method of transport is the blood. Blood flows to every part of the body, travelling through a complex network of tubes.

The network that carries our blood is made up of tubes, or vessels, called arteries, veins and capillaries. Blood is pumped around this network by the heart. Arteries are the largest and strongest vessels. They divide into smaller and smaller vessels. The smallest ones are called capillaries.

Collection and delivery

Capillaries are so small that they can fit between cells. Their walls are so thin that food and oxygen from the blood can pass straight through into the cells. Waste from the cells passes back into the blood to be carried away. The capillaries join up again, making larger tubes, which in turn join to become veins. Blood travels more slowly as it makes its way back to the heart. Larger veins have valves inside them to keep blood moving in the right direction.

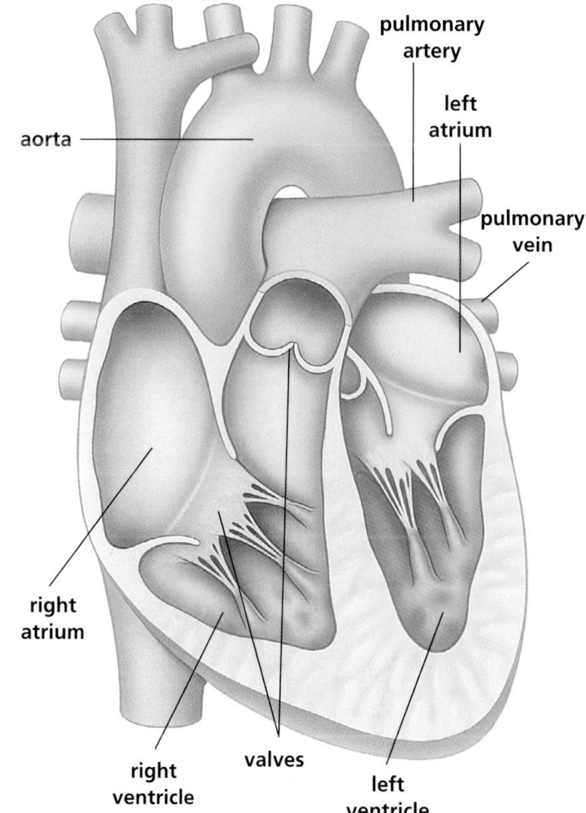

▶ The heart has four chambers. The upper chambers, the atria, pump blood to the ventricles. The lower chambers, the ventricles, are larger and pump blood out of the heart. The left ventricle pumps blood all round the body.

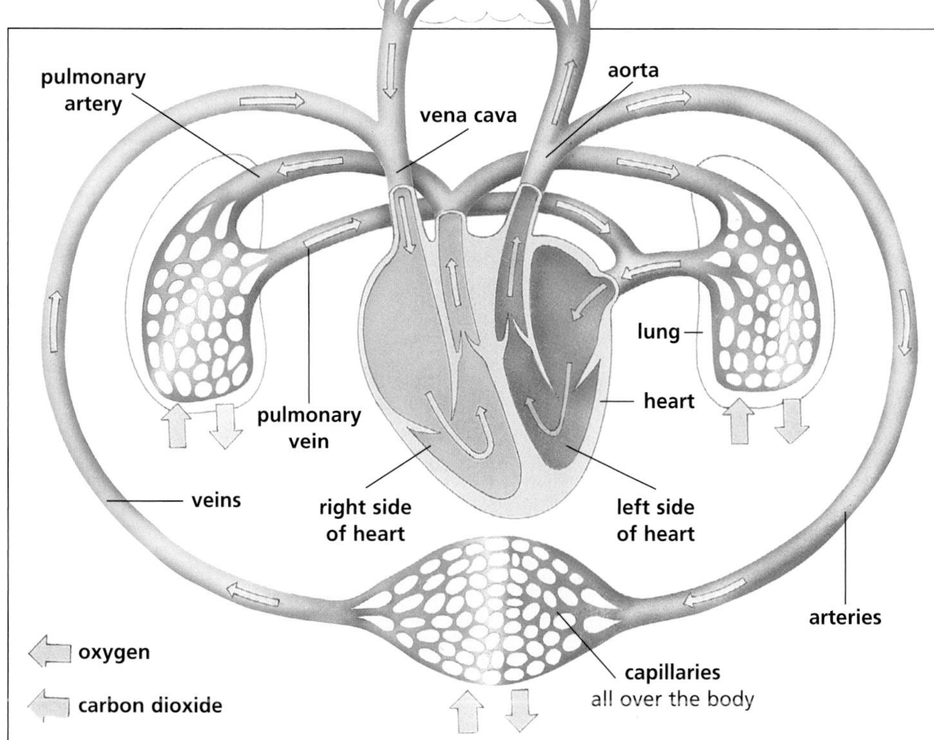

THE HEART

Your heart is made up of two separate pumps. The right-hand pump receives blood from the body and sends it to the lungs through the pulmonary arteries. In the lungs, the blood picks up oxygen. Then it returns to the left side of the heart through the pulmonary veins.

The left side of the heart then pumps this oxygenated blood through arteries to organs and muscles all over the body. Through capillaries in the organs and muscles, the blood gives up its oxygen and collects waste carbon dioxide.

When it has done this, the blood returns in veins to the right side of the heart, to be sent to the lungs for more oxygen.

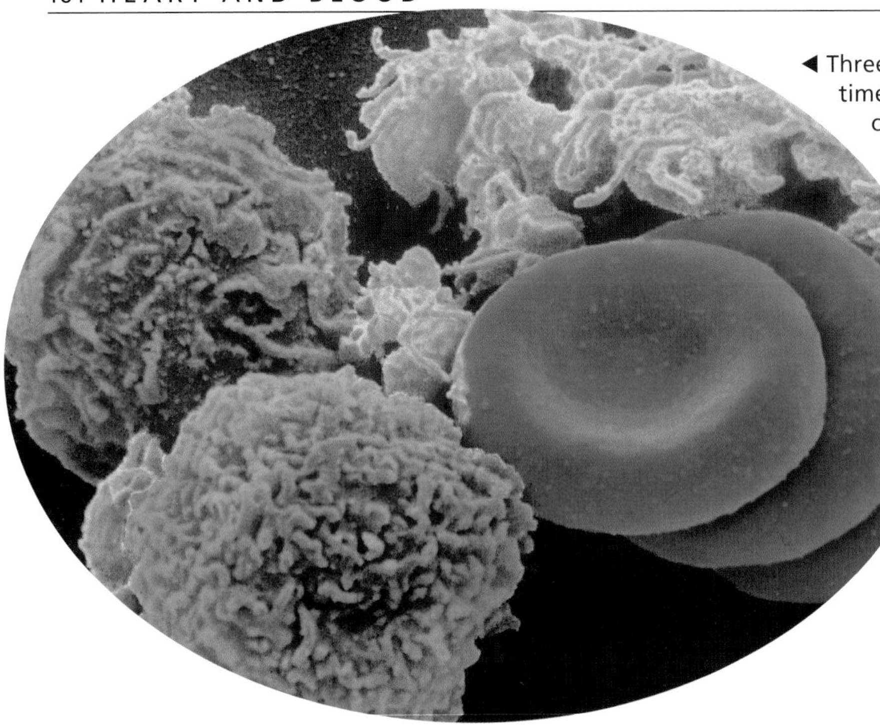

◀ Three different types of blood cell magnified many times. In this picture, the white blood cells are coloured blue. The cells coloured pink are platelets. Platelets help to seal cuts in the skin. They clump together to form clots and produce a mass of fibres (shown here in orange) that trap red blood cells and dry to form a scab.

What is blood?

Almost half of the blood in your body is made up of red blood cells. These tiny red discs contain a substance called haemoglobin. This picks up oxygen in the lungs and releases it into the cells, which need it for energy.

Blood also contains a smaller number of white blood cells – about one for every 500 red cells. Their job is to fight infections. All the blood cells are swept along in a liquid called plasma, which contains dissolved chemicals and carbon dioxide. Fresh supplies of blood cells are continually made in the bone marrow.

The pump that never tires

The driving force that keeps your blood moving is your heart. The heart is made of a special type of muscle called cardiac muscle, which never gets tired. Day and night, every beat is a muscle contraction that forces about 60 millilitres of blood on its way. The heart of an adult at rest beats about 70 times a minute, but this can double during exercise.

Like any active muscle, the heart needs a good supply of blood. Sometimes the blood vessels to the heart become narrow or blocked. This causes a heart attack. Smokers and people who are overweight have a higher risk of heart attacks than others.

Find Out More

- Bones and muscles
- Digestion
- Health
- Immune system
- Lungs and breathing
- Oxygen

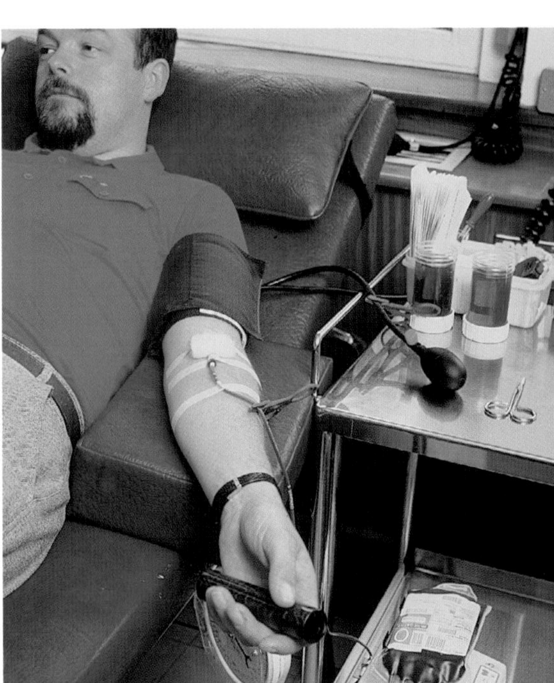

▶ A blood donor gives about 500ml of blood, which can be stored for a few weeks. The blood can be given to another person of the same blood group.

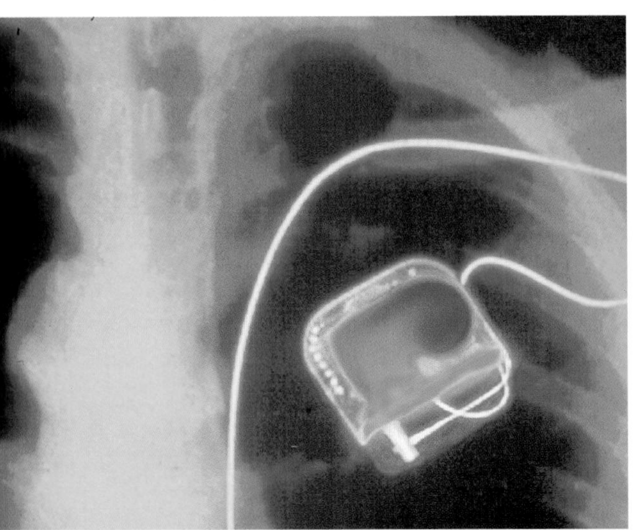

◀ Sometimes the heart's natural pacemaker, which controls heart rate, fails because of heart disease. The person in this X-ray has had an artificial pacemaker implanted in their chest, which allows them to lead a normal, active life

Your heart beats non-stop, 24 hours a day, 7 days a week. If you live to be 70, that comes to over 2.5 billion heartbeats!

Heat

If you hold the wooden handle of a spade, and then touch the metal, the metal feels colder than the wood, even though the two materials are really the same temperature. This is because of the way heat flows.

Your fingertips are warmer than the metal. Heat flows easily into the metal from them, because metal is a good conductor. As they lose heat, your fingertips get cooler and they feel cold. Heat does not flow easily into wood, which is a poor conductor. That's why your fingertips stay warm when they touch it.

HOW HEAT FLOWS

In a kitchen, heat usually comes from burning gas or electricity. The heat has to flow into food to cook it. Heat flows in three ways – conduction, convection and radiation.

Heat from a gas flame or electric hotplate enters the base of the saucepan. It flows through the metal, and into the water in the pan, by conduction.

Heat flows through the water by convection. Currents of hot water rise from the base of the pan and carry heat to all the water.

Red-hot wires heated by electricity toast bread in a toaster. The hot wire gives out heat rays that heat everything they meet. This kind of heat flow is called radiation.

▲ Most materials contract when they get colder, but water expands as it freezes to ice. This makes ice less dense than water, which causes ice to float in water, like this iceberg.

Gain and loss

Heat is a form of energy, and everything has a certain amount of heat. An object gets hotter if heat flows into it and it gains more heat. If heat flows away, an object gets colder.

Everything is made of atoms and molecules that are moving. When heat flows into something, it makes these particles move faster. When heat is lost, they slow down.

Heating up

Rub your hands together quickly: they soon feel warm. The friction makes the particles in your skin speed up, and it gets hotter. Striking a match produces enough heat in this way to cause the head of the match to burst into flame.

The Sun is our main source of heat. Heat rays radiate out from the Sun. Solar heating systems store the Sun's heat and use it to warm buildings and heat water.

Find Out More

- Energy
- Engines and turbines
- Fire
- Refrigeration
- Temperature

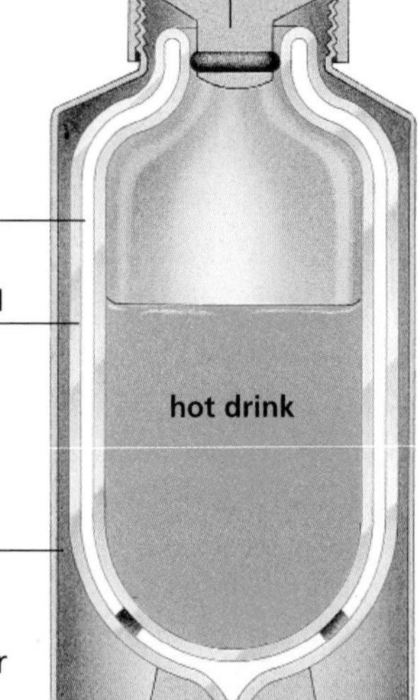

We make heat for our homes in two main ways. We burn fuel, such as gas in a cooker or coal in a fireplace, or we pass electricity through a wire – that is how electric fires work.

Your body also makes its own heat, as it consumes food and drink. This heat keeps you warm and keeps your body working.

▲ Air gets most heat from the ground, not directly from the Sun. The warm air rises, and birds like this condor ride on the spiralling current.

▶ The container in a vacuum flask has a near-vacuum between its two walls – nearly all the air has been pumped out. Vacuums are very good insulators, so little heat can get in or out.

Bigger and smaller

Heat not only makes particles move faster. It also makes them move apart, which is why a heated object expands. When Concorde is flying, its hull gets very hot and expands by about 25 centimetres!

In the same way, when something gets colder, the particles slow down and move together, so the object contracts and gets smaller.

Heating a container of gas raises its pressure as the gas particles move faster and strike the container walls with greater force. A car engine burns fuel to make hot gases, and the hot, high-pressure gases drive the engine's moving parts. A jet plane's engine works in the same way. Both of these types of engine are known as heat engines.

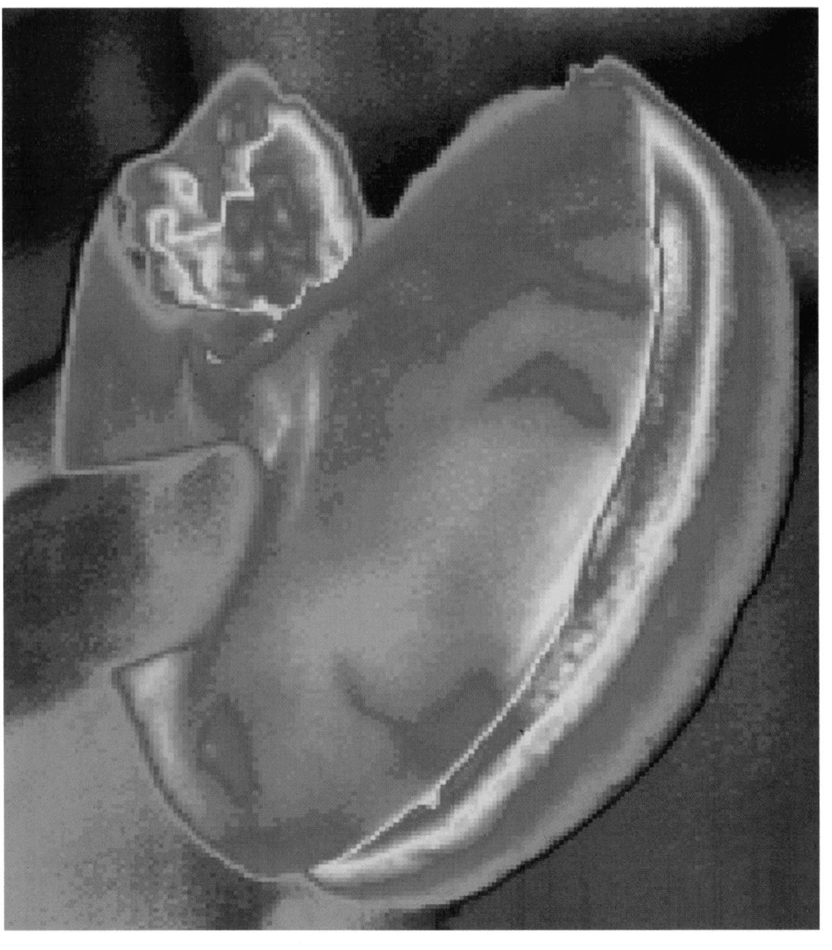

▶ In this thermograph (heat picture) of a person holding a burger, hotter and colder parts appear in different colours. The hottest parts, such as the burger itself, show up red. Parts coloured blue or purple, such as the bun, are the coldest.

Helicopters *see* Aircraft

Helium

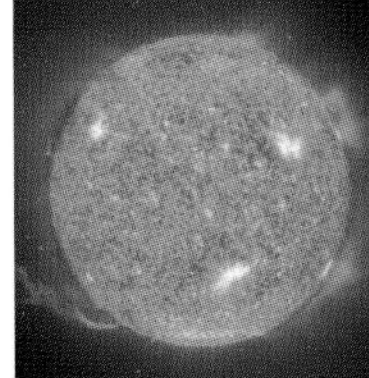

There is helium gas in the air you breathe – but only a tiny amount. In every 200,000 litres of air, there is only 1 litre of helium. But after hydrogen, helium is the commonest element in the Universe. Helium is created in the massive nuclear reactions that make the stars shine.

Helium is the lightest element, after hydrogen. It belongs to a group of unreactive elements called the noble gases. The other members of the group are neon, argon, krypton, xenon and radon. The noble gases are all present in tiny amounts in the Earth's atmosphere.

Properties

You cannot see or smell the noble gases. Scientists used to think that none of them ever reacted with any other elements, and as result they were called the 'inert gases'. However, chemists have now made compounds of xenon, krypton, and radon, so the name of the group has been changed to the 'noble' gases.

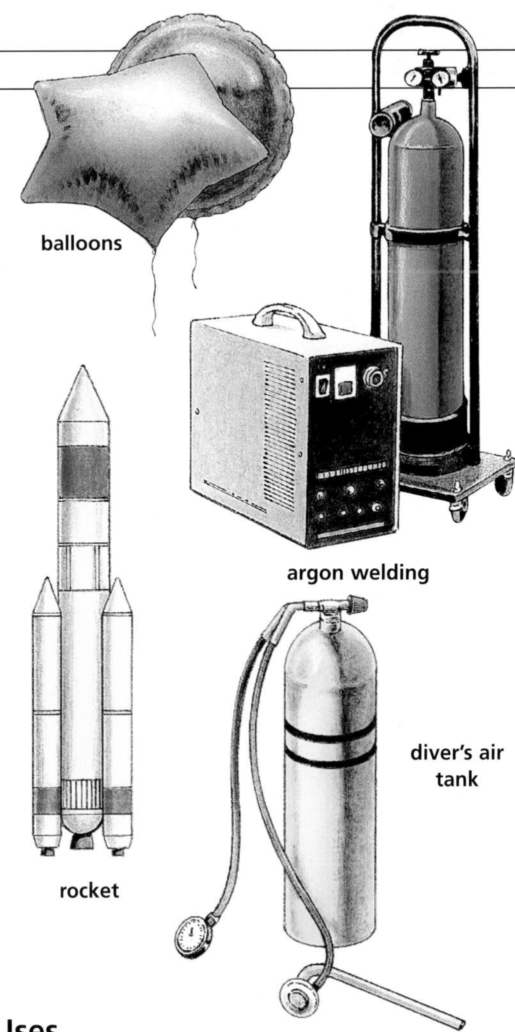

▶ Helium has many uses. It is so light that it is used to fill airships and balloons. It is also used to pressurize the hydrogen fuel in rockets, and the air in divers' air tanks. Argon welding is used to join pieces of aluminium or stainless steel.

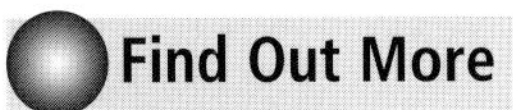

Find Out More

- Lights and lamps
- Nuclear energy
- Periodic table
- Rockets
- Stars

Uses

Apart from radon, which is radioactive, the noble gases are used in lighting. When a glass tube is filled with a noble gas and an electrical charge passes through it, the gas glows. Neon glows orange-red, for example, while krypton glows bluish-white.

The noble gases are also used to provide an unreactive atmosphere for certain processes such as welding metals.

The noble gases have very low boiling points, and are used to study matter at low temperatures. Liquid helium is the coldest substance – the gas only becomes liquid at –268.9 °C.

Helium was discovered in 1868 when scientists studied light coming from the Sun. They named the new element after helios, the Greek word for the Sun.

◀ This lighting display uses glass tubes filled with noble gases, which glow with different colours when an electrical charge passes through them.

Hibernation *see* Animal behaviour • **Hormones** *see* Glands and hormones • **Hovercraft** *see* Ships and submarines

Human reproduction

At the moment of birth, a new baby emerges from its mother's body to begin a life of its own. But the baby's life really began nine months earlier, when a sperm cell fertilized an egg. Over the months that followed, the egg divided, grew and developed from a single cell to become a new human being.

Sperm cells are released into a woman's body during sexual intercourse. They then set off on a journey, swimming through the woman's womb, into the fallopian tubes that lead to the ovaries, in search of an egg. Of the 300 million or so sperm that set off, only a few hundred reach the egg. If one of these sperm succeeds in fertilizing the egg, the woman becomes pregnant.

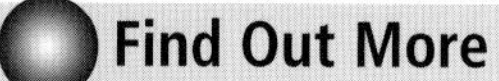

Find Out More

- Cells
- Genetics
- Growth and development
- Sex and reproduction

▲ A sperm fertilizes an egg. Even though it is much smaller than the egg, it will penetrate the outer layers and fuse with the egg cell underneath.

The developing baby

Once an egg has been fertilized, it begins to grow and develop. In just a week it will become a ball of over 100 cells. At first the cells are all alike, but soon they change to form the muscles, bones, blood, heart, eyes and ears of the baby.

After eight weeks the baby is less than three centimetres long, but it has all its important organs in place. The baby continues to grow for the next seven months. It floats gently in a bag of fluid, which protects it from bumps and jolts, and it receives nourishment from its mother via the umbilical cord.

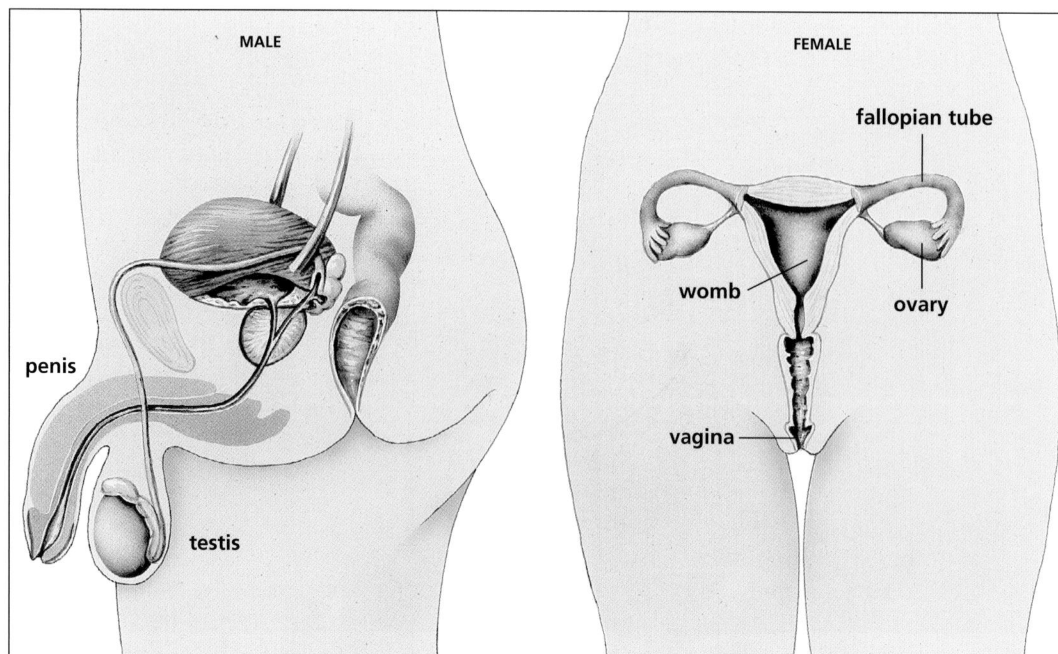

HUMAN SEX ORGANS

The human sex organs. The man produces sperm cells in his testes. The woman produces eggs in her ovaries, which release one egg each month. During sexual intercourse, the man's penis becomes erect, and he puts it into the woman's vagina. He releases sperm from his penis into her vagina. From here the sperm swim towards the egg. If one of them succeeds in joining with the egg, the woman becomes pregnant.

During its development a baby is protected inside its mother's body. As its muscles develop, she can feel the baby moving inside her. When nine months have passed the baby fills the space and cannot move very much.

Birth

After nine months, the baby's development is complete. Birth begins when the mother's hormones stimulate the neck of the womb to open. More hormones urge the muscles of the womb to contract, gradually pushing the baby down the vagina.

Powerful contractions push the baby out of the mother's body, into the outside world. Most babies are born headfirst and take their first breath almost immediately. A newborn baby is dependent on its parents or carers for milk, warmth and protection for many months after it is born.

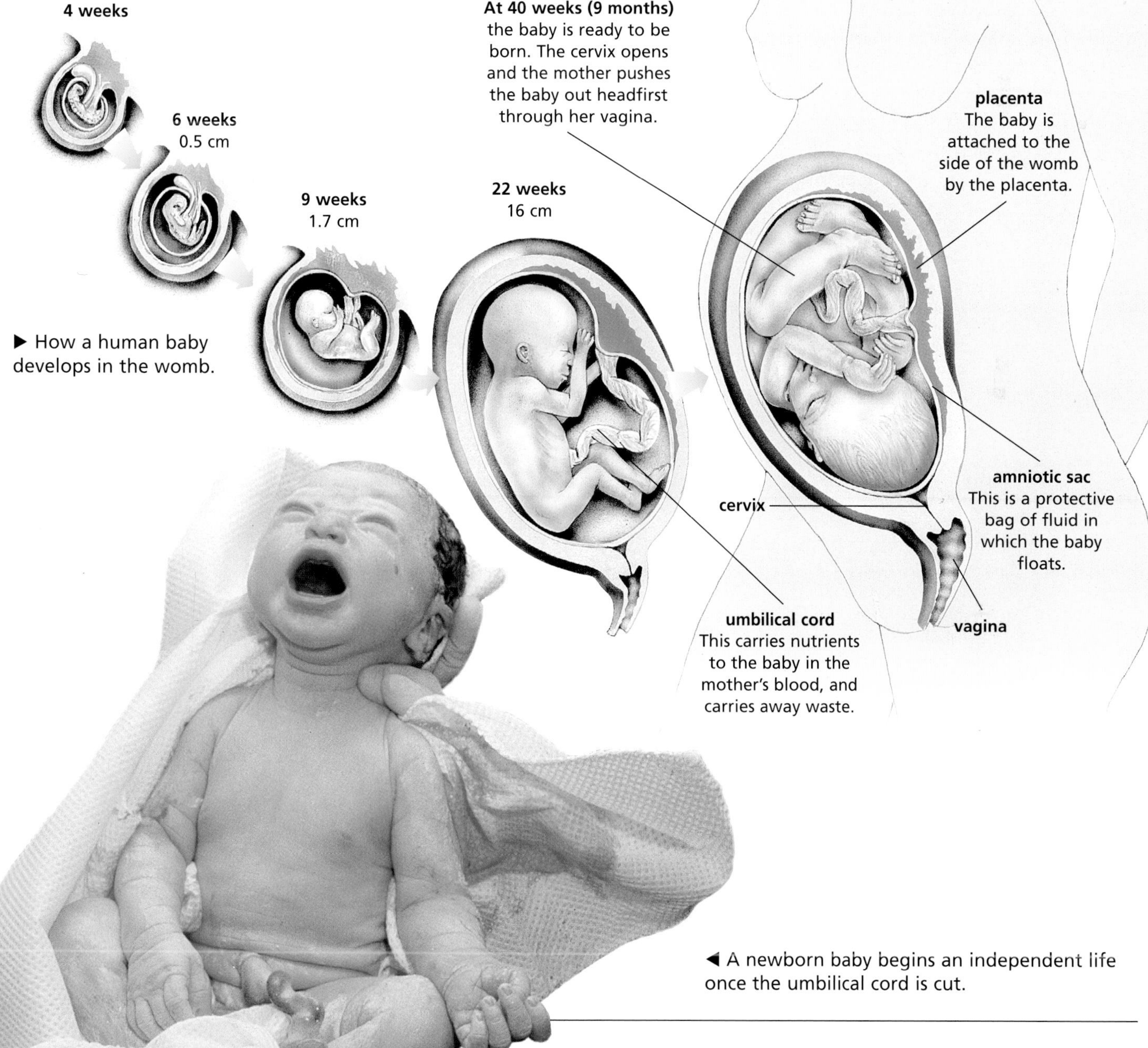

▶ How a human baby develops in the womb.

◀ A newborn baby begins an independent life once the umbilical cord is cut.

Humans

▶ The skeleton of Lucy. This almost complete skeleton was named *Australopithecus afarensis* after the Afar region of Ethiopia where it was found.

In 1974, the remains of a 3-million-year-old female skeleton were discovered in Ethiopia. Scientists called her Lucy, and she forms the closest link we have between apes and human beings.

Lucy was an Australopithecine – a southern ape. The evidence from Lucy's skeleton suggests that, unlike the apes, she walked upright, just as we do. Remains of other Australopithecines have been found in Kenya, Tanzania and South Africa. Their teeth, jaws and many other features are very similar to our own.

Early humans

Scientists have found many other fossil remains of our ancient relations in Africa. *Homo habilis* ('handyman') flourished over a million years after Lucy, in East Africa. *Homo habilis* walked upright, was probably about the same size as a 12-year-old boy is today, and had a larger brain than the Lucy. *Homo habilis* were probably the first creatures to make tools, which is why they are known as 'handy'.

Homo erectus

Homo erectus means 'upright man'. These people lived about a million years ago. They walked upright and used tools. They also used fire to keep warm, which made it possible for them to live in cooler climates. Their remains have been found near Beijing in China and in Europe.

Homo sapiens

About 200,000 years ago a new group of humans evolved in Africa and moved north. These were *Homo sapiens* ('wise man'), and they were very similar to us. They lived in groups, and hunted large animals such as deer and mammoths. We know they

▼ Humans developed through a number of stages over the last 3 million years. Here are the main stages.

Lucy (Australopithecine) probably looked something like this. She walked upright, but probably not with the same kind of stride as we do.

Homo habilis used cutting, scraping and hammering tools.

Homo erectus people were the first to use fire.

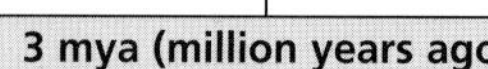

3 mya (million years ago) | **2 mya** | **1.5 mya**

communicated with each other from the pictures and symbols they drew.

Neanderthals

Neanderthal people were a group of *Homo sapiens* who lived in Europe and the Middle East between 80,000 and 30,000 years ago. They were probably the first people to bury their dead. Scientists think that the Neanderthals are more closely related to us than any of the other early humans that have been found.

Modern humans

About 100,000 years ago modern humans – *Homo sapiens sapiens* (us) – evolved in Africa, and began to spread around the world. They gradually replaced all other groups of people, including the Neanderthals.

Neanderthal people probably performed ceremonies for their dead.

Homo sapiens were the first humans to use paintings and carvings to communicate.

1 mya **present day**

For thousands of years our ancestors got their food from wild plants and animals. They moved from place to place with the seasons. Then, around 10,000 years ago, people in different parts of the world started to farm. They planted crops and began to tame and keep animals. Many now settled in villages, where they lived throughout the year. Over time such settlements grew into complex societies.

So what is a human?

One small but significant thing that makes humans different from apes is our long thumb. All primates have 'opposable thumbs' – thumbs that can bend across the palm – but the human thumb is especially long. This makes it possible for us to carry out delicate tasks. Another advantage that we have over our ape cousins is our large brain. We are probably the most intelligent animal that has ever lived on Earth. This has allowed us to make tools, to create cultures, and to develop language.

Our ideas and memories do not die with us, but survive in forms such as painting, books and film. We have made huge changes to the Earth's environment. We have built our homes in every part of the world from the frozen Arctic Circle to the hottest desert.

▲ These rock engravings in Algeria are 7000 years old. Paintings done by early humans have been found from as far back as 40,000 years ago.

Find Out More

- Brain and nerves
- Farming
- Life
- Mammals
- Speech and language
- Tools

In prehistoric times, people lived to an average age of only 18 years. Romans in AD 600 lived to about age 30, on average. In the year 2000, people in the developed world could expect to live to an average age of over 70.

Building bodies

A human body is made of millions of tiny building blocks called cells. A cell is the basic unit of all living things. We have about 50 million million cells in our body. Most cells are so small that it would take 100,000 to cover a pinhead. All cells have the same basic contents, but their shapes vary according to their jobs. Nerve cells are long and thin so that they can carry electrical messages to and from the brain.

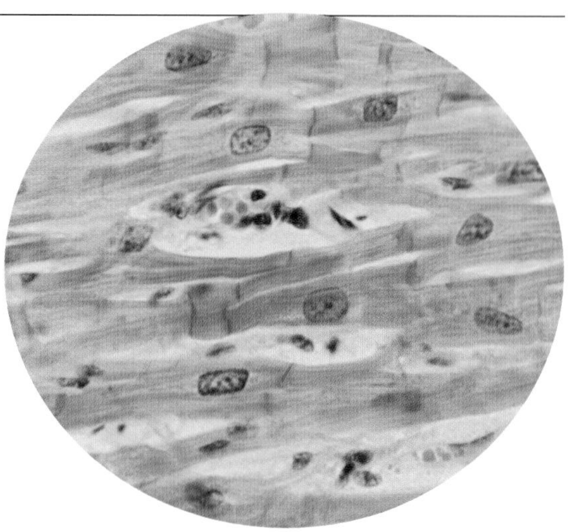

▶ A close-up of heart-muscle tissues. You can see the individual cells. Every cell has a nucleus, which contains the genetic material – the instructions for making a complete human being.

▼ The different systems of the human body.

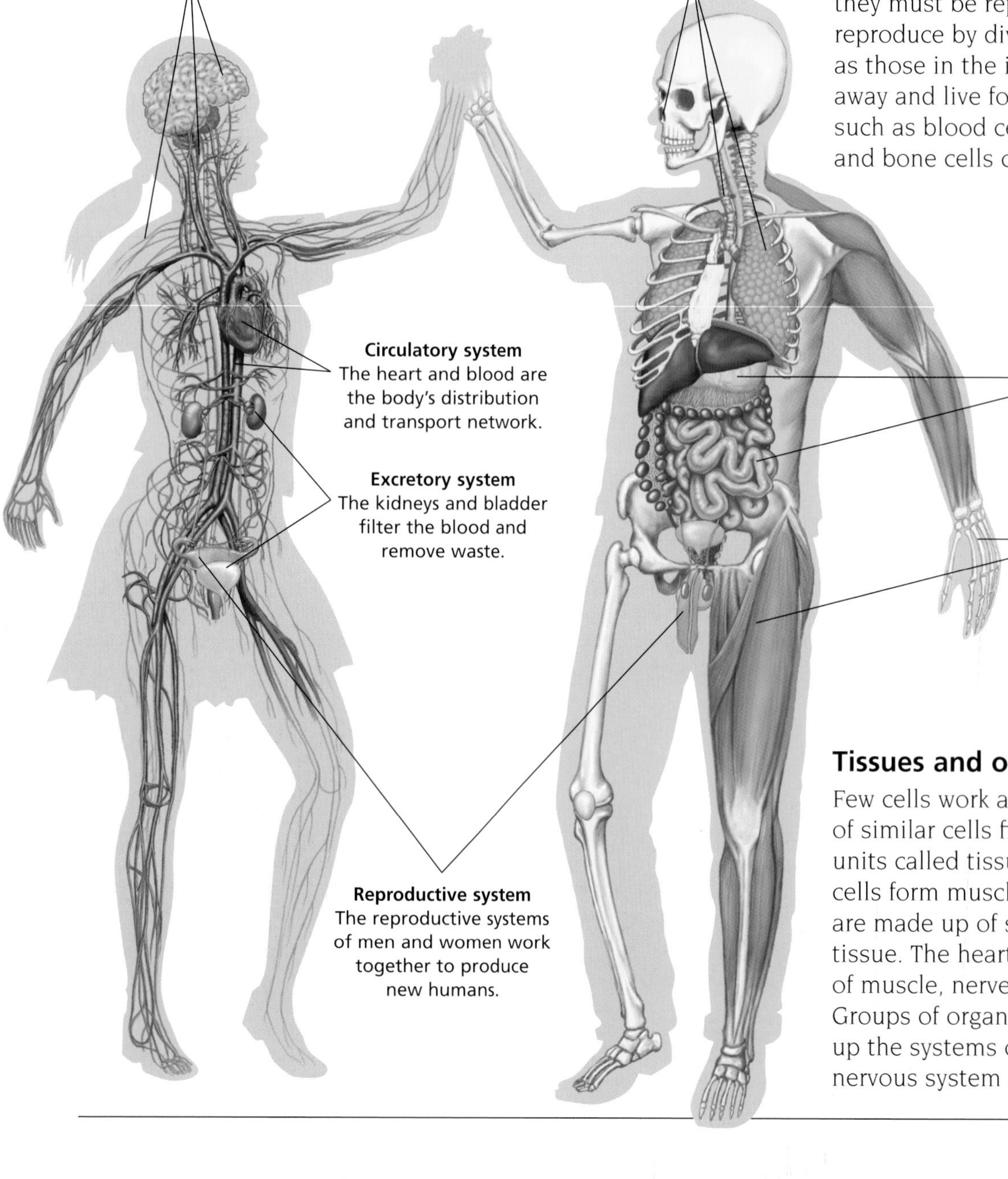

Nervous system
The brain, spinal cord and the network of nerves are the body's communication system.

Respiratory system
The nose, windpipe and lungs work together to extract the oxygen we need from air.

Circulatory system
The heart and blood are the body's distribution and transport network.

Excretory system
The kidneys and bladder filter the blood and remove waste.

Digestive system
Breaks down our food so that we can absorb the nutrients we need.

Bones and muscles
These keep us upright and make it possible for us to move.

Reproductive system
The reproductive systems of men and women work together to produce new humans.

More cells

When we grow, we produce more cells. If we are injured and cells are damaged, they must be replaced. Most cells reproduce by dividing in two. Some, such as those in the intestine, are easily worn away and live for only a few days. Others, such as blood cells live for a few months and bone cells can last for 30 years.

Tissues and organs

Few cells work alone in the body. Groups of similar cells fit together and work as units called tissues; for example, muscle cells form muscle tissue. The body's organs are made up of several different kinds of tissue. The heart, for example, is built up of muscle, nerve and connective tissues. Groups of organs that work together make up the systems of our body, such as the nervous system and the digestive system.

Human senses

▶ Ears contain the mechanism for hearing and give us our sense of balance. After the eyes, our ears are probably our most important sense organs.

An eagle can spot a scampering rabbit from nearly 5 kilometres away. A person would struggle to see it just 1 kilometre away. Eagles' eyes have five times more light-sensitive cells than ours. But even our eyes have more than 130 million light-sensitive cells in an area the size of a postage stamp.

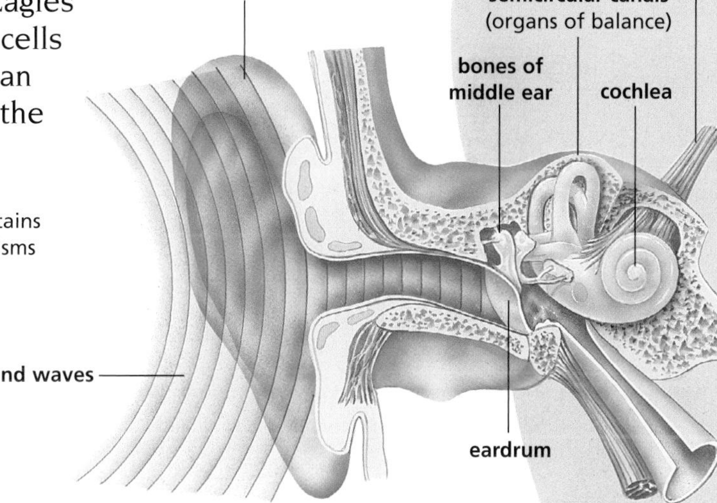

The ear contains the mechanisms for hearing.

Sight is our most important sense. About 80 per cent of everything we know about the world reaches us through our eyes. Our eyes and other sense organs pick up information about the outside world. They send messages to the brain, which uses the information to work out what is happening around us. Different sense organs detect different things, but they all send their messages as tiny electrical signals through a network of nerves.

What can you see?

By day, the world is full of light energy, which pours from the Sun in a never-ending stream. Our eyes use this light to give us information about our surroundings. A lens at the front of the eye focuses light from outside to create a tiny picture of the world inside the eye. The inner eye is covered by a layer of light-sensitive cells called the retina. The cells send messages to the brain when light falls on them. The retina contains two types of cell – rods and cones. Rods respond to dim light, but see only shades of grey. Cones only work in bright light, but enable us to see in colour.

If you cover one eye, you will find it is hard to judge how close or far away things are. This is because each of our eyes has a slightly different view of the world. The brain uses the two views to put together a three-dimensional picture.

Hearing

The ear detects vibrations in the air, which we call sounds. Inside the ear, a series of tiny bones magnify them. In the inner chamber of the ear, called the cochlea, the vibrations send waves of movement through a fluid. The cochlea is lined with thousands of sensitive hairs. Nerve cells attached to each hair send out signals as the movement of the fluid bends the hairs. Other sensors in the ear tell us which way up we are, and help us to balance.

Scientists have recently discovered a new taste which they have called umami. It is a savoury, meaty flavour and may be the fifth taste which humans can identify.

◀ Most of the time our eyes work well, but they can be fooled. How many cubes can you see in this picture? Depending on how you look at it, you might count six or seven.

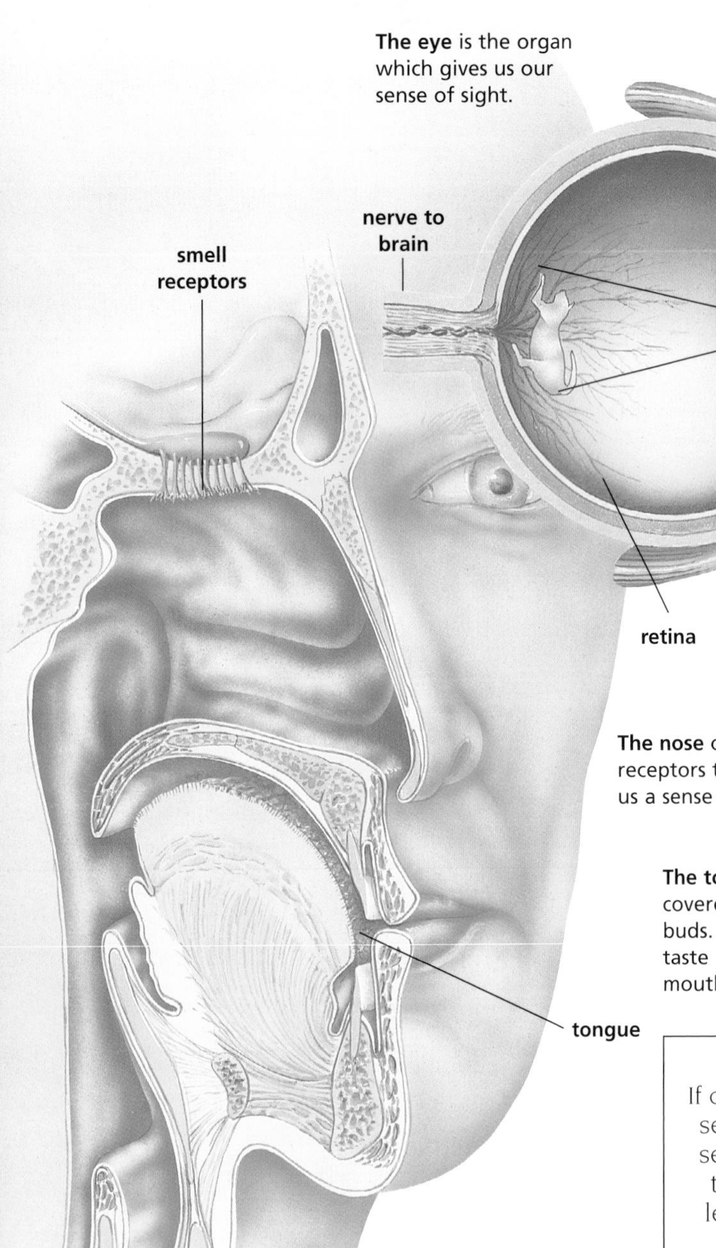

Find Out More
- Brain and nerves
- Ears
- Eyes
- Light
- Mirrors and lenses
- Senses
- Sound

◀ Our sense organs for sight, smell and taste are all on the front of the head.

Touch

We can learn a lot about the world from our sense of touch. Our skin contains millions of touch sensors, of many different kinds. Some can detect pressure, some can feel if something is hot or cold, and pain receptors sound the alarm if we touch something that is too hot, or cold, or sharp.

Inside our muscles, we have special touch sensors. These fire off as a muscle moves, and help the brain to keep track of exactly what each part of the body is doing.

BRAILLE

If one sense has been damaged, people often learn to use their other senses more acutely. Blind people use their sense of touch to get a sense of the size, shape and texture of an object. They can also use touch to read a special kind of writing called Braille, in which the letters are patterns of dots raised from the paper. Braille is named after its inventor, the Frenchman Louis Braille (1809–1852).

Taste and smell

Smell and taste receptors in our nose and tongue work closely together. We learn this from experience. When we have a blocked nose, our food does not taste as good, because we cannot smell it as well as taste it.

Both smell and taste receptors respond to chemicals. We can distinguish four different tastes – sweet, sour, bitter and salt. Bitterness receptors are the most sensitive, possibly because poisons are bitter-tasting. Our noses can identify a wide variety of different smells.

Hydraulics *see* Pressure • **Hydroelectric power** *see* Water power • **Hydrofoil** *see* Ships

Hydrogen

Hydrogen is the lightest of all the elements (the substances from which all matter is made). It is also the commonest element in the Universe. It is found in everything, from the stars and galaxies in space to the water you drink and the food you eat, and every part of your body.

Hydrogen in its pure form is a non-poisonous gas. You cannot see, smell or taste it. On the Earth hydrogen is rarely found on its own. When mixed with oxygen in the atmosphere it forms a highly explosive mixture that ignites with a single spark. In this process, the hydrogen combines with the oxygen to form water – water molecules have two atoms of hydrogen and one atom of oxygen.

▶ Hydrogen is a powerful fuel. The main engines of the Space Shuttle are powered by hydrogen.

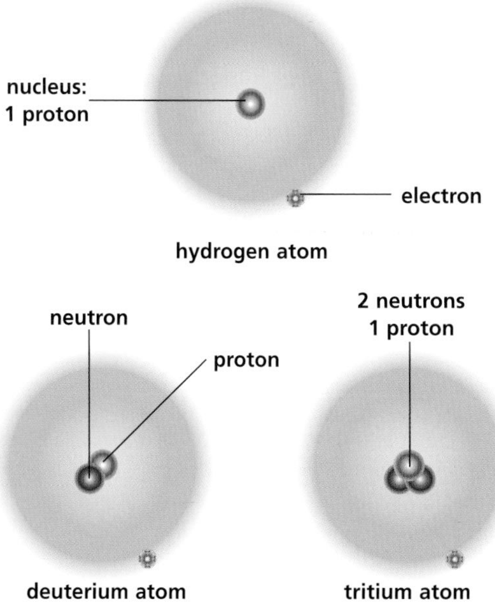

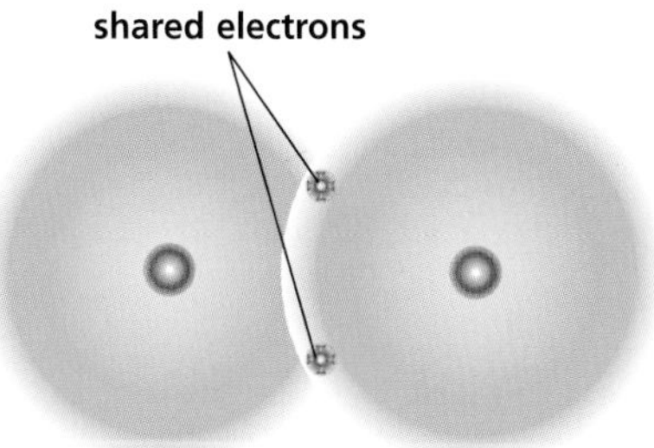

◀ Hydrogen is so light because its atoms have only one proton and one electron. However, there are some kinds of hydrogen (deuterium and tritium) that are heavier. These types are used to make hydrogen bombs. Hydrogen gas is made up of molecules, each containing two hydrogen atoms.

Hydrogen compounds

Hydrogen combines with other elements in numerous ways, making millions of different chemical substances. In food it is present in carbohydrates, vitamins, proteins and fats. Nearly every chemical from which your body is made contains hydrogen. And our most important fuels – coal, oil and natural gas – are compounds made up mainly of carbon and hydrogen.

Uses of hydrogen

Industry gets most of its hydrogen from natural gas. Hydrogen is used to make farm fertilizers, margarine and plastics.

Because it is so light, hydrogen was once used to fill airships. But in the 1930s there were some terrible accidents when airships caught fire. Airships now use helium gas, which does not burn. The fact that hydrogen does burn so explosively, however, makes it a good fuel for space rockets. In the future it may also be used to fuel cars and trucks – the only exhaust fumes would be water vapour!

Find Out More

- Atoms and molecules
- Nuclear energy
- Oil and gas
- Periodic table
- Rockets

Hydrogen bombs *see* Nuclear energy

Ice caps and glaciers

Almost the entire continent of Antarctica is covered in ice. Two huge ice sheets, up to 3 kilometres thick, flow very slowly from the centre of the continent out towards the sea. As the ice flows, it grinds up the rocks below, carries pieces to the ocean, and dumps them in. As the ice sheet melts, huge chunks break off into icebergs that float out to sea.

Ice sheets (also called ice caps) and glaciers are thick masses of ice that flow over land.

Rock made of ice

If snow falls in the winter, but doesn't completely melt during the summer, it gradually piles up. As it piles up, the snow gets packed tighter and tighter. Just as loose sediments turn into solid rock, so loose snow turns into solid ice. Eventually, the pile of ice and snow gets so thick that it starts to flow. A glacier has formed.

Glaciers and ice caps can form anywhere that it is cold and snowy, from the high mountains near the Equator to low elevations near the Poles. They can be as small as a few hundred metres across, or as large as a continent.

▶ This satellite photo over Antarctica shows Byrd Glacier (right) and a smaller glacier (top left) flowing from the coast into the permanently frozen Ross Ice Shelf (top).

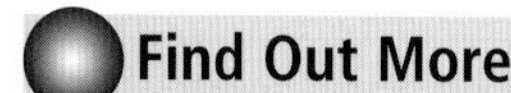

Find Out More

- Erosion
- Rivers and lakes

Flowing rock

Gravity makes glaciers flow. Inside the glacier, the ice crystals change shape and slide past each other. Glaciers in the mountains flow downhill, whereas huge ice sheets spread outwards under their own weight. In relatively warm areas, there is a lot of water in the glacier. It collects at the base, and then acts like grease so the glacier can slide down the mountain. Warm glaciers can move a few metres every day. Polar glaciers, however, are so cold that they are frozen to the rock beneath them. They move much more slowly, just a few centimetres each day.

▼ Glaciers play a big part in shaping many landscapes. As the glacier moves, the ice scrapes away the rock beneath it and on either side. High up on the mountain the glacier carves cirques (hollows) between mountain ridges, while lower down it gouges out U-shaped valleys. The crushed rock is pushed out at the sides and snout of the glacier as moraines (big piles of stones and boulders) or deposits of even smaller rock particles.

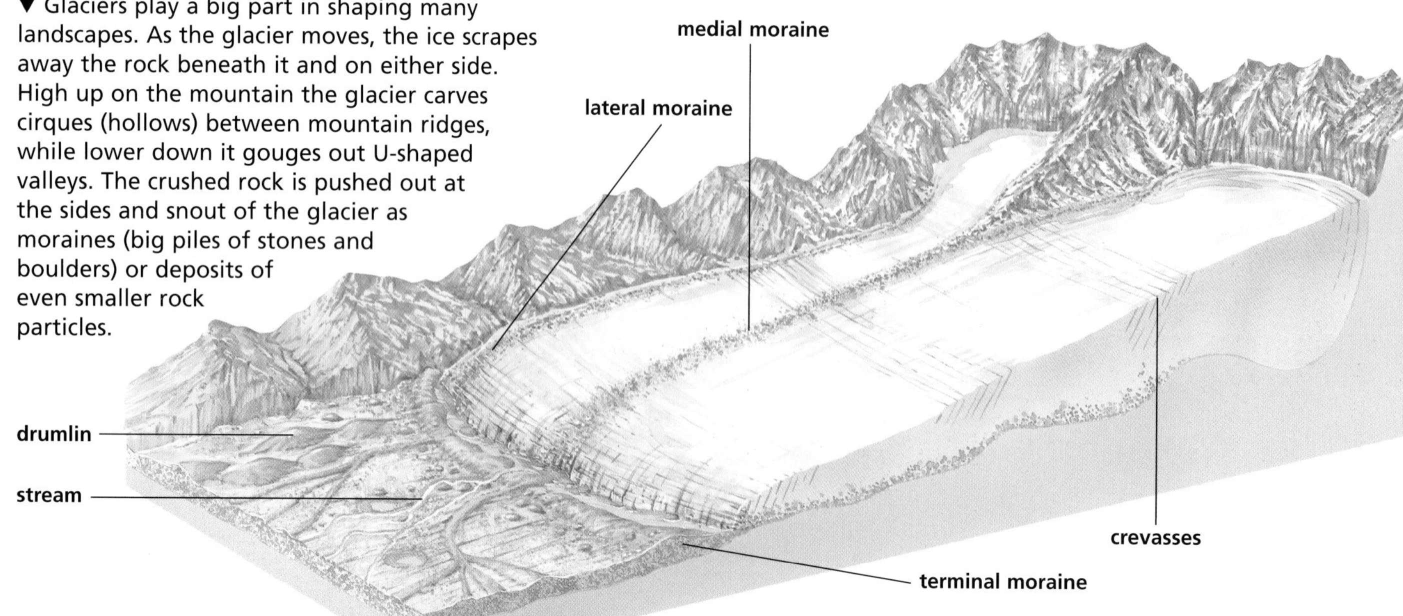

Immune system

Our waterproof, protective skin keeps out most of the millions of unwanted bacteria and viruses that try to invade our bodies every day. Even if the skin is cut or the intruders get in through the nose or mouth, our immune system provides an army of defenders ready to deal with them. Failure can mean disease and illness.

The skin is not only a physical barrier, it also has an array of chemical weapons to help fight invading germs. Oil from the skin contains substances that kill bacteria, and inside the nose, sticky mucus traps and destroys invaders we inhale. Ears contain wax to do a similar job, and the stomach produces a chemical cocktail of acid to kill bacteria we eat with our food.

▲ The lymph system produces antibodies and white blood cells in the spleen and lymph nodes. The lymph nodes, or 'glands', swell up when you have an infection. The thymus gland and the tonsils also help fight infection.

ALLERGIES

Like all our body systems, the immune system is finely tuned. Sometimes a person may become so sensitive to an everyday substance that they develop an allergy to it. Dust or pollen, for instance, may be dealt with like dangerous invaders as the body launches an all-out attack. Pollen grains can cause hay fever, which is a typical allergic reaction. Sufferers develop red, itching eyes, a runny nose and often sneeze uncontrollably. Some foods, including peanuts, contain chemicals that produce a severe allergic reaction in some people that has to be treated in hospital.

▶ Hazel trees produce vast amounts of pollen which can affect some hay fever sufferers in spring.

Find Out More

- Cells
- Diseases
- Heart and blood
- Medicine
- Skin and hair

In the 1990s the World Health Organization estimated that 80 per cent of the world's children were being vaccinated against diphtheria, tetanus, polio and tuberculosis. These diseases have killed millions of children in the past.

IMMUNIZATION

Immunization is a way of preparing the body to fight serious diseases. When you are given a vaccine against a disease, a tiny amount of a bacterium or virus is allowed to enter your body. This triggers your immune system, which produces antibodies and memory cells that will protect you against the disease for many years.

▼ This girl in Iran is being vaccinated against the tropical disease leishmaniasis.

Next line of defence

A cut in our skin is like a door into the body for invading germs. Damaged cells release a substance called histamine that causes redness and swelling. The redness causes a slight increase in temperature, which helps to kill bacteria. Blood vessels widen and white blood cells leak out of them and move into action.

White blood cells and antibodies

We have several different types of infection-fighting white cells in the blood. Two of the most important are lymphocytes and macrophages. Lymphocytes produce special chemicals called antibodies to fight bacteria and viruses. Each invader is slightly different, and each antibody is exactly matched to destroy just one type. Macrophages engulf the dead and dying bacteria and viruses and slowly digest them.

Some antibodies and some special memory cells stay in the blood after we have recovered from an infection. The memory cells quickly alert the immune system and step up antibody production if we meet the same invader again.

▼ The bone marrow produces both lymphocytes and macrophages. It produces thousands of different kinds, each effective against a different disease. When an invader gets into the blood, millions of copies of the cell that is effective against that invader are produced.

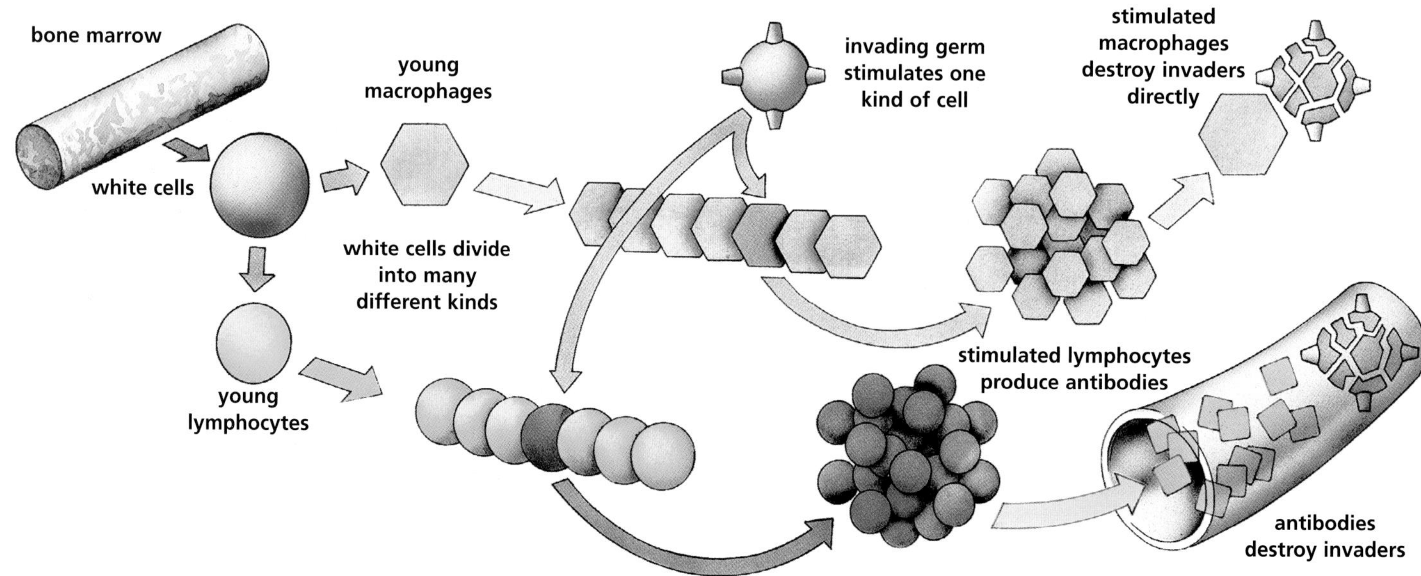

Industry

Two workers stand on either side of a car production line. A conveyor moves a partly built car between them. They pick up a wheel and fix it to the front axle with nuts. They pick up another wheel and fix it to the rear axle. Then another car comes by, and they repeat the process.

▲ Today robots may work on assembly lines alongside people. These are not the human-like robots we call androids, but machines with mechanical arms that can move and grip things in the same way as human arms and hands. They often do the dirty jobs, like welding and paint spraying.

This way of working is called an assembly line. A product is made (assembled) from a series of parts added in turn. Different workers carry out different stages of the assembly. Because each worker carries out the same simple action all the time, he or she can do the job quickly.

Mass production

Assembly lines are widely used in industry to manufacture goods – anything from matches to aircraft. Manufacturing literally means 'making by hand'. But most goods today are machine-made in factories.

Making large quantities of goods using machines and assembly lines is much cheaper than making things by hand. The process is called mass production.

Automation

Some of the key machines used in industry are machine tools – machines that can make identical parts. If the parts are the same, they will fit together and the products can be made on an assembly line.

In many industries machines work automatically, controlled by a computer. For example, a computer may control a laser cutter that cuts a machine part from a sheet of metal. Where a number of machines need to work on a product in turn, it is automatically transferred from one machine to the next. This is called automation.

In 1913, US car manufacturer Henry Ford (1863–1947) began using moving conveyors on assembly lines. The time needed to make a car chassis (basic frame) was cut from 12 hours to 1½ hours.

REVOLUTION IN INDUSTRY

Until about 250 years ago, most goods were made at home and sold locally. We call this kind of industry a cottage industry. But then people invented machines that speeded up spinning and weaving. In 1771, Richard Arkwright in England put many of these machines in a building and employed people to operate them. It became the first factory. Other people followed suit. At much the same time James Watt improved the steam engine, which then went into widespread use to power the factory machines. A revolution in working methods had begun, which we call the Industrial Revolution.

Find Out More

- Farming
- Mining
- Paper
- Resources
- Technology
- Textiles

▶ Primary industries produce raw materials such as oil, fish and wheat. Secondary industries make the raw materials into products that people (consumers) use.

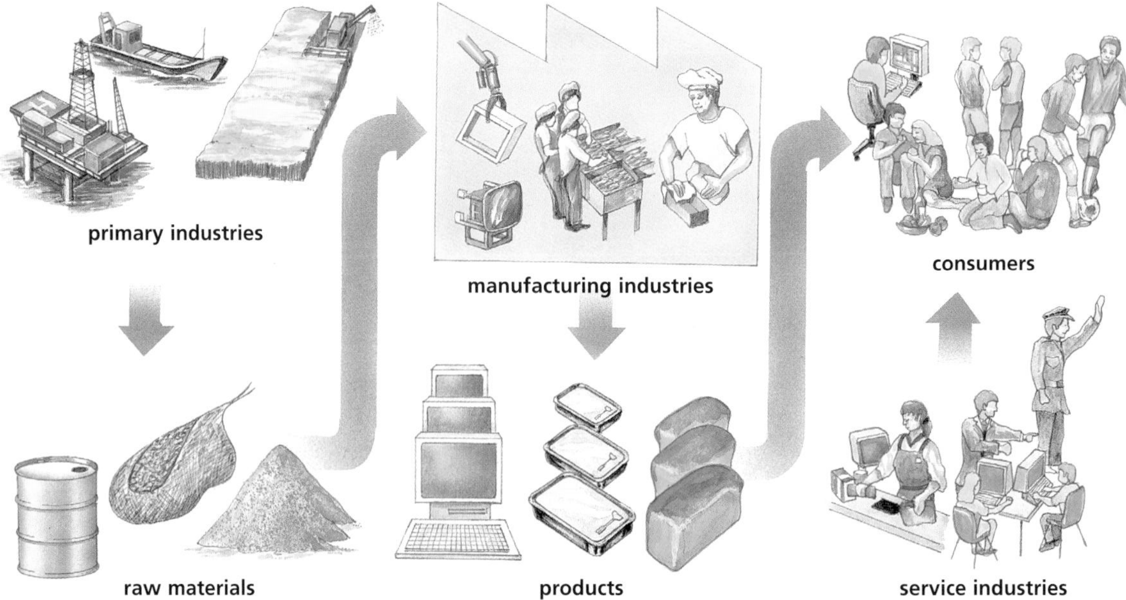

Primary and secondary

Manufacturing industries take raw materials, such as oil, rocks, wood or crops, and transform them into things such as fuels, metals, furniture and food.

The industries that provide these raw materials are known as primary industries. Mining, farming, forestry and fishing are all primary industries.

Manufacturing industries make use of materials that the primary industries provide. They are known as secondary industries. Some industries make products that we buy, but others, such as the chemical industry, make materials that are sold to other manufacturers.

▼ Molten steel pours from a furnace. Made from iron, steel is by far the most important metal used in industry to build machines and structures.

At your service

After the goods have been produced, they have to be sold. The industries that sell the products of manufacturing are known as tertiary industries. They are also called service industries, because they provide a service to consumers (the people who buy and use the products). Shops and supermarkets are service industries.

Any business that provides a service to the public is known as a service industry. Examples include banking, nursing and information technology (work with computers).

As manufacturing industries become more automated, they provide fewer jobs for people. Gradually, more and more people are working in the service industries.

Infections *see* Diseases • **Information technology** *see* Computers • **Infrared** *see* Electromagnetic spectrum

Insects

Cockroaches are a biological success story. They eat almost anything, including glue, paper, soap, ink and shoe polish. They can even live for three months on just water.

Cockroaches have lived on Earth for about 300 million years – since before the dinosaurs. They are just one species in the incredibly successful group called insects.

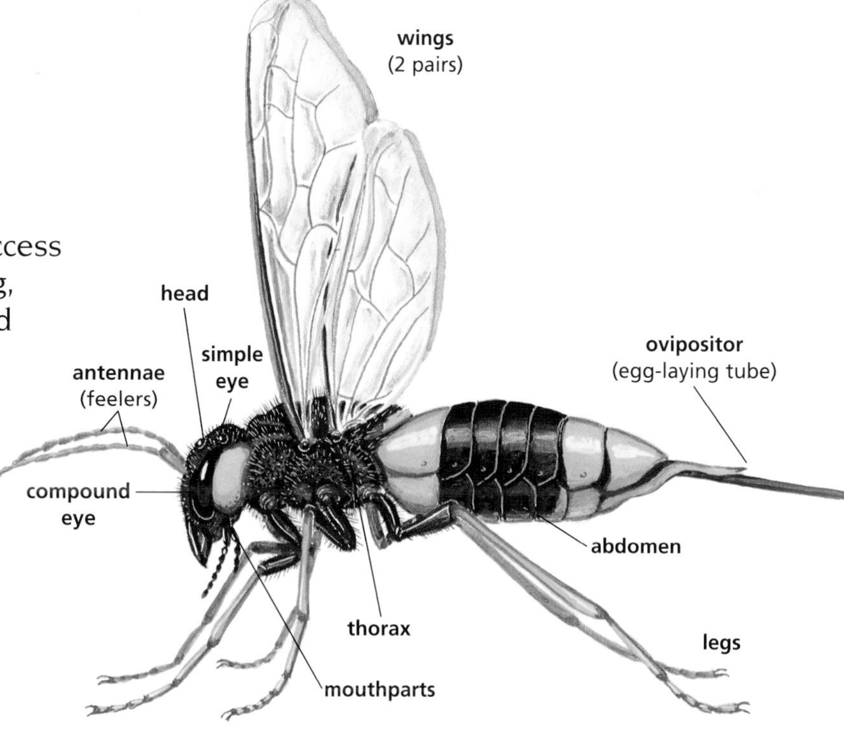

▲ A typical insect, such as a wasp, has six legs and three parts to its body – the head, the thorax and the abdomen. Most insects also have wings and feelers called antennae on the head.

There are more kinds of insect than of all other forms of life put together. Over 1 million different insects have been named and there may be 10 million more.

Keys to success

Insects have survived so well partly because they are small and breed quickly. And their tough, waterproof, flexible outer skeleton is another important key to their success. The skeleton has allowed insects to dominate almost every habitat except the open sea.

The one drawback of having an outer skeleton is that it does not stretch as an insect grows. So insects have to shed, or moult, their skeleton in order to grow.

Small is good

Most insects are less than 25 millimetres long. Their small size allows insects to live in small spaces and survive on very little food. The smallest insects are fairy flies less than a quarter the size of a pinhead, while the largest insects are not much bigger than a person's hand.

Insect size is limited by the outer skeleton, which can only support light weights, and by the breathing system, which would not work in a large animal.

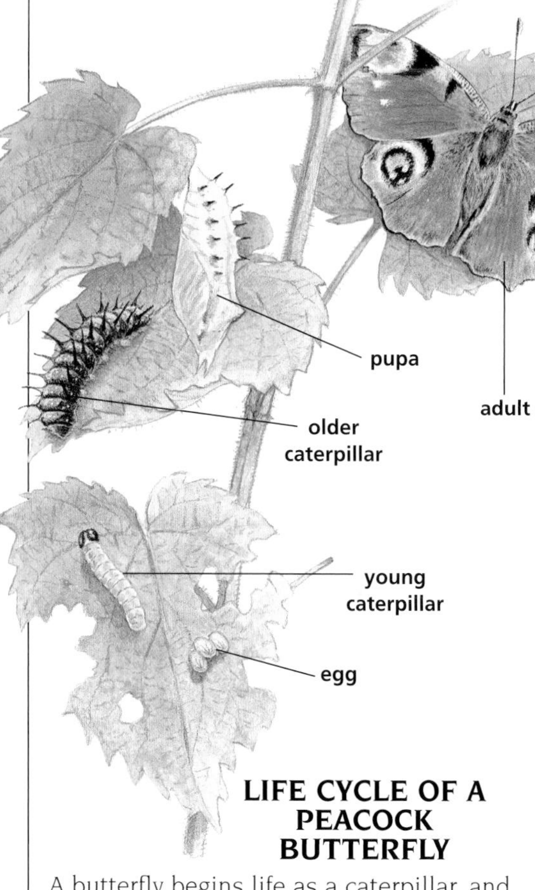

LIFE CYCLE OF A PEACOCK BUTTERFLY

A butterfly begins life as a caterpillar, and changes completely as it grows to become a butterfly. This change is called complete metamorphosis. Other insects look rather like their parents when they hatch. They get bigger and grow wings as they develop. This change is called incomplete metamorphosis.

Find Out More

- Animals
- Classification
- Invertebrates
- Life

In a field the size of a football pitch, there are about 200 million insects in the grass and soil.

Internet

The internet connects you to people, businesses and organizations all around the world. You can listen to faraway radio stations, download music from new bands, or play computer games. And you can find out almost anything you might want to know.

Few inventions have changed people's lives as much as the internet. Long-lost families have been reunited by it. Some people have found life-saving information on it. All these amazing developments have been made possible by a communications network that goes all over the world.

What is the internet?

The internet is a vast network of computers, connected to each other in a variety of ways. The original internet was a small computer network, set up in the 1960s by American military scientists who wanted a reliable way of communicating with each other in emergencies. The network soon grew, as scientists realized how useful it could be.

Many large organizations are connected directly into the internet. But smaller users, such as people with PCs at home, connect to organizations called Internet Service Providers (ISPs). The ISPs run special 'server' computers that pass on internet information.

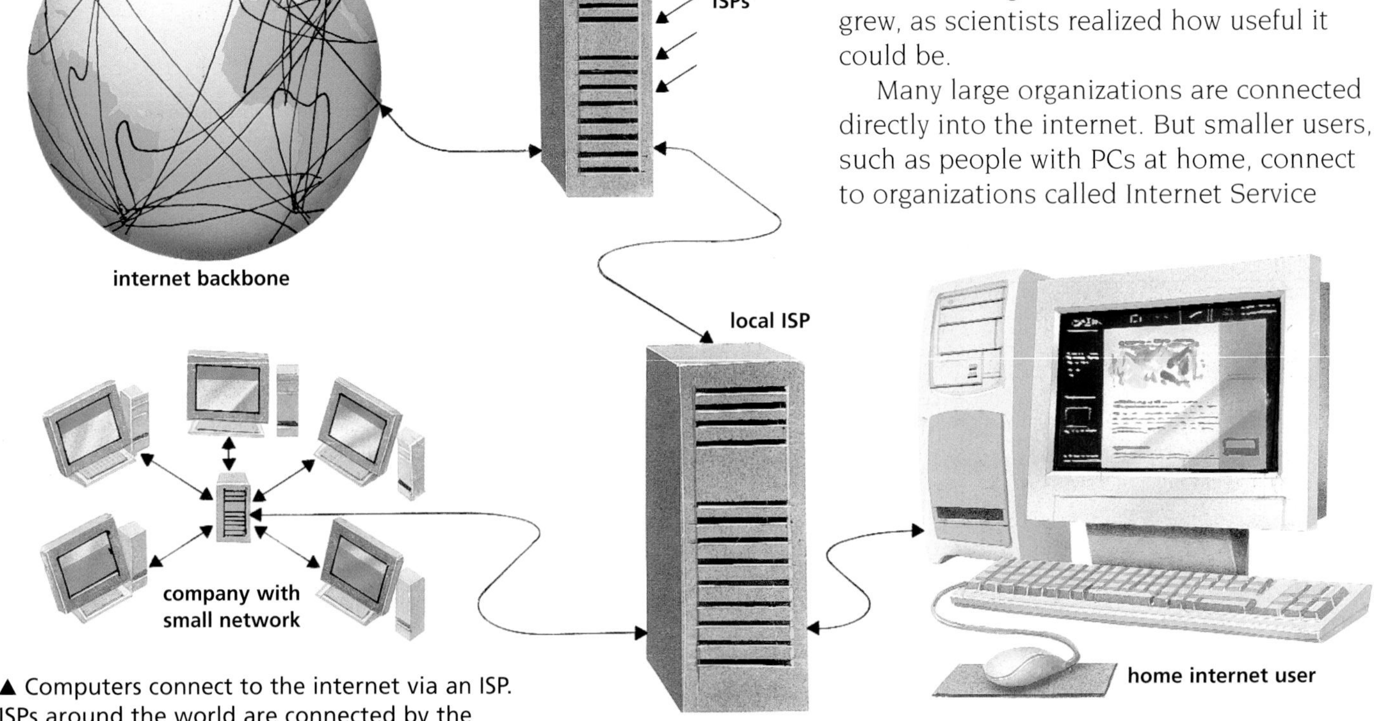

▲ Computers connect to the internet via an ISP. ISPs around the world are connected by the internet's 'backbones'. These are fibre-optic cables carrying information that span the globe.

▼ The internet is now available on some mobile phones. Accessing pages is slow, but phones are getting faster all the time.

Email and web pages

Sending messages by electronic mail (email) is one of the most popular things on the internet. All you need is a modem (a device that connects your computer to the telephone network) and an email program. You can write messages as long or as short as you like. And you can 'attach' all sorts of other computer files – a picture, a movie, a sound file or a computer program.

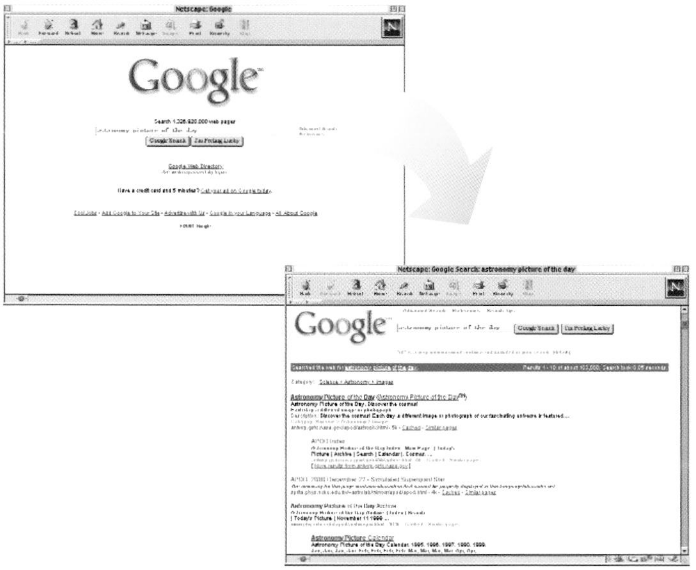

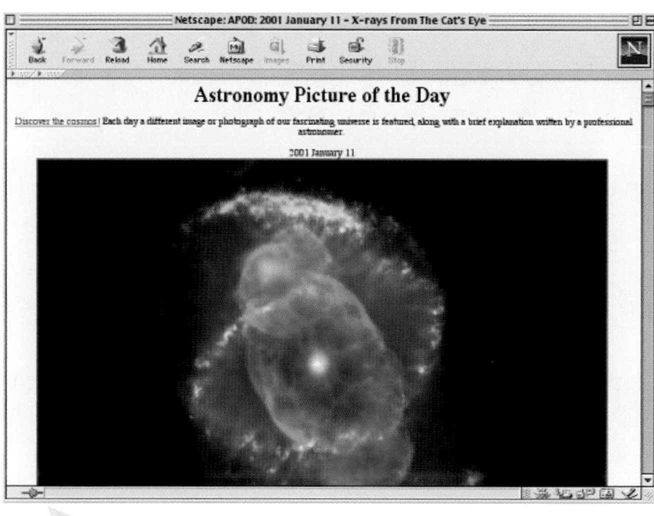

The internet also has billions of pages of information in the form of 'web' pages. To help you find your way around all this information, there are websites called search engines that help you find the pages you're interested in. If you are interested in dinosaurs, for instance, you can enter the word 'dinosaur', and the search engine will give you a list of sites on that subject.

Another very useful internet idea is the newsgroup. This lets people with a common interest send emails to whole bunches of like-minded people. There are many thousands of such groups on an area of the internet called the usenet.

▲ How a search engine works. Suppose you want to find out about a website you have heard of, Astronomy Picture of the Day. Typing in 'astronomy picture of the day' gives a list of websites with these words in. And clicking on the first site in the list takes you to the website itself.

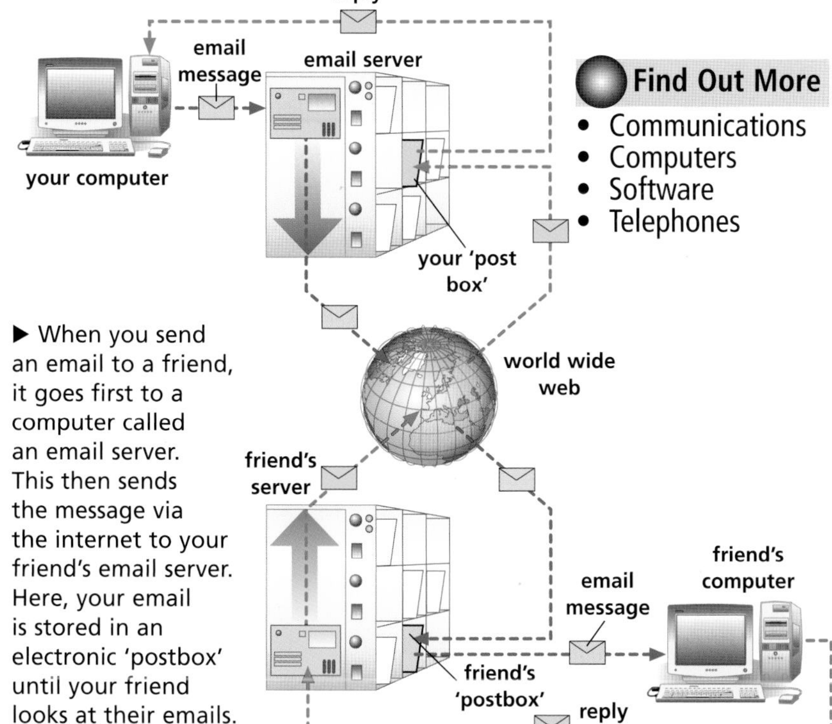

▶ When you send an email to a friend, it goes first to a computer called an email server. This then sends the message via the internet to your friend's email server. Here, your email is stored in an electronic 'postbox' until your friend looks at their emails.

Find Out More

- Communications
- Computers
- Software
- Telephones

Internet shopping

The internet is also becoming important for business. Home shopping sites let you order groceries with an email and have them delivered. You need never go to a supermarket again.

But the net also threatens businesses such as record companies. A lot of music is now available on the internet, and people can make digital copies of songs and swap them for free. So bands and record companies constantly try to stop this 'piracy' happening.

THE WORLD WIDE WEB

The world wide web was invented to make scientists' lives easier. They needed a quick way of telling others around the world what research they were doing – and a quick way to see what research others were doing. So Tim Berners Lee (born 1955) and his colleagues at the European Particle Physics Laboratory (CERN) in Switzerland, invented the Hypertext Transfer Protocol (http). This makes it possible to look at pages of information from an Internet server on a PC. The web took off so fast after its launch in 1992 that it contained more than a billion pages by 2000.

Invertebrates

A cloud of black ink suddenly spreads through the sea water. It forms a 'smoke screen' that hides a squid as it darts quickly away from danger. Squid are the fastest swimming invertebrates, or animals without backbones.

Squid are also the largest invertebrates – giant squid can grow up to 18 metres long. But most invertebrates are small animals. It is only in the sea, where the water provides support, that they can grow into giants.

▶ Corals have a hard skeleton that supports and protects the soft living coral. Millions of coral skeletons build up to form coral reefs.

Invertebrate groups

Invertebrates are an incredibly diverse collection of animals. Ninety-nine per cent of all animals are invertebrates. They live all over the world – in the sea, in fresh water and on land. There are probably between 3 and 15 million kinds, or species, although only about a million species have been identified. They include sponges, worms, starfishes, snails, insects and crabs.

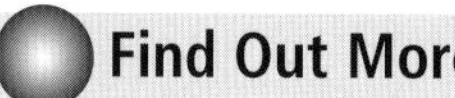

Find Out More
- Animals
- Classification
- Insects

Skeleton on the outside

Many invertebrate groups have hard external skeletons. These provide a strong, rigid surface to which muscles can be attached. Invertebrate skeletons are often divided into segments, allowing the animal to twist, turn and squirm along more easily.

▼ Molluscs are the second largest group of invertebrates after arthropods (see next page).

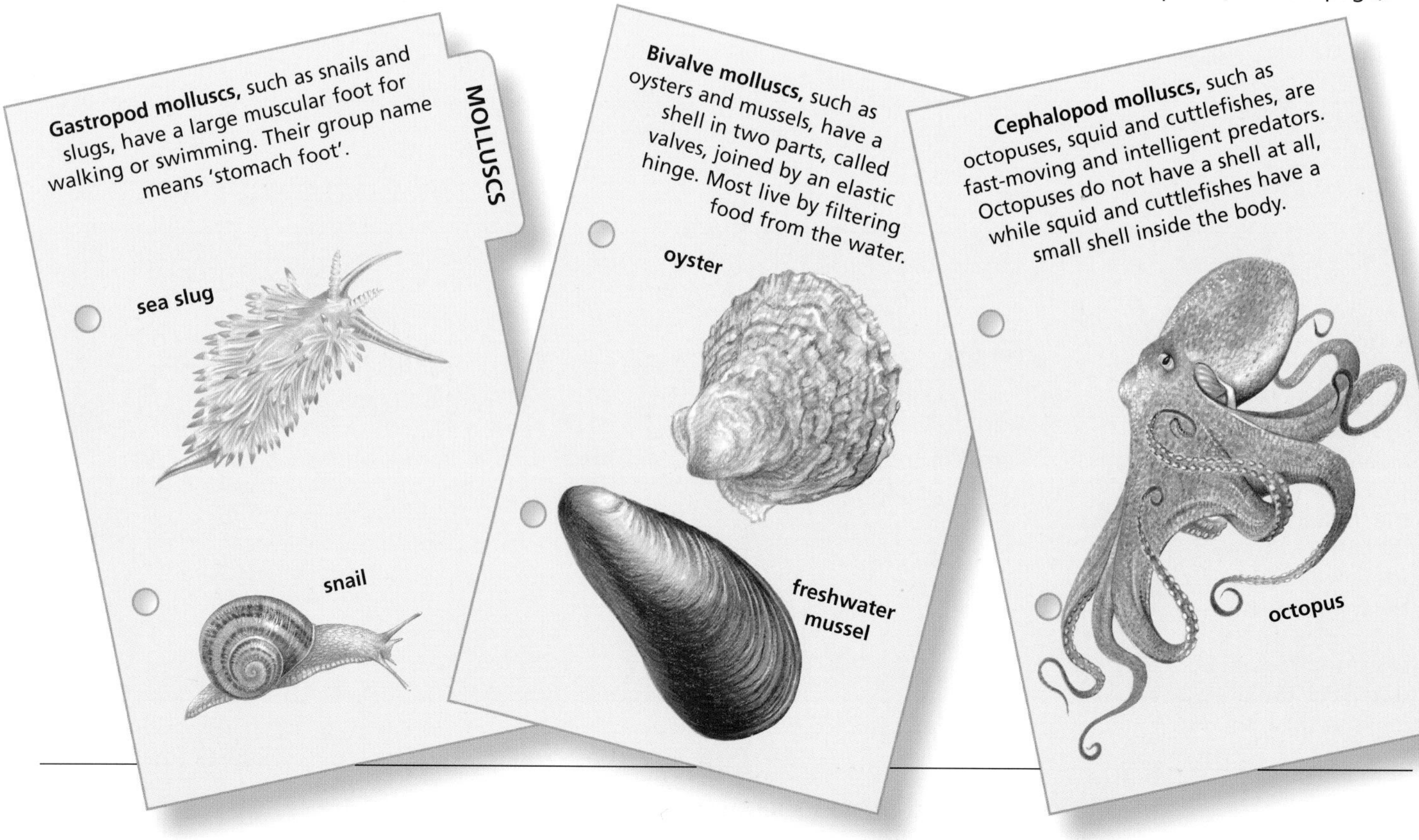

MOLLUSCS

Gastropod molluscs, such as snails and slugs, have a large muscular foot for walking or swimming. Their group name means 'stomach foot'.

sea slug

snail

Bivalve molluscs, such as oysters and mussels, have a shell in two parts, called valves, joined by an elastic hinge. Most live by filtering food from the water.

oyster

freshwater mussel

Cephalopod molluscs, such as octopuses, squid and cuttlefishes, are fast-moving and intelligent predators. Octopuses do not have a shell at all, while squid and cuttlefishes have a small shell inside the body.

octopus

A major advantage of the external skeleton is that it acts as a suit of protective armour. The shell of a snail, or the hard wing cases of a beetle, help to protect the soft body of the animal inside them.

Spiny skins

Starfish and sea urchins are part of a big group of invertebrates called echinoderms, which means 'spiny-skinned'. Unlike any other animals, they have skeletons made of hard plates just beneath the skin. Most also have lots of small tube-feet with suckers on the end.

The bodies of many echinoderm's have no front or back. Instead, they are based on a circular plan. Often an echinoderm's body is made up of five symmetrical parts, arranged like the spokes of a wheel.

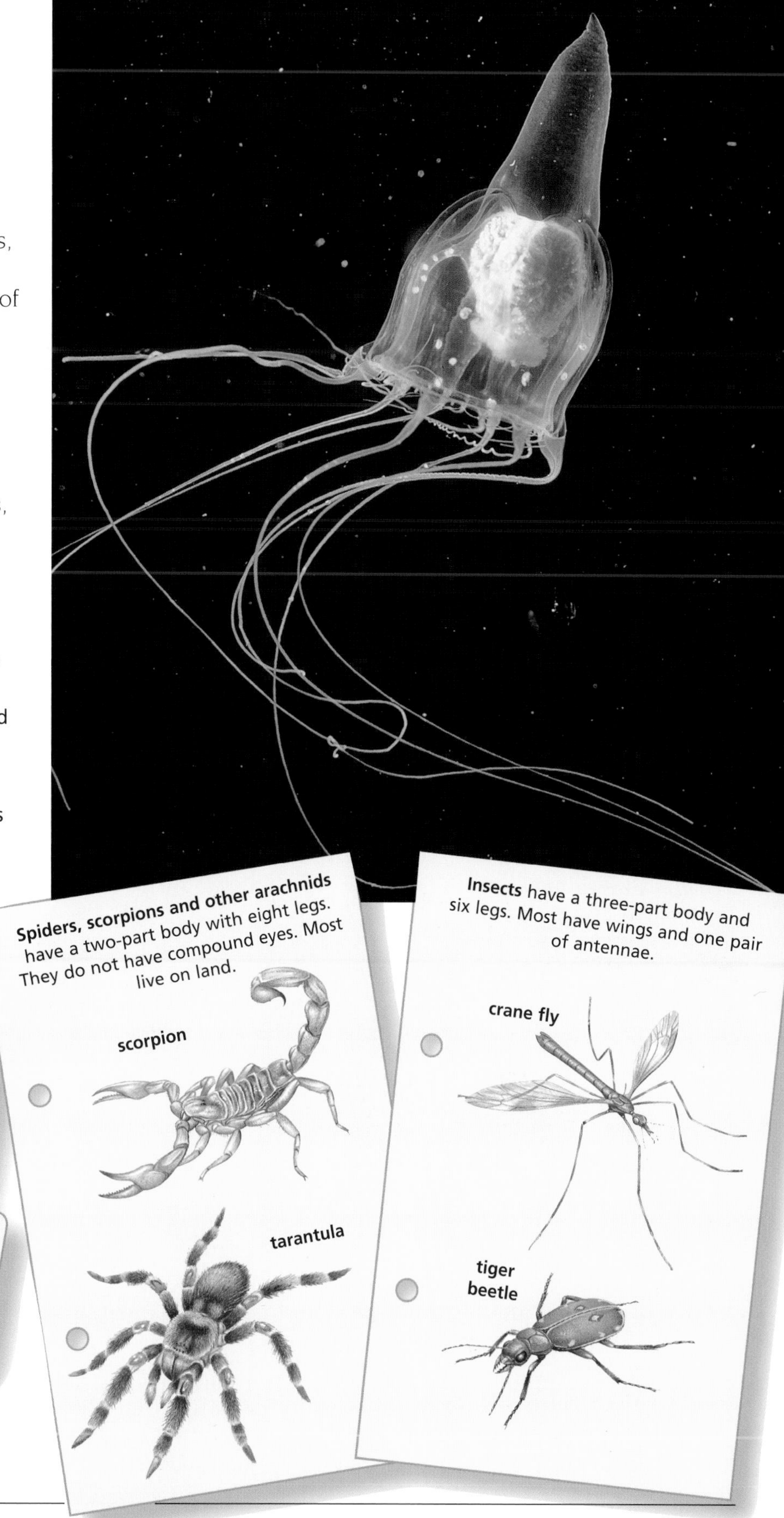

▶ The body of a jellyfish is 95 per cent water. It does not have a skeleton and is supported entirely by the sea water it lives in. A jellyfish uses the stings on its tentacles to defend itself from predators and catch food. The stings are armed with spines like miniature harpoons and are often loaded with poison.

▼ More than 75 per cent of all animals are arthropods. All arthropods have jointed bodies protected by a tough outer case.

Ion *see* Crystals • **Ionosphere** *see* Atmosphere

Iron and steel

Pure iron is quite a weak metal and is not particularly hard. But if you add a tiny amount of carbon to it, it becomes both strong and hard. It turns into the most useful metal we know – steel.

The world uses more iron (in the form of steel) than all the other metals put together. Yearly iron production is around 600 million tonnes, nearly 60 times as much as aluminium, our next most important metal.

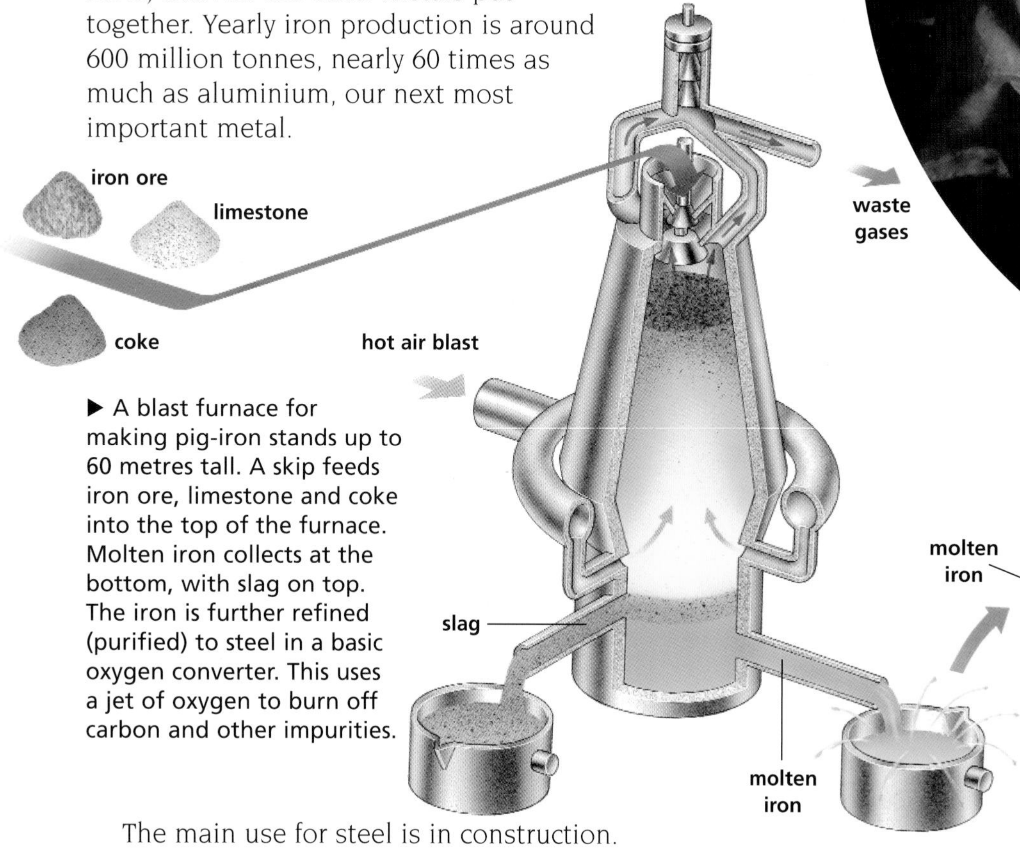

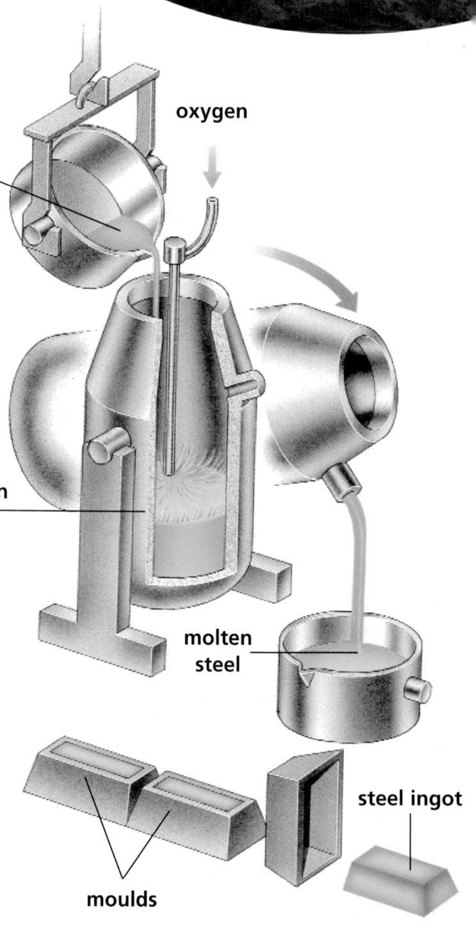

iron ore
limestone
coke
hot air blast
waste gases
slag
molten iron
molten iron
oxygen
basic oxygen converter
molten steel
steel ingot
moulds

▶ A blast furnace for making pig-iron stands up to 60 metres tall. A skip feeds iron ore, limestone and coke into the top of the furnace. Molten iron collects at the bottom, with slag on top. The iron is further refined (purified) to steel in a basic oxygen converter. This uses a jet of oxygen to burn off carbon and other impurities.

The main use for steel is in construction. It is used to build bridges and skyscrapers and all kinds of machines and vehicles. Most tools are made from steel; so are most cans. Cutlery is usually made from stainless steel. This is one of many steel alloys, which contain a mix of other metals.

Extracting the iron

Iron is found throughout the world, but not in metal form. Instead, it is found as an ore – the iron is found within rocks, combined with other elements. There are several iron ores, including magnetite and haematite.

Find Out More

- Alloys
- Buildings
- Magnetism and electromagnetism
- Resources

◀ Wearing protective clothing and using a long rod, a worker takes a sample of molten iron from a blast furnace.

Iron is extracted from iron ore by smelting – heating it to a high temperature, along with other materials. Smelting is carried out in a blast furnace, so called because hot air is blasted into it. The excess carbon quickly burns off, and the impurities form a slag.

Reducing the ore

Iron ore is fed into the blast furnace together with coke and limestone. The hot air being blasted in makes the coke burn fiercely, and temperatures rise as high as 1600 °C. As the coke burns, carbon monoxide gas is produced. This combines with the oxygen in the iron ore, leaving behind iron metal.

At such a high temperature, the iron is molten (liquid) and trickles down to the bottom of the furnace.

Meanwhile, impurities in the ore combine with the limestone to form a molten slag. This is lighter and floats on top of the iron. From time to time, both the iron and the slag are removed. In this state, the iron is known as pig-iron.

HENRY BESSEMER

The Romans were making a kind of steel over 2000 years ago. But steel only began to be easily and cheaply made in 1856. In that year, the English industrialist Henry Bessemer (1813–1898) invented a way of producing steel by blowing air through molten pig-iron to burn out the impurities. Bessemer's process led to the mass-production of cheap, good-quality steel. This made possible new kinds of building and ship, and greatly improved the railways. The basic oxygen converter used in steelmaking today is a refinement of Bessemer's furnace.

▼ Red-hot molten steel is poured into a container. The steel has been produced using the basic oxygen process, which changes pig-iron into steel with the help of a blast of oxygen.

The first iron people used was metal that fell to Earth from outer space, in meteorites.

When the molten iron leaves the furnace, it flows along a channel into moulds. These moulds are called pigs, because they are clustered round the channel like a group of suckling piglets around their mother.

Refining the iron

Pig-iron still contains many impurities, especially excess carbon (from the coke). They must be removed before the metal can become really useful. Refining, or purifying, the metal, takes place in other furnaces.

Most pig-iron is refined by the basic oxygen process. The iron is poured in its molten state into a conical vessel called a converter. Then a high-speed jet of oxygen is blasted into it. Most of the carbon quickly burns off, while other impurities form a slag. In a typical converter, up to 400 tonnes of pig-iron can be converted to steel in about half an hour.

The best-quality steels, such as stainless steels, are made in electric-arc furnaces. Usually, these steels are made using steel scrap, rather than molten iron. The steel is heated to high temperature by means of an electric arc, a kind of giant electric spark.

Irrigation *see* Farming • **Isotopes** *see* Atoms and molecules • **IT** (information technology) *see* Computers

Jet engines

▼ Flames roar from the engine of this jet fighter. They come from the afterburner, which burns more fuel in the exhaust to increase power when needed.

Only two centuries ago, it could have taken you a whole day to travel to the nearest city – the fastest stagecoach could not top 300 kilometres in a day. Nowadays, an airliner covers this distance in 20 minutes! Every large city in the world is no more than a day's journey away.

Most airliners cruise at speeds of up to about 1000 kilometres per hour. Supersonic aircraft can travel up to three times as fast. The jet engine makes economical high-speed travel possible. It produces great power without being very heavy.

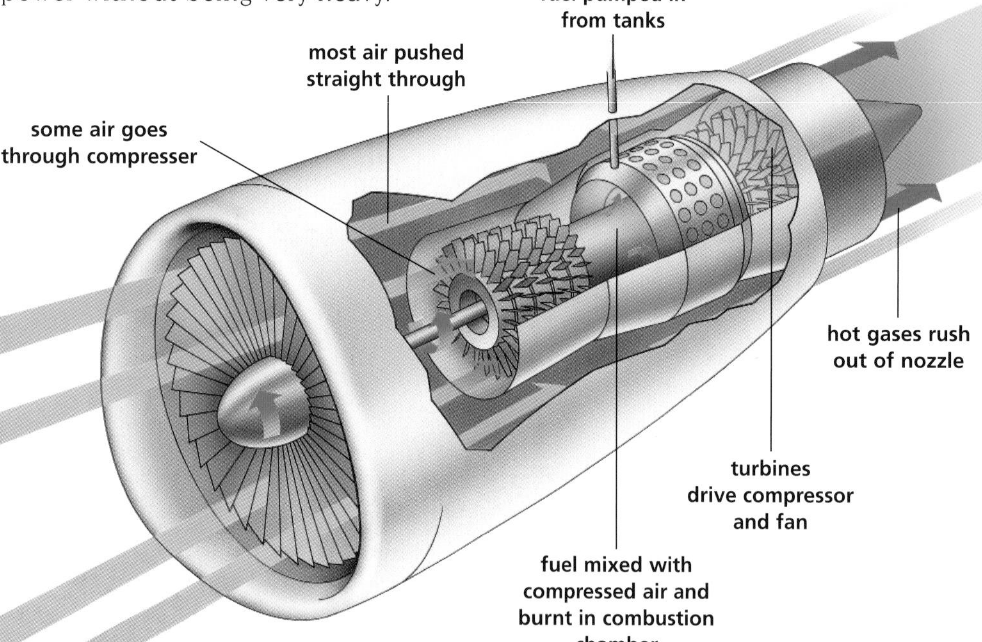

◀ Inside a turbofan jet engine. A huge fan sucks in air. Turbofan engines are much more efficient than turbojets. Some of the air is compressed, then heated in the combustion chamber to increase the pressure even more. This jet of hot air then shoots out of the back of the engine, turning a turbine to power the compresser and the fan as it goes. The rest of the air drawn in by the fan goes around the chamber and out of the back adding an extra 'push' of cooler air.

How a jet engine works

There are three main types of jet engines – turbojets, turbofans and turboprops. A turbojet engine is the basic model. It sucks in air at the front, burns fuel to heat the air, and expels the hot gases from the rear of the engine. The gases leave the engine in a powerful jet, thrusting the engine – and the aircraft– forwards with a strong force.

These days, most airliners use turbofan engines, in which a large outer shell surrounds the jet engine. A turbofan engine produces more power because more air flows through it. The shell surrounding the engine also makes it less noisy. Turboprop engines are often used in helicopters. The turbine drives a shaft connected to the rotors.

Find Out More

- Aircraft
- Engines and turbines
- Fuels

Jupiter

JUPITER DATA
Diameter at equator: 142,984 km
Average distance from Sun: 778.3 million km
Time taken to spin on axis: 9.9 hours
Density (water = 1): 1.3
Time taken to orbit the Sun: 11.86 years
Moons: over 50 discovered to date (2003)

Ferocious winds blowing at 400 kilometres per hour race around Jupiter's Great Red Spot. This is an immense storm that has been raging for more than 300 years on the Solar System's largest planet. Jupiter is 11 times larger than the Earth. Two planet Earths could fit side by side inside the Great Red Spot alone.

Jupiter is the fifth planet out from the Sun. Colourful bands of swirling clouds circle Jupiter. They are driven along by winds of up to 700 kilometres per hour, which are whipped up because the planet is spinning very quickly. The clouds are made of frozen crystals of water, ammonia and other chemicals, floating in an atmosphere of hydrogen and helium.

◀ An image of part of Jupiter, taken in 1994. Pieces of Comet Shoemaker-Levy 9 crashed down a few days before and the darker areas towards the bottom of the picture mark one of the impacts.

▼ There is no solid surface on Jupiter. Going down through the atmosphere, the gas gradually becomes thicker until it merges into the vast ball of liquid around Jupiter's small rocky core.

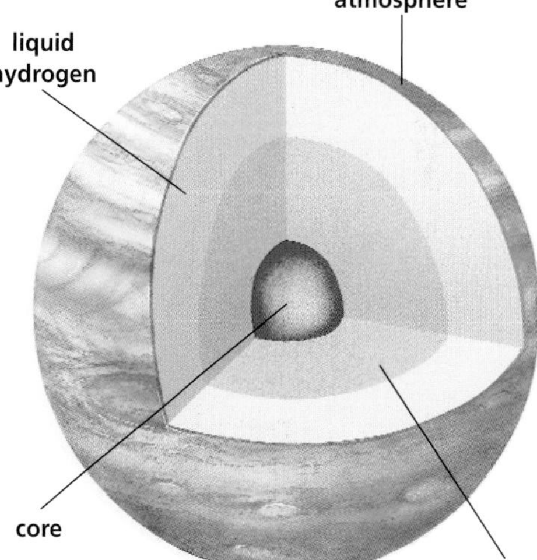

Inside Jupiter

Jupiter contains twice as much material as all the other planets put together. Most of it is hydrogen, though right at the centre of the planet there is a rocky core. Beneath the atmosphere, the hydrogen is squeezed by Jupiter's powerful gravity and made into a liquid.

Deep inside Jupiter, the liquid hydrogen is rather like a molten metal. It can conduct electricity and it makes Jupiter very magnetic. Jupiter's magnetism is 4000 times stronger than the Earth's. One effect of the magnetism is to turn Jupiter into a strong radio transmitter. Its signals can be picked up by radio telescopes.

◀ A view of Jupiter showing the Great Red Spot.

◀ Jupiter's volcanic moon, Io. The volcanoes produce the material sulphur. Sulphurous chemicals give Io its colourful appearance, shading it cream, yellow and orange.

▶ Europa's cracked and ridged surface shows signs of a liquid ocean of water underneath a thick crust of ice.

◀ Jupiter's moon Ganymede. Gigantic Ganymede has some cratered parts, but also has lighter coloured areas, where there are grooves rather than craters.

▶ Callisto is the most cratered world in the Solar System. Like Ganymede and Europa, it is made up of ice and rock.

Jupiter's four largest moons – Io, Europa, Ganymede and Callisto – are known as the Galilean moons, because the astronomer Galileo Galilei was the first to observe them.

Space missions to Jupiter

The first spacecraft sent to explore Jupiter were *Pioneer* 10 and 11, launched in 1973 and 1974. They were followed by *Voyager* 1 and 2, which both flew past Jupiter in 1979 and sent back spectacular images. The *Voyager* pictures revealed that Jupiter, like all the giants, is surrounded by faint narrow rings made out of very fine dust. They also captured three small moons previously unknown to astronomers.

The *Galileo* spacecraft arrived at Jupiter in 1995. Instead of flying past like the earlier craft, it went into orbit so it could study the planet and its moons for several years. *Galileo* released a small probe that parachuted down into Jupiter's atmosphere. Its instruments collected information about the temperature, the pressure and the chemical composition, which was radioed back to Earth.

Jupiter's moons

Astronomers know of over 50 moons orbiting Jupiter. Most are very small, with diameters of only a few kilometres, but some are much larger. The four largest can be seen through a small telescope. In order from Jupiter they are called Io, Europa, Ganymede and Callisto. Ganymede is the largest moon in the Solar System. At 5268 kilometres across, it is even larger than the planet Mercury.

Fire and ice

Io is an extraordinary world speckled with numerous active volcanoes that often spew out sulphurous chemicals. Nearby Europa is completely different. It has a thick crust of ice, but it is broken up in places and crossed by ridges, as if liquid water has oozed up from beneath and then frozen. It might even be a place where life could have started.

Find Out More

- Magnetism and electromagnetism
- Planets
- Solar System
- Space astronomy
- Sun

Kangaroos *see* Mammals • **Kepler, Johannes** *see* Solar System

Kidneys

Nearly two-thirds of your body is water. You gain water as you eat and drink. But you lose about a litre and a half each day through sweating, breathing and in the urine. Our kidneys have the delicate task of keeping the balance between water coming in and water going out exactly right.

The amount of water our bodies lose or gain depends on the outside temperature and on what we are doing. If it is hot we sweat, and unless we drink plenty of water, we will need to conserve the water inside us. If it is cool and we have plenty to drink, we will need to get rid of water.

Find Out More

- Heart and blood
- Water

▼ On the right of this photograph you can see a large, branched kidney stone. Kidney stones can block the flow of urine from the kidneys.

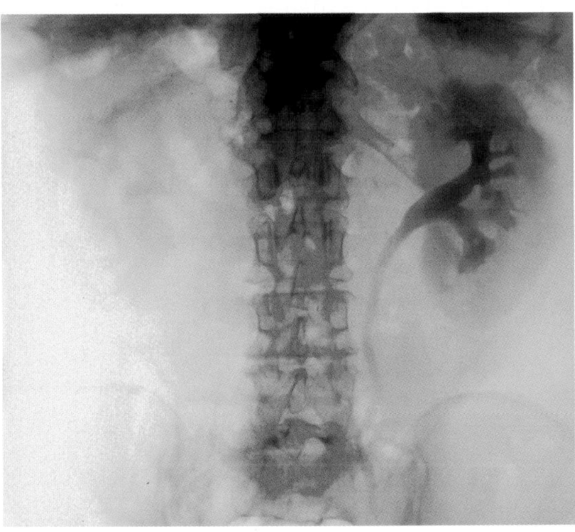

Filtering the blood

As well as balancing the water in our bodies, the kidneys filter and clean out the blood. Each kidney is made up of millions of tiny filtering units called nephrons. The nephrons can filter about 4 litres of blood every 5 minutes. Each day about 200 litres of water leaves the blood and passes into the filters. Most of it is then reclaimed and returns to the blood. Only about a litre per day stays in the nephrons, to leave the kidney and flow into the bladder as urine.

Waste disposal

As well as water, urine contains unwanted salts and urea, a waste substance made by the liver. Urea is poisonous, so the kidneys remove all of it from the blood.

The liquid which leaves the kidneys as urine is about 96 per cent water and just 4 per cent salts and urea. Urine runs down two tubes called the ureters from the kidneys into the bladder. This is a stretchable bag where the urine can be stored. The bladder can hold about half a litre before we must empty it.

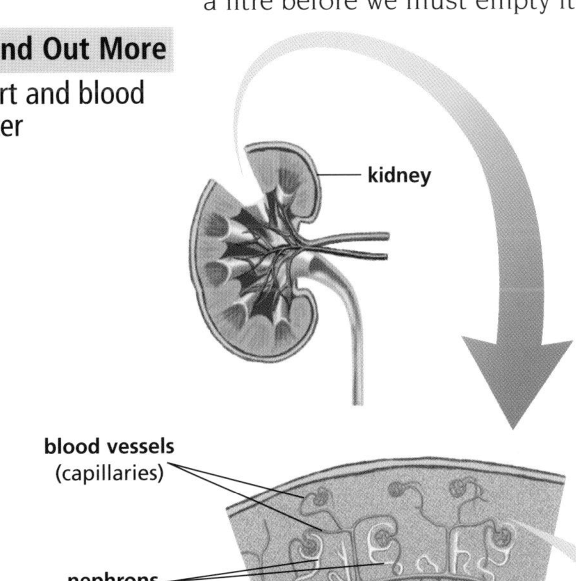

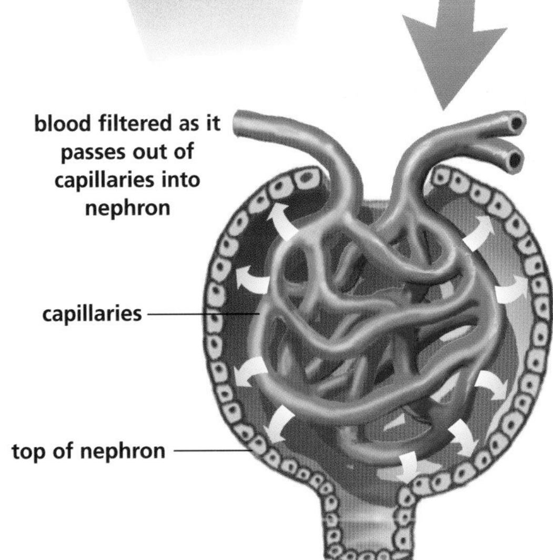

▶ The kidneys are just under the ribs in your back. Below and between them is the bladder. The kidneys contain millions of long, U-shaped tubules called nephrons. Capillaries which surround each nephron reabsorb all the useful materials and most of the water. Unwanted substances pass to the very end of the nephron.

Lasers and holograms

On the Moon is a mirror the size of a tea tray. It was left there by the first astronauts on the Moon. This tiny target is used to reflect back a laser beam sent from Earth – a distance of nearly 400,000 kilometres!

Lasers are useful for all sorts of jobs, because they are so controllable. Doctors direct their heat to weld (fix) retinas in place at the back of the eye, reshape the cornea and seal leaking blood vessels.

Lasers are also used to drop bombs with great accuracy – a laser-guided missile can demolish a target leaving neighbouring buildings untouched.

Surveyors and builders sometimes need to line things up very accurately – for example, if they want to measure heights or mark where a wall should be. A laser is the ideal tool for this, too.

Find Out More

- Compact discs
- Construction
- Lights and lamps
- Weapons

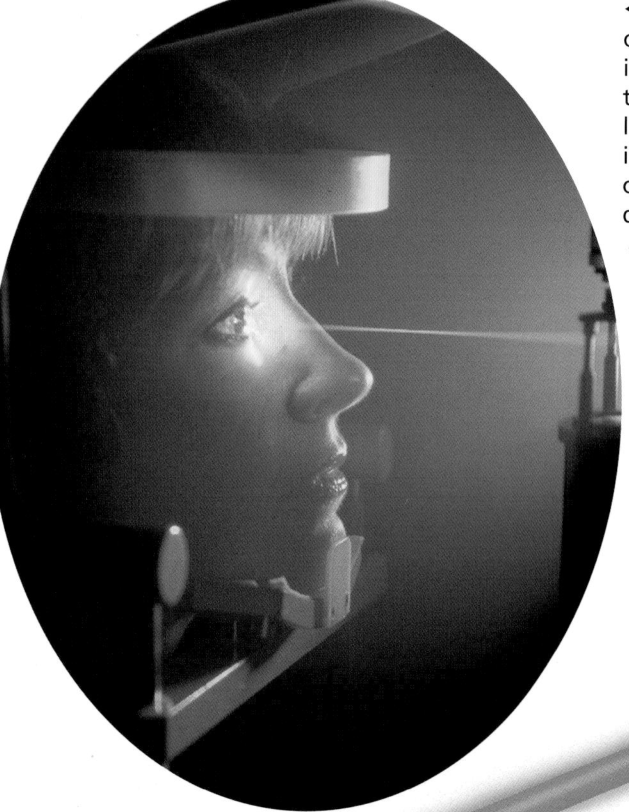

◀ Lasers have a variety of uses in eye surgery, including re-attaching the retina (the layer of light-sensitive cells inside the eye) if it comes loose. Patients do not need an anaesthetic for this treatment.

Straight lines

Lasers are a special source of light called coherent light. This means that all the light waves they produce are in step with each other and travel in the same direction. This is different from a light bulb, which produces light travelling in all directions.

▼ The ruby laser was the first laser invented, in 1960. A high-intensity light produces a bright flash to start the laser. Atoms of chromium within a rod of artificial ruby are excited by this light flash, and emit red light.

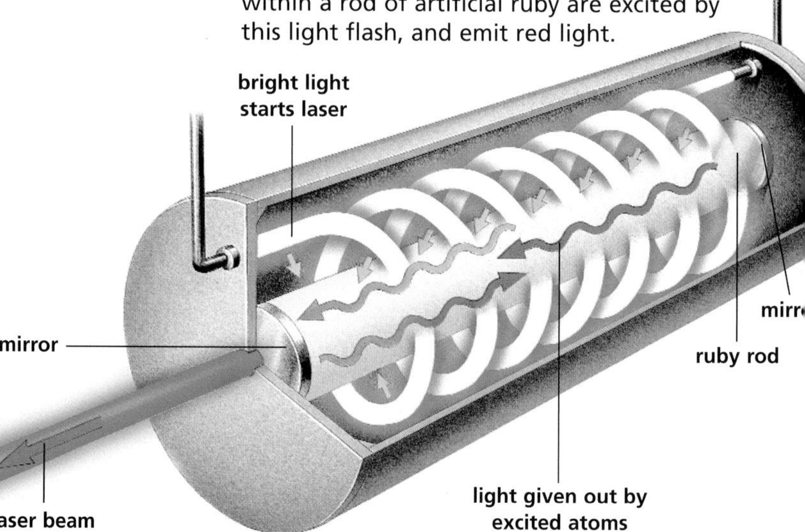

◀ This green laser beam is used to create an artificial 'star' high in the atmosphere. Astronomers can measure changes in the shape of this 'star' caused by the atmosphere, then use this information to improve their images of real stars.

Another difference is that a light bulb will seem dimmer if you stand a long way from it. This is because the light spreads out – the further away you are, the less light enters your eye. Laser light hardly spreads out at all. It can be sent a very long way – to the Moon and back – without becoming much dimmer.

Heat and colour

Concentrated light from the Sun can set fire to a piece of paper. A powerful laser can do the same, because all the energy in the light is concentrated into one small spot. Very powerful lasers can even cut through metal. Laser cutters guided by computers are used by manufacturers to carve pieces of metal very precisely into complicated shapes.

Light is a kind of wave. The white light from a light bulb is a mixture of light of many different colours, each of which is a different wavelength. Laser light, however, is a single, pure colour. Each type of laser produces light of one particular wavelength.

'Laser' stands for 'light amplification by stimulated emission of radiation.' In other words, a light source is made stronger (amplified) by rays (radiation) that are given off (emitted) by atoms that have been given extra energy (stimulated).

How lasers work

A laser works by making an atom produce light, and forcing the atom next to it to make the same light. It's rather like having a row of dominoes standing up – if you knock one over, the rest fall in sequence.

Lasers have either a crystal inside them or a tube containing a gas or liquid. There is a mirror at either end. Electricity (or a flash of bright light) is used to give energy to the atoms in the laser material. They get rid of this energy by sending out light waves. This triggers other atoms to send out the same waves. The light builds up inside the crystal and reflects from a mirror back down the crystal again, triggering more atoms as it goes. The light carries on again, back and forth, getting steadily stronger. One of the mirrors is not perfectly reflecting, and the laser beam eventually escapes at this end of the tube.

THE MAGIC OF HOLOGRAMS

In 1947, the British physicist Dennis Gabor (1900–1979) worked out how it would be possible to record a three-dimensional image on photographic film. No one was able to try out his ideas until the 1960s, when the laser was invented. The first hologram was made in 1962, but a laser had to be shone through the film to make the picture visible. Advances since then have made it possible to make holograms that can be seen in normal light. Holographic images are used on credit cards to make them less easy to copy.

Lateral lines *see* Fishes • **Latitude** *see* Maps • **Lenses** *see* Mirrors and lenses • **Levers** *see* Machines

Life

Imagine travelling back in time 4000 million years. You would find a very different Earth, with no plants, no animals, no bacteria, no viruses. No life at all. Only the crackling electricity of lightning storms, the intense heat and fumes of volcanic eruptions and the boom of meteorites hitting the Earth. There would be no oxygen for you to breathe and nothing to shield you from the Sun's powerful radiation. Yet somehow, in this hostile environment, the first incredible spark of life began.

No one knows for sure how this happened, but scientists think that energy from sunlight and lightning strikes triggered the formation of chemicals that could copy themselves. This may have taken place in the chemical 'soup' that existed in the oceans, in shallow pools or around volcanoes. The next crucial step was when the self-copying chemicals became trapped in 'bubbles' of oil, which held them together. These tiny blobs of chemicals were the beginnings of the first living cells.

mya = millions of years ago

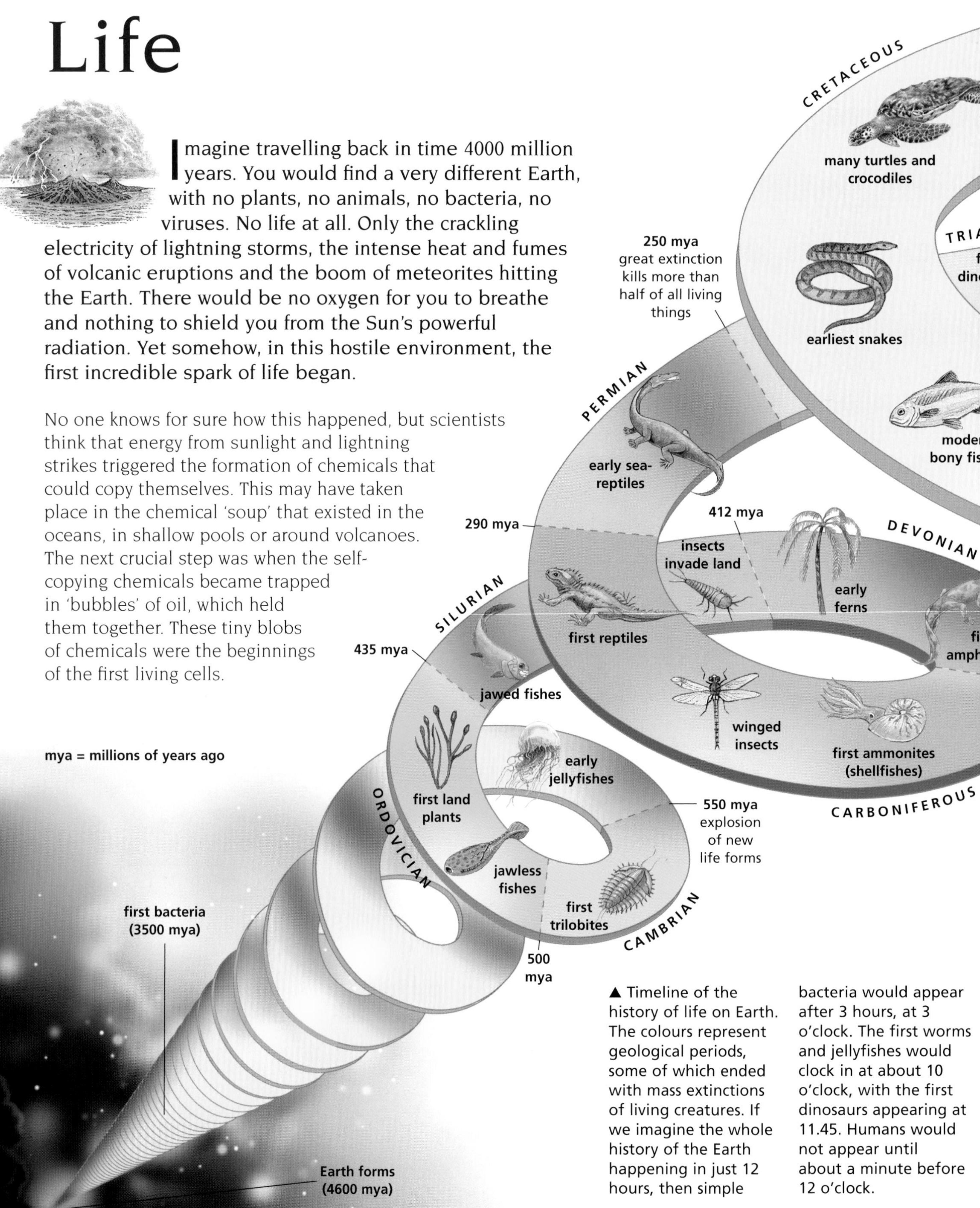

▲ Timeline of the history of life on Earth. The colours represent geological periods, some of which ended with mass extinctions of living creatures. If we imagine the whole history of the Earth happening in just 12 hours, then simple bacteria would appear after 3 hours, at 3 o'clock. The first worms and jellyfishes would clock in at about 10 o'clock, with the first dinosaurs appearing at 11.45. Humans would not appear until about a minute before 12 o'clock.

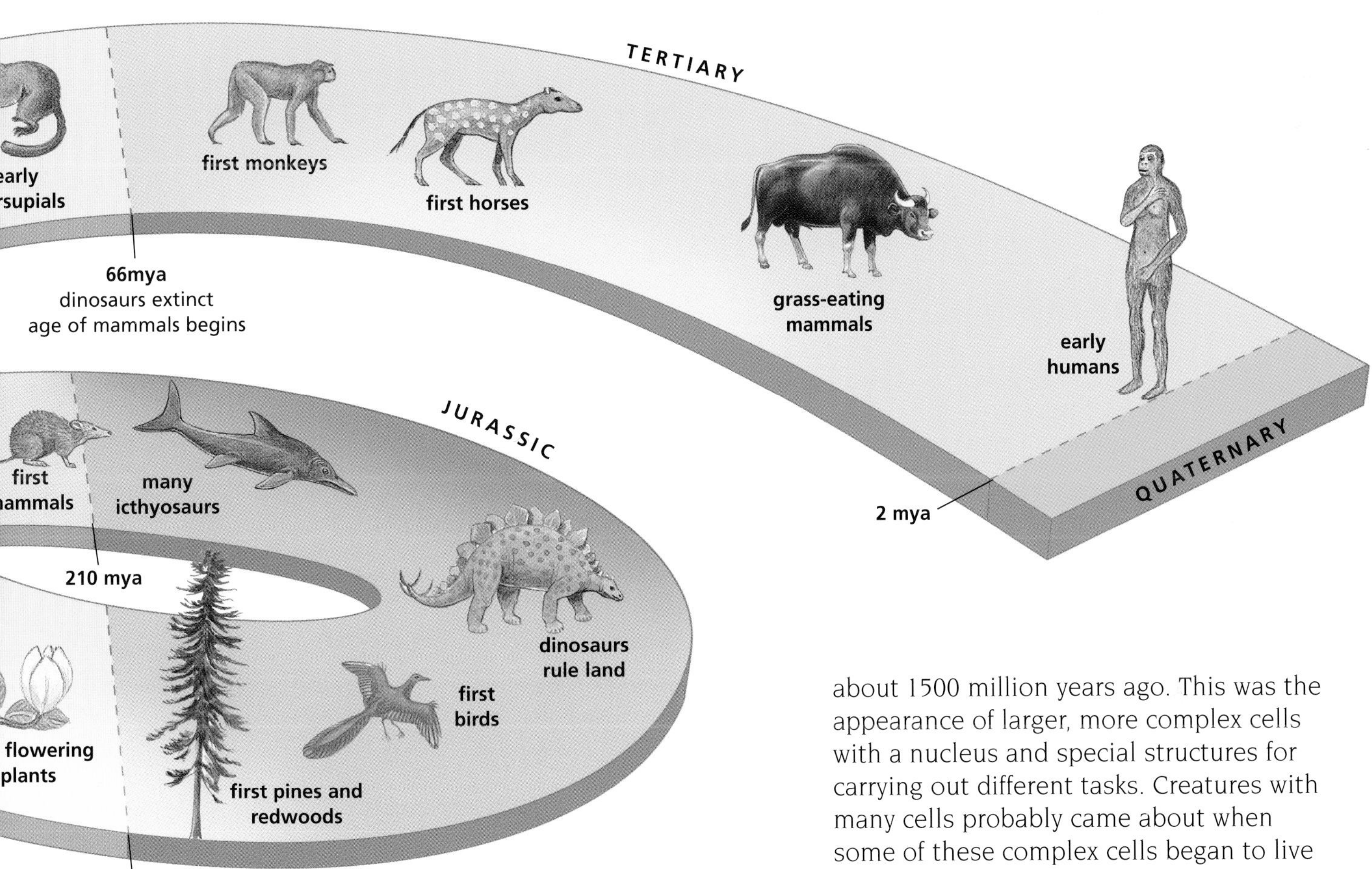

360 mya

What is life?

From the very first simple cells that lived on the Earth to the complex trees and tigers of today, all living things have certain things in common. They reproduce by making copies of themselves, they feed, they get energy from their food, they get rid of wastes and they respond to the world around them.

The first life forms

For almost 2000 million years after life began on the Earth, the only forms of life were microscopic, one-celled creatures similar to the bacteria of today. Some of them eventually began to use light from the Sun to make food, giving off oxygen in the process. As the oxygen built up in the atmosphere, it shielded the Earth from some of the Sun's harmful radiation.

Changing cells

The extra oxygen triggered the next milestone in the development of life, about 1500 million years ago. This was the appearance of larger, more complex cells with a nucleus and special structures for carrying out different tasks. Creatures with many cells probably came about when some of these complex cells began to live together in organized colonies, perhaps about 1000 million years ago, or earlier.

Animal explosion

Around 600 million years ago, life really took off. There was a huge explosion of animal life in the oceans, and the ancestors of probably all the modern animal groups we know today came into being. Over hundreds of millions of years, some simple animals without backbones, which looked like jellyfishes or worms, developed into animals with backbones, including the first fishes.

Life on land

Another great landmark in the development of life happened about 400 million years ago, when life moved on to the land. Plants were first to make the move, followed by insects and other small animals, and finally 'walking fishes' called amphibians. From amphibians developed the first large land animals, the reptiles – such as the dinosaurs – and later birds and mammals, including humans.

Find Out More

- Animals
- Cells
- Earth
- Fossils
- Geological time
- Plants

Lifts *see* Buildings

Light

We are bathed in light. From a distance of 150 million kilometres the Sun sends light streaming down on us. Our eyes have evolved to make use of this light. Light also helps to keep us warm.

Light is a form of energy that travels very quickly. Burning sticks, hot coals and light bulbs all give off light. The Sun gives us most of the light that we use.

Seeing is the main way humans use light. The eye collects light heading towards it. Special cells inside the eye sense the light and send signals to the brain. Somehow the brain turns these signals into pictures.

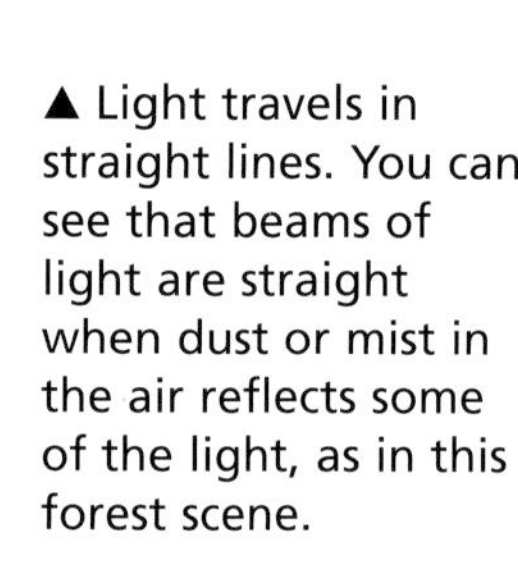

▲ Light travels in straight lines. You can see that beams of light are straight when dust or mist in the air reflects some of the light, as in this forest scene.

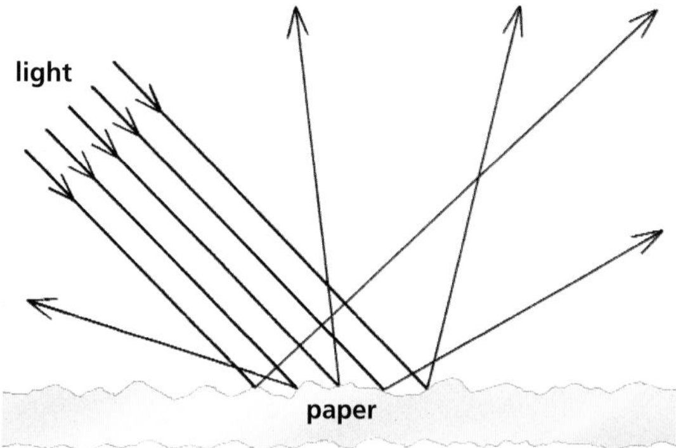

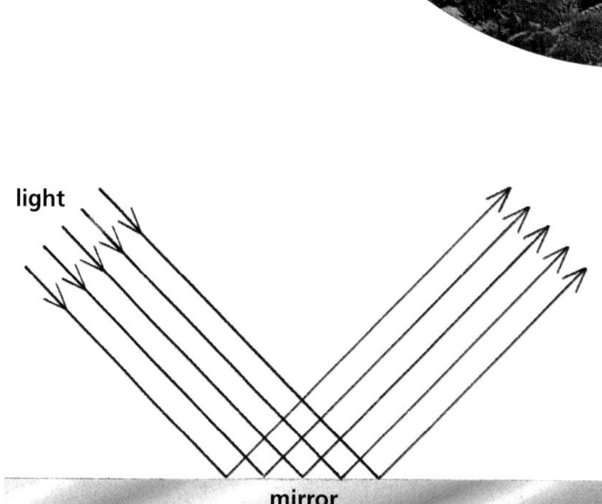

▲ Most smooth surfaces, such as paper, are actually quite uneven, and reflect light in all directions. Very smooth and shiny surfaces, such as mirrors, reflect light in a more orderly way.

Dull, shiny or see-through?

When light hits an object, some of the energy is taken in (absorbed). The rest either bounces back (reflects) or travels straight through the object. Glass and water are transparent (see-through) as they let light travel straight through them without absorbing much energy. Objects that you cannot see through reflect and absorb light.

Shiny objects with a smooth surface reflect light very well. Dark, rough objects do not reflect very well, so they absorb most of the light hitting them. The energy absorbed from light warms the object up. This is partly why we get hot on a sunny day in summer.

▶ Very still water is smooth enough to act as an excellent mirror. These mountains in South America are reflected in the still lake.

WAVE BASICS

The British physicist Thomas Young (1773–1829) proved that light consists of waves.

Wave motion consists of a series of peaks and troughs (a). Every wave has a wavelength: the distance the wave travels between two peaks (one complete cycle). The height of each peak or trough is the amplitude of a wave.

The frequency of a wave is the number of cycles the wave goes through every second. The bottom wave (b) is twice the frequency of the top one. Higher frequency waves have shorter wavelengths.

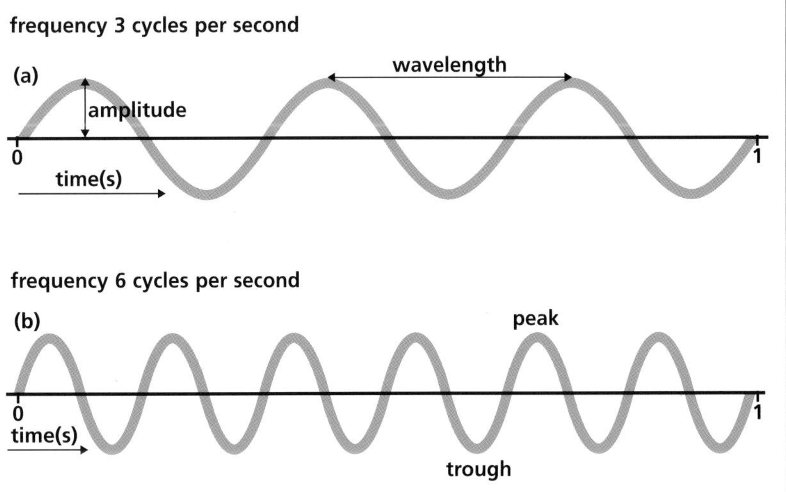

Light waves

Light travels as a series of tiny waves. When a lamp makes light, the energy streams out like ripples crossing a pond. The distance between two peaks in a series of ripples is called the wavelength. Light waves also have a wavelength. The wavelength of light is very small – you could fit 2500 of the smallest light waves in just one millimetre.

▲ In this puppet theatre from Indonesia, the puppets are held between the light source and a semi-transparent screen. The puppets block the light, making dark shadows on the bright screen.

Colours

When we see white light, we are actually looking at many colours mixed together.

These colours can be split up so we can see them. A rainbow is made when drops of water separate the colours in sunlight. The same thing can be done using a prism (a triangular piece of glass). The pattern of colours is called a spectrum.

Most objects are coloured because of the way they reflect light. White objects reflect all the colours. Black objects hardly reflect any light at all. Coloured objects reflect back some of the colours, but absorb others.

Each colour is light of a different wavelength. Red light has the longest wavelength, while violet light has the shortest. Waves with a longer wavelength than red light are invisible: they are called infrared (IR) waves. At the other end of the spectrum, invisible ultraviolet (UV) waves have wavelengths shorter than violet light.

Bending light

If you hold a straight stick so that it has one end under water, you will see that the stick does not look straight. Light coming from the end of the stick is bent as it comes out of the water.

If you stand on top of a cliff above a beach and watch the waves angling in, you may notice that they sometimes bend as they reach the shore. Waves slow down as the water gets shallower, and because the waves are coming in at an angle, one end is slowed down first. This makes the waves bend.

Light can be bent in the same way: this is called refraction. Light travels more slowly in glass than in air, so when light rays hit a piece of glass at an angle, they bend. The lenses and prisms we use in spectacles, cameras and binoculars all bend light in this way.

In space, light travels 9461 million million kilometres in a year. Astronomers call this distance a light year. They use it to measure the distances to stars and galaxies.

Find Out More

- Colours
- Electromagnetic spectrum
- Lights and lamps
- Spectrum
- Waves and vibrations

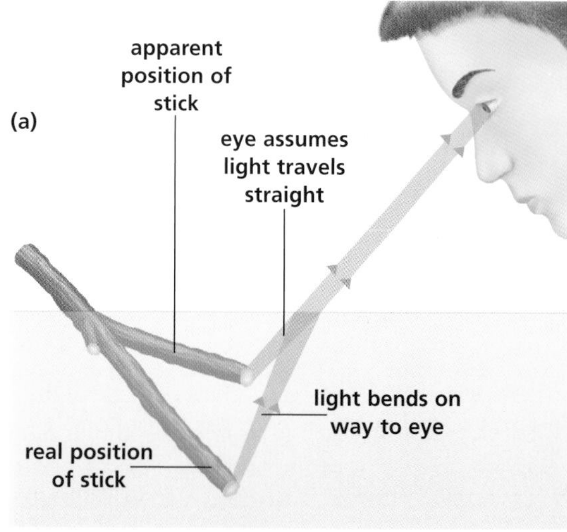

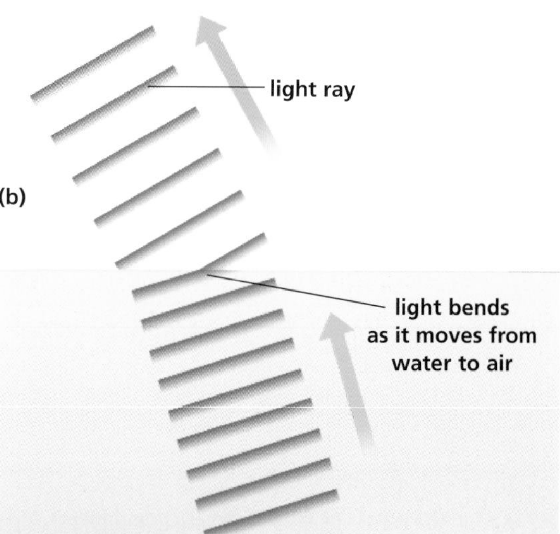

▶ If you put one end of a straight stick in water, it appears to bend where it enters the water (a). This is because light rays from the underwater end of the stick bend as they move from water into air (b). This fools the eye into seeing the end of the stick nearer to the surface than it actually is.

THE FASTEST THING WE KNOW OF

When you switch on a torch, you don't have to wait for it to light something up. This is because light travels very quickly – 300,000 kilometres in a second. At that speed you could travel round the world seven times every second.

When light comes from a very long way away, it takes some time to get to us. Light from the Sun takes over 8 minutes to reach the Earth. But light from the most distant galaxies takes billions of years to reach us.

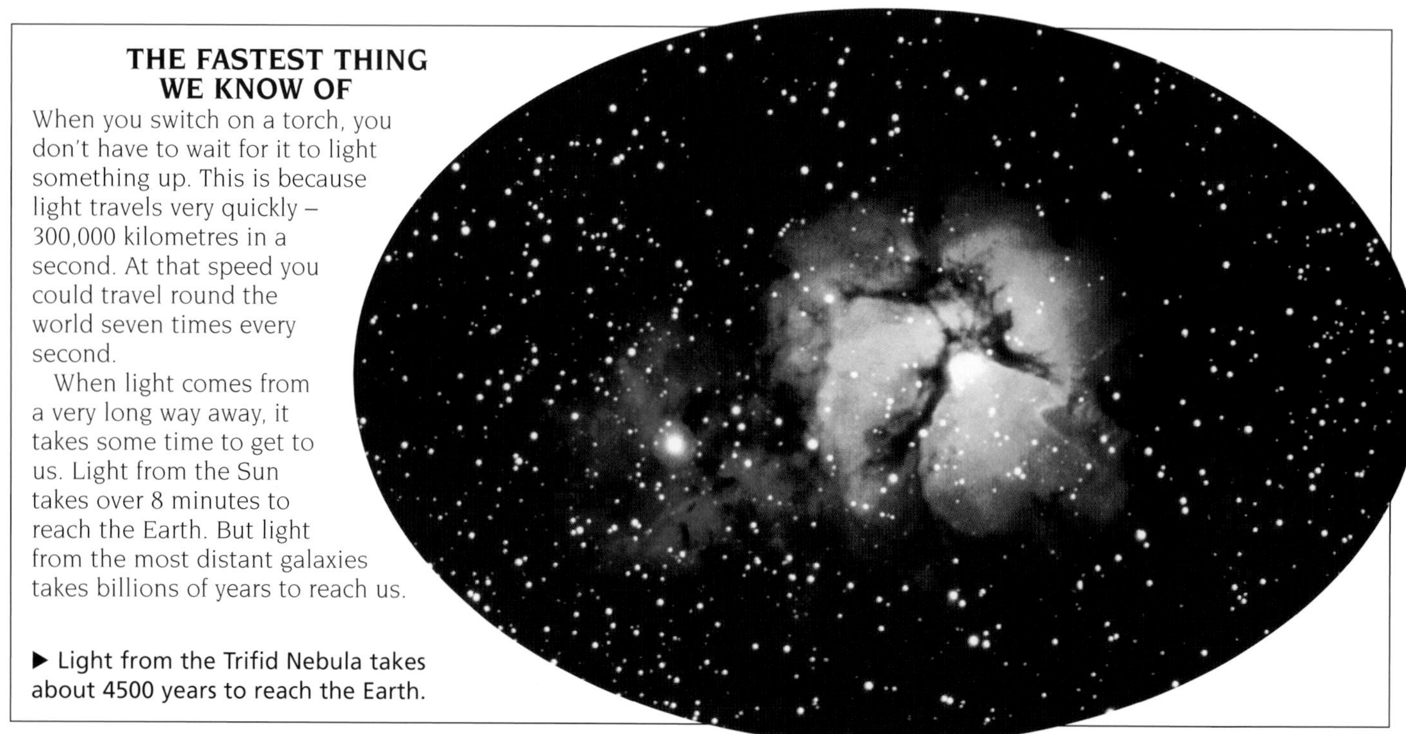

▶ Light from the Trifid Nebula takes about 4500 years to reach the Earth.

Lighthouses *see* Mirrors and lenses • **Lightning** *see* Thunder and lightning

Lights and lamps

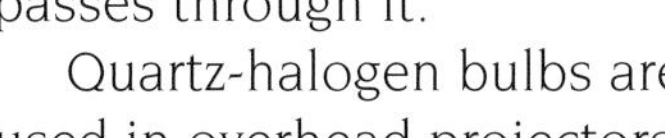

The Sun is like a huge nuclear furnace that pours out light and heat. Without it, all life on Earth would die. But modern life does not stop when the Sun goes down. We have lights in our homes, headlamps on our cars and torches to carry around.

In the past, people burned materials such as wax or oils for light, but they produced a fairly poor light, and could not be used again. Most modern lighting is electric.

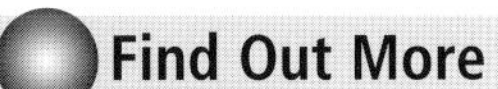

Find Out More

- Chlorine
- Circuits
- Lasers and holograms
- Light

Electric light

The simplest electric lights contain a coil of thin wire called a filament. It is made of tungsten, a metal with a very high melting point. This filament is inside a sealed glass bulb, filled with a small amount of a gas that stops it catching fire. The filament glows brightly when a current passes through it.

Quartz-halogen bulbs are used in overhead projectors and spotlights. The bulbs are made from quartz rather than glass, because they work at a higher temperature. They also produce more light and use less power than ordinary bulbs.

A fluorescent light is a glass tube containing a small amount of gas. When an electric current passes through the gas, it produces ultraviolet (UV) light. As we cannot see UV light, the inside of the tube is coated with a material called phosphor, which glows when UV hits it. It is this glow that we see.

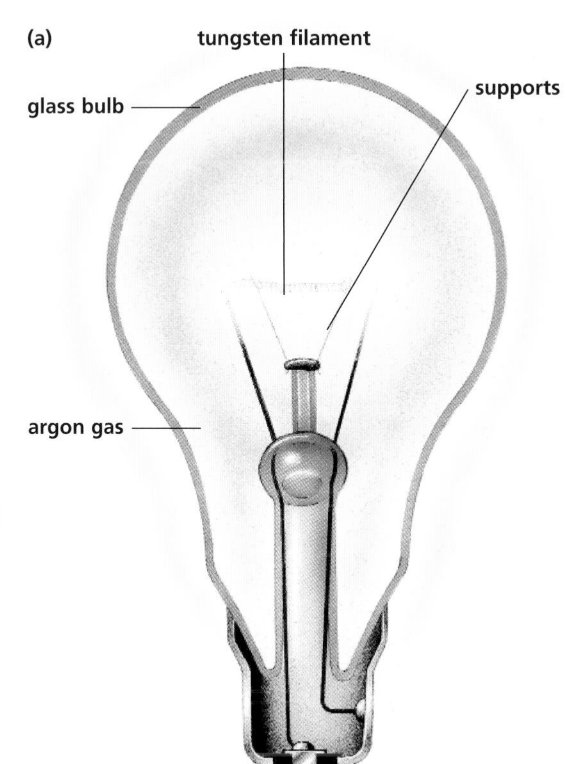

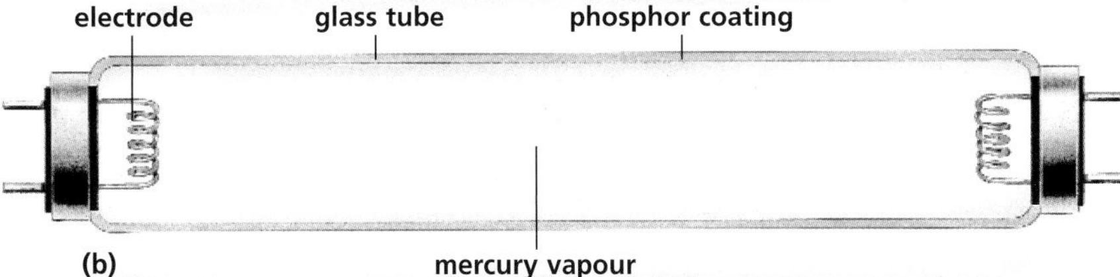

▲ Cutaways of an ordinary filament light bulb (a) and a fluorescent tube (b). A fluorescent tube produces four times the light of a light bulb of the same power.

◀ Glow-worms make their own light from chemical reactions. Scientists are studying them – and using the chemicals they produce – to make new light sources.

Light years *see* Constellations • **Limestone** *see* Rocks • **Liquid crystals** *see* Hardware, computer

Liquids

The liquid we are all most familiar with is water. All forms of life depend on water. But there are also other important liquids. For example, we use oil (in the form of petrol and diesel) to supply cars and other machines with energy, and also to help machines run smoothly. And many metal objects are made by first melting the metal, then pouring the molten liquid into a mould of the desired shape.

Unlike solids, liquids do not have a fixed shape. They can flow, and take up the shape of whatever container they are in. Liquids aren't normally as strong as solids – you can easily push your hand through a still liquid. However, unlike a gas, you cannot squeeze a liquid to make it take up less space – just try pushing a cork into a bottle that is full to the brim!

▼ A pond skater can walk on the surface of a pond because the surface of a liquid behaves like an elastic skin. The force that causes this is called surface tension. The pond skater is not heavy enough to break this 'skin'.

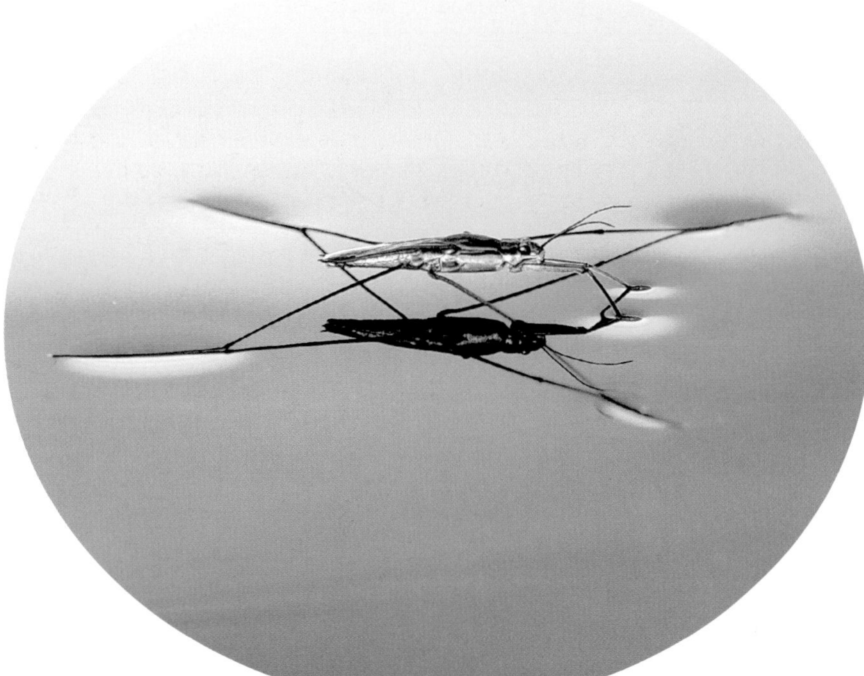

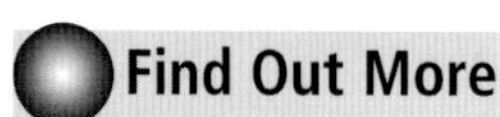

Find Out More

- Atoms and molecules
- Gases
- Matter
- Metalworking
- Mixtures and solutions

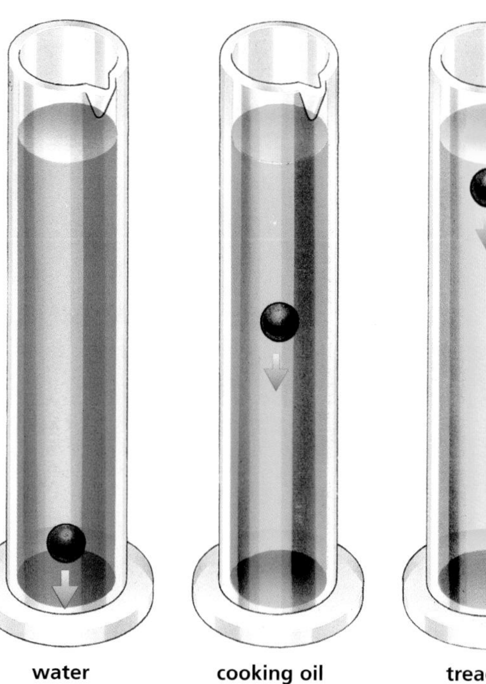

▲ Some liquids are thicker than others. Thicker liquids like honey or treacle flow more slowly than thinner liquids like water. Thicker liquids are said to have a higher viscosity. If you drop a ball bearing or marble into different liquids, you will see that it falls more slowly through liquids with a higher viscosity.

Particles in motion

Like all forms of matter, liquids are made up of tiny particles such as atoms and molecules. Liquids can flow and change shape because – unlike in a solid – the particles can move around each other, like marbles in a bucket.

If you cool a liquid enough, it will freeze into a solid. If you heat up a liquid, the particles move faster. Faster particles on the surface of the liquid evaporate – they escape from the surface. If you heat up the liquid more, it will boil – bubbles of gas form in the liquid, which eventually all turns into gas.

At high pressures, liquids are anything but soft. Engineers can use very fine, high-pressure jets of water to slice through metal.

Lithium *see* Sodium • **Litmus paper** *see* Acids and alkalis • **Litre** *see* Measurement

Liver

The liver is the body's chemical factory. It is the largest organ in the body, and one of the busiest – it carries out more than 500 different tasks. One of its main jobs is to process the nutrients we absorb from our food.

The liver has many different roles. It produces a substance called bile, one of the digestive juices. It recognizes many harmful drugs and poisons, and renders them harmless before they can do any damage. And it recycles old red blood cells.

Import control

Four-fifths of the blood going to the liver comes directly from the digestive system. The liver removes some nutrients from the blood, passing on only those we need for our daily needs. If we have too much glucose from sugary or starchy foods, the liver will take up sugar from the blood and store it. These stores can be quickly released if sugar levels get low.

The liver also absorbs and stores fat and some vitamins. It uses one of these vitamins, vitamin B12, for making new red blood cells. The liver also recycles old red blood cells. Some of the chemicals from these old cells are used to make the bile, which is stored in the gall bladder.

Some nutrients that the liver receives cannot be stored at all. If there is too much protein or vitamin C, for example, the liver must remove them altogether. It converts excess proteins into urea, which is sent to the kidneys and leaves the body in urine.

By the time blood leaves the liver, it has the correct balance of nutrients for all the body's needs.

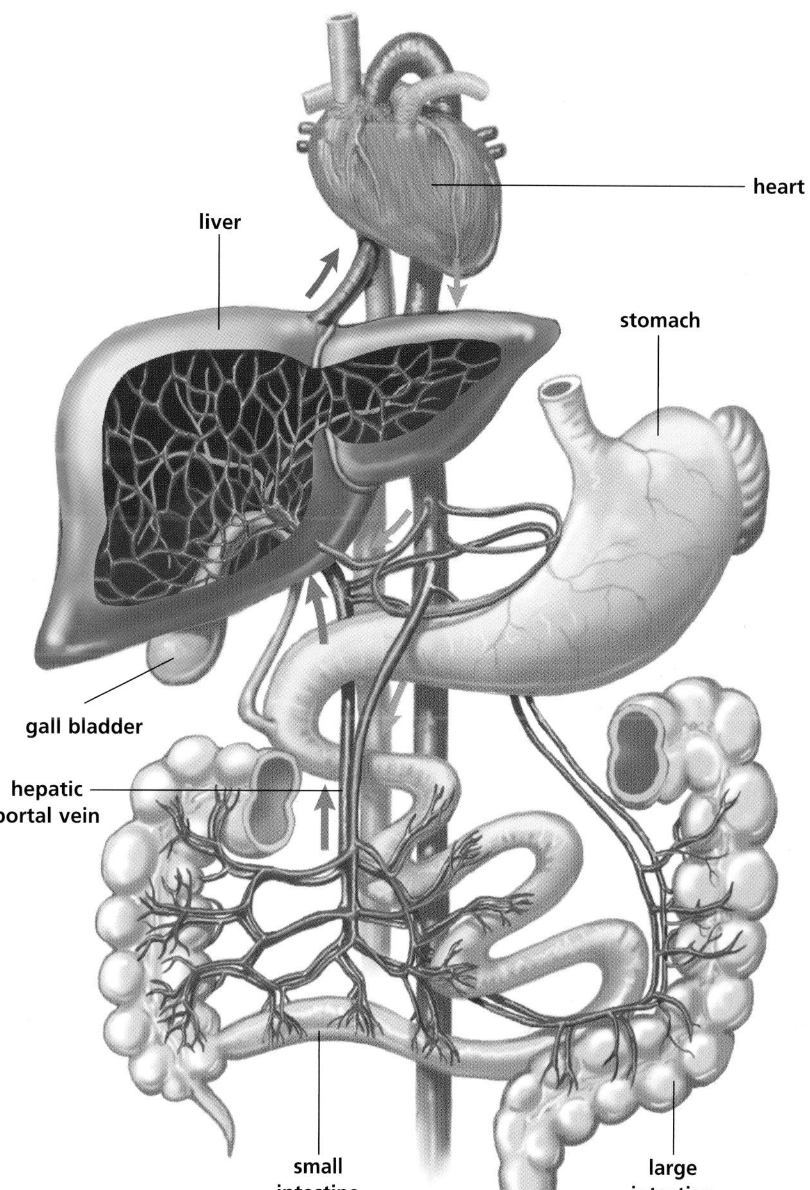

▲ Blood from the digestive system arrives at the liver in the hepatic portal vein. Once the liver has processed the blood, it passes into the main blood system. Bile from the liver is stored in a small sac called the gall bladder.

▼ Jaundice is a yellowness of the skin, which is caused by diseases of the liver or gall bladder.

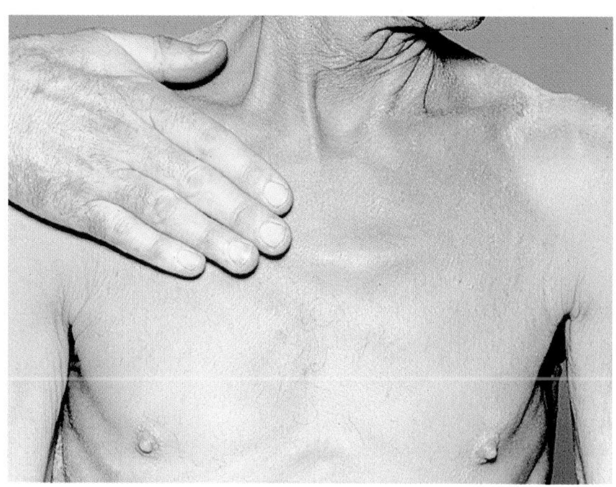

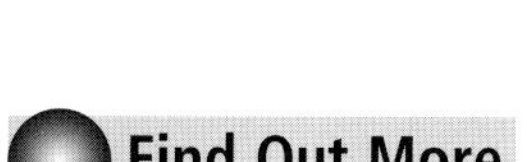

- Diet
- Digestion
- Heart and blood
- Kidneys

Lungs and breathing

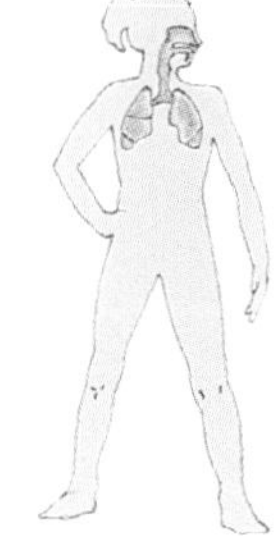

From the day we are born to the day we die, we breathe every few seconds. We may take as many as 20,000 breaths a day. We breathe air because we need a constant supply of the oxygen it contains to fuel our activities. Our lungs extract the oxygen, and send it via the blood to all our cells.

Your body needs energy to power the activities of every cell. Energy comes from the food you eat. It is released during respiration, a chemical process that takes place in every cell. Respiration uses oxygen and produces carbon dioxide as a waste product. Breathing in draws in the oxygen, and breathing out gets rid of the waste carbon dioxide.

Find Out More

- Bones and muscles
- Cells
- Heart and blood
- Oxygen

LUNG DISEASES

People who live in places where the air is polluted, or who smoke, are more likely to suffer from lung diseases. Bronchitis is a disease in which the linings of the air passages (bronchi) become inflamed. In asthma, the muscles in the bronchi contract, and restrict the flow of air. One form of asthma treatment is to use an inhaler containing a drug that relaxes the muscles of the bronchi.

In and out

Your nose, windpipe, lungs and chest muscles make up your breathing system. Lungs have no muscles of their own, so the muscles of the chest do the work of breathing.

▼ As we breathe in, the diaphragm is lowered and the ribs move up and out to draw air into the lungs.

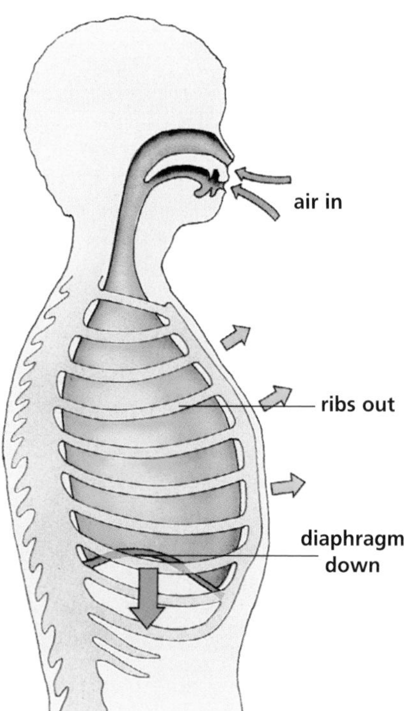

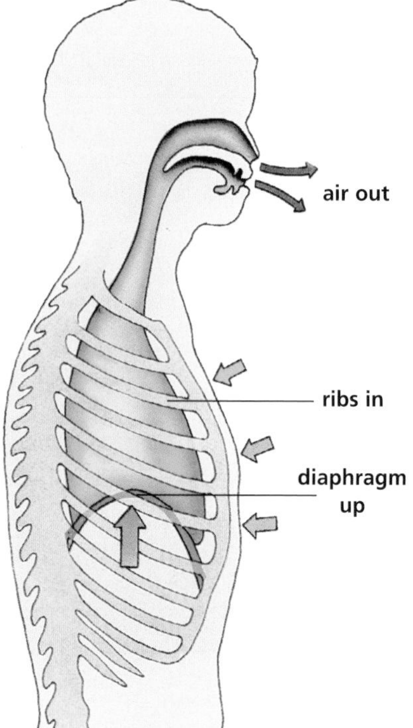

Most important of all is the diaphragm, a flat sheet of muscle covering the floor of the chest. As the diaphragm pushes downwards, it reduces pressure on the lungs and creates more space inside your chest. Air rushes in to fill the lungs. During gentle breathing, the diaphragm moves only a centimetre or two. As you exercise, it may move 6 or 7 centimetres. When you take a really deep breath, muscles between the ribs lift them upwards to make even more space in your chest.

Breathing out is the reverse of breathing in. Muscles lower the ribs, and the diaphragm arches upwards. The lungs are squeezed, and air and carbon dioxide are forced out.

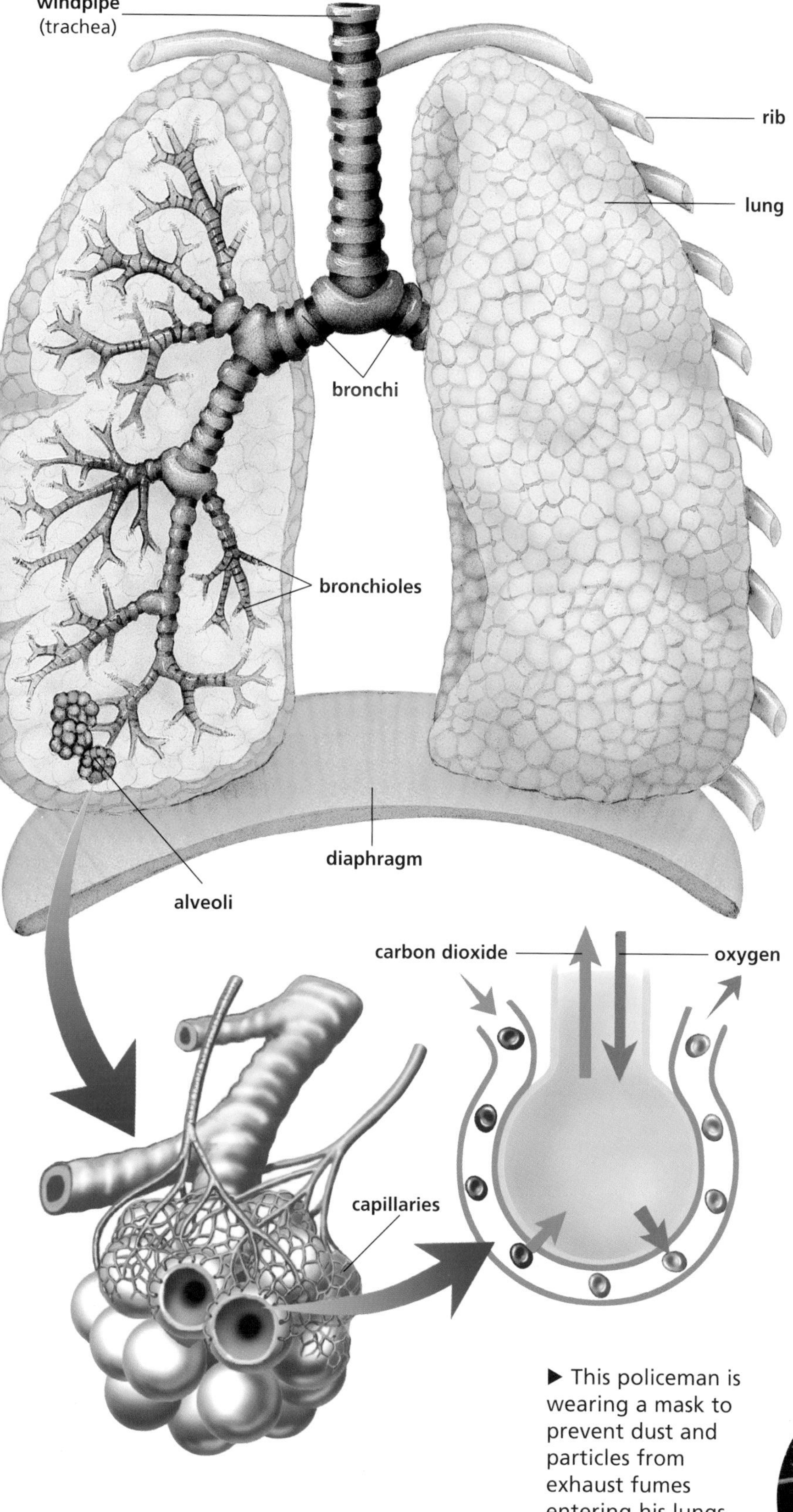

◀ Air enters the lungs through the nose and mouth, and passes down the windpipe. The windpipe divides into two bronchi, which in turn divide into bronchioles and finally into alveoli. Each of your lungs has over 200 million alveoli.

▲ Oxygen is exchanged for waste carbon dioxide through the thin walls of the alveoli. Alveoli are arranged in groups which resemble bunches of grapes.

After vigorous exercise you may breathe up to 10 times faster than when you are resting, to get all the oxygen your body needs.

Inside the lungs

Air travels to the lungs through the nostrils and down the windpipe, or trachea. Inside the lungs it passes into smaller and smaller branching passageways. Each tiny passageway ends in a group of air sacs called alveoli. Hundreds of millions of aveoli make up the lungs. It has been estimated that if they were flat, they would cover a tennis court. An adult's lungs hold about 5 litres of air.

The walls of the alveoli are thinner than tissue paper, and are covered with tiny blood vessels, or capillaries. Oxygen easily seeps through these capillaries into the blood, while carbon dioxide from the blood goes in the other direction.

Keeping the lungs clean

The air around us is often dirty, and dirt and dust can harm the alveoli. So the air is cleaned on the way to the lungs. Hairs in the nose catch the largest particles. Smaller particles are trapped in the windpipe, and air passages by a sticky liquid called mucus. The mucus passes up to the throat and is swallowed or sneezed or blown out.

▶ This policeman is wearing a mask to prevent dust and particles from exhaust fumes entering his lungs.

Machines

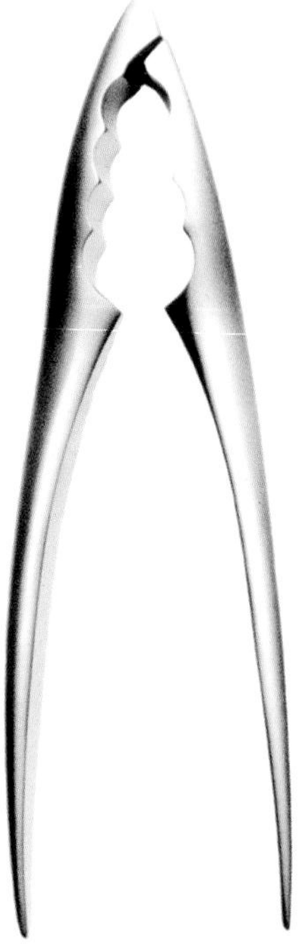

▶ Nutcrackers are a kind of lever. The hand is much further from the hinge than the nut, and this magnifies the effort of the hand so that it becomes strong enough to crack the nut.

Imagine being hungry and thirsty, and having only canned food and drinks in corked bottles – but no can opener or corkscrew to open them. You would have to use your bare hands – a difficult and dangerous business! Every day, tools make all sorts of tasks possible.

All sorts of tools, such as can-openers, corkscrews, hammers and spanners, are operated by hand. They work by increasing the amount of force you can exert with your hands or fingers. These devices are simple machines.

Powered machines, such as cars and excavators, have engines and motors to produce force. But they may also contain simple machines, such as levers and gears, to increase the amount of force driving the wheels, buckets or other parts.

Greater effort required

Every machine needs a force to drive it, and this driving force is called the effort. The machine magnifies the effort and applies it to a load, which may move.

You can lift the side of a car using a jack. The effort is the light force of your hand turning the jack handle, while the load is the great weight of the car. The jack greatly increases the force of your hand until it is equal to the weight of the car and raises it.

Find Out More
- Energy
- Engines and turbines
- Forces
- Motion
- Tools

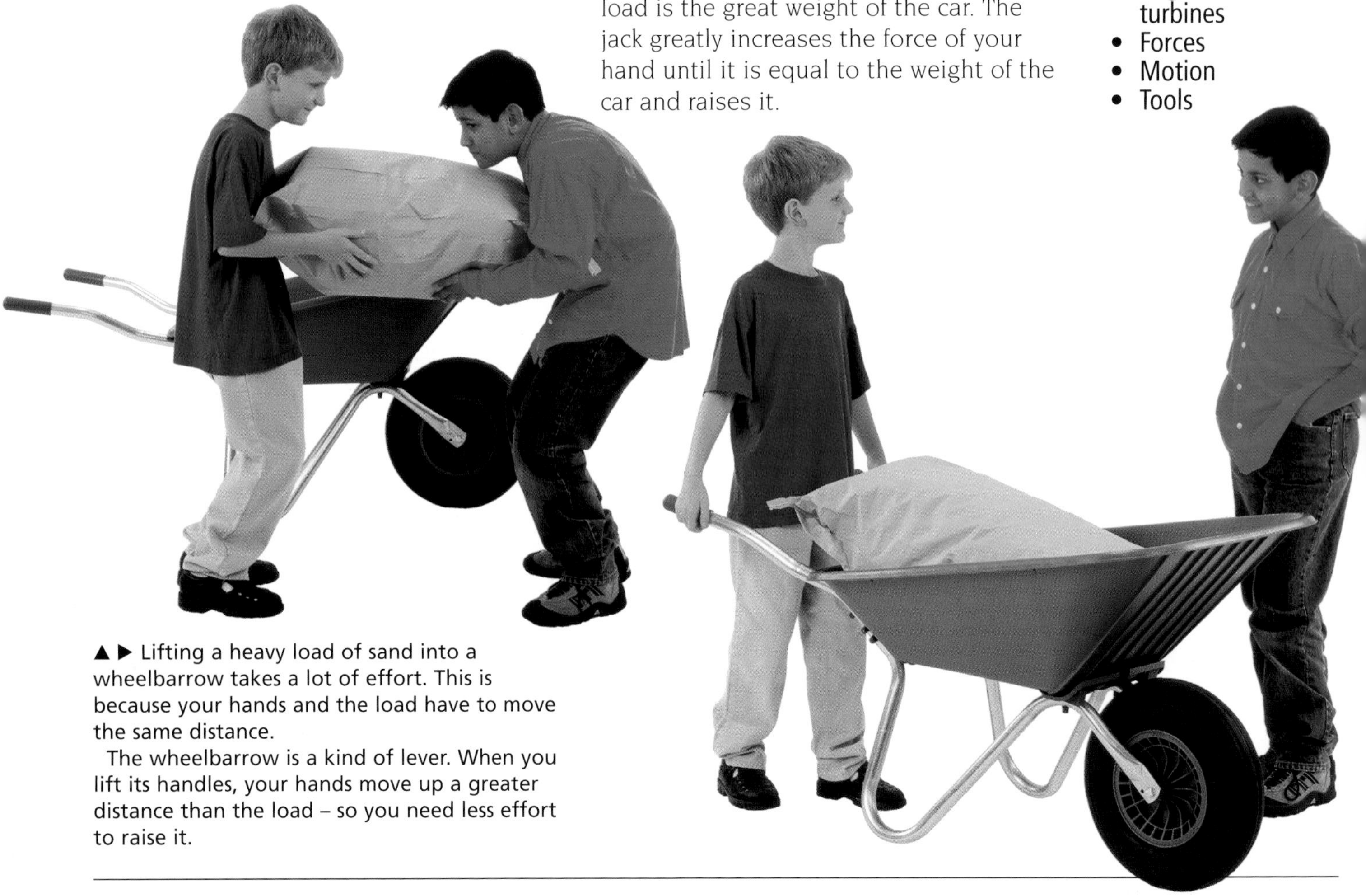

▲ ▶ Lifting a heavy load of sand into a wheelbarrow takes a lot of effort. This is because your hands and the load have to move the same distance.

The wheelbarrow is a kind of lever. When you lift its handles, your hands move up a greater distance than the load – so you need less effort to raise it.

LEVERS

You can use a lever to raise a heavy load, using an effort equal to only half the load, if the effort is twice as far from the pivot as the load. But the load moves only half as far as the end of the lever where the effort is being applied.

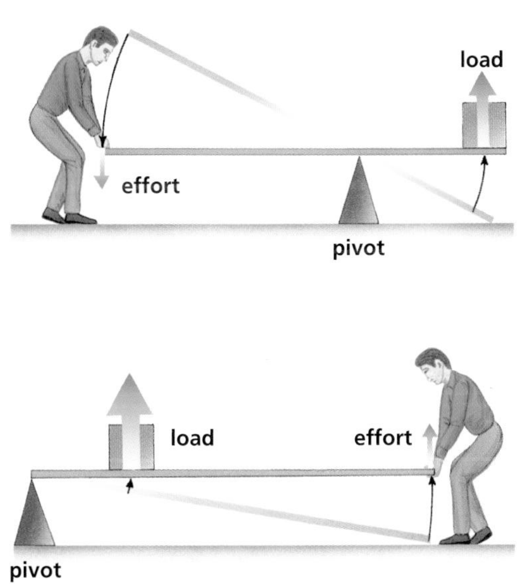

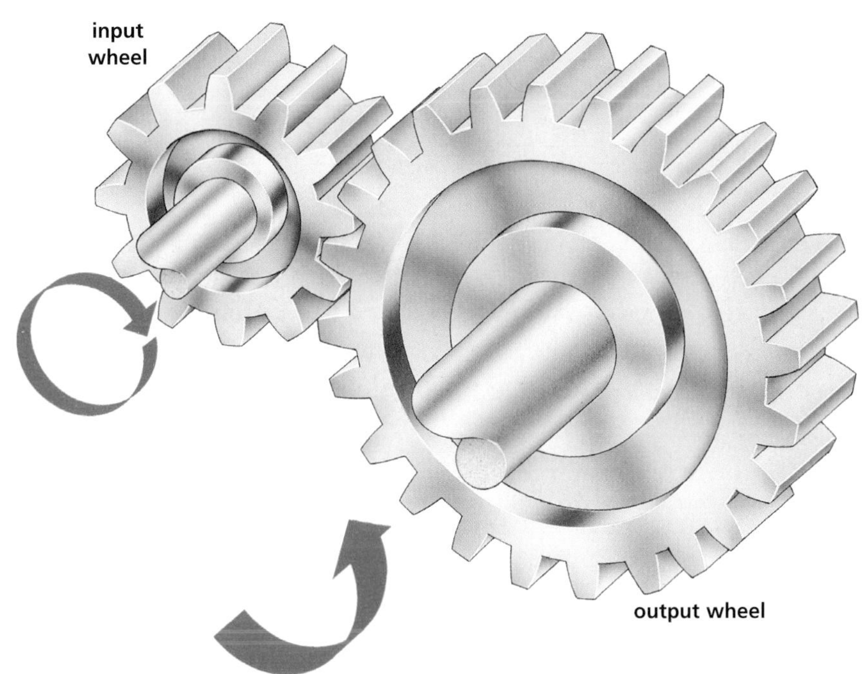

▲ Principles of gearwheels: the small gearwheel turns the larger gearwheel more slowly, but with more force in the opposite direction.

The jack works because you have to turn the handle many times to raise the car's wheel just off the ground. Your hand travels a greater distance than the car rises. Simple machines trade force and distance like this. By moving a greater distance than the load, the light effort is magnified to match the heavy load.

Levers and gears

The most common kinds of simple machines are levers and gears. Levers are rods or bars used to move things. You push one end to exert a force at the other end of the lever or another part of it. Pliers, nutcrackers and bottle openers are levers, and pianos, bicycle brakes and excavators use levers. Spanners and screwdrivers are levers that move in a circle.

Car and bicycle gears contain toothed wheels that mesh together or are connected by a chain. The gearwheels are different sizes and rotate at different speeds, so that they can increase or decrease the force. You can ride up a hill in low gear on a bicycle because you pedal more quickly and this increases the force that turns the back wheel.

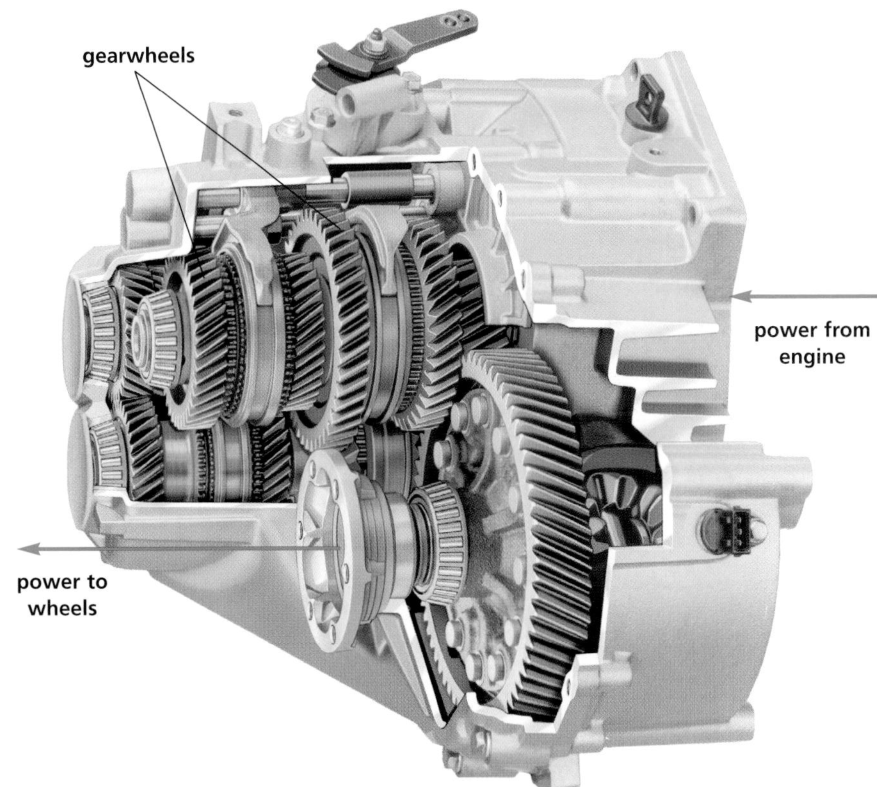

▲ The gearbox in a car connects a shaft from the engine to a shaft that turns the wheels. Changing gear makes different gearwheels connect the shafts so that the engine can turn the car's wheels at different speeds and with different amounts of force.

Mach number *see* Sound • **Magma** *see* Volcanoes • **Magnesium** *see* Sodium

Magnetism and electromagnetism

Without magnetism many things we take for granted today would not exist. The electricity that powers all the electrical items in your home, for example, comes from generators that use huge magnets to create electric current. And in your television, the picture is moved and changed many times each second by magnets inside the TV tube.

▲ If you scatter tiny iron filings around a magnet, they line up along the lines of magnetic force around the magnet. More filings collect at the poles than anywhere else. A compass needle will also point along the lines of magnetic force.

Magnetism is a force that is found in nature and has been known about for thousands of years. Before scientists discovered how it worked, it was thought to be a magical power. Magnetism is closely related to electricity and can do important work for us.

Quite repulsive

A magnet can attract other objects or repel other magnets (push them away) without touching them. All magnets are surrounded by an invisible magnetic field, where their magnetism can be felt. The field is strongest in two places on the magnet, called the north and south poles. On a bar-shaped magnet, the poles are at either end.

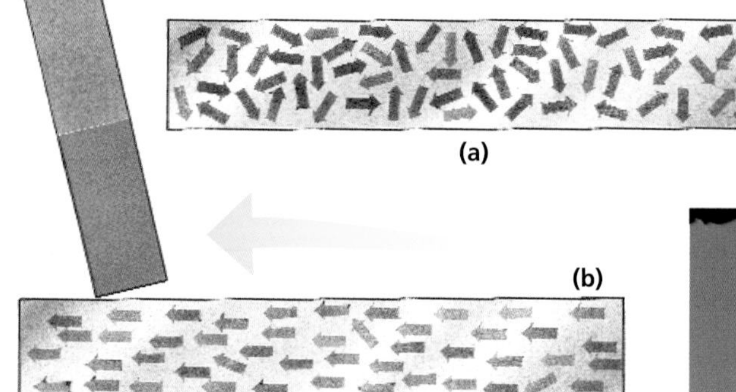

▲ A magnetic material like iron contains many tiny magnetized areas called domains. If the material is not a magnet, these domains point in different directions (a). But by rubbing another magnet on the material, the domains can be lined up, and it becomes a magnet (b).

◄ A compass needle is a small bar magnet whose north pole lines up with the Earth's magnetic field, showing us where north is.

Magnification *see* Microscopes, Mirrors and lenses

Magnets can only attract things that also contain magnetic materials. Iron is the most common magnetic material. An iron-rich rock called magnetite, or lodestone, was one of the first natural magnets discovered. Other magnetic materials include nickel and cobalt. It is the arrangement of the electrons (the tiny particles inside atoms) in a substance that makes it magnetic or not.

Perhaps the best-known use for magnets is in compasses. Compass needles always point to the north. But why? The answer was found by William Gilbert, an English scientist, in 1600. He discovered that a compass needle is in fact a magnet, and that the Earth itself has a magnetic field, with one magnetic pole near the North Pole, and the other near the South Pole.

MICHAEL FARADAY

Michael Faraday (1791–1867) has a special place in the history of physics and engineering because his discoveries led to so many inventions. He was one of the greatest experimental scientists of all time.

Faraday invented the first electric motor, and discovered the theory of electromagnetic induction. This showed that a magnet pushed into a coil of wire generated an electric current in the coil.

Modern electric generators all use induction to make electricity. Faraday also discovered that an electric current in one wire can cause a current to flow in another wire.

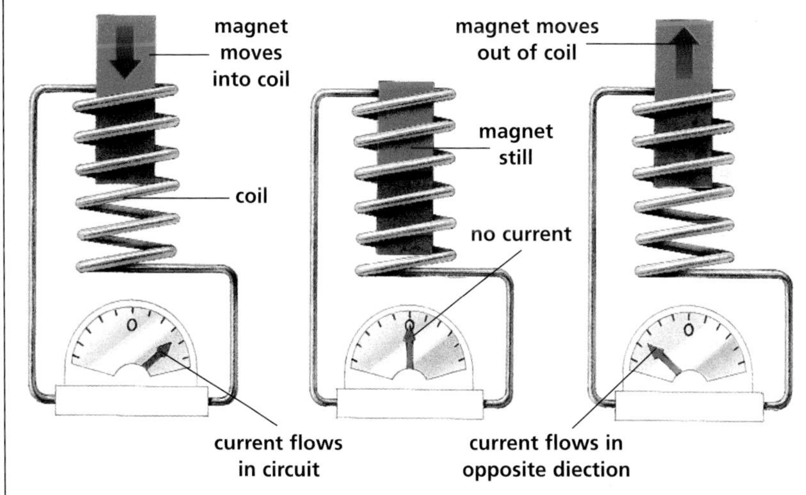

◀ Powerful electromagnets can be turned on to pick up scrap metal, then turned off to dump the metal. Similar electromagnets are used to lift and dump old cars into crushers.

Find Out More

- Electricity
- Electricity supply
- Electric motors

Electrickery

Because magnetism depends on the behaviour of electrons, there are strong connections between electricity and magnetism. This was first noticed in 1820, by the Danish scientist Hans Christian Oersted, who saw that a current flowing through a wire made a nearby compass needle move. Later, André Ampère in France discovered that electric currents in wires can attract or repel each other, just like magnets.

Today, these principles are used to make a powerful type of magnet called an electromagnet. An electromagnet is made by passing an electric current through a coil of wire, usually wound around an iron core. When the current is switched off, the electromagnet loses its magnetism. Electromagnets are used in many electrical machines, such as generators and motors. In the home, small electromagnets work electric doorbells.

Mainframe (computer) *see* Computers • **Malaria** *see* Diseases

Mammals

A group of peccaries shuffles through the forest, unaware of the danger lurking ahead. A jaguar crouches, still and silent, by the side of the track, its spotted coat making it almost invisible in the fading light. At the last moment, the jaguar pounces, grasping a peccary's throat in a suffocating bite.

▲ Seal pups that are born on the ice feed on their mother's very rich milk. This helps them to grow fast and become independent before the ice breaks up.

Cats like the jaguar belong to the same group of animals that we do – mammals. Mammals are generally more intelligent than other animals and are the only animals to have fur or hair. The young of most mammals are born live, although a few mammals lay eggs. Females feed their young on milk produced in special mammary glands on their own bodies.

Worldwide mammals

There are about 4000 different kinds, or species, of mammal. They live all over the world, from icy polar regions to baking deserts and tropical forests. They are able to do this because, like birds, they are warm-blooded. Their body stays at the same high temperature, regardless of the temperature around them.

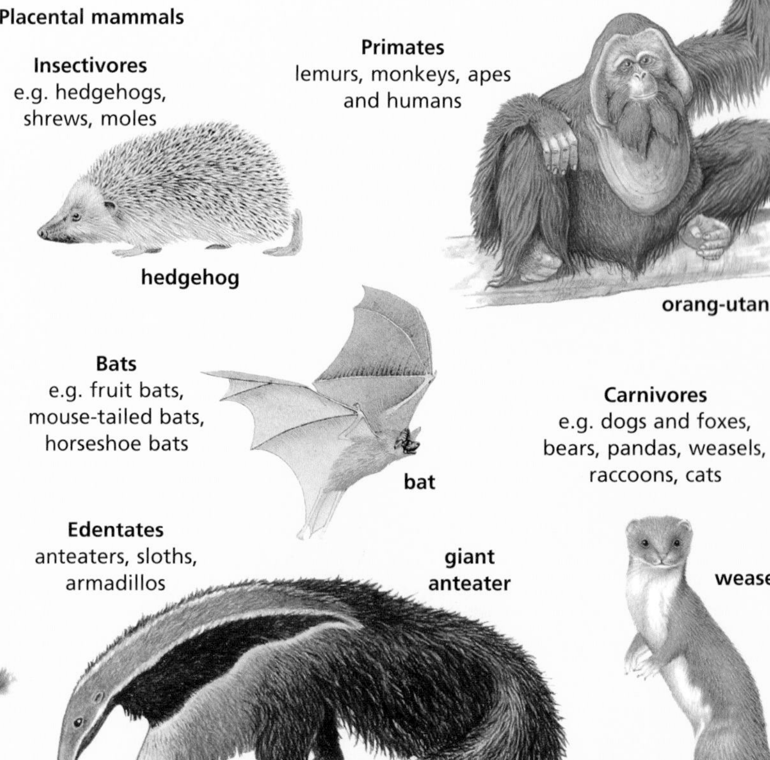

▲ ▶ Living mammals are classified into 21 groups, or orders, based on features that they have in common. The main orders are shown above. The biggest order is the rodents, with 1,700 species.

Mammal young

Mammals are divided into three groups, according to the way their young develop.

Placental mammals give birth to well-developed young. Inside the mother's body, the young are nourished through a special organ called the placenta. Marsupials give birth to tiny young, which finish their development in a pouch on their mother's body. Monotremes (platypuses and echidnas) hatch out of eggs.

Find Out More

- Animals
- Classification
- Life
- Sex and reproduction

Sky and sea

The only true mammal fliers are bats. There are hundreds of different bats. They make up one quarter of all mammal species. A bat's wings are made of thin flaps of skin stretched between long finger bones.

Swimming around in the oceans are mammals such as whales, dolphins, sea cows and seals. Their ancestors used to live on land, but they have now made the sea their home. Dolphins, whales and sea cows spend their whole lives in the sea. Seals, sea lions and walruses come out of the sea to breed.

◀ Most mammals have three kinds of teeth: incisors for cutting, canines for gripping and tearing, and molars for grinding up food.

Pinnipedes
seals, walruses, sea lions

walrus

Proboscids
elephants

elephant

Even-toed ungulates
e.g. pigs, camels, deer, giraffes, cattle

red deer

Rodents
squirrels, mice, beavers, rats, voles, chipmunks, porcupines

chipmunk

Odd-toed ungulates
horses, tapirs, rhinoceroses

rhinoceros

Whales
dolphins, porpoises, whales

blue whale

Lagomorphs
rabbits, hares, pikas

hare

Mankind *see* Humans • **Manufacturing** *see* Industry and manufacturing

Maps

When most people think of maps, they think of the road maps they use to find their way around, or political maps that show where countries, cities and towns are in the world. You can actually make a map of just about anything, from the galaxies in the Universe to the ant hills in your back garden.

A map is a drawing or an image of a place that highlights specific information about the area.

There are many different kinds of map. Physical relief maps show the shape of the land, by marking land at different elevations (heights) above sea level. The map of South Africa on the opposite page is of this type. Geological maps (such as the one below) show what rocks are on the Earth's surface or just beneath the soil. Climate maps show how climates vary from one part of the world to another.

Find Out More

- Navigation
- Rocks
- Satellites

◀ This is a geological map of England, Wales and part of Scotland. Geologists use such maps to work out the geological history of a particular place, to plan building projects, and to find important natural resources such as coal.

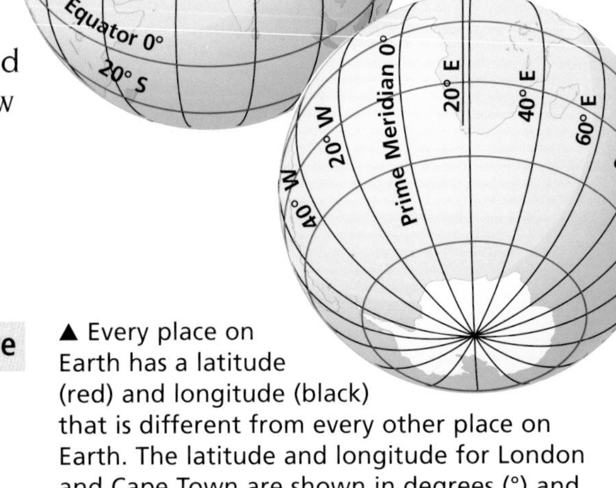

▲ Every place on Earth has a latitude (red) and longitude (black) that is different from every other place on Earth. The latitude and longitude for London and Cape Town are shown in degrees (°) and minutes (′). (There are 60 minutes in a degree.)

Latitude and longitude

To make it easier to describe where things are on the Earth, people have divided the surface into a grid. Longitude lines, also known as meridians, run from the North Pole to the South Pole. Latitude lines, also called parallels, are like rings around the Earth that run parallel to the Equator.

Latitude and longitude are measured in *degrees* rather than kilometres or miles. Latitude is measured in degrees north or south of the equator. Longitude is measured in degrees east or west of the Prime Meridian. The Prime Meridian is the line of longitude that runs through Greenwich, England.

Maps for all occasions

It would be confusing (and impossible) to put every bit of information about a place on one map, so we have hundreds of kinds of maps.

People use maps for many things. For example, hikers use topographic maps to plan their routes. Mining companies use geological maps to decide where to explore for important minerals. Meteorologists make weather maps every three hours in order to track storms and other weather systems.

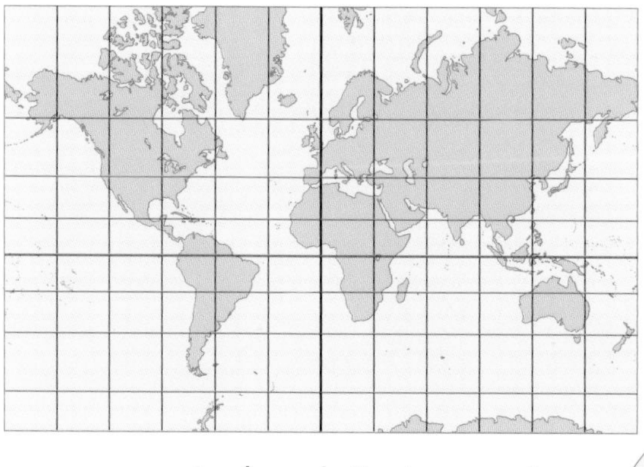

Mercator projections are useful for navigating because the directions are not distorted. But things at the north and south edges look much bigger than they really are.

A **polar projection** is a map whose centre is at the North or the South pole. The shapes of things are right, but things at the edge of the map look bigger than they really are.

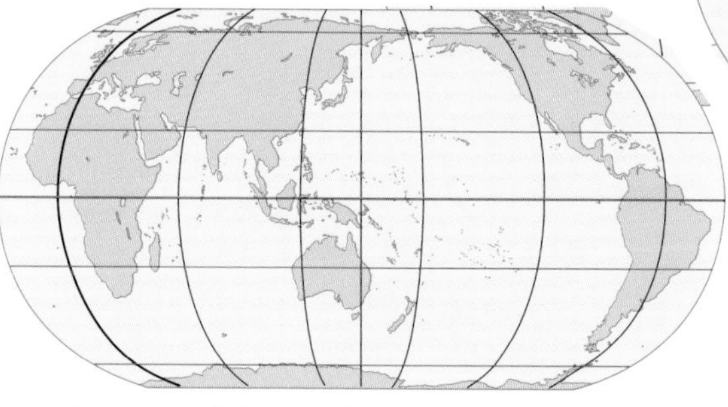

In an **Eckert projection,** the scale of the areas is the same everywhere on the map. However, both the shapes and directions are distorted.

▲ All maps of the Earth show a slightly distorted view. The problem is that the Earth is a sphere, but maps are flat. People have developed different kinds of maps for different uses. Each is accurate in some ways and distorted in other ways.

▲ This Digital Elevation Model (DEM) shows part of the western USA: the long, flat, green strip is the Central Valley of California. Such images are made using computer programs that put together millions of elevation (height) measurements taken from aircraft, satellites and surveyors on the ground. Each colour represents a different elevation.

READING MAPS

The map on the right is a topographical (physical relief) map of South Africa. To read this map, you need to know which direction is which, how big an area is shown, and what the symbols mean.

As on most maps, north is towards the top, with west to the left, east to the right and south towards you. Sometimes there is an arrow pointing north to remind you.

To show how big an area is shown, there is a scale bar. This shows that every centimetre on the map represents 16 million centimetres (160 kilometres) on the ground.

The different elevations (heights) above sea level are shown in different colours on the map. The key (or legend) tells you what the different colours mean. It also shows what the symbols used on the map mean.

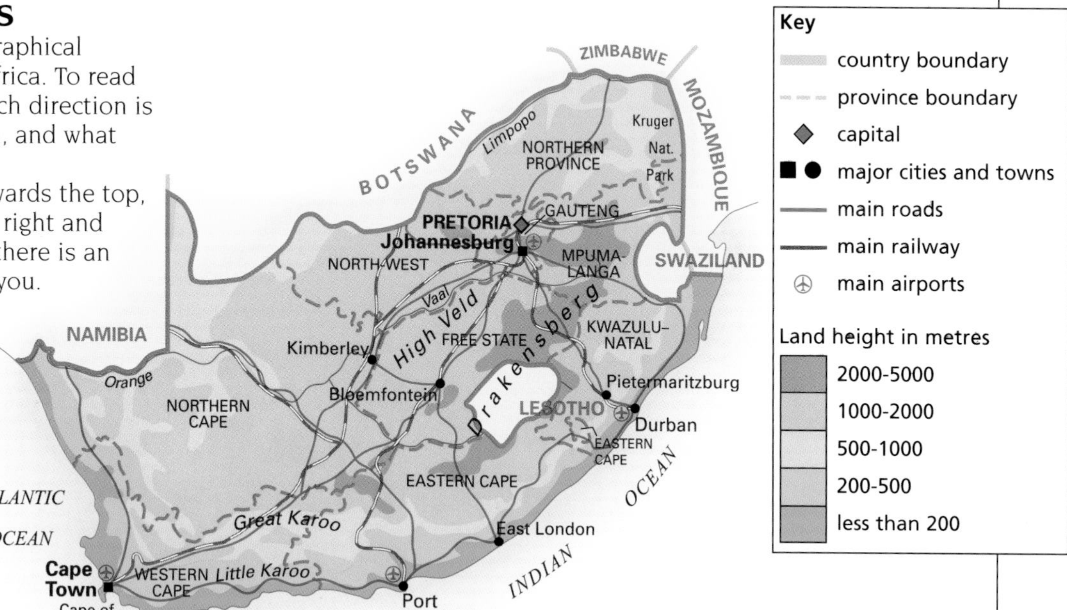

Marconi, Guglielmo *see* Radio • ***Mariner*** (space probe) *see* Space astronomy

Mars

A bleak desert landscape stretches to the horizon on every side. The rust-coloured surface is littered with boulders but there is no sign of life. This place might be somewhere on Earth, but it is Mars.

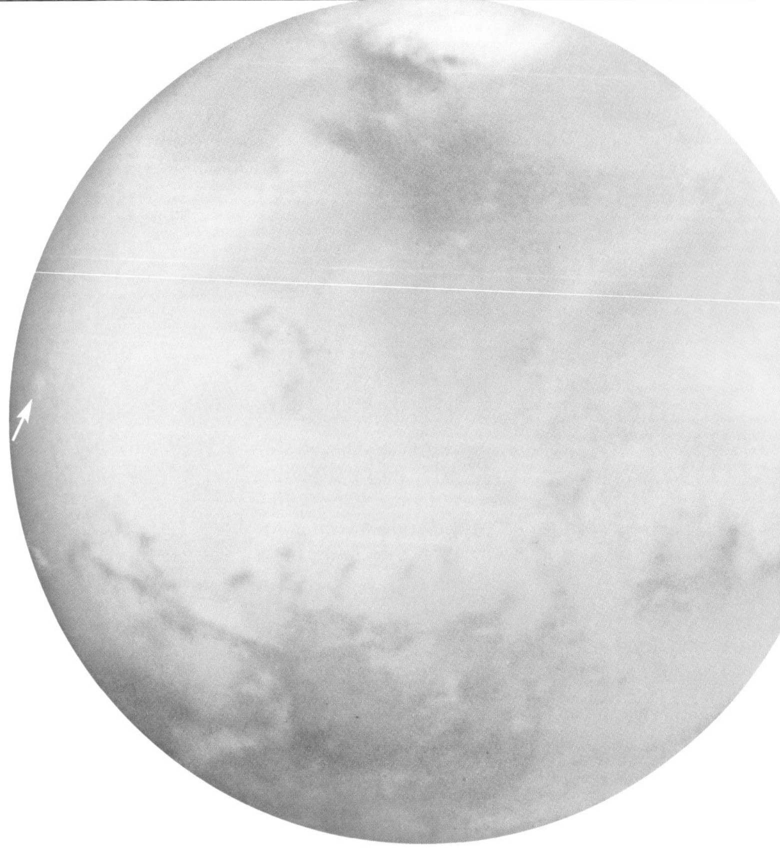

▲ This view of Mars was taken by the Hubble Space Telescope in 1995. On the far left (arrowed), the peak of a volcano pokes through early morning mist made of water ice crystals.

Mars is the fourth planet out from the Sun. It is visible in our night sky, glowing orange-red, for a few weeks about every two years. Mars is the planet most like Earth. Its polar caps grow and shrink with the seasons. There is an atmosphere and weather. Mist forms in the morning and clouds sometimes shroud the tops of mountains. Strong winds whip up great dust storms.

But Mars is not a friendly place for life. The atmosphere is mainly carbon dioxide and very thin: the Earth's atmosphere is 100 times denser. Temperatures can reach 20 °C on a summer afternoon, but are mostly much lower, less than –23 °C on average.

In this environment, any liquid water would evaporate directly. However, there could be ice trapped in the rocks underground, and there is permanent water ice over the north pole. The frost that settles on the polar caps in winter is solid carbon dioxide, or 'dry ice'.

MARS DATA
Diameter at equator: 6796 km
Average distance from Sun: 228 million km
Time taken to spin on axis: 24.6 hours
Density (water = 1): 3.9
Time taken to orbit the Sun: 1.88 years
Moons: 2

▼ This panoramic view of a dried-up flood plain on Mars was taken by the space probe *Mars Pathfinder* in 1997. The red colour of the rocks is due to iron oxide: rust.

Martian history

Mars was a very different planet 1000 million years ago. At that time it had active volcanoes, a thicker atmosphere and flowing water. Long snaking valleys were cut by streams. Massive floods wore away parts of the ground and carried rocks about.

Several vast volcanoes rise over the plains in the northern hemisphere. None of them are active any longer. Olympus Mons is the largest volcanic mountain in the Solar System.

▶ Olympus Mons seen from orbit by *Viking* spacecraft. Mars has lower gravity than the Earth because it is a smaller planet. The low gravity helped Olympus Mons pile up to a stupendous height after many eruptions.

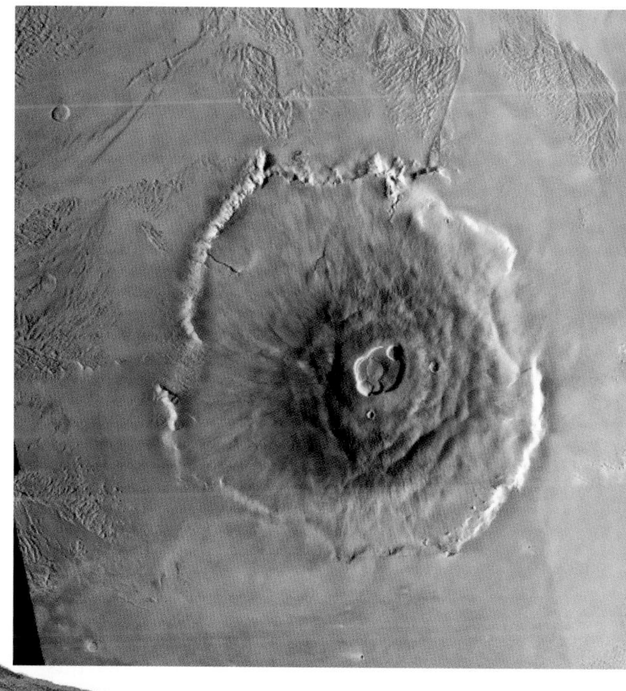

Mount Everest

Olympus Mons

Hawaiian islands

sea level on Earth

Canyons and craters

A huge system of canyons, called the Mariner Valleys, extends for 5000 kilometres near the equator. These great chasms are 6 kilometres deep on average. They formed when volcanic activity caused large areas of Mars's surface to bulge upwards. The Mariner Valleys are where the surface rocks cracked apart under the strain.

There are many craters on Mars. Most are in the southern hemisphere. In the north, craters have been covered up by flows of volcanic lava.

▲ The Martian volcano, Olympus Mons is 600 kilometres across and 25 kilometres high. The cliffs around its base are 6 kilometres high. Earth's largest volcano, Mauna Loa in Hawaii, rises just 10 kilometres above the surrounding seabed.

Is there life?

For a long time, people imagined there could be life on Mars. However, by the 1960s astronomers realized that there could be no liquid water there, which is needed by life as we know it.

If there ever was life on Mars, when it was warmer and wetter, there may be fossils waiting to be discovered. And it is just possible that some microscopic life could exist underground.

Find Out More

- Planets
- Solar System
- Space astronomy
- Sun
- Volcanoes

MARTIAN MOONS

Mars has two small moons, Phobos (right) and Deimos. Phobos is 28 kilometres long and Deimos 16 kilometres long. They could be asteroids captured by Mars's gravity. Both moons are very dark and covered in impact craters. Deimos looks smoother because it is covered by a layer of dust.

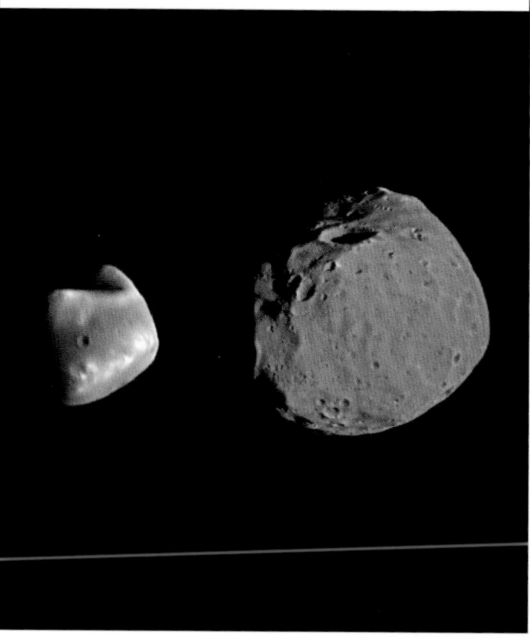

Marsupials *see* Mammals • **Mass** *see* Gravity

Mathematics

Draw a circle with a diameter of one centimetre. Now measure its circumference (the distance around the edge). You will find that it is just over 3 centimetres. This value is known as pi (π). You get the same number if you divide the circumference of any circle by its diameter. Mathematicians have used computers to calculate π to billions of decimal places, but an exact value will never be reached.

▲ Computers have made it possible to speed up most mathematical calculations enormously. This CM-5 supercomputer can carry out 10 billion separate instructions every second.

Calculating π is just one aspect of mathematics. Mathematicians also study the properties of numbers, shapes, lines and the space which objects fill. They explore the patterns present in numbers, and try to understand why these patterns occur.

Mathematics is an essential tool in all other sciences. It has been called the language of science. Scientists record their measurements as numbers, they use mathematical equations to help them draw conclusions from experimental results, and they use maths to try and predict the results of new experiments.

THE NUMBER LINE

Different sets of numbers have different names. They can all be shown, in theory, on a straight line called a number line. Positive and negative whole numbers are called integers. Numbers with fractional parts fall between the integers.

Rational numbers are numbers that can be written as fractions, for example $5/2$ or $3/4$. Irrational numbers are not equal to any fraction. An example is π. Although it is an irrational number, π has a place on the number line. This can be found by drawing a circle of a diameter of 1 unit, placing it on the line and rolling it exactly one revolution along (see diagram).

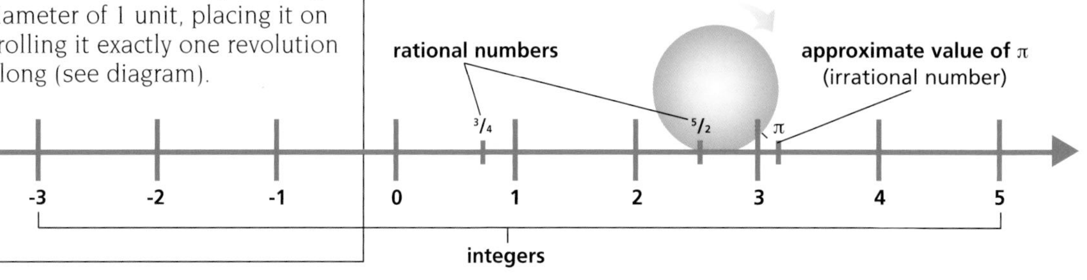

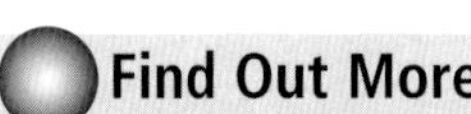

Find Out More

- Geological time
- Measurement
- Moon
- Relativity
- Seasons
- Sun
- Waves and vibrations

Numbers

Mathematics starts when we learn to count and to calculate with numbers.

Today we normally count using the decimal or base 10 system. With just 10 digits (0, 1, 2, 3, 4, 5, 6, 7, 8, 9), plus the decimal point (used for parts of whole numbers), we can write any number we wish, no matter how large or small. We can do this because the value of each digit in a number depends on its position. Each place is worth 10 times the one on its right. So, for example, 3510 is shorthand for

thousands	hundreds	tens	ones
3	5	1	0

Other number systems are also possible. Computers, for example, operate using the binary (base 2) system with just two digits: 0 and 1. In a binary number, each place is worth two times the one on its right. For example:

eights	fours	twos	ones
1	1	0	0

in binary means 1 eight + 1 four + 0 twos + 0 ones – in decimal numbers, 12.

▶ Fractals are complex geometric shapes that have the property of 'self-similarity'. This means that smaller versions of the overall shape appear again and again within the shape – each part, when magnified, will look basically like the whole object. Many natural objects – for example, ferns or the patterns of a tree's branches – have fractal shapes. Fractal geometry also makes it possible for computers to create beautiful, complex patterns like the one shown here.

Arithmetic

The four basic ways of combining numbers in arithmetic are addition (+), subtraction (–), multiplication (x) and division (÷). Mathematicians call these processes operations, and the signs are called operators. Squaring a number (multiplying a number it by itself) is another example of a mathematical operation.

In addition and multiplication, the order of the numbers does not matter:

$2 + 3 = 5$	AND	$3 + 2 = 5$
$3 \times 4 = 12$	AND	$4 \times 3 = 12$

In subtraction and division, however, the order of the numbers is important:

$4 - 1 = 3$	BUT	$1 - 4 = -3$
$10 \div 5 = 2$	BUT	$5 \div 10 = \frac{1}{2}$ (0.5)

Geometry

Geometry is the study of the properties of lines, angles and shapes. The ancient Greek mathematician Euclid first taught geometry more than 2000 years ago. The important properties of a shape include the number of sides it has, the lengths of the sides, and the angles between the sides.

▼ An angle is a measure of turn. A complete turn is 360°. A right angle (a) is a quarter turn, or 90°. An acute angle (b) is less than 90°, while an obtuse angle (c) is more than 90°. A reflex angle (d) is more than a half turn, or 180°.

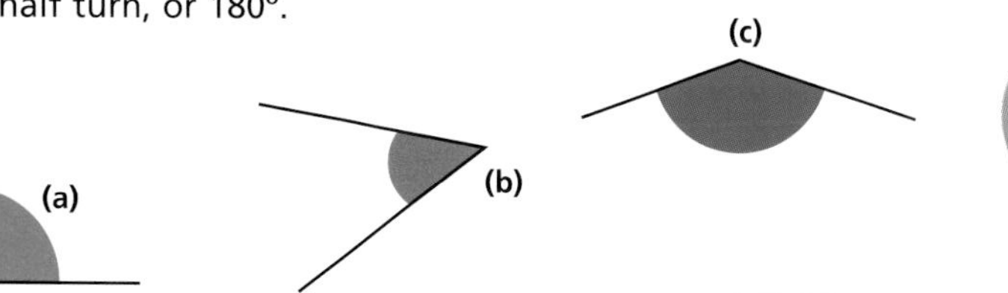

Topology

Imagine drawing a doughnut shape, a disc and other shapes on a rubber sheet. Then imagine stretching the rubber to distort the shapes. What properties of the shapes stay the same? Does the area of each shape change? Do the lengths of the sides change? What about the number of sides, or the number of edges?

Topology is about studying which properties of shapes remain unchanged when the space they fill is stretched and distorted. This branch of mathematics is important in the study of the origin and structure of the Universe.

▼ The distorted ring still has a hole through the middle, while the disc is still solid.

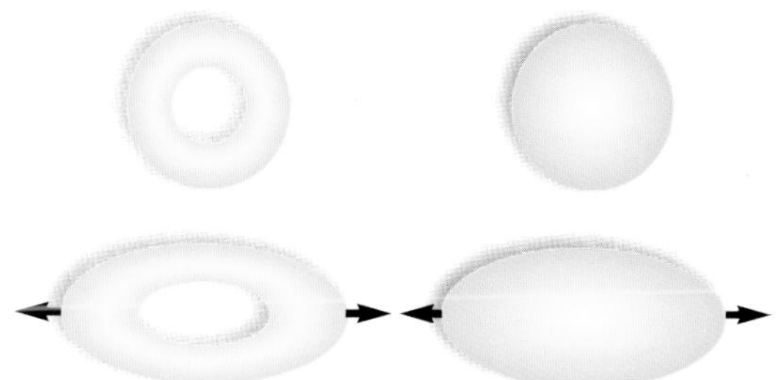

Take a long, rectangular strip of paper. You'll see that it has four edges and two sides. Now give the paper a half-twist and fasten the two narrow ends together. If you draw a line all the way round this twisted loop, you will find it only has one side. Run your finger along the edge, and you will see it has only one edge, too. This amazing loop with a twist is called a Mobius strip.

Algebra

In algebra, mathematicians use symbols to represent quantities. For example, the letter a might be used to represent the length of a rectangle, while b could be its breadth. The rules of algebra allow mathematicians to explore the relationships between quantities using these symbols instead of specific numbers. They can then prove results that apply in general, not just to the numbers they might first have chosen.

a h b right angle

◀ Pythagoras's theorem says that the square of the lengths of the two shorter sides of any right-angled triangle add up to the square of the length of the longest side. If you count the number of small squares in the larger squares drawn on sides *a* and *b* of this triangle, they equal the number on side *h*.

Statistics

Statistics is the branch of mathematics concerned with collecting and interpreting data (information given in numbers) about people and events. Examination results, the effectiveness of new drugs in curing disease and weather measurements are all examples of data that can be better understood using statistics. Using statistics, mathematicians can work out, for example, whether a school's exam results in a particular year are generally better or worse than the results for previous years.

Probability theory is a mathematical way of working out the chances of something happening or not. Probability is given on a scale from 0 (impossible) to 1 (certain). For example, the probability of tossing heads with a fair coin is $^1/_2$, the probability of throwing a double six with a pair of fair dice is $^1/_{36}$. Probability theory is important in the assessment of risk, for example in launching a rocket or building a new power station.

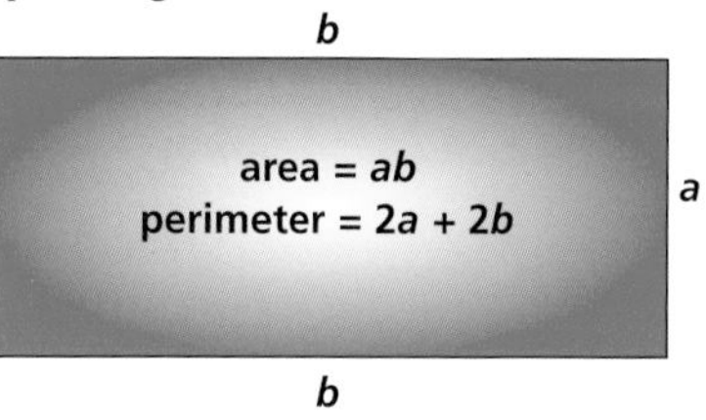

▲ The equations 'area = $a \times b$' (this can be written ab) and 'perimeter = $2a + 2b$' show how to calculate the area and perimeter (the distance round the edge) for any rectangle from its length and breadth.

SET THEORY

The theory of sets is a type of algebra. A set is the collection of all numbers or objects with a certain property in common. The diagram below (called a Venn diagram) shows two overlapping sets. A is the set of odd numbers less than 10. B is the set of square numbers less than 10. The region where the two sets overlap is called the intersection (∩). The set that contains the members of both sets is called the union (∪).

$A = \{1,3,5,7,9\}$
$B = \{1,4,9\}$
$A \cap B = \{1,9\}$
$A \cup B = \{1,3,4,5,7,9\}$

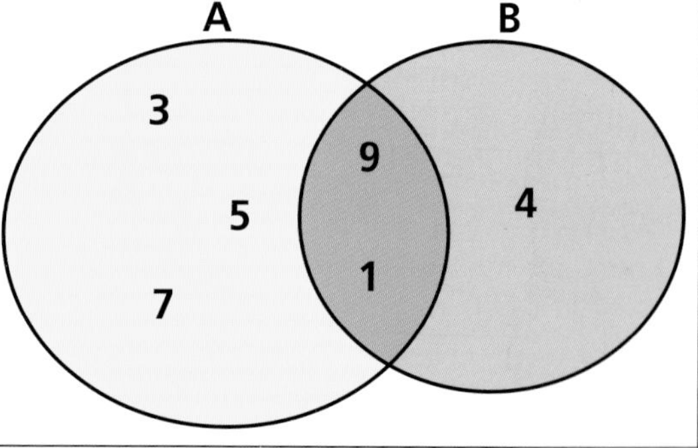

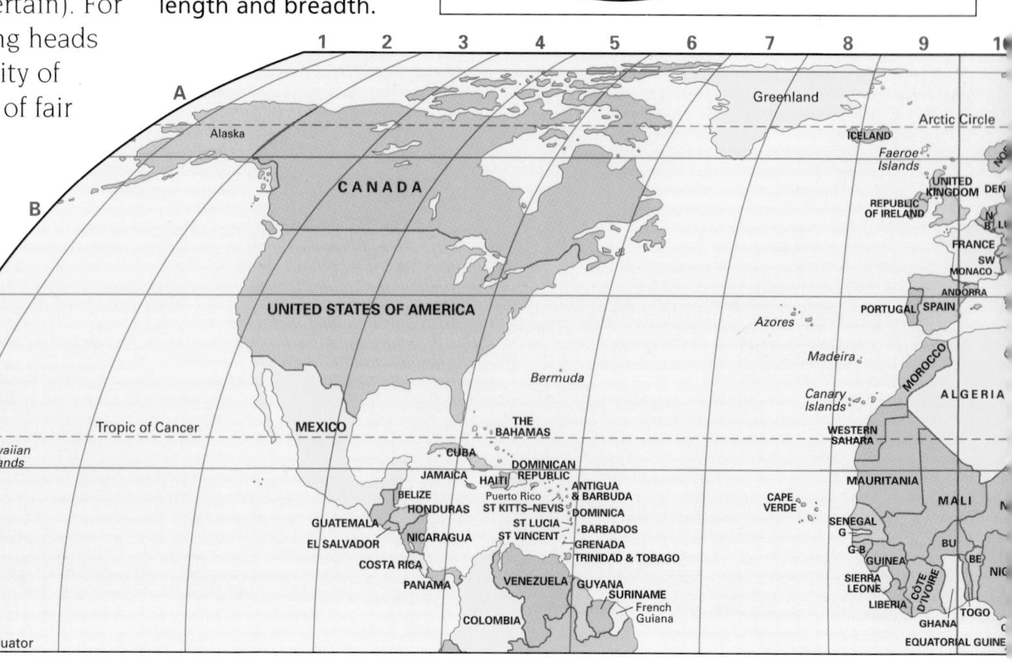

▶ In co-ordinate geometry, points in space are located on a grid made up of lines called axes. An everyday use of co-ordinate geometry is for finding places on a map. On this map, the co-ordinates for Venezuela are D6.

Matter

Everything around us is made of matter, from the tiniest grain of sand to the Sun in the sky. Rock, metal, wood and plastic are all made of matter. So is this book. So are you. But matter is not just solid stuff. Liquids and gases are also made of matter, so the water we drink and the air we breathe are matter as well. Scientists call solids, liquids and gases the three states of matter.

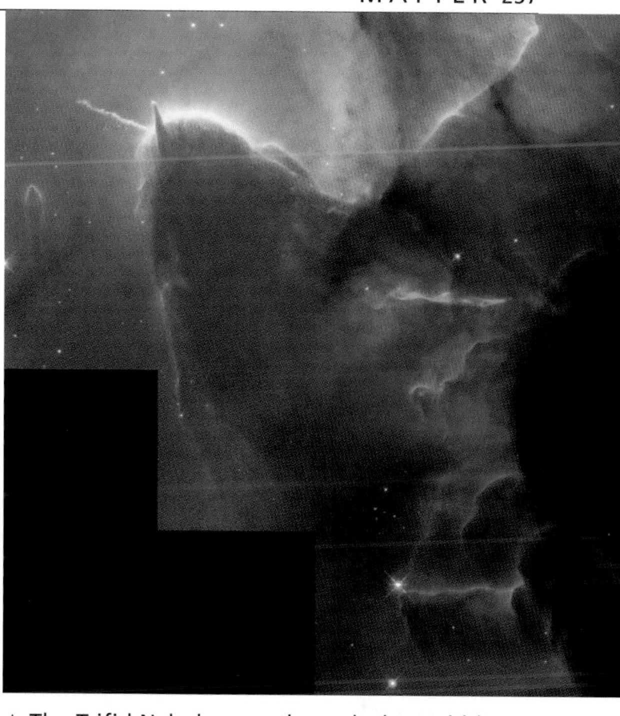

▲ The Trifid Nebula seen through the Hubble Space Telescope. Using telescopes we can see much of the matter in the Universe – planets, stars, asteroids, galaxies and nebulae. Astronomers have calculated that in outer space there is also mysterious 'dark matter' that we cannot see.

All matter is made up of tiny particles called atoms. Sometimes atoms join together to form bigger particles called molecules. Atoms and molecules are much too small to see with the naked eye.

Mass, volume and density

We work out how much matter there is in an object by measuring its mass. Mass is measured in kilograms or grams. All matter has mass. All matter also occupies space – it has volume. Volume can be measured either in cubic metres or in cubic centimetres. The volume of liquids is usually measured in litres.

Some small objects, such as a stone on a beach, have a lot of mass for their volume (their size). Some large objects, such as a hot-air balloon, have very little mass for their size. How much mass an object has for its size is called its density. The stone has a high density, while the balloon has a low density.

The states of matter

All matter can exist in three different states: solid, liquid or gas. In nearly all substances, the solid state is the densest state, while the liquid state is less dense and the gaseous state the least dense.

Whether a substance is a solid, liquid or gas depends mainly on the temperature.

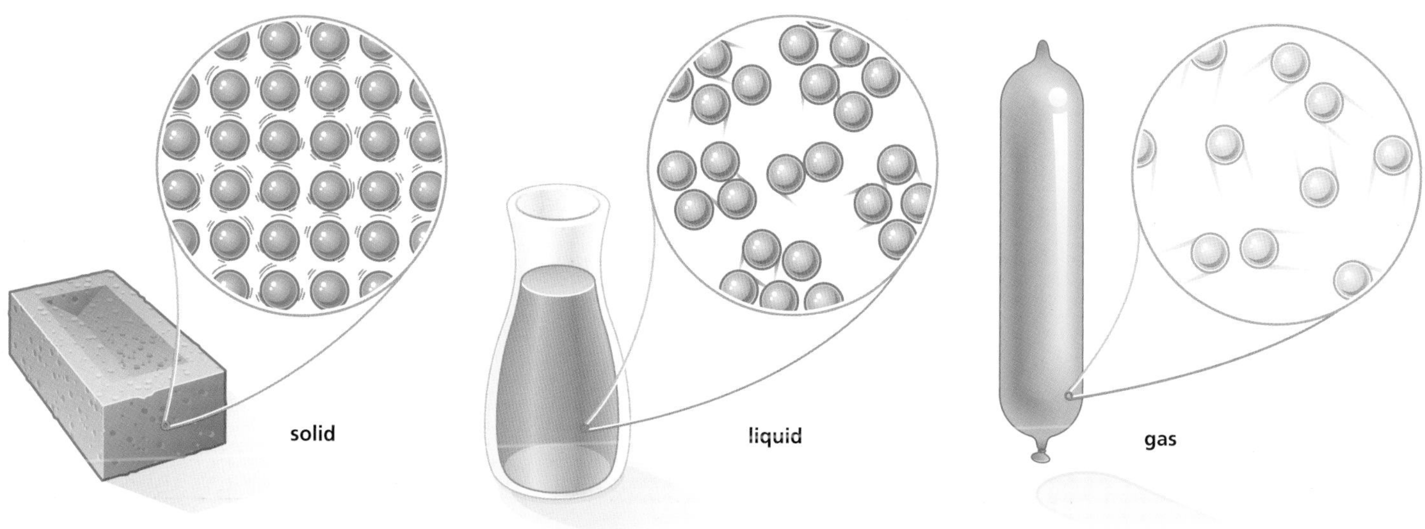

▼ The particles in any substance move around in all directions. In a solid they vibrate about a fixed point. In a liquid the particles move around more freely. In a gas they move around even more than in a liquid.

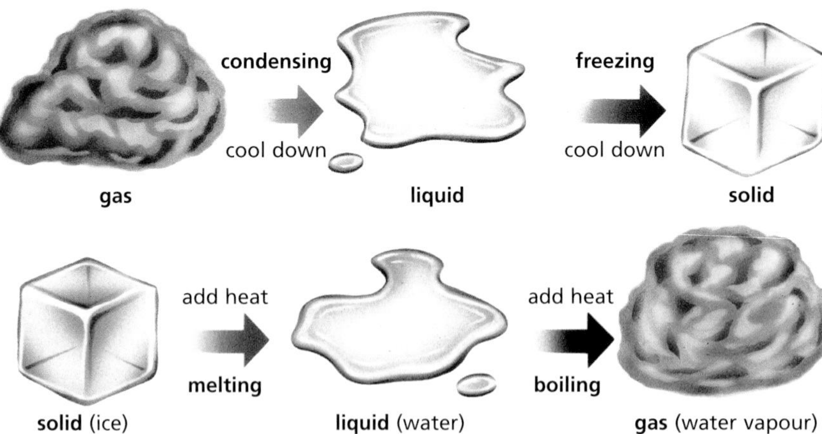

◀ Nearly all substances expand when they melt. An exception is water, which actually expands when it freezes as ice. However, like all other substances, water expands when it becomes a gas.

Most metals are normally solids, but if you heat them to a very high temperature they turn into a liquid. If you heat them even more, they turn into a gas. Substances that are gases at ordinary temperatures, such as oxygen, become liquid at very low temperatures. Oxygen becomes liquid at 183 degrees Celsius (°C) below the freezing point of water (0 °C). Water itself is the only substance that is commonly found in all three states.

Changing states

Substances mainly change state because of changes in temperature. Changing from a solid to a liquid is called melting. Most substances expand when they melt. Changing from a liquid to a gas is called boiling. All substances expand when they turn into gases. Changing from a gas to a liquid is called condensing. Changing from a liquid to a solid is called freezing. Water freezes at 0 °C and boils at 100 °C.

When you heat a substance, you are giving it energy. When you cool it, you are taking away energy. Particles of matter (such as atoms and molecules) are always moving. They need energy to do this. How fast and freely they move depends on how much energy they have.

In a gas, the particles are free to fly around fast, like the ping-pong balls in a lottery machine. They bump into each other and will fill every corner of a container.

If you cool a gas, its particles slow down. Eventually they become so slow that they don't bounce off each other so quickly when they hit each other. They can almost stick together, and the gas becomes a liquid.

If you cool a liquid to below its freezing point, its particles become even less energetic. The liquid becomes a solid. In a solid the particles are close together, and only move a little about fixed points.

The matter in us, and in our Sun and planets, came from a huge cloud of 'stardust' – the remains of a giant star that blew up billions of years ago in a huge explosion called a supernova.

Find Out More

- Air
- Gases
- Liquids
- Solids
- Water

Pressure and changing state

Pressure as well as temperature can affect whether a substance changes state. For example, the gas propane can be turned into a liquid by compressing (squeezing) it. If there is less pressure than normal, a liquid will turn into a gas more easily. For example, if you heat up water high on a Himalayan mountain where there is less air pressure than usual, the water will boil at a lower temperature. This means that it is impossible to make a good cup of tea in high mountains, because you can't get the water hot enough!

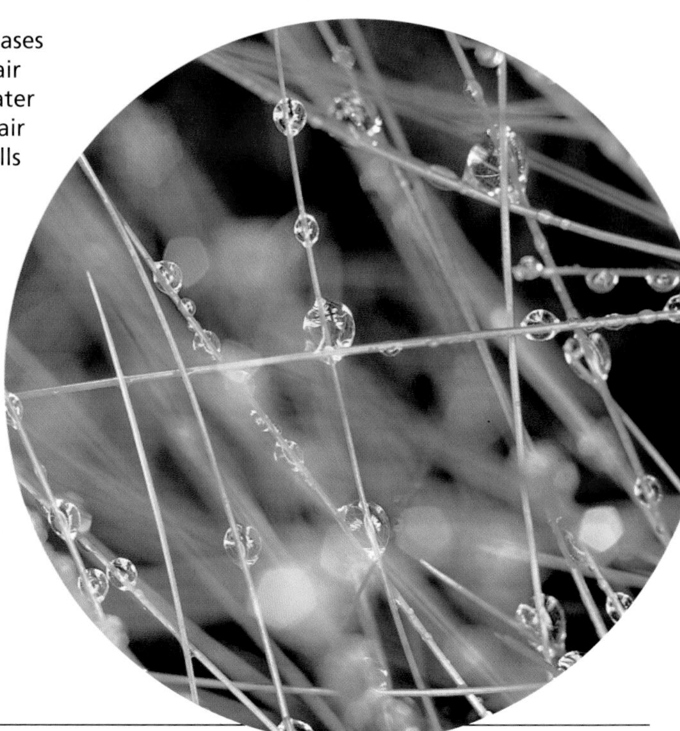

▶ One of the gases present in the air around us is water vapour. As the air temperature falls in the early morning, some of this water vapour condenses (turns to liquid) as tiny drops of liquid water – dew.

Maxwell, James Clerk *see* Electromagnetic spectrum

Measurement

How big is that insect? How heavy is that rock? How fast does a light wave move? How hot is molten steel? These are typical questions that scientists need to answer when they carry out their work. They find out the answers through measurement.

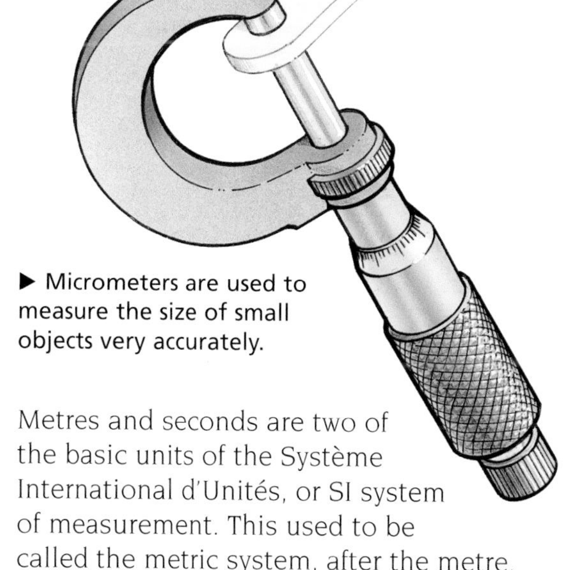

▶ Micrometers are used to measure the size of small objects very accurately.

If you want to be able to compare one set of measurements with another, it helps to use the same kind of units. In science, everyone uses the metre for measuring length and the second for measuring time.

▲ The metric system was first introduced in France, in about 1800. These illustrations show some of the new metric measures in use: the litre, the gram, the metre, the are (a unit of area, equal to 100 square metres), the franc (currency) and the stère (a unit of volume, equal to one cubic metre).

▼ The forward flight deck of the space shuttle orbiter *Atlantis*. Flat panel screens on the main flight console show flight and engineering information, measuring such things as pressure, temperature, fuel levels and speed. Because the flight deck has so many panels, it is nicknamed the glass cockpit.

Metres and seconds are two of the basic units of the Système International d'Unités, or SI system of measurement. This used to be called the metric system, after the metre.

The French Academy of Sciences laid down standards for the metric system in the 1790s. Most countries have adopted this system, but a few, including Britain and the United States, still use some units of what is called the English, or Imperial system. These units are based on measures such as the pound, the foot and the inch.

Kilograms and kelvins

Other basic units of measurement in the SI system are the kilogram, the kelvin and the ampere. The kilogram is used to measure mass (the amount of matter in a body), the kelvin to measure temperature, and the ampere to measure electric current.

Most other units of measurement can be expressed in terms of these basic ones. For example, velocity (speed) is measured in metres per second; while density is measured in kilograms per square metre.

Keeping standards

Each of the basic units of measurement is defined in a precise way. This is so that everyone knows exactly what is meant by a metre, a kilogram, a second, and so on.

A metre used to be defined as the length of a platinum alloy rod kept in Paris, France. But now it is defined as the distance light travels in a vacuum in a certain amount of time (1/299,792,458 of a second). This is very precise and never-changing because light always travels at the same speed in a vacuum.

A second used to be measured as a fraction of the time taken for the Earth to spin once on its axis. But this varies slightly, so the second is now defined precisely in terms of the radiation given out by atoms of caesium, which always vibrate at the same rate. One second is the time taken for 9,192,631,770 vibrations.

Of the original standards adopted for the metric system, only the standard of mass is still current. The standard kilogram is a platinum alloy cylinder about 40 mm high and wide. Many countries hold exact copies of this cylinder.

Find Out More
- Electromagnetic spectrum
- Forces
- Mathematics
- Science
- Temperature
- Time

SI unit	What it measures	Imperial unit	Conversion
metre (m)	length	yard (yd) feet (ft)	1 m = 1.094 yd (3.281 ft) 1 yd (3 ft) = 0.9144 m
kilogram (kg)	mass (weight)	pound (lb)	1 kg = 2.205 lb 1 lb = 0.4536 kg
second (s)	time		
litre (cubic decimetre, dm^3)	volume	pint	1 litre = 1.760 pints 1 pint = 0.5682 litres
newton (N)	force	poundal (pdl)	1 N = 7.233 pdl 1 pdl = 0.138 N

The scientific unit of force, the newton, is named after Isaac Newton, who is said to have thought up his ideas about gravity while watching an apple fall. Weight is a force and, roughly speaking, one newton is about the weight of an apple.

GIGABYTES AND NANOMETRES

Scientists often have to measure very tiny and very big quantities, and they express these in terms of multiples (numbers of times bigger) or sub-multiples (number of times smaller) of the basic units. A prefix (the part of the word before the unit itself) indicates the number of times bigger or smaller than the basic unit.

For example, we measure distances in kilometres. The prefix 'kilo' means one thousand, so a kilometre is a thousand metres. Some computers have a memory measured in gigabytes (billions of bytes), while light wavelengths are measured in nanometres (billionths of metres). A full list of prefixes is given in the table.

Prefix	Times bigger or smaller
tera (T)	1,000,000,000,000 (1000 billion)
giga (G)	1,000,000,000 (1 billion)
mega (M)	1,000,000 (1 million)
kilo (k)	1000
hecto (h)	100
deca (da)	10
deci (d)	1/10
centi (c)	1/100
milli (m)	1/1000
micro (μ)	1/1,000,000 (1 millionth)
nano (n)	1/1,000,000,000 (1 billionth)
pico (p)	1/1,000,000,000,000 (1000 billionth)

◀ A mass spectrometer is a very sensitive measuring instrument that helps scientists to measure the amounts of different chemical elements in a substance. Each of the peaks on the computer screen represents a different chemical.

Medicine

In the past, doctors were too expensive for ordinary people, who would visit a barber, a tooth-puller or a herbalist for treatment. A barber would be happy to do minor operations as well as haircuts. There were few effective treatments for illnesses, and people died of diseases which are easily cured today. One of the most popular cures was applying leeches to suck blood from the patient.

Today we understand much more about how the body works and what causes illness. Diagnosis – a doctor's assessment of what is wrong with a patient – has become much more accurate. Advances in technology have led to new equipment and better treatment.

▶ A small sample of blood for testing is taken from a vein in a patient's arm using a syringe.

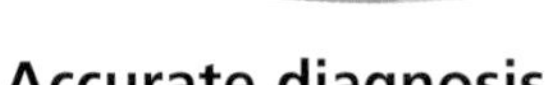

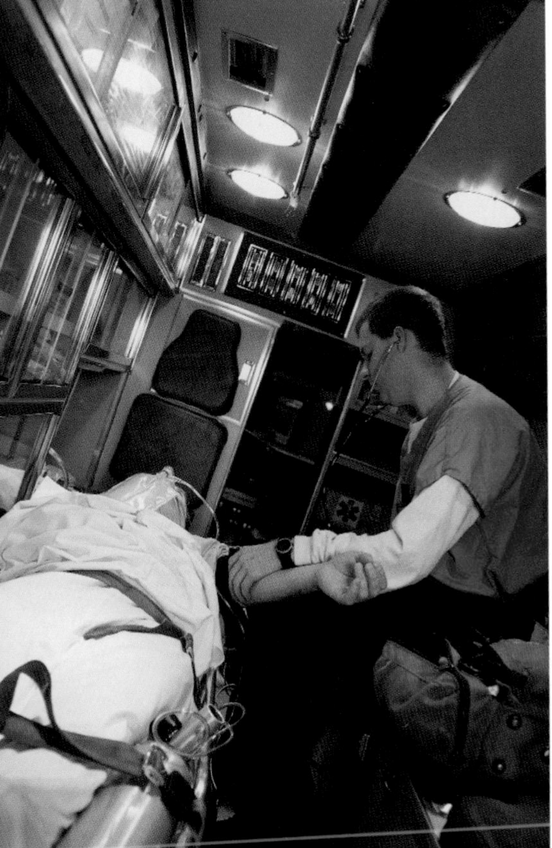

◀ Paramedics are specially trained to give emergency treatment in well-equipped ambulances as a patient is being taken to hospital.

Accurate diagnosis

Doctors still use simple ways to find out what is wrong. A view inside the mouth can reveal signs of infection, and unusual blood vessels in the eye can be a sign of the disease diabetes. Stethoscopes, first used in 1816, magnify the body's breathing and heart sounds so that the heart and lungs can be checked.

Doctors can also take samples of urine and blood, and send them for testing. Such tests can reveal the presence of bacteria and other substances, which help to pinpoint what is wrong.

Technical support

Advances in technology mean that many babies born prematurely (early) have a good chance of survival. They are kept in incubators where nurses care for them. Special sensors monitor the baby's breathing and heart beat.

Patients who are seriously ill may go into an intensive care unit. Here, artificial ventilators can take over their breathing, while tubes deliver drugs directly into their bloodstream. Sensors monitor the patients all the time, checking their breathing and heart rate through electrodes connected to their chest.

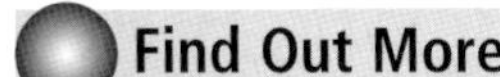

Find Out More

- Cancers
- Diseases
- Health
- Heart and blood

Clean and safe

Medical equipment must be clean and free of germs. Most surgical instruments, such as scissors and forceps, made of stainless steel, can withstand being sterilized. Most are sterilized in a device known as an autoclave, which heats them to over 100 °C. Many everyday items such as gloves and sterile syringes are made of disposable plastic, which is hygienic and can be thrown away.

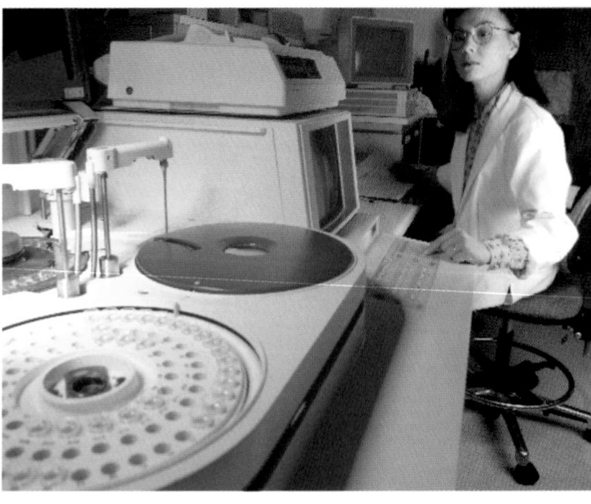

▶ A machine used for analysing blood samples. Such machines can carry out a whole range of tests on a small sample of the patient's blood. The results of the tests help the doctor to diagnose a patient's illness.

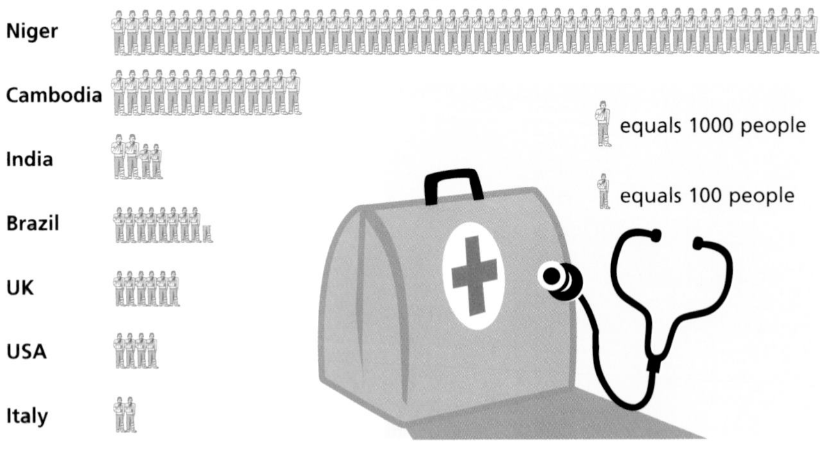

▲ This graph shows the number of people per doctor in different countries. In developed countries such as the USA, most people have access to a doctor. But in places like Niger, in Africa, there is only one doctor for every 53,000 people.

Medicines and cures

Drugs and medicines are used to cure diseases or to relieve symptoms. Most traditional remedies relied on herbs. Modern drugs are produced and refined in large factories, although many were first discovered from natural sources. Aspirin, for example, came from the bark of a willow tree.

One of the most important medicines discovered in the 20th century was antibiotics, which kill bacteria. The first to be found was penicillin.

▼ A medical centre in Venezuela. Such centres mean that people living in remote areas can get vaccinations and other medical support.

Complementary medicine

Complementary medicine means any treatment that isn't one of the standard, traditional treatments used by most doctors. Here are some examples.

Acupuncture is an ancient Chinese therapy that stimulates nerves by inserting needles through the skin. It can be used as a treatment or as an anaesthetic for certain operations. Aromatherapy treatments use fragrant plant oils and massage to treat many conditions from strains to cancer. Homeopathy is a form of treatment in which patients take tiny doses of substances that produce similar symptoms to their illness.

▶ A woman receiving acupuncture to the face. Acupuncturists believe that there are lines of energy criss-crossing the body. By inserting needles into the skin at points where energy lines cross, they aim to re-balance the energies of an ill patient.

Health centres

Today, patients can be treated with painkillers, antibiotics and a full range of other drugs. Some doctors and patients prefer a combination of these medicines with older treatments such as acupuncture and homeopathy. Doctors who work in health centres may have the support of physiotherapists, chiropodists, nurse practitioners and herbalists to treat their patients.

HIPPOCRATES

Hippocrates was the most famous doctor of ancient Greece. He was born around 460 BC. He understood that sickness was due to natural causes, rather than evil spirits or star signs, and that patients might recover if they rested, exercised, and ate proper food. Today, doctors take an oath in which they promise to help their patients. This is called the Hippocratic oath.

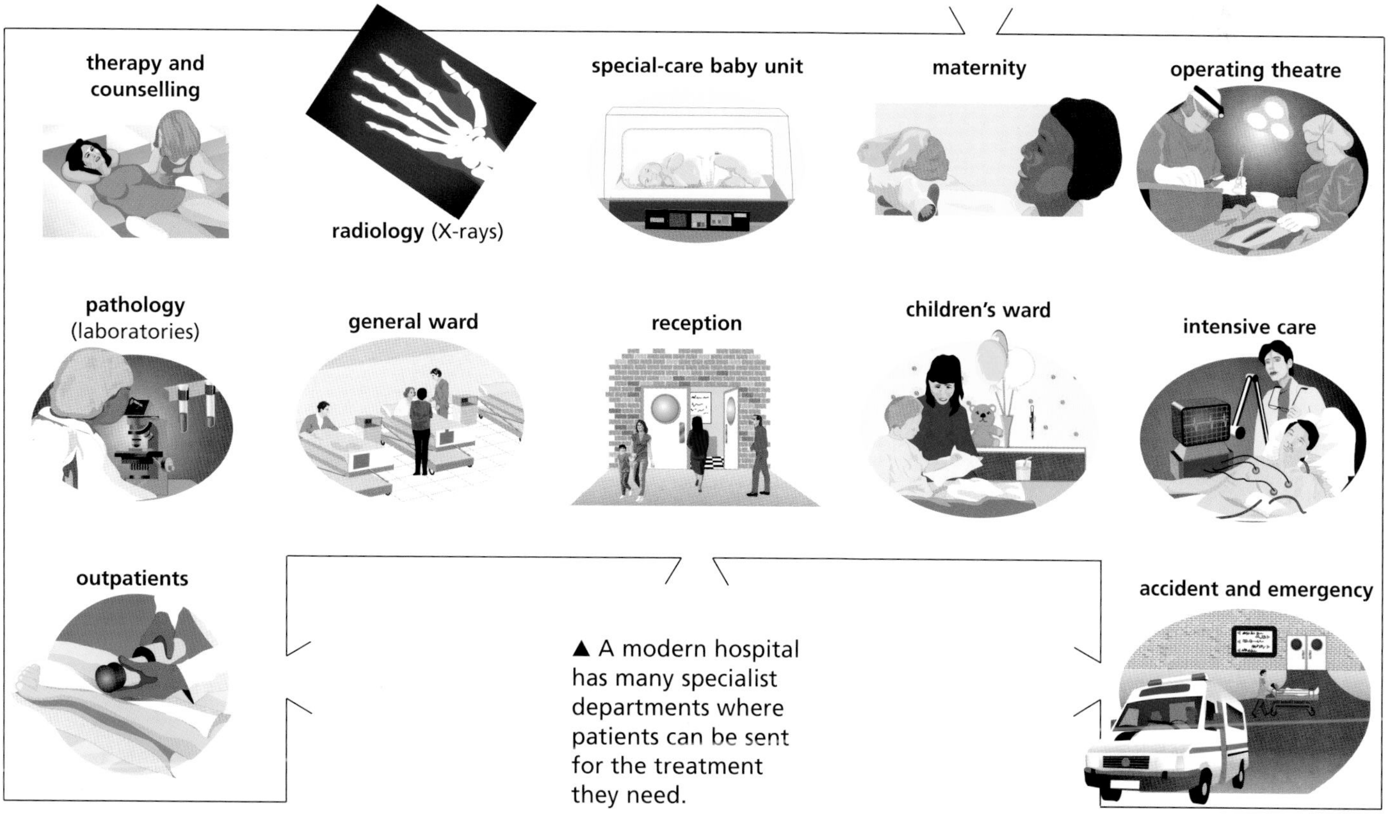

therapy and counselling

radiology (X-rays)

special-care baby unit

maternity

operating theatre

pathology (laboratories)

general ward

reception

children's ward

intensive care

outpatients

accident and emergency

▲ A modern hospital has many specialist departments where patients can be sent for the treatment they need.

Melting *see* Matter • **Memory** *see* Mind • **Mendel, Gregor** *see* Genetics

Mercury

A huge Sun beats down from Mercury's sky. Its fierce heat bakes the rocky surface and the temperature soars to 450 °C, hot enough to melt lead. But when the Sun goes down a big chill sets in on the planet closest to the Sun.

Temperature swings on Mercury are greater than those on any other planet. With no atmosphere to hold in the heat, the surface cools down to −180 °C at night. There could even be ice near Mercury's poles, shaded from the Sun inside deep craters.

Mercury spins very slowly while speeding around the Sun. This has a strange effect. In the time between one sunrise and the next, Mercury completes two orbits. That takes 176 Earth days, so days and nights are very long, which is why the temperatures are so extreme.

▶ The only close-up pictures of Mercury were taken by the spacecraft *Mariner 10*, which flew past three times in 1974–1975. This illustration is based on the Mariner photos.

MERCURY DATA
Diameter at equator: 4878 km
Average distance from Sun: 57.9 million km
Time taken to spin on axis: 58.6 days
Density (water = 1): 5.4
Time taken to orbit the Sun: 88.0 days
Moons: 0

Hide and seek

Mercury is difficult to observe. Though bright, it is always near the Sun and mostly hidden in the glare. But every few weeks it dodges out far enough to be spotted for a few days at dusk or dawn. Through a telescope, Mercury usually looks like a half-moon or crescent. We see these different shapes, or phases, because Mercury is closer to the Sun than us.

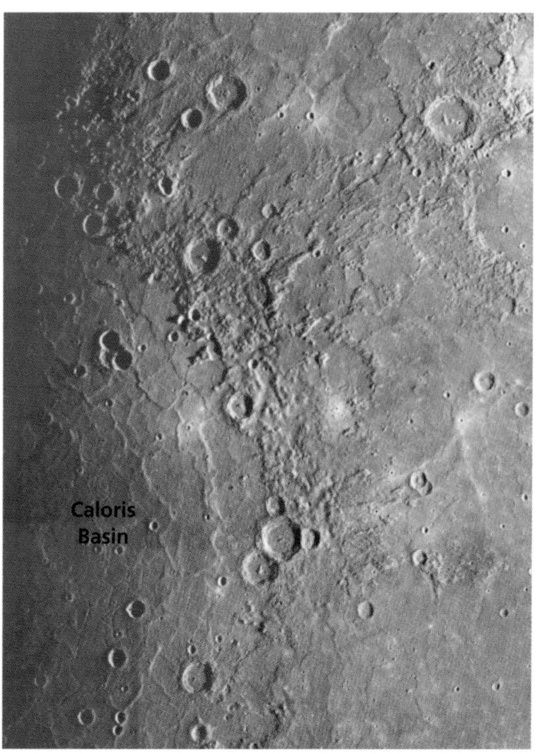

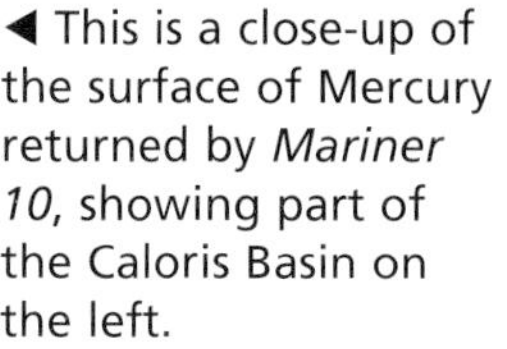

◀ This is a close-up of the surface of Mercury returned by *Mariner 10*, showing part of the Caloris Basin on the left.

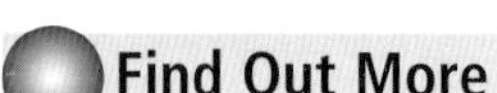

Find Out More
- Orbit
- Planets
- Solar System
- Space astronomy
- Sun

A battered surface

Mercury's surface is peppered all over with thousands of craters where meteorites once rained down. One enormous impact by a rock about 100 kilometres across created the Caloris Basin. Surrounded by several rings of mountains and partly filled in, it is 1300 kilometres wide.

Long ridges cross the surface with cliffs up to 3000 metres high. They formed over 3000 million years ago when Mercury shrank as it cooled down.

Mercury's surface rocky layer is much thinner than Earth's. Beneath it is a huge iron core, about 1900 kilometres across.

Mercury (metal) *see* Metals, Periodic table

Metals and non-metals

For some two million years, early humans used tools made of stone. Then, about 5000 years ago, people discovered how to extract metal from rocks and to make metal tools. To begin with, people used copper and bronze (an alloy, or mixture, of copper and tin). Then came iron, and finally steel.

Most of the elements – the substances from which all things are made – are metals. Metals have many properties in common, but non-metals have a wide variety of properties. Several of the non-metals, such as carbon and oxygen, are present in large quantities in living things. But our bodies need only tiny amounts of metals such as iron and zinc.

▼ Steel is very strong for its weight. It is the main structural material in the London Eye in the UK. The big wheel is 135 metres high.

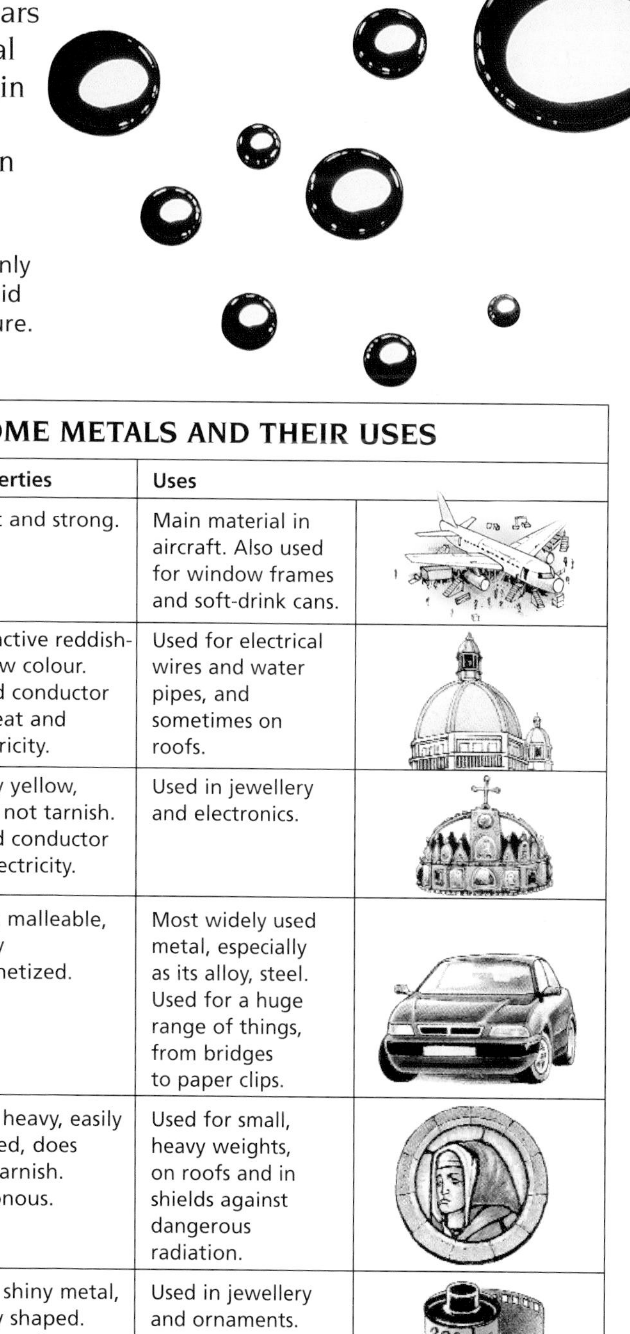

▶ Mercury is the only metal that is a liquid at room temperature.

SOME METALS AND THEIR USES		
Name	**Properties**	**Uses**
Aluminium	Light and strong.	Main material in aircraft. Also used for window frames and soft-drink cans.
Copper	Attractive reddish-yellow colour. Good conductor of heat and electricity.	Used for electrical wires and water pipes, and sometimes on roofs.
Gold	Shiny yellow, does not tarnish. Good conductor of electricity.	Used in jewellery and electronics.
Iron	Grey, malleable, easily magnetized.	Most widely used metal, especially as its alloy, steel. Used for a huge range of things, from bridges to paper clips.
Lead	Soft, heavy, easily shaped, does not tarnish. Poisonous.	Used for small, heavy weights, on roofs and in shields against dangerous radiation.
Silver	Pale, shiny metal, easily shaped. Best conductor of electricity.	Used in jewellery and ornaments. Light-sensitive silver compounds used in photographic film.
Uranium	Heavy and radioactive.	Used as a fuel to produce nuclear energy.

Properties of metals

All the metals (apart from mercury) are solids at room temperature. They all have a crystalline structure, although the crystals are much too small to see with the naked eye. Pure metals are shiny when polished. Metals are good conductors of electricity and heat. Many of them are quite strong – you can squeeze them or stretch them and they won't break. But metals are malleable – you can shape them by hammering or rolling them. Many are also ductile – you can draw them out into thin wires.

Despite these similarities, there are differences among the metals. Metals such as tin, lead and aluminium, are softer, weaker and melt at lower temperatures than metals such as iron and copper.

▶ Many non-metals do not conduct electricity well. Non-metallic materials such as ceramics, glass, plastics and rubber are used as insulators – like the glass insulators on these high-voltage cables.

Find Out More

- Alloys
- Conductors and insulators
- Elements and compounds
- Iron and steel
- Metalworking
- Periodic table

SOME NON-METALS AND THEIR USES

Name	Properties	Uses
Carbon	Exists as diamond, graphite or soot.	All forms of life on Earth are based on carbon compounds.
Chlorine	Greenish, poisonous gas. Highly reactive.	Used to disinfect swimming pools and drinking water. Compounds include table salt.
Helium	Very light, non-reactive gas.	Used to fill airships, and in the air breathed by divers.
Hydrogen	The lightest element. A gas in its pure form.	Huge numbers of important compounds, including water and most of the chemicals that make up living things.
Neon	Invisible, unreactive gas.	Used in strip lighting.
Nitrogen	Invisible gas.	The main gas in air. Compounds important in all living things, and in fertilizers.
Oxygen	Invisible gas.	Essential to respiration (breathing), and to combustion (burning).
Phosphorus	White, red or black solid.	Used in matches. Some compounds found in living things, and others used as fertilizers.
Sulphur	Exists as various kinds of yellow solid.	Used in matches, gunpowder and in vulcanizing (strengthening) rubber. Many important compounds.

Some metals, such as sodium and potassium, are highly reactive, while others, like gold and platinum, are unreactive.

Gold is one of the few elements that is found in its pure state in nature. Many other metals are only found in minerals in rocks, where they are combined with non-metals. For example, the main iron minerals are compounds of iron and oxygen.

Metals can be made stronger by melting them together to make alloys. Steel is an alloy of iron and carbon (a non-metal). Stainless steel contains the metals chromium and nickel.

Properties of non-metals

Some of the non-metallic elements are also very reactive – especially the halogens, such as chlorine. Other non-metals, the noble gases such as helium, are the least reactive of all the elements.

The non-metals include gases such as oxygen and nitrogen, solids such as carbon and sulphur, and one liquid, bromine. Some solid non-metals can have different forms, called allotropes. The allotropes of carbon include diamond and graphite. Non-metals are generally poor conductors of electricity, although graphite is an exception.

The metalloids

A few elements have properties in between metals and non-metals. These are the metalloids. The metalloids silicon and germanium are semiconductors – they can be treated with chemicals to change how well they conduct electricity. Semiconductors are important in electronics.

Metalworking

The blacksmith is heating a strip of iron on a fierce fire. A horse waits patiently nearby. When the iron is red-hot, the blacksmith places it on an anvil. Then he begins hammering it into the shape of a horseshoe. He is carrying out the earliest method of shaping metal, called forging.

▶ A red-hot sheet of metal is rolled in a steel mill. Hot rolling is usually followed by cold rolling, which improves the surface finish.

Forging is still one of the main ways in which metal is shaped. But these days, forging is carried out in factories, using mechanical hammers. They have a heavy ram that shapes metal when it drops onto it from a height. This method is called drop forging. Usually, the metal is hammered into a shaped mould, or die. In an alternative method using a forging press, metal is shaped by a squeezing action rather than by sudden blows.

Moulding metal

Another ancient way of shaping metal is by casting. The metal is heated until it is molten (liquid). Then it is poured into a shaped mould. It takes the shape of the mould when it cools and sets hard. Many castings are produced using moulds made from wet sand. Mould-makers can make large and complicated shapes, such as ships' propellers. Sand moulds have to be broken up to release the castings.

Many objects, however, are made in permanent moulds, called dies, which can be used over and over again. This method,

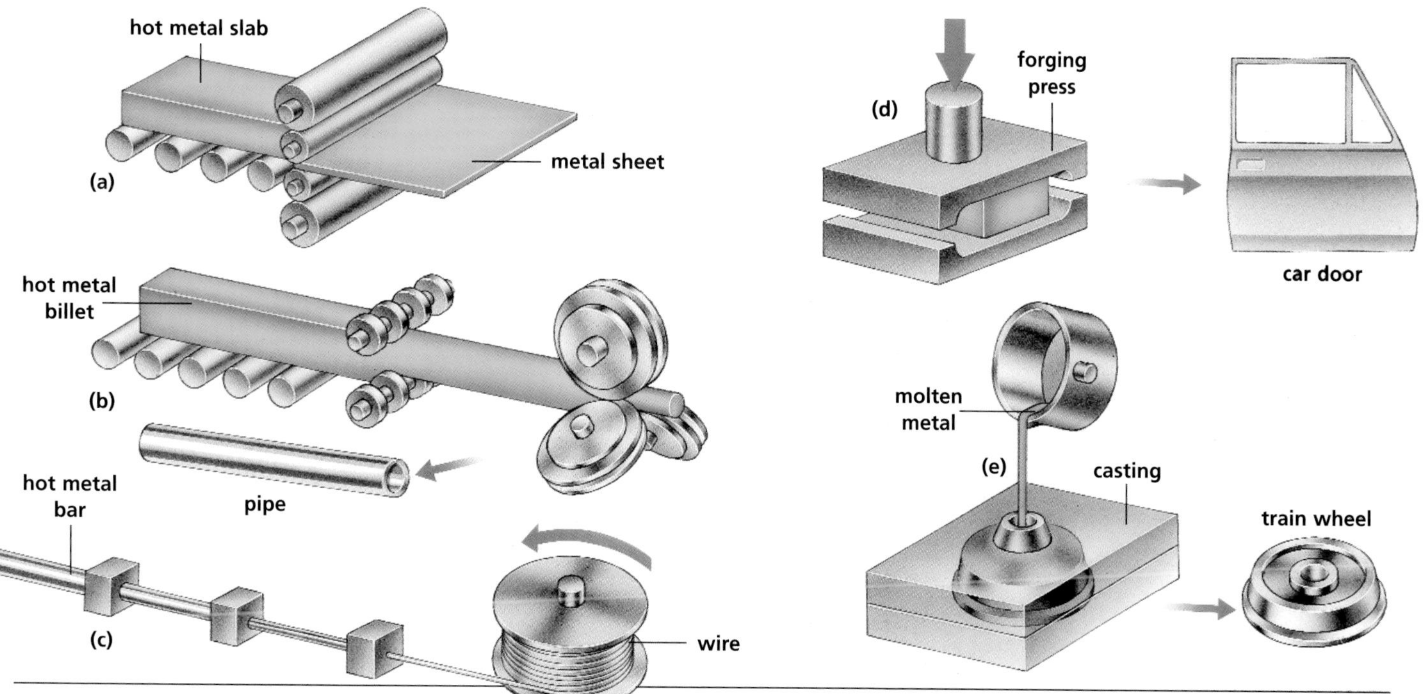

▼ Metal can be shaped in many different ways, including rolling (a, b), drawing (c), forging or pressing (d) and casting (e).

known as die-casting, is widely used for mass-producing small castings for toys and domestic appliances.

Rolling along

Huge amounts of metal are used in the form of plate or sheet, to make things like ships' hulls and car bodies. These products start life as thick slabs, which are made thinner and longer by rolling.

This is done in rolling mills. Here, red-hot slabs are passed back and forth through sets of heavy rollers. As the metal passes through each set, it gets thinner and longer. A thick slab originally 10 metres long would typically end up as a sheet 2 millimetres thick and 1.5 kilometres long.

After hot rolling, sheet is often rolled cold. This is done to give it an accurate thickness and a harder finish.

Pressing and stamping

One main use for sheet steel is for car bodies. The sheet is shaped cold on hydraulic presses, similar to but smaller than forging presses. Smaller versions of the drop forge are used to shape small objects, such as coins, from cold metal. They force metal into shape in dies, a process called stamping.

Other methods use dies for shaping. Rods and tubes may be made by extrusion, which involves forcing metal through holes in dies. Wire is made by drawing metal through sets of dies with smaller and smaller holes.

▼ A welder joins pieces of metal that have been heated and softened using an electric arc.

Find Out More

- Electricity
- Iron and steel
- Metals and non-metals
- Tools

▶ A huge hydraulic press is used to make a shaft for a steam turbine (a kind of engine used in power stations). The press can exert a force of 4000 tonnes on the hot metal.

Electrical arcs (large sparks) can form underwater as well as in air. This means that electric arc welding can be used to join pieces of metal underwater.

Joining up

Metal pieces often need to be joined together to make large objects, such as ships' hulls and pipelines. Welding is the most common method.

In welding, the edges of the parts to be joined are first softened by heating them to high temperatures. Then molten metal from a filler rod is added. The added metal bonds with the softened metal. This fills in the gaps and produces a strong joint when it cools. Gas welding uses a burning gas torch to heat the metal. Arc welding uses an electric arc to heat it.

Soldering is another method using molten metal (solder) to form joints. It is used mostly to join wires in electrical circuits. Soldering is carried out at much lower temperatures than welding, and joints are not as strong.

Metamorphosis *see* Insects • **Meteorology** *see* Weather

Meteors and meteorites

The Earth is constantly pelted by dust and bits of rock from space. On any dark night you could see a brilliant streak of light flash across the sky for a second or two, as a grain of dust burns up.

Streams of dust from comets circle around the Sun. Every year, the Earth ploughs through some of these streams on about the same dates, and we get showers of meteors (often called 'shooting stars'). The Eta Aquarid shower in May, for example, is caused by dust from Halley's Comet. Not all meteors come in showers, though. One-off meteors might be seen anywhere on any night.

Large dust grains burn up as they speed through the atmosphere about 100 kilometres up. But every year, millions of tonnes of very fine space dust drifts down on to the Earth without burning up.

Find Out More

- Asteroids
- Comets
- Solar System

▲ This photograph of the sky was taken over a period of time during a meteor shower called the Leonids. The streaks that radiate outwards are meteor trails.

Meteorites

Sometimes, quite large rocks from space reach the ground. They are called meteorites. Some are stone, some metal, and some a mix of both. Not many are seen to fall, but there are certain places in the world where meteorites have lain undisturbed over many years and can be collected. Many have been recovered from the ice of Antarctica.

Careful study shows most meteorites have come from the asteroid belt, but a very few are definitely rocks that were once part of the Moon or Mars.

IMPORTANT METEOR SHOWERS

Name	Date seen
Quadrantids	4 January
Eta Aquarids	4 May
Perseids	12 August
Geminids	13 December

▼ A fragment of an iron meteorite. Some meteorites are made up of a particular mixture of iron and nickel, which produces the criss-cross pattern as seen here.

▼ Meteor Crater in Arizona, USA, was created when a 40-metre-wide iron meteorite crashed to Earth about 50,000 years ago. The crater is 1.2 kilometres across and 200 metres deep.

Microbes *see* Bacteria and viruses

Microchips

Computers might be powerful, but the bits that do all the hard work are tiny. The 'brains' of a computer are made of microchips, each one a flat sliver of silicon smaller than a fingernail. Microchips can contain millions of unbelievably small electronic parts.

▲ Each tiny square on this silicon wafer is one microchip. The wafer measures about 30 cm across.

But it's not just computers that use microchips. You'll find them in almost every electronic gadget you can think of. In a car, they may help control the braking system. They could even be in your toaster, controlling how brown the toast gets. But what has made microchips so popular?

▲ This magnified photo shows one mircochip from the wafer.

Cool, cheap, light and fast

The electronic circuits that were used before microchips were invented used lots of separate parts all wired together. These included transistors, which switch signals on and off, resistors, which oppose currents, and diodes, which let current go one way only.

But in large electronic circuits the wiring gets hot and can burn out. And all those separate parts are quite big – a transistor is about the size of a jelly bean – so conventional circuits need a lot of space.

Microchips overcome these problems by using laser light and special chemicals to 'grow' tiny circuits on a thin wafer of very pure silicon. The special chemicals, called dopants, are used to alter the electrical properties of the silicon in different ways, making tiny areas that behave like transistors, or resistors, or diodes. No wires are needed – the different parts can be grown side by side. The result is a tiny circuit that stays cool. And because all the parts are so close, the chip works very fast.

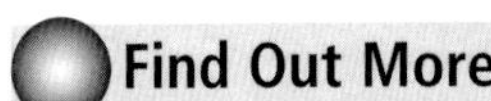

Find Out More

- Acids and alkalis
- Circuits
- Computers
- Conductors and insulators
- Electronics

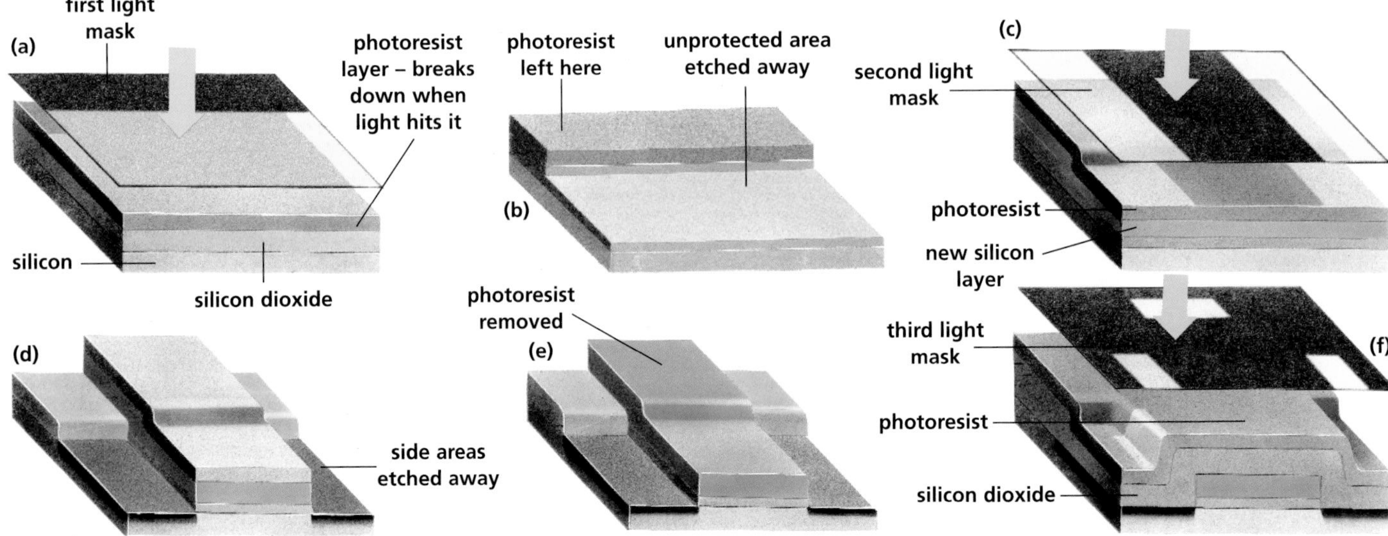

A chip off the block

To make a chip, the circuit first has to be designed. Engineers have to design chips using computer design software because there are simply too many components to draw by hand. The first microprocessor chip had 2300 transistors, but today's chips can have more than 30 million!

Once it has been told what the microchip should do, the designer's computer works out which components are needed and how they should connect up.

Laser stencils

The microchip is made in several layers, so when the design is correct, a picture of each layer is printed onto a series of glass 'masks'. These masks are used like stencils. The first mask is placed over the silicon wafer, then a laser is shone through it.

The wafer is coated with a tough coating that is sensitive to light. The areas where the laser hits the coating are changed, and can be washed away with an acid. Dopant chemicals are then injected into the chip. Where the coating has been washed away the dopant can reach the silicon below. In this way, the different dopants can be placed on exactly the right areas to form the electronic circuit.

Making contacts

Components in the chip are connected together by metal tracks laid down after the circuit parts have been made on top of the chip. There can be many layers of these connectors, separated by glass 'insulator' layers.

When the chip is finished, it is sawn off the wafer and placed in a plastic package. Thin wires are stretched from the chip to contacts that stick out of the package. The chip is then tested – if it works, it is ready to be soldered onto a circuit board.

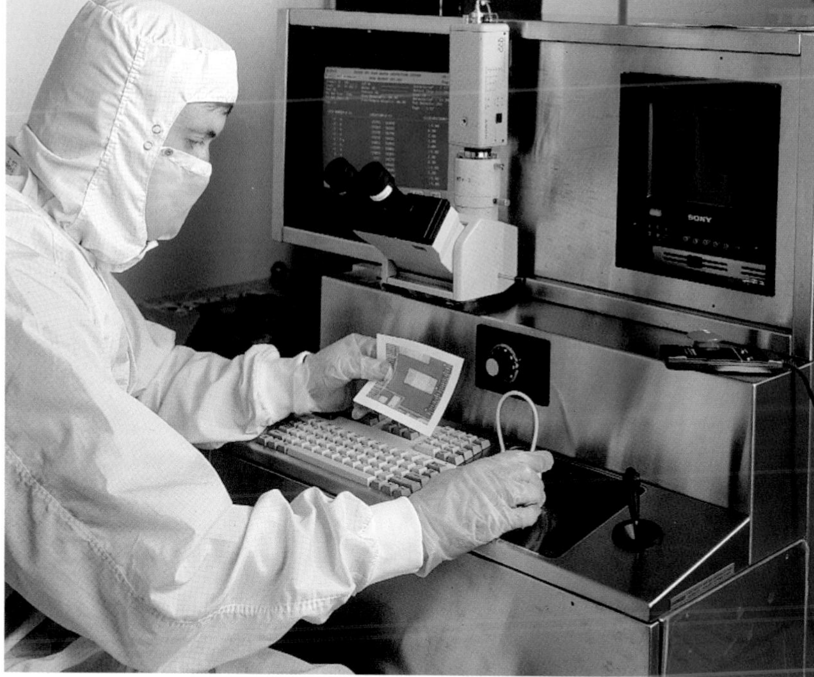

▲ The slightest impurity can ruin a microchip, so the people who make them and test them have to wear special suits and masks, and work in dust-free 'clean rooms'. The chips are made in a vacuum, so that the dopants do not become contaminated by impurities in the air.

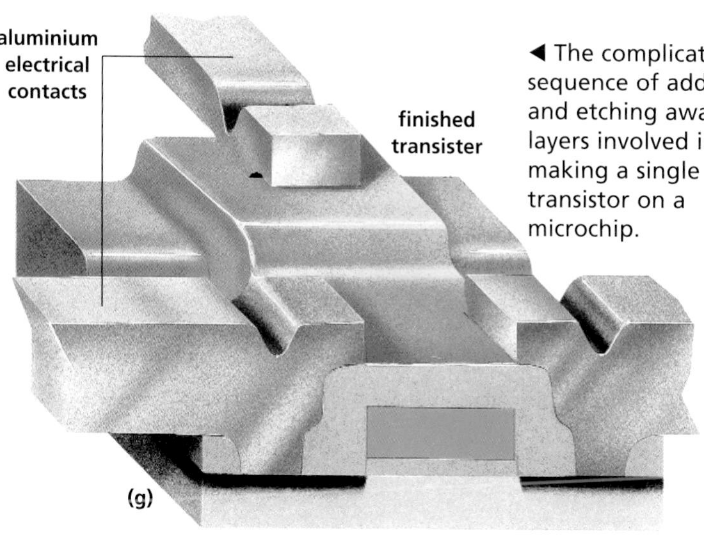

◀ The complicated sequence of adding and etching away layers involved in making a single transistor on a microchip.

THE FIRST MICROCHIPS

The American Jack Kilby (born 1923), working for the company Texas Instruments, was the first to develop an integrated circuit. In 1964 he worked out how to make more than one transistor in a sliver of a material called germanium. By 'growing' the transistors together at the same time, he found he could connect them together internally without wires. In 2000, Jack Kilby was awarded the Nobel Prize for Physics, for his part in developing integrated circuits.

Around the same time another American, Robert Noyce (1927–1990), working for Fairchild Semiconductors, made a similar microchip from silicon. Silicon ultimately became the standard microchip-making material.

Microcomputers *see* Computers • **Microlight** (aircraft) *see* Aircraft • **Microorganisms** *see* Bacteria and viruses

Microphones and speakers

Be careful what you say! Spies use special microphones to hear conversations from a long way away. The same microphones can also record birdsong from a distance. Later, the tape can be played back through a loudspeaker.

cone
coil
magnet

▲ How a loudspeaker works. The loudspeaker coil is attached to the cone. An electric signal passing through the coil causes it to be attracted to or repelled from the magnet. This pushes and pulls the cone, making sound waves.

Microphones turn sounds into a pattern of electricity (an electric signal). Loudspeakers do the opposite: they turn electric signals into sounds that you can hear.

The need to shake

Sound is made by something shaking (vibrating). These vibrations shake up the air to make a sound wave.

Microphones have a moving part that can be shaken by a sound wave. Often this is a thin disc called a diaphragm. Different types of microphone use different methods for turning the vibrations of the diaphragm into electric signals.

In loudspeakers, electric signals produce vibrations in something that can shake up the air. Most loudspeakers have cones that vibrate. A telephone's speaker uses a metal diaphragm rather than a cone.

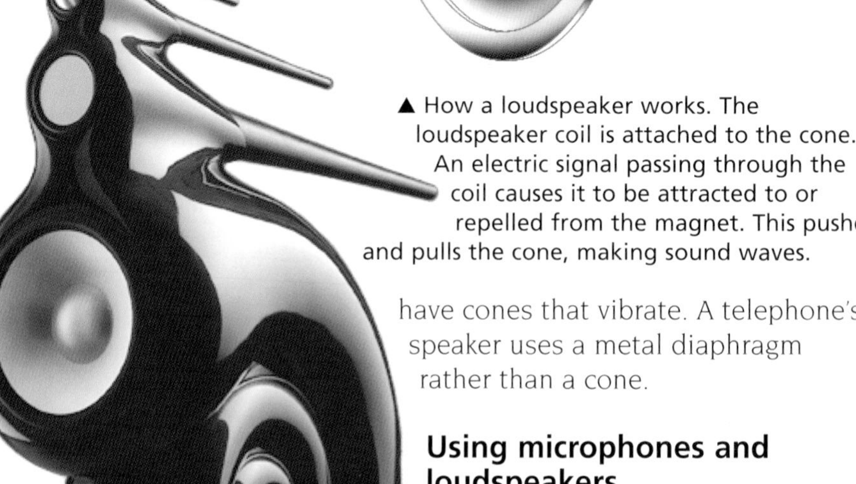

▶ The shell-shaped Nautilus speaker is designed to give outstanding sound quality, adding nothing and taking nothing away from the pure sound. It stands more than a metre high, and weighs 110 kg.

Using microphones and loudspeakers

Microphones and speakers have many uses. Hearing aids use small microphones to collect sound. The sounds are then amplified and played back through a loudspeaker in the earpiece. Microphones and speakers are used for music concerts, and there is a loudspeaker in every TV. Telephones and most computers have built-in microphones and speakers.

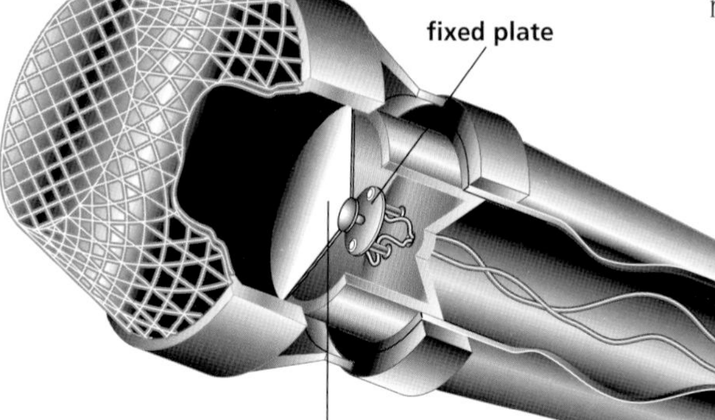

▶ How a condenser microphone works. Two thin plates carry an electric charge across them, which varies depending on how far apart the plates are. Sound causes one plate to vibrate. This changes the distance between the two plates, causing similar changes in the charge on the plates.

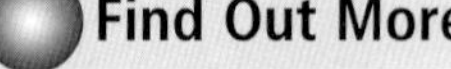

Find Out More

- Magnets and electromagnetism
- Sound
- Sound recording

Microscopes

Imagine being the first person to look at bacteria and tiny insects through a microscope. You would have seen creatures to rival the scariest horror-movie monsters!

An ordinary (light) microscope makes very small things appear larger than life. It uses two lenses fixed at either end of a metal tube. The lens at the far end (the objective lens) collects light from the object and focuses it to make an image inside the tube. You look through the other lens (the eyepiece), which acts like a magnifying glass to enlarge the image made by the objective. Together, these two lenses can magnify the object by as much as 2000 times.

▼ A compound (many-lensed) microscope.

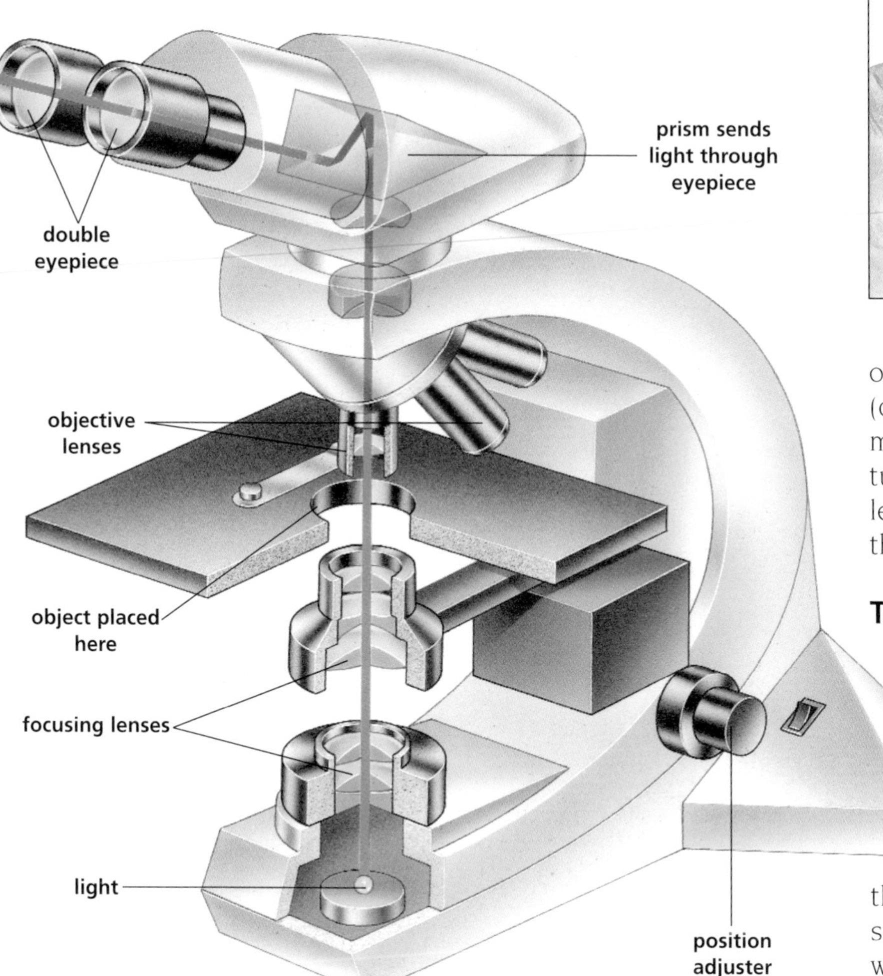

FIRST SIGHT

Anton van Leeuwenhoek (1632–1723) was a Dutch fabric merchant without much formal education – yet he was very good at grinding lenses. He made microscopes with a single tiny lens (see below) that were at least 10 times better than any others at the time. Using them, he made some remarkable biological discoveries – bacteria, blood cells and the 'little animacules' in people's saliva. As he could not draw well, he paid someone else to sketch the things he found with his microscopes.

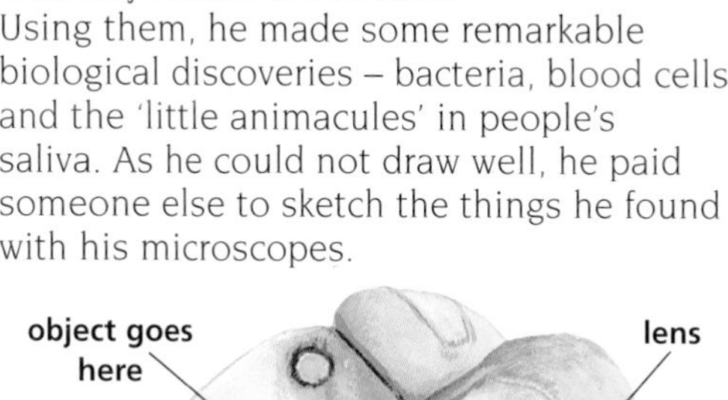

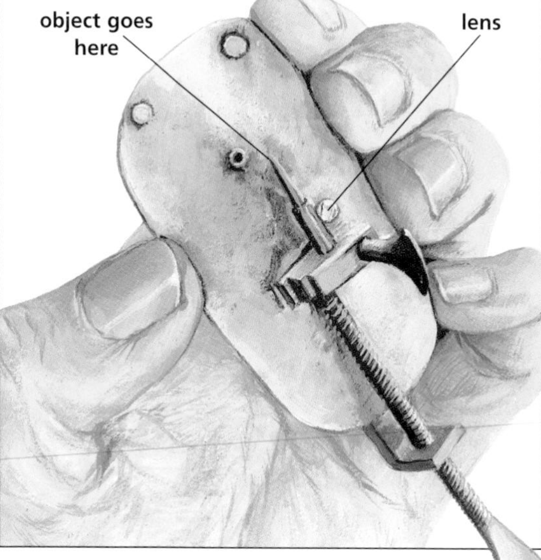

Compound microscopes have several objective lenses of different curvature (degrees of being curved). These are mounted on a disc at the far end of the tube, which is turned to bring a selected lens in line with the eyepiece. This changes the magnification of the microscope.

The see-through object

Microscopes are generally used to look at things that are so tiny that they could never reflect enough light into the objective lens to be seen. The object to be viewed has to be transparent and have light shining through it. This is fine for things like bacteria and cells, but objects such as rock samples have to be sliced wafer-thin for the light to get through.

Microwaves *see* Communications, Electromagnetic spectrum, Radar and sonar • **Migration** *see* Animal behaviour

◀ ▼ Three photographs showing a cell's genetic material.

(a) A photograph of a dividing cell, magnified about 200 times. The genetic material is in the chromosomes (A).

The object is placed on a strip of glass (the slide) and positioned so that light passes through it. If the object is in a liquid, a tiny puddle is trapped between the slide and a small glass square (the cover slip).

Simple microscopes may have a mirror that is tilted to direct light onto the object, but larger ones usually have built-in lamps. They might also have a camera instead of an eyepiece, so that the object can be photographed.

The limits of light

There is a limit on how much a microscope that uses light can magnify an object, and how small an object can be seen through it. This is because light travels as a wave. Have you ever noticed that water waves will bend round rocks if the rocks are small enough? The same thing can happen with light. If the object is very tiny, the light waves bend round it, so it cannot be seen. To achieve really high magnifications and see minute objects, you have to use an electron microscope.

Electron microscopes

Electrons are tiny particles of matter that come from atoms. They have an electrical charge, so magnets can be used to change the way they move. An electron microscope uses a beam of electrons instead of light, and uses magnets to focus the electron beams instead of the lenses used in a light microscope.

Some electron microscopes send electrons through a transparent object. These are called transmission electron microscopes. Others (scanning electron microscopes) bounce electrons off the object's surface while sweeping the beam back and forth. A computer examines how electrons bounce off the surface and build up a detailed picture. Electron microscopes can magnify objects by up to a million times.

(b) Electron micrograph of a single chromosome pair, magnified over 10,000 times. These are X and Y chromosomes (sex chromosomes). Females have two X chromosomes; males have an X (top) and a Y chromosome, as shown here.

(c) A scanning tunnelling microscope image of a section of DNA, the material chromosomes are made from. The image is magnified over $1\frac{1}{2}$ million times. DNA has a double-helix (spiral) structure. The row of orange/yellow peaks in the centre are the individual turns of the helix.

State of the art

Scanning tunnelling microscopes (STMs) are the newest kind of microscope. An STM has a tiny, ultra-fine probe that is moved across the surface of an object. Electrons from the atoms on this surface jump onto the probe tip as it passes. By counting these electrons, it is possible to make an image of the surface capable of showing individual atoms.

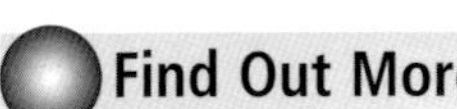

Find Out More

- Atoms and molecules
- Light
- Mirrors and lenses
- Waves and vibrations

Milky Way *see* Astronomy, Constellations, Galaxies

Mind

Our brain is so astonishingly complex, it's not surprising that no one really knows how we think and learn. There are more than 100 billion nerve cells in the brain, each one connected to thousands of others.

Communication between the cells never stops; each one can send up to 300 electrical signals every second.

We do know that as we grow and learn, new pathways are made between groups of nerve cells. The more we use a pathway, the more efficient it becomes and the more easily we can use it. This is how we learn a new skill or remember information. Your brain changes all the time as it adapts to new inputs and learns new skills.

Learning and remembering

People learn in many different ways, and learning goes on throughout our lives. We learn by trial and error: babies pick up a rattle and discover that shaking it makes a noise. As we grow up, we use the same method to find out which tin is full of biscuits and which is empty. If all our problems had to be solved by trial and error, even everyday tasks would take a long time. Learning from past experience is important. We remember which key opens a door – we do not have to try each key in the bunch every time.

We also learn by imitating others and practising what we have seen people do or heard them say. This is how we learn to speak and how we learn new languages. We can also learn about what other people have done at one remove, for instance by reading, watching television or surfing the Internet.

▲ This child will learn by trial and error as she plays with the shapes.

Find Out More

- Brain and nerves
- Cells
- Glands and hormones
- Growth and development

MEMORY GAME

Imagine you are going shopping and you need to remember to buy six things. Think of a story that links these things – it can be as silly as you like. The story will help you to remember the list. A story to link the items in this list might go like this:

1. You are eating **sausages** and they taste odd – they are covered with **stamps**.

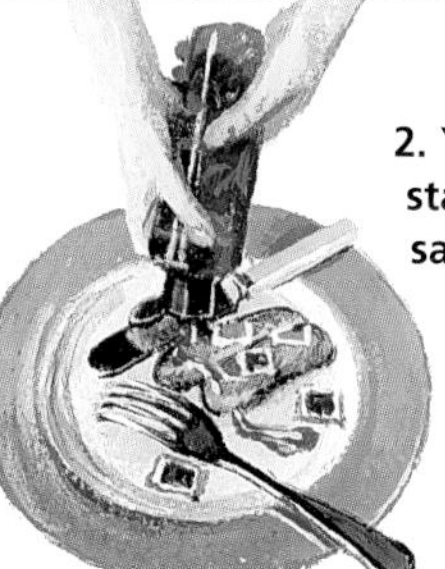

2. You wash the **stamps** off the **sausages** with **shampoo.**

Shopping list
sausages
postage stamps
shampoo
chocolate
a comic
a birthday card

3. The **sausages** turn into **chocolate**. You settle down to eat the **chocolate** and read your **comic.**

4. A **birthday card** falls out of the **comic** and you remember it is your birthday.

▶ Emotions can be shared by large groups of people. You can see by their faces and gestures that these people are happy.

▼ Throughout the night your brain is active, sorting and storing the day's events. Brain waves show patterns of activity in different parts of the brain.

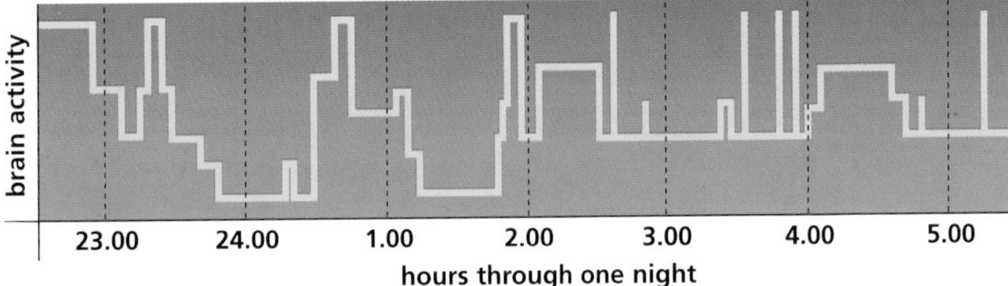

Feelings and emotions

Emotions are strong feelings such as love, hate, anger and grief. These feelings begin in the brain but often they affect the whole body. When we are angry or frightened, the brain releases hormones to prepare us to take action. If we are sad or very happy, we may burst into tears.

The brain also releases other chemicals that affect the way we feel, such as endorphins and seratonin. Endorphins are sometimes called the body's own painkillers and affect the way we feel pain. Serotonin reduces anxiety and makes us feel calmer and able to cope.

Sleep

A baby sleeps for about 16 hours a day, and an adult for about eight hours. Your brain is still active when you are asleep, but in a different way. It does not register the usual messages from your senses, but it is busy dreaming. REM or rapid eye movement sleep is the period when the sleeper's eyes move as though they are watching something. Most dreaming takes place during the REM phase.

Minerals

Deep underground, hot, liquid rock is turning solid. As it cools, atoms of silicon and oxygen are attaching to each other, creating quartz. At the surface a salty lake is drying up and tiny cubes of salt are forming from the sodium and chlorine in the water.

◀ ▲ Different minerals can grow from the same elements depending on where they form. Near the Earth's surface, carbon atoms make soft, black, sooty-looking graphite. But 100 km deep in the Earth's mantle where the pressures are high, the same carbon atoms form hard, clear diamonds.

Quartz and salt are both minerals. Minerals are the building blocks of rocks. Every mineral has a specific chemical make-up. For example, every crystal of quartz contains two atoms of oxygen for every atom of silicon. Every molecule of salt is made of one sodium atom and one chlorine atom. Rocks such as granite, however, are not minerals. There is no single recipe for granite.

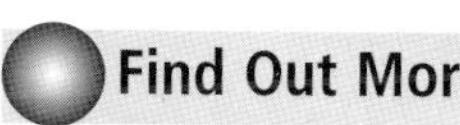
Find Out More

- Atoms and molecules
- Crystals
- Resources
- Rocks

Crystals of all shapes and sizes

Every mineral has a crystalline structure. This means that all of the atoms and molecules in the mineral are arranged in a particular three-dimensional pattern. Some minerals, such as quartz, form large crystals that we can see. In other minerals the crystals are too small to see with the naked eye.

Identifying minerals

Geologists can identify most minerals by properties such as colour, shape, hardness, density and the way they break. Gold is easy to tell from fool's gold (the mineral pyrite) because it is much denser and softer. Salt breaks into cubes, while mica peels off into thin sheets. But some minerals are so similar that you have to use a high-powered microscope to tell them apart.

▲ This rock contains crystals of the blue mineral malachite. All minerals are crystalline. Sometimes they form large crystals that are easy to see, but some mineral crystals, like the malachite crystals here, are so small that they are only visible under a microscope (inset).

▶ Some minerals fluoresce, or glow, under ultraviolet light. The minerals shown here are zinc minerals from Franklin, New Jersey, USA. Miners used to use an ultraviolet light to find the areas rich in these minerals.

Minidiscs *see* Sound recording

Mining

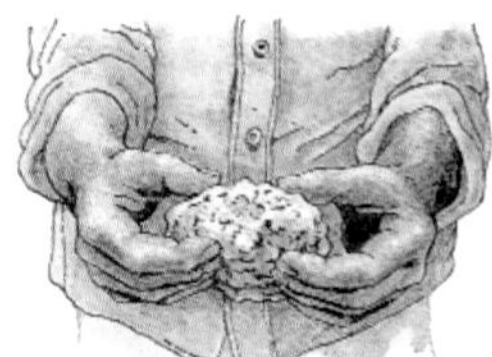

In a tunnel nearly 4000 metres underground, the air is full of dust after an explosion. The temperature is 50 °C. Stripped to the waist, miners are loading shattered rock onto wagons. They are risking their lives to dig out one of the most precious metals on Earth – gold.

Many metals are mined, or dug out of the Earth's crust, underground. They include copper, zinc, lead and nickel. These metals are found in minerals, or ores, in the rocks. To mine these ores, shafts are sunk vertically down into the ground. Tunnels are then driven horizontally across to reach the ore deposits. Explosives are used to break up the rocks containing the ores, then the pieces are transported to the surface.

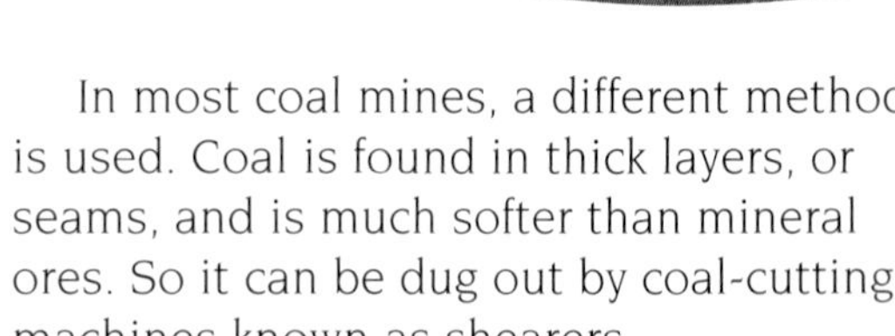

▶ In a silver mine in Mexico, miners drill holes in the rock, into which they will place explosives. The explosives will break up the rock, which contains the silver ore.

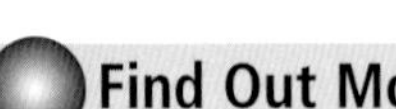

Find Out More

- Coal
- Explosives
- Gold and silver
- Oil and gas
- Resources
- Salts

In most coal mines, a different method is used. Coal is found in thick layers, or seams, and is much softer than mineral ores. So it can be dug out by coal-cutting machines known as shearers.

Keeping cool

Large mines have hundreds of kilometres of tunnels on many levels, fanning out from many shafts. Some of the mines have lifts and railways to transport the miners to the ore deposits. Some shafts have hoists, or skips, to lift out the ore or coal. Other shafts are used for ventilation to supply fresh, cool air for the miners to breathe.

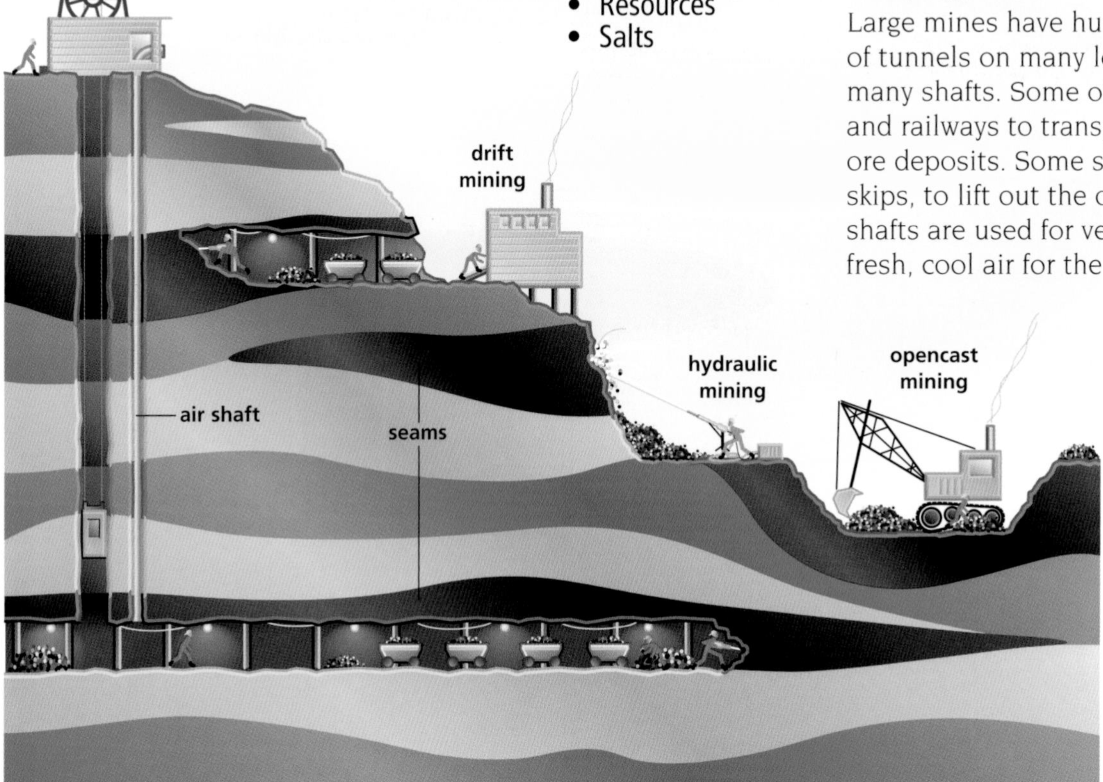

◀ Different methods of mining are needed to reach mineral or coal deposits. Opencast mining digs out surface deposits. Hydraulic mining breaks up soft deposits with water jets. Underground deposits can be reached from hillsides or through shafts.

On the surface

It is cheaper and safer to mine on the surface of the ground. Fortunately, quite a few ore deposits are found on or near the surface. They include iron and copper ores and also the aluminium ore bauxite. Many coal seams are found near the surface too.

Mining at the surface is called opencast mining. Mining begins by stripping off any soil, or overburden, covering the deposit. This is done by huge excavators, such as drag-lines. If the ore or coal deposit is soft, it can be dug out and loaded into wagons or trucks. If it is hard, it must first be broken up by explosives.

Quarrying is the name given to the surface mining of rock, such as chalk, limestone and marble. Marble is widely used for decoration in building work. It has to be removed carefully by driving wedges into natural cracks in the rock.

Flash in the pan

Gold is found deep underground, and on the surface in 'placer' deposits, in stream and river beds. In the early days of gold mining, miners would 'pan' for gold using a shallow pan. They would swirl material from the river bed around in the pan with some water. The lighter, gravelly material would wash away, leaving the heavier gold behind. Today, mechanical panning methods are used.

The Bingham Canyon copper mine in Utah, USA, is the world's largest man-made hole. Covering an area of 7 square kilometres, it is nearly a kilometre deep.

Tin ore (cassiterite) is also found in placer deposits, particularly in Malaysia. The ore is dug out by huge dredges. These are floating platforms which use a conveyor belt of buckets to dig up material from the sea or river bed.

▲ Cassiterite (tin ore) is dug out from opencast mines in Malaysia, as well as from placer deposits.

◀ Gold miners use hoses to suck up mud and gravel from the bed of the Madre de Dios river, Peru. The mixture is fed through a device called a sluice box. Heavy specks of gold fall to the bottom, while the lighter mud and gravel flow back into the river.

Out of a hole

Resources can also be taken from the ground by drilling. For example, holes are drilled down to deposits of crude oil, or petroleum, which are then piped back to the surface.

Borehole mining is used to extract underground salt deposits. Water is pumped into a hole bored into the solid salt. It dissolves the salt and is then pumped back to the surface as brine, a mixture of water and salt. Evaporating the brine recovers the salt. Sulphur can be mined in a similar way, using very hot water to melt the deposit.

Mirrors and lenses

You are the captain of a ship on a foggy night. You know there are rocks about, so you are glad to see the bright light from a lighthouse. Lighthouses don't just use a big light bulb. There is also a curved mirror to reflect the light forwards and a curved lens to bend it into a powerful beam.

Mirrors reflect light well because they are smooth and shiny. The earliest mirrors were probably polished metal, but now we use coated glass.

Flat mirrors have a shiny aluminium coating on the back of a piece of glass. When you look in a flat mirror, your image seems to be behind the mirror. It is also the wrong way round. Ambulances have words written backwards on them so they can be read the right way round in a car's mirror.

▶ Polishing the main mirror for the Hubble Space Telescope. This huge mirror is used to gather light from distant galaxies. To get a sharp image the mirror has to be very, very smooth. The engineers making it wear masks and special suits to keep off every speck of dust.

Curved mirrors

Behind the bulb in a torch there is a shiny curved surface. It reflects light from the bulb forwards in a beam. Shapes that curve inwards like this are called concave. This is the sort of mirror used in lighthouses. Concave mirrors are also used in some

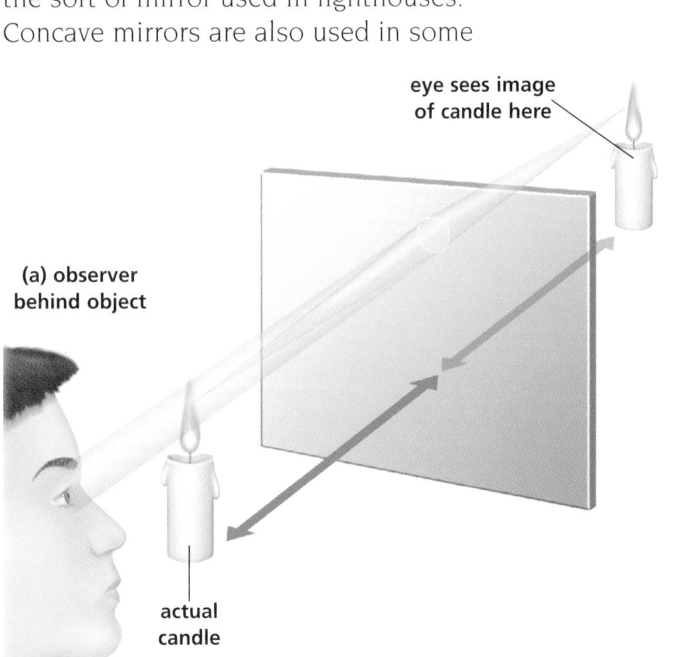

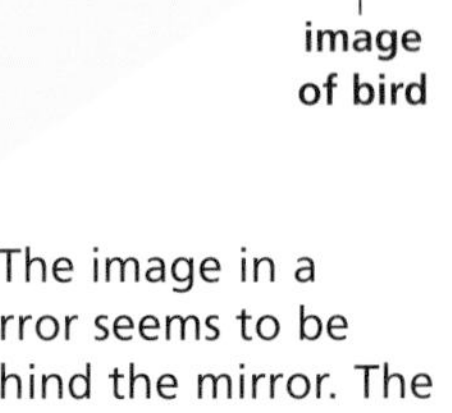

◀ The image in a mirror seems to be behind the mirror. The eye cannot tell the difference between the light reflected off the mirror and that coming from a real object the same distance away as the image.

telescopes, because they are very good at collecting light.

Convex mirrors curve outwards. They let you see a very wide picture. You sometimes see them placed at difficult road junctions so drivers can see what is coming round the corner.

Lenses

If you look at a flower under a magnifying glass, it seems much bigger. The same lens can also be used to make a picture. If you were to hold it up in front of a window, you could make a picture of the window on a piece of paper. The picture would be smaller than the window and upside-down. A camera uses a lens in just this way to make a picture on a film. The picture does not have to be smaller. A projector uses a lens to throw a very large picture on a screen.

Cameras, magnifying glasses and projectors all use lenses that are fat in the middle and thin at the edges. This shape is called convex. Convex lenses bend light so that it comes together. They are also sometimes called converging lenses.

Some lenses are shaped so they are thin in the middle and fat at the edges. These are concave lenses, and they make light spread out. Such lenses are also known as diverging lenses. Concave lenses are used in spectacles for short-sighted people, who cannot see things that are a long way away.

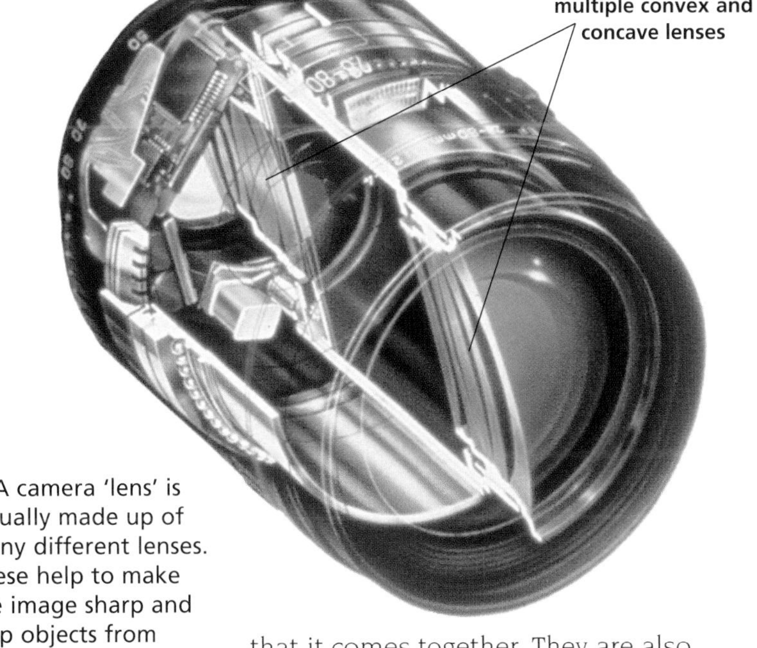

▶ A camera 'lens' is actually made up of many different lenses. These help to make the image sharp and stop objects from having a halo of colours around the edges.

Find Out More

- Cameras
- Eyes
- Light
- Microscopes
- Movies
- Photography
- Telescopes

Special lenses

The lens in our eye is the one we use most often. It has the wonderful ability to get fatter and thinner. Without this, we would have trouble focusing on objects.

A single lens makes pictures that are slightly blurry. Sometimes the colours are not quite right either. To get round this problem, camera and projector 'lenses' are actually made up of several lenses.

▲ A convex (converging) lens bends light so that it narrows to a point. A concave (diverging) lens spreads light out.

Missiles *see* Weapons • **Mitosis** (cell division) *see* Cells

Mixtures and solutions

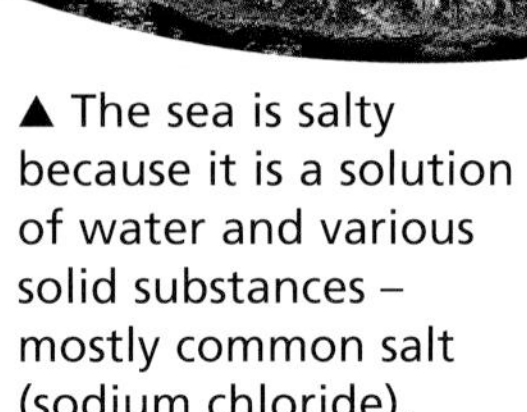

In the natural world, most things are made of lots of different substances mixed up together. Rocks are mostly mixtures of minerals, usually various kinds of tiny crystals. Sand on the beach is often a mixture of tiny grains of rock and fragments of seashells. The air we breathe is a mixture of gases, mainly nitrogen and oxygen. The sea is a special kind of mixture called a solution, in which substances such as salt are dissolved.

▲ The sea is salty because it is a solution of water and various solid substances – mostly common salt (sodium chloride).

Mixtures are different from chemical compounds. For example, if you mix together iron filings and talcum powder, the mixture behaves in the same way as the two separate substances. The iron filings are still magnetic, and the talcum powder still absorbs water.

But if iron reacts chemically with oxygen in the air, a completely different chemical results – iron oxide (rust). Iron oxide is not magnetic, is reddish in colour and is much weaker than iron.

Separating mixtures

You can separate the ingredients of mixtures in various ways. Filtration is one common method. This is like passing the mixture through a sieve. If you need to separate really tiny particles from a liquid, then you need a material with even tinier holes – like filter paper. Another way of separating mixtures is to let the less dense ingredients float to the top. For example, cream floats to the top of milk, where you can skim it off.

◀ As part of the process of purifying iron and other metals, the metal is heated to melting point. The lighter impurities float to the top of the liquid and can be skimmed off as scum.

Some industrial processes use a technique called fractional distillation to separate mixtures of liquids. The liquid mixture is heated in a device called a fractionating column. Different liquids vaporize (turn to gas) at different temperatures. Those that vaporize most easily rise to the top of the column, while those with higher boiling points rise less far. This is how crude oil is refined into products such as jet fuel and petrol.

Modems *see* Faxes and modems • **Molecules** *see* Atoms and molecules • **Molluscs** *see* Invertebrates

▼ Your blood is a mixture of water, cells, and various chemicals. Scientists can separate the blood cells from the liquid in a blood sample by spinning it at high speed. This forces the heavier cells to the bottom of the test tube, while the liquid is left at the top.

Solutions

Solutions are a special kind of mixture, in which one substance (the solute) is dissolved in another (the solvent). If you put sand in water and stir it up, the sand will eventually settle on the bottom. But if you stir salt into water, the salt will dissolve – it will remain evenly spread throughout the water.

Common salt is a chemical compound, sodium chloride. When a solid crystal of salt is dropped into water, molecules (tiny particles) of water gather on the surface of the crystal. They pull at the sodium and chloride particles, separating them from each other. Eventually each particle is surrounded by water molecules and the salt is dissolved.

The substances in solutions can be solids, liquids or gases. Beer and wine are solutions of two liquids – water and alcohol. Fizzy drinks are fizzy because carbon dioxide gas is dissolved in them. When you release the pressure by opening the drink, the gas fizzes out of solution.

▲ One way of making real coffee is to mix hot water and coffee grains. But if you drank it like this you would get a mouthful of gritty grains! So the mixture is separated by filter paper. This has tiny holes which are too small for the grains to get through.

Saturation and separation

A solvent can only dissolve a certain amount of a substance. If you go on pouring salt into a glass of water, eventually no more salt will dissolve and salt crystals will pile up at the bottom of the glass. When this happens, the solution is said to be saturated.

You can separate a solution of salt and water by heating the solution until the water has all boiled away. You will be left with salt crystals. You can separate the water and alcohol in wine or beer by fractional distillation – alcohol boils at a lower temperature than water.

▼ How a grain of salt dissolves in water. Solid salt (sodium chloride) is made up of tiny charged particles (ions) of sodium (positively charged) and chlorine (negatively charged). Water molecules are attracted to these ions, and surround each one.

salt particle

chloride ion

sodium ion

water molecules

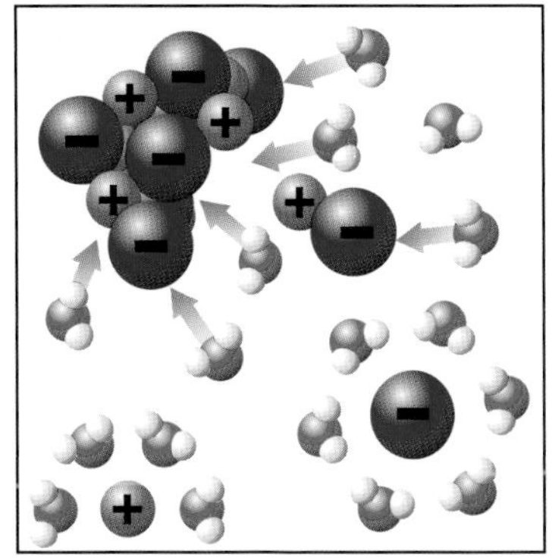

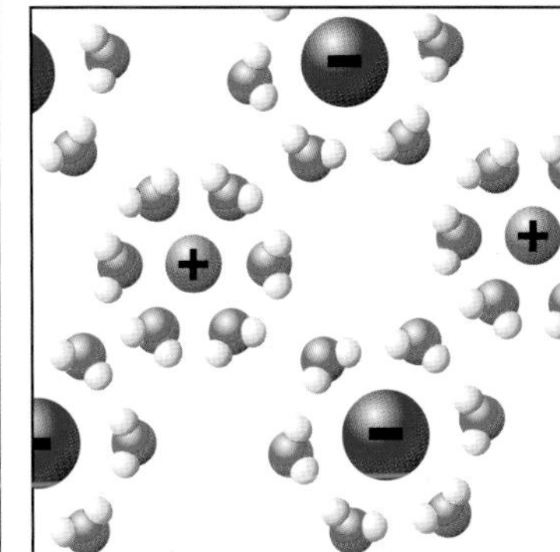

Find Out More

- Atoms and molecules
- Chemical analysis
- Elements and compounds
- Oil products
- Salts

Momentum *see* Motion • **Monsoons** *see* Rain and snow • **Months** *see* Time

Moon

On 20 July 1969, astronauts Neil Armstrong and Buzz Aldrin landed on the Moon and became the first people ever to go there. They found themselves on a bleak lifeless world with crunchy grey soil under their feet. The Sun shone from a completely black sky overhead.

The Moon is planet Earth's natural satellite. Other planets have moons that orbit them, too. Our Moon is a barren ball of rock about one quarter the diameter of the Earth. It has no atmosphere, no liquid water and no life. Hardly anything has changed on the Moon for thousands of millions of years.

Even without a telescope, you can see dark and bright areas. The dark regions formed when molten rock welled up into great basins on the surface thousands of millions of years ago. They were named *maria* (Latin for 'seas') on early maps of the Moon, but they are really rocky plains. The first astronauts to land touched down on the Sea of Tranquillity. The lighter parts of the Moon's surface are mountainous highland areas.

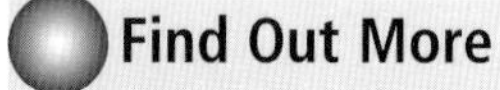

Find Out More

- Astronauts
- Earth
- Gravity
- Orbits
- Space travel

▲ Astronaut James Irwin with the lunar rover during the *Apollo 15* mission to the Moon. The lunar rover was used on the later Moon missions to explore large areas around the landing site.

Craters everywhere

The Moon is littered with craters. They were gouged out by rocks crashing down from space. Most were made soon after the Moon formed. Larger rocks called asteroids

MOON DATA
Diameter: 3476 km
Average distance from Earth: 384,400 km
Mass: 0.012 Earth's mass
Time taken to orbit the Earth: 27.33 days
Time taken to spin on axis: 27.33 days
Time between new Moons: 29.53 days

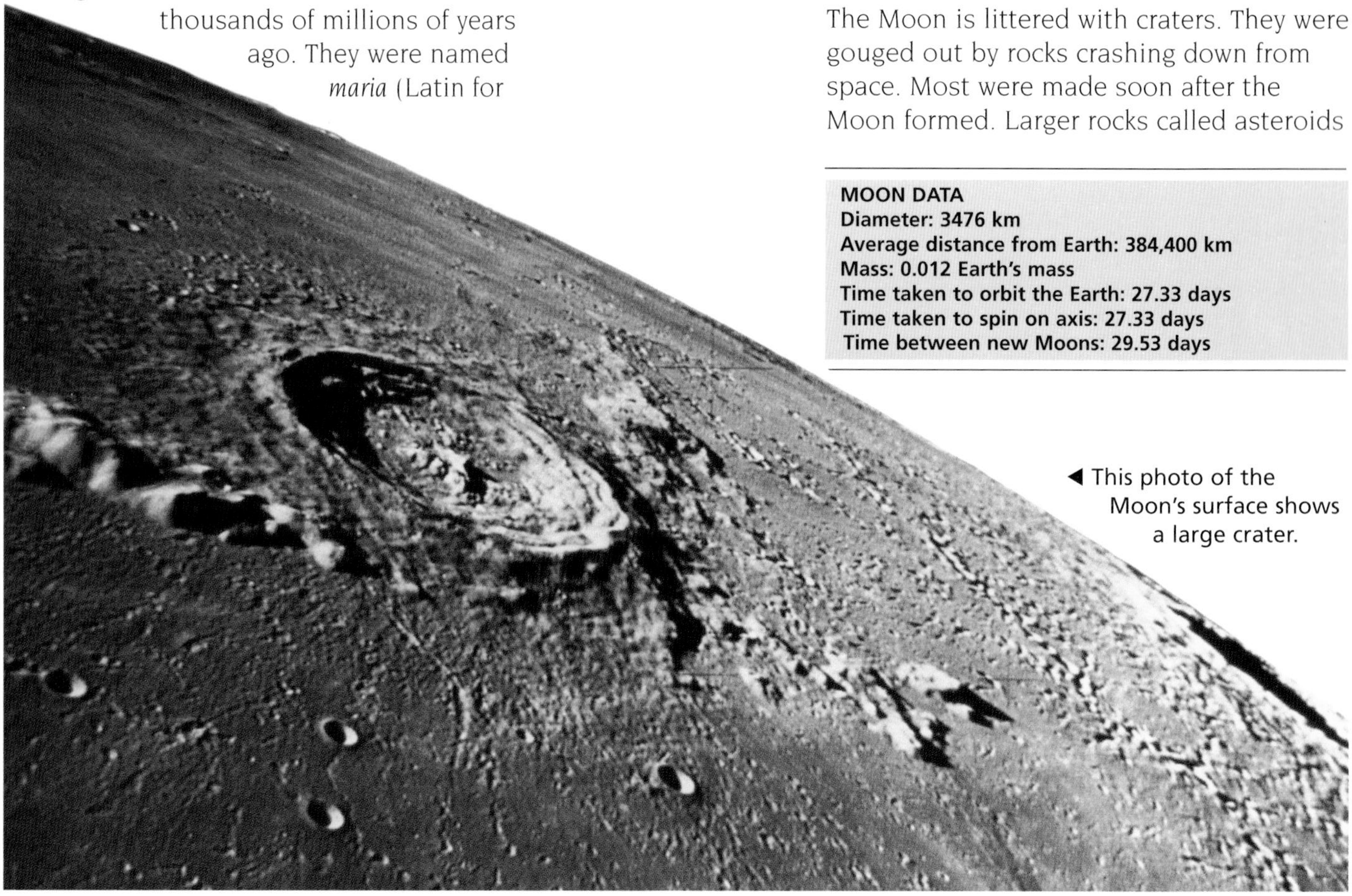

◀ This photo of the Moon's surface shows a large crater.

produced the basins that later became the 'seas'. There are fewer craters on the 'sea' areas than in the highlands.

Crater sizes range from a few centimetres up to about 100 kilometres. A few are even wider. The largest crater on the Moon is called Bailly and is 295 kilometres across.

Near and far

The Moon orbits the Earth at a distance of about 385,000 kilometres. The Moon's gravity is less than a fifth of the Earth's, but because it is so close, its gravitational pull is the main cause of the Earth's tides. The Moon takes the same time to orbit the Earth as it does to spin once on its axis. This means the same side of the Moon, known as its near side, always faces the Earth. Spacecraft have returned images of the Moon's far side. It has many craters but far fewer 'sea' areas.

THE MOON'S PHASES

Sunlight makes the side of the Moon facing the Sun shine. On this part of the Moon it is daytime. The other half is in darkness and here it is night. As the Moon travels around the Earth, we see different amounts of its sunlit half. Night by night, the shape of the Moon seems to change from a thin crescent to a complete disc and back again. The shape of the Moon is called its phase.

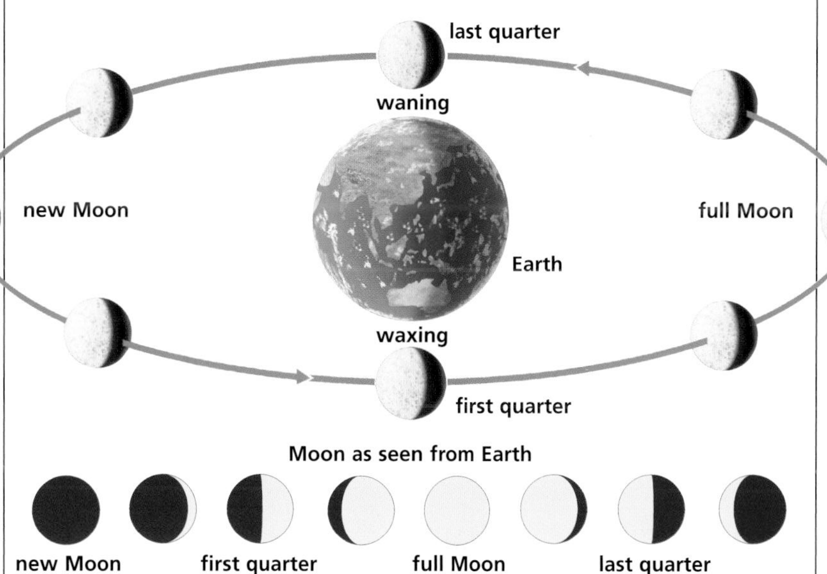

How the Earth got its Moon

Astronomers have long puzzled about where the Moon came from. The most popular idea is that a large asteroid crashed into the Earth very soon after it first formed. The huge impact spewed vast amounts of rock into space. Some of it circled around the Earth. Then the pull of gravity caused some of the rock fragments to come together and form the Moon.

The Apollo missions

Six crews of American astronauts made successful Moon landings between July 1969 and December 1972. The commander of each mission remained in orbit round the Moon, while the lunar module undocked and took two astronauts down to the surface.

When the astronauts had finished working on the surface, the lunar module launched them back into orbit. They rejoined the command and service modules, which carried all three astronauts back to Earth.

The Apollo astronauts collected 400 kilograms of Moon rocks in all and carried out a variety of experiments. The last three crews took an electric powered Lunar Rover, or Moon buggy, to ride in so they could explore farther afield.

Cold Sea
Bay of Rainbows
Sea of Shadows
Sea of Serenity
Sea of Crises
Ocean of Storms
Sea of Tranquility
Copernicus
Sea of Fertility
Sea of Clouds
Sea of Nectar
Sea of Moisture
Tycho

▶ A map of the Moon showing the names of some of the main features. The easiest crater to spot is Tycho. It is 85 km across and has a mountain peak in the centre.

Morse code *see* Communications • **Mosses** *see* Plants

Motion

Kick a ball. You can feel the force that you use to start it soaring through the air. But why does the ball keep moving through the air? This puzzled people for centuries, for the answer seems unbelievable. The answer is that nothing keeps it moving – it goes by itself.

To get anything moving, a force must push on it or pull on it. But once something is already moving, like a ball soaring or rolling, it does not need a force to continue moving. It carries on of its own accord, moving effortlessly in the same direction and at a constant speed. You continue to move unaided when you slide on some ice or roll along on skates...until you hit a wall!

Find Out More

- Engines and turbines
- Forces
- Friction
- Gravity
- Orbits

Speed, turn, slow or stop

Once an object is moving, it will not speed up (accelerate), slow down or change direction unless another force acts on it. This happens all the time. A soaring ball is slowed by the air, which exerts a backward force called friction as the ball moves through it. The ball also slows down and soon stops rising because the force of gravity pulls it down. At the same time, the force of a gust of wind may blow the ball to one side and change its direction.

If a force pushes or pulls on one side or one end of an object, or if two forces act on both sides or both ends, then the object turns. You grip the ends of the handlebars of a bicycle to turn them.

More weight, less speed

Have you ever tried to push a car to get it moving? Even though the car can roll easily, it needs several people to push it and takes a lot of force to get it going. This is because the car is very heavy. The more you all push, the faster it goes. Slowing and stopping a heavy object needs a lot of force too, so a car has powerful brakes.

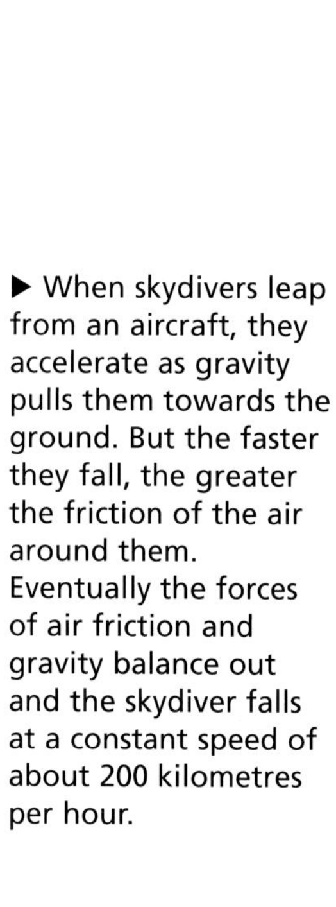

▶ When skydivers leap from an aircraft, they accelerate as gravity pulls them towards the ground. But the faster they fall, the greater the friction of the air around them. Eventually the forces of air friction and gravity balance out and the skydiver falls at a constant speed of about 200 kilometres per hour.

Pushing back and moving forwards

How do you jump? You push down on the ground with your legs. But surely, to move upwards, you need a force that pushes you up? Where does that force come from? It comes from the ground, which pushes you up as you push down on it. Forces always act in pairs like this.

Out of this world

Movement is different in space. The Earth, stars, planets and moons were moving as they formed and cannot stop. Space is empty, and there is no air to produce friction and stop them. In the same way, spacecraft and satellites enter space at high speed and, if they do not return to Earth, will continue to move for ever.

You are never at rest. The Earth moves through space, circling the Sun at a speed of 108,000 kilometres per hour, and carrying you along with it.

▼ As the water spurts from a high-power hose, it pushes back on the nozzle. It takes a lot of strength for the firefighters to hold the nozzle steady and stop it pushing them back.

▼ A ride on a bicycle involves several different forces as you start off, speed up, turn, slow down and stop.

You push off and pedal to start moving. The force of your legs goes to the back wheel, which turns and moves the bicycle forwards. The bicycle speeds up.

You reach a steady speed on the flat. A backward force called friction comes into action as the bicycle moves. It equals the forward force on the back wheel. There is no overall force so the bicycle's speed is constant.

Travelling downhill, the force of gravity pulls you forwards, and you do not need to pedal.

Travelling uphill, gravity pulls you backwards. You have to pedal hard to produce enough forward force to overcome gravity.

You swivel the handlebars to turn the bicycle. A sideways force moves the front wheel to the side and you change direction.

You apply the brakes. The brakes produce a backward force on both wheels of the bicycle, and you slow down and stop.

Motorways *see* Roads • **Moulding** *see* Metalworking, Plastics

Mountains

Eighty million years ago, India was an island continent 5000 kilometres south of mainland Asia. Th…

The … Tibet, and volcanoes …

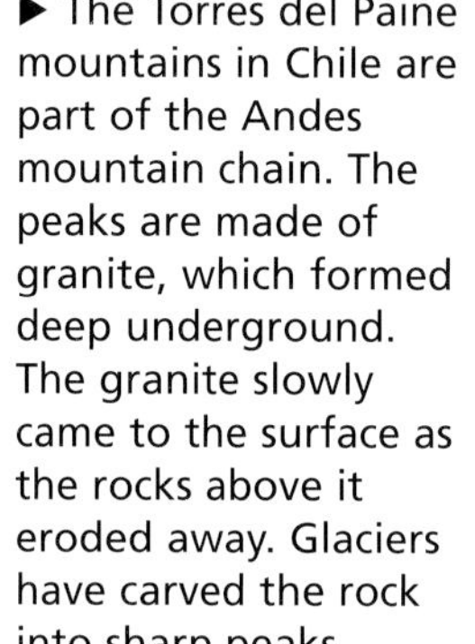

▶ The Torres del Paine mountains in Chile are part of the Andes mountain chain. The peaks are made of granite, which formed deep underground. The granite slowly came to the surface as the rocks above it eroded away. Glaciers have carved the rock into sharp peaks.

Eventually, the Indian continent crashed into mainland Asia, squeezing and breaking the rocks and folding them into contorted shapes. As the rocks piled on top of each other, the continent got thicker. Rocks that had formed on the bottom of the sea were thrust upwards and became part of the highest mountain range on Earth – the Himalayas.

How mountains form

There are two main kinds of mountain ranges: volcanic mountains, and fold and thrust mountains. Both kinds form over millions of years as the broken pieces of Earth's surface (the tectonic plates) collide with each other.

Volcanic mountain ranges, like the Cascades in the USA and the Andes in South America, form where the ocean floor dives beneath the edge of a continent. The rocks beneath the continent melt and then erupt as lava and ash. Over millions of years, the volcanoes grow to form long, tall mountain chains.

Fold and thrust mountains, like the Himalayas in Asia and the Appalachians in the USA, form when two land masses crash into one another. As they collide, the rocks crumple and get pushed up into mountain ranges.

Find Out More

- Continents and plates
- Rocks
- Volcanoes

Shaping mountains

Once mountains begin to form, they are shaped by other forces such as running water, glacier ice and gravity. At one time, the Highlands of Scotland were as tall and jagged as the Alps. But as they got older, they wore down. Many ancient mountain ranges are now just low hills or flat plains of folded rocks.

▼ Thrust mountains and fold mountains form when two continents collide. Fault block mountains form when a continent has been stretched.

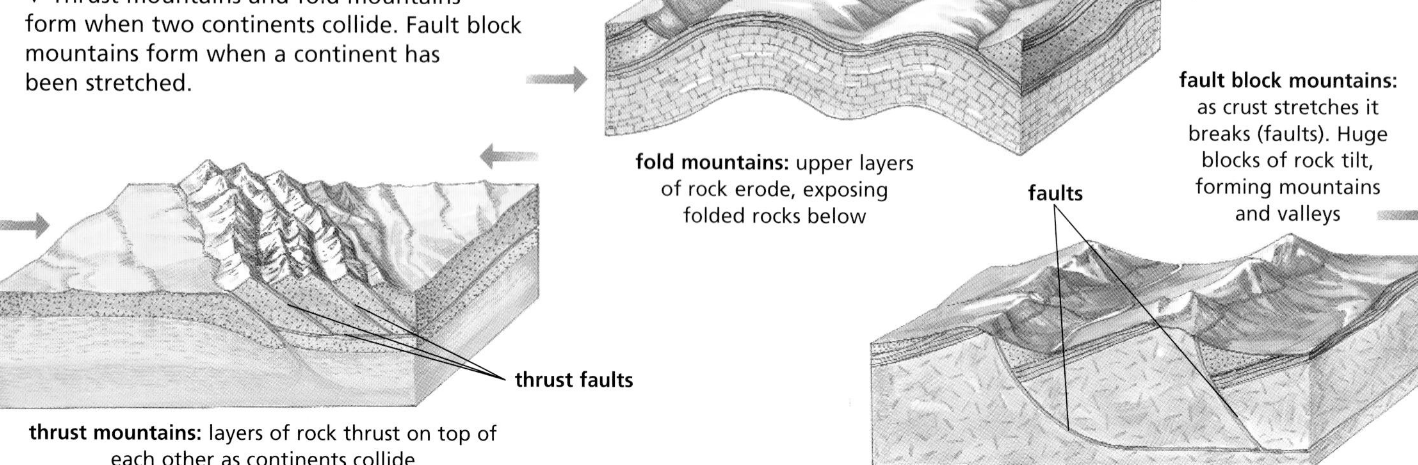

fold mountains: upper layers of rock erode, exposing folded rocks below

fault block mountains: as crust stretches it breaks (faults). Huge blocks of rock tilt, forming mountains and valleys

thrust mountains: layers of rock thrust on top of each other as continents collide

Mouse (computer) *see* Hardware, computer

Movies

A good film takes us out of ourselves

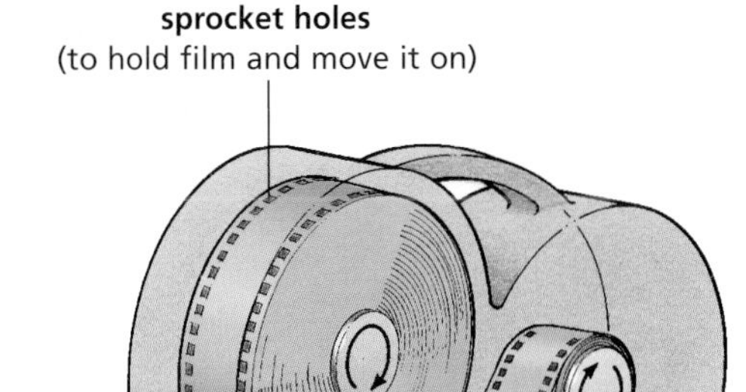

A movie is a series of still images projected onto a screen very quickly. You see it as a smoothly changing picture because the images are timed to trick your eye. Your eye will continue to see an image for about a twentieth of a second after it has disappeared (this is called persistence of vision). So the eye is still 'holding' the last image when the next one appears.

Filming a movie

Movie cameras capture the light coming from moving objects and use it to freeze an image – quickly, so the images are not blurred by the object's movement. The lens captures the light and directs it onto a film. (Movie film is light-sensitive, like ordinary camera film.) The rotating shutter cuts off the light at regular intervals, to break the action up into a series of images.

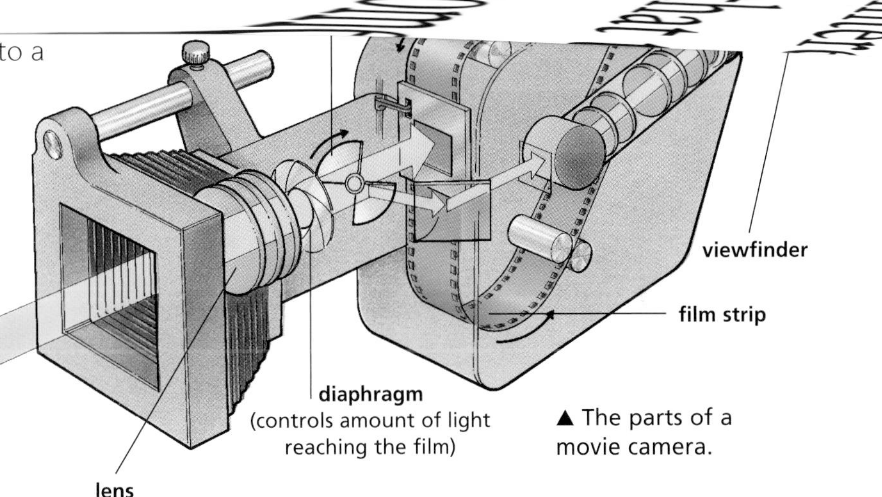

▲ The parts of a movie camera.

▼ These photographs of a cat falling were taken by photography pioneer Etienne-Jules Marey in the 1890s. He wanted to try to capture the illusion of movement in still images.

Projecting the movie

The projector at the cinema contains a lamp and a lens to direct light through the film and onto a screen.

With 24 frames being projected each second, a movie uses a lot of film. This is cut into lengths called reels. Cinemas use two projectors. As soon as one completes its reel, the other starts up.

▼ A thaumatrope is a cardboard disc with an image on each side. If you spin the disc, the two images merge to make a single picture. The thaumatrope shows how your eye can be fooled by fast-moving pictures.

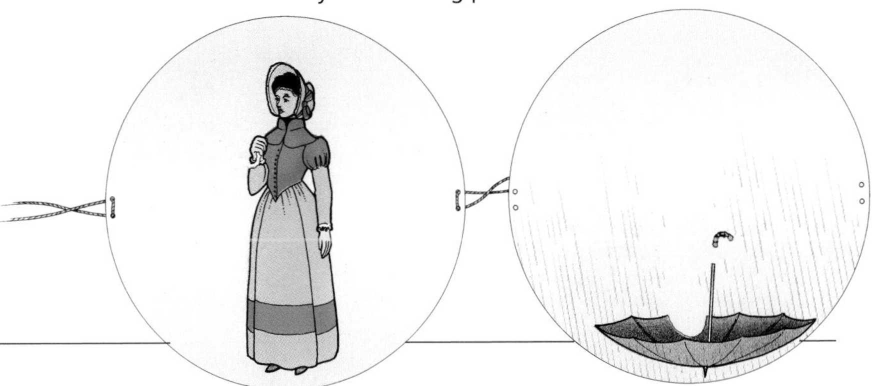

TIME-LAPSE PHOTOGRAPHY

A movie camera takes 24 frames every second. If you take one frame every hour, but project the film back at the normal speed, you can see a day's worth of frames every second! This means you can film something changing extremely slowly, such as a flower unfurling.

Cinema shows 24 frames a second, but TV shows 25. So, when you watch 25 minutes' worth of movie on television, you see it slightly fast – in only 24 minutes.

Find Out More

- Cameras
- Photography
- Sound recording
- Television

Sound

The movie soundtrack is on the same film as the pictures, sometimes as a patterned strip of light and dark down the edge. The projector shines light through this strip onto a light-sensitive circuit. This converts the pattern into an electrical signal, which is then turned into sound by an amplifier and loudspeaker.

Cartoons that move

Traditional-style cartoons and animations use models, puppets or lots of drawings, but modern animation is usually made using powerful computers. Feature-length cartoons can take years to produce.

As with an ordinary film, a series of images, each one slightly different from the one before, creates the illusion of movement. Puppeteers spend hours patiently moving the bodies of their puppets between each frame. Cartoonists create lots of drawings, each with a tiny change.

Traditional animation can be speeded up by using transparent plastic sheets called cells. The background artwork can remain the same while cells with drawings of the moving characters are placed on top.

▼ The 1933 movie *King Kong* had some of the best special effects of its time. King Kong himself was a model, and in this scene he is set against a 'futuristic' background.

Music

People have been making music

orchestra, accompanied by a washing machine and vacuum cleaner!

Music is a collection of noises that have been arranged to sound interesting. It can make you happy, sad, relaxed or excited. Some people enjoy singing or playing musical instruments. Others just like to listen to recordings or live musicians.

Sounds are made by objects that are shaking back and forth (vibrating). These vibrations can be very quick, or rather slow. Fast vibrations make sounds that have a high pitch. Slow vibrations make low-pitched sounds.

Each vibration has a certain frequency. This is the number of vibrations that occur every second. The frequencies of sounds that go well together form a pattern. A sound of one frequency always goes very well with a sound of twice that frequency. Patterns like this make music.

▶ A singer with the flamenco group Los Activos. The human voice is the simplest musical instrument. The air in the throat is set vibrating by tiny strings called vocal cords.

Find Out More

- Sound
- Waves and vibrations

Musical notes

Musical sounds are organized into notes. The pitch of every note is a certain frequency. A scale is a sequence of notes. Most scales used in Western music start with a note of one frequency and end with the note of twice that frequency. These two notes are an octave (eight notes) apart.

Harmony is created when two or more notes with different pitches are sounded together. The length of a note can vary too. The mix of long and short sounds adds rhythm, which is a very important element in all music.

Musical instruments

All musical instruments make vibrations. They are designed so the vibrations produce musical notes. There are three main types of instrument. String instruments make notes from vibrating

◀ Each key on a piano plays a different note. Several notes played at the same time produce a chord.

strings. Wind instruments have to be blown in some way. Percussion instruments have to be struck by something.

Sounds different

A guitar and a violin sound very different, even if they are playing the same note.

When an instrument makes a note, lots of different vibrations are produced. One of these vibrations will make the pitch of the note. It will be the loudest. Any other vibrations will be much quieter. The sound that we hear is made up of all these vibrations.

A violin will make one collection of vibrations. A guitar will make a slightly different collection. This is why they sound different.

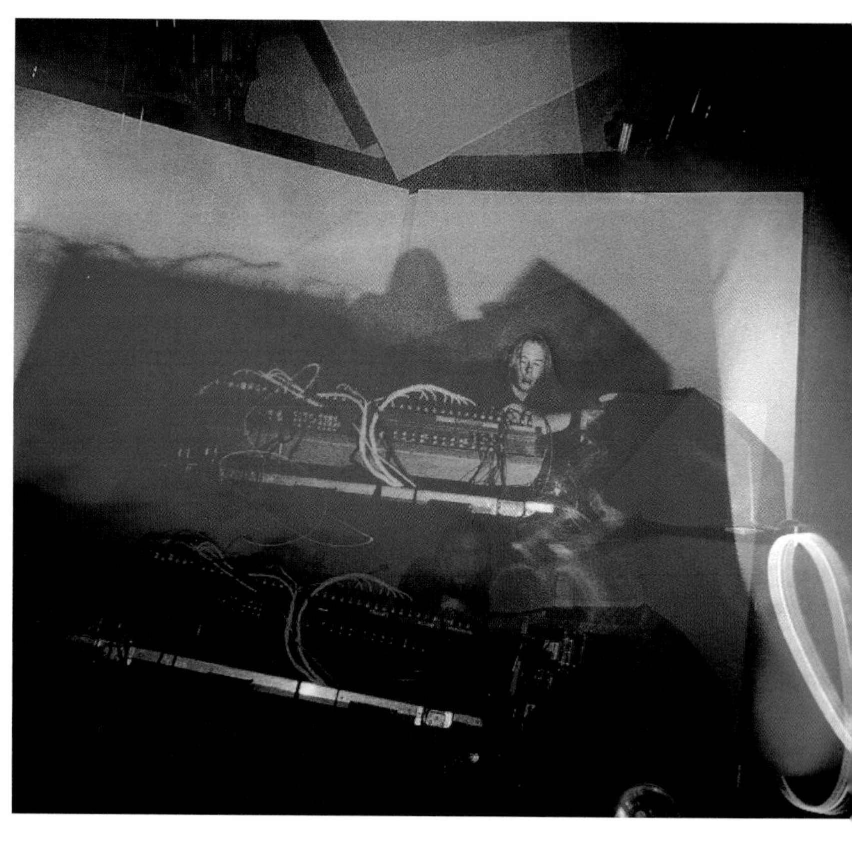

▶ Electronic instruments make electric wave patterns similar to the sound waves produced by other instruments. These are then turned into sounds by loudspeakers. They can also take recorded samples of real sounds and change them in many different ways.

◀ How different kinds of musical instruments produce their sound.

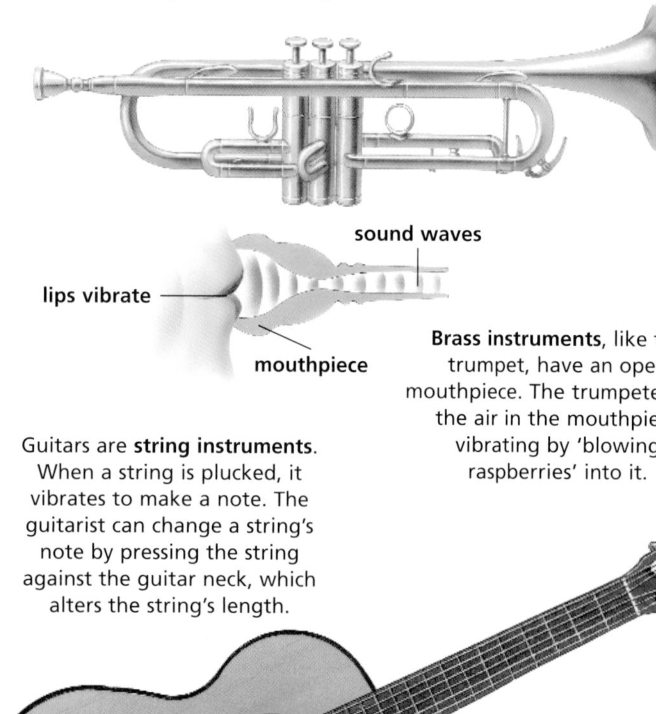

Brass instruments, like the trumpet, have an open mouthpiece. The trumpeter sets the air in the mouthpiece vibrating by 'blowing raspberries' into it.

Guitars are **string instruments**. When a string is plucked, it vibrates to make a note. The guitarist can change a string's note by pressing the string against the guitar neck, which alters the string's length.

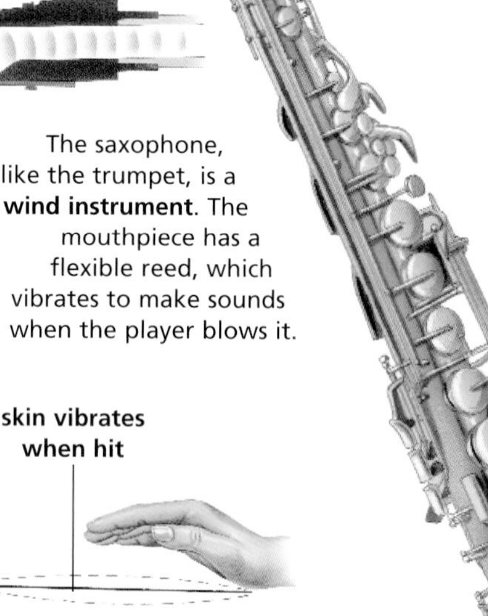

The saxophone, like the trumpet, is a **wind instrument**. The mouthpiece has a flexible reed, which vibrates to make sounds when the player blows it.

Drums are **percussion instruments**. Hitting the skin with a hand or a stick sets up vibrations in the skin, which makes a sound.

Mutations *see* Genetics • **NASA** *see* Space travel • **Natural gas** *see* Oil and gas • **Natural selection** *see* Evolution

Navigation

How do you find your way at night if you don't

stars always point to the Pole Star, which points the way north.

Years ago, people used to find their way around by looking up at the sky. By day they looked at the Sun and by night at the stars. Today, other objects in the sky help us navigate. They are navigation satellites. Most planes and ships now use satellite navigation. It is also available for walkers and for use in cars.

Other systems

Before satellite navigation came into use, ships and planes – and walkers too – relied on other methods, such as maps and compasses. Navigators also had devices such as the sextant, to measure the positions of the Sun and stars.

GPS NAVIGATION

GPS stands for 'Global Positioning System'. The system uses 24 NAVSTAR satellites, each orbiting at the same height (just over 17,000 kilometres) above the Earth, and transmitting special radio signals. A GPS receiver anywhere on the Earth's surface can pick up signals from at least five of these satellites

far away each satellite is, and hence its own position.

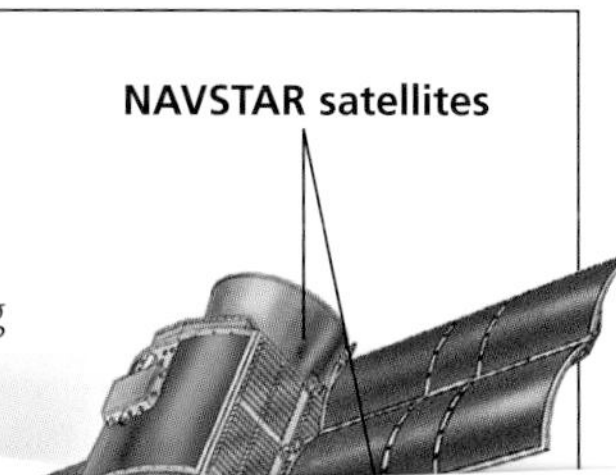

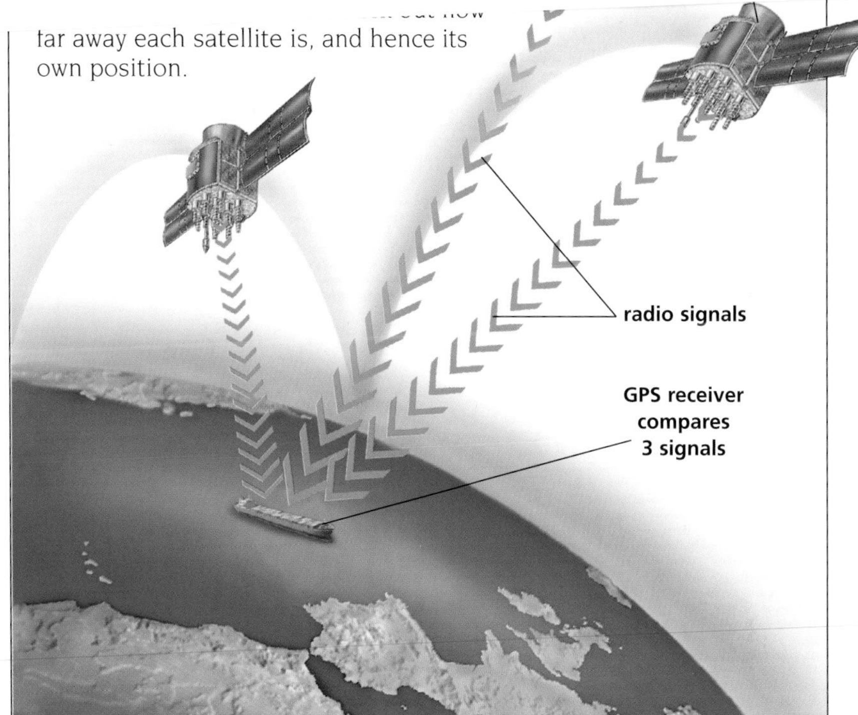

◀ This in-car navigation system does not show the car's position. However, it can show detailed route maps and give up-to-date information on local traffic hold-ups.

Find Out More

- Magnetism and electromagnetism
- Radar and sonar
- Satellites

Inertial navigation systems are used in planes, ships, submarines, missiles and spacecraft. These systems provide a constant check on a vehicle's position by sensing every change in speed and direction it makes.

Latitude and longitude

The position of any object on the Earth's surface is pinpointed by its latitude and longitude. The latitude tells you how many degrees the object is north or south of the Equator. Longitude is how many degrees the object is east or west of a line through Greenwich, England.

In atlases, the maps have grid lines on them. These are lines of latitude (running from left to right) and longitude (running from top to bottom).

Nebulas and clusters

Little swarms of glittering stars and shining clouds coloured pink and blue are dotted all through the Milky Way. These clusters and nebulas are some of the most beautiful sights in the sky.

The space between the stars is not completely empty. There are scatterings of gas molecules and tiny grains of dust. In some places the gas and dust have collected into immense, dark clouds.

Clouds between the stars and around individual stars are called nebulas. If there is a bright star nearby, a nebula shines. Ultraviolet starlight makes gas glow with its own light. Dust clouds shine because they reflect starlight.

Though dark nebulas do not give out any light, they may stand out as silhouettes against stars and glowing gas farther away. Unlike light, infrared radiation and radio waves can travel from inside dark nebulas to be picked up by telescopes on Earth.

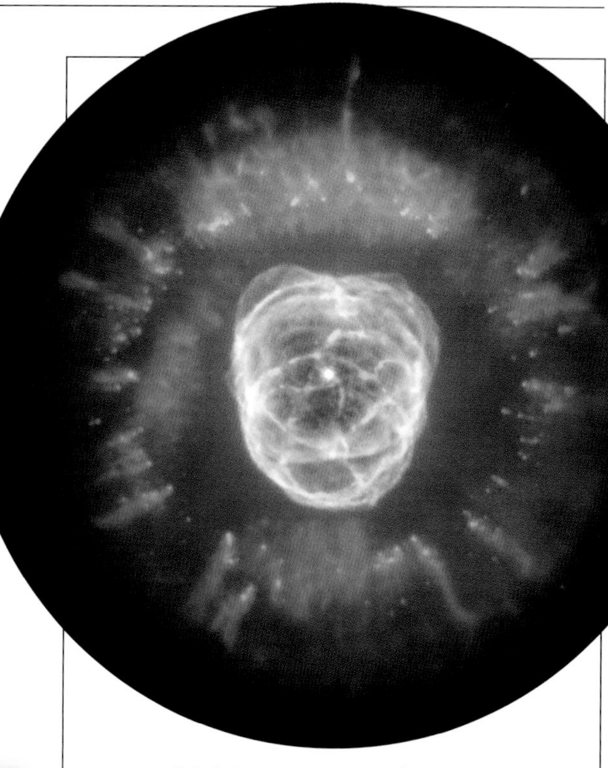

▶ The Eskimo Nebula, an example of a planetary nebula.

There is enough gas between the stars in the Milky Way to make 10 million Sun-sized stars.

PLANETARY NEBULAS

When a small or medium-sized star reaches the end of its life, it expands and the outer layers of gas are blown off into space. Nebulas of this kind are called 'planetary nebulas'. The name has nothing to do with planets: it was invented by the astronomer Sir William Herschel, because this type of nebula reminded him of planets.

◀ The Horsehead Nebula. The shape like a horse's head is a column of gas and dust projecting out of a large dark nebula into the bright glowing nebula next to it.

Nebula nurseries

New stars are born inside dark nebulas. The powerful radiation given off by massive new stars opens up bubbles in the nebula and makes the gas glow. Most of the gas is hydrogen, which glows pink.

Bright nebulas are always near to young stars. A newly-formed star cluster can often be seen at the centre of a bright nebula. They are called open clusters. They contain between several hundred and several thousand stars.

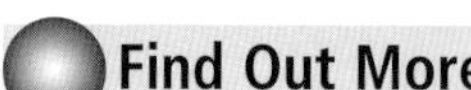

Find Out More

- Gas
- Light
- Stars

◀ The Pleiades. About 500 stars belong to this open star cluster, but only the brightest can be seen in this picture. The cluster is travelling through an interstellar cloud

▼ The centre of a globular cluster of stars. This particular cluster is nicknamed the starfish, because of the bright stellar 'arms' that curve away from the centre.

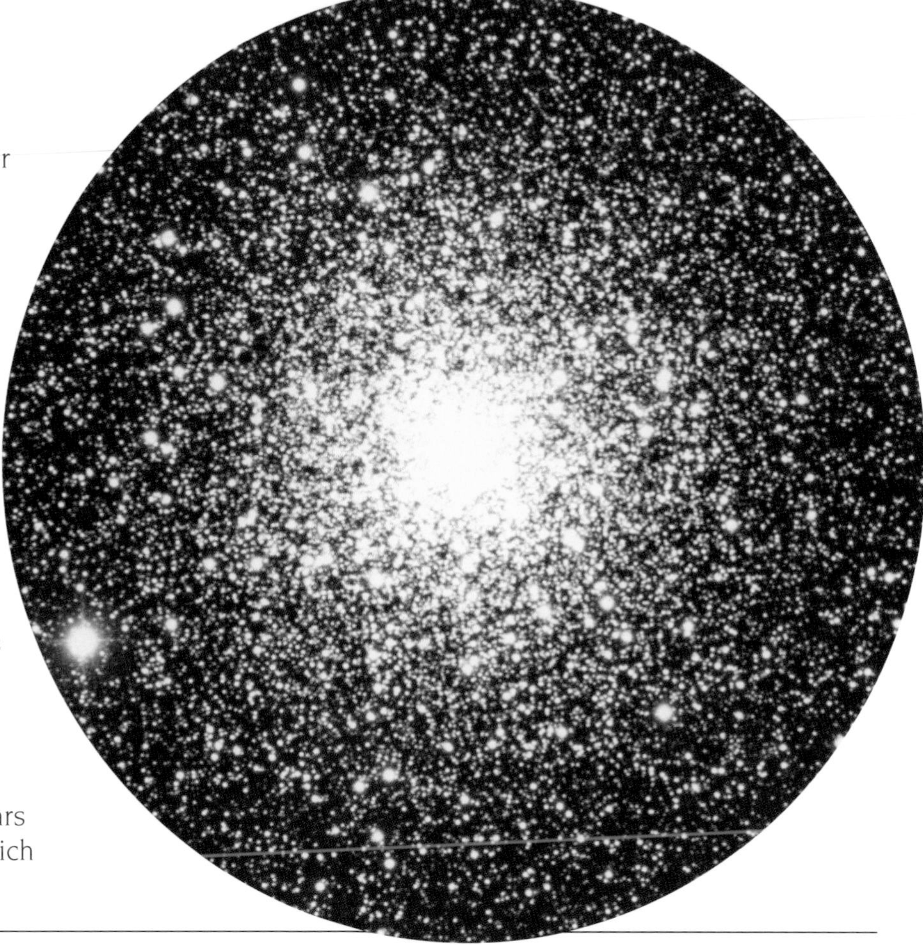

Star clusters

After a while, the gas around a new star cluster disperses into space, so most open star clusters do not have nebulas around them. The stars in an open cluster may become separated. Many of the stars we see in the sky are no longer clustered together.

A star cluster to look out for is the Pleiades, or Seven Sisters, in the constellation Taurus. You can see it with the naked eye. This cluster formed 50 million years ago – more recently than the dinosaurs died out on Earth. The Pleiades have moved away from the cloud where they were born and have ploughed into another one.

As well as open clusters, there are star clusters of a different kind, known as globular clusters. Shaped like balls, they have hundreds of thousands of stars crammed into a small region. All the globular clusters in our own galaxy, the Milky Way, are very old. Many contain stars that formed 10,000 million years ago, which makes them twice as old as our Sun.

Neon *see* Helium, Lights and lamps

Neptune

Windy weather is always the forecast for Neptune. Almost the whole planet is swept by jet streams blowing many times faster than any winds on Earth.

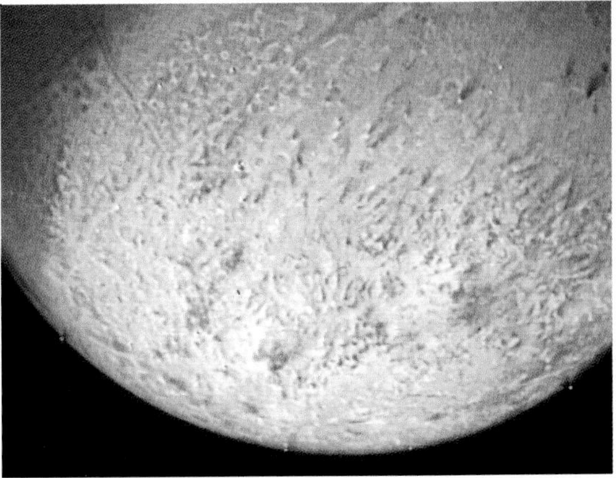

▲ Neptune's largest moon, Triton. This close-up image was taken by *Voyager 2*.

Eighth planet from the Sun, Neptune is about the same size as Uranus, and very similar inside. But much more goes on in Neptune's atmosphere than on Uranus. Stormy dark spots appear. Bands and patches of cloud are constantly changing. Both planets look blue because of methane gas in their atmospheres.

Neptune was discovered by Johann Galle in 1846 at the Berlin Observatory. Mathematicians were able to predict where it should be found because of the way its gravity affects Uranus's motion. The Voyager 2 spacecraft discovered that Neptune has several dark, narrow rings.

Triton

Seven small moons and one large one, Triton, orbit Neptune. Triton's diameter is 2705 kilometres, about four-fifths the size of the Earth's Moon. Though two-thirds of it are rock, its surface layer is icy. At a temperature of –236 °C, it is the coldest place ever recorded. It has a very thin atmosphere, which is mainly nitrogen.

When Triton's icy crust is warmed by the Sun, pockets of gas form in the frozen nitrogen. They erupt, sending geysers 8 kilometres high shooting upwards. Particles carried by the gas drift in the wind. Then they fall, leaving dark trails across the surface.

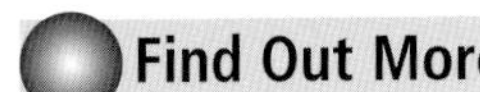

Find Out More

- Planets
- Solar system
- Uranus

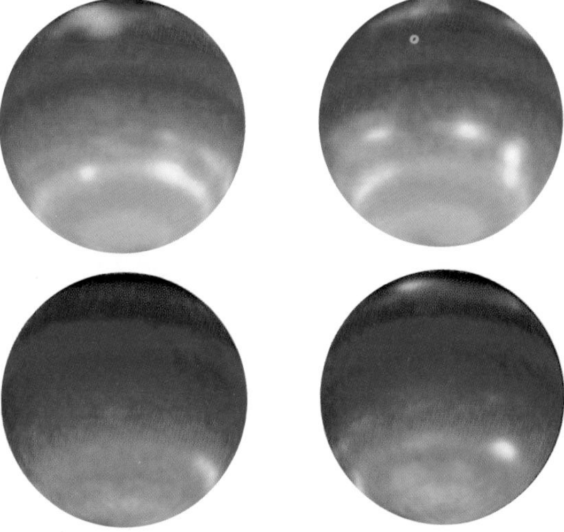

▲ Pictures from the Hubble Space Telescope show that dark spots and bright clouds come and go regularly in Neptune's atmosphere. The clouds are made of frozen crystals of methane.

NEPTUNE DATA
Diameter at equator: 49,532 km
Average distance from Sun: 4498 million km
Time taken to spin on axis: 16.1 hours
Density (water = 1): 1.64
Time taken to orbit the Sun: 165.8 years
Moons: 8

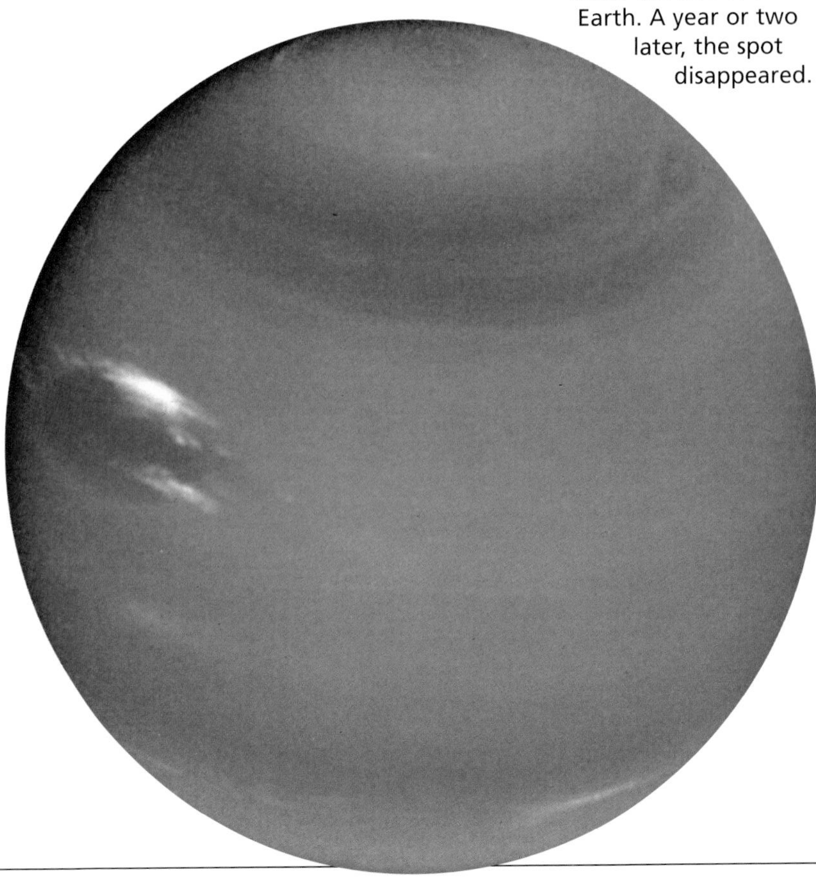

▼ Neptune as it looked when *Voyager 2* flew past it in 1989. The dark oval is where a storm formed. Called the Great Dark Spot, it was more than twice the size of the Earth. A year or two later, the spot disappeared.

Nerves *see* Brain and nerves • **Neutrons** *see* Atoms and molecules, Nuclear energy • **Newton, Isaac** *see* Gravity

Nitrogen

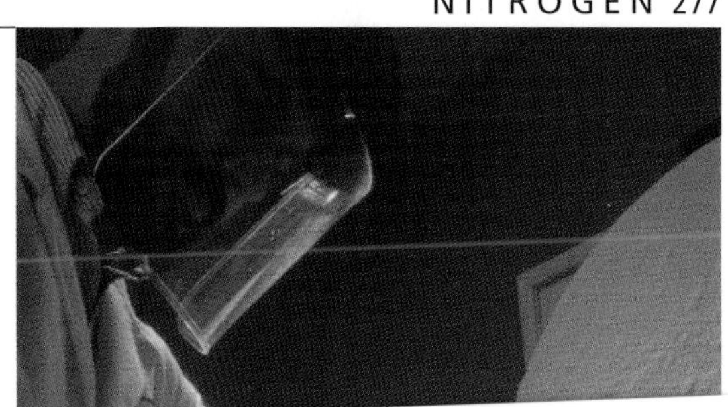

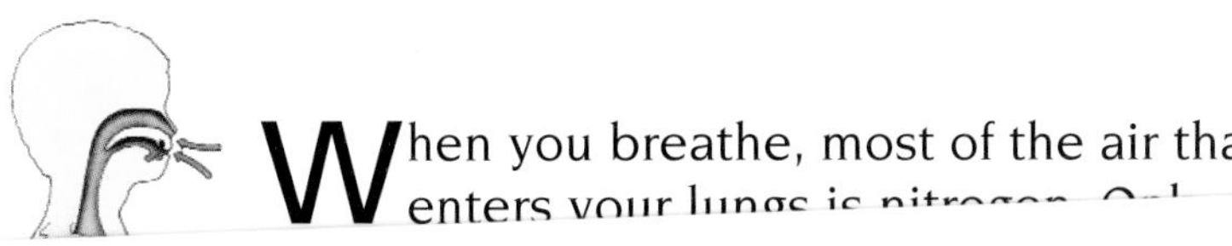

When you breathe, most of the air that enters your lungs is nitrogen.

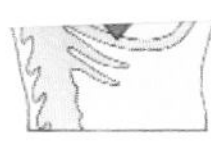

body is actually made of chemical compounds that include nitrogen.

Pure nitrogen is a non-poisonous gas. You cannot see it, smell it or taste it. At room temperature it does not react with other chemicals. But nitrogen can combine with other elements to make many important compounds.

▶ Liquid nitrogen being used to preserve bone marrow. Nitrogen gas becomes a liquid at around −196 °C.

Nitrogen compounds

Ammonia is a compound of nitrogen and hydrogen. It is made in factories, and is used to make fertilizers, explosives, and rocket fuels. Nitrogen is also found in all kinds of other chemicals, including nitric acid, which is important in industry. Some of the main pollutants in vehicle exhausts are nitrogen oxides.

Find Out More

- Explosives
- Fertilizers
- Gases
- Lungs and breathing
- Periodic table

In living things, nitrogen is combined with carbon, oxygen and hydrogen in a number of complicated chemicals called amino acids. Amino acids link together in different ways to make lots of even more complicated chemicals called proteins. The cells in your body are largely made of proteins, and proteins have many other important functions in all living things.

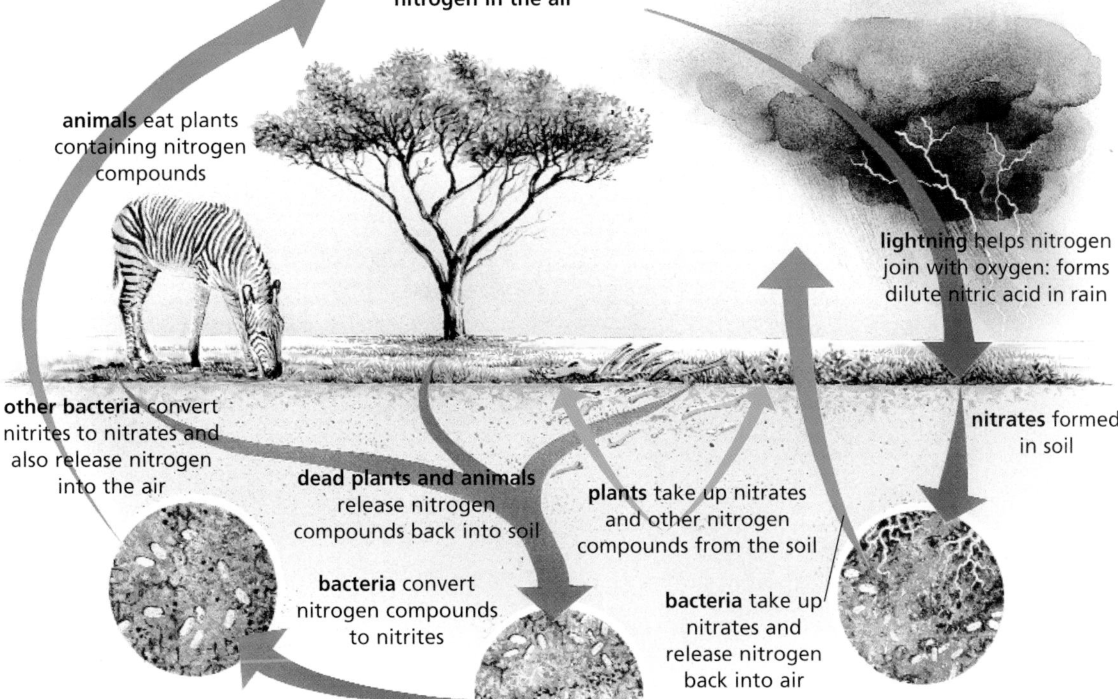

Because it is so unreactive, nitrogen is often added to food packages, such as crisp packets, to help keep the food fresh.

◀ The nitrogen cycle. Plants and animals can't get the nitrogen they need to make proteins directly from the air. In the nitrogen cycle, with the help of various kinds of microbe, nitrogen moves from the air into plants and animals and back again, helping to sustain life as it does so.

Noble gases *see* Helium • **Noise** *see* Sound

Nuclear energy

Atoms are the tiny particles from which all matter is made. They are so small that 4000 million of them would fit across the full stop at the end of this sentence. Yet vast amounts of energy are locked up in every atom. Scientists have used this energy to make bombs with awesomely destructive powers. More peacefully, this energy is used to produce electricity, or to power ships and submarines.

The tiny particle at the centre of every atom is called the nucleus. It is made up of smaller particles called protons and neutrons. We call the energy we tap from atoms nuclear energy because it comes from the nucleus of the atom.

Splitting atoms

The most common substance used to produce nuclear energy is a heavy metal called uranium. It gives out energy when its atoms split. This process is a kind of nuclear reaction, called fission. Nuclear fission releases vast amounts of energy – much more than in any chemical reactions, even fire or explosions. One kilogram of uranium fuel can produce the same amount of energy as 55,000 kilograms (55 tonnes) of coal.

Scientists first used nuclear energy to make atomic bombs, like the ones dropped on Japan in 1945 at the end of World War II. Before that, the biggest bombs contained less than half a tonne of ordinary explosives. The first atomic bomb dropped on Japan exploded with the force of 20,000 tonnes of ordinary explosives.

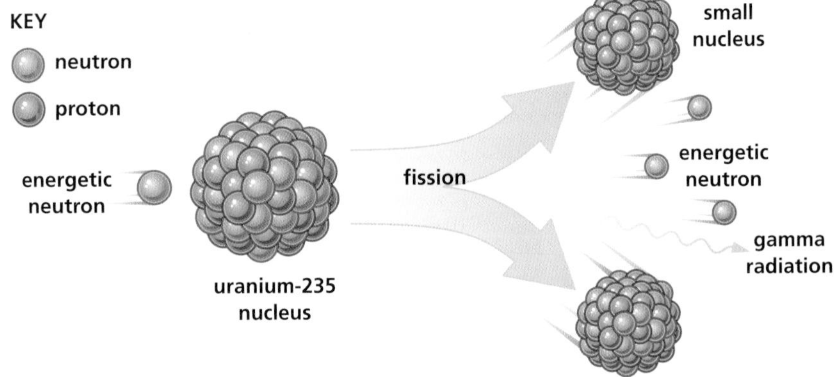

▲ In the fission of uranium, a neutron hits the nucleus of a uranium atom and splits it in two. Several neutrons are released, along with enormous amounts of energy. Each neutron released from the fission reaction can go on to split other uranium nuclei in a chain reaction, releasing more and more energy.

◀ A US Navy Trident missile is launched from the nuclear-powered submarine Ohio during practice manoeuvres off the coast of Florida. Trident missiles are designed to carry a nuclear warhead that explodes with the power of 100,000 tonnes of TNT (a conventional explosive).

In the years that followed World War II scientists worked to use nuclear energy for peaceful purposes. The first nuclear power station – Calder Hall, Cumbria, UK – started to produce electricity in 1956.

The nuclear reactor

The main part of a nuclear power station is the reactor. The nuclear 'fuel', uranium, is packed into the centre, or core, of the reactor. This is where nuclear fission takes place. A coolant (cooling substance) passes through the core and carries away the heat produced by fission. It is led away to produce steam. The steam is used to drive turbines that generate electricity.

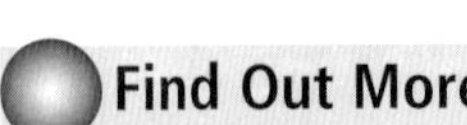

Find Out More

- Atoms and molecules
- Energy
- Engines and turbines
- Power stations
- Radioactivity

The reactor is controlled by control rods. These are pulled out or pushed in to make the nuclear reaction go faster or slower. If something goes wrong, the rods are automatically pushed right in to shut the reactor down.

Radiation danger

Nuclear power stations are 'cleaner' than ordinary power stations burning oil, gas or coal to produce steam, because nuclear power stations do not produce gases that pollute the air. But not many new ones are being built, beacause they suffer from a serious drawback. Uranium fuel and substances produced in nuclear reactors are radioactive – they give off penetrating radiation that is dangerous to living things.

For this reason, nuclear reactors are built with thick steel and concrete walls to stop the radiation escaping. But this isn't the end of the problem. Nuclear reactors produce dangerous radioactive waste, which could harm people, animals and the environment. Some of the waste will have to be stored for thousands of years before it becomes safe. It is often buried deep underground, embedded in glass blocks.

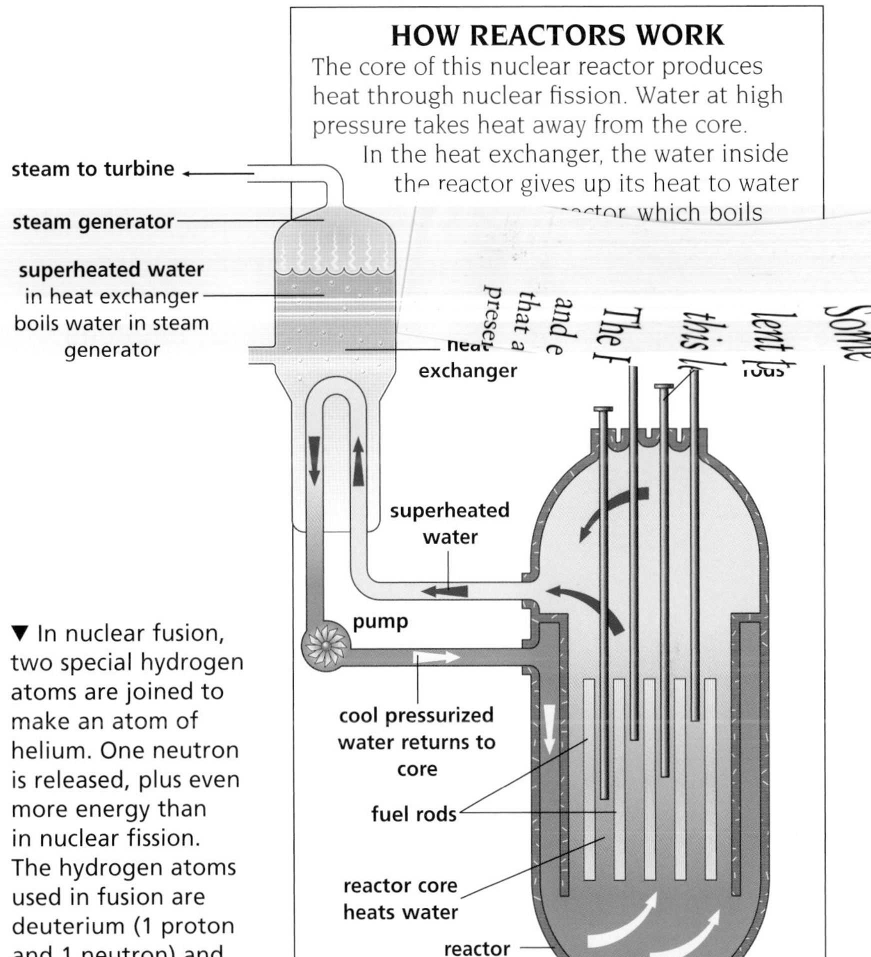

HOW REACTORS WORK

The core of this nuclear reactor produces heat through nuclear fission. Water at high pressure takes heat away from the core.

In the heat exchanger, the water inside the reactor gives up its heat to water ... which boils

▼ In nuclear fusion, two special hydrogen atoms are joined to make an atom of helium. One neutron is released, plus even more energy than in nuclear fission. The hydrogen atoms used in fusion are deuterium (1 proton and 1 neutron) and tritium (1 proton and 2 neutrons).

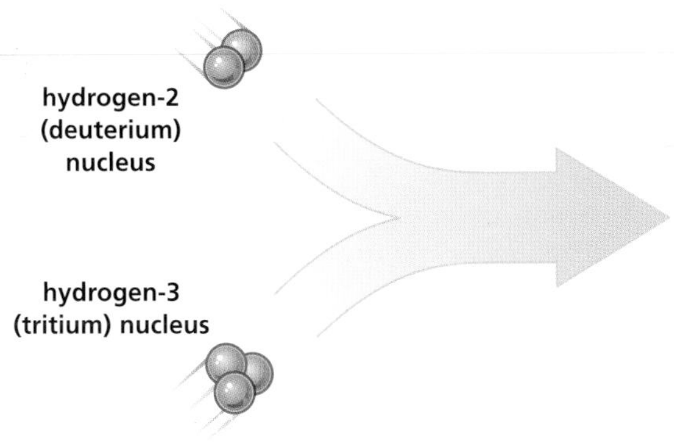

Scientists have already used nuclear fusion on Earth to make bombs – hydrogen bombs. Hydrogen bombs explode with the force of tens of millions of tonnes of ordinary explosives. Unfortunately, scientists have not yet managed to control nuclear fusion to produce power for peaceful uses.

Powering the Sun and the stars

Nearly all life on Earth depends on heat and light energy from the Sun. The energy that powers the Sun and the other stars, making them shine, comes from a different kind of nuclear reaction called fusion. In nuclear fusion, energy is not produced when atomic nuclei split, but when they join together (fuse). In the commonest fusion process, pairs of hydrogen atoms fuse together to form atoms of another element – helium.

▶ A scientist takes a dead fish from a lake near Chernobyl, in Ukraine. In 1986 there was a serious accident at the nuclear power station there. Radioactive material escaped and spread over a vast area.

Nylon *see* Fibres • **Observatories** *see* Telescopes

Ocean life

At the slightest hint of danger, a porcupine fish swallows a lot of water and swells up like a balloon. This makes its sharp spines stick out. Few predators would risk swallowing such a prickly mouthful.

Porcupine fish live on coral reefs, which are home to almost a third of all fish species. These reefs are built up over thousands of years from the skeletons of tiny animals called corals. The coral structures provide a huge variety of places for fishes and other animals to feed, hide and shelter.

Floating food

In areas of the ocean where there are no coral reefs, the basic source of food is the clouds of microscopic floating plants called phytoplankton. These live only in the top 100 metres or so of the oceans, where there is enough light for them to grow. Feeding on the plant plankton are tiny animals called zooplankton.

Plankton cannot swim against the tides and ocean currents, so they drift wherever the water takes them. Larger sea animals, from fish and birds to huge whales, feed on these drifting masses of plankton.

Find Out More
- Ecology
- Fishes
- Oceans

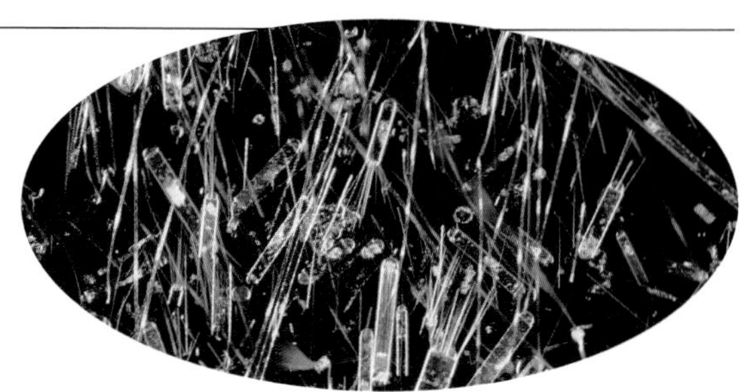

▲ Phytoplankton thrive in nutrient-rich waters where there is plenty of sunlight for photosynthesis. They are most abundant in shallow water.

Life in the deeps

Plants live only in the sunlit surface waters of the oceans, but animals live at all levels. In deep water, animals have to cope with darkness, cold and crushing water pressure. They feed on each other, or on the dead animals, food scraps and droppings that rain down from the sunlit world above.

▲ Coral reefs form in warm, shallow waters. The waters around a reef teem with life. Sea anemones (1), starfishes (2) and crabs (3) live on its surface. Small fishes such as seahorses (4), damsel fishes (5), parrot fishes (6) and clown fishes (7) dart in and out of crevices. Long, thin trumpetfishes (8) hunt for fishes head down, while moray eels (9) hide in the coral to surprise their prey. Manta rays (10) and jellyfishes (11) float above the coral.

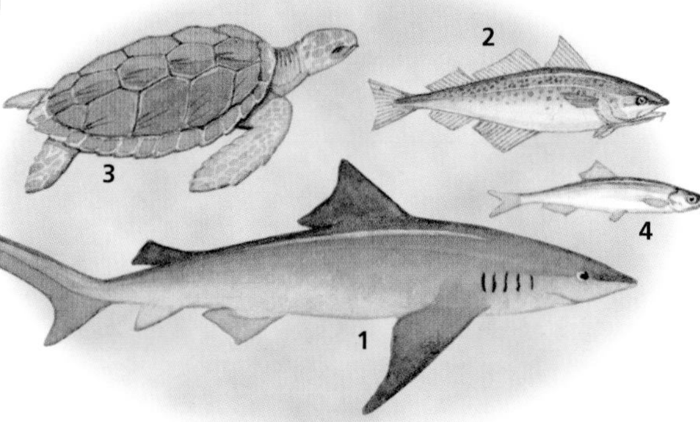

▶ Many larger sea-dwelling animals live in the open ocean. These include fishes such as the bull shark (1) and tuna (2), sea mammals such as whales, and other creatures such as squid and turtles (3). They often make long journeys in search of food. The much smaller anchovy (4) lives in large shoals near the coasts.

◀ Bottom-dwelling animals often stay in one place and wait for their food to come to them. Some, like the hatchet fish (1) and anglerfish (2), swim along with their large mouths open. The brittle star (3) finds food with its long, thin arms.

Oceans

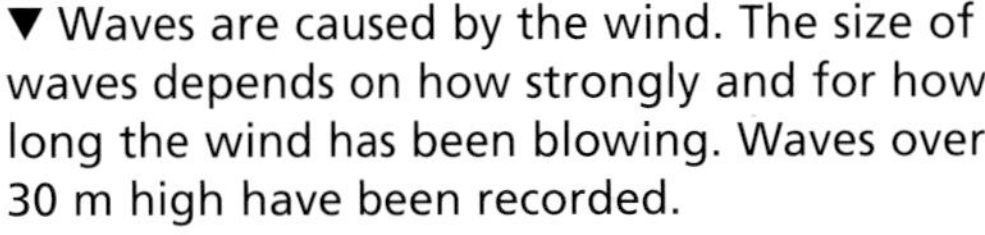

▼ Waves are caused by the wind. The size of waves depends on how strongly and for how long the wind has been blowing. Waves over 30 m high have been recorded.

Giant worms, blind shrimps, beds of clams and webs of primitive bacteria grow around springs of scalding hot water jetting out of the sea floor. These hot springs contain minerals that feed the animals and form strange pinnacles of rock. This is the scene on some parts of the ocean floor, 3 kilometres below the surface.

The world ocean is made up of all five oceans on Earth – the Atlantic, Pacific, Indian, Arctic and Southern oceans. Altogether, they cover almost three-quarters of Earth's surface.

Find Out More

- Climate
- Coasts
- Continents and plates
- Tides
- Water cycle

Salt water

There are a billion billion tonnes of salt water in the ocean. Ocean water is salty because it is full of minerals dissolved in it. Some of the minerals are brought from the continents by rivers and winds. Others come from the hot springs at the bottom of the ocean. If the entire ocean evaporated, it would leave a layer of salt 50 metres thick. Much of this salt would be sodium chloride – common table salt.

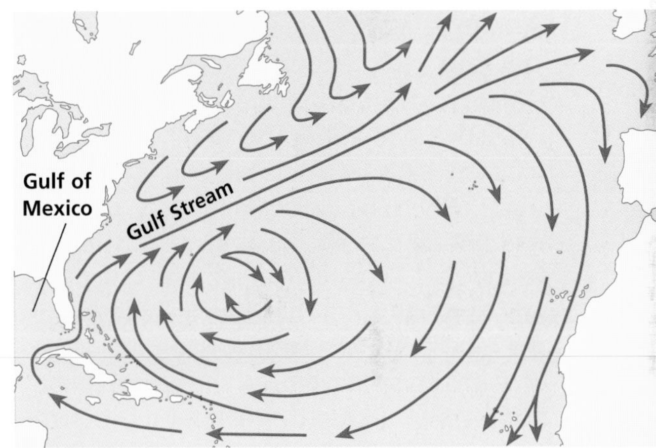

▶ The Gulf Stream is a current of warm surface water that flows from the Gulf of Mexico north-east towards Europe.

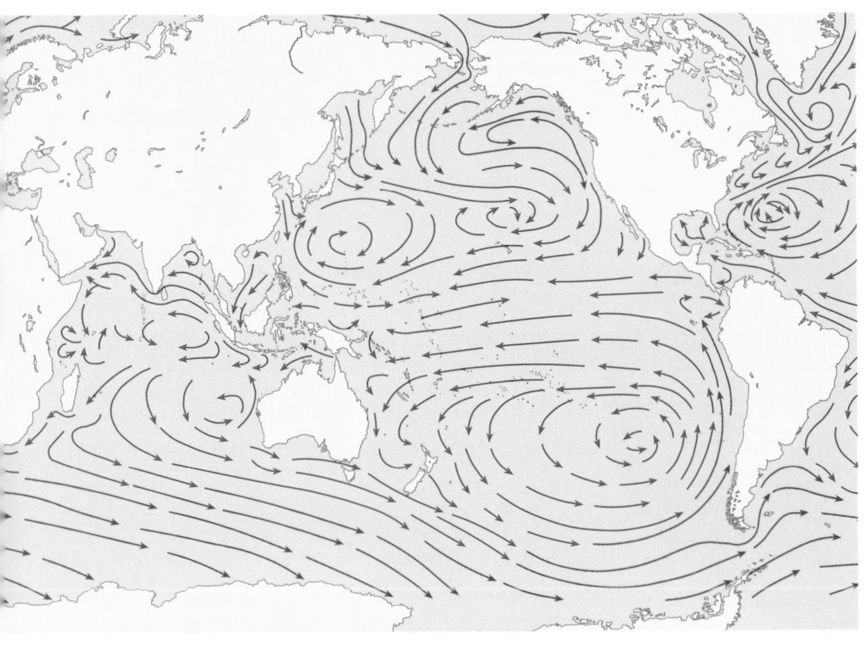

Currents

Ocean water flows around the Earth in great rivers called currents. Currents on the ocean's surface are driven by the winds. They travel in more or less the same direction that the wind most commonly blows.

There are also currents that flow from the surface towards the sea floor and down along the ocean bottom. These currents flow because parts of the oceans are colder than others, and parts are saltier than others. Cold, salty water is denser than warm, fresh water, so it sinks. Once the water warms up or gets diluted with less salty water, it will rise back to the surface.

◀ This map shows the surface currents in different parts of the ocean. Currents of warm water are in red, cold currents are in blue.

▶ Atolls are coral islands that grow on the cones of underwater volcanoes. This is why atolls form in a circle. They are made from the skeletons of corals, tiny underwater animals that live together in huge numbers.

Surface currents are important because they bring warm water to cool places. For example, the Gulf Stream brings warm water from the Gulf of Mexico to Britain and the rest of north-west Europe. Without the Gulf Stream, Britain would be as cold in winter as north-east Canada. Deep currents are also important, because they bring nutrient-rich water from the bottom of the ocean up to the surface where fish feed. Because currents are driven by wind and heat, they change from season to season and when the Earth's climate changes.

Ancient water

The ocean is almost as old as Earth itself. Geologists think that when Earth first formed, it got so hot that most of it melted. Many minerals are partly made of water. When the minerals melted, water was released to the Earth's surface through volcanoes. Some volcanoes may still be spewing out water that has never been on the Earth's surface before. Another source of water could have been the comets that bombarded the Earth when it was young.

▼ A 'black smoker' – a hot spring in the dark world of the ocean floor. Scientists think that life on Earth may have first evolved round such springs deep under the oceans.

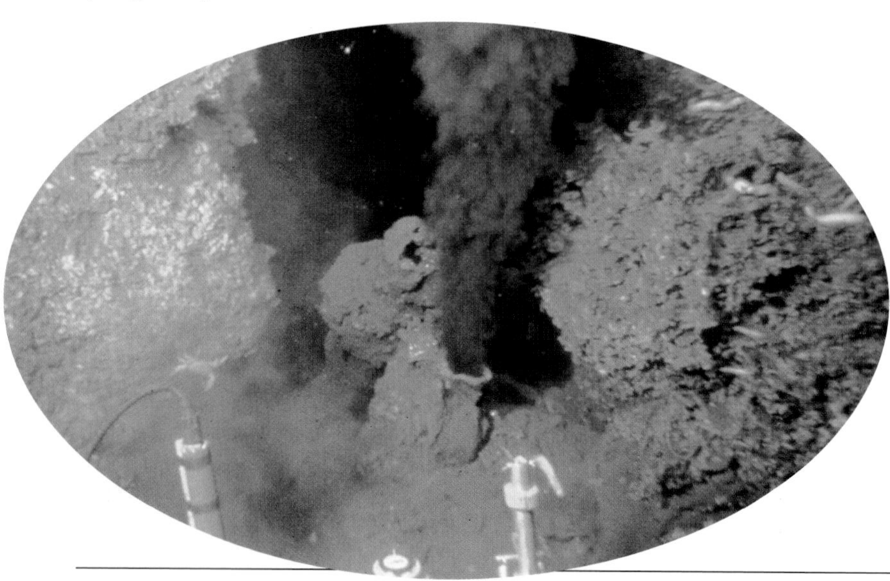

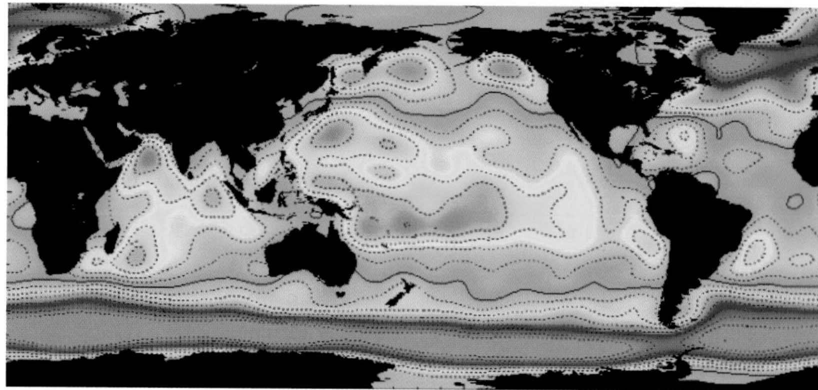

▲ A map of the height of the ocean surface compared to average sea level. Sea-surface height depends on such things as the shape of the sea floor, ocean currents, water temperature and the weather. Red indicates the highest sea levels, purple the lowest.

The ocean crust

The rocky crust beneath the oceans is quite different from the continental crust. The ocean crust is only about 10 kilometres thick (the continents are 35 kilometres thick). It is made almost entirely of the igneous (volcanic) rocks, basalt and gabbro. On top of the rocks is a layer of clay and mud made of sediments that have washed off the continents, and of skeletons of tiny sea creatures.

Octaves *see* Music • **Octopuses** *see* Invertebrates • **Oesophagus** *see* Digestion

Oil and gas

If you could dig deep, far below the ground you might find a liquid, so dark and so precious that it is sometimes called 'black gold'. It is crude oil. It is a valuable fuel that powers transport and machines, and it also contains a whole range of useful chemicals.

Crude oil, often called petroleum or simply oil, lies sealed in cavities in rock deep under the land and under the seabed. In these deposits, there may also be large quantities of natural gas, mainly methane.

Oil and gas deposits formed over millions of years from the buried remains of animals and plants that lived in ancient seas.

Find Out More
- Fuels
- Oil products

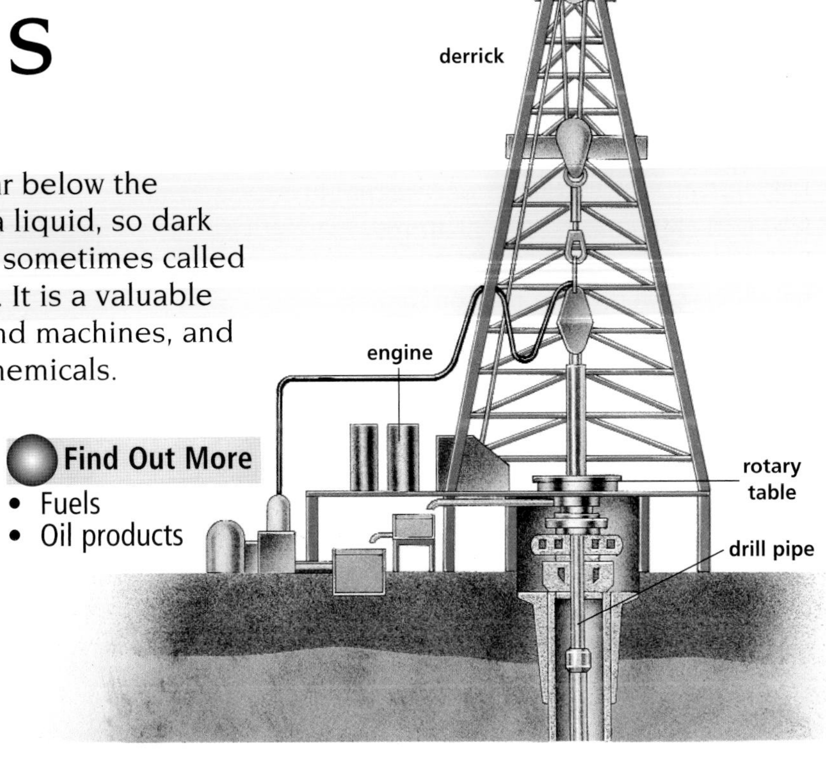

Drilling for oil

Experts search for deposits of oil and gas by studying the layers of rock deep beneath the land and seabed. They locate cavities where deposits are likely to lie. But the only way to be sure is to drill for oil or gas.

On land, a drilling rig is set up. This lowers a sharp drill into the ground. In soft ground, the drill can dig down 60 metres every hour.

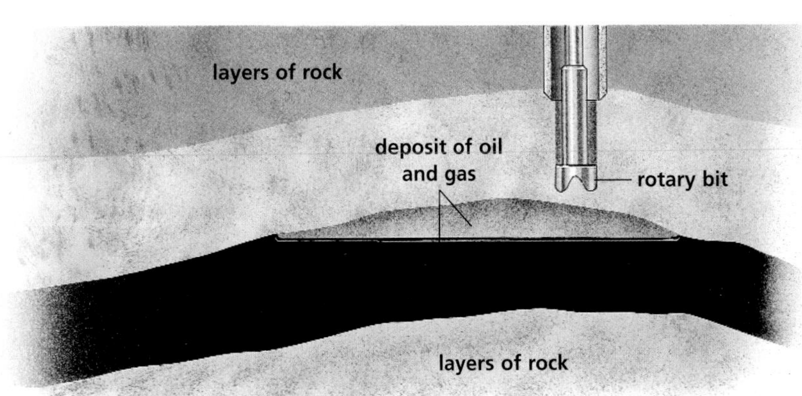

▲ An oil rig drills a deep shaft into the ground to find a deposit of oil or gas. The deposit may be hundreds of metres down.

At sea, a drilling rig is built on tall legs that go down to the seabed. If the water is too deep, the rig floats at the surface. The rig sends a drill down through the water to the seabed, and drills down into it.

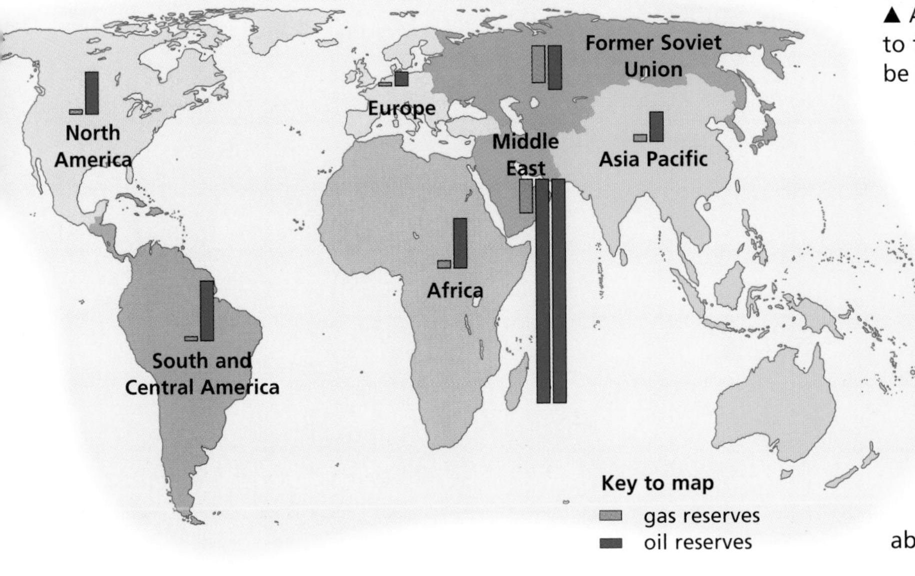

◀ Saudi Arabia and other countries of the Middle East have almost half the world's known reserves of oil. The United States has about 20 per cent and Europe, including Russia, about 15 per cent. These reserves are expected to last for about 50 more years.

Striking oil

If the drill meets a deposit, the oil or gas flows back up the shaft or is pumped up. The shaft becomes an oil well or gas well.

On land, the oil rig is taken down and the top of the well is fitted with pipes to take the oil or gas away. At sea, the rig is removed and a production platform towed out to the drilling site. This may be a huge tower that stands on the seabed and supports a platform above the water. Or the production platform may float. Pipes go down from the platform to the oil well on the seabed.

▼ At an oil refinery the crude oil is separated into many different products. The main ones are fuels (such as liquid petroleum gas (LPG), petrol, paraffin and diesel), lubricating oils, and bitumen for surfacing roads.

▲ Oil deep below the seabed flows up shafts to a production platform. There the oil is treated to remove water and also waste gas, which may burn off in a flare. The oil is piped or sent by tanker to a refinery, which may also receive oil pumped up from oil wells on land.

Using oil and gas

Tankers and pipelines carry the oil to oil refineries. The crude oil contains lots of useful substances, including diesel, petrol and kerosene. At the refinery, these different substances are separated out.

Tankers and pipes take gas to gas terminals, too. There the gas is purified and then piped direct to homes and factories, or bottled for use in places with no direct gas supply. In homes, gas is used for cooking and heating. It is also used as a source of heat for industry, and some power stations burn gas to produce electricity.

▶ After refining, products such as liquid petroleum gas (LPG) and petrol are stored in huge tanks before being pumped into road tankers, oil drums or canisters for delivery.

The world's production of oil is about 27,000 million barrels per year (one barrel is 159 litres of oil). This is enough oil to fill approximately 10 million public swimming pools.

Oil products

The bar of the pole vault is set at 6 metres. The athlete sprints towards it, long pole in hand. He digs the pole into the ground and launches himself into the air. The pole bends right over, looking as though it will break, but then straightens. It helps throw the vaulter over the bar, with millimetres to spare.

No natural material, like wood or metal, could be used for such a vaulting pole. It would not be light enough, flexible enough or strong enough. The pole is made of fibreglass, a plastic material that is reinforced (strengthened) by having long glass fibres running through it. Such a material is called a composite. Another type of composite uses carbon fibres to strengthen the plastic. It is used, for example, to make tennis rackets.

Composites and plastics are examples of synthetic materials. These are manufactured from chemicals made in factories, not from natural materials. Thousands of different products are synthesized from chemicals these days – not only plastics, but also dyes, drugs, detergents, explosives, fibres, pesticides, and so on.

Sources of synthetics

Most synthetic materials are manufactured from organic chemicals, which are carbon compounds. These compounds are called 'organic' because it was once thought that they could only be produced by living things (we now know this is not true).

▲ Oil refineries are run mainly from the control room, where workers can monitor the various processes. Everything works automatically, under computer control.

◀ In an oil refinery, crude oil is processed into many different products, including petrol, kerosene and diesel oil.

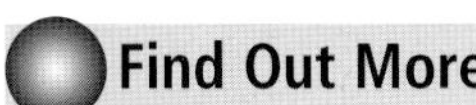

Find Out More

- Atoms and molecules
- Coal
- Oil and gas
- Plastics
- Polymers

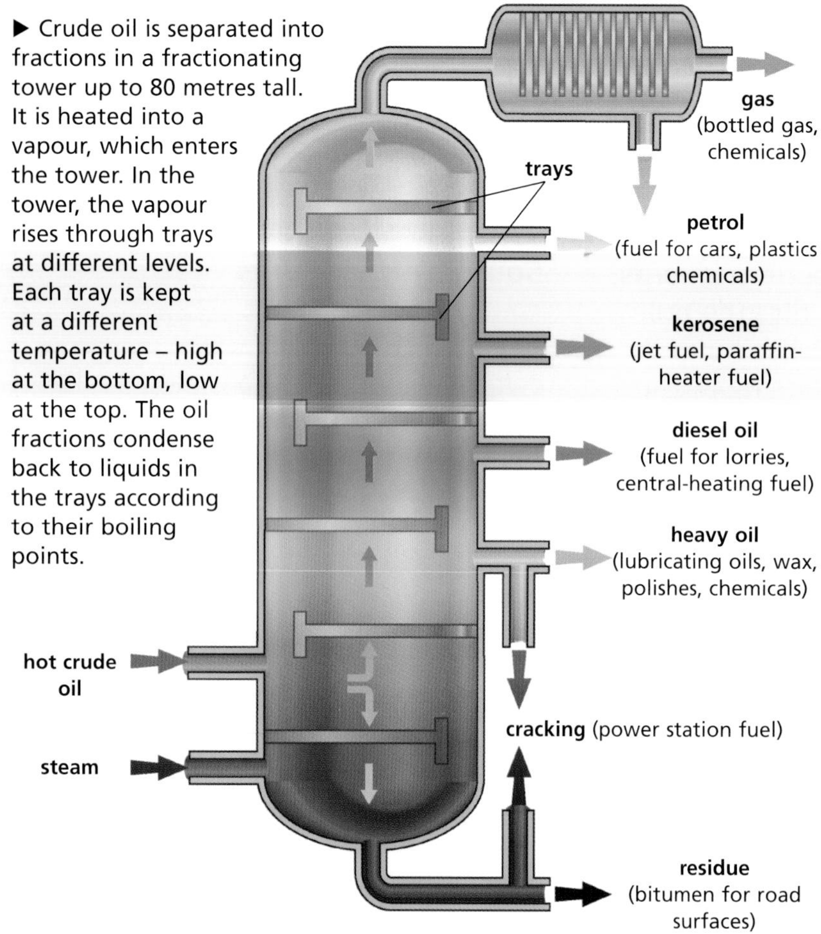

▶ Crude oil is separated into fractions in a fractionating tower up to 80 metres tall. It is heated into a vapour, which enters the tower. In the tower, the vapour rises through trays at different levels. Each tray is kept at a different temperature – high at the bottom, low at the top. The oil fractions condense back to liquids in the trays according to their boiling points.

Living things contain thousands of different carbon compounds, and it is from the remains of living things that we get our organic chemicals. We get them mostly from crude oil (petroleum), which scientists believe is the remains of tiny creatures that died and decayed millions of years ago.

Crude oil is a mixture of hundreds of different carbon compounds. They are called hydrocarbons because they are made up of carbon and hydrogen. Their molecules (basic units) have a backbone of carbon atoms joined together in chains or rings.

Sorting out

The hydrocarbon mixture that is crude oil is of little use as it is. The hydrocarbons have to be sorted out before they become useful. Fortunately, this is quite easy because they all have different boiling-points. This means that they can be separated by distillation. In this process, a substance is heated so that it evaporates (turns to vapour). Then the vapour is allowed to cool and condense (turn back into liquid).

Distillation is just the first stage in processing, or refining, the oil. It separates the oil into various parts (fractions). Some of these fractions can be used directly as fuels. Other fractions and gases provide the starting-point for making a wide range of chemicals, often called petrochemicals.

Get cracking

Heavy oil fractions can be made into more useful products by cracking. This is a process by which the large molecules in the heavy oil are broken down into smaller ones. This produces lighter oils, fuels and gases. In turn, the gases can be converted into fuels and chemicals. This is done by polymerization, a process of building up larger molecules from smaller ones. Together, these and the many other processes that take place in an oil refinery, make it possible to use every part of the crude oil.

▼ Crude oil is such a valuable source of chemicals that it seems almost a waste to burn it as fuel. A tank of petrol takes an average family car about 500 kilometres. But we could convert that fuel into chemicals, which could be used to make any of the products shown here.

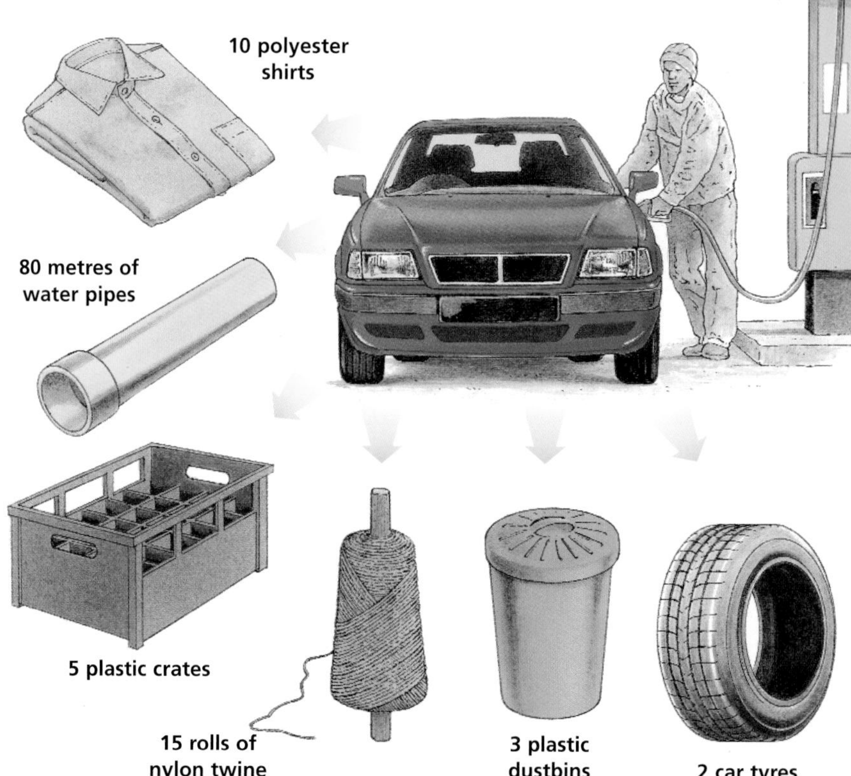

Orbits

Everything, everywhere, is moving. Out in space, satellites, moons, planets and stars are in non-stop motion. Inside the atoms that make up everything, tiny particles are moving non-stop, too. All these things move in the same way – in orbits.

An orbit is a circular or oval path around a centre of some kind. Man-made satellites and the Moon orbit around the Earth, while the Earth and other planets orbit the centre of the Solar System, the Sun. Stars, including the Sun, go round and round the centre of the group of stars which is called the Galaxy.

In every atom, one or more electrons go round the nucleus, a particle at the centre of the atom.

▶ Spacecraft meet in space high above the Earth as a new section called *Unity* (foreground) is added to the International Space Station (centre). The incoming spacecraft fires its rocket engines to go faster and so reach the same orbit as the station.

◀ Tie an object firmly to some string and whirl it around. You pull on the string to keep it in an orbit around your hand. Likewise, gravity between the Sun and Earth pulls on the Earth to keep it in orbit around the Sun.

Find Out More

- Atoms and molecules
- Gravity
- Motion
- Space shuttle
- Space travel

A central pull

All orbiting things, from tiny electrons to huge stars, keep to their paths because a force comes from the centre and pulls them into an orbit. Out in space, this force is gravity. Inside atoms, this is electrical force.

Without these central forces, all the satellites, moons, planets and stars would leave their orbits and fly off into space. And all atoms would blow apart as electrons left their orbits.

Reaching orbit

Large rockets launch satellites and spacecraft into Earth's orbit. They must reach orbital velocity – a speed of 28,000 kilometres per hour – to stay in orbit, or they crash back to Earth. Once in orbit a satellite needs no power, because there is no air friction in space to slow it down.

At a speed of 40,000 kilometres per hour ('escape velocity') a spacecraft can escape from Earth's orbit altogether, and go into orbit around the Sun.

Ores *see* Mining, Resources • **Organic farming** *see* Farming • **Oxidation** *see* Reactions, chemical

Oxygen

When you breathe in, about a fifth of the air that rushes into your lungs is oxygen. Without this oxygen we would die of suffocation. But scuba divers don't carry pure oxygen in their air tanks. Too much oxygen can be poisonous.

Pure oxygen is a gas. You cannot see it, smell it or taste it. As well as existing in its uncombined form in the atmosphere, oxygen is the commonest element in the rocks and minerals that make up the Earth's crust. Combined with hydrogen, oxygen makes water, which covers two-thirds of the surface of the Earth.

Combining with oxygen

When oxygen combines with other materials, the common process is called oxidation. When something burns, it is combining with the oxygen in the air. This process is called combustion. It is a kind of chemical reaction, and heat energy is given out. When pure hydrogen burns, it combines with oxygen to make water.

There isn't always a fire when oxygen combines with other elements. For example, when iron is exposed to the air, it slowly reacts with the oxygen to form iron oxide – rust.

Without plants to renew the oxygen supply in the air, we would soon run out of oxygen. The Amazon rainforest produces a fifth of all the oxygen made by plants.

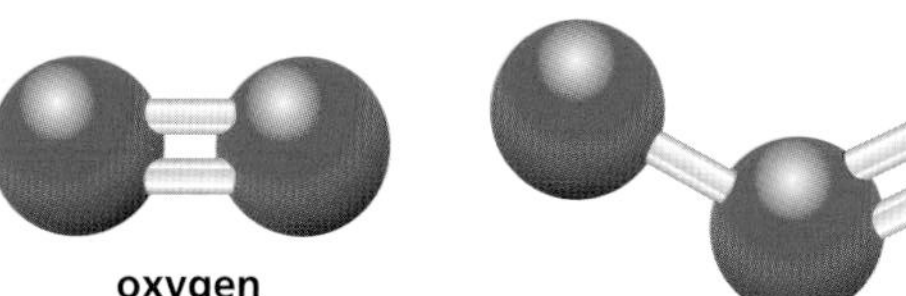

◀ Molecules of oxygen gas have two oxygen atoms, while the molecules of its bigger relative ozone have three.

▲ In a fire, the material that is burning is actually combining with oxygen in the air.

Uses of oxygen

Oxygen is used in many important industrial processes – in steel-making, for example, and in the preparation of nitric and sulphuric acids. Oxygen compounds are used in the manufacture of materials such as plastics. Oxygen's power to burn, or oxidize, other materials is used in welding, explosives, rocket fuels, and even in treating sewage.

Respiration

Most living things need oxygen – only some kinds of bacteria can live without it. We use oxygen to release energy from food. This process, called respiration, takes place in the cells of our bodies. Carbon dioxide and water are given out as the waste product of respiration. Land animals breathe in oxygen from the air, but fish have gills so they can extract (take) oxygen from water. Plants also need oxygen, but they produce more oxygen than they use.

Oxygen is a waste product of photosynthesis, the process by which plants make sugary food from carbon dioxide, sunlight and water.

Ozone

The oxygen gas we breathe is made of molecules containing two atoms of oxygen. But there is another kind of oxygen gas in which the molecules have three oxygen atoms. This gas is called ozone. Ozone is poisonous, but there is normally only a very small amount in the air we breathe.

However, polluting gases from car exhausts can react with sunlight to make ozone, causing some people to have breathing difficulties.

Ozone is, however, very important to us. High up in the Earth's atmosphere there is a thin layer of ozone, which protects us from the Sun's harmful ultraviolet radiation. This layer has been damaged by various man-made chemicals, including the CFCs (chlorofluorocarbons) that were used in aerosol sprays. Although CFCs are no longer so widely used, the ozone layer will take many years to recover.

▲ High up in the atmosphere, the air is thinner and there is much less oxygen. At these great heights, fighter pilots and mountaineers need to breathe from bottles of oxygen.

Find Out More

- Air
- Fire
- Lungs and breathing
- Plants
- Pollution

▶ In an oxyacetylene torch, oxygen gas makes the acetylene fuel burn very fiercely. This produces enough heat to cut metals, or to weld pieces of metal together.

THE DISCOVERY OF OXYGEN

Until the late 18th century, no one knew why things burned – although there were plenty of theories. Then, in 1772, the Swedish chemist Carl Wilhelm Scheele (1735–1804) discovered oxygen. But Scheele did not announce his discovery for several years – until after the British chemist Joseph Priestley announced in 1774 that he had discovered oxygen. However, it was left to the French chemist Antoine Lavoisier to realize that oxygen was an element, and that when things burn they are reacting with oxygen.

◀ Antoine Lavoisier (1743–1794)

Paints and varnishes

Left to themselves, wood rots and iron rusts when exposed to the weather. But give them a thin coat of paint, and they can last for centuries.

Paint is a liquid mixture containing colouring matter, which dries to form a thin, tough film. This film decorates the surface underneath and protects it from attack by water, air and insects.

The substance that forms the film is called the vehicle, or binder. The colouring is provided by pigments. To make the mixture flow easily when applied, it is dissolved in a solvent, often called thinners.

▶ Wearing a mask as protection against poisonous fumes, a worker spray-paints the side of a car.

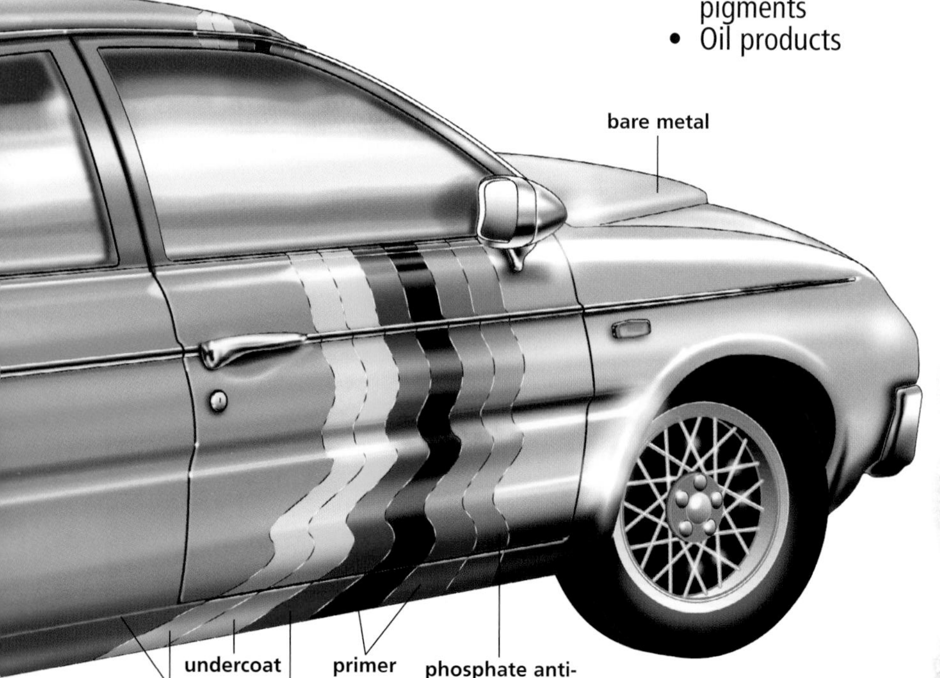

▼ Many coatings are needed to build up the shiny paintwork on a car body. First, the body is dipped in phosphate solution to help it resist corrosion. Then it is given one or two coats of primer, followed by a base coat, an undercoat and one or more top coats. The final coats are baked, or stoved. (Colours shown are not actual colours of different coatings.)

Find Out More
- Colours
- Dyes and pigments
- Oil products

Early paints used natural oils like linseed oil as a vehicle. Modern paints use synthetic resins, which are kinds of plastics. In the oil paints generally used for painting outside, the usual solvent is white spirit, a product we get from oil refining.

A strong bond

After the paint has been applied, two processes take place. The solvent evaporates, and the binder reacts with the oxygen in the air. As a result, the molecules of the binder join up to form a rigid polymer, or plastic material – the paint film.

Many paints these days use water as a solvent, and so are cleaner to use and cause no air pollution – unlike some oil-based paints. One kind of water-based paint is an emulsion. In an emulsion, the vehicle particles do not dissolve, but are spread out in the water as very fine droplets.

A clear, hard varnish called shellac is made from the secretions of the tiny red lac insect from Thailand. At certain times of year, lac insects swarm in huge numbers on trees, literally feeding themselves to death. But before she dies, each female lays her eggs on the tree, protecting them with a clear material called lac. This is later harvested and made into shellac.

Palaeontology *see* Fossils

Paper

As you read these words, you are looking at a material that started life in a forest in the wilds of Canada or Scandinavia. You are looking at paper, which is made from the wood of trees.

Paper is one of the greatest inventions of all time. It has allowed ideas and knowledge to be written down and passed on from generation to generation. Even in this electronic age, we are using more paper than ever before. Each year an area of forest the size of Sweden has to be cut down for papermaking.

▶ A worker in a paper-mill takes a sample of wood pulp from a roller. The sample will be tested for quality.

Pulping

The first stage of papermaking is to turn the wood from logs into a mass of fibres, called pulp. The cheapest pulp is made by shredding the wood using a rotating grindstone. It is used to make newsprint, the paper newspapers are printed on. Better-quality pulp is made by treating wood chips with chemicals. The chemicals release the wood fibres (cellulose) by dissolving the substance that binds them together (lignin).

logs
de-barking
chipping
digester turns chips to pulp
wood pulp washed and bleached
beater frays wood fibres
water added
pulp
wire mesh belt
pressing rollers
heated rollers
dryer
heavy rollers give smooth finish (calendaring)
paper roll

◀ In the paper mill, logs are first chipped, then mixed with chemicals to make pulp. The pulp then goes to the paper-making machine. Excess water drains away, then the damp paper is pressed, dried and further rolled to smooth the surface.

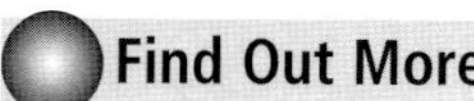

Find Out More

- Forests
- Wood and timber

Papermaking

At the paper-mill, the wood pulp first goes to a machine that beats the fibres and makes them frayed and flexible. The beaten pulp then goes into a mixer, where certain materials are added. They may include china clay to give the paper more weight; a glue-like material to make the paper easier to write on, and pigments to add colour. The thoroughly mixed pulp is then fed to the papermaking machine.

Parachutes *see* Textiles, Space shuttles • **Parasites** *see* Diseases • **Pasteur, Louis** *see* Diseases

Periodic table

Elements are the basic substances that everything on the Earth and in the Universe is made of – including us. Your body is mostly made of the elements carbon, hydrogen, and oxygen. Elements cannot be split into simpler substances. About 90 different elements are found in nature, and scientists have managed to make several more.

Although each element is different, some elements behave in a similar way to other elements. In the 19th century, chemists struggled to discover a pattern in the 60 or so elements then known. Then, towards the end of the century, the Russian chemist Dmitri Mendeleev found a pattern. This pattern, which is still used today, is called the periodic table.

Using this table, Mendeleev predicted that certain unknown elements would be discovered to fill the gaps in the table. When these elements were later discovered, scientists found they behaved as Mendeleev had predicted they would.

CREATED IN A DREAM

Dmitri Mendeleev

The French chemist Antoine Lavoisier (1743–1794) knew about 33 elements. He tried to arrange them in a table in 1789. He classified the gases, metals, non-metals and earth elements. By the time of the Russian chemist Dmitri Mendeleev (1834–1907), 65 elements were known. Mendeleev is said to have had the idea for organizing elements into a periodic table in a dream. He realized that there were gaps in his table, and even predicted the chemical properties of these missing elements.

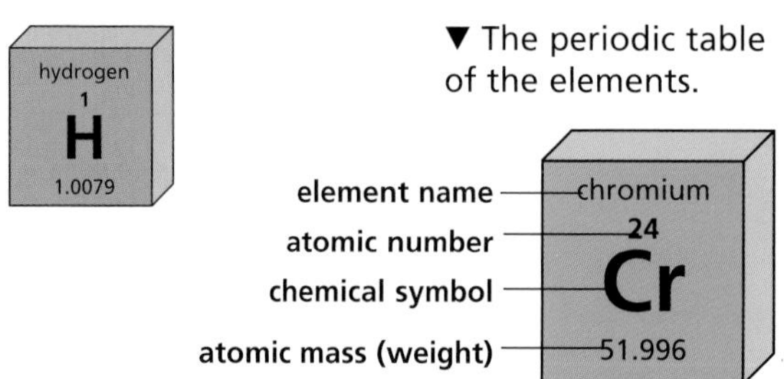

▼ The periodic table of the elements.

lithium 3 **Li** 6.941	berylium 4 **Be** 9.0122
sodium 11 **Na** 22.990	magnesium 12 **Mg** 24.305
potassium 19 **K** 39.098	calcium 20 **Ca** 40.078
rubidium 37 **Rb** 85.468	strontium 38 **Sr** 87.62
caesium 55 **Cs** 132.91	barium 56 **Ba** 137.33
francium 87 **Fr** (223.02)	radium 88 **Ra** (226.03)

scandium 21 **Sc** 44.956	titanium 22 **Ti** 47.867	vandium 23 **V** 50.942	chromium 24 **Cr** 51.996	manganese 25 **Mn** 54.938	iron 26 **Fe** 55.845	cobalt 27 **Co** 58.933	nickel 28 **Ni** 58.693	copper 29 **Cu** 63.546	zinc 30 **Zn** 65.39
yttrium 39 **Y** 88.906	zirconium 40 **Zr** 91.224	niobium 41 **Nb** 92.906	molybdenum 42 **Mo** 95.94	technetium 43 **Tc** (97.907)	ruthenium 44 **Ru** 101.07	rhodium 45 **Rh** 102.91	palladium 46 **Pd** 106.42	silver 47 **Ag** 107.87	cadmium 48 **Cd** 112.41
lutetium 71 **Lu** 174.97	hafnium 72 **Hf** 178.49	tantaium 73 **Ta** 180.95	tungsten 74 **W** 183.84	rhenium 75 **Re** 186.21	osmium 76 **Os** 190.23	iridium 77 **Ir** 192.22	platinum 78 **Pt** 195.08	gold 79 **Au** 196.97	mercury 80 **Hg** 200.59
lawrencium 103 **Lr** (262.11)	rutherfordium 104 **Rf** (263.11)	dubnium 105 **Db** (262.11)	seaborgium 106 **Sg** (266.12)	bohrium 107 **Bh** (264.12)	hassium 108 **Hs** (269.13)	meitnerium 109 **Mt** (268.14)	ununnilium 110 **Uun** (272.15)	unununium 111 **Uuu** (272.15)	ununbium 112 **Uub** (277)

lanthanum 57 **La** 138.91	cerium 58 **Ce** 140.12	praseodymium 59 **Pr** 140.91	neodymium 60 **Nd** 144.24	promethium 61 **Pm** (144.91)	samarium 62 **Sm** 150.36	europium 63 **Eu** 151.96	gadolinium 64 **Gd** 157.25	terbium 65 **Tb** 158.93	dysprosium 66 **Dy** 162.50	holmium 67 **Ho** 164.93	erbium 68 **Er** 167.26	thulium 69 **Tm** 168.93	ytterbium 70 **Yb** 173.04
actinium 89 **Ac** (227.03)	thorium 90 **Th** 232.04	protactinium 91 **Pa** 231.04	uranium 92 **U** 238.03	neptunium 93 **Np** (237.05)	plutonium 94 **Pu** (244.06)	americium 95 **Am** (243.06)	curium 96 **Cm** (247.07)	berkelium 97 **Bk** (247.07)	californium 98 **Cf** (251.08)	einsteinium 99 **Es** (252.08)	fermium 100 **Fm** (257.10)	mendelevium 101 **Md** (258.10)	nobelium 102 **No** (259.10)

Different kinds of atom

All the elements are made up of tiny particles called atoms. Mendeleev knew that different elements had atoms with different weights. Scientists now know that the atoms of different elements also have different structures.

The small particle at the centre (nucleus) of an atom contains even smaller particles called protons and neutrons. Other tiny particles called electrons whizz round the nucleus. In any atom there are the same number of electrons and protons.

Each element has a different size of atom. The atomic number in the periodic table tells you how many protons there are in an atom of the element. The electrons are arranged in 'shells' around the nucleus. The way an element behaves depends on how many electrons there are in the outermost shell.

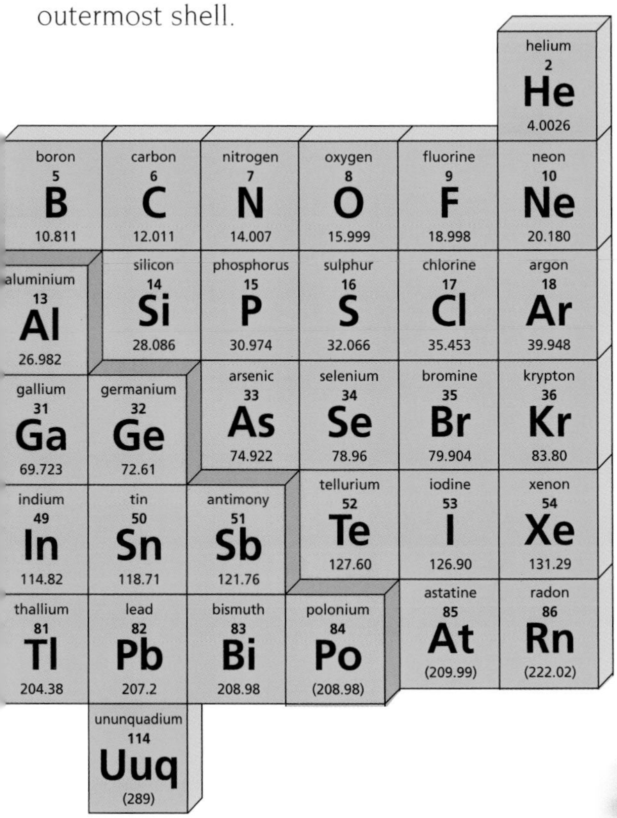

					helium 2 **He** 4.0026
boron 5 **B** 10.811	carbon 6 **C** 12.011	nitrogen 7 **N** 14.007	oxygen 8 **O** 15.999	fluorine 9 **F** 18.998	neon 10 **Ne** 20.180
aluminium 13 **Al** 26.982	silicon 14 **Si** 28.086	phosphorus 15 **P** 30.974	sulphur 16 **S** 32.066	chlorine 17 **Cl** 35.453	argon 18 **Ar** 39.948
gallium 31 **Ga** 69.723	germanium 32 **Ge** 72.61	arsenic 33 **As** 74.922	selenium 34 **Se** 78.96	bromine 35 **Br** 79.904	krypton 36 **Kr** 83.80
indium 49 **In** 114.82	tin 50 **Sn** 118.71	antimony 51 **Sb** 121.76	tellurium 52 **Te** 127.60	iodine 53 **I** 126.90	xenon 54 **Xe** 131.29
thallium 81 **Tl** 204.38	lead 82 **Pb** 207.2	bismuth 83 **Bi** 208.98	polonium 84 **Po** (208.98)	astatine 85 **At** (209.99)	radon 86 **Rn** (222.02)
	ununquadium 114 **Uuq** (289)				

Understanding the periodic table

The periodic table is set out in groups (the columns going up and down) and periods (the rows going across the table). All the elements in a group behave in a similar way. For example, the column on the far left is the group of the most reactive metals. The group includes sodium (atomic number 11) and potassium (19), which react violently if put in water, whereas rubidium (37) is even more reactive, bursting into flames if exposed to air. In complete contrast, the column on the far right is the group of noble gases – the elements that are least reactive. The group includes several gases, such as helium (2) and neon (10), that are found in small quantities in the air we breathe.

If you look across the table from left to right, each period (row) starts with a so-called alkali metal, followed by an alkaline earth metal. For example, in the third period sodium (Na) is an alkali metal, while magnesium (Mg) is an alkaline earth metal.

There are many more metals than non-metals in the periodic table. Many of the commonest metals, such as iron and copper, fall in a large block known as the transition metals (coloured green in the diagram). The non-metals fall to the right of a ziz-zag dividing line (coloured blue in the diagram). Among the non-metals, the last but one column is a group of highly reactive elements called the halogens. The halogen in period 3 is chlorine (Cl). Next to chlorine, in the far-right column, is the unreactive noble gas argon (Ar).

There have been hundreds of attempts to improve on the Mendeleev-style periodic table, including three-dimensional and circular tables. None of them have displaced the 'long-form' that we use today, which was based on Mendeleev's first table.

THE FOUR CLASSICAL ELEMENTS

Earth
Cold and dry.

Water
Cold and wet.

Air
Hot and wet.

Fire
Hot and dry.

▲ Old symbols for various 'elements' (air, fire, earth and water were thought to be elements, but we know now that this is not the case). In the Middle Ages, people called alchemists tried to turn metals such as lead into gold. They made several important chemical discoveries during their experiments.

Find Out More

- Atoms and molecules
- Elements and compounds
- Metals and non-metals
- Reactions, chemical

Pesticides

The stem of the beautiful rose is covered with greenfly feeding on the sap, while ladybirds and lacewings feed on them. The gardener sprays the rose with insecticide and soon the greenfly die. But the ladybirds and lacewings fly off – they are not affected.

Insecticides are one kind of pesticide, a chemical that kills harmful organisms on farms and in homes and gardens. The other main types of pesticide are herbicides, designed to kill weeds, and fungicides, which kill fungus diseases.

Some minerals and plant extracts are used as pesticides. Sulphur and copper sulphate, for example, are used to treat fungus diseases.

Most pesticides are synthetic, made mainly from petroleum chemicals. They are often compounds containing chlorine and phosphorus. The trouble is that they may kill not only harmful pests but also useful ones. They may also build up in the environment. This happened widely in the 1950s and 1960s, when a pesticide called DDT was used on a large scale. It was later found to be poisonous to birds and other animals.

Being selective

DDT and similar substances have now been banned in many countries to protect the environment and wildlife. New pesticides have been developed that break down rapidly after they have been used and so are not a long-term danger.

Pesticides have also been developed that are selective in their action, like the insecticide that kills aphids but not ladybirds. Selective lawn herbicides kill broadleaf weeds but leave the thin blades of grass untouched.

Sometimes pests can be controlled without using chemicals. Parasites or other organisms that naturally prey on the pests are used. This method is known as biological control.

▲ A crop-sprayer flies low to spray insecticide over a field of rape.

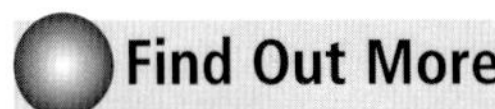

- Ecology
- Pollution

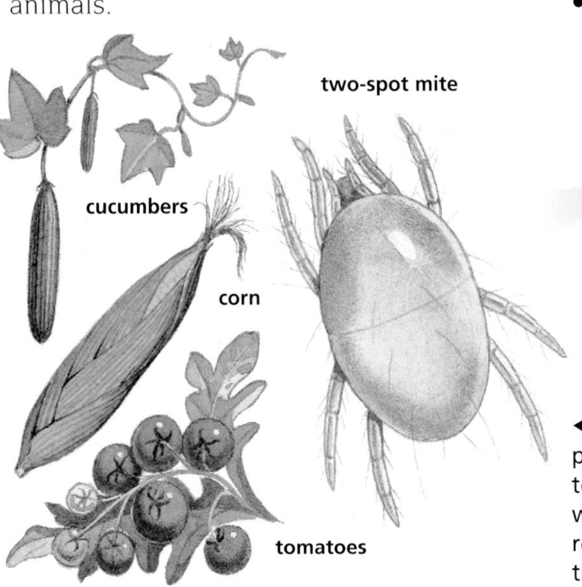

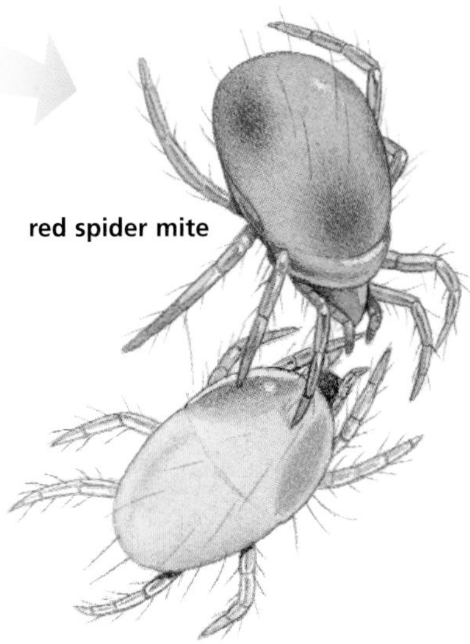

◀ Two-spot spider mites are a serious pest on food crops such as cucumbers, tomatoes, maize (corn) and hops. One way to control these pests is to release red spider mites, which catch and eat the two-spot mites.

Petrochemicals *see* Oil products

Petrol and diesel

Foresters need chainsaws that are powerful enough to cut down big trees, but also light and portable. Only one kind of engine is suitable for the saw – a petrol engine. It carries its own fuel supply and is light yet powerful.

Petrol and diesel engines power all sorts of vehicles, from cars and motorcycles to diesel trains, boats and small aircraft. Being light and portable, petrol engines are also used to drive machines such as lawnmowers and chainsaws.

Inside a petrol engine

A petrol engine contains one or more cylinders in which a piston moves up and down. It produces power by burning petrol in the cylinders. The intense heat causes air in the cylinders to expand violently, driving down the pistons. The pistons turn a crankshaft, which drives the wheels, propeller or other mechanism.

The petrol engine in a car is a four-stroke engine. The piston repeats a cycle of four movements in which it goes up and down twice. Motorcycles and other light machines often have simpler, two-stroke engines. The piston repeats a cycle in which it goes up and down once.

▲ A chainsaw has a rotating chain lined with sharp teeth that cuts into the wood. It is driven by a small but powerful petrol engine, and can cut through a thick trunk or branch quickly and easily.

Diesel engines

A diesel engine works in the same way as a petrol engine, except that it needs no spark plug to ignite the fuel. The air is strongly compressed, which causes it to heat up. Fuel is then added, and it immediately ignites in the hot air.

Find Out More

- Cars and trucks
- Engines and turbines
- Fuels
- Global warming
- Pollution

inlet valve
piston
cylinder
spark plug
petrol – air mixture
connecting rod
outlet valve
crankshaft

Induction stroke. On the first stroke, the piston goes down and sucks air into the cylinder through the inlet valve.

Compression stroke. On the second stroke, the fuel injector squirts petrol into the cylinder as the piston rises and compresses the petrol – air mixture.

Power stroke. The spark plug ignites the compressed mixture. The hot gases produced expand and force down the piston on its third, power stroke.

Exhaust stroke. On the fourth stroke, the piston rises and pushes the waste gases out of the cylinder through the outlet valve.

◀ A four-stroke petrol engine repeats a cycle of four strokes, or movements, in which the piston goes up and down the cylinder twice. Car engines usually have four cylinders, each on a different stroke at any time.

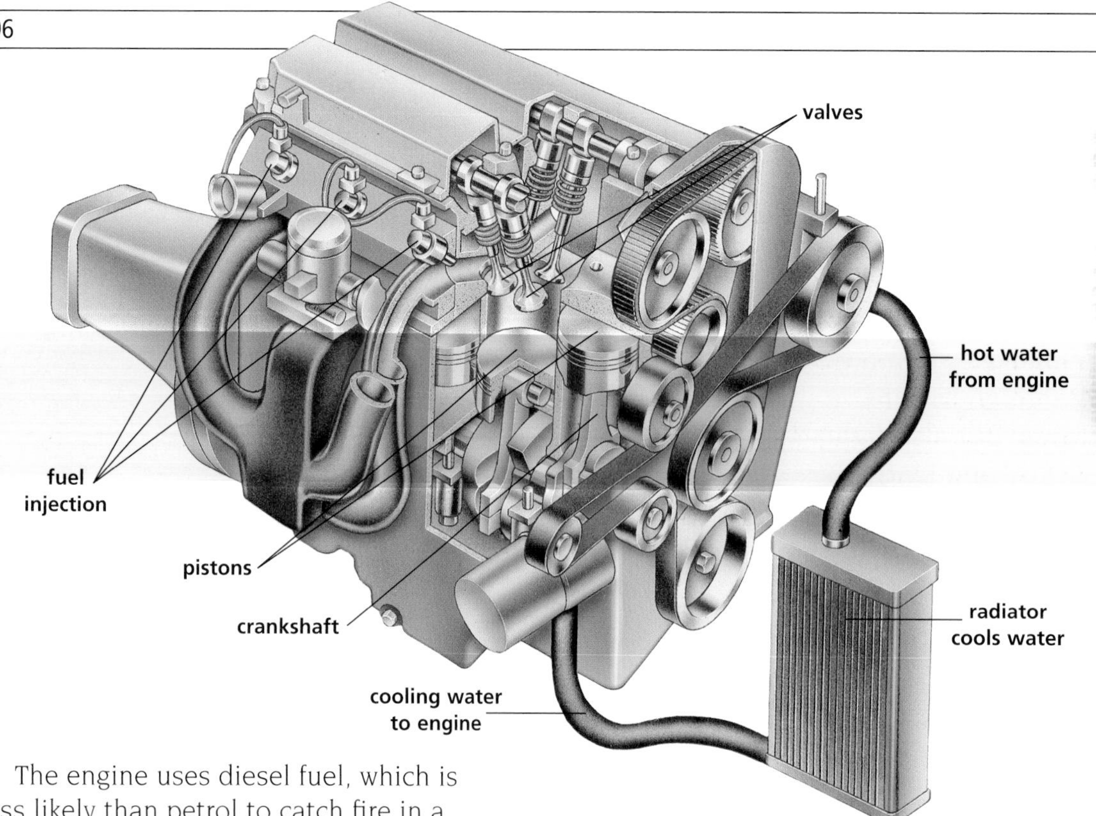

The German engineer Rudolf Diesel developed the diesel engine. He patented his invention in 1892.

◀ A diesel engine has no spark plugs. Instead, the injected fuel is compressed until it is hot enough to ignite by itself.

The engine uses diesel fuel, which is less likely than petrol to catch fire in a crash. Diesel engines are simpler in construction, more robust and more fuel-efficient. Unfortunately, they cause more pollution than petrol engines.

Outside the engine

Around a petrol or diesel engine are several systems that make the engine work.

The injection system controls the supply of fuel to the cylinders, squirting in more when the vehicle needs to go faster. In petrol engines, the ignition system makes the fuel ignite at the right moment to give the most power.

The exhaust system leads waste gases away from the cylinders into the atmosphere. The fuel ignites with a bang, and the exhaust system has a silencer that reduces this noise. The waste gases are polluting, and the catalytic converter in the exhaust system makes most of the polluting gases harmless. It does not remove carbon dioxide, though, which causes global warming.

▼ In Thailand, many boats have a petrol or diesel engine and propeller mounted at the end of a long steering handle. This makes it easy to turn the boat quickly. However, the boats are very noisy.

Petroleum *see* Oil and gas • **Phosphate** *see* Fertilizers

Photocopiers

Long ago, the only way to make copies of books was to write them out by hand. This was a job that monks were specialists in. Their work was beautiful – but took years to do. With modern photocopiers we can make hundreds of copies in minutes.

A photocopier 'reads' a piece of paper that you put onto it and prints a new copy. It uses light to read the paper, and static electricity and ink to make the copy. The process is called xerography, a word meaning 'dry writing'.

To use a photocopier, you place a page upside-down on a glass screen. The photocopier moves a light across the page from beneath. The light is reflected off the white parts of the page, but not off the black parts (the writing or image). A lens directs the reflected light onto a flexible belt, which has already been given a positive electric charge. Where light falls on the plate, the charge leaks away.

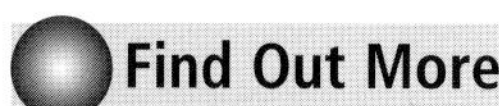

Find Out More

- Electricity
- Printing

There is now a 'copy' of the image on the belt, written in electrical charge.

Toning up

A black powder called toner is sprinkled onto the belt. The toner has a negative electric charge. It sticks to the positively charged parts of the belt, but does not stick to the rest.

Next, a piece of paper is pressed against the belt, on top of the toner. Another electric charge transfers the toner onto the paper. At this stage, the toner is on the paper in the pattern of the original writing, but it is not fixed. It can easily be smudged or blown away.

Finally the paper is warmed by heated rollers. This melts the toner particles, forming a sticky ink which quickly dries on the paper. The copy is now ready to be pushed out of the machine.

▼ A modern photocopier is a complex device. Light from the page being copied is projected onto a belt (or drum) charged with electricity. Where the page was light, it causes the electrical charge to leak away. The dark areas of the page keep their charge, and black toner powder sticks to these areas. The toner is transferred to a sheet of paper, then fixed by heat.

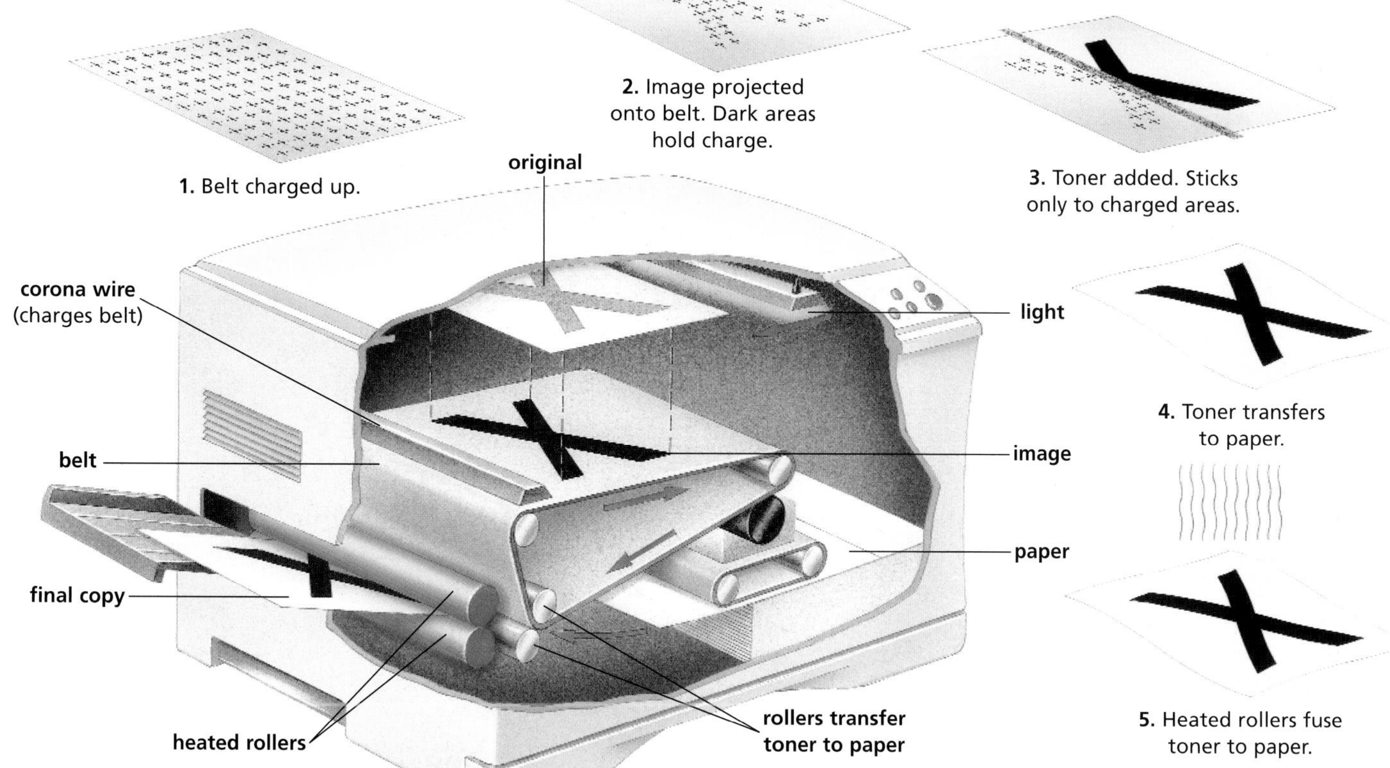

Photography

We all enjoy photographs of our parties and holidays, but photography has serious uses as well. There have been haunting images of starvation in Africa as well as pictures taken on the Moon. We have even photographed the moment when a human life begins.

Photographs are made in three steps. First light is allowed to fall on a film. Next the film is turned into a negative (a picture in which the dark parts of an object look light, and the light bits look dark). Finally a print is made from the negative. The print is the photograph that we look at.

In a digital camera, the picture is recorded electronically, not on film. The photograph is printed by the type of printer that you would use with a computer.

Taking a photograph

A black-and-white film is made from thin plastic, coated with a light-sensitive chemical containing silver.

To take a picture, you open the camera's shutter to let in light. This is called exposing the film. Where a lot of light hits the film, the chemical is changed by the light. In darker areas, there is less change.

Making a negative

Turning an exposed film into a negative is called developing. There are three stages.

First of all, the film is dipped in a liquid called the developer. The developer reacts with the exposed chemicals in the film, making them release tiny pieces of silver.

▶ When you press the shutter button on a camera, the shutter opens and light falls briefly on the film (a). There is now an image of the scene on the film, but it can't be seen (b). Developing the film (c) produces a negative version of the scene on the film (d). The negative is put in an enlarger (e), and printed onto photographic paper. Now the light and dark areas on the photo correspond to the light and dark areas in the original scene (f).

In the camera, photographic film is exposed to light from the object.

(a)

object being photographed

light from object

lens focuses light on film

The film is developed to make a negative image.

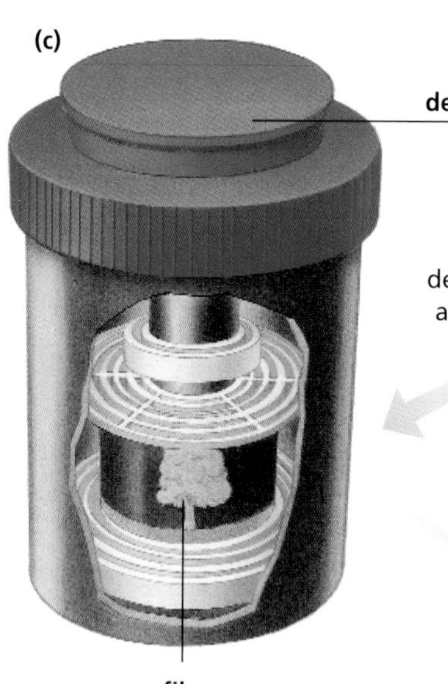

(d)

negative

An enlarger is used to make the image bigger. It shines light through the negative onto paper. This can be done in dim red light – bright white light would turn the light-sensitive paper white, and the image would be lost.

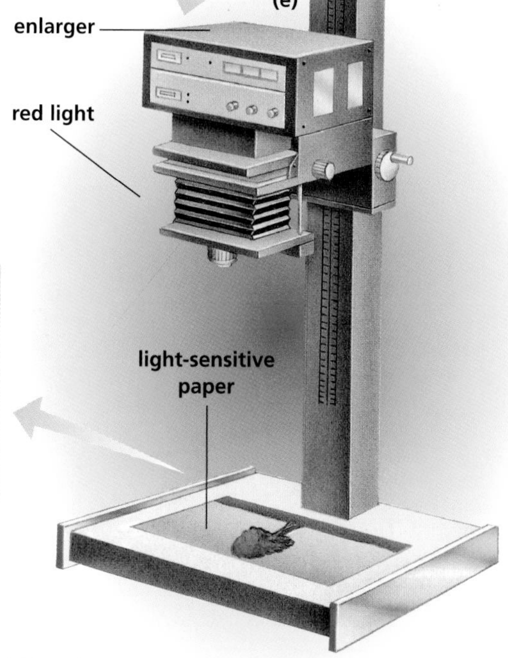

Photosynthesis *see* Plants • **Physics** *see* Science • **Pipelines** *see* Tunnels and pipelines

Where lots of the film chemical has been exposed, there will be many spots of silver.

Next the film is dipped in another chemical called fixer. The fixer reacts with the chemicals on the film, making them easy to wash off. It also sticks the pieces of silver firmly on the film. Finally the film is washed in water to rinse away all the unused chemicals.

The film is now transparent in some places, and dark in others where the silver has built up. The dark places are where the most light fell when the film was exposed, so the result is a negative image (black where the scene was bright, light where the scene was dark).

Printing

Pictures are printed on special paper with a light-sensitive coating. To do this, you shine light through the negative onto the paper. Where the negative is black, not much light gets through and the paper is not exposed. The transparent parts of the negative let a lot of light onto the paper, exposing the light-sensitive coating.

The paper is then developed by a three-stage process, just like the negative was. At the end of this, the paper has black areas (where silver has built up) and white parts (no silver and the paper shows through) in the right places. It is now a positive image.

▲ A photograph taken in about 1843 by the Englishman William Fox Talbot (1800–1877). The first ever photograph was taken in 1826 by the Frenchman Nicéphore Niepce, but it was Talbot who invented the modern method of making a negative from which many prints can be made.

COLOUR PHOTOGRAPHY

Developing and printing colour photographs is a bit like doing black-and-white ones – three times over.

The colour film has three layers: one is sensitive to red, one to green and one to blue. These are the three primary colours of light – our eyes and brains can be given the sensation of any colour just by mixing red, green and blue light in different amounts.

The negative made from the exposed colour film is called a colour-reversed negative. Colour prints are made by passing first red, then green, then blue light through the negative onto special paper that also has three sensitive layers. The print ends up with the right combination of colours.

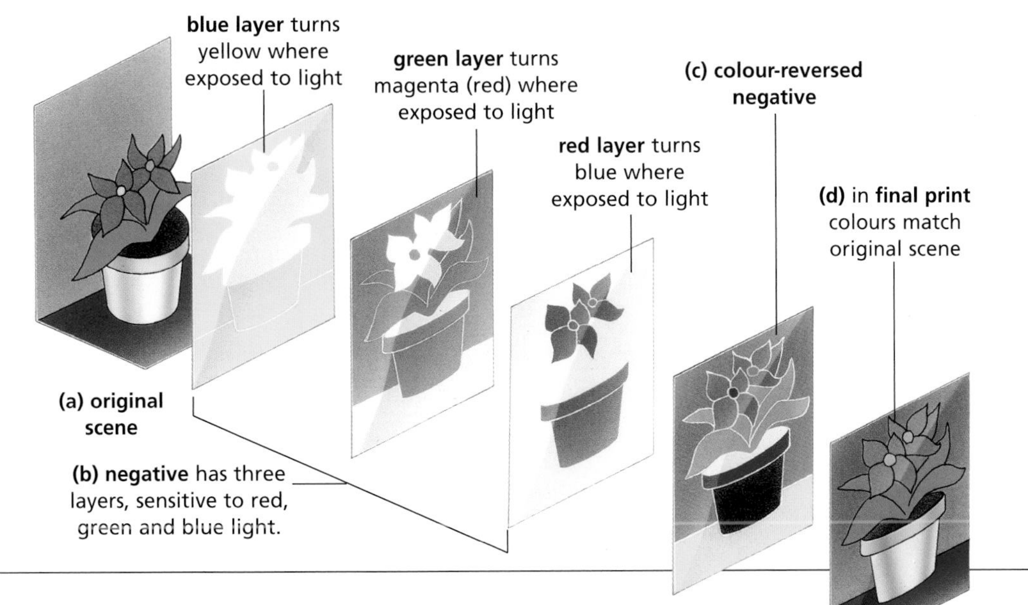

Find Out More

- Cameras
- Colours
- Gold and silver
- Light
- Movies

Pixels *see* Computer graphics and design

Planets

On a clear night you may spot a planet shining brightly – perhaps Venus, Jupiter or even Mars. The planets do not give out any light of their own. They shine because they reflect the light of the Sun.

To ancient astronomers, the planets were all the heavenly bodies that moved around in the sky while the stars stayed in the same places. 'Planet' comes from a Greek word meaning 'wanderer'. Today astronomers use the word 'planet' to mean a world in orbit around a star.

Our Solar System has nine major planets orbiting the Sun. They are Mercury, Venus, Earth, Mars, Jupiter, Saturn, Uranus, Neptune and Pluto. They all travel around the Sun in the same direction and all spin on their axes, but apart from that they are a strange assortment. Jupiter is 60 times larger than Pluto. Four are rocky, four mostly gas and liquid, and one icy.

▲ There is evidence that many other stars also have planets around them. One of the first to be discovered was a large planet orbiting the star Tau Boötis. This artist's impression of the planet shows it with a moon, although astronomers do not yet know if it has one.

▼ A comparison of the sizes of the planets (their diameters) of our own Solar System in relation to the Sun. The planets are shown in their correct order from the Sun, but the distances between them are not to scale.

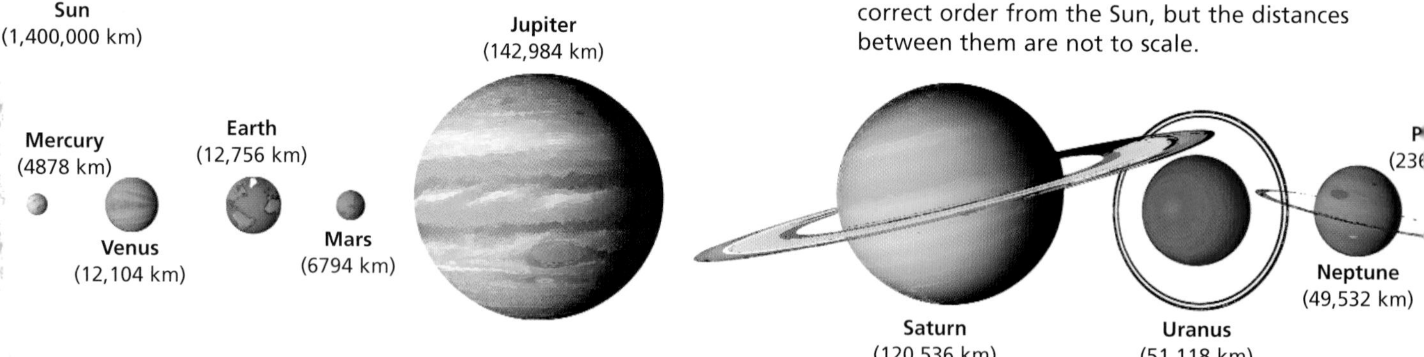

Different kinds of planets

In the Solar System, there are three other planets that are rocky like Earth: Mercury, Venus and Mars. They are sometimes called the terrestrial planets. The four giant planets – Jupiter, Saturn, Uranus and Neptune – are completely different. They have small rocky cores but are covered by deep layers of liquid and gas.

Pluto is different again. It is made of a mixture of ice and rock, and is by far the smallest planet. Pluto is more like some of the large moons orbiting the giant planets. These large moons are really no different from planets, but they happen to go round a planet rather than the Sun. Jupiter's moon Ganymede and Saturn's moon Titan are both larger than Mercury.

Find Out More

- Solar System
- Stars
- Sun

Plankton *see* Ecology, Ocean life

Plants

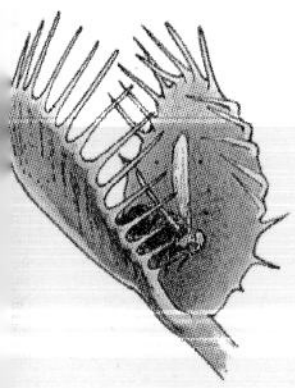

A fly spots some sugary sap on a leaf and buzzes down for a snack. But it turns out to be a terrible mistake. The fly touches tiny trigger hairs on the surface of the leaf, which snaps shut in a fraction of a second. Trapped in its leafy prison, the fly is dissolved and turned into a soupy meal for the well-named 'Venus fly trap'.

Most plants cannot move as quickly as the Venus fly trap. Plants react much more slowly than animals do to changes in their surroundings. But in many ways, plants are more successful than animals. They have lived on the Earth for longer, and were the first living things to move out of the oceans onto the land. And without plants, all animals, including humans, would die.

Food factories

Plants can make their own food, but animals cannot. Animals either eat plants or other animals – which themselves live off plants.

The process plants use to make their food is photosynthesis. During photosynthesis, plants use the energy in sunlight to turn carbon dioxide gas from the air and water from the soil into food. They use a green chemical called chlorophyll to trap the Sun's energy, which is why most plants are green.

▶ The giant sequoia or redwood trees of California, USA, are among the biggest living things on Earth. The tallest one is over 112 m – as high as the American Statue of Liberty. The heaviest weighs as much as 4800 average-sized cars!

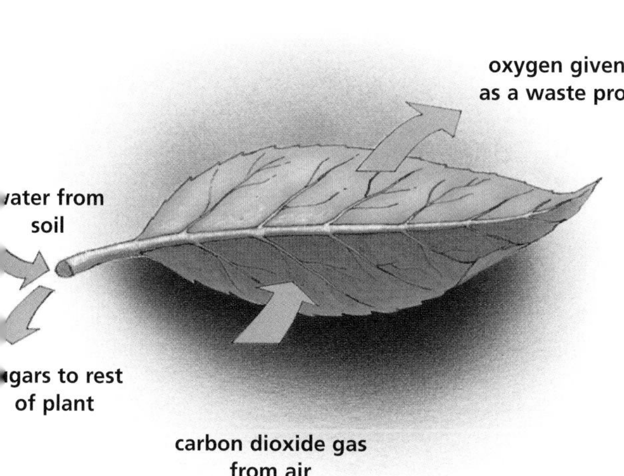

◀ A plant makes sugary food inside its leaves in a process called photosynthesis. During photosynthesis, plants also produce oxygen gas, which all animals need to breathe to stay alive.

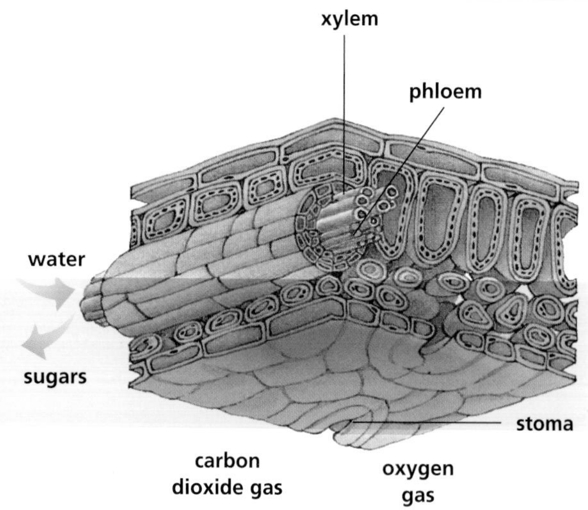

◀ A cross-section through a leaf. Tiny holes called stomata allow gases to pass in and out. Running through the roots, stems and leaves are two kinds of tube. The xylem carries water and minerals and the phloem carries food.

Plant structure

A typical plant has roots to anchor it in the ground. The roots take up water and minerals from the soil. A stem or trunk links the roots to the leaves and holds them up so that they can collect sunshine and air for photosynthesis and breathing.

Plant groups

Scientists have identified more than 270,000 different kinds, or species, of plant. They are divided into four main groups according to how they reproduce: mosses and liverworts; ferns; conifers (plants with cones); and flowering plants. More than 80 per cent of all plants are flowering plants.

Spore plants

Ferns, horsetails, mosses and liverworts reproduce by means of spores. These dust-like particles are simpler than seeds and do not have a food store. They consist only of genetic material (DNA) inside a protective coat. Spore-producing plants appeared on Earth before flowering plants. They can only live and reproduce in damp places.

Seed plants

The purpose of a flower is to make seeds, which spread away from the parent plant and grow into new plants. Conifers also produce seeds, which develop on woody cones. A seed contains the tiny beginnings of a plant and a food store, all surrounded by a tough outer coat. Seeds can stay dormant ('asleep') for years before growing. This helps them to survive cold or drought.

▶ Plants are divided into four main groups according to how they reproduce.

Mosses and liverworts
- live in damp places and produce spores
- most have no roots and no tubes inside them
- about 16,000 different kinds

Ferns
- live in damp places, especially rainforests, and produce spores
- have rigid stalks containing tubes, leaves called fronds and fine roots
- about 10,000 kinds of ferns, horsetails and clubmosses

▼ A fern spore grows into a tiny, heart-shaped prothallus, which produces sperm and egg cells. A sperm has to swim through moisture on the surface of the prothallus to fuse with an egg cell before a new fern can develop.

2. Spore cases form on fully grown ferns.

spore case on undersi[de] of leaf

prothallus

egg orga[n]

rhizoids

sperm or[gan]

3. Prothallus produces sperm and egg cells.

sperm

egg

prothallus

4. Sperm joins with egg on surface of prothallus to form fertilized egg.

new fern plant

prothallus

1. New fern plant grows from fertilized egg.

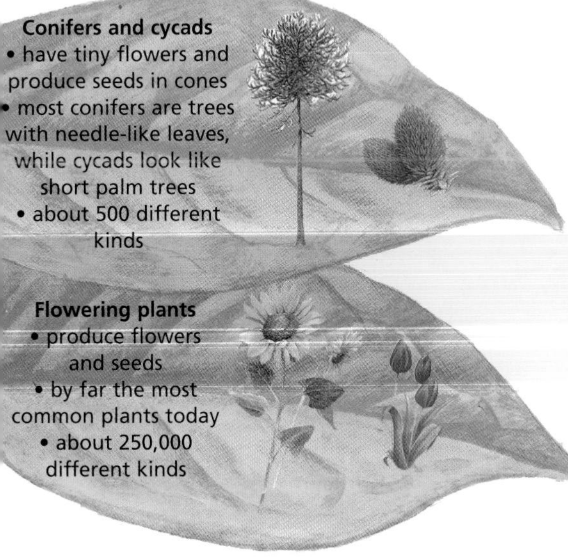

Plants with cones

A typical conifer produces separate male and female cones. The male cones produce pollen and the female cones produce egg cells. Ripe male cones open to release clouds of pollen, which are carried by the wind to female cones. There the pollen joins with (fertilizes) the egg cells. Seeds then develop within the female cone. The seeds of conifers are not completely enclosed within fruits, as are the seeds of flowering plants.

Flowering groups

The largest group of flowering plants is called the dicotyledons, or dicots for short. Most common flowers and vegetables are dicots, as are all broad-leaved trees such as oaks. The sprouting seeds of a dicot have two seed leaves – 'di' means two and cotyledon means seed leaf. Dicot leaves come in many shapes, with their veins forming a network through the leaf. The flower parts usually occur in multiples of four or five.

The oldest trees alive today are bristlecone pines. Some bristlecones started to grow in the White Mountains of California over 4600 years ago. These trees were in their prime when the first Pharaohs were ruling ancient Egypt. When Christ was born, they were already 2600 years old.

The other main group of flowering plants is called the monocotyledons, or monocots. Grasses, palms, lilies, orchids and tulips are all monocots. They have long, narrow leaves with parallel veins and flower parts that occur in multiples of three.

Plants with flowers

From grasses and apple trees to daffodils and orchids, flowering plants are a very varied group of plants. They evolved together with insects, and many flowers depend on insects to carry their pollen. The bright colours and scents of flowers, and the sugary nectar within them, attract animals (usually insects), which then carry away pollen on their bodies. Flowers that use the wind to carry their pollen, such as grasses, tend to be small, and dull.

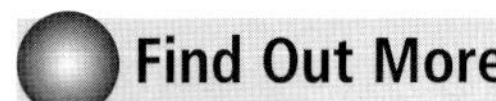

Find Out More

- Animals
- Classification
- Ecology
- Energy
- Life
- Sex and reproduction
- Wood and timber

▼ In a flower, the male sex cells are in the pollen grains, which are held in sacs called anthers. Pollen lands on the female part of a flower, the stigma. The pollen grain grows a tubule down from the stigma to the ovary. There it fertilizes a female sex cell to make a seed.

Plastics

Chemists make plastics in much the same way as we make daisy-chains. They link together chemicals with short molecules (basic units) in chains to make long molecules. If a short molecule was the length of a daisy stalk, a plastics molecule would be up to 3000 metres long.

CELLULOID AND BAKELITE

A US inventor named John Hyatt (1837–1920) made the first successful plastic in 1870, when he was trying to make an artificial ivory for billiard balls. His invention was made from the cellulose in wood and was called celluloid. The modern plastics industry was born in 1909, when the US chemist Leo Baekeland (1863–1944) made Bakelite while trying to produce new varnishes. Bakelite was the world's first synthetic plastic.

John Hyatt

Leo Baekeland

All the materials we call plastics are made up of long molecules. It is these long molecules that make plastics so special. Most other materials have short molecules, made up of just a few atoms joined together. In a plastics molecule, tens of thousands of atoms may be joined together.

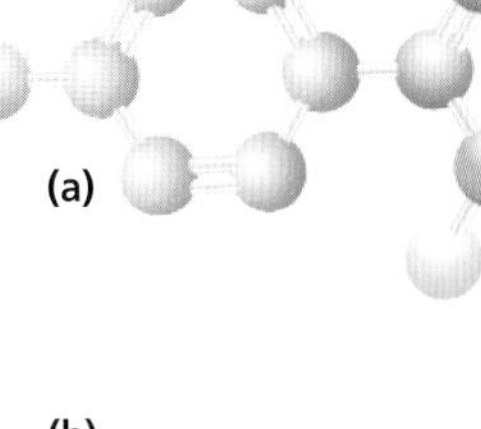

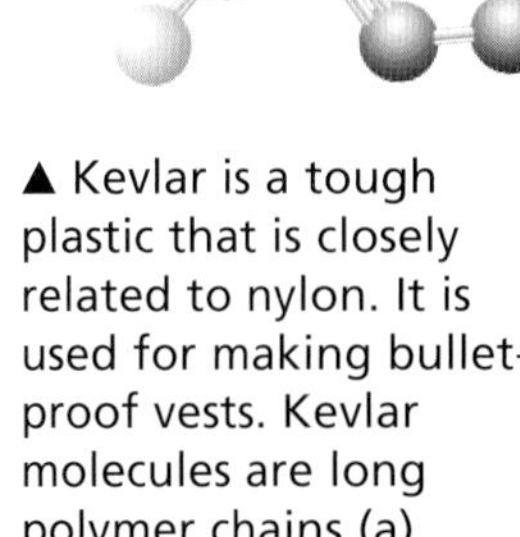

▲ Kevlar is a tough plastic that is closely related to nylon. It is used for making bullet-proof vests. Kevlar molecules are long polymer chains (a), made up of individual units (b) that contain two carbon rings.

◀ A technician in a plastics factory checks the production of plastic tubing. Wide tubing like this is used to make dustbin bags and plastic sheets.

There are substances in nature that have long molecules, including rubber and wood. But we don't call them plastics. Plastics are synthetic substances, manufactured from chemicals. An important property of many plastics is that they are easy to shape by heating.

We find plastics everywhere. We drink from plastic cups, fry food in non-stick plastic-coated pans, wrap goods in plastic bags, and wear plastics in the form of synthetic fibres. Drainpipes, squeeze bottles, heat-proof surfaces, floor coverings, tyres and superglues are just a few of the many other products made from plastics that we come across every day.

Many parts

Another general name for plastics is 'polymers'. The word means 'many parts'. This tells us that plastics are made by stringing many small parts (short molecules) together. The chemical process of making plastics is called polymerization.

Find Out More

- Carbon
- Oil products
- Polymers
- Reactions, chemical

Plastic surgery *see* Surgery • **Plate tectonics** *see* Continents and plates

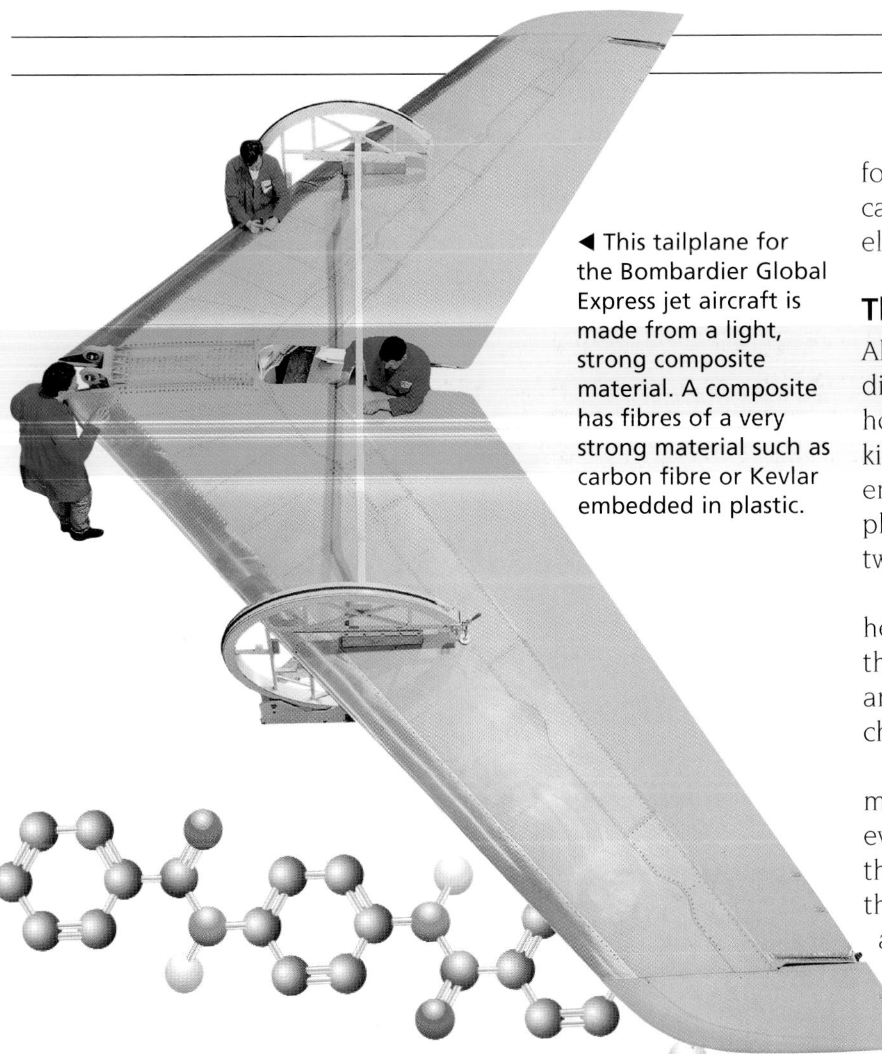

◀ This tailplane for the Bombardier Global Express jet aircraft is made from a light, strong composite material. A composite has fibres of a very strong material such as carbon fibre or Kevlar embedded in plastic.

In almost all plastics, the long chains that form the molecules are linked together by carbon atoms. Carbon is the only chemical element that can link together in this way.

Thermoplastics and thermosets

All plastics are shaped by heating, but react differently to heat afterwards. If you place a hot saucepan on the plastic worktop in the kitchen, nothing happens. But place it in an empty polythene washing-up bowl, and the plastic will melt. This happens because the two plastics are different types.

Polythene softens and melts when heated. It is a type of plastic called a thermoplastic. Many other common plastics are thermoplastics, including PVC (polyvinyl chloride), polystyrene and nylon.

The worktop plastic does not soften or melt when heated, although it will burn eventually. It is a type of plastic called a thermoset. The worktop is made from a thermoset called melamine-formaldehyde, after the substances it is made from. The first synthetic plastic, Bakelite, was made from phenol and formaldehyde.

SHAPING PLASTICS

Plastic is usually shaped by a process of moulding. Warm plastic may be blown into shape in a mould (a), or molten (liquid) plastic may be injected into a mould (b). Plastic packaging material is often formed from a sheet of plastic, sucked into a mould using a vacuum (c). To produce rods and tubes, molten plastic is forced through a hole, or die, in a process called extrusion (d). Plastic sheet used for kitchen worktops is made by laminating. This involves pressing sheets of plastic and filler material together and heating them.

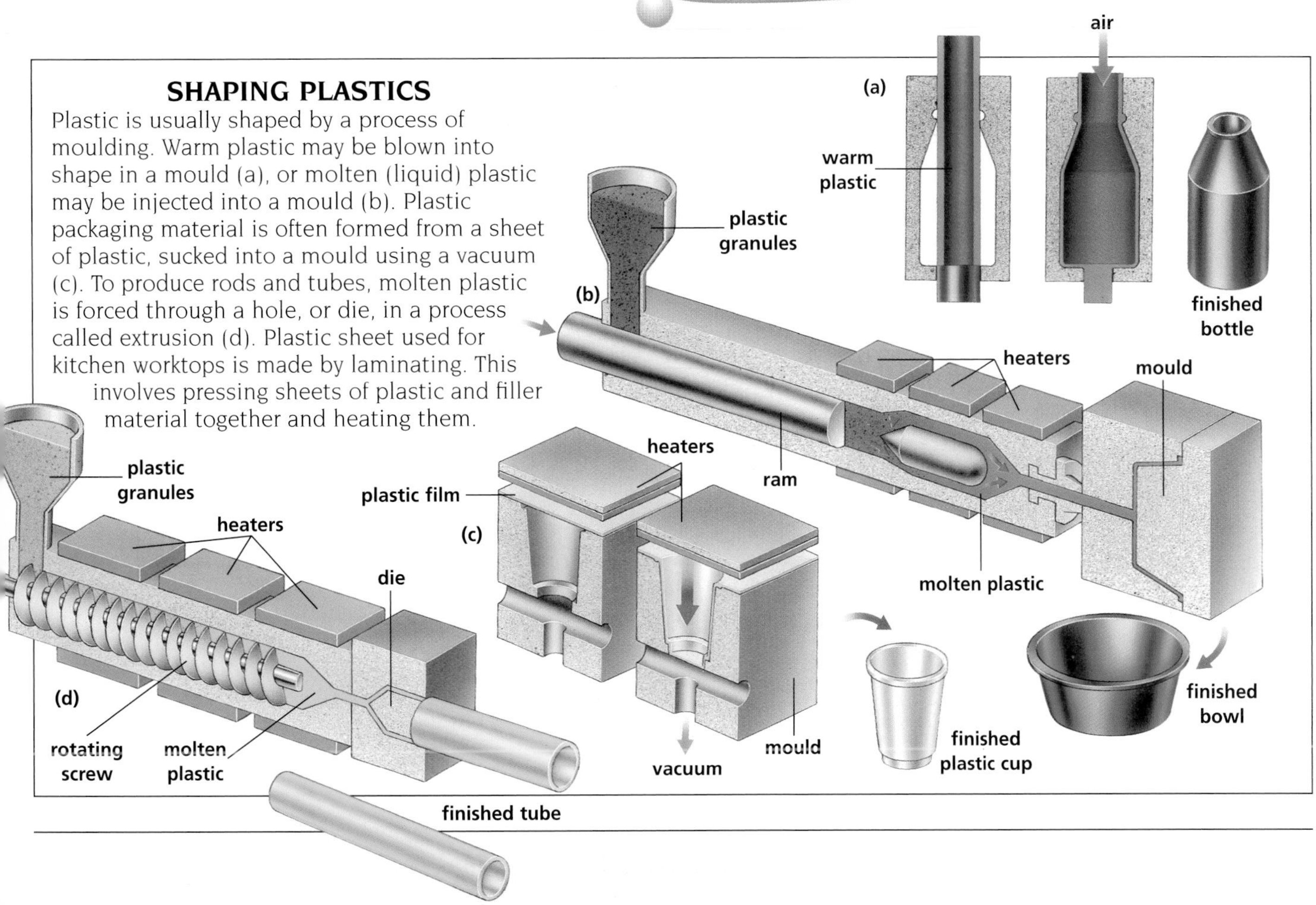

Pluto

As soon as the American Clyde Tombaugh announced the discovery of the ninth planet in 1930, astronomers realized that Pluto was an oddity in the Solar System.

Pluto's orbit is different from those of the other planets. Its long, elliptical shape means that Pluto is sometimes nearer the Sun than Neptune. Its distance from the Sun varies between 7400 and 4400 million kilometres. Neptune and Pluto can never collide, though. In the time it takes Neptune to make three trips around the Sun, Pluto orbits exactly twice, so they never meet.

Pluto is by far the smallest planet but it is not rocky like the other small planets. Inside it is a mixture of ice and rock, with a thick layer of frozen water over the top. The world most similar to Pluto is Neptune's moon, Triton. Like Triton, Pluto has a very thin atmosphere of nitrogen.

Charon

Pluto's moon Charon was discovered in 1978. Then in 1992, astronomers started to find many miniature ice planets orbiting beyond Neptune. Charon could have become Pluto's moon when two of these small objects collided billions of years ago. A great crash could also explain why Pluto's axis is tilted by 58 degrees.

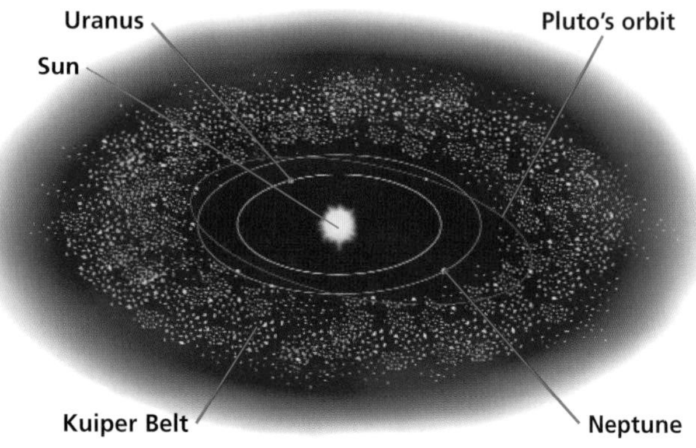

◀ Pluto is the largest known member of a family of thousands of icy miniature planets, which orbit the Sun in a belt beyond Neptune. This belt is called the Kuiper Belt.

▶ Pluto is a tiny planet, smaller across than the United States. Pluto's moon Charon is half as big. The distance between them is only one and a half times the Earth's diameter. Charon orbits Pluto in 6.4 days. The same side of Charon always faces Pluto.

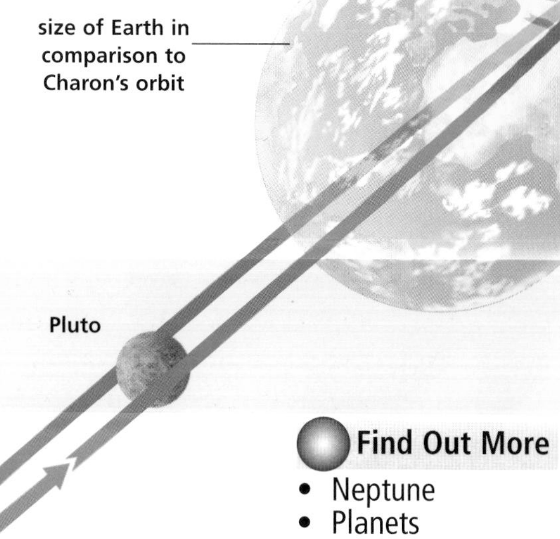

Find Out More

- Neptune
- Planets
- Solar System

▼ The small photo is the most detailed picture ever taken of Pluto and Charon. It was made by the Hubble Space Telescope and shows just vague dark and light patches. The big picture shows what we think they may look like from other evidence. No spacecraft has yet visited Pluto.

PLUTO DATA
Diameter at equator: 2360 km
Average distance from Sun: 5900 million km
Time taken to spin on axis: 6.39 days
Density (water = 1): 1.83
Time taken to orbit the Sun: 247.7 years
Moons: 1

Polar life

Every year, a small bird called the Arctic tern makes an amazing journey. It travels over 35,000 kilometres from one end of the world to the other and back again. By making this journey, it escapes from the freezing winter weather in both polar regions.

The North Pole is surrounded by the frozen Arctic Ocean, whereas the South Pole is surrounded by a frozen continent – Antarctica. Few animals, apart from polar bears, can survive on the Arctic ice, but the treeless lands around the Arctic – the tundra – come alive in summer, as animals visit to feed and breed there. In contrast, there is hardly any ice-free land around Antarctica, but the huge variety of life in the oceans during the summer attracts hordes of penguins, whales and seals.

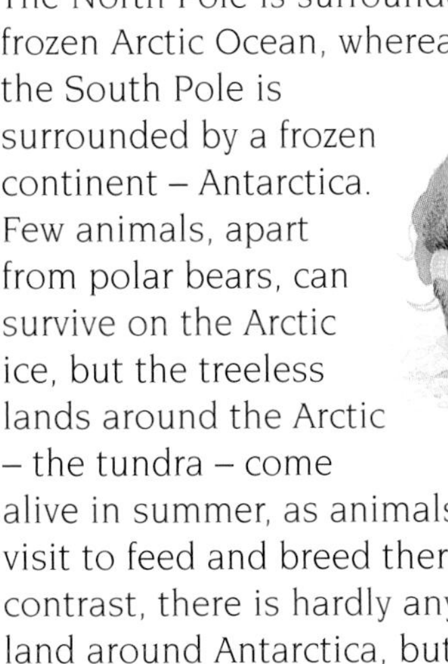

◀ If musk oxen are attacked by wolves, they often form a circle with the young protected in the middle. Musk oxen live on the Arctic tundra all year round.

▲ Low-growing carpets of purple saxifrage cover the Arctic tundra with stunning sheets of colour during the summer months.

Find Out More
- Climate
- Ecology
- Ice caps and glaciers

Polar plants

Polar plants hug the ground to stay out of the biting winds, and form low, rounded cushions to help trap moisture. In the short summer, plants burst into flower and quickly produce seeds. Many of these seeds survive the winter buried in the soil.

Fur and fat

Polar animals have thick fur or dense feathers to trap the body's warmth. Fur or feathers may turn white in winter for camouflage against the snow. Many animals also have a dense layer of fat in the skin. This traps body heat, and also acts as a energy store when food is hard to find.

▼ The largest bears in the world, polar bears, hunt for seals beneath the Arctic ice. Their big paws have rough, non-slip soles to help them grip slippery snow and ice.

Pollution

The year 2000 began badly for the environment. In January, oil smothered and killed over 150,000 sea birds on the north-west coast of France. In February, cyanide poisoned hundreds of tonnes of freshwater fish in Hungary's Tisa River. In March, raw sewage killed thousands of sea fish in a lagoon near Rio de Janeiro, Brazil.

▶ This cormorant was just one of the many victims of a huge oil spill that took place off the Shetland Islands in 1993.

Oil, deadly chemicals and sewage are three of the things that can pollute or poison our environment and our water.

The oil that smothered the birds in France came from a wrecked oil tanker. At any time, hundreds of oil tankers are sailing the world's seas, together carrying millions of tonnes of oil. When tankers get holed in collisions, or run aground on rocks, vast amounts of oil can pour into the sea and drift ashore. All kinds of sea- and shore-life are affected, from shellfish to seals. Some animals may be saved by washing them with detergent, but most perish.

DISASTER AT BHOPAL

The world's worst chemical disaster happened in the Indian city of Bhopal in 1984. An explosion at a chemical plant making insecticides (below) released a cloud of deadly gas into the air. Because the gas was twice as heavy as air, it did not drift away, but formed a 'blanket' over the surrounding area. It attacked people's lungs and affected their breathing. Eventually, as many as 3000 people died and many thousands more had their health ruined.

▼ The environment is under attack from all directions.

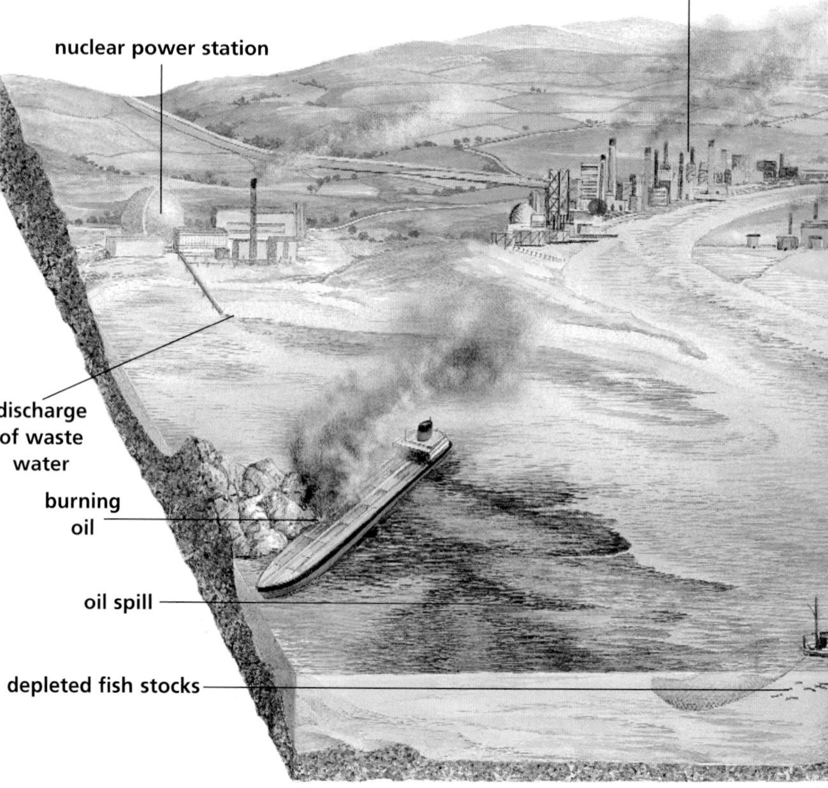

▲ The sun sets behind a blanket of smog hanging over Mexico City. Smog, a mixture of smoke and fog or chemical fumes, pollutes many of the world's big cities.

Chemical attack

The cyanide that slaughtered the fish in Hungary came from a gold mine, where it was used to extract gold. Many industries produce poisonous waste products. Usually they are treated to make them harmless before they are released back into the environment.

Chemicals from farming also affect the environment. Farmers apply chemical fertilizers such as nitrates to the land. Sometimes they apply too much, and the surplus chemicals get washed by rain into rivers. Eventually, they can get into our drinking water.

More deadly than nitrates are the pesticides farmers use to protect their crops from insect and weeds. Many pesticides are persistent, which means that they remain active for a long time, and can be poisonous to other animals.

Polluting the air

The air can become polluted too. One of the main causes of air pollution is the car. When car engines burn their fuel, they give off fumes, such as nitrogen oxides, carbon dioxide and soot. These fumes may cause breathing problems.

Raining acid

Power stations and factories burn fuels such as coal and oil to produce energy. They too give off fumes that pollute the air, including sulphur and nitrogen oxides. These oxides combine with oxygen and moisture in the air to form sulphuric and nitric acids. When it rains, the rain is acidic.

Acid rain falls into lakes and rivers, and can make them too acid to support plant and animal life. Acid rain also kills trees. Lifeless lakes and dying forests are already found in parts of northern North America and northern Europe.

In a greenhouse

The carbon dioxide that factories and cars produce when they burn their fuels builds up in the Earth's atmosphere. It makes the atmosphere act rather like a greenhouse and trap more of the Sun's heat. This is causing world temperatures to rise, or global warming.

Chemicals called chlorofluorocarbons (CFCs), found in sprays and refrigerators, increase the greenhouse effect. They also attack the layer of ozone in the Earth's upper atmosphere, which protects us from much harmful radiation from the Sun. If the ozone layer thins too much, it will let through more of this dangerous radiation.

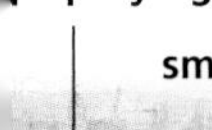

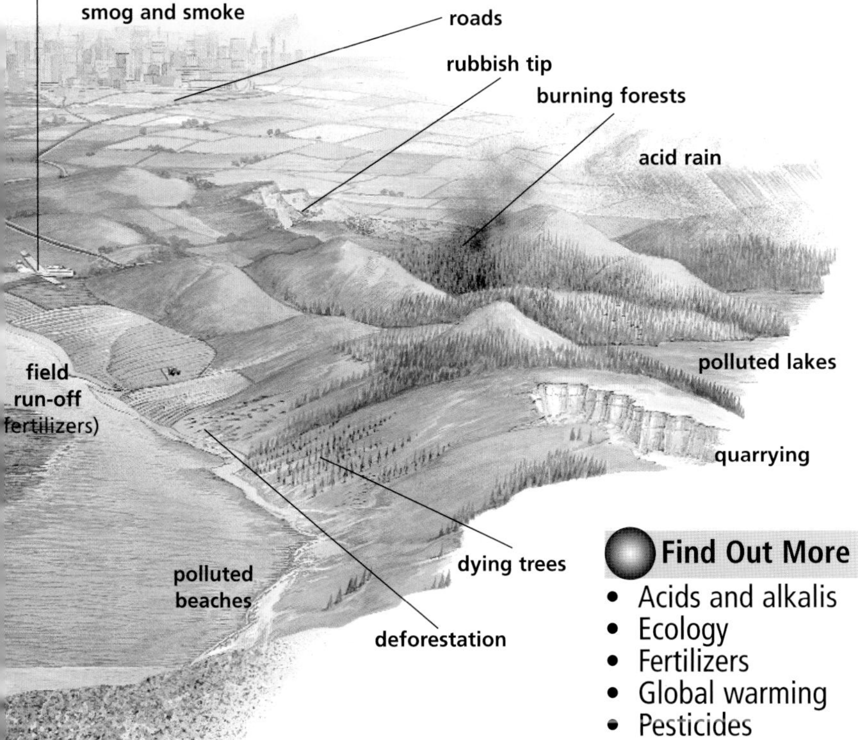

Find Out More
- Acids and alkalis
- Ecology
- Fertilizers
- Global warming
- Pesticides
- Waste disposal

Polymers

The tiny fibres in this paper, the starch in the bread you eat and the muscles you're using to hold this book all have one thing in common. It's the same thing that links car windscreens, nylon thread and the outsides of telephones and ballpoint pens.

▲ A piece of human hair seen through an electron microscope. Hair is made of a protein called keratin. All proteins, the building blocks of living things, are polymers.

All these things are made of polymers. Polymers are a special kind of molecule. All chemical compounds (substances) are made of molecules. Many molecules are small and simple, but a polymer forms a long chain made up of thousands of repeating building blocks, called monomers (poly- means 'many' and mono- means 'single').

◀ The high-performance clothing and equipment used by these climbers in the Himalayas is nearly all made from synthetic polymers.

Proteins – the complicated chemicals that make up your muscles and much of the rest of your body – are all polymers. They are made from chains of simpler chemicals called amino acids.

DNA, the molecule that stores your genetic code in every cell of your body, is also a polymer. Rubber is another natural polymer.

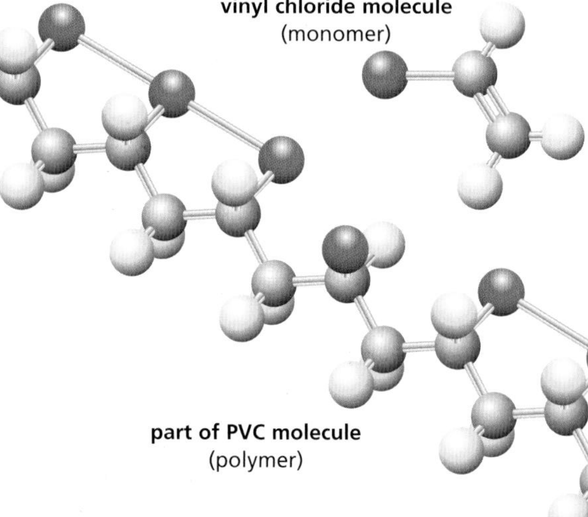

▼ PVC (polyvinyl chloride) is a common polymer used to make water pipes, window frames, flooring and many other products. The repeating unit (monomer) in PVC is vinyl chloride.

Natural polymers

In nature, polymers are found in many carbohydrates, such as starch and cellulose. Cellulose is the fibrous material in plants. It is made up of many units of glucose (a simple sugar).

Find Out More

- Atoms and molecules
- Elements and compounds
- Plastics
- Rubber

Artificial polymers

All plastics, from nylon to PVC, are polymers. The first plastic was celluloid, made in 1869 from the cellulose in cotton fibres. In 1909 another plastic, bakelite, was made by joining up smaller molecules to make a big polymer molecule.

Since then, a huge range of artificial polymers has been made. They have all kinds of uses because they can be shaped, they are strong and lightweight, and they can be made with many different properties.

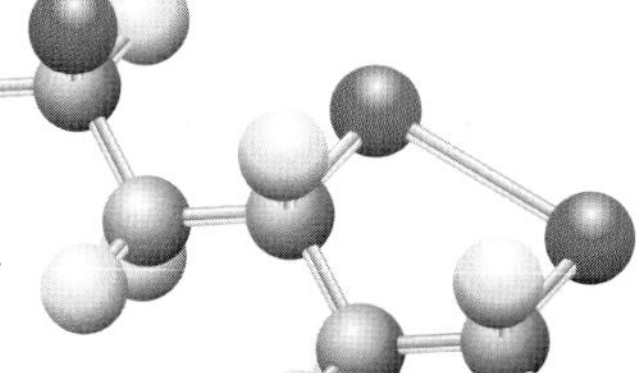

Potassium *see* Sodium • **Pottery** *see* Ceramics • **Power** *see* Energy

Power stations

Switch on your TV and it flickers into life. But have you ever considered where it gets its power from? Huge, fuel-hungry power stations dotted around the country make electricity and send it to our homes through cables. One power station generates enough electricity to supply thousands of homes.

▶ White, cloud-like plumes of water vapour rise from cooling towers at a power station in Cheshire, UK.

Most modern power stations make electricity by burning fuel to heat water. Heating water creates steam, which is used to turn the blades of giant turbines – just as blowing on a child's toy windmill makes it spin round. The spinning turbines drive huge machines called generators, which produce electricity.

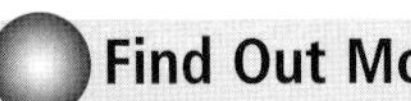

Find Out More

- Electricity supply
- Fuels
- Generators
- Nuclear energy
- Pollution

Choice of fuels

There are several types of fuel that a power station can use to heat water. Those most often used in today's power stations are coal, gas, oil or nuclear fuel. Coal, gas and oil are known as fossil fuels, because they formed from the remains of plants and animals over millions of years.

In conventional power stations, fossil fuels are burned to heat vast quantities of water. In nuclear power stations, however, nuclear fuels such as uranium are used to make electricity. The uranium is not burnt

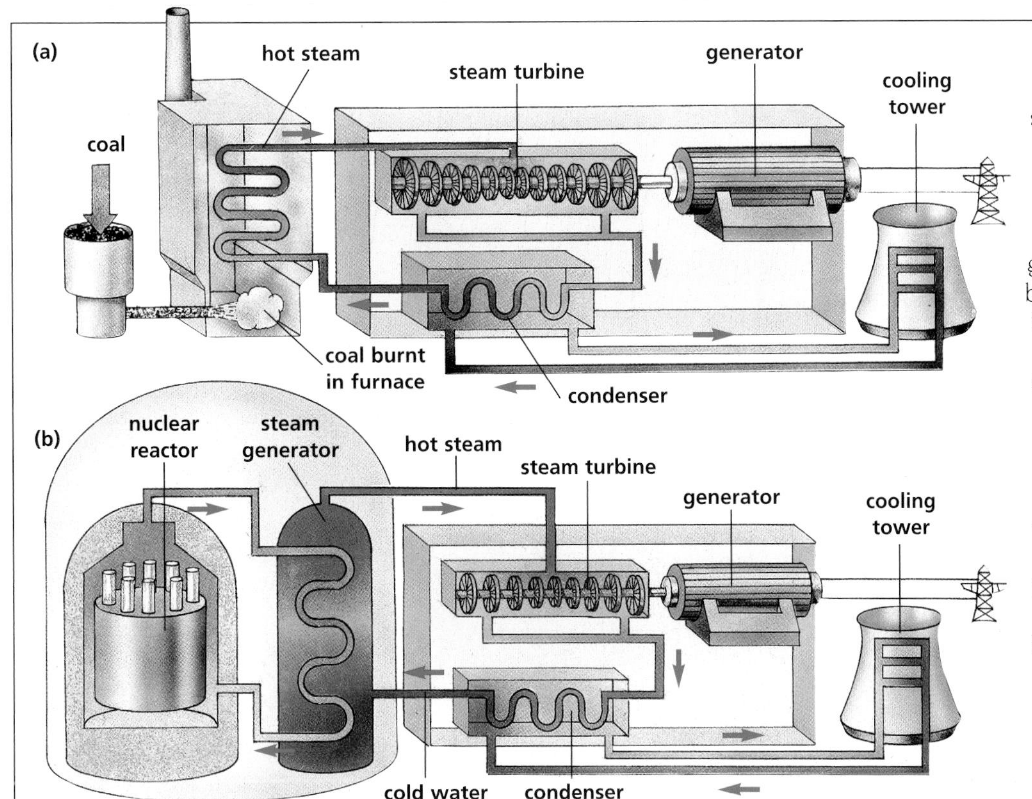

POWER STATIONS

A coal- or oil-fired power station (a) contains a furnace, where the fuel is burned to heat water and make steam. The steam drives a turbine attached to an electricity generator. The steam is turned back into water in a condenser, then goes back to the furnace to be heated again. The condenser is cooled with cold water, which is then itself cooled in a cooling tower.

In a nuclear power station (b), the energy to heat the water and make steam comes from a nuclear reactor. The reactor heats the water in the steam generator through a heat exchange system, so that no radioactivity can get into the steam powering the turbines.

in a furnace. Instead, its atoms are broken apart in a process called nuclear fission. This process creates large quantities of heat, which is used to produce high-pressure steam.

Burning fossil fuels in power stations creates pollution that causes damage to the Earth's atmosphere. It may cause acid rain, for example. Nuclear power stations cause no air pollution, but they produce wastes that are radioactive (give off dangerous radiation).

Alternative energy

Because using fuel to make electricity damages the environment, scientists have found different (alternative) ways of generating electricity. Hydroelectric power stations are one way of doing this. They use the power of the water that cascades down a waterfall or a dam, to turn a turbine – without making harmful waste materials.

▲ Some people think they are an eyesore, but wind farms provide energy without damaging the environment.

▼ A model of what was probably the world's first power station, built by Thomas Edison (1847–1931). Edison invented light bulbs in 1879, and realized that many people would want electric light in their homes. He decided that he would have to set up power stations to provide electricity for them. So he designed the first power station at Pearl Street in New York. The station was 'switched on' in 1882.

Wind is also a harmless source of power. Armies of giant windmills – called wind farms – are springing up both on land and at sea. The propellers of the windmills spin round and turn generators when the wind blows. The electricity the windmills generate can also charge batteries, which then supply power when the wind drops.

Power from the sun is another great hope for the future. At present solar power is expensive, but scientists are trying to find ways of producing it more cheaply. Geothermal energy is also being examined. This involves using the tremendous heat trapped in the Earth's crust – perhaps 15 kilometres below ground – to heat water and drive turbines.

Pregnancy *see* Human reproduction • **Prehistoric life** *see* Fossils, Humans, Life

Pressure

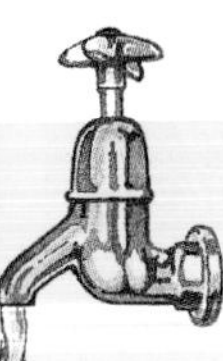

Try to stop the water gushing from a tap by covering the spout – and you will probably end up soaked! That is because the flow of water is too strong to stop.

The water in the tap has a high pressure. It pushes against the inside of the tap with a large amount of force. Water comes out with great force when the tap is turned on.

DOWN DEEP

In 1960, two people descended 11 kilometres to the deepest part of the ocean in an underwater craft called *Trieste*. The pressure of the water there was equal to a weight of just over a tonne on every square centimetre of the cabin (a square centimetre is about the same size as a thumbnail). The cabin had to be very strong to resist this enormous pressure.

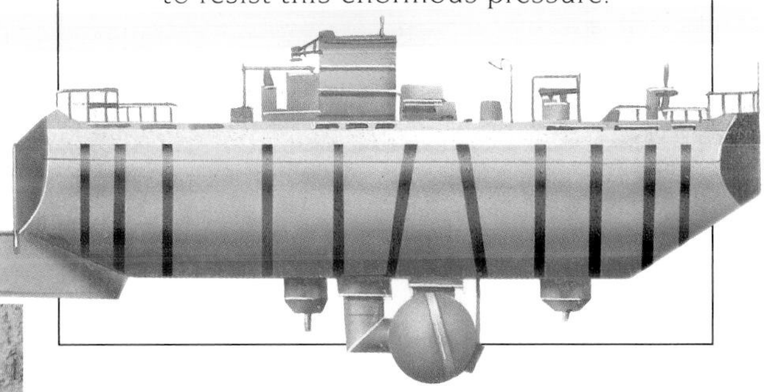

Using pressure

Bicycles, cars and other road vehicles all run on air! The high pressure of the air in the tyres holds the wheel rims above the road surface. Pumps inflate tyres by raising air pressure so that air flows through the valve into the tyre. The valve stops the high-pressure air from escaping.

◀ An excavator works by hydraulics. A pump raises the pressure of hydraulic fluid and sends the fluid through hoses to moving parts such as the bucket, which it drives with great power. The driver controls the fluid's movement to make the bucket scoop up dirt.

Raising pressure

The pressure in a tap is high because the pipe leading to the tap goes back to a tank above it. The weight of all the water in the pipe and tank gives it pressure. If the tank is not higher than the tap, a pump may raise the pressure of the water.

Gases, such as air, also have a certain pressure just as water does. The weight of all the air above you presses in on your body. When you breathe in, the pressure of the surrounding air makes it flow into your lungs.

Solid things exert pressure too. Your weight makes your feet press down on the ground with a certain amount of pressure.

▶ When you suck through a straw, you expand your lungs to lower the air pressure inside them. The outside air pressing on the drink is at a greater pressure, and forces the drink up the straw into your mouth.

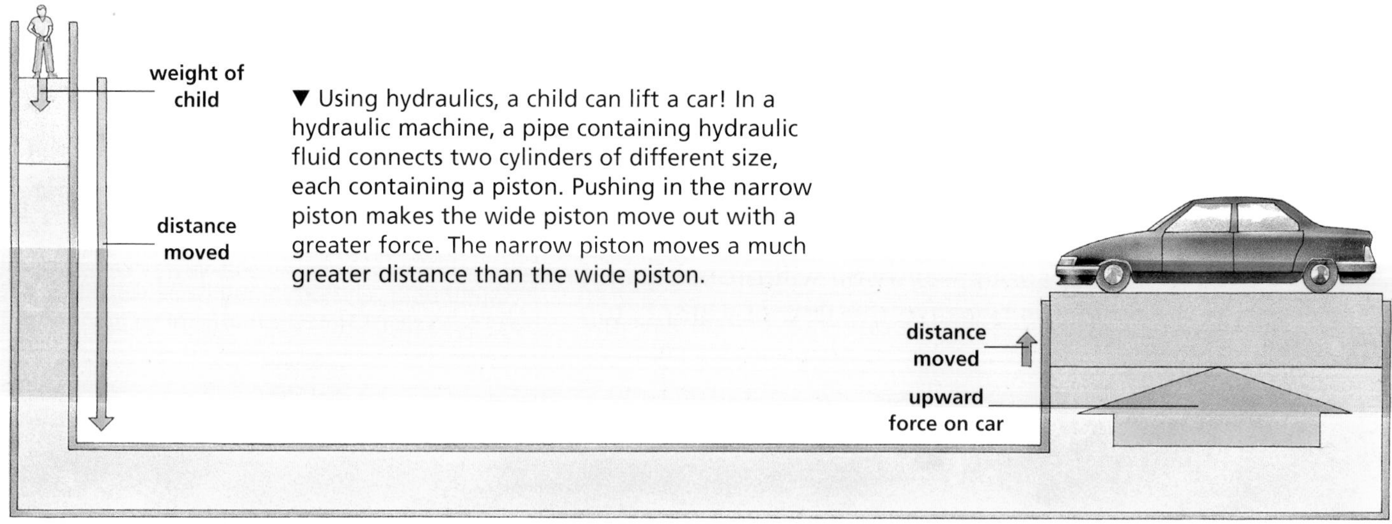

▼ Using hydraulics, a child can lift a car! In a hydraulic machine, a pipe containing hydraulic fluid connects two cylinders of different size, each containing a piston. Pushing in the narrow piston makes the wide piston move out with a greater force. The narrow piston moves a much greater distance than the wide piston.

Find Out More

- Atmosphere
- Flight and flow
- Floating and sinking
- Forces
- Lungs and breathing

Pumps raise the pressure of water in fountains to make the water spurt upwards. Pneumatic machines, such as road-mending drills, use air pressure, while hydraulic machines, such as car brakes and diggers, use liquid pressure. For both types of machine, pumps produce high-pressure air or liquid to drive the moving parts.

No pressure

Pumps can also remove air from a container to reduce the pressure inside. There is a vacuum in the container when the air has gone. The walls of a vacuum flask contain a vacuum, which keeps food or drink inside the flask hot or cold for several hours.

▶ A diver carries a cylinder of compressed (squashed) air in order to breathe underwater. This limits the time of the dive – it is not safe to breathe high-pressure air for very long.

Primates *see* Mammals • **Printed circuits** *see* Electronics

Printing

There was a time when all books were made of paper and words were printed on the pages. But no longer. Electronic books are now available that you read on a book-size screen. At the touch of a fingertip, you can change the size of the letters, put in a bookmark, make notes or look up words in the built-in dictionary.

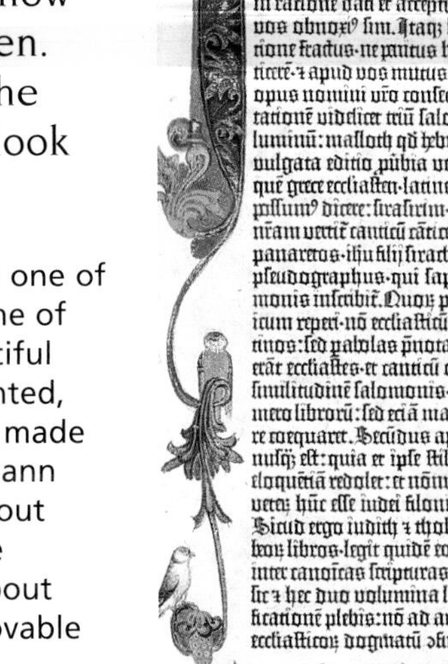

▶ A page from one of the first and one of the most beautiful books ever printed, the Latin Bible made by German Johann Gutenberg (about 1400–1468). He printed it in about 1455, using movable metal type.

Books printed on paper will still be with us for a long time. But methods of producing them are becoming increasingly electronic. Not so long ago, authors wrote their text (words) with a typewriter. Mistakes were marked on the paper copy, then a typesetter set the text in metal type (the lettering used in printing). Finally, a printing plate was made from the type.

Today, most authors write their text using a word-processor program on a computer. They send it to their editors on computer disk or by email. It may stay in electronic form through all the editing and design stages, until it gets to the printer, who makes the printing plates from an electronic file.

Scanning the pictures

Illustrations to go with the text are also stored in an electronic form. Professional photographers are increasingly using digital cameras, and many artists produce their artwork on a computer using illustration software. Photographs and illustrations on paper are converted into electronic form by a scanner.

A scanner works by scanning a laser beam across every part of a picture. This process records information about the colour and intensity of each tiny section of the picture in electronic form. When the

Find Out More

- Colour
- Computers
- Lasers and holograms
- Photocopiers
- Photography

◀ The four stages in printing a colour picture. The yellow plate is printed first (a), followed by the cyan plate (b), then the magenta (c). The black plate prints last, producing the full-colour picture (d).

Programs (computer) *see* Software • **Proteins** *see* Diet, Genetics • **Protons** *see* Atoms and molecules

picture is printed, this information is converted into patterns of dots for printing. Pictures have to be printed as tiny dots. You can see these dots if you look closely at a printed photograph in a newspaper or a book.

With a colour picture, four separate scans are made to produce four different images: one yellow, one cyan (blue), one magenta (red) and one black. This process is called colour separation. It depends on the principle that any colour can be made up from a combination of the colours yellow, cyan and magenta. Printing plates are made from these separations. (The fourth, black plate improves the look of the final picture.)

Printing processes

In the oldest printing method, called letterpress, raised letters were coated with ink and then pressed against a sheet of paper. Most printing now is done by a method called offset lithography (litho).

image on plate

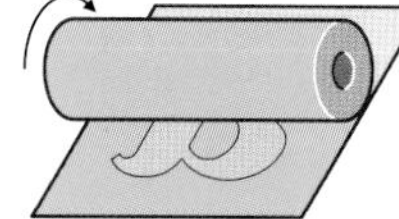

roller wets plate

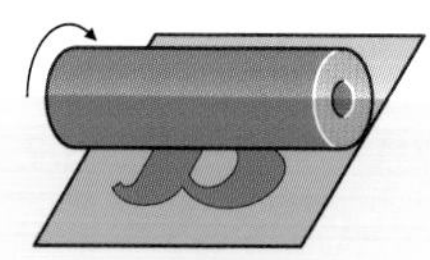

inking

inked type transferred to paper

◀ In litho printing, a flat plate carries the type image. A roller wets all the plate except for the image, then another roller spreads ink, which sticks only to the type area. The inked image is then transferred to paper.

High-speed litho printing presses, fed by a continuous supply (web) of paper, can print 1000 copies every minute.

In litho printing, an image of everything to be printed in a particular colour is transferred photographically to a printing plate. The image is then treated so that sections that need to be dark attract greasy printing ink.

On the printing press, the plate is clamped to a cylinder, then wetted and inked in turn. The image areas repel the water but attract the ink. The cylinder revolves and transfers the ink image via another cylinder to the paper.

PRODUCING A MAGAZINE ARTICLE

A reporter and a photographer are covering a fire. This is the story of how technology helps to turn their words and pictures into a magazine article.

1 Reporter records story on tape, types it up and emails it to magazine office.

2 Photographer takes pictures to go with story and sends them via an ISDN line (fast telephone link).

3 Designer designs pages of article on computer using text and photographs.

4 Magazine editors check finished page layouts produced by colour printer.

5 Pages sent to printer as electronic files, which printer uses to make printing plates.

Pulsars *see* Stars • **Quarks** *see* Atoms and molecules • **Quasars** *see* Galaxies

Radar and sonar

Around a busy airport, the skies are full of planes. Some have just taken off. Others are coming in to land. Some are 'stacked up', circling and waiting to land. Yet air-traffic controllers know exactly where each plane is, and can make sure that there are no collisions, thanks to radar.

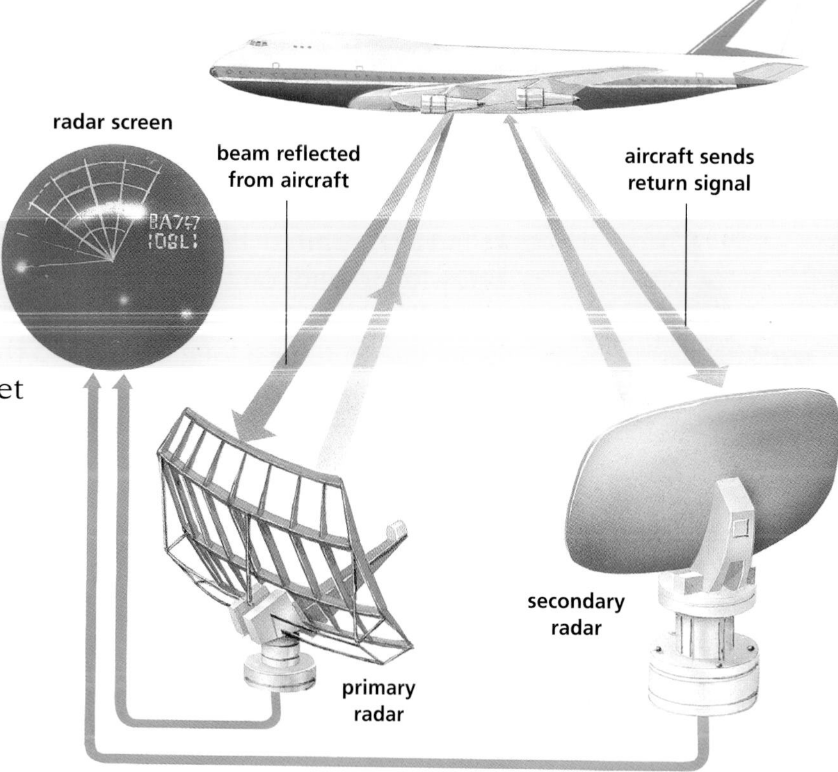

▲ Two kinds of radar system operate at airports. *Primary radar* finds the position of an aircraft by sending out a radar beam and detecting the echo as it reflects back from the plane. *Secondary radar* sends out a beam to a special device on the aircraft. This sends back a signal giving the plane's height and identification number.

Radar detects objects by bouncing radio beams off them. It uses very short radio waves called microwaves, which can 'see' through clouds and in the dark.

Radar has many uses besides air traffic control. Ships use radar to avoid collisions at night or in bad weather. Astronomers use radar to map the surface of planets, and police use hand-held radar 'guns' to check the speed of motorists. Rain reflects radar beams, so weather scientists and aircraft can use radar to spot storms.

In a radar system, a rotating aerial sends out narrow beams of microwaves. When a beam hits an object (a plane, say) it is reflected back as a kind of echo. The longer the echo takes to return, the further away the plane is. On the radar screen, a bright spot shows the position of the plane. A signal picked up by another aerial from the plane's own radar gives the plane's identification number and height.

Seeing with sound

Radar signals cannot travel through water, so ships and submarines use a kind of 'sound radar', called sonar, to measure depth and to detect things in the water.

The sound waves used are ultrasonic, which means that they are too high-pitched for the ear to detect. Hospitals use ultrasound scanners to produce sound 'pictures' of a baby still inside its mother.

Find Out More

- Navigation
- Sound
- Ultrasound

◀ The Air Traffic Control Centre at San Francisco International Airport. The round green radar screens show the position of aircraft flying within about 80 kilometres of the airport.

Radiation *see* Radioactivity, Electromagnetic spectrum

Radio

It is 12 December 1901. In St John's, Newfoundland, on the east coast of Canada, a team of people are struggling to raise a long aerial into the stormy skies. Supported by balloons and kites, the aerial is at last raised. Miraculously, it picks up faint signals – the letter S in Morse code. The signal comes from Poldhu in Cornwall, England. It is the first international radio broadcast.

▲ Clockwork radios work without an electricity supply or batteries. The clockwork spring turns a generator, which makes electricity.

The driving force behind the first transatlantic radio transmission was the Italian inventor Guglielmo Marconi. He had been experimenting with sending radio, or 'wireless', messages for six years. In December 1901 he proved that radio could be a new way for the whole world to communicate.

Today, radio stations in every country broadcast programmes to billions of people. And two-way radio links connect mobile phones, aircraft with airports, ships with the shore, and spacecraft with Earth.

Find Out More

- Circuits
- Communications
- Electromagnetic spectrum
- Microphones and speakers
- Waves and vibrations

How radio works

In a radio studio, microphones make an electrical 'copy' of the sound being recorded. This is called a sound signal. The sound signal is combined with a more powerful signal called the carrier wave. The combined signal goes to a transmitter, a metal antenna on a tall mast that sends out the signal as radio waves. The radio waves travel through the air to your radio receiver, where an electrical circuit, called a demodulator, extracts the original sound.

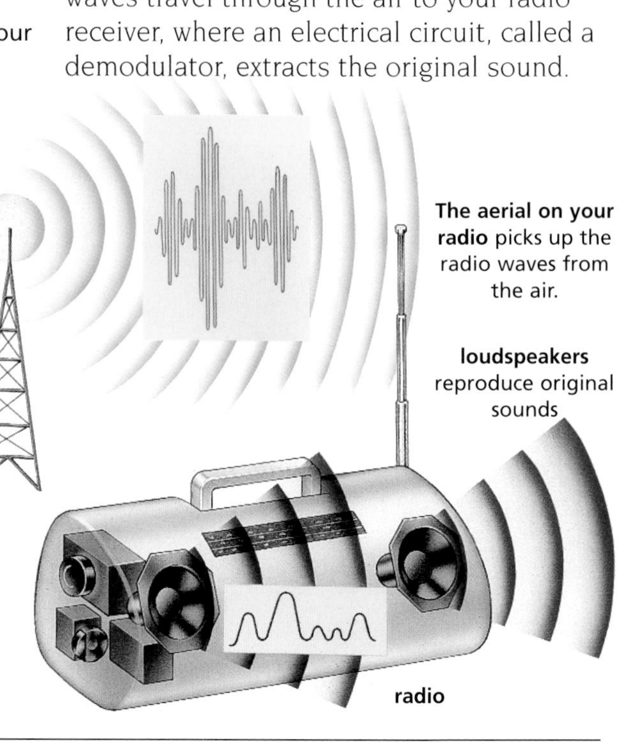
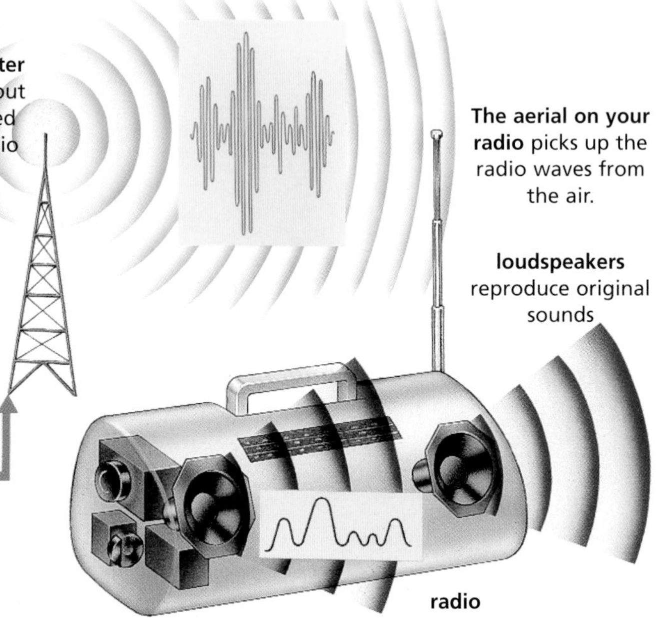

▼ How a radio broadcast reaches your radio at home.

Radioactivity

In 1945, near the end of World War II, an atomic bomb was dropped on the Japanese city of Hiroshima. Some 80,000 people died in the terrible explosion. But many more died later from an invisible danger – the radioactivity produced as the bombs exploded. The radioactivity caused all kinds of diseases, including cancers that only appeared many years later.

▶ Marie Curie (1867–1934) worked with her husband Pierre (1859–1906) on the study of radioactivity. They won the Nobel Prize in 1903 for their discovery of the radioactive elements polonium and radium. Marie died of a disease caused by radioactivity.

Radioactivity is what happens when the atoms of certain unstable elements, such as the heavy metal uranium, break down to atoms of more stable elements. As they do this, they give off radiation.

Types of radiation

When radioactive materials break down, they send out tiny particles, smaller than atoms. These are called alpha particles and beta particles. They also send out gamma rays, which are a kind of wave, like light waves but carrying much more energy.

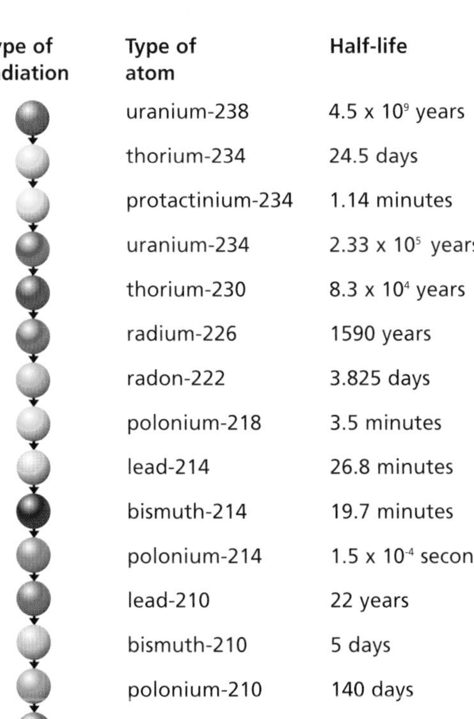

Type of radiation	Type of atom	Half-life
∝	uranium-238	4.5 x 10^9 years
β	thorium-234	24.5 days
β	protactinium-234	1.14 minutes
∝	uranium-234	2.33 x 10^5 years
∝	thorium-230	8.3 x 10^4 years
∝	radium-226	1590 years
∝	radon-222	3.825 days
∝	polonium-218	3.5 minutes
β	lead-214	26.8 minutes
β	bismuth-214	19.7 minutes
∝	polonium-214	1.5 x 10^{-4} seconds
β	lead-210	22 years
β	bismuth-210	5 days
∝	polonium-210	140 days
	lead-206	stable

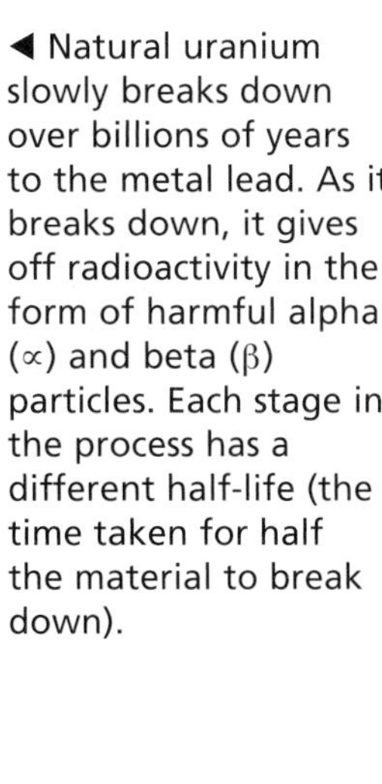

◀ Natural uranium slowly breaks down over billions of years to the metal lead. As it breaks down, it gives off radioactivity in the form of harmful alpha (∝) and beta (β) particles. Each stage in the process has a different half-life (the time taken for half the material to break down).

All forms of radioactivity can be dangerous, but some are more penetrating than others. Paper can block alpha particles, but only a sheet of light metal will stop beta particles. To block gamma rays you need a thick sheet of lead. Doctors use small doses of gamma rays to destroy some kinds of cancer.

Dangers and uses

Nuclear power stations produce lots of dangerous radioactivity, but this is carefully contained behind thick walls, and radioactive waste is buried deep underground. Lots of natural materials are slightly radioactive, but mostly not enough to be harmful. For example, plants and animals take in small amounts of radioactive carbon from the atmosphere. Radioactive materials break down at regular rates, so archaeologists can tell how old many things are by measuring the amount of radioactive carbon that is left in them.

Scientists use radioactive substances in other kinds of research. For example, they can trace the passage of a harmless radioactive substance through the body using a Geiger counter, a device that detects radioactivity.

Find Out More

- Atoms and molecules
- Electromagnetic spectrum
- Nuclear energy

Radio telescopes *see* Astronomy, Telescopes • **Radiography** *see* X-rays • **Railways** *see* Trains

Rain and snow

Every summer, India, Bangladesh and the rest of southern Asia are drenched by the rains of the summer monsoon. Warm, moist air blows in from the Indian Ocean and brings hundreds of centimetres of rain to the mountains and plains.

▲ As water droplets fall through a cloud they gradually gather even more droplets. A falling raindrop would be made up of about one million droplets.

Rain falls when clouds can no longer hold their moisture. Clouds are made of water vapour, tiny water droplets, ice crystals and dust. If the droplets and crystals are very small and far apart, the air holds them up. But if the droplets are close together, they start to join. Eventually the droplets become too big and heavy to stay up in the cloud, and fall as rain.

Cooling clouds

The main reason why rain falls from clouds is because the clouds cool off. This happens when they rise higher up in the atmosphere, perhaps because the clouds are warmer than the air around them, or in order to get over a mountain.

When the air cools, the water vapour in the clouds condenses (turns to liquid) and droplets form. The same thing happens on a can of cold drink on a hot day, when water vapour from the air condenses and forms water droplets on the side of the can.

Snow, sleet and hail

Most clouds contain ice crystals as well as water droplets. As the air cools, the ice crystals grow, until they get so big that they fall to the ground. If the air is less than 0°C all the way from the cloud to the ground, we get snow.

Sleet forms when raindrops partly freeze as they fall to the ground. Hail forms in storm clouds, when a piece of dust gets covered in layers of ice. The hailstone may grow by being blown back up into the cloud and covered in more ice. This can happen again and again, until sometimes the hailstones grow as big as golf balls!

Find Out More

- Climate
- Clouds
- Water
- Water cycle
- Weather

▶ The monsoon rains in India. Although the monsoon causes flooding that is sometimes disastrous, the people living in monsoon regions rely on the rains. The monsoon rains water their crops, and the floods add important materials and minerals to the soil.

Rainbows *see* Colour, Spectrum • **Rainforests** *see* Forests • **RAM** (Random-Access Memory) *see* Computers

Reactions

Chemistry doesn't just happen in scientific laboratories. Chemical reactions are going on all around you. For example, rusting, burning, cooking and breathing all involve chemical reactions.

A chemical reaction is a process in which a substance is changed chemically when it interacts with another substance. In the course of the reaction, chemical bonds between the atoms are made or broken. The substances you start with at the beginning of the reaction are called the reactants. The results of a reaction are new substances, the products. You can reverse some kinds of chemical reaction, but not others.

▶ Firework displays involve very fast, explosive chemical reactions. Different substances added to the gunpowder make the colours. Copper compounds, for example, give blue colours, while sodium compounds give yellow.

Reactions all around us

When iron rusts, it is slowly reacting with oxygen in the air. The product is iron oxide (rust). Iron oxide is a reddish, crumbly solid – very different from either iron (a strong grey metal) or oxygen (an invisible gas).

Lots of different reactions go on in cooking. When you fry or boil an egg, for example, the clear sludgy stuff round the yolk turns firm and white. A chemical reaction has taken place.

A whole series of complicated chemical reactions take place after we breathe in oxygen. One of the products is carbon dioxide gas, which we breathe out. There are many other reactions going on all the time inside us, involving thousands of different biological chemicals.

Chemical reactions are very important in many industries. They are used to make a huge range of products, from fertilizers and explosives to cleaning fluids and dyes. Some industries use living things as

◀ The iron in the metal bodies of old cars slowly reacts with oxygen in the air to make iron oxide – better known as rust.

miniature chemical factories. For example, yeast (a kind of microscopic fungus) helps to make bread and beer. Scientists now use bacteria to help make some medicines and even plastics.

Using and giving out energy

All chemical reactions use or give out energy – usually in the form of heat. Reactions that produce more energy than they take in include combustion (burning) reactions. When a substance burns, it is actually reacting with oxygen and giving off heat.

Reactions that take in more energy than they give out include the process used by plants to make their own food. Plants use the energy from sunlight to change carbon dioxide and water into glucose (a type of sugar) and oxygen.

The energy involved in reactions isn't always in the form of heat. Reactions where there are flames also give off energy in the form of light. Even more violent reactions, such as explosions, give off sound energy as well. Similarly, some reactions may be started by energy from electricity, light or sound – even by a blow from a hammer.

▲ The light from these fireflies is produced by a chemical reaction in the bodies of the insects.

Find Out More

- Chemical analysis
- Chemicals
- Elements and compounds
- Explosives
- Fire

Some reactions work better if a substance called a catalyst is present. A catalyst helps the reaction to take place, but the catalyst itself does not change.

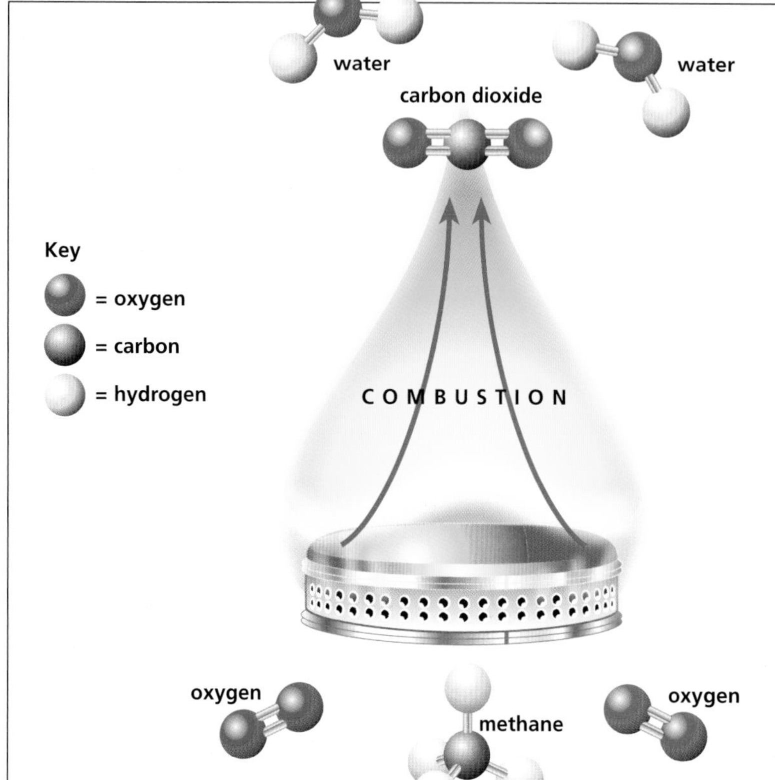

ANATOMY OF A REACTION

When methane burns on the top of a gas cooker, it is reacting with oxygen in the air to form carbon dioxide and water vapour. This chemical reaction can be written as an equation. The equation is a shorthand description of what happens in the reaction.

$$CH_4 + 2O_2 = CO_2 + 2H_2O$$

The chemical symbols indicate the different substances involved in the reaction. Methane is made up of carbon atoms each linked to four hydrogen atoms (CH_4). Carbon dioxide is a carbon atom linked to two oxygen atoms (CO_2). Water is made up of oxygen atoms joined to two hydrogen atoms (H_2O), and oxygen gas is pairs of oxygen atoms (O_2). Burning is one example of a very common type of chemical reaction involving oxidation. Rust formation is another example: iron reacts with oxygen in the air to form rust. And the process by which the body breaks down food to get energy is a whole series of oxidation reactions.

Recycling

Next time you drink a can of cola or fizzy lemonade, spare a thought for the can. It is made of aluminium, and the metal has probably been used before. It might once have been cooking foil, milk-bottle tops, or even part of an aircraft wing.

Aluminium is one of the materials that are recycled, or used again. Glass, paper and plastics are also widely recycled.

Reasons for recycling

There are good reasons for recycling. Recycling reduces the huge amount of waste we produce, which has become one of the world's biggest problems.

Another reason for recycling is to save energy – and money. For example, it takes large amounts of electricity to extract aluminium from its raw material, bauxite. Re-melting aluminium waste uses much less energy.

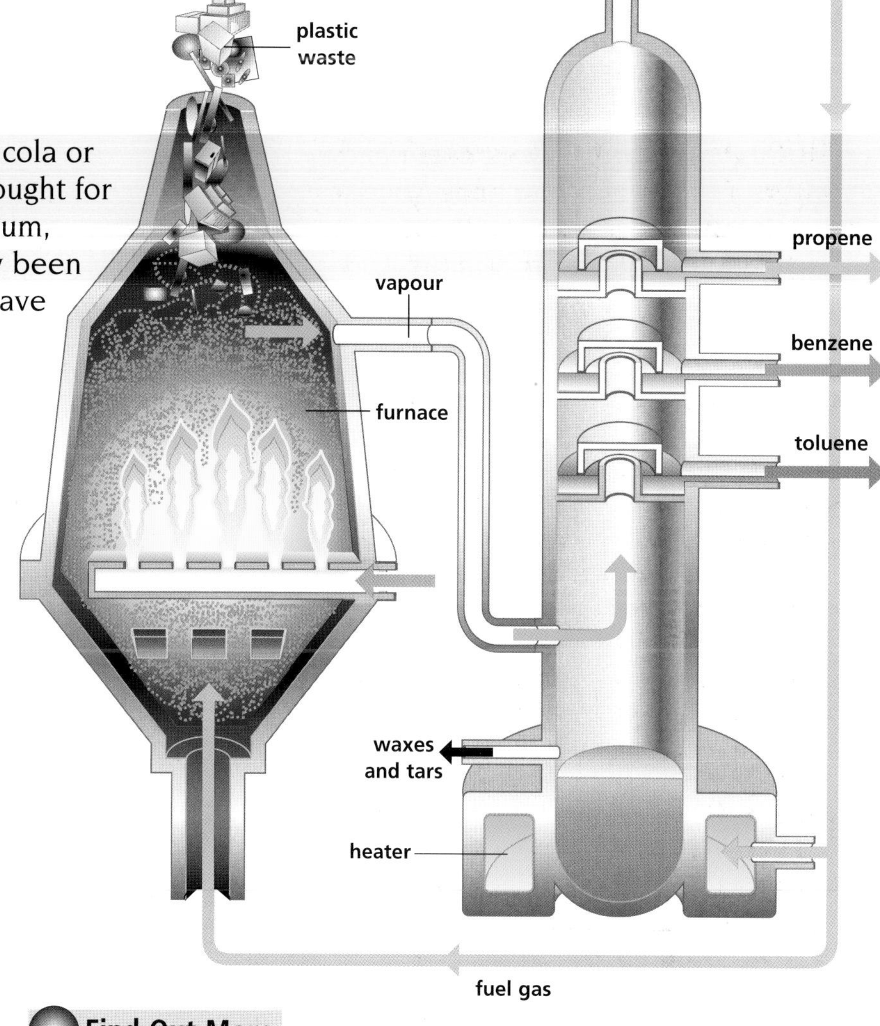

▲ At present, recycling plastic is difficult and expensive. Plastics waste is heated in the absence of air until the materials turn to vapour. The vapour goes to a distillation tower, where the various substances in the vapour are separated out.

Gone for ever

Recycling also saves Earth's resources. Paper, for example, is made from wood pulp, which comes from trees. Recycling paper means cutting down fewer trees.

Trees are a renewable resource – we can keep growing them. But with most raw materials, once we have used them up they will be gone for ever. Oil, for example, will almost certainly run out later this century. This is why we need to recycle plastics, which are made from oil.

Find Out More
- Oil products
- Paper
- Plastics
- Resources
- Waste disposal

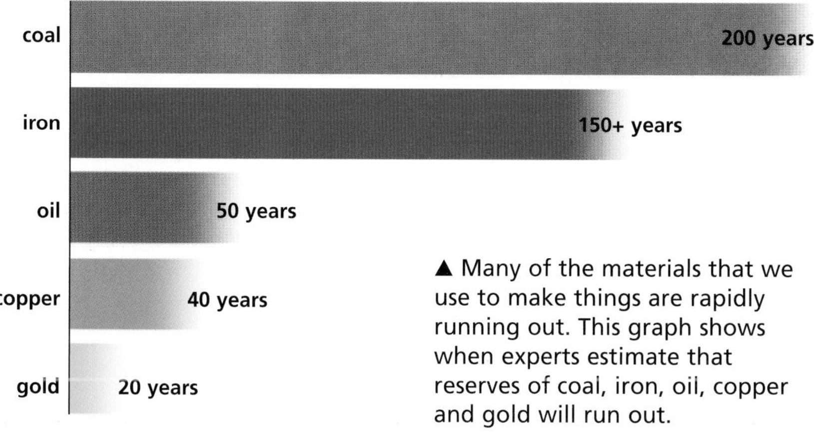

▲ Many of the materials that we use to make things are rapidly running out. This graph shows when experts estimate that reserves of coal, iron, oil, copper and gold will run out.

Rotting away

Nature is very good at recycling many materials. Worms, insects, fungi and bacteria can convert some waste into chemicals that enrich the ground and help new growth. Metals, glass and most plastics cannot be broken down in this way. However, some plastics that do decompose are now being developed.

Red dwarfs and giants *see* Stars • **Reflection, refraction** *see* Light • **Reflexes** *see* Brain and nerves

Refrigeration

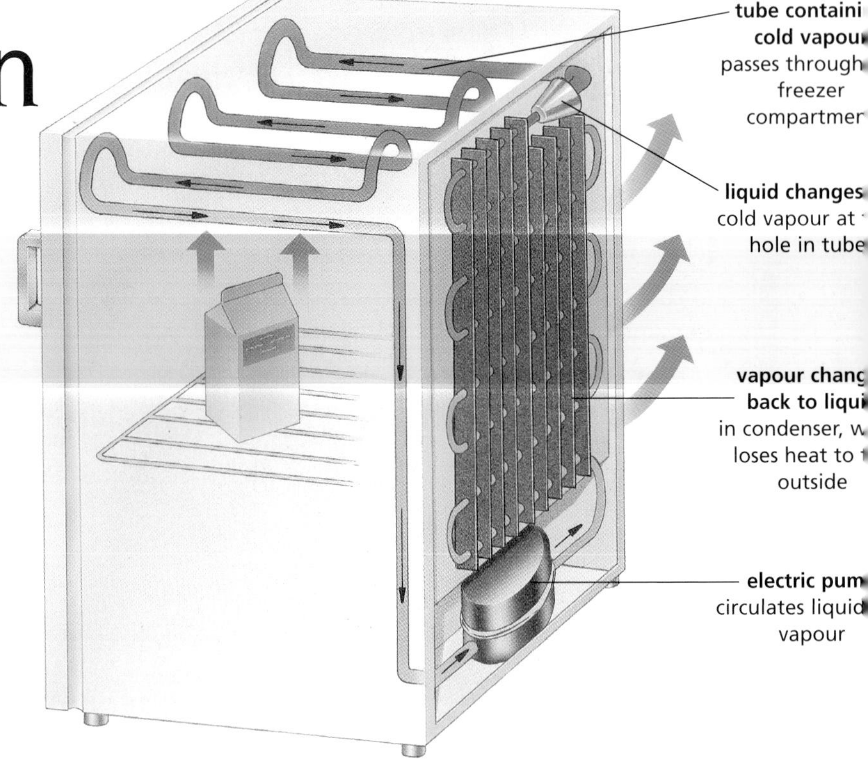

▲ A refrigerator takes heat from inside the freezer compartment, and transfers it to the warm condenser outside. Cold air descends from the freezer compartment to cool the whole interior.

Wet your finger and blow on it. Your finger gets cold before it dries. Refrigerators work in a similar way to keep food and drinks cool.

Blowing air over a wet finger makes the water quickly evaporate or dry up. Water loses heat as it evaporates. It takes this heat from your finger, which gets colder.

Refrigerators and freezers use evaporation to remove heat from food and drinks. A refrigerator cools food and drinks to a temperature just above freezing. This keeps them fresh for a few days, because bacteria do not multiply so fast at low temperatures, so the food does not decay. In a freezer, food is frozen to a temperature of about –18°C, and this preserves it for a long time, because bacteria cannot multiply at all below freezing.

How a refrigerator works

Inside a refrigerator is a tube containing a liquid called a refrigerant. The liquid passes through a tiny hole inside the tube, which makes it evaporate and become a vapour. It gets very cold, and takes heat from inside the refrigerator so that the contents are cooled.

The tube, now containing cold vapour, goes to the rear of the refrigerator. The refrigerant changes back into a liquid, which makes it gain heat. The heat taken from the food warms the tube, which is why the back of the refrigerator is warm. Then the liquid refrigerant returns to the inside to evaporate and cool again.

Freezers and air conditioning units work in the same way as refrigerators.

Find Out More

- Heat
- Matter
- Temperature

▼ The cold tubes of a refrigeration system pass through the base of an ice rink to keep the ice frozen.

Cryogenics is the study of very low temperatures. Some materials become superconductors when extremely cold. They lose all electrical resistance and can conduct very strong electrical currents.

Relativity

If you could travel in a super-fast spacecraft at 99 per cent of the speed of light to the star Sirius and back, $17\frac{1}{2}$ years would pass on Earth before you returned. But time would slow down on the journey. On your return, you would be only $2\frac{1}{2}$ years older!

The theory of relativity says that, to an outside observer, time is seen to slow down for moving things. They have to move very fast – near to the speed of light (300,000 kilometres a second) – for time to slow very much. No spacecraft can move this fast, but fast-moving particles show that relativity really is true.

Find Out More
- Energy
- Light
- Stars

The ultimate speed limit

Time is not the only quantity to change for fast-moving things. To an outside observer the mass of an object increases as it moves faster, and its length decreases.

The theory of relativity says that the mass of an object would become infinitely great if it moved at the speed of light. Infinite mass is impossible. Therefore, nothing can move at or faster than the speed of light.

Creating energy

Relativity also explains that mass changes into energy. This means that a material can be destroyed and turn into energy, such as heat and light. It explains how the Sun shines. It produces immense heat because gas at its centre is changing into huge amounts of energy.

Nuclear reactors in nuclear power stations work in this way too. They convert a small amount of nuclear fuel into a huge amount of heat energy. The heat is then used to generate electricity.

GREAT IDEAS

Albert Einstein (1879–1955), who was born in Germany and also lived in the United States, explained relativity. He published the first part of his theory, special relativity, in 1905. This shows how time slows for moving things and how mass changes into energy. The second part, general relativity, followed in 1915. It says that matter, such as stars, makes space curve, causing light rays to bend. It explains how black holes exist in space.

▼ Einstein worked out his theory of relativity after it had been found that the speed of light is always the same, no matter how fast the person measuring it is moving. If the train driver and the person on the ground both measured the speed of the light coming from the signal, they would get the same result, even though the train is rushing towards the light.

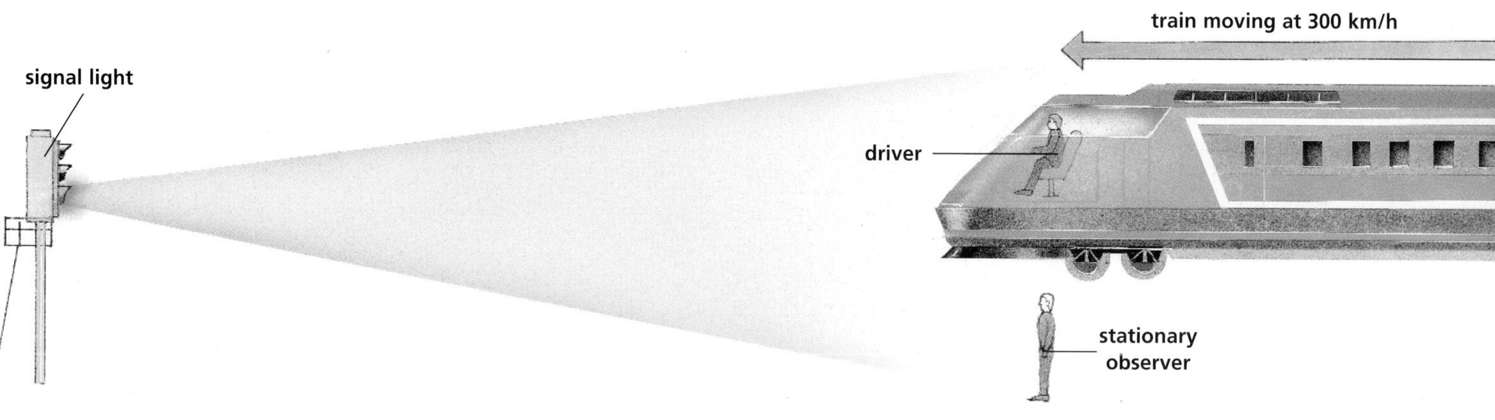

Renewable resources

In a tiny desert village in Rajasthan, India, an ordinary-looking lamp post shows how energy use is changing. This village has no electricity supply, but the lamp stores the Sun's energy by day to light the village at night. In the future, all people will need everlasting sources of energy like this.

We need energy sources to power all our machines and for cooking and heating in our homes. The Sun's energy, or solar energy, is one of several renewable energy sources that produce energy all the time.

At present we mainly use fuels to produce energy. Once burned, fuels are finished – they are not renewable. Our sources of fuel will run out in the future, and people will then depend on renewable energy.

Energy crisis

The world's known reserves of oil and gas are likely to run out by 2050. Today's nuclear power stations may have closed by then. Few new nuclear power stations are being built, as many people consider them too dangerous, although scientists hope that power from nuclear fusion will soon be a reality. Coal will remain the only available fuel, and it could be used to make other fuels such as petrol. Known coal reserves will last for hundreds of years.

Using more renewable energy will cut back on fuel and make reserves last longer. Unlike fuels, renewable energy does not cause pollution and global warming, and it will reduce this damage too.

▼ This experimental car is powered by the Sun. It is covered with solar cells that use sunlight to generate electricity and power the car's electric motor. Solar cells are likely to become an important source of energy in the future.

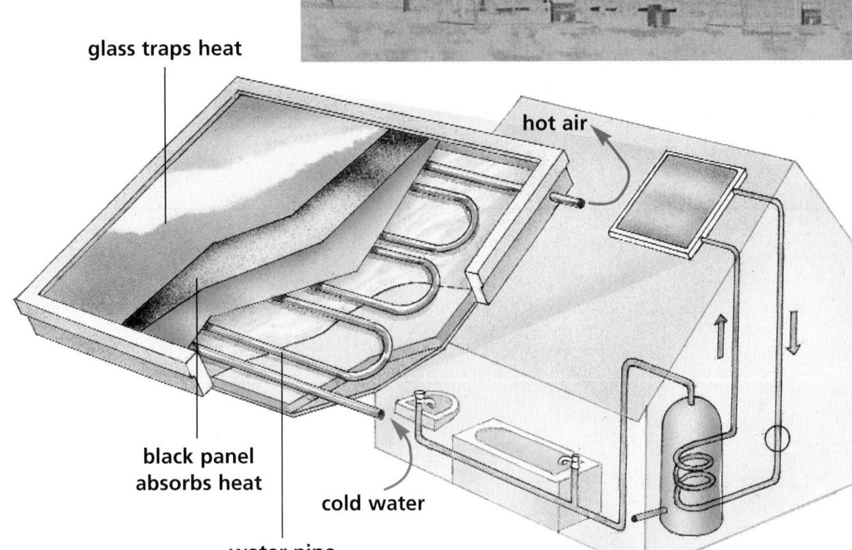

▲ Inside a solar heating panel is a layer of black material, which gets hot when the Sun shines on it. The material heats water flowing through a pipe in the panel. The hot water goes to heat the house or supply hot water to taps. Using solar heating cuts electricity or fuel costs.

Everlasting energy

There are five main kinds of renewable resources. Hydroelectric power stations,

◀ This wind farm has rows of giant turbines. The wind spins the blades of each rotor, which drives an electricity generator at its hub. The photo has been 'cross-processed' to show the structure of the turbines more clearly.

Find Out More

- Energy
- Engines and turbines
- Fuels
- Global warming
- Water power

which generate electricity from flowing water, produce the most energy.

Solar power taps the Sun's energy in two ways. Solar panels, often on roofs of houses, face the Sun and absorb solar rays of heat and light. Some panels tap the Sun's heat to warm a house or provide hot water. Photovoltaic panels or solar cells turn the Sun's rays into electricity, which may be stored in a battery for use later.

Geothermal power taps the energy inside the Earth. In some places, underground rocks are very hot. Water is heated by piping it through the hot rocks. In Iceland, most homes are heated in this way.

Wind turbines tap the energy of moving air. The wind turns the blades of the turbine, which drive an electricity generator. Wind turbines line high ridges or coasts in windy regions. Wind power is being used in many countries, particularly Germany, India, Denmark and Spain.

Wave machines of various kinds tap the energy of water as it rises and falls in waves and convert the energy into electricity. This renewable resource is still undergoing development.

▼ Geothermal power stations may be built where hot rocks lie close to the surface, for example in volcanic regions. Hot water in the rocks is brought to the surface through a bore hole. There the hot steam drives steam turbines that power electricity generators.

electricity generator
steam turbine
steam separator
steam cools to water
hot water rises through bore hole
cooling tower
cold water returned to ground

More to come

Renewable resources do not produce much energy and are unlikely ever to meet all our energy needs. The International Energy Agency has forecast that by 2010, 3 per cent of all our energy will come from hydroelectric power and only 1 per cent from other renewable resources. Coal, oil and gas will provide 90 per cent of our energy.

One reason for this is that generating electricity by solar power is costly. But as the fuels needed to produce electricity become rarer, they will also be more expensive. Then the use of solar power should increase.

Reproduction *see* Human reproduction, Sex and reproduction

Reptiles

A cobra rears up and spreads its hood wide. It draws its coils tightly together, ready to lunge forward and sink its poisonous fangs into an enemy or its prey.

▲ A chameleon shoots out its tongue with lightning speed to catch an insect. The sticky tip of its tongue traps the insect.

Snakes are an unusual group of reptiles with no legs, eyelids or external ears. They are closely related to lizards, which usually have four legs and long tails. Less than a quarter of all snakes use poison (venom) for attack and defence. Other snakes kill by squeezing and suffocating animals tightly in their strong coils.

▲ Turtles may lay up to 150 eggs in a hole they dig on a sandy beach.

Reptile groups

The other main reptile groups, besides snakes and lizards, are turtles and tortoises, and crocodiles and alligators. There were many other reptile groups in the past, including the dinosaurs.

Reptiles have a scaly skin, which stops their bodies from drying out. Unlike amphibians, they can live in dry places. Reptiles are most common in warm places, because their bodies rely on their surroundings for warmth.

Waterproof eggs

One of the most important differences between amphibians and reptiles is that reptiles lay their eggs on land, while amphibians lay their eggs in the water. Even reptiles that live in watery places, such as crocodiles and turtles, lay their eggs on land. Reptile eggs are sealed with a special membrane, the amnion, that stops them drying out. Most reptile eggs have soft, leathery shells, but tortoises, crocodiles and geckos lay eggs with hard shells.

The basilisk lizard can walk – or rather run – on water to escape predators. It relies on its speed, wide feet and fringed toes to stop it sinking below the surface.

Find Out More

- Animals
- Classification
- Life
- Sex and reproduction

▼ A crocodile opens its powerful jaws ready to clamp them around the throat of a wildebeest. A crocodile's teeth are brilliant for gripping prey but no good for chewing. So a crocodile swallows its food whole.

Resistance *see* Circuits

Resources

Every hour of every day oilfields around the world pump some 500 million litres of crude oil, or petroleum, out of the ground. Oil is one of the most valuable resources, or substances we need to produce the materials we use in our everyday lives.

Oil is valuable for two reasons. One, it can be made into fuels, such as petrol. In fact, it is one of our main energy resources, along with natural gas and coal. Two, oil can be converted into useful chemicals. From these chemicals, many different products can be made, such as plastics, paints and pesticides.

Minerals are very important resources too. They are the substances that make up the rocks in the Earth's crust. In some places, there are concentrations, or deposits, of useful minerals, which can be obtained by mining.

The vital ores

By far the most valuable of these deposits are materials called ores. These are the minerals that we can process into metals. Our modern civilization could not exist without metals. They enable us to build the many machines used in industry, transport and in our homes.

▶ Natural deposits of sulphur are often found around volcanic vents (openings). Sulphur is used to make many things, including gunpowder, insecticides and fertilizers.

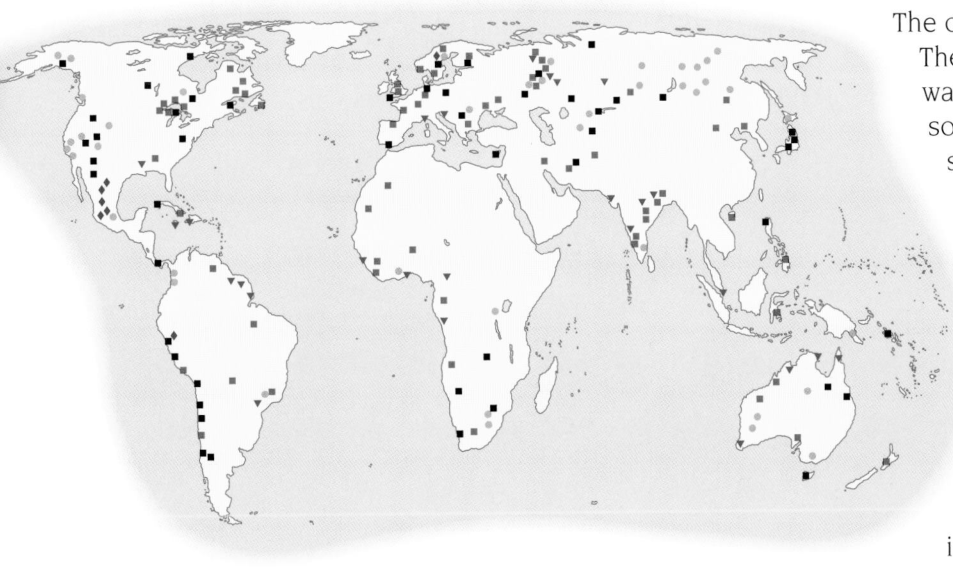

▼ This map shows where major deposits of mineral ores are found around the world. Some ores, such as iron, are found widely. Others, such as aluminium, are found only in a few places.

Key
- ▾ aluminium
- ▪ copper
- ● gold
- ▪ iron
- ♦ silver

Other useful resources

Many other minerals and mineral mixtures are useful for industry. Limestone is used to make cement and in iron-making furnaces. The sand on the seashore is one of the main ingredients of glass. Clays are used to make bricks and pottery.

Many minerals can form crystals, which have regular shapes and flat surfaces. Some crystals are very beautiful and provide us with sparkling gems – diamonds, sapphires, rubies and emeralds are the most prized.

Sea sources

The oceans are another valuable resource. They are full of minerals, dissolved in the water. The main one is common salt, or sodium chloride. This is extracted from sea water on a large scale.

Sea water also contains magnesium salts. Most of the world's magnesium is extracted from sea water by a process known as electrolysis, which involves passing electricity through it.

Up in the air

Even the air we breathe is a useful source of chemicals for industry. Air is a mixture of many gases, the chief

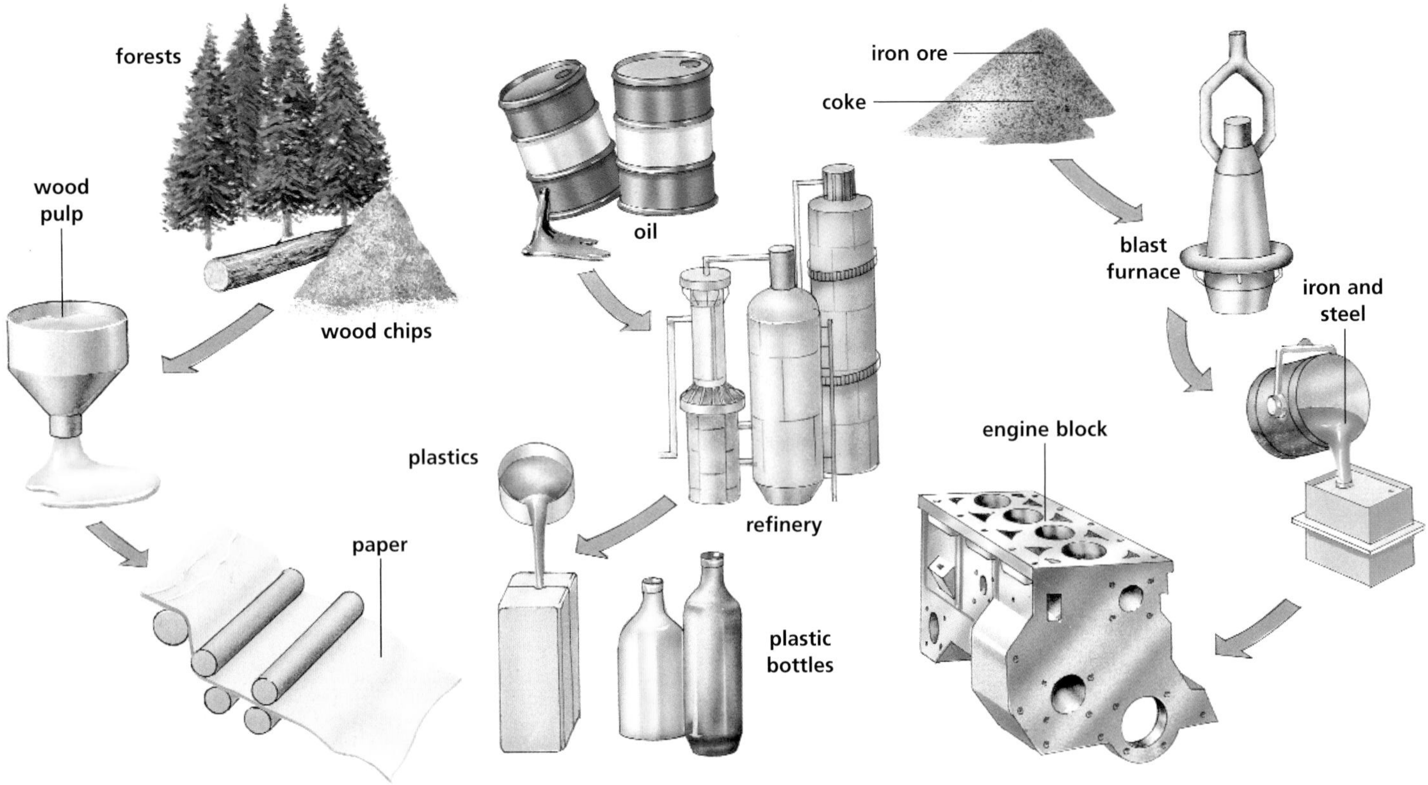

▲ Many of the products that we use every day have been made using natural resources.

ones being nitrogen and oxygen. Both these gases are widely used in industry. Nitrogen, for example, is used to make fertilizers,while liquid oxygen is used as a propellant in rockets.

The air is also the main source of the noble, or inert, gases. The most common of these gases, argon, is used to fill electric light bulbs. Because argon is inert, or unreactive, it helps to prevent the bulb's white-hot wire filament from burning up.

Living resources

Living things can also be an important resource. Forests provide us with wood. Farms and plantations give us useful crops such as rubber and cotton. Other crops, such as rape, sunflowers and flax, are grown for the oil contained in their seeds.

Properly managed, forests and farms can continue to produce wood and crops year after year. They are known as renewable resources. Oil, coal, gas and mineral deposits are not renewable. They took hundreds of millions of years to form, and once they have been used up, they will be gone for ever. This is why it is vitally important that we do our best to look after these precious resources.

Find Out More

- Ceramics
- Crystals
- Metals and non-metals
- Minerals
- Oil and gas
- Recycling
- Wood and timber

▼ Rainforests are rich in natural resources, including wood. By means of a process called photosynthesis, they also supply most of the world's oxygen.

Rivers and lakes

In a remote region of southern Siberia lies the deepest lake on Earth, Lake Baykal. Baykal is 630 kilometres long and over 1500 metres deep. It holds more fresh water than any other lake or river on Earth.

The other main sources of Earth's fresh water are rain and snow, groundwater (water in the rocks and underground), and rivers and streams.

Rivers and streams

When rain falls on land, it runs over the ground or through the soil and gathers with other rainwater in low areas, where it forms streams. Small streams join to make larger streams, and then eventually come together to form rivers. The rivers run until they empty into the sea or a lake.

There are many large rivers on Earth, and endless numbers of smaller rivers (tributaries) that feed them. Even in deserts there are dry stream-beds (called wadis or arroyos) that drain water off the desert when it rains.

Changing courses

Rivers are always changing. They not only change themselves, but also shape the land around them. They scour out an ever-deeper channel in some places, making valleys, and deposit (drop) mud, sand and gravel in others. The river channel can move back and forth across a valley, becoming more winding or straightening out. If there is a lot of rain upstream, the river will cut a wider channel or flood the banks. Once in a while, usually during a flood, part of a river will jump over to a completely new course. How fast a river changes depends on how much water is flowing, how fast it is flowing, and what kind of rock it is flowing over.

▲ A satellite image of the Mississippi River in the USA. It is a meandering river, which changes its course as it erodes its banks on one side, and deposits mud on the other. You can see signs of old river channels in the fields on either side of its current course.

Lakes

If water gathers in a hollow and doesn't quickly evaporate, sink into the ground, or run off in a stream, a lake forms. The hollows in which lakes form can be made in different ways.

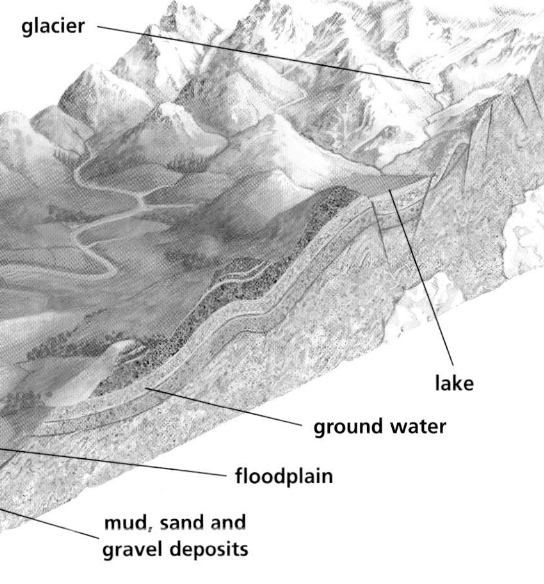

▶ Rivers can take different forms, and they vary along their course from the mountains to the sea. This illustration shows a meandering river.

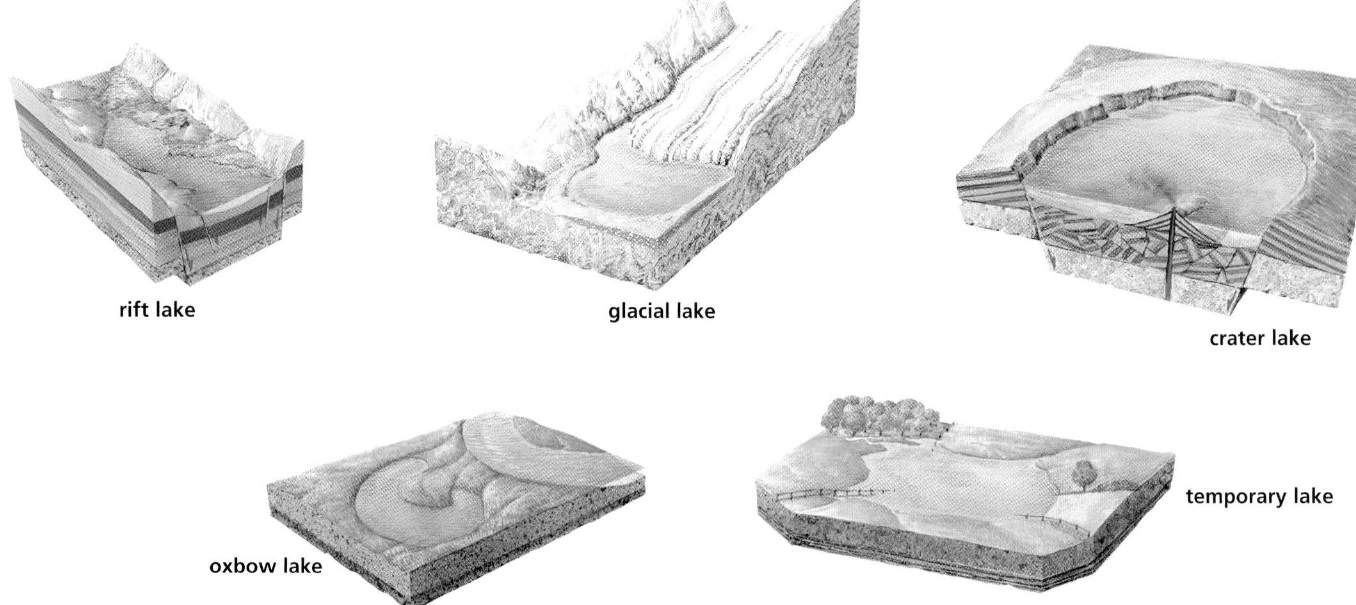

▲ Different types of lake. Lakes form in low areas where water collects.

Glacial lakes

The most common kind of lake is a glacial lake. Glacial lakes such as those in the Lake District of England or the Great Lakes area of North America fill depressions that glaciers scoured out of the land thousands of years ago.

Rift-valley lakes

Long, deep lakes such as Lake Baykal and Lake Tanganyika in eastern Africa fill rift valleys. Rift valleys form when a continent starts to rip apart. The continental crust (the surface layer of the Earth) stretches and breaks. Then blocks of the crust drop down to form a depression.

Crater lakes

Crater Lake in Oregon, USA, fills a volcanic caldera. When volcanoes erupt, lava erupts out of the ground, leaving an empty chamber below. The land drops down to fill the chasm, forming a large crater called a caldera, which can then fill with water. Small crater lakes can form at the tops of volcanoes that have blown their tops off. Lakes also fill impact craters, where meteorites have hit the Earth and exploded, creating a hole in the ground.

Temporary lakes

Just as there are temporary rivers on Earth, there are temporary lakes. The Lake Eyre Basin is a huge low area in the desert of Australia. Lake Eyre fills with water only once every 10 or 20 years when it rains hard for a few days. It then dries up within a few weeks. Lakes that come and go with the rains are known as playa lakes.

There are more than 70 lakes beneath the ice sheets in Antarctica. The largest one, Lake Vostok, is 230 km long and 50 km across. It lies 4 km beneath the ice.

Groundwater

There is about 70 times more water in the ground than in all the lakes, rivers and streams on Earth combined. Groundwater is water that seeps into the ground and then collects in the spaces between grains in rock such as sandstone. It flows through the rock, in some cases for millions of years, before coming back out of the ground as a spring. Even in the driest parts of the world, where there are no permanent rivers or lakes, there is groundwater.

Find Out More

- Coasts
- Continents and plates
- Erosion
- Ice caps and glaciers
- Water cycle

▶ Glacial lakes fill depressions (low areas) that were scoured out by glaciers that moved across the land during the last Ice Age.

RNA *see* Genetics

Roads

There is a road that starts in north-west Alaska and runs south through North America, into Central America and on into South America. It then heads east and finally ends in Brasília, the capital of Brazil. It is the Pan-American Highway, which stretches for an astonishing 24,140 kilometres.

Every year more than 50 million new vehicles – cars, vans, trucks and buses – flood on to the world's roads, adding to the hundreds of millions already there. Road systems are continually being improved. Old roads are widened and new ones built.

Under construction

Before people start to build a road they have to decide on a suitable route. This often needs to be agreed with local government, local people and environmental groups.

Once agreement is reached, the route can be cleared and levelled. The next step is to build the bridges, tunnels and junctions.

Most roads are paved with a mixture of crushed stone and tar, called tarmac or asphalt. The road has a rounded top surface, or camber, to allow rainwater to run off. Drains along the edge carry the water away.

Motorways

Motorways are a type of road specially designed to handle large volumes of high-speed traffic. They have no traffic lights, roundabouts or junctions – drivers can only stop on a motorway if their vehicle breaks down. Motorways are built as level and as straight as possible so that traffic does not have to slow down for corners or hills.

▲ Motorways are built so that other roads pass over or under them at cleverly designed intersections. Some of these intersections become very complex.

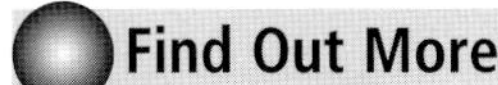

- Cars and trucks
- Construction
- Transport

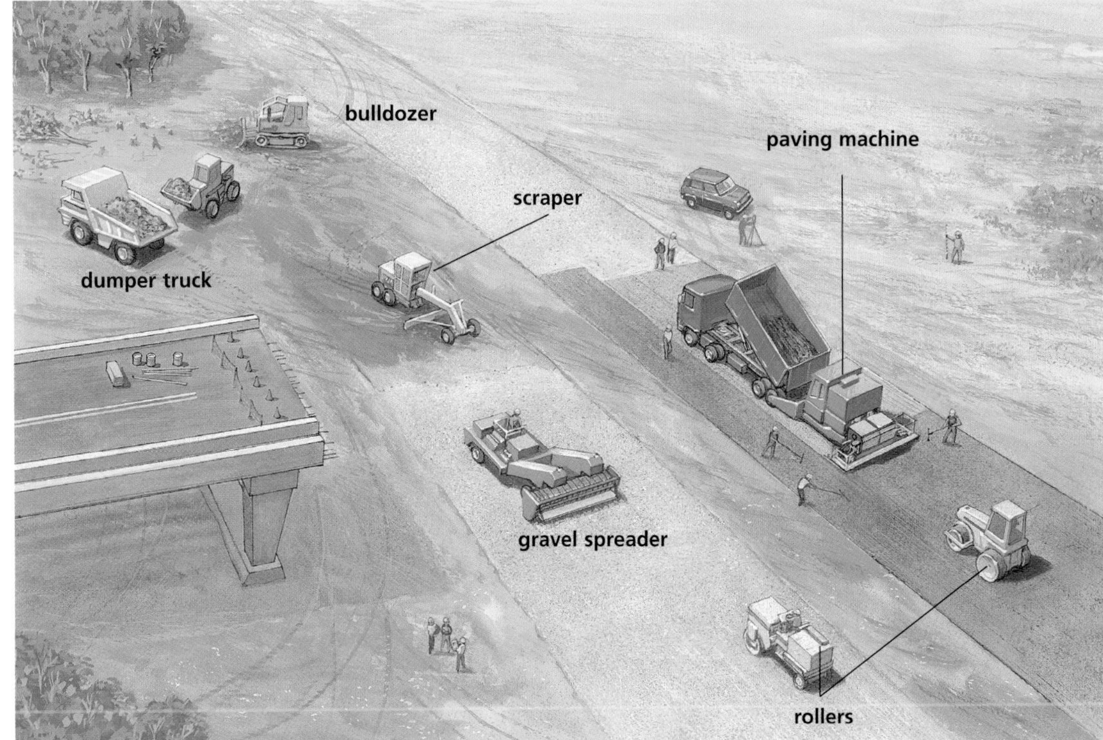

▶ Road-building uses many machines to prepare the ground and lay the surface. Bulldozers and scrapers clear the ground; dumper trucks remove soil and bring in crushed stone for the foundations and tarmac for the surface. Paving machines spread the tarmac, while rollers compact it and roll it flat.

Robots and AI

'Shape shifter' robots can design themselves – and even recycle themselves. A computer designs the robot's parts, which are then 'printed out' by a machine called a 3-D printer. When the robot has finished the task it was built for, it melts itself down, and the plastic is used for another robot.

A robot is an automatic machine that does jobs under the control of its computer brain. The great advantage of a robot is that it doesn't make mistakes or get tired, and it can work just about anywhere.

Robot workers

Robots are used to do jobs that are too dangerous or boring for people to do. In factories, robots carry out tasks that have to be done over and over again, 24 hours a day. Robots are also used for dangerous tasks like getting broken or worn-out parts from nuclear reactors, or finding and disarming bombs.

The basic parts of a robot are a controller (the robot's 'brain'), sensors (these tell the robot about the outside world) and effectors (its 'hands').

▼ The basic parts of a robot arm. Most robots will have pressure sensors – a sense of 'touch'. They might also have camera 'eyes', and microphone 'ears', or other non-human sensors like infrared vision. Most robots have an arm that can be fitted with several different effectors.

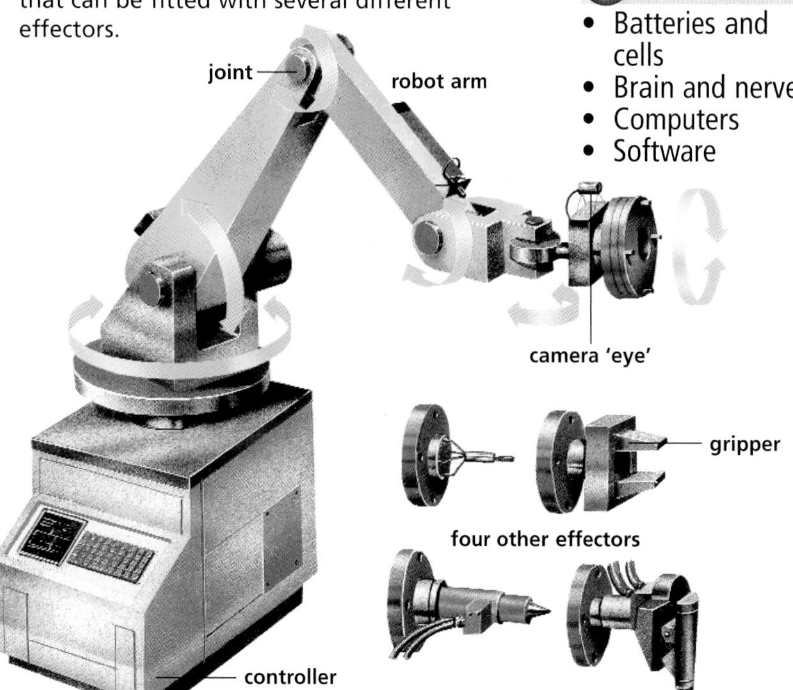

▼ One way artificial intelligence researchers test out their ideas is to build robotic football players. But robot footballers aren't going to take over from humans for a while yet. Most games are decided by the number of own goals each team scores!

Find Out More
- Batteries and cells
- Brain and nerves
- Computers
- Software

Smart and smarter

A robot making things in a factory can be 'trained' by a human operator. It learns by copying the movements the human makes. But robots of this type are limited to doing only a handful of tasks.

Artificial intelligence (AI) researchers are now trying to make robots more clever, so that they can do a wider range of jobs. A major aim is to build robots that can work out for themselves how to do things. Experimental robots have been made that can learn and 'evolve' new ways of doing tasks.

Soon, robots will be in our living rooms. A vacuum cleaner that can wander around a room on its own, sucking up dust and dirt, is being developed. But because trailing a power cord might trip people up, it is battery powered.

Rockets

The most exciting part of a firework display comes as rockets zoom up into the night sky and burst high above in cascades of colour. All spacecraft get to space and travel there in the same way. Only a rocket engine can carry them up and out into space.

▲ Firework rockets carry a cluster of stars that burn in bright colours. These ignite and burst out when the rocket uses up its solid fuel and is high in the air.

The rocket engines of a spacecraft, such as the space shuttle, work in the same way as a firework rocket. They both burn fuel called a propellant very quickly to produce huge amounts of hot gases. As these gases rush out from the exhaust of the engine or tail of the rocket, they exert a powerful force on the engine or rocket and drive it forwards or upwards.

Beyond the air

Most kinds of transport have engines that burn fuels, such as petrol, diesel fuel or paraffin. Fuels need a gas called oxygen to catch fire and burn. This oxygen comes from the air.

Rockets are different. They carry their own oxygen, and so can work beyond the atmosphere where there is no air.

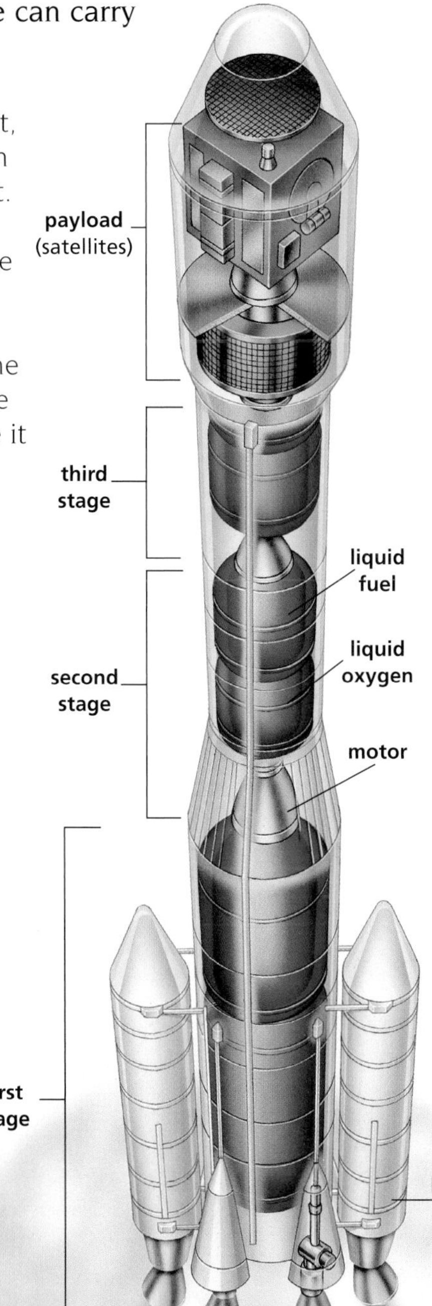

▶ The *Ariane* rocket is a huge rocket that launches a payload such as a satellite into space. It has three sections called stages that fire in turn. When its fuel is used up, each stage falls away and the next stage takes over. Only the payload and third stage reach space. Using stages saves fuel.

Rocket fuels

Firework rockets and many space rockets that launch spacecraft use fuel made of powder. In this solid fuel is a substance containing oxygen, which enables the fuel to burn. A solid-fuel rocket engine continues to burn until the fuel is used up.

In all spacecraft and many rocket launchers, two liquids are pumped to the engine, where they catch fire and burn. In most liquid-fuel engines, one liquid is liquid oxygen and the other is a liquid fuel such as liquid hydrogen.

Liquid-fuel rocket engines can run for an exact time, then shut down and start again later. This enables spacecraft to change orbit in space, and to return to Earth.

Find Out More

- Engines and turbines
- Fire
- Fuels
- Space shuttles
- Space travel

Rocks

▲ This pink granite is made of mineral crystals. These are pink feldspar, white feldspar, clear quartz and black mica.

Rocks are the Earth's history books. They tell us what a place was like millions of years ago. They show us what the weather was like, what animals and plants were alive, whether it was desert or swamp, land or sea, mountains or plains. Everything we know about the Earth's history comes from studying rocks.

A rock is a natural, solid piece of a planet, moon or asteroid. Most rocks are made of minerals, but some are made of dead plants and animals.

The three types of rock

Geologists group rocks into three categories: igneous, sedimentary and metamorphic. Each type forms in a different way.

▲ Granite is an igneous rock that forms deep underground when hot, liquid rocks cool and harden.

▲ Sandstone is a sedimentary rock made of small grains of sand that settled out of water or air.

Igneous rocks

Igneous rocks start out as hot liquid rock called *magma*. As the magma cools, mineral crystals begin to grow in it, and the liquid hardens. Sometimes magma turns solid underground. These rocks are called *plutonic*. Granite is a type of plutonic rock. Other times magma flows out on the surface before it turns solid. This kind of igneous rock is called *volcanic*. Basalt is the most common volcanic rock.

◀ Gneiss is a metamorphic rock. It began as a sedimentary rock, but after millions of years of being heated and squeezed, it turned into gneiss.

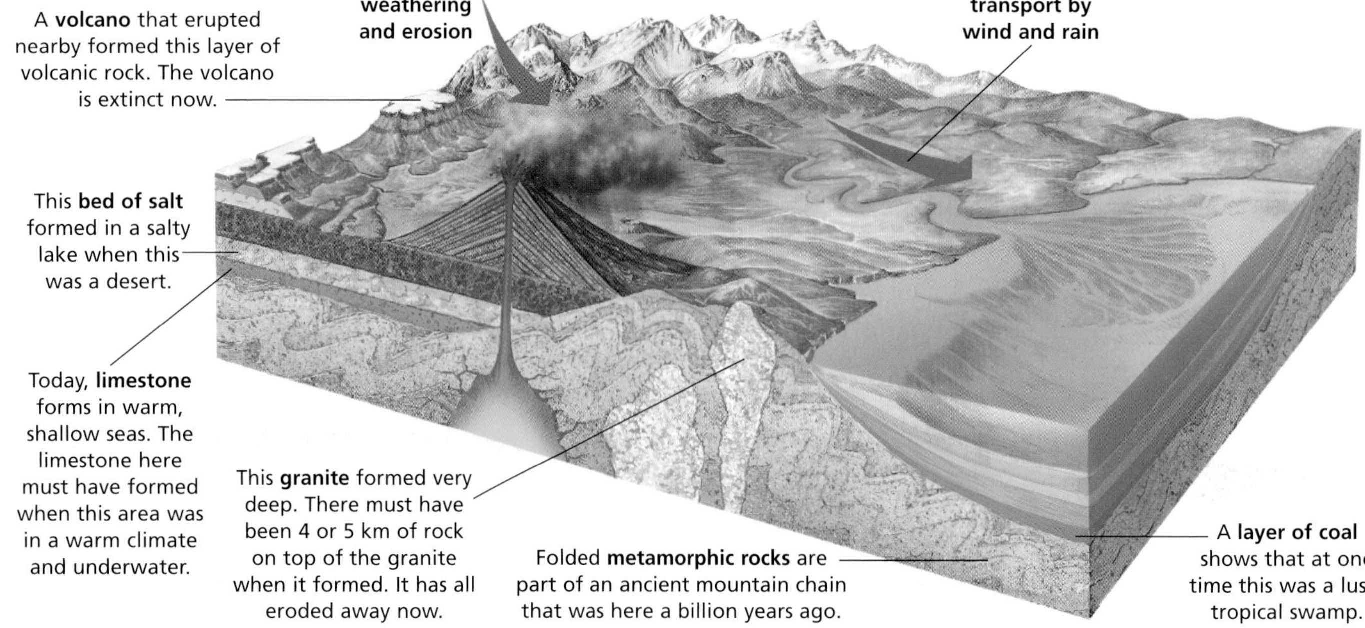

THE STORY OF A ROCK

Over millions of years rocks change or break down, and eventually become new rocks. This is called the *rock cycle*. Below is one example of a rock cycle.

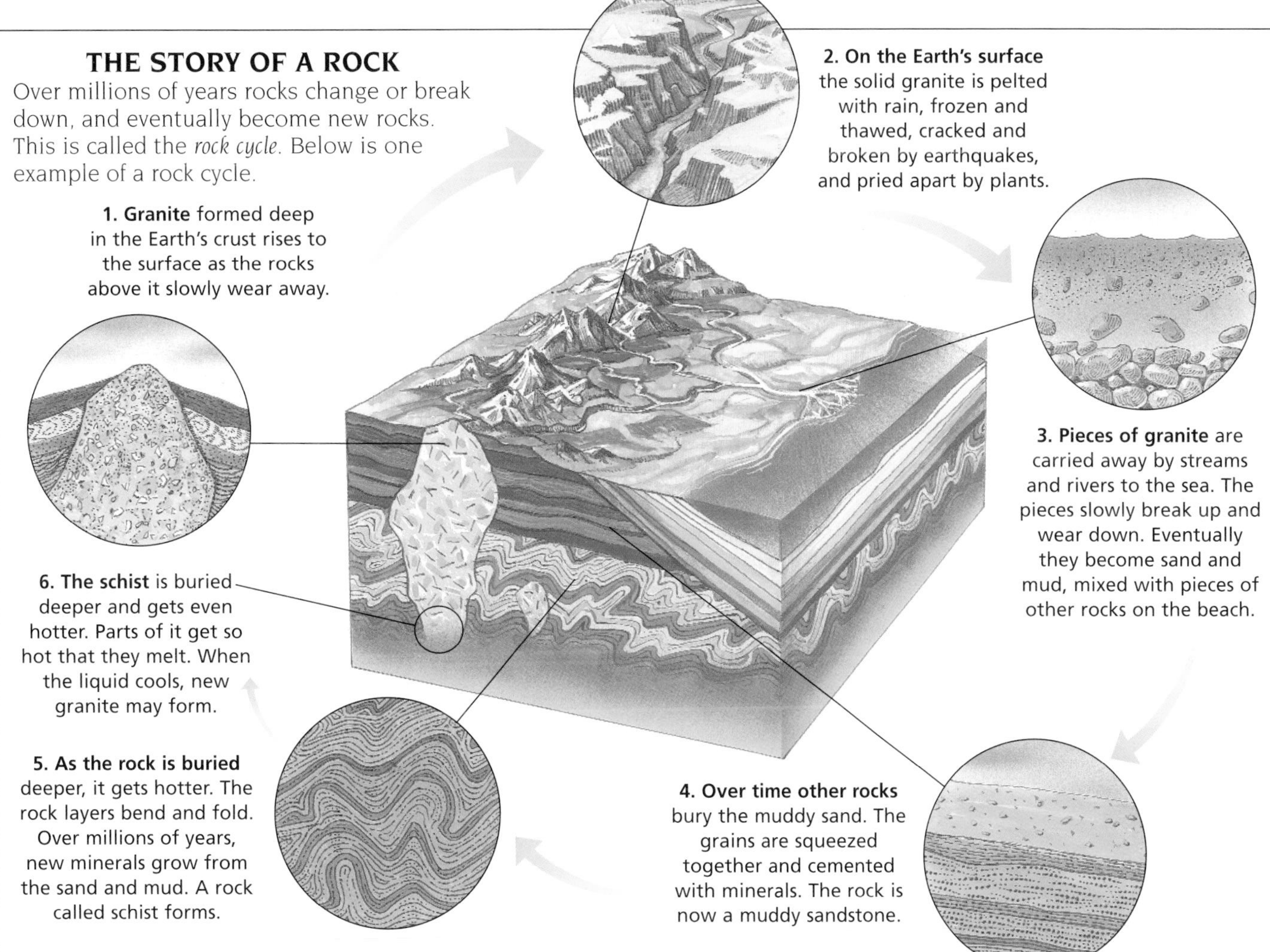

Sedimentary rocks

Loose pieces of rock such as pebbles, sand and mud are called sediments. Most sediments form when other rocks break down and erode (wear) away. Sediments are carried by rivers down to lakes or the sea, where they settle on the bottom. As more sediments settle on top of them, they are slowly squeezed together, eventually turning into sedimentary rocks. Sandstone is a sedimentary rock.

Some sedimentary rocks come from living things. Limestone is made of shells and skeletons of tiny sea creatures. Coal starts out as layers of dead swamp plants.

Metamorphic rocks

Metamorphic rocks are rocks that have been changed (*metamorphosed*) by heat and pressure. The heat and pressure can come in many ways. Heat from magma or hot igneous rocks can bake other rocks nearby. When rocks get buried, the weight of the rocks above squeezes them and the heat from inside the Earth cooks them. Rocks can also get squeezed when continents crash into each other.

Examples of metamorphic rocks include slate, which is metamorphosed shale, a sedimentary rock made from mud. Other examples include marble, which is metamorphosed limestone. Most metamorphic rocks take millions of years to form.

Find Out More

- Earth
- Geology
- Minerals
- Resources
- Volcanoes

◀ Though this rock was found on dry land, the ripple marks on it show that it formed in shallow water. Geologists can use rocks like these to work out what a place was like when the rock formed.

Rubber

The dare-devil girl dives off the high bridge and plunges towards the river far below. Down she goes until she is only a few feet above the water. But she doesn't plunge in because she is bungee-jumping. An elastic rope attached to her feet pulls her back up.

The elastic rope is made of rubber. Being elastic is only one of rubber's useful properties. It is also airtight and waterproof, and absorbs shock well. These properties make it suited to two of its main uses – for motor tyres and footwear.

Rubber can be natural or synthetic. Both natural and synthetic rubber are made up of long molecules, which are folded back on themselves rather like a spring. They unfold when the rubber stretches, then spring back when released.

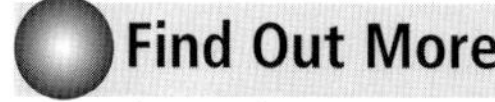

Find Out More

- Oil products
- Plastics
- Polymers

▲ Once the different parts of a tyre have been assembled, they are fused together, and the rubber is hardened, in a tyre press. Here, a tyre press releases a new tyre, still steaming, from its mould.

Making rubber

Natural rubber is prepared from the white milky sap, or latex, of rubber trees. Synthetic rubber is made from chemicals obtained from petroleum, or crude oil. These chemicals form long chains, or polymers, when they react together, producing a substance similar to natural latex.

Some latex is made into products such as rubber gloves, but most is processed further. One of the most important processes is called vulcanization. This involves adding sulphur and heating the rubber. This makes it harder and tougher.

▼ Making natural rubber, and its use in manufacturing car tyres.

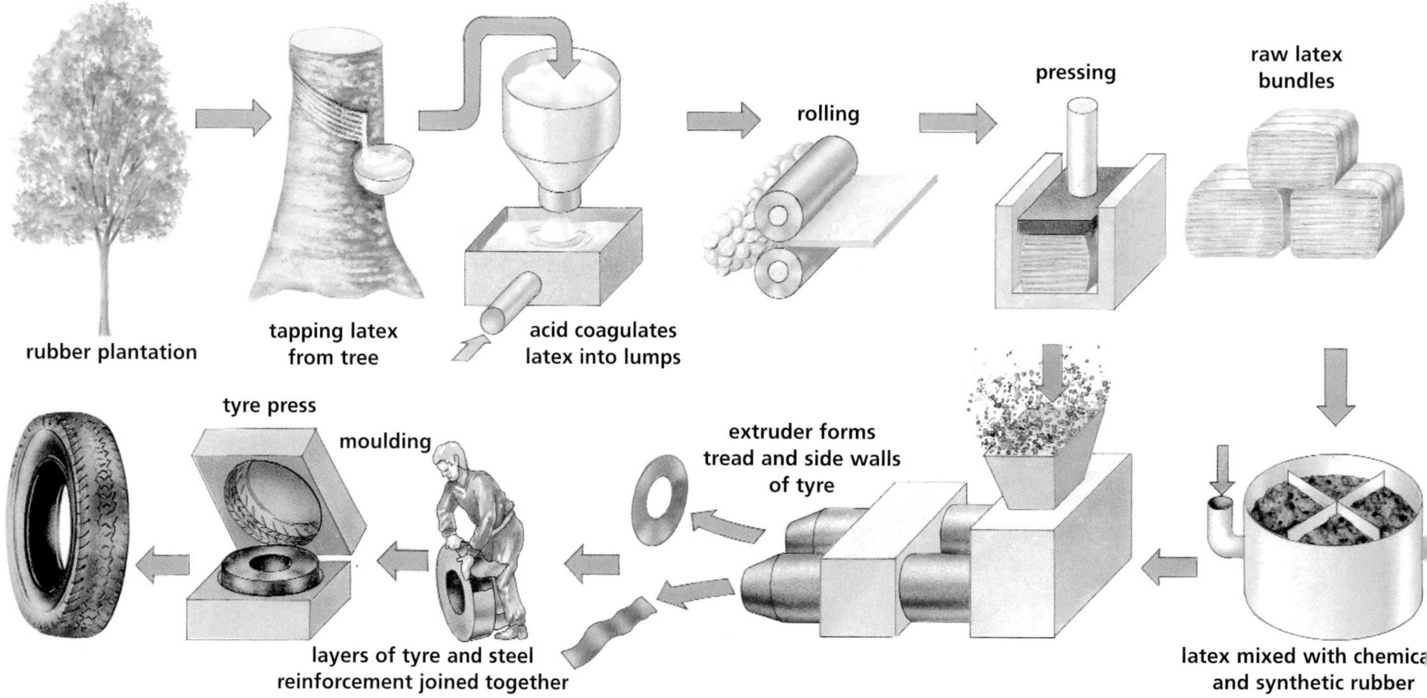

Rust *see* Reactions, chemical • **Rutherford, Ernest** *see* Atoms and molecules

Salts

Common salt – the white powdery stuff you sprinkle on your chips – is the most widely used mineral in the world. But common salt is just one of a large number of chemical substances called salts.

Most salts are crystalline solids that can dissolve in water. They generally melt only at high temperatures – common salt becomes a liquid at 801 °C.

Salts are made up of tiny, electrically charged atoms, or ions. Salts usually consist of a metal ion (this has a positive charge) and a non-metal ion (this is negatively charged). For example, common salt is sodium chloride – sodium ions (metal) and chloride ions (non-metal).

Find Out More
- Acids and alkalis
- Atoms and molecules
- Crystals
- Metals and non-metals
- Mixtures and solutions

Making salts

Salts are the result of mixing two other kinds of chemical, acids and alkalis. For example, if you mix hydrochloric acid and sodium hydroxide (also known as caustic soda, an alkali), you get sodium chloride and water.

Most common salt comes from deposits deep underground. Salt is also obtained from the sea in hot countries. Sea water is trapped in shallow pools, and the water evaporates leaving salt crystals.

▼ A crystal of common salt seen through a microscope.

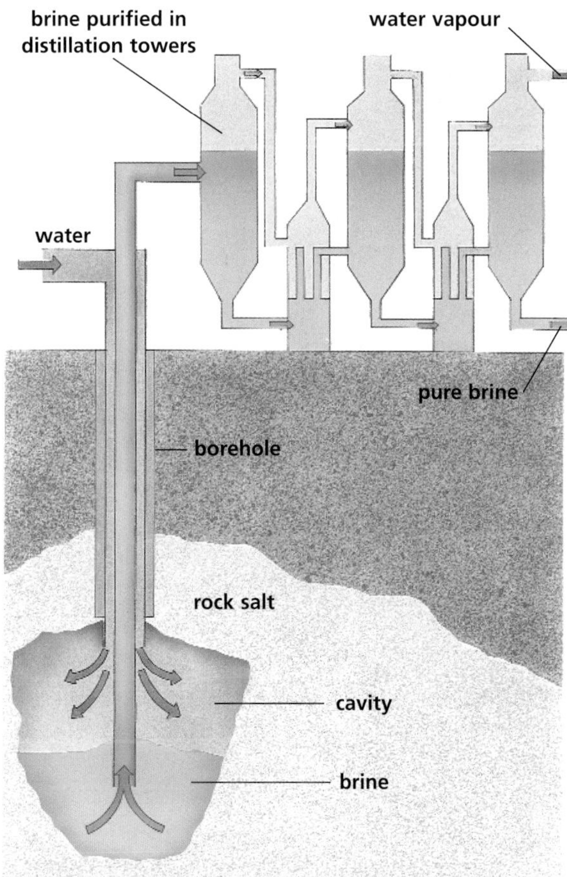

▲ Salt can be mined by a process called solution mining. A borehole is drilled into the rock salt and two pipes are inserted, one inside the other. Water is pumped in through the outer pipe, and dissolves the rock to make brine. The brine is pushed out of the ground through the inner pipe.

Uses of salts

Common salt has been used for thousands of years to preserve and flavour foods. It is used in the manufacture of dyes, paper, pottery, leather, medicines and chemicals. Other salts also have a huge range of uses. For example, copper sulphate is used in sprays to kill fungi attacking crops. Various salts containing silver are light-sensitive and are used to coat photographic film. Many other salts are used in medicine and in all kinds of industries.

Sandstone *see* Rocks

Satellites

Hundreds of kilometres above our heads, a swarm of tiny 'moons' travels silently in space. They are artificial moons, or satellites. They circle endlessly around the Earth in a constant path, or orbit.

▲ APSTAR is a modern communications satellite, used to send TV, radio and telephone signals around the world.

Up in space, satellites do many things to help us down on Earth. Communications satellites relay (pass on) all kinds of communications signals. These signals include TV programmes, telephone calls and e-mail messages. Weather satellites take pictures of clouds and measure conditions in the air.

Remote-sensing satellites take pictures of the Earth's surface in light of different colours. These pictures show up details that cannot be seen in ordinary photographs. Astronomy satellites carry telescopes into space, where they can see more clearly. Navigation satellites help ships to travel across the oceans and aircraft to find their way in the sky. They are even used by walkers in wild places.

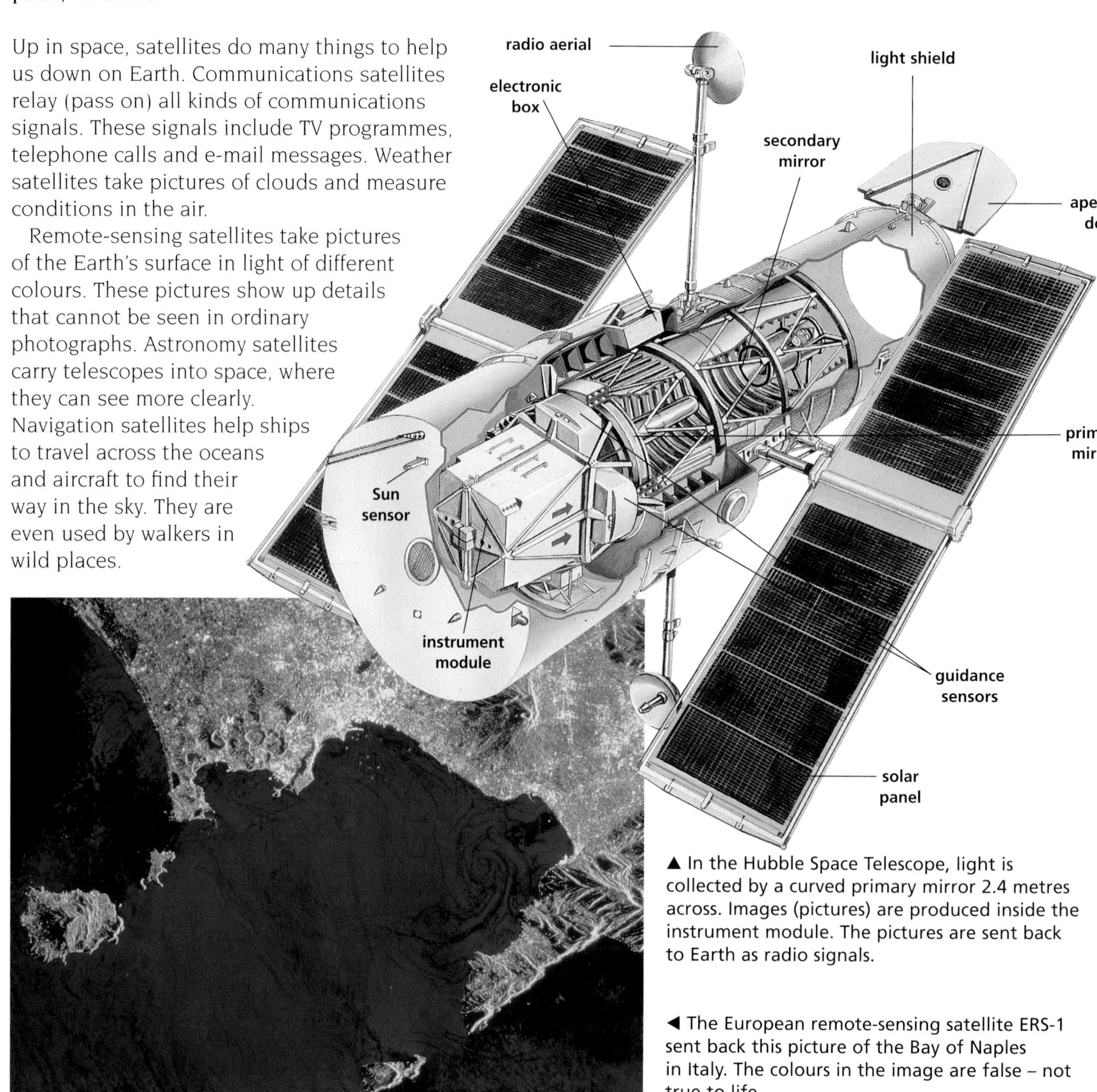

▲ In the Hubble Space Telescope, light is collected by a curved primary mirror 2.4 metres across. Images (pictures) are produced inside the instrument module. The pictures are sent back to Earth as radio signals.

◀ The European remote-sensing satellite ERS-1 sent back this picture of the Bay of Naples in Italy. The colours in the image are false – not true to life.

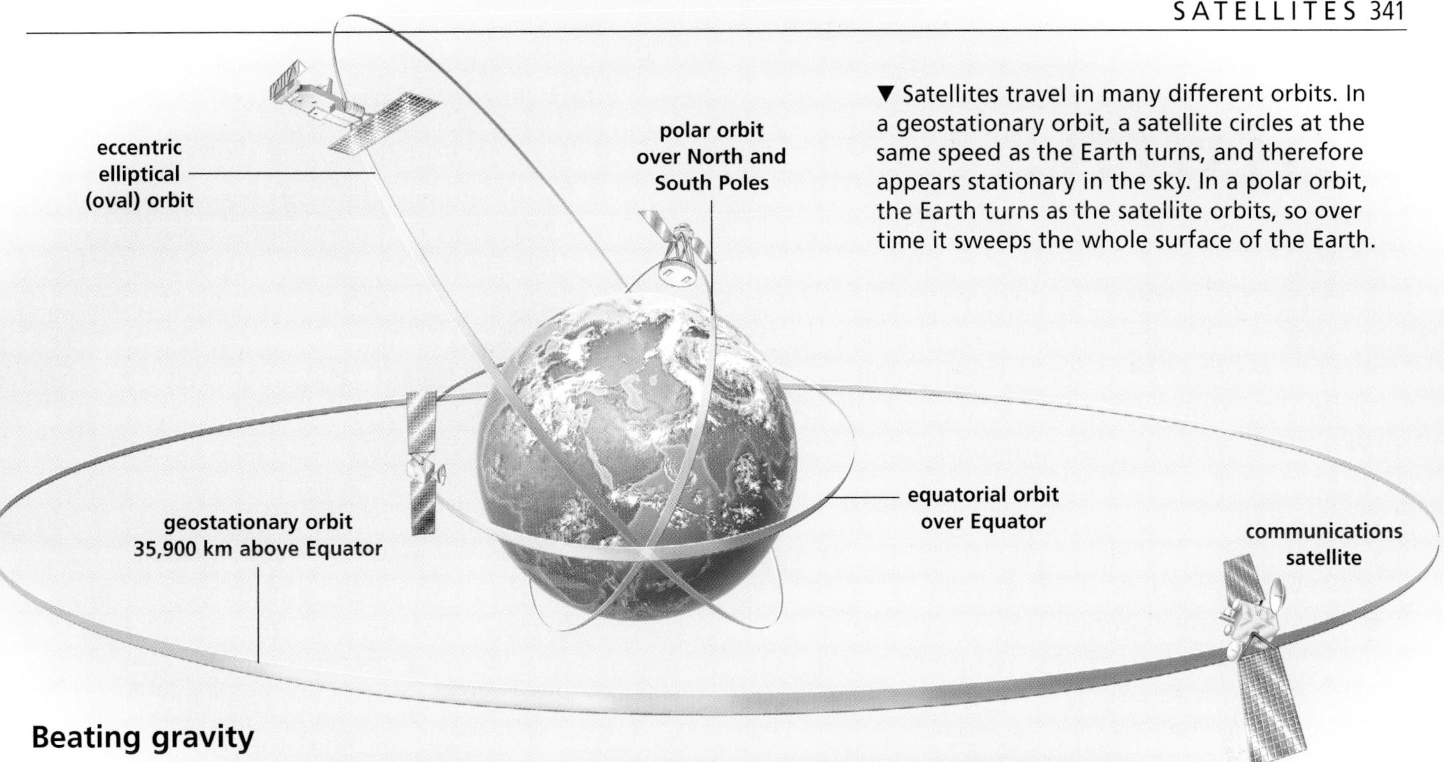

▼ Satellites travel in many different orbits. In a geostationary orbit, a satellite circles at the same speed as the Earth turns, and therefore appears stationary in the sky. In a polar orbit, the Earth turns as the satellite orbits, so over time it sweeps the whole surface of the Earth.

Beating gravity

To launch things into space, we must somehow overcome gravity, the powerful pull of the Earth. How do we do this? We can get a clue by throwing a ball. If we throw the ball gently parallel with the ground, it travels only a little way before it falls down under the pull of gravity. But the faster we throw it, the farther it travels before it falls back to the ground.

If we could throw the ball at a speed of 28,000 kilometres an hour, a strange thing would happen. It would fall at the same rate as the Earth curves. In other words, it would stay the same height above the Earth. It would become a satellite of the Earth.

Real satellites have to be launched from the Earth at this very high speed, which is called the orbital velocity. To reach such a speed, satellites have to be launched by powerful rockets. Rockets are the only engines that can work in space.

What satellites are like

Satellites are built from light but strong materials. They come in many shapes and sizes. For example, the scientific satellite *Lageos* is a sphere only about 60 centimetres across. However, the Hubble Space Telescope is more than 13 metres long and weighs 11 tonnes.

Satellites carry all kinds of equipment – instruments to measure different kinds of radiation, other instruments to measure magnetism, telescopes, cameras and a radio. The radio sends the information and pictures from all the other equipment back to a control centre, or ground station, back on Earth.

All the equipment on satellites works by electricity, usually produced by solar cells. These are batteries that work by sunlight. The panels you see on many satellites are made up of thousands of solar cells.

Find Out More

- Communications
- Gravity
- Orbits
- Rockets
- Space travel

◀ This dish aerial on the ground sends and receives radio signals to and from a communications satellite in orbit high above. Intelsat, the world's biggest communications satellite network, uses ground stations in over 100 countries to pass on communications around the world.

Saturn

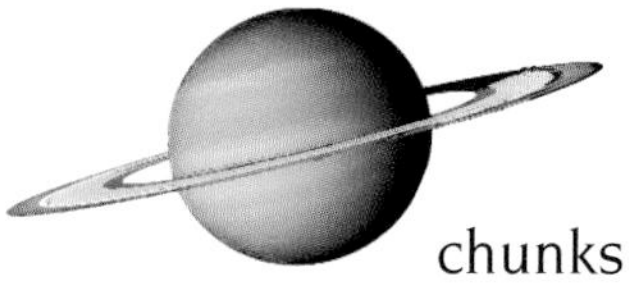

Saturn's rings are spectacular. Though solid-looking, they are swarms of icy chunks orbiting Saturn like countless miniature moons. Saturn's beautiful rings make it easy to forget that the planet itself, second largest in the Solar System, is magnificent.

Like Jupiter, Saturn is a giant planet, made up mostly of liquid and gas. Its material is so light overall that Saturn would float in an ocean of water large enough to take it!

The clouds in Saturn's atmosphere lie under a layer of haze, which makes them look rather fuzzy. Saturn's rapid spin creates winds of up to 1600 kilometres per hour dragging the clouds into bands circling the planet. Saturn spins so fast that it bulges out around its equator. It is 11 per cent wider at its equator than between its poles.

Find Out More

- Planets
- Solar System
- Space astronomy

▼ This view of Saturn was taken by the Hubble Space Telescope in 1996. The large white spot close to the rings indicates a storm.

▼ Saturn's bright A and B rings are separated by a space called the Cassini Division. There are smaller gaps in the A and C rings. The rings are made up of pieces of ice, rock and dust.

shepherd moons

Enke Gap

Cassini Division

A ring

B ring

C ring

Stormy weather

Most of the time, Saturn's appearance changes very little. About every 30 years, storms break out when bubbles of warm gas rise up through the atmosphere. We see them as large white spots because clouds of frozen ammonia crystals form over the storm areas. Since it takes Saturn about 30 years to orbit the Sun, the storms seem to be linked to Saturn's seasons.

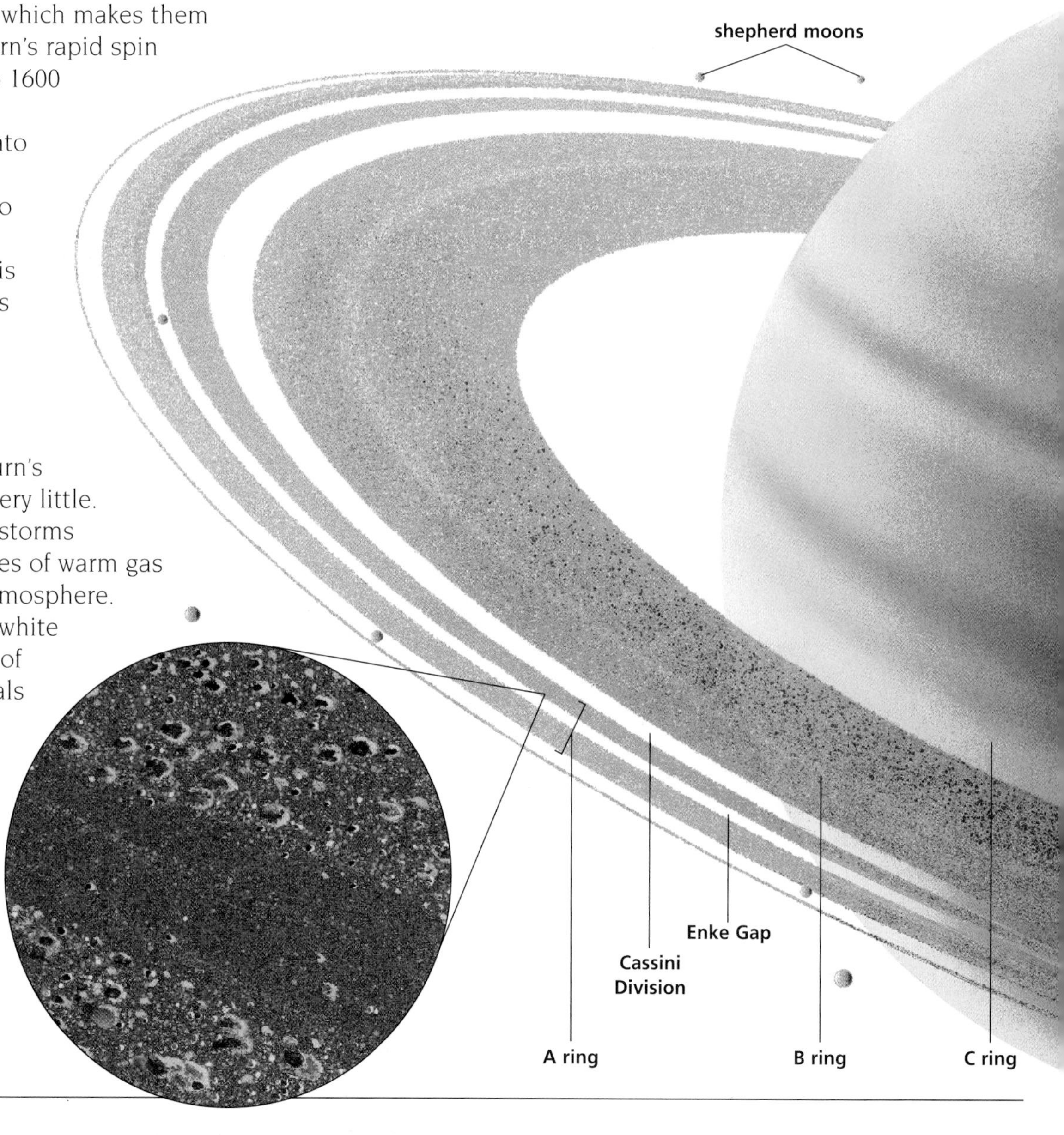

▶ A close-up view of one of the rings.

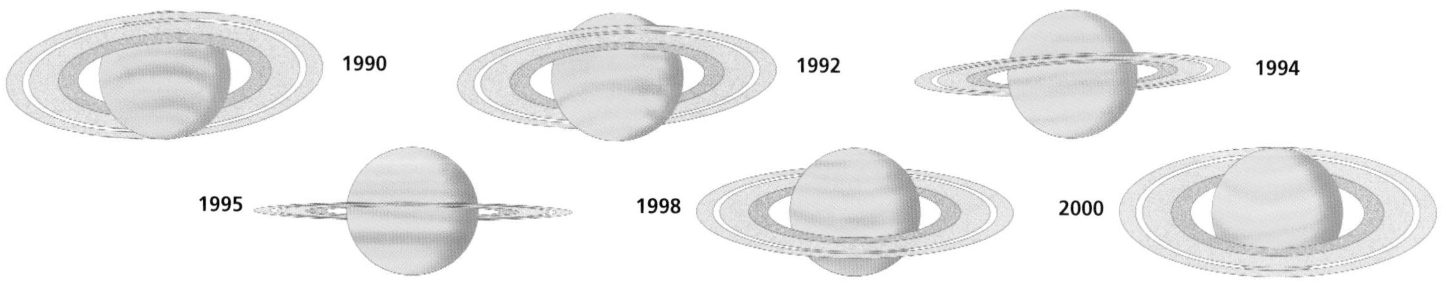

▲ Our angle of view of the rings changes as Saturn travels around the Sun. Most of the time they are easy to see with a small telescope. Every 15 years the rings seem to close up until they are edge-on to us. Since they are only a few metres thick, they become invisible for a while.

Rings

The icy lumps that make up Saturn's rings are frozen water with rock and dust mixed in. They range from pieces the size of a golf ball up to house-sized boulders. A few may be a kilometre across.

The three brightest rings are called A, B and C. Beyond them, dimmer and dustier rings extend outwards nearly 500,000 kilometres from Saturn's centre. Another dim ring, labelled D, lies closer to Saturn inside the C ring.

What look like gaps between the rings are not completely empty, but they contain far fewer objects. They are kept clear by the gravity of some of Saturn's moons. Two tiny moons, Pandora and Prometheus, keep the narrow F ring in place. For this reason they are called 'shepherd moons'.

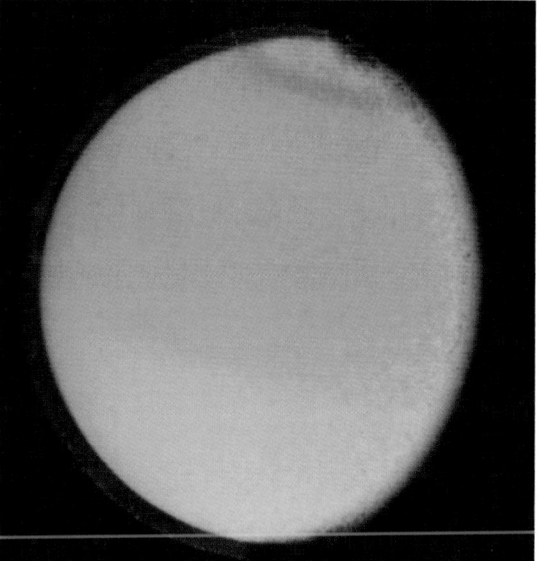

◀ Saturn's largest moon, Titan, has a thick atmosphere. The surface is hidden by orange haze.

Moons

The 13 moons nearest Saturn orbit within the ring system. Some of them actually share orbits, in twos and threes, though they avoid colliding with each other.

All the moons seen by the *Voyager* spacecraft are icy, with craters. Some also have smooth plains. The most mysterious is Titan. It is the second largest moon in the Solar System after Jupiter's moon Ganymede, but its surface is completely hidden by a blanket of smog. It is the only moon with a thick atmosphere.

Titan's atmosphere is half as thick again as the Earth's and, like the Earth's, is made mainly of nitrogen. But it also includes methane, the natural gas used for fuel on Earth. Astronomers suspect there could be lakes on Titan made of liquid methane and ethane. At the temperature of Titan (–180 °C) these chemicals will be liquid while water will be frozen rock hard.

▼ The icy surface of Saturn's moon Enceladus is brighter than any other in the Solar System. It may be kept fresh by deposits of frost spewed out from ice volcanoes. Parts of the surface are cratered. There are also smooth plains where the craters have been covered.

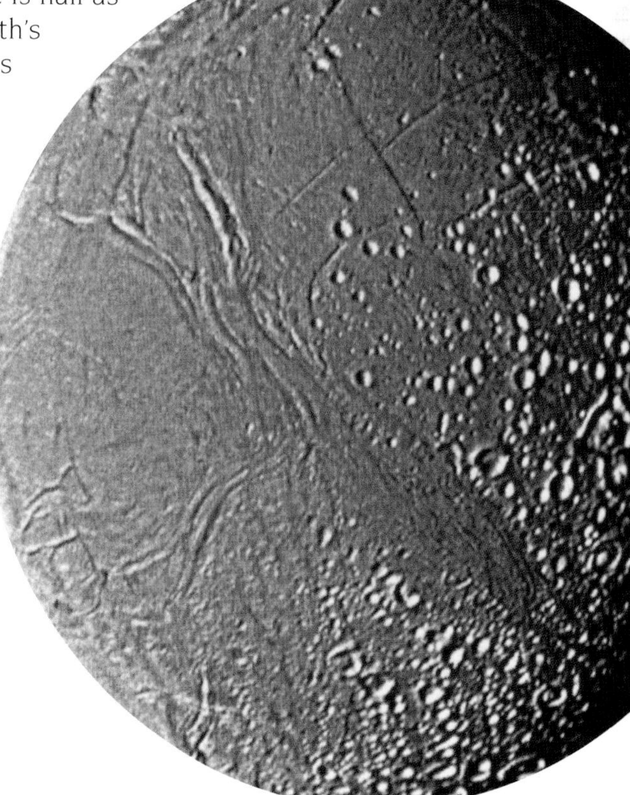

SATURN DATA
Diameter at equator: 129,660 km
Average distance from Sun: 1427 million km
Time taken to spin on axis: 10.5 hours
Density (water = 1): 0.7
Time taken to orbit the Sun: 29.46 years
Moons: 30

Savannah *see* Grasslands • **Scanners** *see* Medicine, X-rays

Science

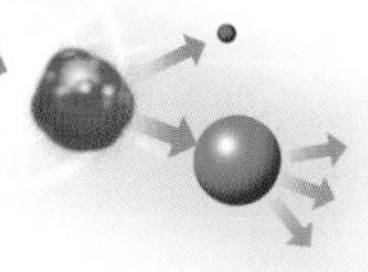

In a 27-kilometre long underground tunnel circling Geneva, Switzerland, streams of incredibly tiny atomic particles smash into each other at speeds close to the speed of light. This tunnel forms part of a powerful atom-smasher, or particle accelerator, in which scientists probe into the nucleus (centre) of atoms.

The science that investigates atoms is called nuclear physics. Nuclear physicists carry out their atom-smashing experiments to try to find out how matter (the stuff that everything is made of) is put together. Like all scientists, they are seeking knowledge – the word science means 'knowledge'.

The three main sciences are physics, chemistry and biology. Biology is the science of life. Physics and chemistry study the physical, non-living world. Earth science is the study of the Earth, while astronomy and other space sciences cover everything beyond Earth's atmosphere.

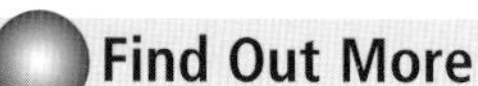

Find Out More

- Astronomy
- Atoms and molecules
- Classification
- Ecology
- Geology
- Mathematics
- Matter
- Measurement
- Weather

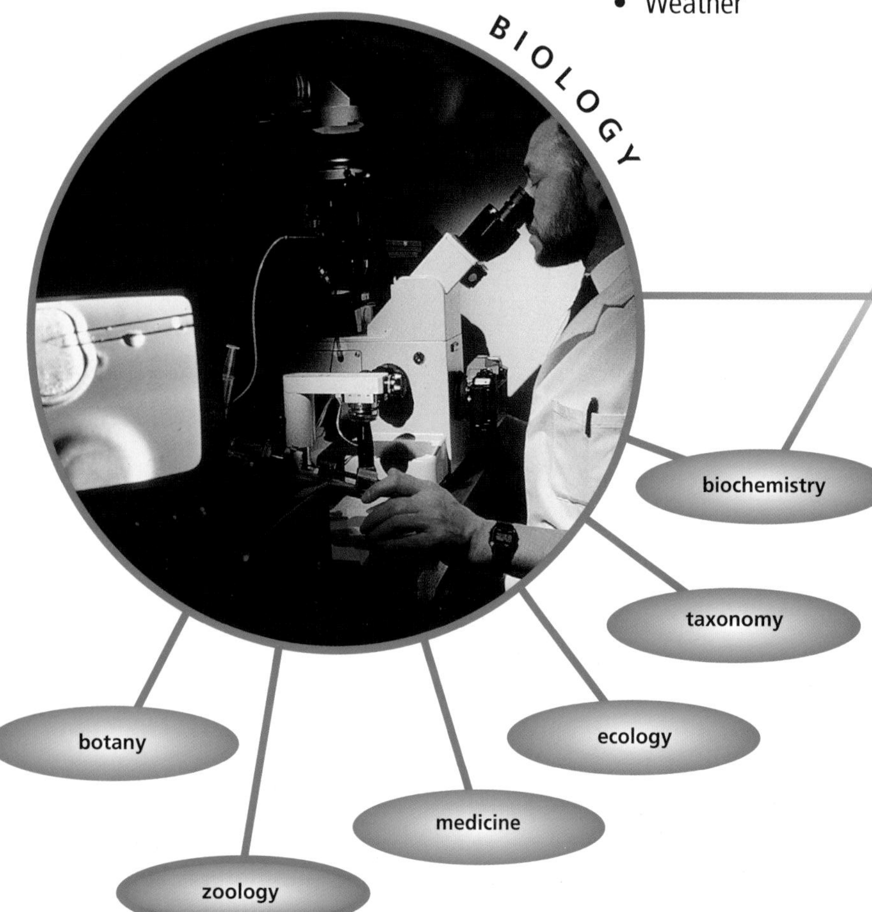

Physics

In physics, scientists study matter, energy and radiation. Everything in our Universe is made of matter. And anything that happens in our Universe involves energy in some form or other – for example, heat, electricity or sound. Visible light, and invisible rays such as radio waves, ultraviolet rays and X-rays, are ways in which energy moves.

Chemistry

In chemistry, scientists study the chemical properties of the different substances that make up our world. They investigate the changes that take place when these substances react together.

Chemists find new ways of splitting up or combining substances to produce more useful products. This process has led to a host of man-made, or synthetic, substances

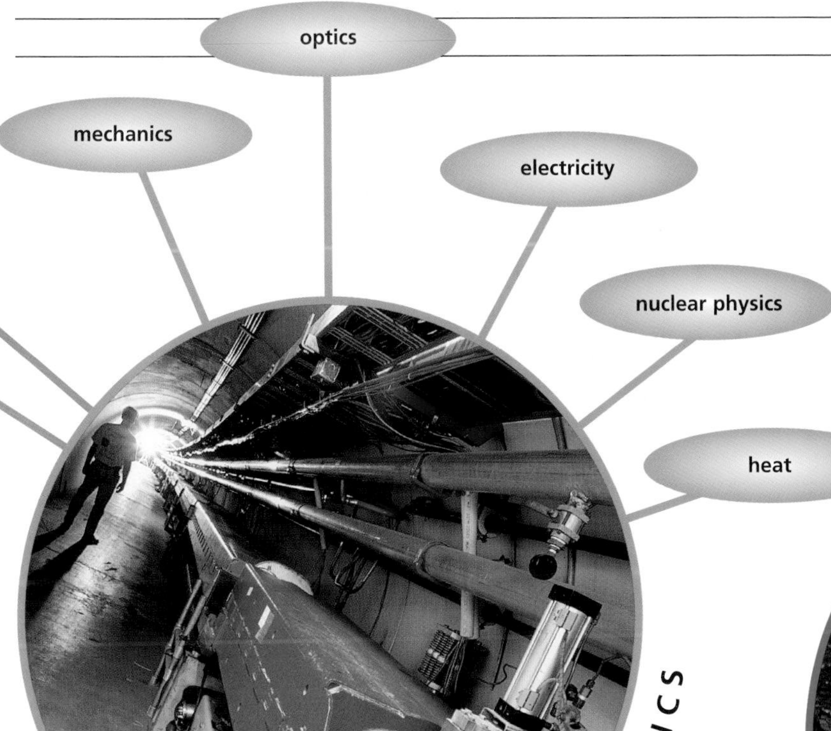

Ecology is the study of living things in their natural environment, and the connections between them. Subjects such as genetics, molecular biology and biochemistry study the processes that take place in living cells. Classification (taxonomy), which means grouping living things into categories, or families, forms an important part of biology.

that have transformed our world. These include plastics and synthetic fibres, detergents and drugs (pharmaceuticals).

Biology

In biology, scientists study living things. Two main biological, or life, sciences are botany and zoology. Botany is the study of plants, and zoology is the study of animals.

SCIENTIFIC METHODS

Scientists in all branches of science set about gaining knowledge in very specific ways. Often they start from an observation – they see something happening. They then put forward an idea, or hypothesis, to try and explain how and why it happens. Afterwards they test the idea by carrying out experiments. Both observations and experiments usually involve making measurements. They give scientists the data, or information, they need to see if their hypothesis is true or not.

If a hypothesis proves to be accurate after a series of experiments, then it may be accepted as a scientific law. But even long-standing laws may be overturned if new data or better explanations are found.

Earth and space sciences

The main Earth science is geology, which deals with the way the Earth is made up and how it changes and has changed in the past. An important part of geology is the study of rocks.

Astronomers study the heavenly bodies – planets, stars and galaxies – and space in general. Using the latest techniques, astronomers are expanding our knowledge of the Universe almost day by day. Space telescopes picture the spectacular deaths of giant stars, while space probes visit planets, moons and even tiny asteroids.

Seashore

Caught in the strong grip of a starfish, a mussel has little chance of escape. The starfish gradually pulls apart the two halves of the shell, using the many rows of 'tube feet' under its five arms. Then it pushes its stomach out through its mouth and digests the mussel's soft body.

Being attacked by predators is only one of the many problems of living on a seashore. The lives of seashore creatures are dominated by the tides that creep up and down the beach.

As the tide flows in, the shore is covered by floating food. But as it flows out again, creatures are exposed to drying winds, strong sunshine, extreme temperatures and the fresh water in rainfall. Many burrow in the sand or mud or shelter under rocks or seaweed or in rock pools. Some, such as shellfish and barnacles, have tough shells, which help to stop them drying out and protect them from the pounding waves.

Find Out More

- Birds
- Coasts
- Ocean life
- Oceans

▲ When barnacles are covered by seawater, they filter food from the water with their feathery legs. At low tide, barnacles seal their legs inside their shells.

▼ Where rivers meet the sea, they form wide, flat, muddy areas called estuaries. At low tide, wading birds, such as this sandpiper, use their long bills to extract worms, snails and other creatures from the rich mud.

Rock-pool life

Rock pools are like tiny, self-contained worlds. The microscopic algae and larger seaweeds in the pool provide food for winkles, limpets and other plant-eaters. The plant-eaters in turn are eaten by meat-eaters such as starfishes, small fishes and whelks. There are also scavengers such as crabs, that eat dead and decaying plant and animal material.

At low tide a rock pool may quickly heat up or cool down, and the water may become very salty as some of it evaporates away. Plants and animals in the pool have to cope with these rapid changes.

▼ Different plants and animals live in different zones on the shore, according to the amount of time they can survive out of the water.

Sea anemones, starfishes and sea urchins (1) live among the seaweeds in the rock pools. These seaweeds include kelp (2), serrated wrack (3) and thong weed (4). Further up the shore live seaweeds such as bladder wrack (5), knotted wrack (6) and spiral wrack (7). Mussels (8), limpets, periwinkles and barnacles (9) have strong shells to protect them. Channelled wrack (10) and lichens (11) flourish on the drier rocks.

Seasons

In the middle of June in the Arctic Circle, the Sun is still out at 2 am. It hasn't dipped below the horizon since March and it won't until September. At the South Pole, in Antarctica, it has been dark for three months and the Sun won't rise for another three.

The temperature, weather and amount of daylight change with the seasons, throughout the year and from place to place. These changes are all to do with the Earth's yearly journey around the Sun.

Earth moving through space

The Earth is tilted on its axis, and the way it is tilted affects the amount of sunlight different areas receive. Between mid-March and mid-September the North Pole leans towards the Sun, and the South Pole leans away from it. From mid-September to mid-March, the reverse is true. Warmer weather and longer days come to the side of the Earth tilted towards the Sun.

▶ Winter is colder than summer because there is less sunlight. The days are shorter and the Sun is lower in the sky. When the Sun is low in the sky, less of its energy reaches the Earth's surface.

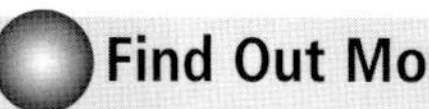

- Climate
- Energy
- Sun
- Weather

Warm and cool, light and dark, wet and dry

Seasons are different in different parts of the world. In temperate latitudes (mid-way between the Equator and the poles), there are four very different seasons: winter, spring, summer and autumn. Near the North and South Poles there are just two seasons: a light season and a dark season, and it stays cool all year.

In the tropics, near the Equator, it is hot all year round, because the Sun is always high in the sky. But many regions near the Equator have a rainy season in the summer and a dry season in the winter.

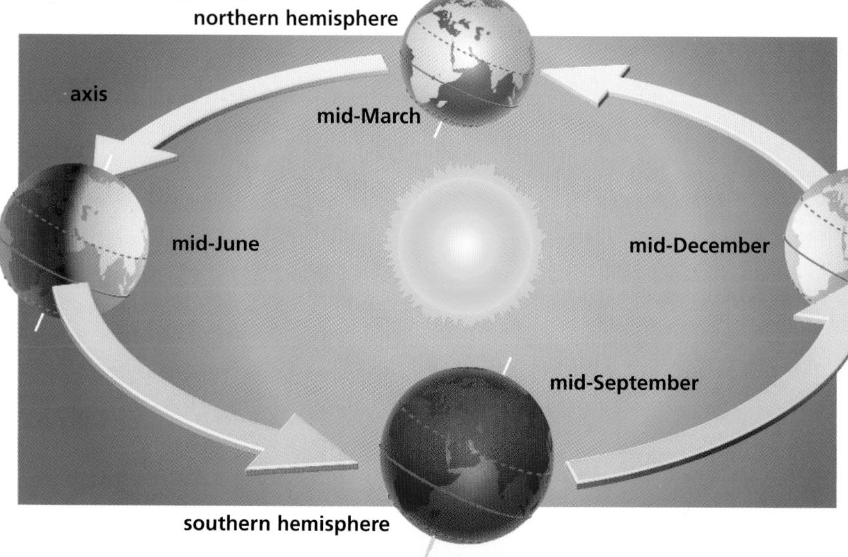

◀ The Earth takes a year to make one orbit around the Sun. From mid-March to mid-September, the North Pole is tilted towards the Sun, and it is warmer in the northern hemisphere. From mid-September to mid-March the South Pole is tilted towards the Sun, and it is warmer in the south.

▼ This time-lapse photograph shows the position of the Sun at one-hour intervals throughout the day near the North Pole in midsummer. Although the Sun dips very low, it never actually sets.

Seaweeds *see* Plants • **Seismology** *see* Earthquakes • **Semiconductors** *see* Conductors and insulators

Senses

Piercing the blackness of an African night comes the strange, child-like cry of a bushbaby. Its sensitive ears pick up the faint sounds of insects moving through the trees, while its enormous eyes focus on its prey in the moonlight. Keeping its feet clamped firmly to the branch, the bushbaby suddenly shoots out its body and hands to grab an insect meal out of the darkness.

Unlike bushbabies, we are creatures of the daytime and rely heavily our sense of sight – on detecting the light bouncing off things around us. It is hard for us to imagine what life must be like for animals that live in a world dominated by other signals, such as smells, sounds, heat or even electricity. We are totally unaware of millions of the smells that dogs can sense and are only able to hear about one third of the sounds that elephants make.

▶ Many bats use their own radar system – called echolocation – to detect flying insects at night. They make high-pitched clicking sounds and use their huge ears to pick up the echoes bouncing back from their prey.

Sight

Nearly all animals have organs that can sense the difference between light and dark. Most animals have eyes, which give them a picture of their surroundings.

Insects have compound eyes, which are made up of hundreds of tiny lenses packed closely together. All mammals have eyes similar to human eyes, containing a single lens. Nocturnal animals, which come out at night, have big eyes to let in as much light as possible. They often have a special layer in the eye that reflects light. This is what makes a cat's eyes shine in the dark.

◀ A fruit fly does not see the world in quite the same way as we do. Its compound eyes have many separate lenses and probably give a blurred picture of its surroundings. But they are good at detecting movement.

Hearing

Most animals pick up sounds with ears in their heads. Animals that rely on their hearing to hunt prey have particularly large ears. The desert fox is an example. Animals that live in water have ears too. Whales, for example, have good hearing and can pick up the sound of other whales singing many kilometres away.

Other animals sense sounds using different parts of their bodies. Among insects, earwigs pick up sounds through the hairs on their pincers, mosquitoes use antennae, and crickets have ears on their legs.

▲ The feathery antennae of the male moon moth have many branches on which the moth can pick up scent particles from the air. A male moth can detect the scent of a female moth from several kilometres away.

▲ The woodmouse uses its long, sensitive whiskers to feel its way through tangled undergrowth and narrow spaces.

Smell and taste

The sense of taste is closely linked with the sense of smell. These two senses allow animals to find food, send smelly messages to one another and avoid things that are harmful. Mammals have a nose for smelling things, but snakes smell with their tongue and moths with their antennae. Many animals use their tongues for tasting things, but octopuses taste with their tentacles and flies taste with their feet.

Special senses

Scientists have only recently begun to discover more about the special senses that certain animals possess that are completely outside human experience. Some animals can detect electricity, magnetism, water vibrations and heat. Birds use their magnetic sense to help them find their way when they migrate.

Most fishes have special lateral lines along the sides of their bodies which help them to pick up vibrations in the water. Sharks can also pick up electrical signals from the muscles of fishes to help them zoom in on their prey with deadly accuracy.

▼ Pit vipers have special heat holes on the side of the face, which pick up the heat given off by warm-blooded prey, such as mice. This helps these snakes to detect their prey in total darkness.

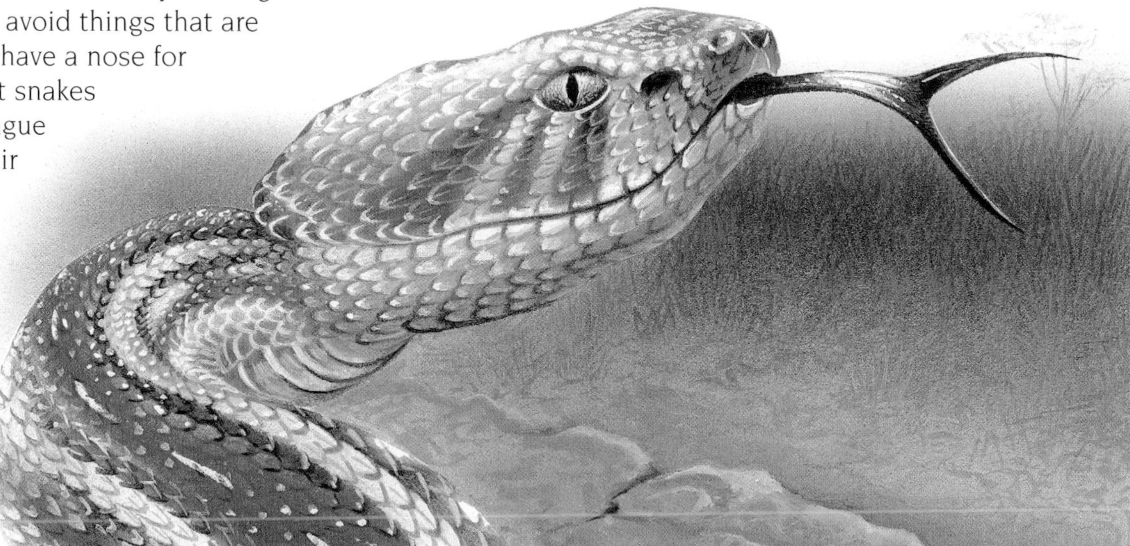

Find Out More

- Ears
- Eyes
- Human senses
- Light
- Sound

Sewage *see* Waste disposal

Sex and reproduction

Take a closer look at a rose bush on a hot summer's day and you may find it is covered with armies of greenfly. The reason there are so many greenfly is that they reproduce amazingly quickly. Female greenfly can give birth to identical female babies without mating with male greenfly. In just two weeks, one female and her daughters can have over 1300 babies.

anemone dividing into two

▲ Anemones reproduce asexually. The anemone copies all its genes and then splits into two, making two genetically identical individuals. Living things made of one cell, such as bacteria and amoebas, also reproduce like this.

Without reproduction, life on Earth would grind to a halt. Reproduction allows living things to replace themselves and increase their numbers. It also allows them to change, or evolve, over time. When they reproduce, living things pass on their genes – the chemical codes inside their cells that control their characteristics – to their offspring.

There are two forms of reproduction: asexual (non-sexual) reproduction and sexual reproduction.

Asexual reproduction

Asexual reproduction is the simplest and quickest form of reproduction. The parent may just split into two or more pieces, or grow an extra part that becomes a new individual. Female eggs may also grow into babies without any input from the male, as happens in greenfly. In asexual reproduction offspring are identical to their parents.

Find Out More

- Animals
- Genetics
- Growth and development
- Human reproduction
- Insects
- Plants

◀ Bees fly from flower to flower, feeding on nectar and pollen. As they do so, some pollen gets caught on the bee's body and is carried from the male parts of one flower to the female parts of another flower. This is called pollination.

After 7 months, one pair of cockroaches could have 164,000 million descendants.

Sexual reproduction

Sexual reproduction involves the joining together of two special sex cells, one from each parent. In animals, the male parent produces sperm cells and the female parent produces egg cells. In plants with flowers or cones, the male cells are called pollen and the female cells are called egg cells. To produce a new individual, a sperm cell or a pollen cell must join with an egg cell. This joining together is called fertilization.

Sexual reproduction mixes up the genes, so each individual is different from its parents, brothers and sisters. This variety is an advantage because some offspring may have a better chance of surviving if conditions change.

▶ Some frogs make a foam nest to protect their eggs but then go away and leave them alone. Animals that do not care for their eggs or young usually produce large numbers of them. Many will die, but a few will survive to pass their genes on to the next generation.

Fertilization

In flowering plants the pollen and egg cells often come from different plants. The egg cells stay put but the pollen travels from one flower to another with the help of the wind, water or animals. This is called cross-fertilization. Pollen may also sometimes fertilize flowers on the same plant. This is called self-fertilization.

In most water-dwelling animals, such as fishes, eggs and sperm are shed into the water and fertilization happens there. Land-dwelling animals usually fertilize the eggs inside the female's body.

Cloning

If you take a cutting and it grows into a new plant, this is a genetic copy of the original plant. The copy is called a clone.

Cloning animals is difficult, and still experimental. One method is to replace the nucleus in an egg cell with one taken from an adult cell. If the egg cell develops into a baby animal, this is a clone of the adult. Cloned animals can have health problems or short lives, and research into human cloning is banned in some countries.

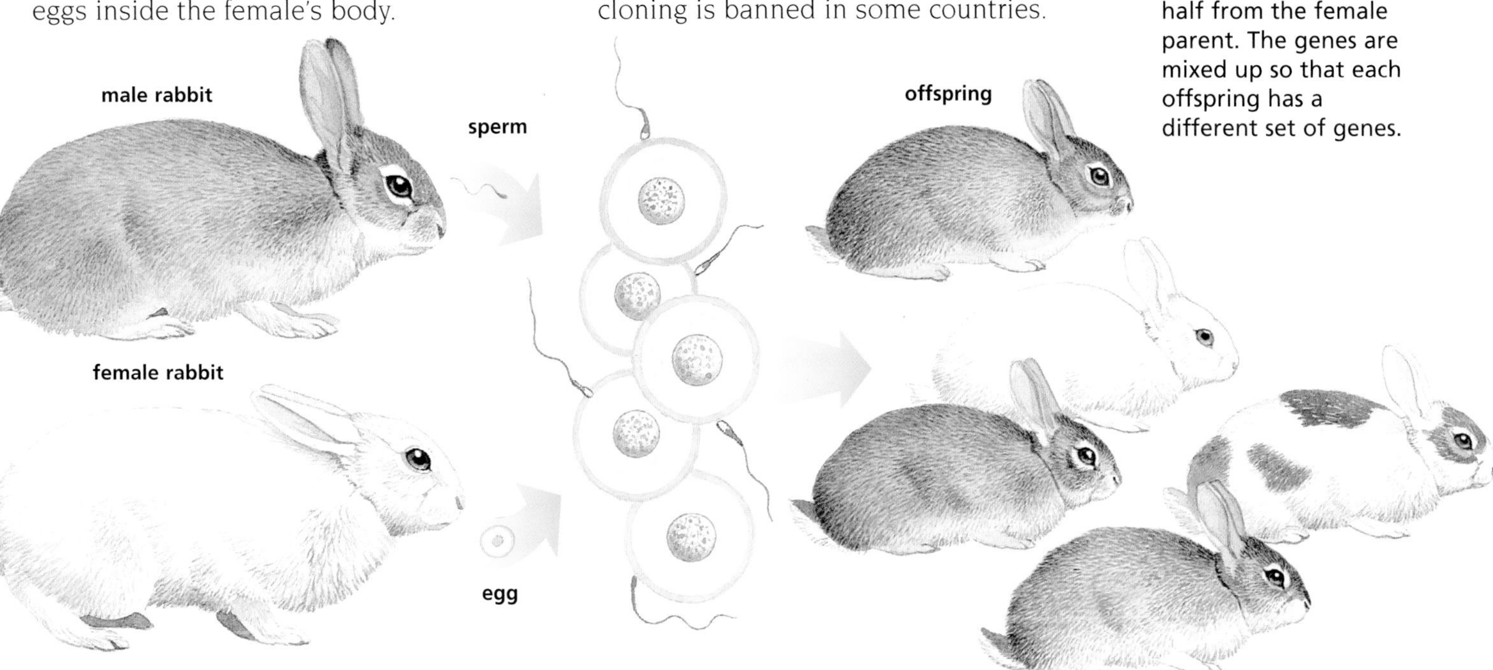

▼ In sexual reproduction, there are two parents, and the offspring receive half their genes from the male parent and half from the female parent. The genes are mixed up so that each offspring has a different set of genes.

Sharks *see* Fishes

Ships and submarines

What floats, is as big as an aircraft carrier, carries over 3,000 passengers, and has an ice rink, a rock-climbing wall, a library and street musicians? The answer is the world's biggest cruise liner, *Voyager of the Seas*, which was launched in November 1999.

▶ A supertanker arrives at an oil terminal. These huge ships are difficult to manoeuvre in the tight space of a harbour. They have to be pushed up to the jetty by small but powerful tugboats.

Cruise liners are now some of the biggest ships being built. The only ships that are bigger are the supertankers that transport oil around the world. They really are huge – nearly 500 metres long, with space for over 500,000 tonnes of oil.

Keeping afloat

How can such huge vessels, weighing many thousand tonnes, float on water? The answer is that an object can float if it displaces (pushes aside) a weight of liquid equal to its own weight. This displaced water creates an upward force, or upthrust, which keeps the object afloat.

Under power

All ships are pushed along by propellers. Most ships use diesel engines to spin the propellers, but a few, including some ice-breakers, submarines and aircraft carriers, are nuclear-powered. In these ships a nuclear reactor is used to heat water in a boiler. The water turns to steam, and jets of steam are then used to turn turbines (large, many-bladed rotors or propellers). The turbines spin the ship's propellers.

Building ships

Ship designers try to make their vessels as streamlined as possible, to reduce water resistance, or drag. Designers test scale models of their craft in water tanks to get an idea of how the real ships will behave.

Most ships are made from strong steel plates welded together on an inner framework. A few ships have hulls made from other materials, such as glass-fibre.

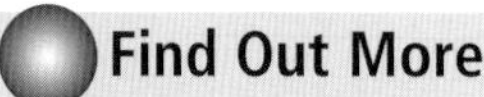

Find Out More

- Flight and flow
- Floating and sinking
- Nuclear energy
- Transport

The inside of the hull is divided into several watertight compartments. This strengthens the hull and provides a safety feature, because individual compartments can be sealed off if they become flooded.

On water wings

Ordinary ships move quite slowly through the water because of the water resistance on their hulls. Craft known as hydrofoils

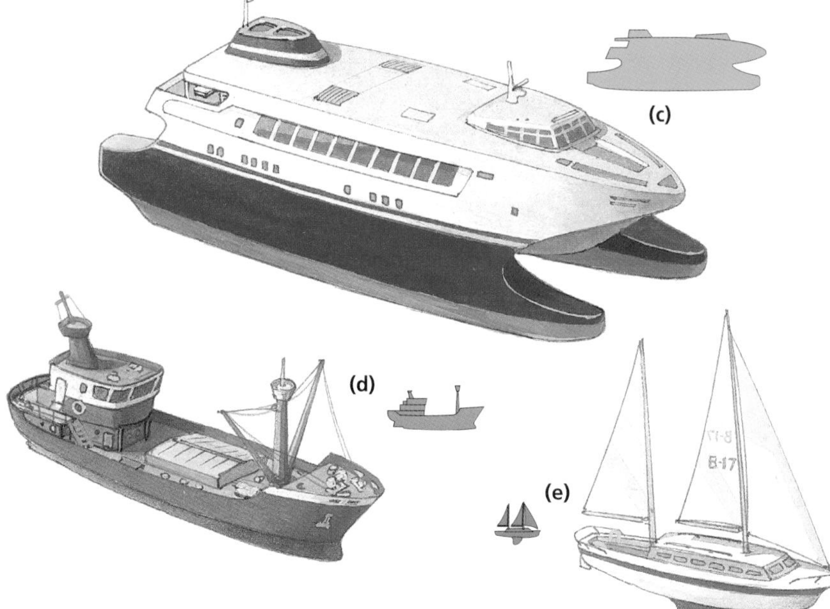

Sight *see* Eyes, Human senses, Senses • **Signals** *see* Communications • **Silicon chips** *see* Microchips

overcome this problem by lifting their hulls right out of the water. A hydrofoil has 'wings', or foils, fitted beneath the hull. When the boat moves forwards, the foils produce a lifting force, just as a plane's wings do in air. The hull lifts clear of the water, and the boat can travel much faster.

Under the waves

Some ships can travel underwater as well as on the surface. Submarines dive underwater or rise to the surface using large ballast tanks, which can be filled with water or air. If the tanks are filled with water, the submarine becomes heavier than the water around it, and sinks. To come up again, air is pumped into the tanks. Air is lighter than water, so the submarine rises to the surface.

Small submarines called submersibles are mostly used for underwater exploration. They are usually powered by electric motors. Large naval submarines are powered by a nuclear reactor. Nuclear submarines can remain submerged for months at a time, but conventional submarines need to surface regularly to recharge their batteries.

▶ This LR5 submersible is a 'lockout' design. It has a sealed diving compartment in which divers can be carried down to the seabed under pressure.

FLOATING ON AIR

Hovercraft glide over the surface on a cushion of air. They can travel at speeds up to about 120 kilometres an hour. A hovercraft looks rather like a huge rubber dinghy, with a 'skirt' around its hull. Powerful fans blow air underneath the craft, and the skirt stops it leaking away too quickly.

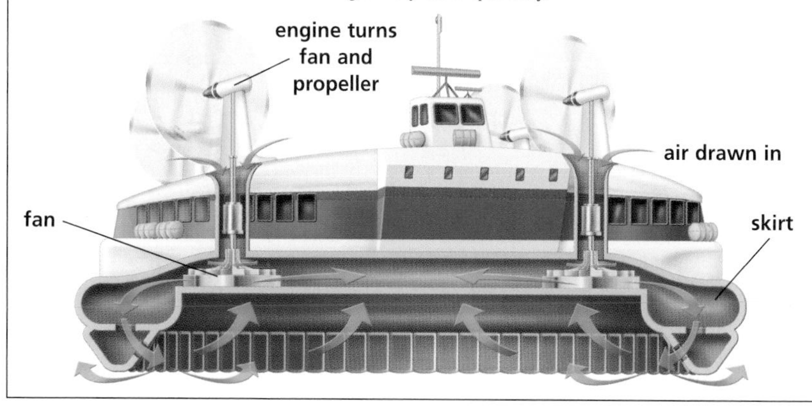

(a)

(b)

◀ Some of the many different types of ship. The small silhouettes with each picture show the relative sizes of each vessel. Container ships (a) are the most common cargo ships. Large passenger ferries (b) are used on the busiest routes. (c) A super-fast trimaran ferry. The trawler (d) is the most common type of fishing vessel. Sailing boats (e) are used mainly for pleasure.

Silk *see* Fibres, Textiles • **Silver** *see* Gold and silver • **Skeletons** *see* Bones and muscles

Skin and hair

Soft and stretchy, but strong and protective, skin covers your entire body. It is a flexible coating that can repair itself. Extra protection comes from a natural sun-blocker made by the skin, and from our fingernails.

Skin is only a few millimetres thick, but it is an effective barrier against the outside world. Skin is waterproof, and as long as it is not cut or scratched it can keep out germs. Cells near the surface divide all the time, producing new cells to heal small wounds and replace skin that wears away.

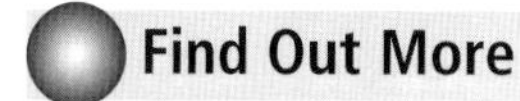

Find Out More
- Brain and nerves
- Heart and blood
- Mammals

▲ Ultaviolet rays from sunlight can do permanent damage to skin. To keep them out, the skin produces a dark pigment called melanin. More melanin means a deeper skin colour, and better protection.

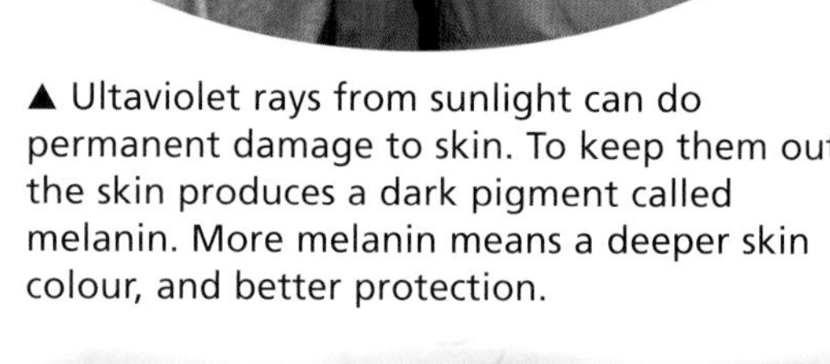

Every one of the 6 billion people in the world has a different fingerprint – the swirling pattern of ridges on our fingertips.

Nails and hair

Both nails and hair grow from roots in the skin. They are made of dead cells hardened with a substance called keratin.

Our prehistoric ancestors had thick, long hair all over the body, which kept them warm. Today we have long hair only on our head. The rest of the body has short, sparse hairs. Each hair has its own tiny muscle to lift it when we are cold.

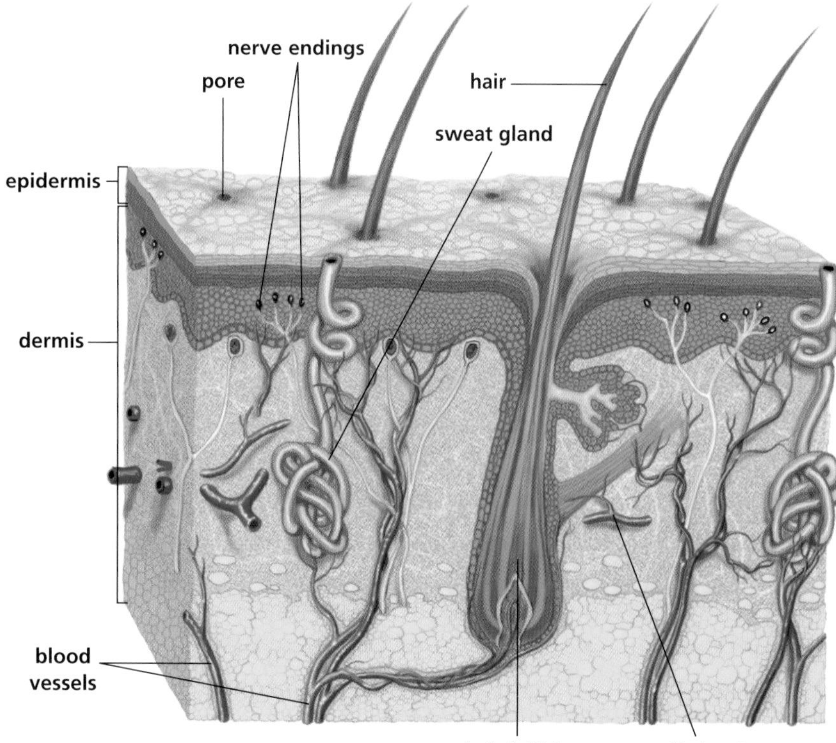

▼ A cross-section through the skin. The skin has two main layers: a thin epidermis on the surface, and a thicker dermis below.

Temperature control

Whether the outside temperature is hot or cold, the temperature inside our bodies stays at 37 °C. Skin helps us to keep to this constant temperature. Around 3 million sweat glands in the skin produce cooling sweat when things get too hot. And in cold weather, tiny blood vessels threaded through the skin shut down, to prevent the warm blood from being cooled.

A delicate touch

Thousands of different sensors just below the skin surface give us our delicate sense of touch. Some tell us if our surroundings are hot or cold; others respond to pain, the light touch of a feather or the pressure of a new shoe. Our lips and fingertips are the most sensitive parts of the body.

Sodium

Some metals, such as sodium and potassium, are so soft that you can cut them with a knife. They are also fiercely reactive – if you put a piece of sodium in water, it will shoot across the surface, fizzing violently. Such metals are never found naturally in their pure state, but they make many stable compounds. For example, common table salt is sodium chloride.

Sodium and potassium belong to a group of highly reactive metal elements. The other elements in the group are lithium, rubidium, caesium and francium. They are all soft, less dense than other metals, and have low boiling points.

Properties

These metals are arranged in a column in the periodic table of the elements, from the least reactive to the most reactive.

At the top is lithium. Lithium is silvery white, and is the least reactive. Sodium comes below lithium, and is also silvery white. Like potassium below it, sodium reacts rapidly with air and violently in water, so it has to be stored under oil. Below potassium is rubidium, which bursts into flames if exposed to air. Francium and caesium, the remaining members of the group, are even more reactive.

Uses

Some medicines contain lithium. It is also used in batteries for things like mobile phones and digital watches.

Both sodium and potassium are essential for all living things. Potassium fertilizers are added to soil to help crops grow. We get most of the sodium we need from common salt – although too much can be harmful. Lamps containing sodium vapour give off a yellowish-orange light, and are used for street lighting.

Caesium is a key element in a car's catalytic converter. It helps to turn some exhaust gases into less polluting compounds.

◀ In some countries with a hot climate, table salt (sodium chloride) is obtained by trapping sea water in shallow pans or lagoons. When the sea water evaporates, 'sea salt' is left behind.

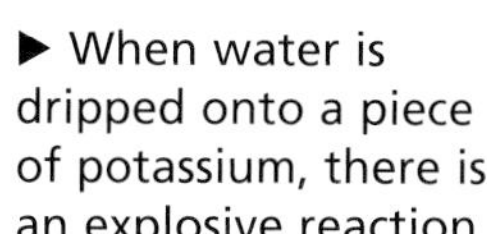

▶ When water is dripped onto a piece of potassium, there is an explosive reaction.

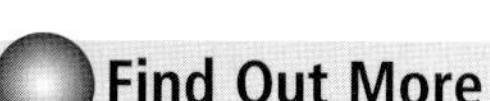

Find Out More

- Batteries
- Fertilizers
- Periodic table
- Salts

Sodium and potassium are used to colour fireworks. Sodium burns with a bright yellow flame, while potassium has a lilac flame.

Software

If you want to bake a really delicious chocolate cake, it's best to follow a recipe. If you follow the instructions carefully, the cake should be great! A computer program can also be thought of as a recipe. It is a list of instructions that makes the computer do the job you want it to.

Computer programs can do really useful things, like control a space rocket, manage your washing machine cycle or change the traffic lights.

A computer's programs are part of its software. The software of a computer is every bit as important as the hardware (the physical parts like the screen and keyboard). If the software is wrong, the program won't work – just like a recipe.

Home on the range

The range of software is staggering. We are all used to word processors, which let us type letters and get them right before we print them out or email them. But PCs can also run programs that let you store information (databases), programs that do calculations (spreadsheets), programs that play music or sounds, ones that let you draw pictures or modify photographs – and of course computer games. There are also many other kinds of software used in science and industry.

One kind of program that has to be designed with extra care is safety-critical software. This is the software that operates aircraft, cars or medical equipment. If safety-critical software goes wrong, people can get hurt.

Not all software is useful. Computer viruses are pieces of software that invade computer systems and cause problems.

▲ Electronic games have been popular since people first began making personal computers. Modern games have sophisticated graphics that can simulate whole environments.

BILL GATES AND MICROSOFT

In the early 1980s, IBM designed a revolutionary computer, the IBM PC (personal computer). It was small enough to sit on a desk. But their computer had no software – so IBM turned to a tiny firm called Microsoft for help. This company was run by a young American called Bill Gates. Microsoft then wrote MS-DOS – the MicroSoft Disk Operating System – for the IBM PC. With every PC sold making money for Microsoft, the firm soon became a huge corporation, and is now the world's leading software maker.

▼ There are many types of computer program. Some are lists of things to do, while others, like this one, describe how a web page should look. Web pages are usually written in Hyper Text Mark-up Language (HTML). The HTML code on the right makes the page shown on the left.

The Yahoo! screenshot is reproduced with permission of Yahoo! Inc. © 2000 by Yahoo! Inc.
YAHOO! and the YAHOO! logo are trademarks of Yahoo! Inc.

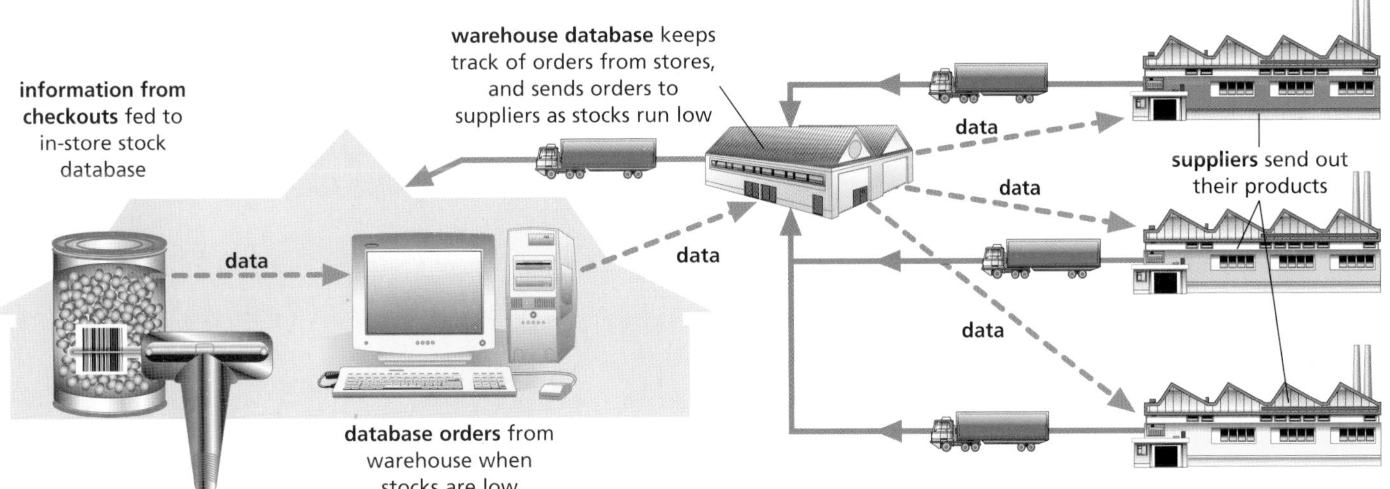

▲ Databases are important programs for many businesses. In a supermarket, databases keep track of what needs ordering at the store, at the warehouse, and at the supermarket's many suppliers.

Some viruses just display cheeky messages, while others erase certain types of file, like pictures or music files. Some viruses erase everything on your computer. Viruses are often spread by email. To fight them, it's important to have up-to-date anti-virus software that stops them working.

◀ Complex software is used to control much of the engine management, and even gear changes, in Formula One racing cars.

Mind your language

Software is written in a computer language. There are many languages – BASIC, Java, and Fortran are a few examples. Each is good at different things. For example, BASIC is a simple language that beginners can learn. Java is a more complex language that makes Internet programs work on many different types of computer. Fortran is a more specialist scientific language. Programmers choose the language for the job in hand.

Some programs can be very long. The program that guides a space rocket into orbit, for instance, can be many thousands of lines long. That's because there are many different pieces of equipment to control, and many pieces of information that need including in the program.

Computer processors cannot understand programs directly. The words and figures in a program have to be converted first into digital instructions that the computer processor can understand. This is done using a system called a compiler.

Bugs and debugging

Because a program is a list of instructions, any mistake in the commands can stop the program working. This could be serious if the software is controlling, for example, the engines on an aeroplane or a computer that does blood tests. So errors, known to computer programmers as 'bugs', have to be removed. Debugging (getting rid of bugs) can take as long as writing the program in the first place.

Find Out More

- Computers
- Computer graphics and design
- Communications
- Hardware
- Internet

Softwood *see* Wood and timber • **Soil** *see* Erosion • **Solar power** *see* Batteries and cells, Renewable energy

Solar System

Nine major planets travel around the Sun, kept in their orbits by the Sun's strong gravity. They are the chief members of the Solar System. Moons circle around seven of them and there are more than 60 moons altogether. The Sun's family also includes many thousands of small objects – asteroids, comets and meteoroids.

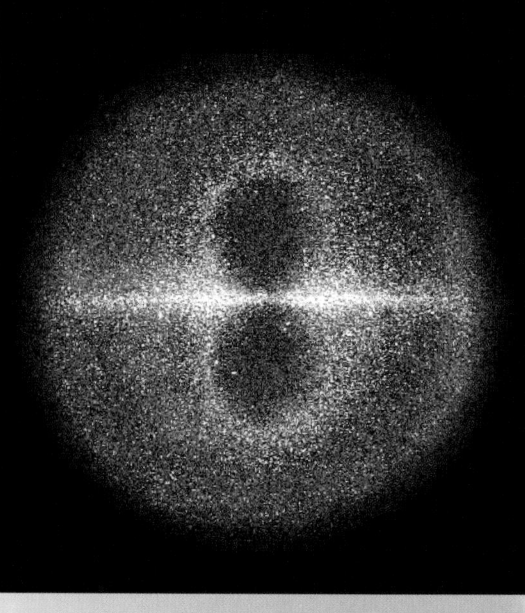

▶ A great shell of comets called the Oort Cloud marks the most remote edge of the Solar System.

The orbits of the planets from Mercury nearest the Sun, out to Neptune, are arranged in space almost in a flat disc, like hoops lying on a table. The paths the planets follow are not circles, though, but ellipses – slightly squashed circles. Pluto is the odd planet out. Its orbit is tilted to the others and is much more stretched out into a long elliptical shape.

Pluto's strange orbit was a mystery. Then in the 1990s, astronomers discovered that Pluto was not the only world beyond Neptune. They found dozens of miniature icy planets orbiting in a doughnut-shaped belt. There are probably thousands of them altogether. So far, none has been found any larger than Pluto.

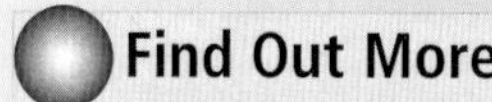

Find Out More

- Asteroids
- Comets
- Planets

KEPLER AND MOVEMENT OF THE PLANETS

Johannes Kepler (1571–1630) was a German astronomer who studied the motion of Mars. He worked out for the first time that the planets follow elliptical orbits rather than circular ones. He also discovered other rules about how they move.

As it travels around its elliptical orbit, a planet's distance from the Sun varies. Kepler found out that a planet moves more quickly when it is nearer the Sun. He also explained how planets farther from the Sun take longer to complete their orbit than those that are closer.

Asteroids and meteoroids

Nearer the Sun, many thousands of rocky fragments orbit the Sun, mainly in a belt between Mars and Jupiter. These are the asteroids, sometimes called minor planets.

Some chunks of rock between the planets are too small even to count as asteroids. They range from large boulders to dust-like bits and pieces. These are called meteoroids. Even the smallest follow their own paths in orbit around the Sun.

The most remote members of the Solar System are comets. Millions of them swarm in a ball-shaped cloud 2000 to 20,000 times further from the Sun than the Earth. At this great distance comets are too faint to be seen. We only see the few comets that come in close to the Earth.

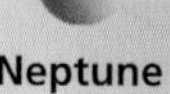

▲ ▶ In this illustration of the Solar System, the orbits of the planets are shown approximately to scale. However, the Sun and the planets themselves are shown much larger – at this scale they would actually be smaller than pinpricks.

IN THE BEGINNING

The history of the Solar System goes back about 4600 million years. When the Sun first formed, it was spinning slowly. A huge disc of gas and dust spread out around its middle (a). Material began to clump together in the disc. Some of the small clumps merged into bigger ones. Sometimes they collided so hard that they broke up again (b).

After millions of years, the largest clumps had become the planets (c). Comets and asteroids are the smaller, leftover pieces. Over time they settled in the zones where they are today. Comets are the most remote members of the Solar System. There are millions of them in a region up to 20,000 times farther from the Sun than the Earth – even farther away than Pluto.

(a)

(b)

(c)

Mars Mercury Sun Venus

Saturn

Earth Jupiter

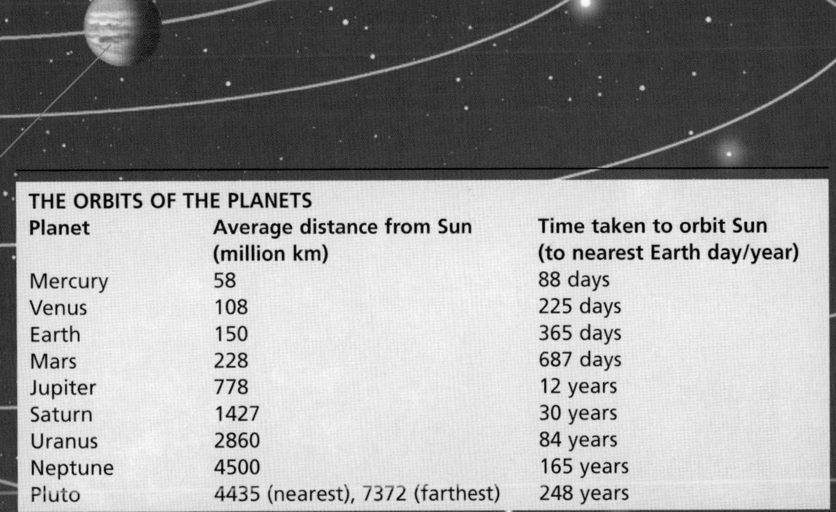

THE ORBITS OF THE PLANETS

Planet	Average distance from Sun (million km)	Time taken to orbit Sun (to nearest Earth day/year)
Mercury	58	88 days
Venus	108	225 days
Earth	150	365 days
Mars	228	687 days
Jupiter	778	12 years
Saturn	1427	30 years
Uranus	2860	84 years
Neptune	4500	165 years
Pluto	4435 (nearest), 7372 (farthest)	248 years

Solids

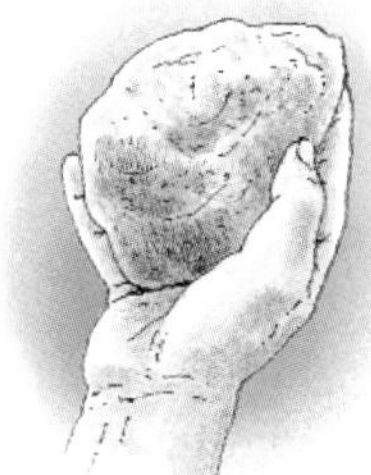

Most of the things we see around us are solids. Rocks, roads, books, pencils, computers, cars, skateboards, knives and forks – these and countless other objects are all made of solid matter. You can pick up a solid object (as long as it's not too heavy!) and turn it around.

Solids have shape and strength – unlike liquids or gases. If you tried to pick up some liquid or some gas, it would just flow away between your fingers.

Find Out More

- Atoms and molecules
- Crystals
- Matter
- Metals and non-metals

▼ Some solids, such as these wooden logs, are less dense than some liquids, so they float.

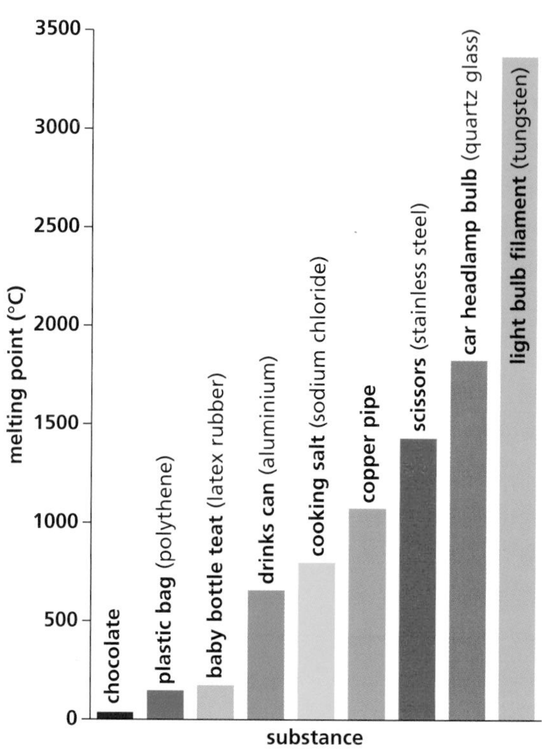

▲ Solids melt at different temperatures, depending on how strongly the atoms within them are held together.

The strength of solids

You can change the shape of some solids – you can bend, stretch, squash or twist them. But it can be hard work – all solids resist forces that try to change their shapes.

This is because the tiny particles (such as atoms) that make up a solid are held together by strong forces of attraction. The particles can only vibrate about fixed points. However, if you heat up a solid enough, the particles move about more quickly and freely – the solid melts into a liquid. Different solid materials melt at different temperatures. Butter will melt in your mouth, but iron only melts above 1500 °C.

Different kinds of solids

The tiny particles that make up some kinds of solids are arranged in a regular, repeating pattern. Such solids are called crystals. Table salt, quartz and diamond are examples of solids with a crystalline structure. In other kinds of solid material the particles are arranged randomly. They are said to have an amorphous (shapeless) structure. Rubber and glass are examples of amorphous materials.

Solutions, Solvents *see* Mixtures and solutions • **Sonar** *see* Radar, Sound

Sound

Hummingbirds hover by flapping their wings very quickly, and their wings shake up the air as they move. The result is a beautiful humming sound.

When someone strums a guitar, you hear a sound. Strumming makes the strings on the guitar vibrate (shake) very quickly. The air carries these vibrations into your ear. Inside the ear, the vibrations are turned into electrical signals that are sent to your brain.

If you twang a ruler, it will wobble up and down. As it does this, it shakes the air particles around it. The shaking particles then make the air particles next to it vibrate as well – the vibrations pass from one set of particles to the next. All of these vibrations are sound waves.

▶ The loudness of a sound is measured in decibels (dB). This scale shows approximate decibel levels for familiar sounds.

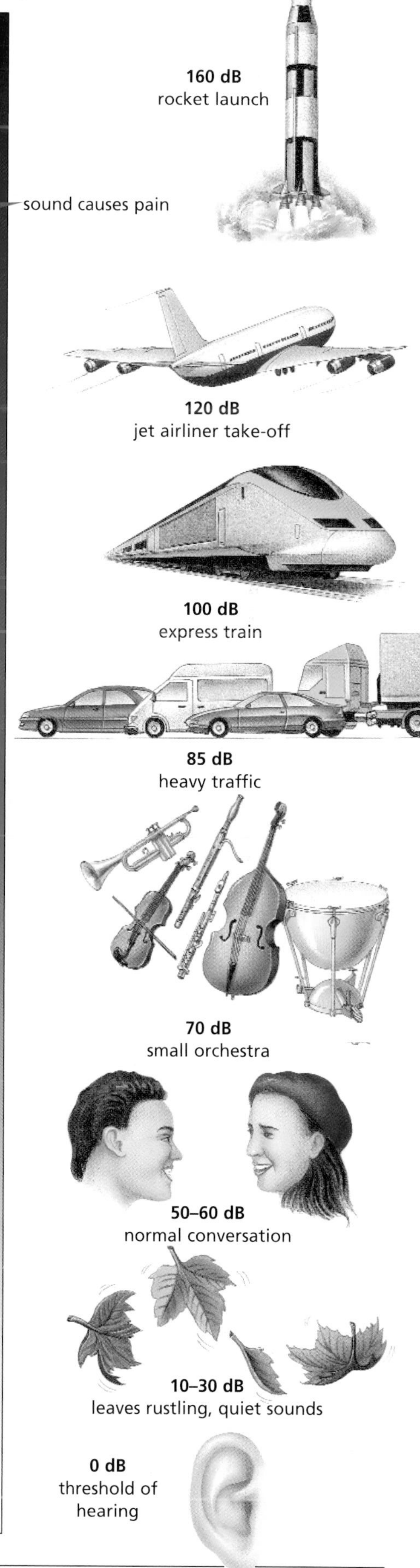

▼ The violent vibrations of this pneumatic drill produce very loud sounds. Workers wear ear defenders to protect their hearing.

Humans make sounds with their voices. To do this, we blow air from the lungs past some tightly stretched cords in the throat (the vocal cords). These cords vibrate and set the air vibrating as well. To be useful, the vibrations must be made louder (amplified). Fortunately, the vibrations make the chest, mouth and throat vibrate as well. All these vibrations together make a sound loud enough to be heard.

High and low, soft and loud

A whistle makes a very high-pitched sound. The vibrations are very fast. A bass guitar makes a very low-pitched sound. Its vibrations are rather slow compared to those made by the whistle.

Every sound has a frequency. This is the number of vibrations made in a second. High-pitched sounds have a high frequency. Low-pitched sounds have a low one.

Humans can hear a range of different frequencies. The lowest sound we can hear has 20 vibrations in a second. The highest sound has 20,000 vibrations in a second. As you get older, you become less sensitive to high-pitched sounds. Some animals, such as bats, can hear much higher-pitched sounds than we can.

Some sounds are very loud, for example when a big truck rumbles past. Other sounds are very soft, such as the rustling of a field mouse. Loud sounds are made by big vibrations. Small vibrations make soft sounds. Listening to very loud sounds for a long time can damage your hearing. For instance, regularly listening to loud music through headphones can be bad for your ears.

Fast and faster

Sound waves travel through the air very quickly – 330 metres per second, or more than 1000 kilometres per hour. At that speed, you could travel the length of three football pitches every second.

Standing at a railway station, you can often tell when a train is coming because the tracks start to buzz. A little time later, you hear the train itself. This is because vibrations made by the train travel through the tracks as well as through the air and the sound travels more quickly through the tracks than through air.

Sound can travel through many different materials, which is why you can sometimes hear your neighbours through the walls! The denser the material, the more quickly sound can travel through it. Submarines

▲ An ambulance speeds towards you, siren wailing. As it passes, the siren note changes, becoming lower. But for the ambulance driver, the sound stays the same. This change in the pitch of a sound as it moves towards or away from the listener is known as the Doppler effect.

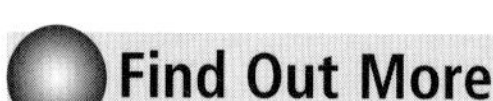

Find Out More

- Aircraft
- Ears
- Senses
- Sound recording
- Waves and vibrations

BREAKING THE SOUND BARRIER

The airliner *Concorde* and many military aircraft can travel faster than the speed of sound: they are 'supersonic'. The jet-powered car *Thrust* SSC travelled at supersonic speeds on land. The scientific term for the speed of sound is Mach 1. The fastest aircraft can fly at Mach 3 – about 3000 kilometres per hour.

People on the ground hear a 'sonic boom' when a supersonic aircraft flies over. This is caused by the aircraft squashing up air in front of it, creating a 'shock wave' that makes a loud sound.

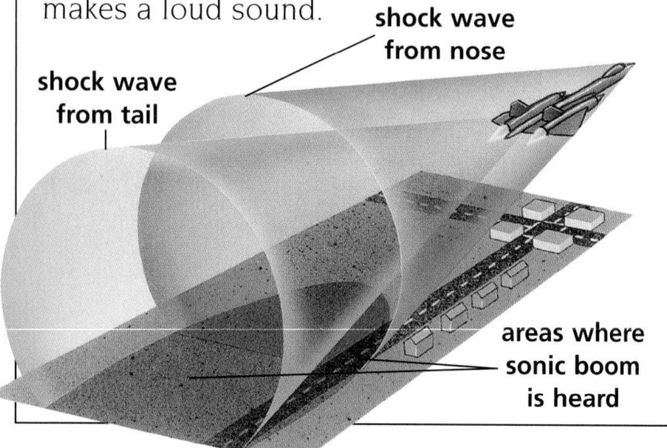

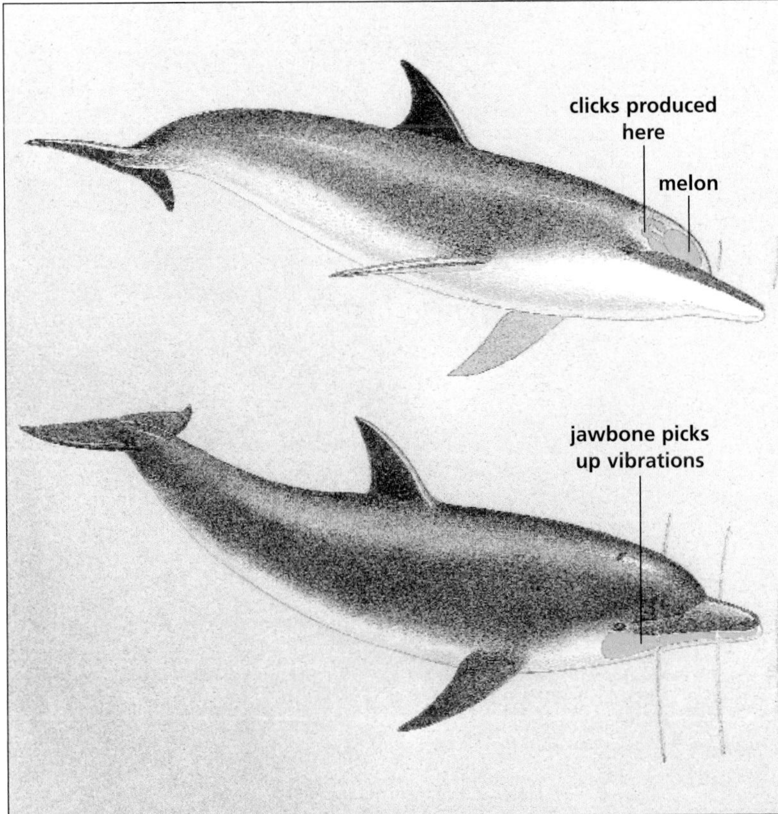

ANIMAL SONAR

Animals such as bats and dolphins can use short pulses of high-pitched sound to find their way around and hunt food.

Dolphins have a sonar system called echolocation. They make clicking sounds in air passages in their nose, which are focused into a 'beam' by an oil-filled organ in the head called the melon.

When the clicks hit an object, they bounce back as echoes. The dolphin picks up the echoes as vibrations in its jaw. The time between the echo and the click tells the dolphin how far away the object is.

By making a continuous stream of clicks and receiving echoes, the dolphin can get information about everything around it. It is like 'seeing' with sound.

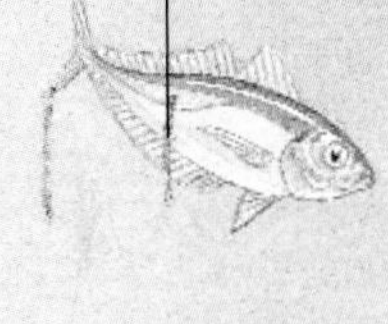

use sound waves in water to detect ships. Water is denser than air, and sound travels five times faster through it. Sound can travel 15 times faster in steel than in air.

Echoes

If you make a loud noise in a large, empty room, you sometimes hear the noise repeated a few times. These repeated noises are echoes. Echoes are made when sound waves bounce off things. The echo arrives back a moment after the original sound.

When a sound wave hits an object, some of it will bounce off or be reflected. But some of the vibrations will be swallowed up (absorbed) by the object.

Soft objects tend to absorb sound, while hard objects reflect sound. That's why a room with no furniture is ideal for making echoes. The hard walls and floor reflect sound, and there are no soft sofas or carpets to absorb it.

▶ An echo-free chamber. The floor, ceiling and walls are made of glass-fibre wedges designed to absorb noise, so that no sounds are reflected.

Sound recording

One of the strangest recordings ever made is winging its way through space. A long way from Earth, two *Voyager* space probes are heading for the stars. They carry recordings of sounds from Earth. Perhaps some day one of them will be found by aliens, who will play it back to hear what our planet is like.

Sounds are made by things that shake (vibrate). These vibrations shake up the air, making a sound wave. If the vibrations stop, the sound dies away. To record a sound, the vibrations have to be caught and changed into something else.

Sounds can be recorded using a microphone. This changes the sound vibrations into an electrical copy of the sound called a signal.

There are many ways of storing signals for a long time. One way is to turn them into patterns of magnetism.

In a recording studio, microphones are used to turn sound waves into electrical signals. These signals are made stronger (amplified) by special electronic circuits. The signals travel down wires to the mixing desk. Electronic instruments make their own electrical signals, which can be sent straight to the desk.

At the mixing desk, a technician controls the signals and mixes them together. Then they are recorded on to a large magnetic tape (the master tape). Copies can be made from the master tape in many different formats, including CD (compact disc), cassette and minidisc. Eventually, music will be sold on computer chips.

▶ This mini hi-fi system can play sounds recorded on cassette, CD or minidisc.

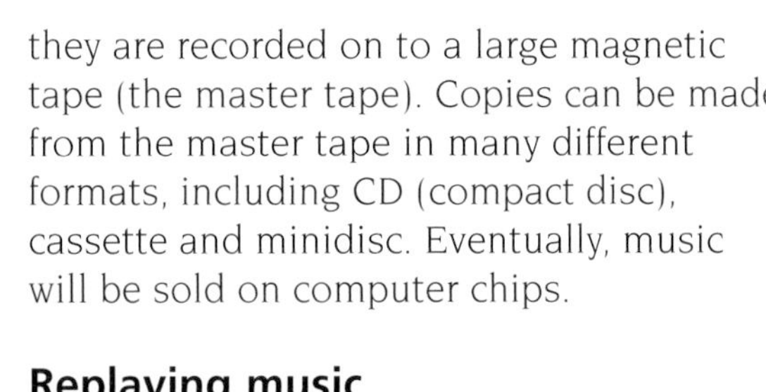

Replaying music

Once the music is stored in some form, it can be played back whenever you want. The player reads the stored music and turns it back into a pattern of electricity. This is then made stronger by an amplifier. From the amplifier, the electrical signals are passed to a set of loudspeakers. These turn the signals into vibrations of the loudspeaker cones, which we hear as sounds.

◀ In a modern recording studio, each instrument or voice is recorded separately on its own 'track'. The recording engineer uses a mixing desk to combine the tracks. He can control how loud each track is. He can also add echo or other effects.

▼ In a stereo recording, the sound is recorded as two slightly different 'tracks'. For example, an instrument may be slightly louder on the left-hand track than on the right. This will make the instrument sound as if it is closer to the left-hand loudspeaker.

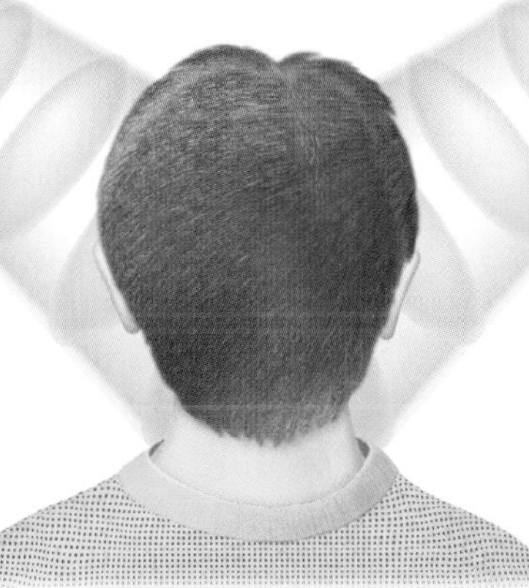

Analogue and digital

The music on the master tape is recorded as a smoothly changing pattern – an analogue recording. The recording on a cassette tape is analogue too.

Analogue recordings are very fragile. They cannot be copied very often or they lose quality. These days most recordings are made digitally.

The first step in making a digital recording is to turn the music into a pattern of numbers (digits). This is called sampling and is done by an electronic circuit. From here, the music can be stored in a variety of ways. On a CD the numbers are stored as a pattern of bumps. On a minidisc, they are stored as spots of magnetism.

The quality of digital recordings is very high. Once the music is in the form of numbers, it can be copied many times without losing any quality.

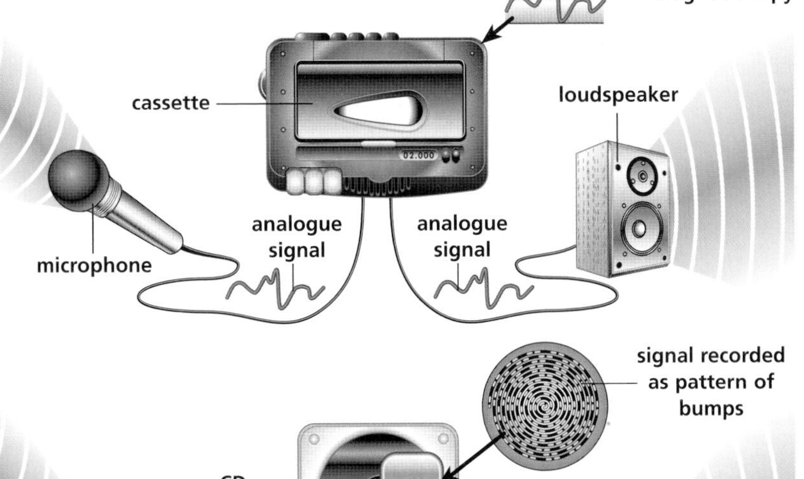

▼ A microphone turns sounds into an analogue (smoothly changing) signal. In a cassette, this signal is copied directly onto tape. In a CD, the signal is digitized and the numbers are recorded as a pattern of bumps.

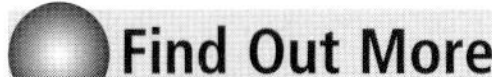

- Compact discs
- Electronics
- Microphones and speakers
- Video equipment

'Hi-fi' is short for 'high fidelity'. Fidelity means faithfulness, and so the name refers to systems that reproduce sounds that are faithful to the original recording.

Stereo

A stereo recording tries to create the illusion that you are listening to real musicians in the room. It does this by tricking your ears. For stereo to work there must be two loudspeakers with some distance between them.

Space astronomy

Space is a wonderful place for observing the stars. Above the Earth's atmosphere the sky is always dark and there are no clouds. The most exciting way to learn about other worlds in our Solar System is to send spacecraft to explore them in close-up.

▲ This miniature rover was carried to Mars by the space probe *Mars Pathfinder*. In this slightly blurred image, relayed direct from Mars, it is studying a rock nicknamed 'Yogi'.

For astronomers, the atmosphere is a nuisance. From the Earth, stars never look truly sharp because the air makes them twinkle. Even worse, the air absorbs invisible kinds of radiation such as X-rays, ultraviolet rays and infrared rays. These kinds of radiation can give astronomers valuable extra information about planets, stars and galaxies.

▶ This picture of the sky shows the remains of an exploded star, known as the Crab Nebula. It was taken by the Chandra X-ray Observatory.

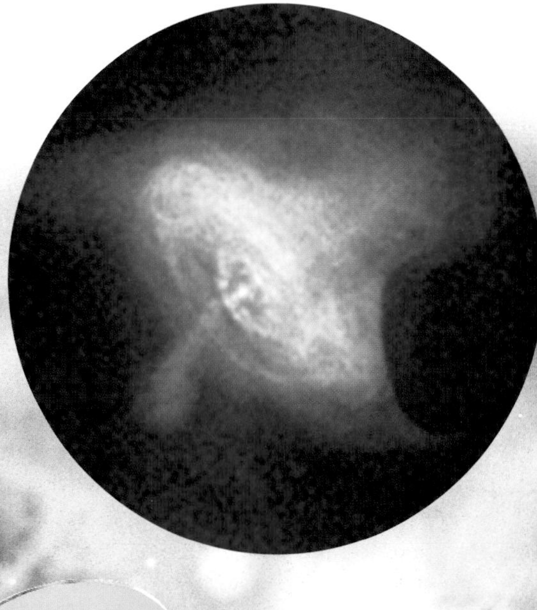

▶ The Chandra X-ray Observatory was launched into an orbit thousands of kilometres above the Earth by the space shuttle *Columbia* in July 1999.

THE HUBBLE SPACE TELESCOPE

The space shuttle *Discovery* carried the Hubble Space Telescope into orbit in April 1990. It circles the Earth every 90 minutes, about 600 kilometres above us.

The telescope's main mirror is 2.4 metres across. It is used to observe ultraviolet and infrared rays as well as visible light. The telescope beams its observations back to Earth as radio signals. The two 'paddles' on either side of the tube are solar panels. They convert sunlight into electrical power. Astronauts have travelled to the telescope on board the space shuttle several times to make repairs and change old instruments for more modern ones.

Find Out More

- Astronomy
- Orbits
- Satellites
- Space travel
- X-rays

Satellites in space

To overcome these problems, many astronomy satellites have been put into orbit around the Earth since the 1960s. Some satellites are launched on rockets. Others are taken on board a space shuttle. Successful ones usually work for several years. These satellites carry special telescopes that are built to pick up each different kind of radiation.

Exploring the Solar System

Every planet in the Solar System, apart from Pluto, has been visited by a spacecraft at least once. There have also been missions to asteroids and comets, and to our own Moon. These interplanetary explorers carry television cameras which beam images back to Earth, and instruments to measure such things as a planet's magnetic field.

Sometimes spacecraft just fly past their targets, returning information for only a few hours. The most successful flyby mission ever was *Voyager* 2, launched in 1977. It toured all four giant planets: Jupiter, Saturn, Uranus and Neptune.

Orbiters, probes and landers

A spacecraft orbiting a planet or moon – called an 'orbiter' – sometimes stays in service for years. The two *Lunar Orbiter* spacecraft, sent to the Moon in 1966 and 1967, made maps of the Moon to prepare for later manned landings. *Mars Global Surveyor* began to make detailed maps of the whole of Mars in 1999.

Galileo was put into orbit around Jupiter at the end of 1995 and stayed there for several years. It released a probe that went down into Jupiter's atmosphere. Venus has also been studied by atmosphere probes, such as *Pioneer Venus* 2, launched in 1978.

Some spacecraft are designed to land softly on a planet's surface. Sometimes landers are released by orbiters, which continue to circle overhead. The two *Viking* space probes, which reached Mars in 1976, released landers that tested the soil for signs of life. These landers also sent back the first pictures from the surface of Mars.

▼ The *Cassini* spacecraft will release a probe when it arrives to orbit Saturn in 2004. The probe will parachute down through the hazy atmosphere of Saturn's largest moon, Titan. Its six instruments will beam back pictures and data.

Space shuttle

The space shuttle is part rocket, part spacecraft and part aircraft. It blasts off the launch pad like a rocket. It manoeuvres in orbit like a spacecraft. And it glides into land like an aircraft. Unlike other rockets, the shuttle can be used over and over again.

The space shuttle has been carrying astronauts into space since 1981. There have been over 100 shuttle flights since then. The shuttle's payload bay (cargo area) can carry satellites such as the Hubble Space Telescope into orbit. It is also used to carry parts of the International Space Station. The cargo bay can also house Spacelab, a complete laboratory where scientists can carry out experiments.

Launch into space

The space shuttle is launched from the Kennedy Space Center in Florida, USA. On the launch pad, the orbiter is mounted on two solid rocket boosters (SRBs) and a huge external fuel tank. On lift-off, the orbiter's main engines and the SRBs all fire at once. Together they have the power of a whole fleet of jumbo jet airliners.

▶ The orbiter *Endeavour* releases a braking parachute after it has touched down on the runway. *Endeavour* is one of three orbiters in use. The others are *Atlantis* and *Discovery*. Two more, *Challenger* and *Columbia*, have been lost in accidents.

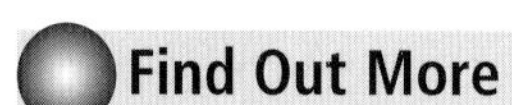

Find Out More

- Astronauts
- Rockets
- Satellites
- Space astronomy
- Space travel

As the orbiter climbs into space, the SRBs and the external tank fall away in turn as their fuel is used up. The SRBs are recovered, but the tank is not.

Down to Earth

At the end of its mission, the orbiter re-enters the Earth's atmosphere, travelling very fast. Air resistance slows the orbiter down, but at the same time makes it heat up because of friction. To keep out the heat, the orbiter is covered with insulation.

About 25 minutes after re-entry, the orbiter glides in to land at Kennedy Space Center.

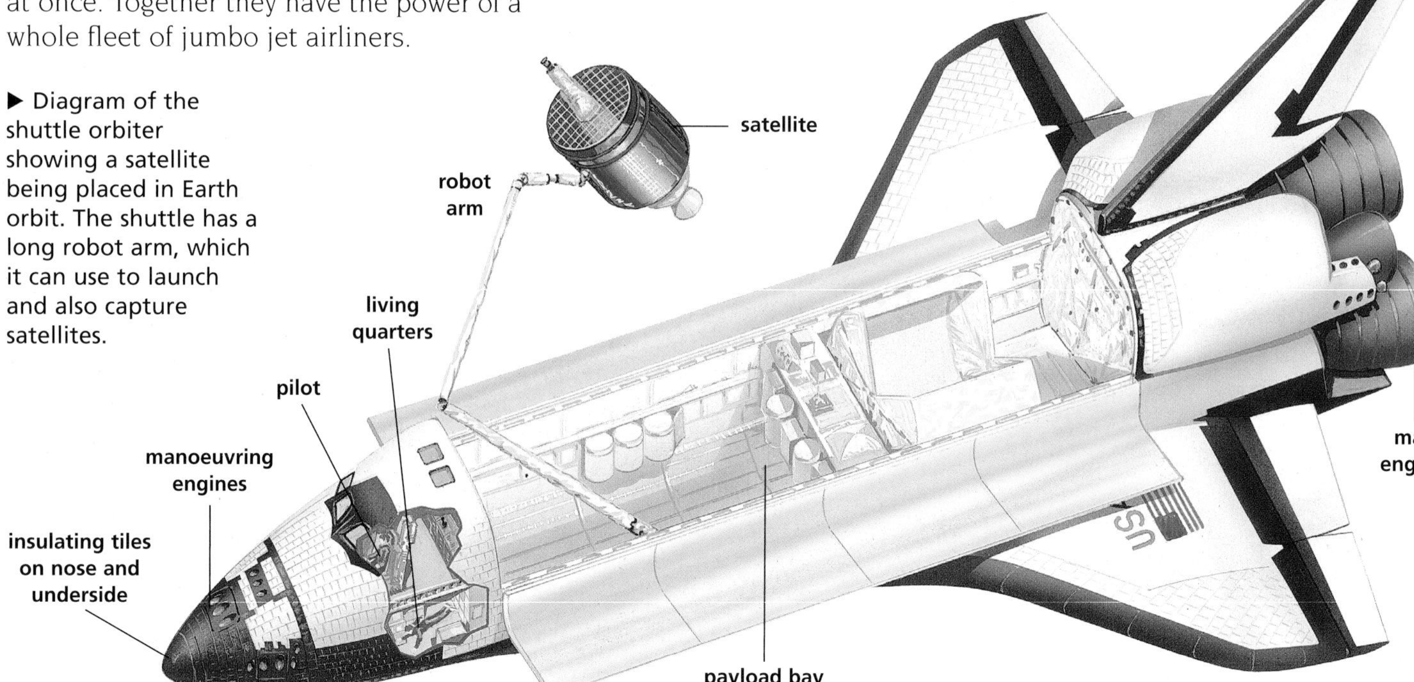

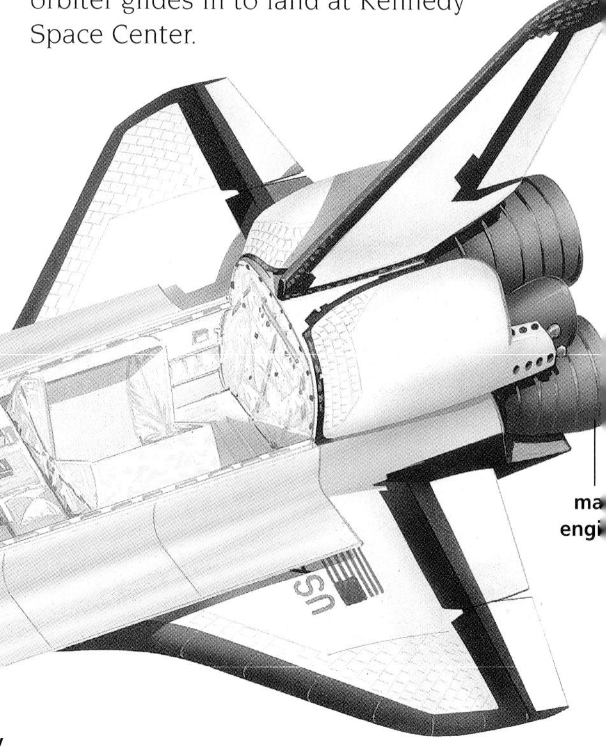

▶ Diagram of the shuttle orbiter showing a satellite being placed in Earth orbit. The shuttle has a long robot arm, which it can use to launch and also capture satellites.

Space stations

Later this century, you could be living and working on a huge space station, watching the Sun rise and set 16 times a day. From there, you might catch a lunar ferry that would whisk you to a base on the Moon, or a spaceship heading for the planet Mars.

Space stations are spacecraft in which astronauts stay in space for a long time. They circle in orbit around the Earth a few hundred kilometres high.

Russia has launched a number of space stations, including *Mir*, launched in 1986. The United States launched the space station *Skylab* in 1973. *Mir* has been the most successful, with astronauts, cosmonauts and scientists from many countries visiting to live and carry out experiments in space.

Find Out More

- Astronauts
- Orbits
- Space shuttles
- Space travel

▲ *Mir* in orbit, photographed by astronauts in a visiting space shuttle. It is made up of a number of parts, or modules. They were launched one by one and put together in orbit. The flat panels that look like windmill sails are solar panels, which convert sunlight into electric power.

The ISS

Today, Russia and the United States are working together with Europe, Japan and Canada on the construction of a large international space station, the ISS.

The ISS is being built bit by bit. Each piece, or module, is carried into orbit, and linked up to modules already there. A Russian Proton rocket carried the first module, named *Zarya*, into orbit in November 1998. Among the other modules of the station are a Russian service module (*Zvezda*), a living quarters, and several laboratories.

In time, the ISS, or a space station like it, may be expanded to become a port for spacecraft, travelling to the Moon and eventually to Mars.

▶ An artist's impression of what the completed international space station will look like. It will be more than 100 m long and weigh about 400 tonnes.

Space travel

On 12 April 1961, Russian pilot Yuri Gagarin became the fastest man alive. Travelling at a speed of nearly 8 kilometres per second, he rocketed into orbit to become the first man in space. He said afterwards, 'The rocket engines were creating the music of the future.'

A Russian schoolteacher named Konstantin Tsiolkovsky first suggested in the early 1900s that rockets could be used for exploring outer space. But it was more than 50 years before rockets were powerful enough to launch objects into space. The first objects launched were satellites. These are spacecraft that circle round and round the Earth in orbit.

Find Out More

- Astronauts
- Satellites
- Space astronomy
- Space shuttles
- Space stations

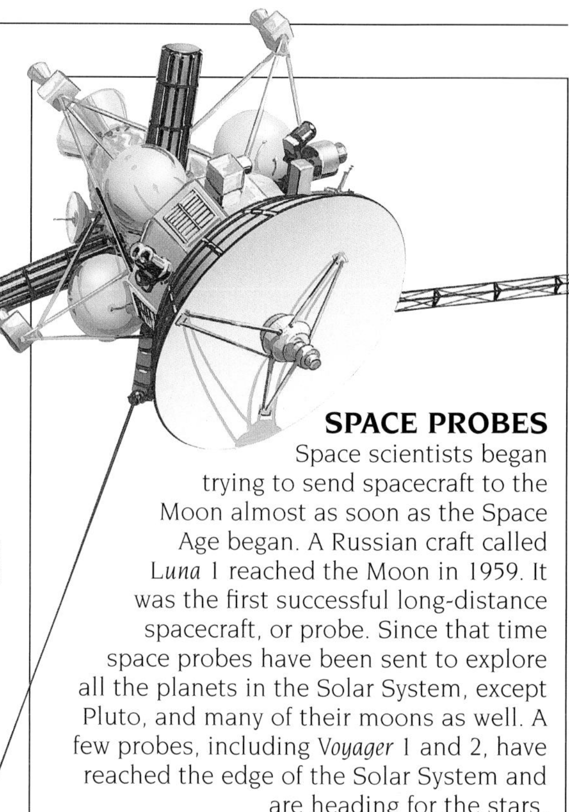

SPACE PROBES

Space scientists began trying to send spacecraft to the Moon almost as soon as the Space Age began. A Russian craft called *Luna* 1 reached the Moon in 1959. It was the first successful long-distance spacecraft, or probe. Since that time space probes have been sent to explore all the planets in the Solar System, except Pluto, and many of their moons as well. A few probes, including *Voyager* 1 and 2, have reached the edge of the Solar System and are heading for the stars.

Human spaceflight

Before Gagarin's pioneering flight, no one knew whether humans would survive travelling in space. But we now know that they can. And they can stay in space for months at a time.

Many countries now launch satellites into space, but only two have launched people – the United States and Russia. In the United States, space activities are controlled by NASA, the National Aeronautics and Space Agency. US astronauts ride into space in the space shuttle, which has been flying since 1981. Russian cosmonauts fly into space in Soyuz spacecraft, which have been operating since 1967.

The US and Russia are working together to build an international space station in orbit, in which astronauts and cosmonauts will work. Europe is working with them through the European Space Agency (ESA). So is Japan through its space agency NASDA.

Human spaceflight is very expensive. So it seems sensible for several countries to share the costs of future missions, such as setting up bases on the Moon and Mars.

MILESTONES IN SPACE TRAVEL

1957
▶ Russia launches the first satellite, *Sputnik 1* on 4 October. *Sputnik 2*, launched a month later, carries the first space traveller, a dog called Laika.

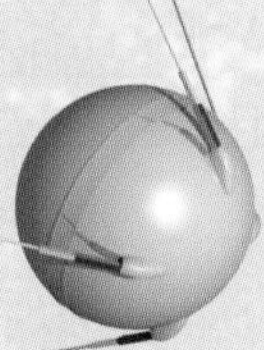

1958
US launches its first satellite, *Explorer 1*, which discovers the Earth's Van Allen radiation belts.

1961
Yuri Gagarin (Russia) becomes the first man in space, travelling once around the Earth in a *Vostok 1* capsule on 12 April.

1962
On 20 February John Glenn becomes the first American in orbit, flying in a Mercury capsule called *Friendship 7*.

1963
▼ Valentina Tereshkova (Russia) flies in *Vostok 6*. She is the first woman to travel in space

1965
On 18 March Alexei Leonov (Russia) makes the first spacewalk from *Voskhod 2*.

1968
Frank Borman, James Lovell and William Anders become the first humans to fly around the Moon in *Apollo 8*.

1969
◀ On 20 July *Apollo 11* lands on the Moon. Neil Armstrong and Buzz Aldrin (pictured here) take the first steps on the surface.

1971
Russia launches the first space station, *Salyut 1*.

1975
▲ Apollo-Soyuz docking. US and Russia mount the first joint mission in space, the Apollo-Soyuz Test Project.

1981
On 12 April the US space shuttle makes its maiden voyage. The orbiter *Columbia* spends just over two days in space.

1986
On 28 January the space shuttle orbiter *Challenger* blows up shortly after lift-off, killing its crew of seven. Also in January, Russia launches the first part of its *Mir* space station.

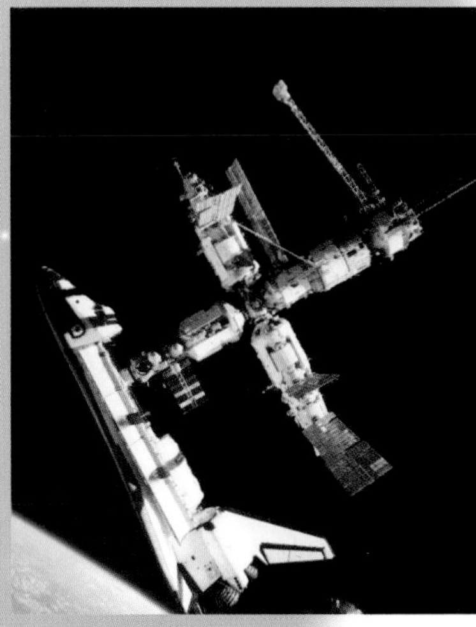

1995
▲ First US space shuttle link-up with Russian space station *Mir*.

1998
◀ *Zarya*, the first module for the international space station (ISS), is launched by Russia.

2000
Astronauts live in the partly built ISS for the first time.

Sparks *see* Electricity • **Species** *see* Classification • **Spectacles** *see* Eyes

Spectrum

The storm is over. After the crashing violence of the thunder and lightning, the graceful arc of a rainbow extends across the sky. The band of colours a rainbow produces is called a spectrum.

When we see white light, we are actually looking at lots of different colours mixed together. White light can be split up so that the separate colours can be seen. A triangular piece of glass (a prism) is very good at doing this as it bends (refracts) light. The different colours bend by different amounts, so they spread out and form a rainbow pattern. Each colour is a different wavelength of light.

Rainbows

Rainbows are made when there are lots of raindrops in the air. The drops reflect light that is coming from behind you. This is why you never see the Sun in the same direction as a rainbow.

When the light enters a raindrop, it splits into colours. The different colours reflect off the back of the raindrop and split up even further as they come out again. Only one colour from each raindrop will reach your eye. However, you see the whole rainbow, because there are millions of drops reflecting light towards you.

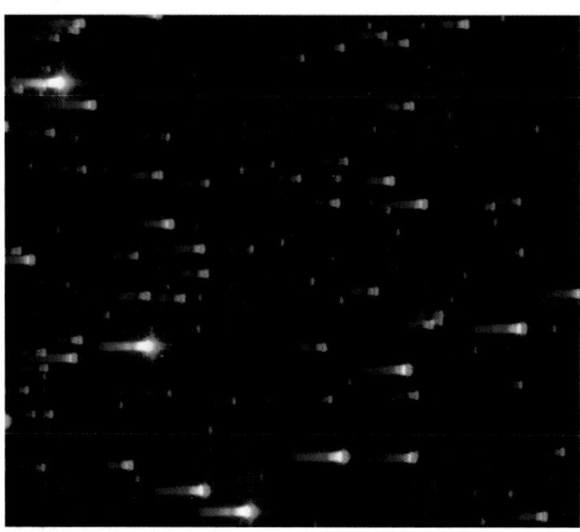

◀ The tiny spectra in this picture are made by stars. The light from the stars was split up by a prism inserted into the telescope used to take the picture. The spectrum for each star is different in detail, as each star produces slightly different light.

▶ A Brocken spectre is a ghostly figure surrounded by a rainbow, sometimes seen by mountaineers. The 'spectre' is actually the viewer's shadow falling on mist or cloud. The halo around it is produced when sunlight is split into tiny rainbows by water drops in the mist or cloud.

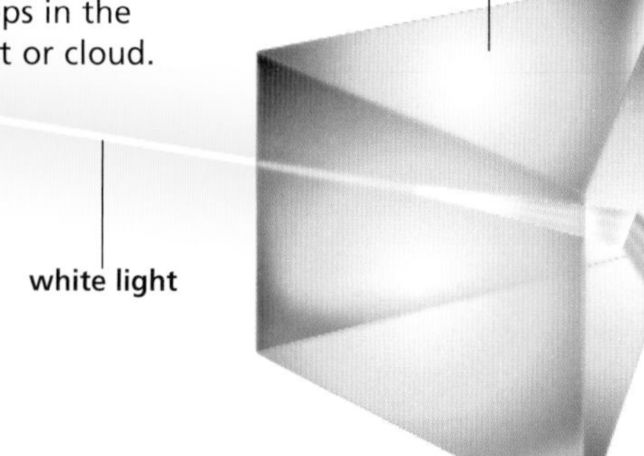

▼ A prism is a triangular-shaped piece of glass that can be used to split white light into a spectrum. White light is partly split as it enters the prism. The colours then travel across the prism in straight lines to be spread even further apart as they leave on the other side.

Find Out More

- Colour
- Electromagnetic spectrum
- Light
- Rain and snow

If you are looking down on a rainbow from high up (from a mountain, for example), you can sometimes see it as a complete circle, not just an arc.

Extending the spectrum

Sunlight contains other waves besides the ones in the visible spectrum. Just beyond the red end of the spectrum is infrared (IR) radiation, with wavelengths longer than red light. We cannot see IR, but it is given off by warm objects. The remote control on a TV uses infrared.

At the other end of the spectrum is ultraviolet (UV) radiation, which has wavelengths shorter than violet light. UV from the Sun gives us a suntan.

Speech and language

Walk into your school playground any morning and you'll hear a babble of conversation. Speech is a really good way of communicating. When we speak, our vocal cords contract and relax very fast, we change the shape of our mouth, and move our tongue, lips and teeth very quickly and precisely. We learn to do all this in the first few years of life.

The speech centre in the left side of the brain controls language. The brain recognizes not only the words that are being spoken, but also identifies who is talking by the sound of their voice.

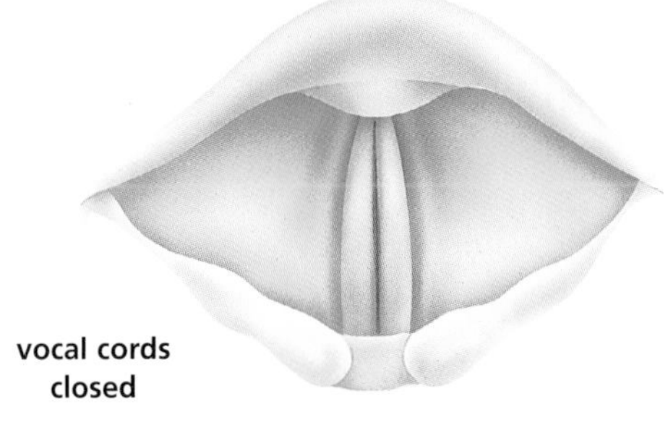

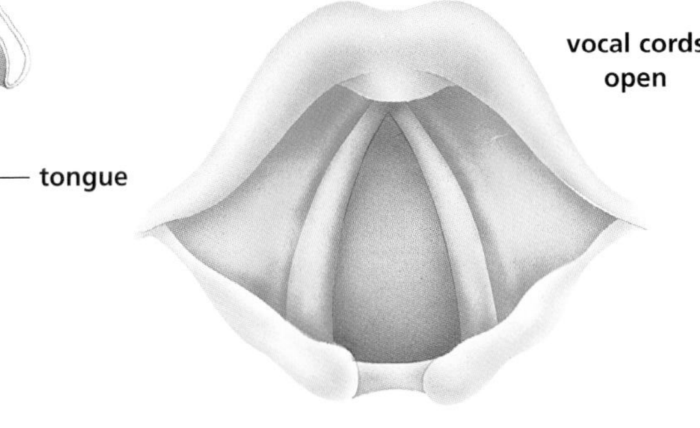

◀ ▲ Our voice box or larynx is at the top of the windpipe. Our vocal chords are stretched across the larynx. Air from the lungs makes the cords vibrate, and muscles pull them tighter or relax them to change the pitch of the sound.

First words

Scientists believe that humans are born with the ability to learn language. At first babies babble, making and listening to their own sounds. As they grow older, they start to imitate what they hear and to put words together. A child's first language will be the one spoken by the people around them.

Grammar is the elaborate set of rules we use to put words together so that they make sense. Even experts are not able to explain all the rules of grammar, and yet by the age of three most children will know how to speak in reasonably correct sentences. As we grow and develop, we learn to use language to express more complex ideas.

Body language

As well as speaking with our voices, we communicate with our hands and bodies. It is quite easy to see when someone is angry, puzzled or surprised just by looking at their face. Some gestures, such as nodding or shaking the head, take the place of words.

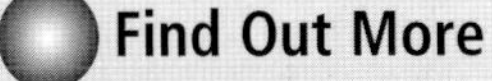

- Brain and nerves
- Communications
- Sound

▼ People who are deaf can learn to communicate entirely through gestures and signs. This person is using sign language to say 'Hello! I am pleased to meet you.'

Hello! I (am)

pleased

to meet

you.

Stars

From red giants to white dwarfs, stars come in a variety of colours and a huge range of sizes. Like our Sun, every star is a giant ball of hot, glowing gas. But because they are so far away, we see them only as pinpricks of light.

Every star keeps shining for millions or billions of years because nuclear energy is generated inside it. But not all stars are identical. They come in different sizes and colours depending on how much material they contain. They also change size and colour as they get older.

The colour of a star tells us its surface temperature. The hottest stars are white or bluish and give off the most intense light, including strong, ultraviolet radiation. The coolest stars look red and their surfaces shine dimly. Many give out more infrared than visible light. Our yellow Sun is a middle-sized star.

X-RAY BINARIES

In some binary stars, one of the pair is normal but the other is a collapsed star. The collapsed star has shrunk to become an immensely dense ball less than 10 kilometres across.

In such a binary pair, the very strong gravity of the collapsed star pulls hot gas away from the normal star as they circle each other. This material collects around the collapsed star, forming a flat disk. At the centre of the disk, extremely hot material falls on to the collapsed star, and energy is given out in the form of intense X-rays.

One kind of X-ray binary consists of a neutron star and a blue giant star (see below).

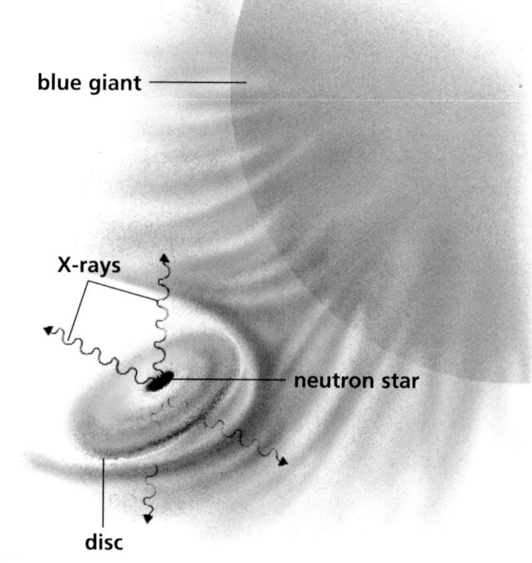

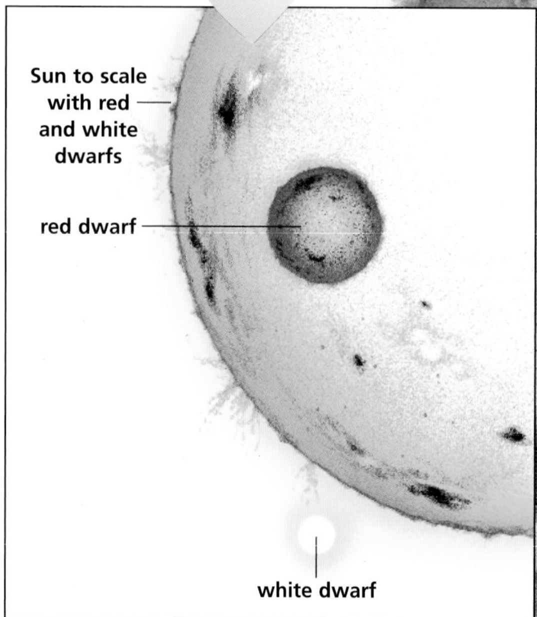

◀ Stars of different kinds, shown to scale. Our yellow-white Sun is a medium-sized star. The blue supergiant was born a giant, but the red supergiant used to be smaller and has swelled up. A red dwarf is an ordinary star, but a white dwarf is the core of a star that was once a red giant.

Double and variable stars

About half of all 'stars' in the sky are really a pair of stars, orbiting around the balancing point between them. They are often called binary stars. If their orbits are edge on towards us, the stars will alternately cross behind and in front of each other. When that happens, the total light from the two stars dips at regular intervals. Star couples like these are called eclipsing binaries.

The brightness of single stars can also change. Such stars are called variable stars. They change for many different reasons. Some giant stars gently pulse in and out every few days in a regular way. Most supergiants also pulsate slowly over several years, though in a pattern that is only partly regular.

Other stars suddenly brighten up or dim in an unpredictable way. One kind of supergiant forms tiny sooty particles in its outer layers. They make the star look much dimmer for a while until they are blown off into space.

▲ The Hubble Space Telescope took this ultraviolet picture of the red supergiant star Betelgeuse, which is 1000 times larger than the Sun. It shows that Betelgeuse is surrounded by a vast cloud of thin, hot gas, rather like our Sun's corona.

SOME SPECIAL STARS

Name	**What's special**	**Constellation**
Sirius	brightest star	Canis Major
Canopus	second-brightest star	Carina
Alpha Centauri	third-brightest star	Centaurus
Proxima	nearest star (4 light years)	Centaurus
Algol	most famous eclipsing binary	Perseus
Mira	famous variable, the first discovered	Cetus

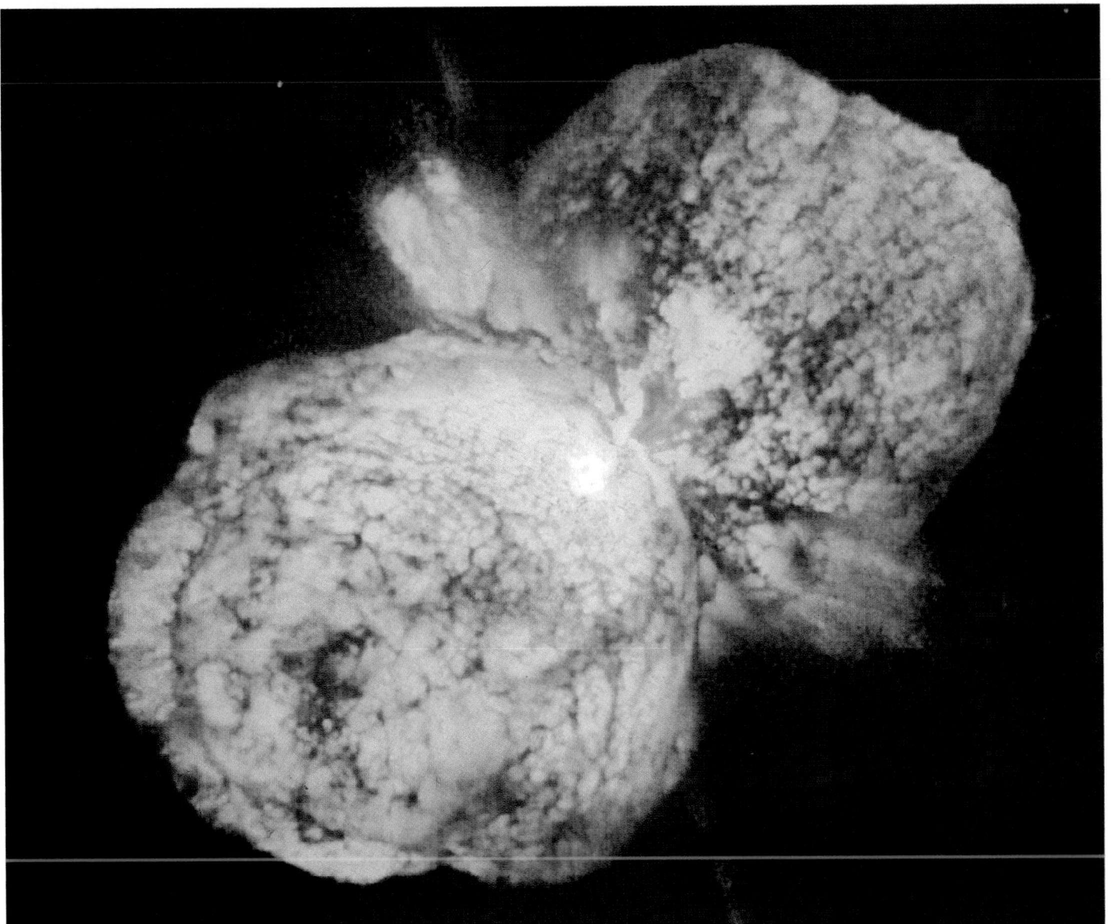

◀ These twin lobes of gas and dust, pictured by the Hubble Space Telescope, are flowing out from one of the most massive known stars, which is hidden inside. Called Eta Carinae, astronomers suspect it may be a double star. It radiates five million times more power than the Sun.

A star's life

Stars do not last forever. They are born and they die. Our Sun is about 5000 million years old now. It has another 5000 million to go before it swells into a red giant and its life as the yellow star we know comes to an end.

New stars are constantly being born to replace ones that die. Clusters of stars usually form together. They begin life in vast clouds of cold, dark gas and dust in space. Gravity pulls the material together into large, rotating clumps. As long as a gas clump is at least a twentieth the size of the Sun, it heats up enough inside to generate nuclear energy and become a star.

For most of their lifetime (often billions of years) stars shine steadily without much change. Smaller stars live much longer than very large ones. But when a star's nuclear fuel begins to run out, the star reacts by puffing up until it becomes a giant or a supergiant. Stars that are less than one and a half times the Sun's mass then blow off their outer layers, leaving a tiny, cooling star called a white dwarf. Stars that are more massive than one and a half

Find Out More
- Constellations
- Galaxies
- Nebulas and clusters
- Sun
- Temperature
- X-rays

▶ The Orion Nebula is a huge, glowing bubble of gas lit up by a group of hot stars that were born only 100,000 years ago. More new stars are being created nearby. Some of them are surrounded by discs of gas and dust, where planets might form.

▼ Different kinds of star have different life cycles. The lives of a small and a large star are shown here.

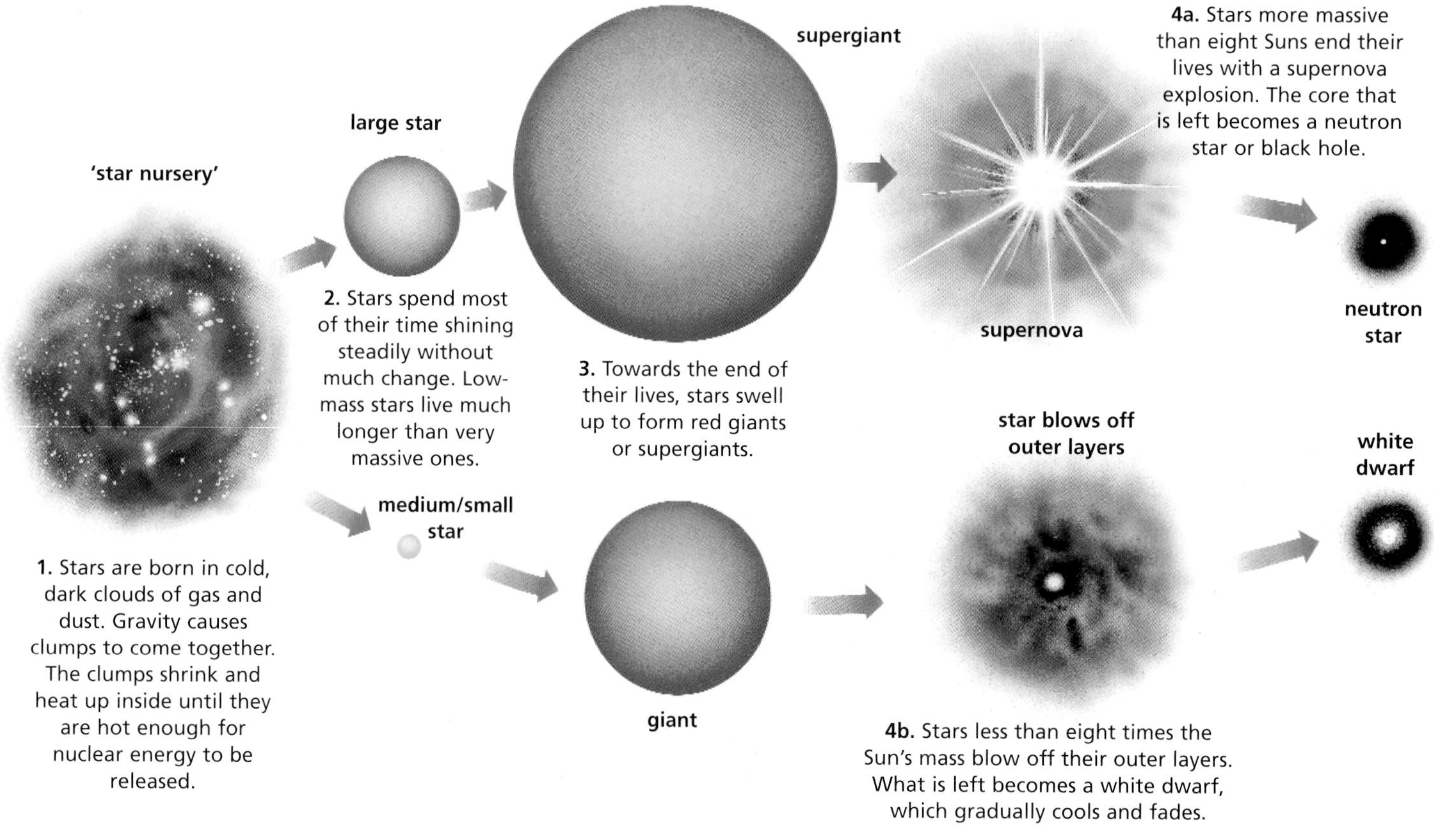

'star nursery'

1. Stars are born in cold, dark clouds of gas and dust. Gravity causes clumps to come together. The clumps shrink and heat up inside until they are hot enough for nuclear energy to be released.

large star

2. Stars spend most of their time shining steadily without much change. Low-mass stars live much longer than very massive ones.

medium/small star

supergiant

giant

3. Towards the end of their lives, stars swell up to form red giants or supergiants.

supernova

4a. Stars more massive than eight Suns end their lives with a supernova explosion. The core that is left becomes a neutron star or black hole.

neutron star

star blows off outer layers

4b. Stars less than eight times the Sun's mass blow off their outer layers. What is left becomes a white dwarf, which gradually cools and fades.

white dwarf

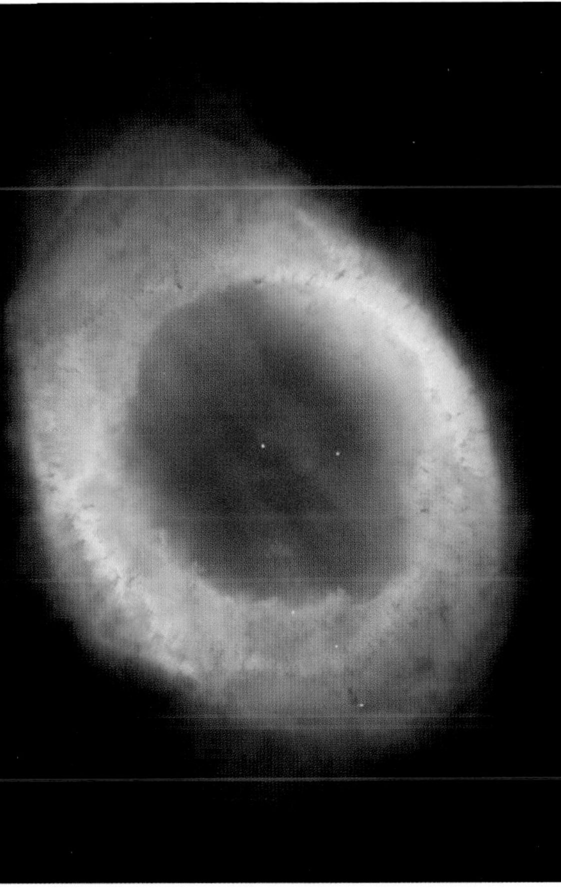

Suns end their lives with a supernova explosion. The leftover core becomes a neutron star, or sometimes a black hole.

Double stars may end in a bright explosion called a nova. A nova can occur when one of the star pair is a white dwarf. The strong gravity of the white dwarf attracts gas over from its companion. The white dwarf cannot take the new gas without becoming unstable. A giant nuclear explosion takes place on the white dwarf's surface, and it suddenly blazes out 10,000 times brighter than it was before.

White dwarfs and neutron stars

The remains left behind when stars die are very strange objects. They collapse in on themselves and become incredibly dense. A white dwarf star, though similar in size to the Earth, has as much mass as the whole Sun. A single teaspoonful would weigh many tonnes.

Neutron stars are even denser than white dwarfs. A neutron star is more massive (weighs more) than the Sun, but all this mass is packed into a ball just 10 kilometres or so across.

Black holes

If a very large star (more than eight times the Sun's mass) becomes a supernova, its core collapses totally. If the core is massive enough, it can form a black hole. A black hole is even more dense than a neutron star. The gravity around it is so immensely strong that not even light can escape. This makes it impossible to see. Black holes are only detected when they are paired with another star. Then, the effects they have can be seen.

◀ The Ring Nebula. The small dot in the centre is the remains of an old star that blew off its outside layers of gas between 5000 and 6000 years ago. It is now a white dwarf. Its ultraviolet radiation makes the nebula glow.

▶ A star in the small neighbouring galaxy called the Large Magellanic Cloud exploded in 1987. It was the brightest, nearest supernova observed since the year 1604.

▼ The Crab Nebula. This tangle of gas was created when a star exploded as a supernova in 1054. What was left of the star's core became a spinning neutron star.

Static electricity *see* Electricity

Steam engines

You boil a kettle of water to make a cup of tea or coffee – power stations boil water on a far greater scale. This generates the supply of electricity that comes to your home and makes your kettle work.

When water boils, it produces a large amount of hot steam. This steam has a lot of energy. Most power stations burn fuel to boil water, and the hot steam goes to huge steam turbines that drive the generators.

Steam turbines

Inside the turbine are sets of blades fixed to a central shaft. The steam drives the blades around, turning the shaft with great power. The turbine shaft drives an electric generator, and the electricity flows through power lines to homes.

Some large ships are powered by steam turbines, which drive the ship's propellers.

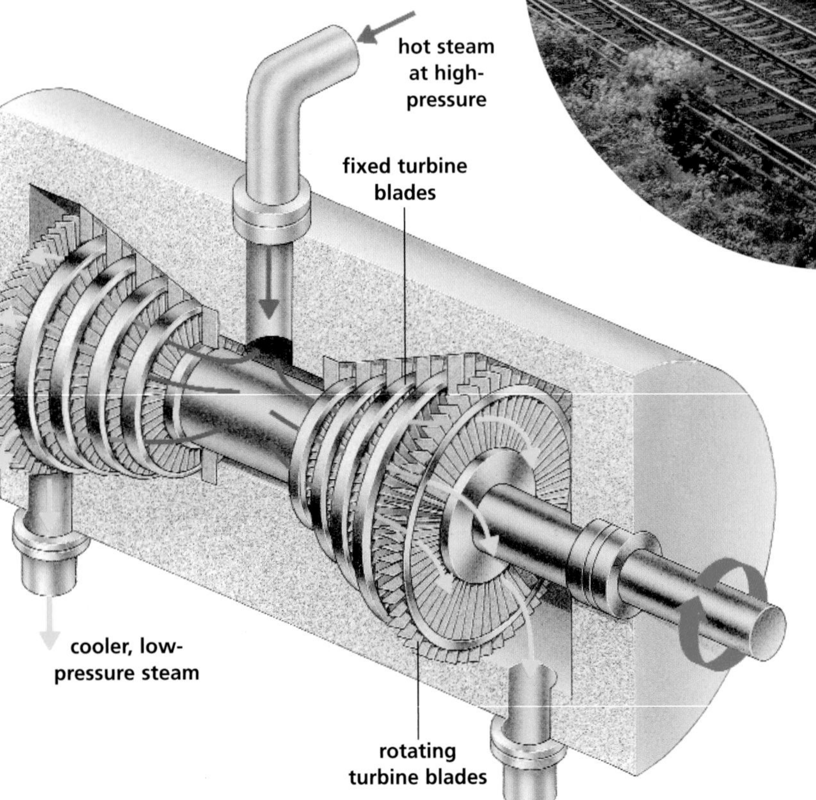

◀ The steam turbine in a power station has several sets of blades all fixed to a central shaft. The steam enters the first set at high pressure and, having turned the blades, leaves at lower pressure. The next sets of blades work at lower pressure. In this way, the turbine uses up nearly all of the energy in the hot steam.

Find Out More
- Engines and turbines
- Power stations
- Trains

STEAM POWER

The steam engine was developed into a powerful, efficient engine by the British engineer James Watt (1736–1819) in 1769. He improved a slow and inefficient engine invented in 1712 by Thomas Newcomen. Units of power are called watts in honour of his achievement.

Steam trains

The steam engines in old locomotives were piston engines. A coal-fired boiler in the locomotive raised steam, which went to cylinders by the wheels. Inside each cylinder, the steam pushed a piston backwards and forwards and the piston drove a connecting rod and crankshaft that turned the wheels.

Steam piston engines once powered factories and ships, too.

◀ The fastest steam locomotive was *Mallard*, which reached a record speed of 203 kilometres per hour in 1938. It is now in the National Rail Museum in York, England.

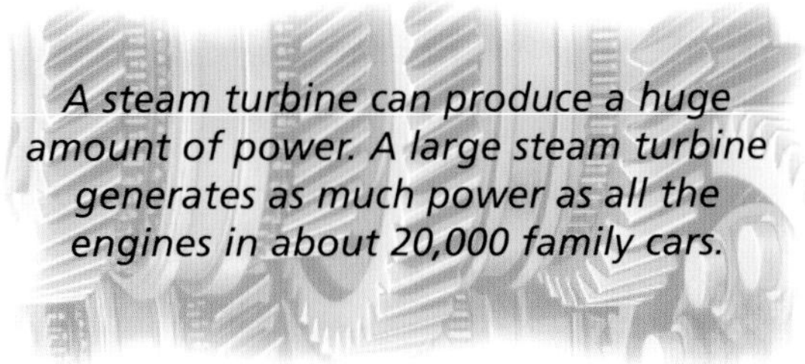

A steam turbine can produce a huge amount of power. A large steam turbine generates as much power as all the engines in about 20,000 family cars.

Steel *see* Iron and steel • **Stratosphere** *see* Atmosphere • **Submarines** *see* Ships and submarines • **Sugar** *see* Diet

Sulphur

If you were foolish enough to stand on the rim of a smoking volcano, you might well smell rotten eggs. The stink is a poisonous gas called hydrogen sulphide – a compound of sulphur and hydrogen. Sulphur is often found around volcanoes and hot springs. For this reason, people used to associate sulphur – or 'brimstone' as they called it – with the underworld and the devil.

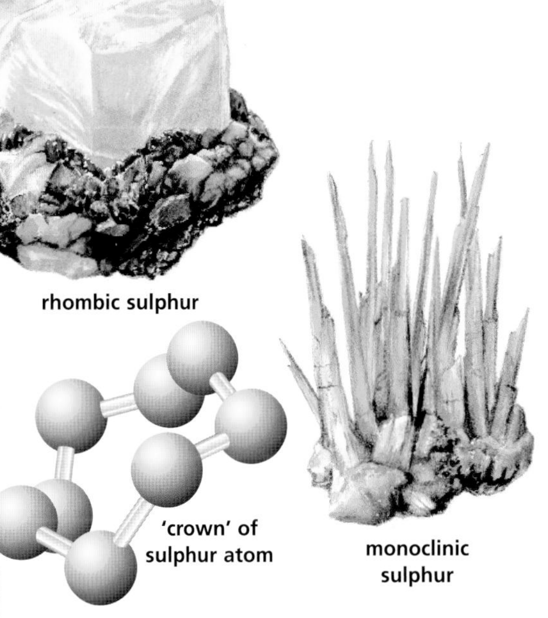

▲ Pure sulphur forms two kinds of crystals, rhombic and monoclinic. Both kinds are made from different arrangements of 'crowns' of sulphur atoms.

Sulphur is a yellow non-metallic element, which is solid at room temperature. It can combine with most other elements. Although some of its compounds are poisonous, others are essential to life.

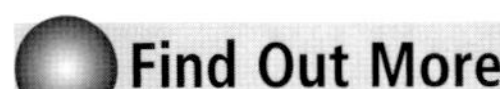
Find Out More

- Crystals
- Elements and compounds
- Rubber
- Volcanoes

Pure sulphur

Pure sulphur has three basic forms, or allotropes. In two of them, the sulphur atoms are arranged regularly into crystal shapes. In rhombic sulphur the crystals are squat, while in monoclinic sulphur they are shaped like needles. The third allotrope is plastic sulphur, which forms when molten sulphur is poured into cold water. Plastic sulphur has no regular shape.

Sulphur is found in many parts of the world, deep underground. It is extracted by drilling a hole and pumping down extremely hot water. This melts the sulphur, which is then blasted to the surface by pressurized air.

▼ Sulphur leaves beautifully coloured deposits around volcanic vents.

Uses of sulphur

Sulphur is an ingredient in matches and gunpowder, and is used to harden rubber – a process called vulcanization. Sulphur is also the basis of many other chemicals, such as sulphuric acid, which is an important raw material in many industries. Some sulphur compounds are important medicines. Others are used by farmers to kill the fungi that attack crops.

When sulphur burns, it makes sulphur dioxide, a poisonous gas. This is produced by coal-fired power stations, and can form damaging acid rain. Sulphur dioxide does have its uses though – for example, as a preservative for jams and other foods.

Sulphuric acid *see* Chemicals

Sun

Shining bright and yellow in the daytime sky, the Sun gives us light and warmth. Most life on Earth needs energy from the Sun to grow and to survive.

The Sun is our very own star – a gigantic ball of glowing gas. It is like the stars that we see in night sky, but much nearer. Among the stars, our Sun is middle-sized and nothing out of the ordinary. But for plants and animals on Earth the Sun is very special. Plants use the energy in sunlight to grow. This process is called photosynthesis. The warmth from the Sun makes our planet a good home for all kinds of living things.

The Sun is mostly made of hydrogen. Like all stars, it generates nuclear energy at its centre. In the process, hydrogen changes to helium – the gas used to fill party balloons. As the hydrogen is turned into helium the Sun gets lighter in weight losing 4 million tonnes every second. The Sun is not about to run out of hydrogen fuel, though. It has been shining for 5000 million years already and will last for around 5000 million more.

▶ The Sun's appearance is constantly changing. The dark patches are sunspots, which last no longer than a few weeks. Sunspots look dark because they are about 1500°C cooler than the surrounding areas.

SUN FACTS
Diameter: 1.4 million km
Mass: 333,000 times Earth's mass
Temperature (surface): 5500 °C
(centre): 15 million °C
Average distance from Earth: 150 million km

A seething surface

The visible yellow surface of the Sun is called the photosphere. It seems to bubble like a cauldron as hot gas surges up and falls back again. The photosphere is surrounded by the Sun's atmosphere. It is made of thin, very hot gas that we do not normally see.

Find Out More

- Hydrogen
- Magnetism and electromagnetism
- Nuclear energy
- Stars

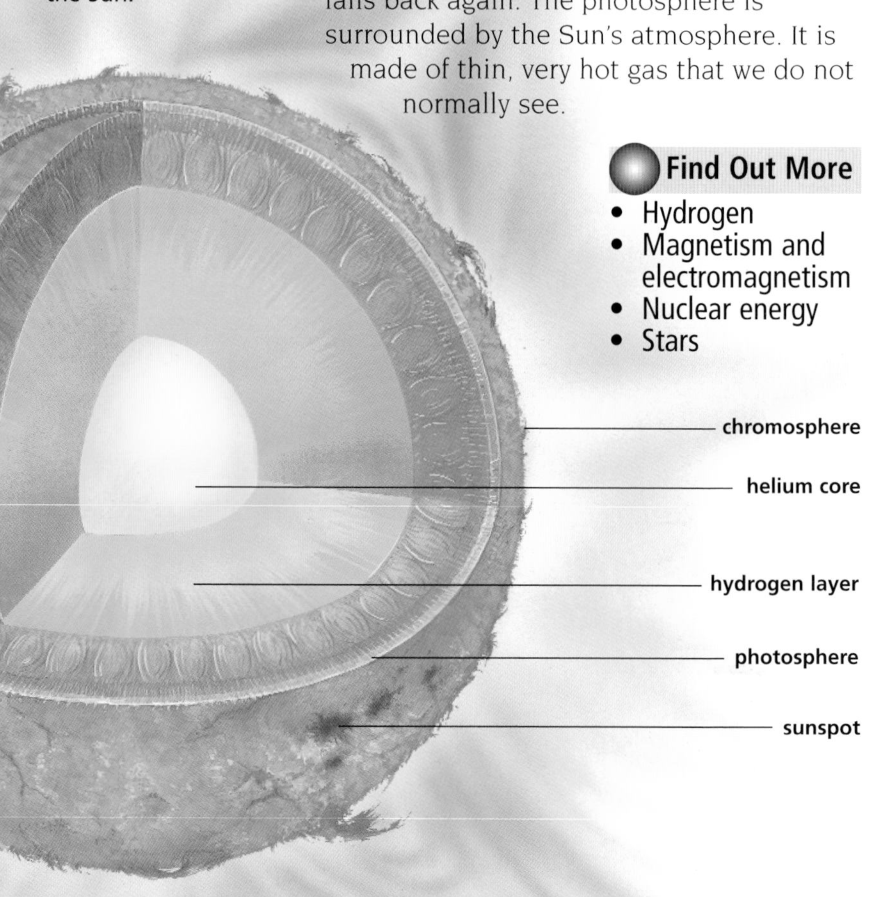

▼ Inside and outside the Sun.

Supercomputer *see* Computers • **Superconductor** *see* Conductors and insulators

Just above the photosphere there is a layer of gas about 5000 kilometres thick called the chromosphere. Sometimes, huge flares explode in the chromosphere. They blast gas particles far into space, even as far as the Earth and beyond. These solar flares can interfere with radio communications on Earth, and are dangerous for astronauts working in space.

The chromosphere merges into the corona, which is the outermost part of the Sun. Temperatures in the corona can be as high as 3 million °C. The corona can be seen when the bright photosphere is hidden by the Moon during a total eclipse. It extends millions of kilometres into space.

▼ A false-colour close-up of a sunspot, taken by the Dutch Open Telescope. These shallow pits on the Sun can be larger than the Earth. Around this sunspot you can see the pattern of the Sun's surface, caused by bubbling gas.

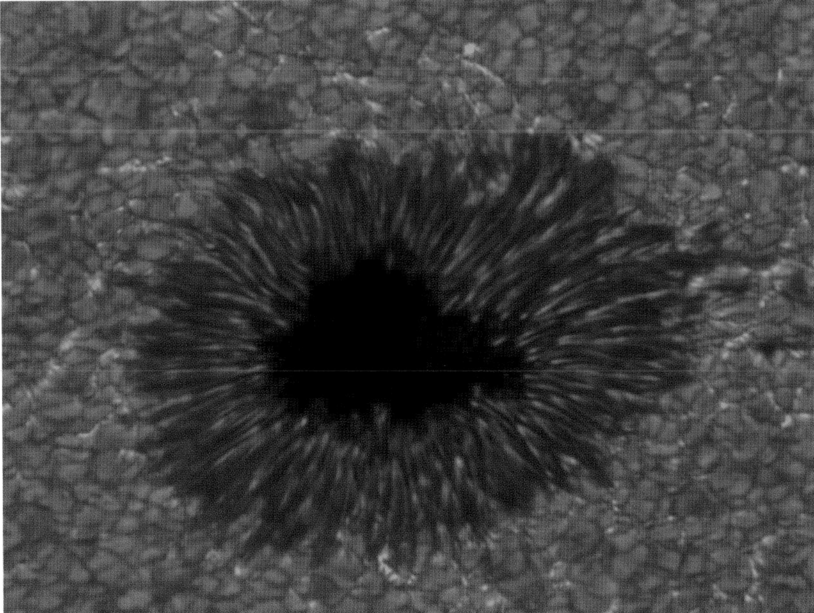

Tiny particles are constantly streaming away from the corona towards the planets, creating a solar wind. The solar wind blows past the Earth at speeds of up to 800 kilometres per second.

The Sun's magnetism

Sunspots are dark, slightly cooler patches on the surface of the Sun. When and where sunspots appear is linked to the Sun's magnetism. Astronomers have noticed that the appearance and disappearance of sunspots follows a regular cycle. Sunspot activity reaches a maximum every 11 years, then falls off. Regular changes in the Sun's magnetic field tie in with this 11-year cycle.

WARNING! Do not look at the Sun, even through sunglasses. Without special equipment you could permanently damage your eyesight.

THE SUN'S MAGNETIC CYCLE

Changes in the Sun's magnetic field happen in a regular cycle of 11 years.

At the start of the cycle (a), lines of magnetic force run north and south between the Sun's poles. At this time there is minimum solar activity.

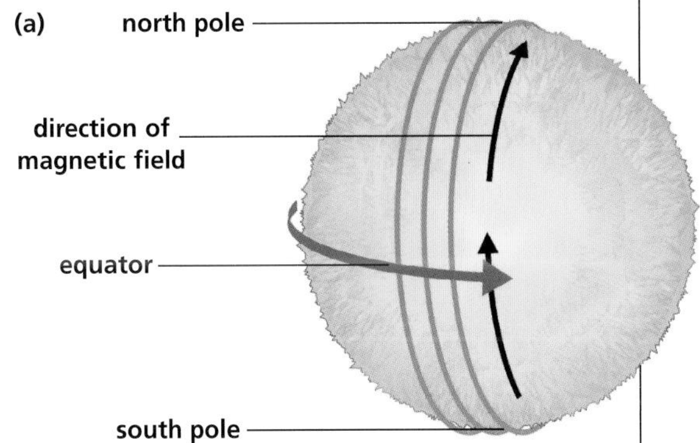

As the Sun rotates, the atmosphere spins faster at the equator than it does at Poles. The lines of magnetic force between the poles begin to bend (b).

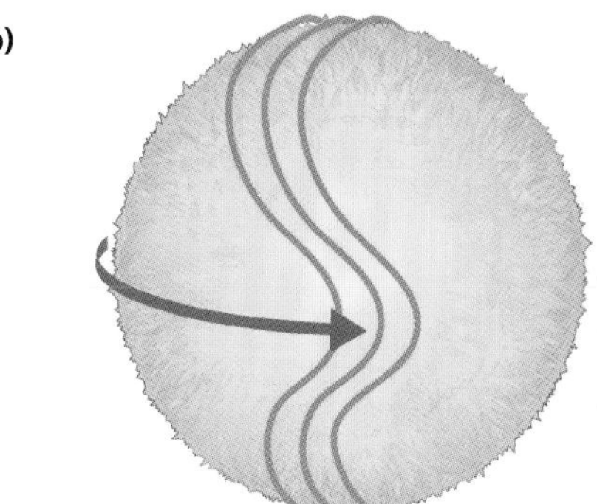

As time goes on, the magnetic field bends more and more. The effect is rather like an elastic band stretching (c).

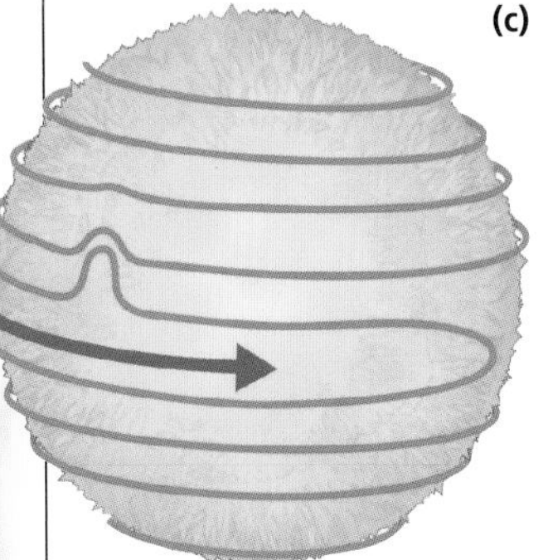

When the magnetic field cannot bend any further, it snaps and twists. This releases energy, causing violent activity to erupt on the Sun. After this maximum, the cycle begins again.

Surgery

Until the 19th century, all operations were carried out without an anaesthetic. Even pulling out a tooth could be unbearably painful. Patients had to be held or strapped down and surgeons had to work fast. Drugs such as alcohol and opium dulled the pain, but patients had to be brave.

The use of ether, chloroform and nitrous oxide, the first true anaesthetics, began in the 1840s. Since then, surgery has developed enormously. Today, before a major operation, patients are given a drug to relax them, then an anaesthetic to make them sleepy or unconscious. For small operations such as having a tooth out, a local anaesthetic is used to numb part of the body.

During some operations, especially those involving the heart, a patient's whole body may be cooled down by ice. As the body's temperature falls all the body's systems slow down. This reduces the risk that the brain will be damaged by a lack of blood or oxygen.

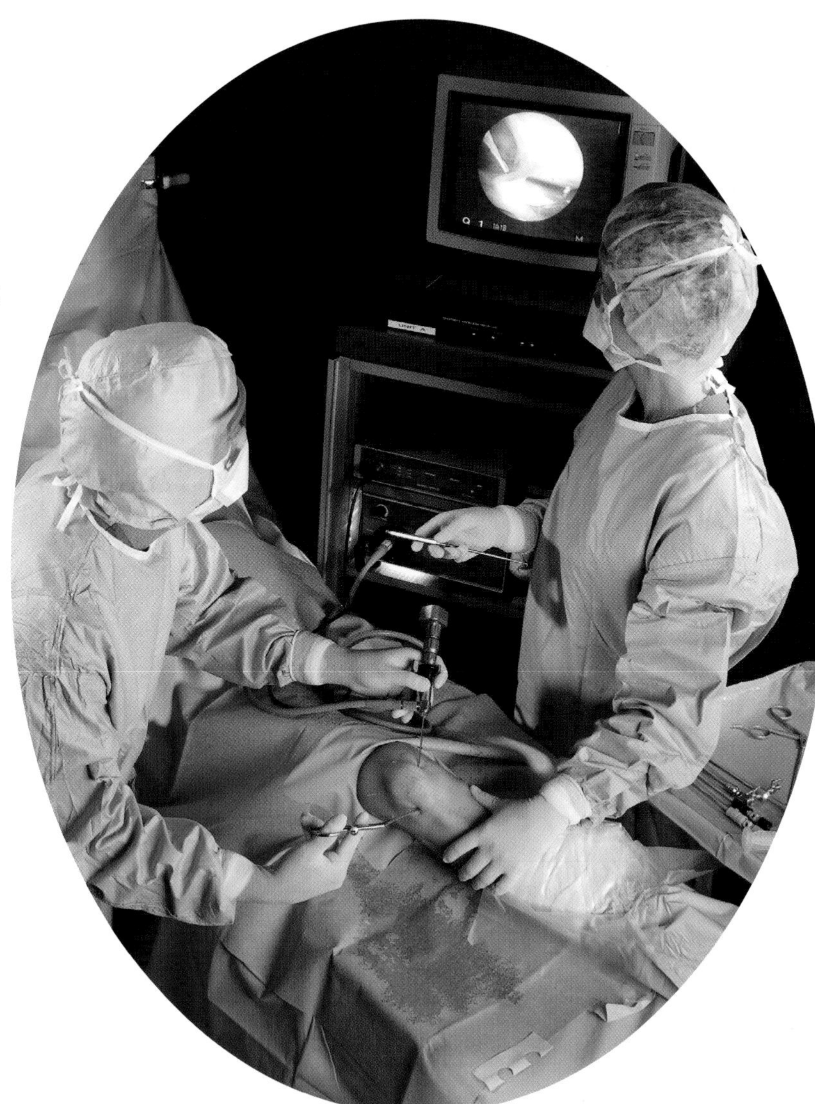

▲ Keyhole surgery. Doctors watch on a screen what they are doing inside the patient.

Keeping clean

Another problem with surgery before the 19th century was infection. Harmful bacteria or other germs got inside the patient's body during the operation, and the patient died of disease. In modern operating theatres every surface and every surgical instrument is sterilized (all bacteria are removed). The clothes and gloves that the surgical team wear are also sterile.

◀ In this picture of 16th century surgery you can see the patient praying and being held down by the doctor's assistant as his leg is cut off. Hot irons are being used to cauterize or seal the wound.

Keyhole surgery

Usually an operation involves making a large cut in the body. Keyhole surgery is a new technique that allows surgeons to perform operations through a small hole. An endoscope, a thin, flexible tube with a light and a camera at the end, is pushed in through a hole in the skin. The endoscope is guided by remote control, and surgeons follow what they are doing on a screen. Endoscopes with special attachments, such as scissors, forceps or a cutting laser, can be used for simple operations.

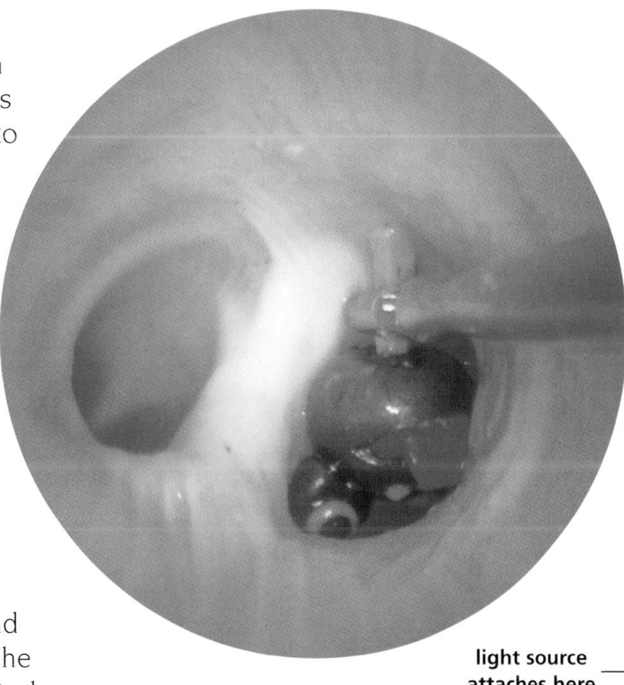

◀ This photograph shows an endoscope removing the top of a martini stirrer that has got stuck in the patient's trachea (windpipe).

Find Out More

- Bacteria and viruses
- Diseases
- Health
- Medicine

Transplants and spare parts

Bone marrow, hearts, lungs, kidneys and the cornea of the eye are just a few of the many body parts that can be transplanted. In a transplant, a damaged or diseased organ is replaced by a healthy organ from someone else, often someone who has been killed in an accident. A few organs, such as kidneys and bone marrow, can be transplanted from living donors.

Sometimes artificial organs can be used to replace weak or damaged body parts. Hip and knee joints can be replaced with plastic or metal substitutes, and artificial eye lenses can be implanted after an operation to remove a cataract.

▼ The parts of an endoscope.

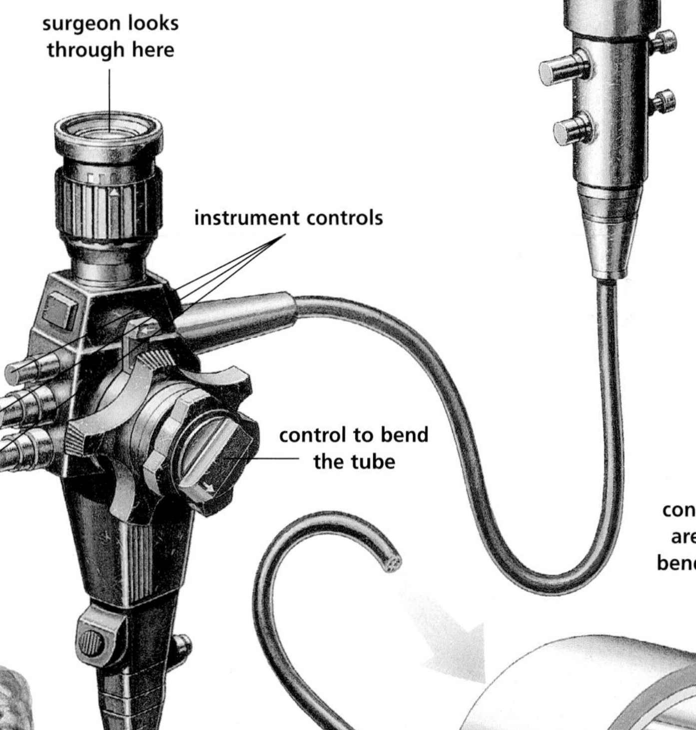

JOSEPH LISTER

When Joseph Lister (1827–1912) was Professor of Surgery in Glasgow in the 1860s, he became concerned about the number of patients whose wounds became infected after operations. He had heard about Pasteur's discovery of bacteria, and decided that bacteria might be causing the infections. So he started to use carbolic acid as an antiseptic. He sprayed it into the air, and soaked his instruments, his patients' skin and his own hands in it. It was unpleasant to use but it worked. The number of infections and deaths fell dramatically. Antiseptic surgery spread rapidly and operations finally became safer.

Technology

Using a scanning tunnelling microscope, which can move individual atoms, scientists have created an incredible new molecule. It is shaped like a propeller and is little more than a millionth of a metre across. When it is heated, the 'propeller' molecule starts spinning. One day, molecules like these will be put together to form micromachines as tiny as specks of dust.

▲ Scientists have already taken the first steps in nanotechnology. This circular pattern was made by arranging individual atoms using a scanning tunnelling microscope.

Rotating propeller-like molecules are some of the products being developed in one of the most exciting branches of modern technology – nanotechnology. It is called nanotechnology because scientists are working with objects – atoms – that are only nanometres across. A nanometre is a thousand-millionth of a metre.

Living with technology

Technology is the means by which we shape the world to suit us. It is often called applied science. Scientists discover things about our world, and technologists find ways of putting these discoveries to practical use. The scientist discovers while the technologist invents.

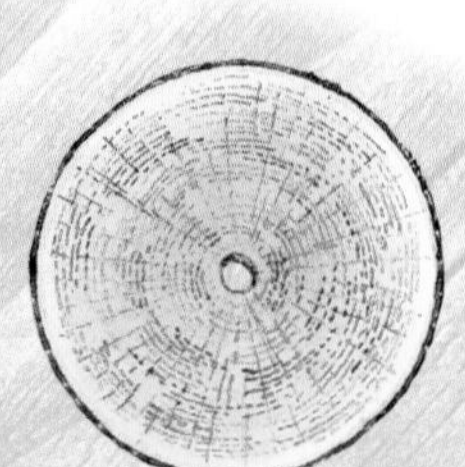

about 3500 BC
Wheel
The wheel first came into use in pottery-making. The first wagon wheels were wooden discs cut from tree trunks.

about 3500 BC
Plough
Farmers in the Middle East first used ploughs drawn by oxen for preparing the ground for sowing seeds.

about 1500 BC
Iron smelting
Metal workers in what is now Turkey were probably the first to build simple furnaces to extract iron from its ores.

about AD 1050
Movable type
The Chinese began printing book pages using separate pieces of type made from baked clay. They could be used again and again.

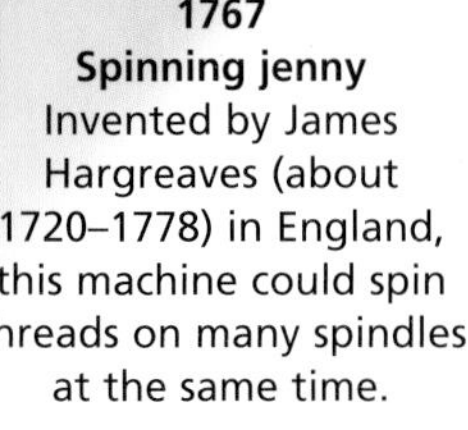

1767
Spinning jenny
Invented by James Hargreaves (about 1720–1778) in England, this machine could spin threads on many spindles at the same time.

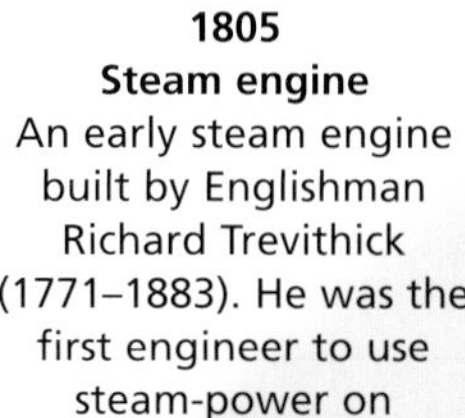

1805
Steam engine
An early steam engine built by Englishman Richard Trevithick (1771–1883). He was the first engineer to use steam-power on a railroad.

In technology, we take natural substances, such as clay and rocks, and transform them into materials that we can use, such as metals, fuels and chemicals.

With metals, we build magnificent structures like skyscrapers and suspension bridges, and machines to transport us and produce the goods we use. We burn fuels, such as oil and gas, in engines to power these machines or to produce electricity in power stations. We make all kinds of things with chemicals, from plastics and paint to medicines and make-up.

Good and bad

Technology can do great things. It can transform grains of sand into microchips, which are the brains behind our computers. It can build spacecraft that can travel billions of kilometres through the Solar System to visit far-distant planets. It can produce antibiotics to fight disease and cars that can travel faster than the speed of sound.

But technology is not all good news. To produce the materials and the machines we need, we are using up vast amounts of the Earth's natural resources, such as metals and other materials from rocks, and fuels such as oil and gas. These resources are limited and will one day run out.

Looking for answers

Technology is being used to try and solve some of the problems it has created. People in many countries are beginning to recycle some materials (use them again) instead of just throwing them away. Scientists are looking at new ways to obtain energy from the wind, waves and Sun because our main fuels – oil, gas and coal – are gradually running out. These alternative energy sources are renewable – they will not run out.

Find Out More
- Coal
- Industry and manufacturing
- Oil and gas
- Renewable energy
- Transport

▼ Some key inventions in the history of technology, from the wheel to the microchip. Technology developed rapidly after the 1700s.

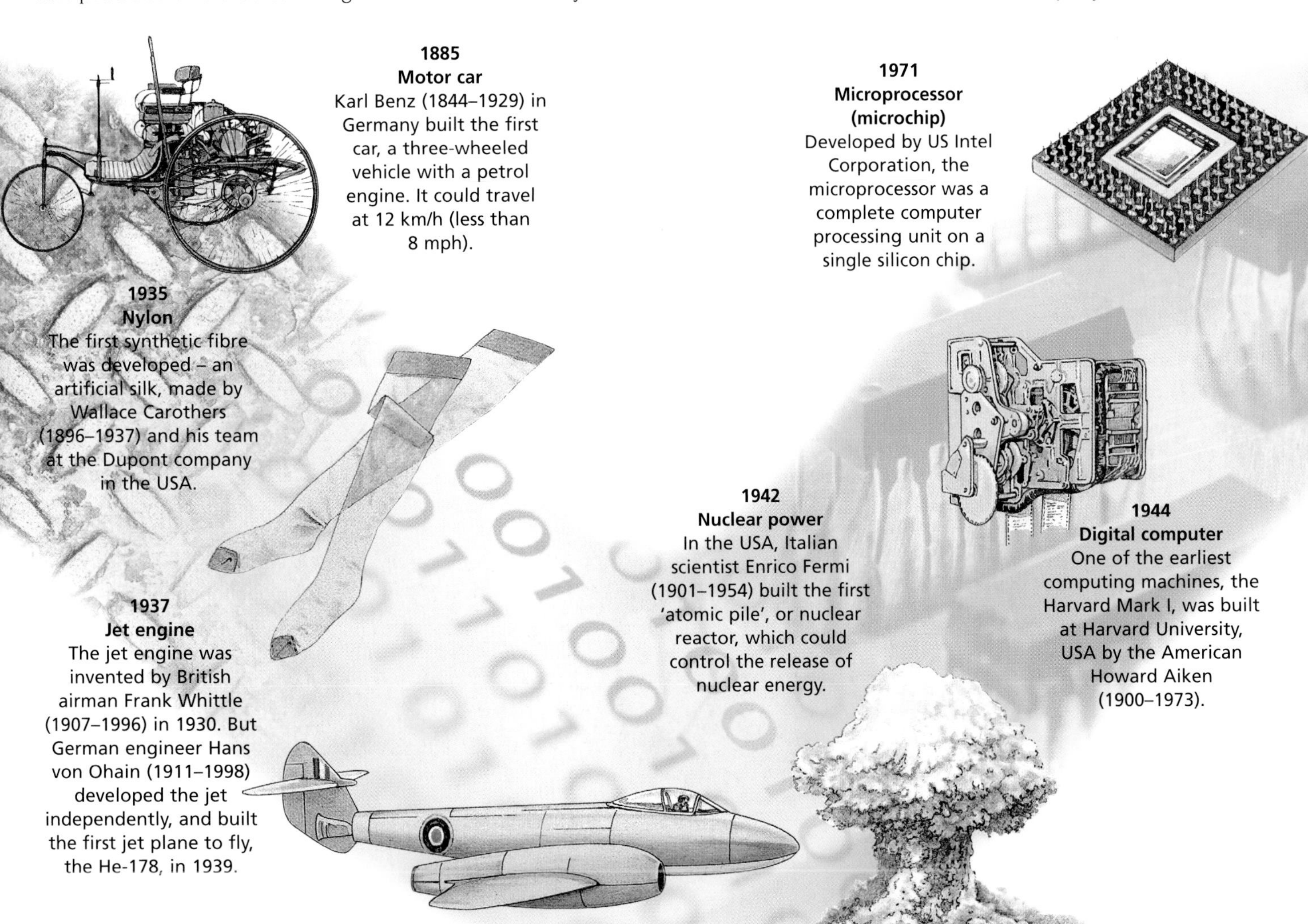

1885
Motor car
Karl Benz (1844–1929) in Germany built the first car, a three-wheeled vehicle with a petrol engine. It could travel at 12 km/h (less than 8 mph).

1971
Microprocessor (microchip)
Developed by US Intel Corporation, the microprocessor was a complete computer processing unit on a single silicon chip.

1935
Nylon
The first synthetic fibre was developed – an artificial silk, made by Wallace Carothers (1896–1937) and his team at the Dupont company in the USA.

1942
Nuclear power
In the USA, Italian scientist Enrico Fermi (1901–1954) built the first 'atomic pile', or nuclear reactor, which could control the release of nuclear energy.

1944
Digital computer
One of the earliest computing machines, the Harvard Mark I, was built at Harvard University, USA by the American Howard Aiken (1900–1973).

1937
Jet engine
The jet engine was invented by British airman Frank Whittle (1907–1996) in 1930. But German engineer Hans von Ohain (1911–1998) developed the jet independently, and built the first jet plane to fly, the He-178, in 1939.

Telecommunications, Telegraph *see* Communications

Telephones

Mobile phones have given people the freedom to make calls from just about anywhere. As a result, they have helped save many lives. Stranded mountaineers, people on sinking boats – even hot-air balloonists in trouble – have all used mobiles to call for help.

Mobiles are a very recent invention. But telephones were invented more than a hundred years ago. Telephones have changed a great deal since the early days, but the way the telephone system works is still basically the same. So just what happens when you make a phone call?

Current voices

When you punch in a phone number, the telephone sends the number to a place called an 'exchange'. The exchange connects you up to the person you want to contact.

When the person you are ringing picks up the phone, you speak into the handset. A microphone in your handset changes

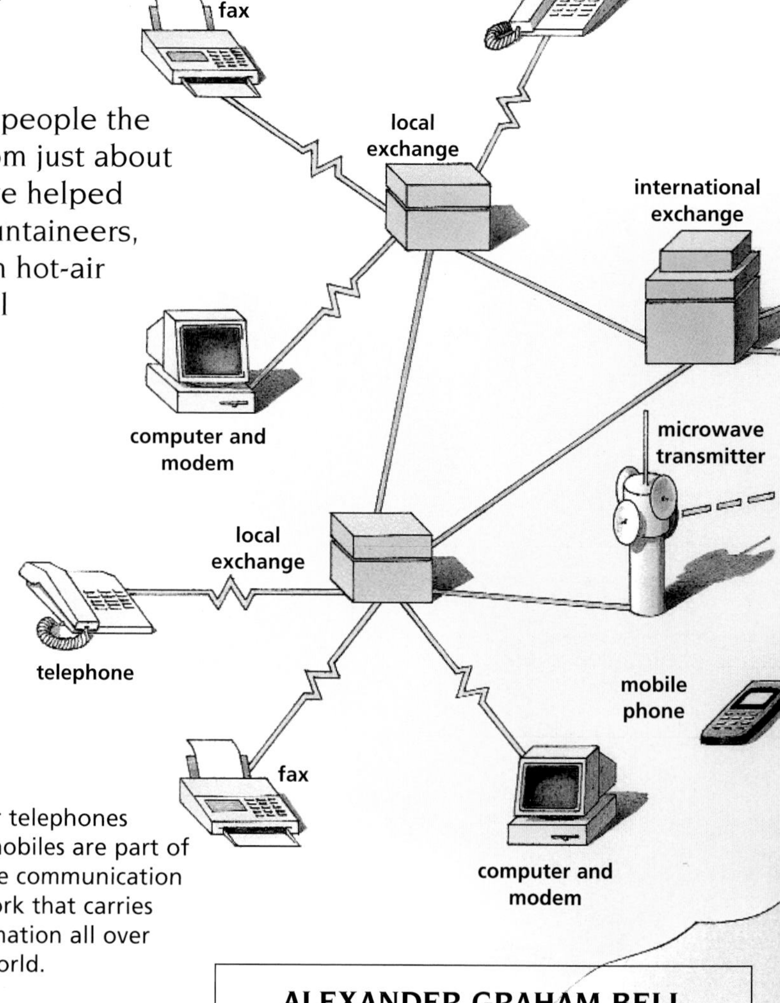

▶ Our telephones and mobiles are part of a huge communication network that carries information all over the world.

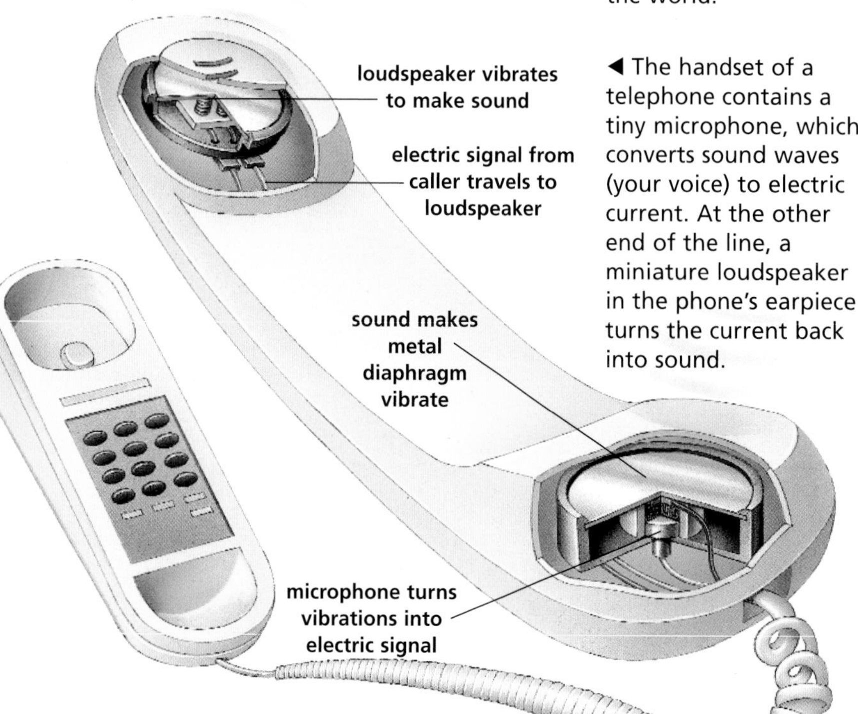

◀ The handset of a telephone contains a tiny microphone, which converts sound waves (your voice) to electric current. At the other end of the line, a miniature loudspeaker in the phone's earpiece turns the current back into sound.

ALEXANDER GRAHAM BELL

Telephones were developed because the Morse code of the telegraph did not let people talk to each other. So engineers and scientists wondered how they could 'squeeze' human voices down the telegraph wires.

The problem was solved by Alexander Graham Bell (1847–1922), a Scot who had emigrated to Canada. He experimented with transmitting sound by electricity and made the world's first telephone call – to his assistant – in 1876. Bell also invented the telephone exchange. The first exchange, with just 20 lines, was installed in Connecticut, USA, in 1877. Britain's first exchange opened in 1879.

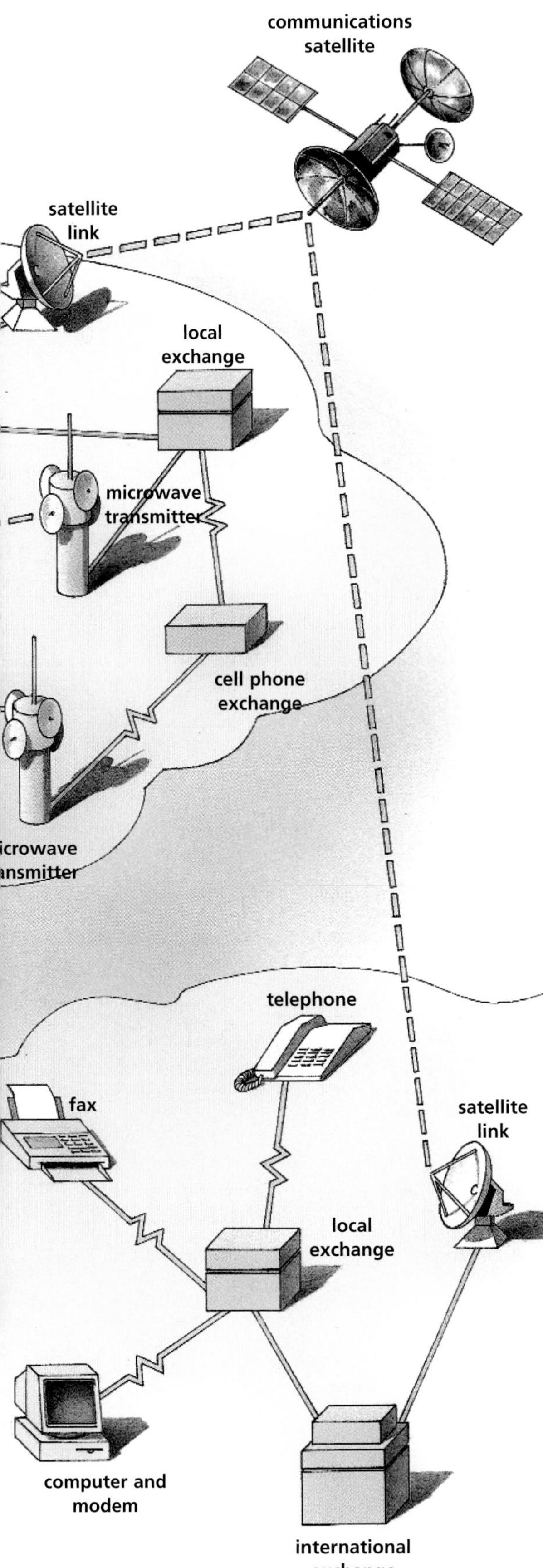

sound waves from your voice into an electric signal. This signal is then sent through the telephone system to the other phone. At the receiving end, the electrical signal drives a tiny loudspeaker in the handset, which reproduces your voice.

But why are telephone exchanges necessary? It's because if every phone in the world was connected to every other, we would be awash in wires. Instead, each phone is connected to a local exchange, which connects in turn to other exchanges.

Early exchanges used operators who plugged your line into the one of the person you were calling. But that was only possible when there were few telephone users. As phones became more popular, automatic exchanges were introduced.

Light fantastic

In modern phone networks, the sound of your voice is not only sent down electrical wires – it is transmitted in many other ways. Many telephone cables are now made up of optical fibres, which can carry more calls than wires. Instead of transmitting the sound of your voice as electrical signals, optical fibres carry the voice information as tiny pulses of light.

Phone networks also use radio waves and microwaves to send information from place to place. Radio links, called relays, are used particularly in places where it's hard to put up telegraph poles. Satellite links, and undersea optical fibre cables, are used to connect phones across the oceans. Telephone networks are also used to transmit information over the internet and to send faxes.

Phones of the future

Modern mobile phones can do much more than just make calls. They can send faxes and emails, store phone numbers and other information, and connect up with your computer and, to a limited extent, the internet.

Videophones let people see each other using built-in cameras and small video screens. You can also use them to watch other kinds of videos, and to surf the internet.

Find Out More
- Communications
- Electricity
- Faxes and modems
- Fibre optics
- Internet
- Microphones and speakers
- Radio
- Sound

▲ A videophone allows two people to have a conversation and see each other at the same time.

Telescopes

Astronomers use telescopes to study the stars, soldiers have small versions mounted on their rifles, and birdwatchers use binoculars, which are like a double telescope.

Telescopes do two jobs. They make things that are far away seem nearer (they magnify them) and they help us to look at things that are too dim to see just with our eyes.

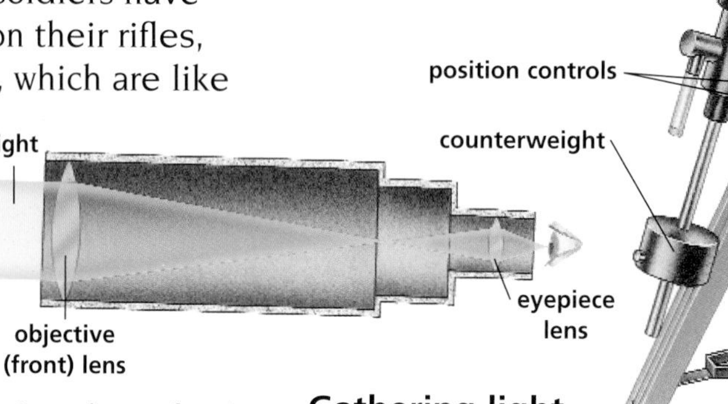

▲ A modern refracting (lens) telescope, and a cutaway view showing how light passes through it.

Refracting telescopes

Lens telescopes are called refracting telescopes because they use a lens to refract (bend) light. A Dutch spectacle-maker called Hans Lippershey probably made the first telescope in 1608. We can imagine that one day he held two lenses up, looked through both of them – and was surprised at what he saw!

Word of Lippershey's discovery soon reached the great Italian scientist Galileo Galilei. In 1609 he made a similar telescope. It had a convex (outward-curving) lens at the front and a concave (inward-curving) eyepiece lens.

Most modern telescopes use a different arrangement. They have a convex lens at the front and another, smaller convex lens as the eyepiece.The front lens is called the objective lens. It gathers as much light as possible and produces an image inside the tube. The second lens (the eyepiece) acts as a magnifying glass and produces a larger version of the image.

Wrong way up

Telescopes with convex lenses at both ends give a wider view than a Galilean telescope, but their final image is upside down. When looking at stars and planets, this isn't a problem, but binoculars and telescopes used on Earth need an upright image. For this, they have reflecting prisms inside to turn the image up the other way.

Gathering light

Being able to see things that are very faint is more important to astronomers than magnification, because even a magnified star still looks like a dot. For this reason, astronomical lens telescopes have to have very big objective lenses. The bigger their lens, the more light they can collect.

The problem with this is that large glass lenses are very heavy. The lens has to be held round the edge, otherwise the support

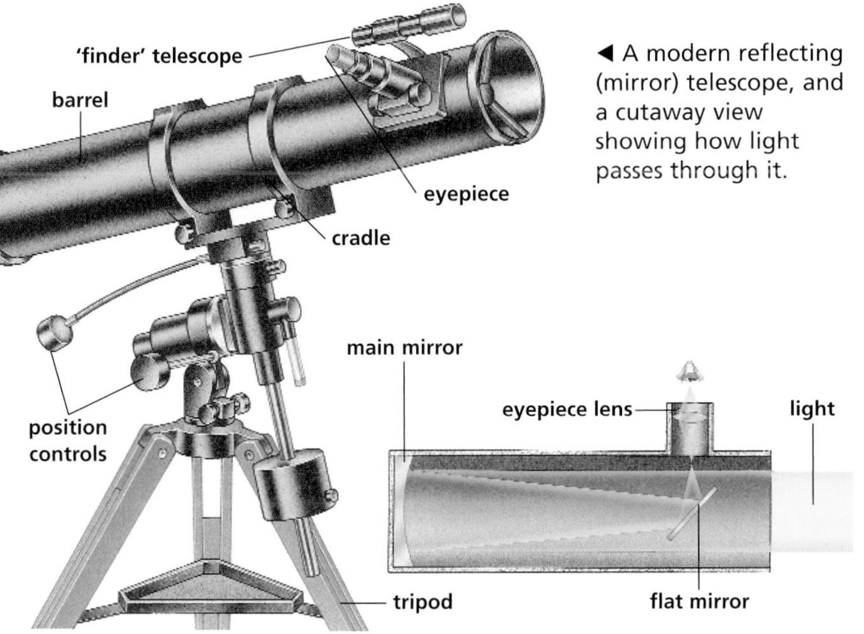

◀ A modern reflecting (mirror) telescope, and a cutaway view showing how light passes through it.

would block the view, and this limits how big a lens telescope can be (the biggest has a lens about 100 centimetres across). To see even fainter objects, a bigger surface to gather the light is needed. Since a lens will not do, a curved mirror is used to gather the light instead.

Reflecting telescopes

One of the most common ways of making a reflecting telescope, or reflector, was first thought up by Isaac Newton in 1672. He used a curved mirror, together with a flat mirror and an eyepiece.

In a Newtonian reflector, the concave main mirror gathers the light and brings it to a focus inside the tube. There, a small flat mirror sends the light to the side of the tube, where it is magnified by an eyepiece.

Mirrors have two advantages when it comes to telescopes. First, as the mirror's reflecting surface is at the front, it can be supported from the back. This is easier than trying to hold a lens by its edge, so the mirror can be much bigger. One of the largest single-piece mirror telescopes is at Mount Palomar in California. Its mirror is 5 metres across – five times bigger than the largest lens telescope.

◀ The highly advanced WIYN telescope is one of several telescopes on Kitt Peak mountain in Arizona, USA. A computer controls the shape of the main mirror and its surface temperature, to ensure the sharpest possible pictures.

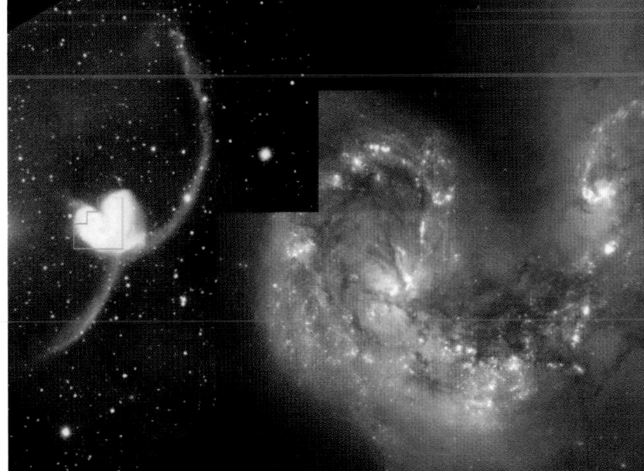

▶ The Antenna galaxy is actually two galaxies colliding together. An image from the Hubble Space Telescope (right) shows in incredible detail new stars being made in the central area. The best ground-based image (left) does not compare.

The second advantage is that a mirror reflects all the colours of light in the same way. A lens will not bend all colours by the same amount, so the image in a lens telescope always suffers from some blurring of colours.

Top telescopes

The Keck I Telescope in Hawaii has a huge main mirror 10 metres across. It is made up of 36 hexagonal pieces 2 metres across. The images from a nearby second telescope (Keck II) are combined with those from Keck I to make an even better image. But ground telescopes will always produce slightly blurred images because of Earth's atmosphere. Being in orbit gives space telescopes such as Hubble a great advantage.

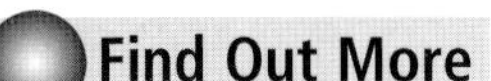
Find Out More

- Astronomy
- Mirrors and lenses
- Space astronomy

Television

When we watch television, we can cheer our favourite sports teams from our living-rooms, or hear news of earthquakes and wars on the other side of the world. We can watch movies, soaps and music videos, too. Satellite, cable and digital TV have added hundreds of extra TV channels. Soon, interactive TV will let us take part in programmes from home.

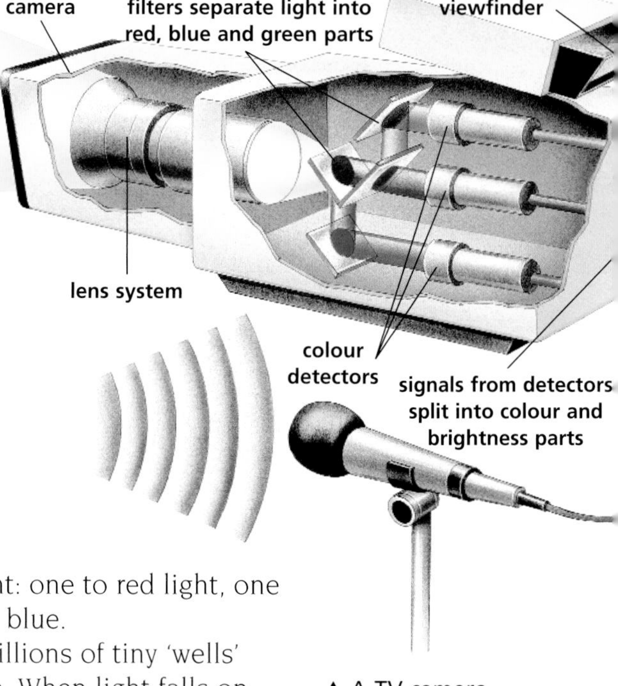

▲ A TV camera captures a moving scene and sends a TV signal to your home via a transmitting aerial or an optical cable.

But have you ever wondered just how those pictures and sounds get on to your TV set? Television is a system that sends and receives pictures and sounds. A television camera records the pictures; a microphone records the sounds. The camera changes the images from light rays into electrical signals. These are sent to your TV set (television receiver). The receiver changes the electrical signals back to light again.

On camera

To make a TV picture, the camera focuses the scene being filmed onto three light-sensitive microchips called charge-coupled devices (CCDs). Each CCD is sensitive to a different type of light: one to red light, one to green and one to blue.

Each CCD has millions of tiny 'wells' sunk into its surface. When light falls on the CCD, each well becomes electrically charged, with a charge equal to the brightness of the light at that point. Together, the three CCDs produce an electric 'picture' of the brightness of red, blue and green light throughout the scene.

A TV camera does not capture a moving scene as whole pictures. Instead, it scans across the scene in a series of lines. The camera scans a complete set of lines 25 times each second.

BAIRD'S BOX

John Logie Baird (1888–1946), a Scot, was the first person to make a moving television picture. He used a mechanical way of scanning each line of his TV picture, using a spinning perforated disc invented by a German scientist, Paul Nipkow. In the UK, the BBC set up the world's first public TV broadcasting company using Baird's device, but it was soon replaced by a better, electronic system.

Sending the pictures

To get the action to your home, the electric 'pictures' from the camera and the sound information from the microphone are collected together into a TV signal. The signal is combined with a carrier wave, a powerful electric current that can be used to create radio waves.

The carrier wave, carrying its TV signal, can be used to send out radio waves from a transmitting aerial on a high TV mast. Your TV aerial then picks up these radio waves. The signal may also travel to your home as flashes of light along an optical cable. Satellite TV programmes are beamed up to a communications satellite in orbit around Earth. The satellite then sends a signal back to Earth, which is picked up by your satellite dish.

Find Out More

- Cameras
- Circuits
- Communications
- Internet
- Microchips
- Satellites

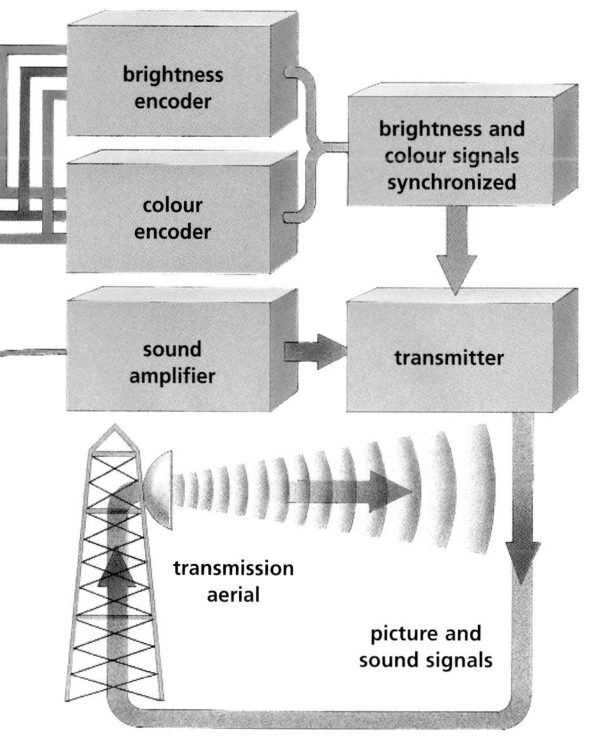

▲ A television programme being filmed in front of a studio audience. Using lighting, sets and special effects it is possible to create all kinds of different scenes in a TV studio.

On screen

Most TVs still use a glass cathode-ray tube (CRT) to display pictures. At the narrow end of a CRT are three electron 'guns'. Each fires a beam of electrons at the TV screen, which is coated with a material called phosphor. Where the beam hits the screen, the phosphor glows. The three electron guns light up red, green and blue phosphor strips on the screen.

The TV signal controls the red, blue and green electron guns. As the beams scan across the screen, the TV signal changes the strength of each beam, recreating the pattern of light and darkness in the original picture. Although the picture is only in three colours, different mixtures of the three cause our eyes to see other colours as well.

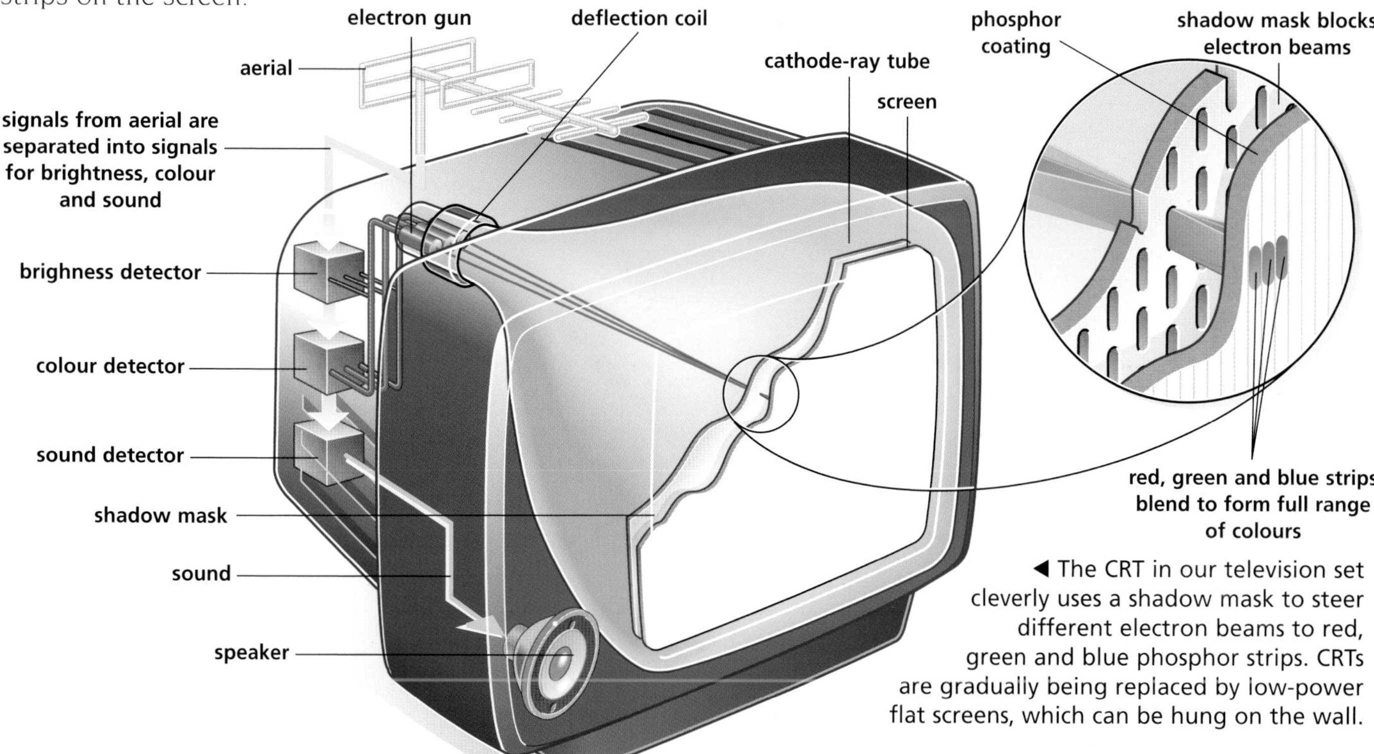

◀ The CRT in our television set cleverly uses a shadow mask to steer different electron beams to red, green and blue phosphor strips. CRTs are gradually being replaced by low-power flat screens, which can be hung on the wall.

Temperature

Why do you shiver when it's cold, and sweat when it's hot? It is your body's way of keeping itself at the same steady temperature. If your temperature changes too much, you feel ill.

When you measure temperature, the number of degrees tells you how hot or how cold something is. If you are well, your body temperature is about 37°C (degrees Celsius or Centigrade). Shivering makes you warmer, and helps to stop your temperature falling lower in cold weather. Sweating cools you down, and stops your body from overheating.

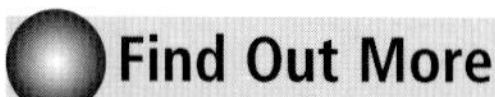

Find Out More

- Fire
- Fuels
- Heat
- Refrigeration
- Space travel

By degrees

A temperature of 37°C is warm. Ice is cold and has a temperature of 0°C, while boiling water has a temperature of 100°C.

Temperatures in degrees Celsius or Centigrade are on the Celsius scale. There is another scale called the Fahrenheit scale. Ice has a temperature of 32°F (degrees Fahrenheit), your body 98°F, and boiling water 212°F.

Thermometers measure temperature. A glass thermometer contains a thin tube in which a liquid moves up and down a scale of degrees to show the temperature. This liquid is usually mercury or coloured alcohol. The liquid rises when it is warmed and drops when cooled. A digital thermometer has a screen that displays the number of degrees.

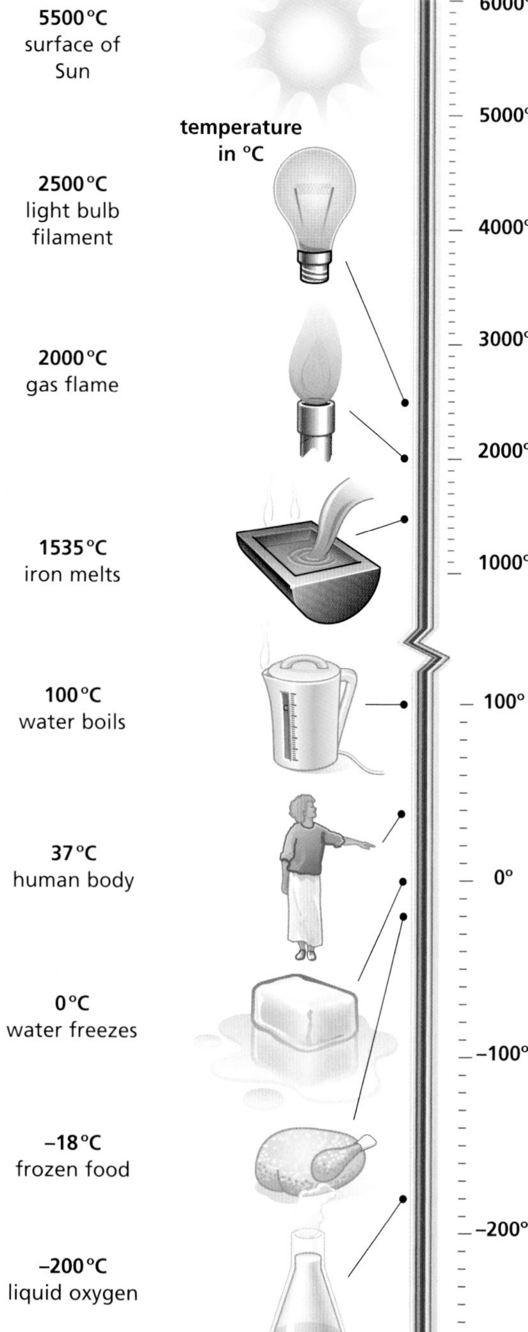

▶ Temperatures range from absolute zero, the lowest possible temperature, up to temperatures of millions of degrees inside the Sun and other stars. Substances freeze, melt or boil at set temperatures.

◀ A clinical thermometer is a special glass thermometer used to measure body temperature. It has a small range of temperature a few degrees above and below normal, which is about 37°C or 98°F.

Keeping warm

A heating system keeps the rooms of a house at a comfortable temperature. It contains devices called thermostats that detect and control the room temperature. The thermostat switches the heating on if the room is too cool, and off when it gets too hot.

Electric kettles also have thermostats. They switch the kettle off when the water gets to the temperature at which it boils.

Tendons *see* Bones and muscles • **Territories** (animal) *see* Animal behaviour

Textiles

The material for an Indian sari may come from a silkworm, or from a cotton plant. Or it may be a synthetic material made from crude oil. The cloth may be plain, or printed, or have woven patterns, sometimes using gold or silver thread.

Sari fabric is just one example of the huge variety of textiles. We use textiles for clothes, for carpets, parachutes, sails and bandages. Textiles can be made from natural fibres, such as cotton, from synthetic fibres such as nylon, or from a mixture of the two.

▶ The thick fleece being shorn from these sheep will be spun into woollen yarn to make clothing.

Fabrics from fibres

The first step in producing most textiles is to draw out and twist bundles of the raw fibres together to form a yarn. This is known as spinning.

Weaving is the main method used to make fabric from yarn. In the weaving process, lengths of yarn are interlaced on a loom to form cloth. Other methods include knitting, in which the yarn is linked in loops, and felting, in which the fibres are tangled together.

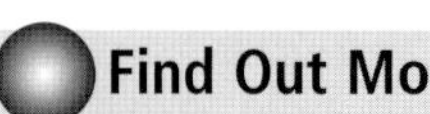

- Fibres
- Industry and manufacturing

Textile properties

In general, textiles made from natural fibres are softer, absorb moisture better and are more heat-resistant than synthetic fabrics. Synthetic textiles are stronger, harder-wearing and more crease-resistant. Many modern textiles are made from a mixture of natural and synthetic materials.

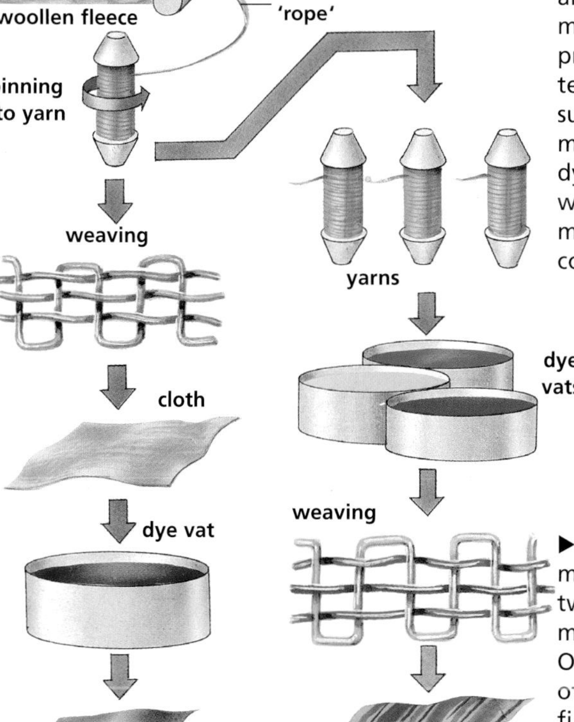

◀ Spinning, dyeing and weaving are the most important processes in making textiles from fibres such as wool. A fabric may be coloured by dyeing it after weaving (left), or it may be woven from coloured yarns.

▶ The threads from silk moth cocoons are twisted together by a machine to make yarn. One cocoon is made up of over 250 metres of fine silk thread.

Theodolites *see* Construction • **Thermometers** *see* Temperature • **Thermoplastics** *see* Plastics

Thunder and lightning

Within a towering storm cloud 18 kilometres up in the air, the winds reach 100 kilometres per hour. Gusts of cold air swoop downwards, while warm, moist air shoots up. As the air churns violently, water droplets and ice crystals collide. Electrical charges build up, then suddenly a brilliant flash of lightning brightens the sky.

Lightning happens when hundreds of millions of volts of electricity flow between thunderclouds and the ground.

Lightning strikes

During a thunderstorm, the base of the thundercloud has a negative electrical charge and the ground has a positive charge. If two places have opposite electrical charges, electricity tries to flow between them to even out the charges. Electricity can move easily through materials like metal, but it has trouble moving through air. Air acts like a dam on a river, keeping the electricity from flowing. In a thunderstorm, the electrical charges build up so much, that the 'dam' of air breaks, and a bolt of 100 million volts of electricity rushes between the clouds and the ground.

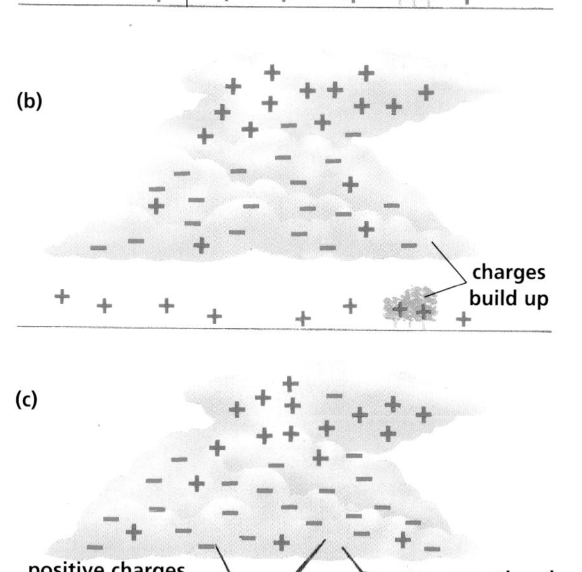

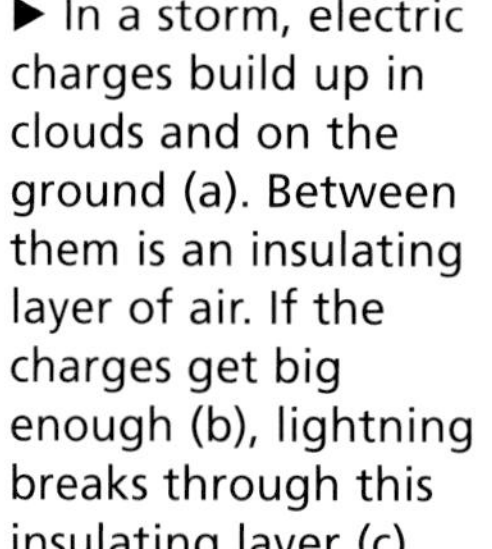

▶ In a storm, electric charges build up in clouds and on the ground (a). Between them is an insulating layer of air. If the charges get big enough (b), lightning breaks through this insulating layer (c).

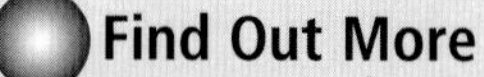

Find Out More

- Clouds
- Conductors and insulators
- Electricity
- Light
- Sound

Since there are different electrical charges within the clouds, lightning can also happen within a single cloud or from cloud to cloud. This sheet lightning causes a bright flash across the sky. Heat lightning is just the light from lightning just over the horizon that is reflected off clouds.

Thunder

Whenever you hear thunder, you can be sure there is lightning somewhere. As a lightning bolt travels through the air, it instantly heats the air around it to more than 30,000 °C. When air is heated, the molecules move apart and the air expands. Lightning makes the air expand so quickly that it creates a sound wave – thunder. Light travels so quickly that we see lightning as it is happening, even if it's very far away. Sound, on the other hand, travels a million times more slowly. It takes thunder about three seconds to travel a distance of one kilometre.

◀ Lightning bolts are huge surges of static electricity that run between clouds and from clouds to the ground.

Thyroid gland *see* Glands and hormones • **Tidal power** *see* Water power

Tides

Throughout the day, on almost every sea coast on Earth, the sea water slowly rises and falls. These rises and falls are called tides. A tide is really a wave, thousands of kilometres long.

Tides are caused by gravity, the force that attracts one object to another. Like the Earth, the Moon and the Sun both have a gravitational pull, which affects the world's oceans and seas.

The pull of the Moon

As the Moon orbits Earth, its gravity forces water into two bulges, one on the side of Earth facing the Moon and the other directly opposite. There are high tides at the two bulges and low tides in between.

As the Earth spins, places move in and out of the bulges. Most places on Earth experience at least one high tide and one low tide every day. This is because the Earth is rotating throughout the day. If you are on a beach, high tide is when the sea comes in and low tide is when it goes out. A tide is really a wave, thousands of kilometres long. On the open ocean, tidal waves travel very fast – at over 1000 km/h.

▶ Spring tides occur when the Sun and the Moon pull the sea in the same direction, making the water rise and fall more than normal. Neap tides occur when the Sun and the Moon pull the sea in different directions, so the difference between high and low tides is less.

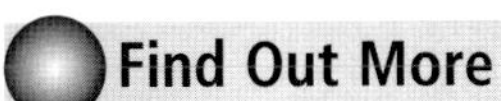

Find Out More

- Earth
- Gravity
- Moon
- Oceans
- Sun

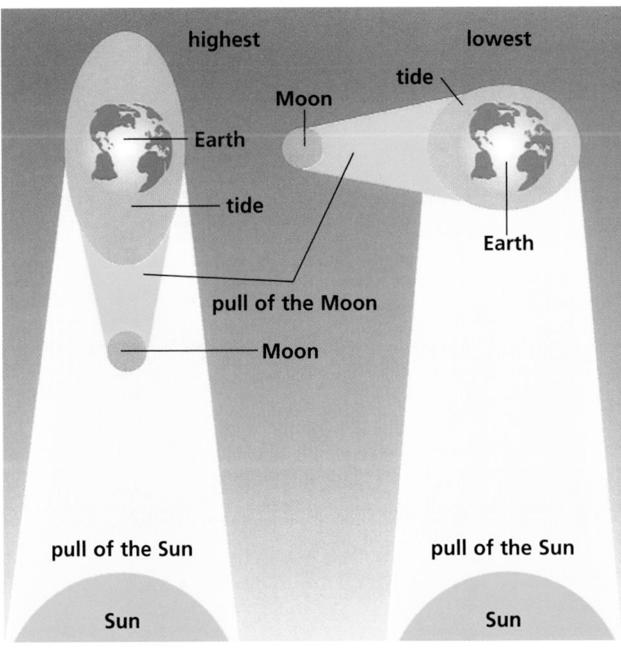

The pull of the Sun

The Sun also pulls on the water, but since the Sun is so much farther away, the pull is not as strong. The high tides are highest and the low tides lowest when the Sun and Moon are pulling in the same direction. This happens when they are on the same side of the Earth or directly opposite each other. When the Moon and Sun pull in different directions the difference between high and low tides is less.

▼ The Thames Barrier is the world's largest tidal flood barrier. It protects London from destructive and dangerous flooding which could be caused when there is a powerful storm in the North Sea at the same time as a high tide.

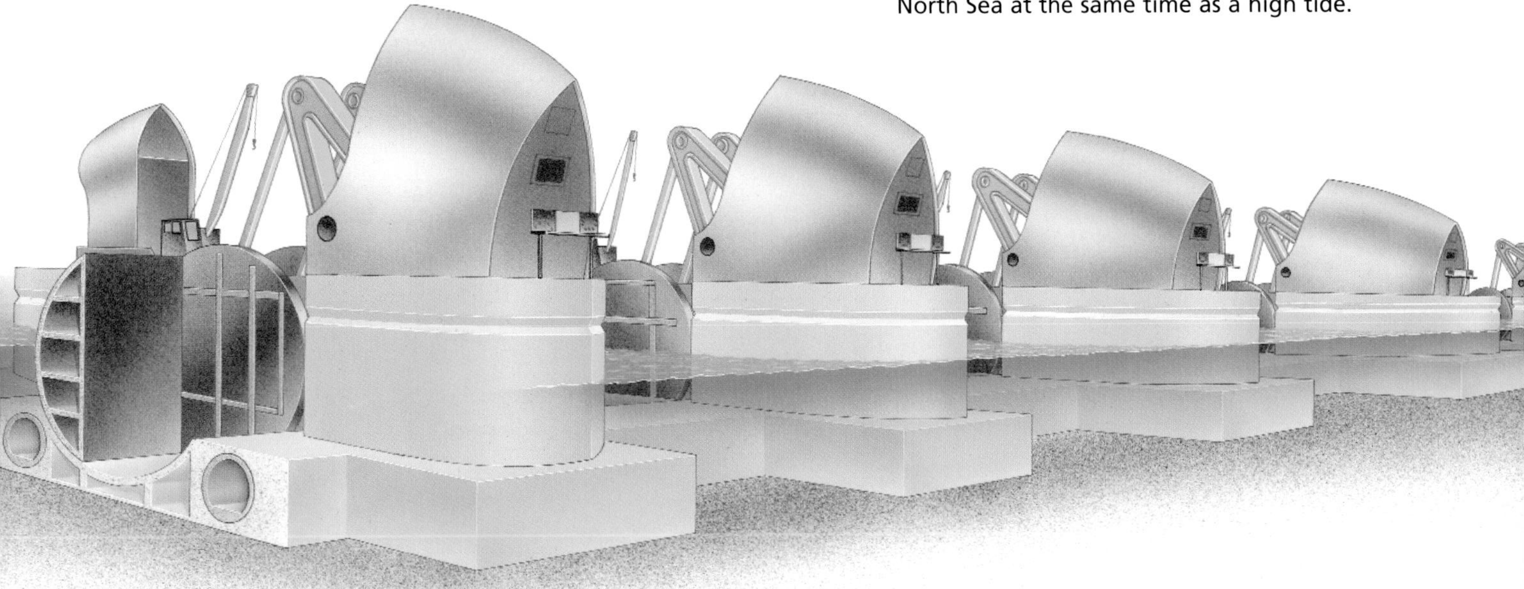

Tigers *see* Classification, Mammals • **Timber** *see* Wood and timber

Time

At noon each day, the Sun is at its highest point in the sky. From here it sinks and travels westwards until sunset. At dawn, the Sun rises in the east, then arcs upwards and westwards until it is noon again.

The period between one noon and the next is always the same. It is one of the great natural divisions of time – the day.

▶ The pointer (gnomon) on a sundial casts a shadow, which moves as the Sun moves across the sky. Sundials keep good time, but they work only on sunny days.

Sun time and Moon time

The time from one noon to the next is called the solar day – the day according to the Sun. But the Sun does not actually move across the sky. It is the Earth that moves, spinning on its axis once a day.

The Earth moves, or orbits, around the Sun, as well as spinning like a top. One complete orbit takes $365\frac{1}{4}$ days. This period gives us our other great division of time – the year.

We get another natural unit of time from the movement of the Moon around the Earth. As it orbits the Earth, the Moon changes in appearance in a regular way, depending on how much of it is lit by the Sun. It goes through these changes, or phases, every $29\frac{1}{2}$ days. This time period is the basis of our month.

Calendars

From the time of the earliest civilizations people have made calendars – systems for organizing time. Early calendars were lunar ones, with time divided into months based on the phases of the Moon. But these calendars had a problem. There are not an

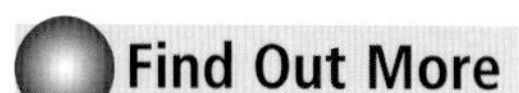
Find Out More
- Geological time
- Measurement
- Moon
- Relativity
- Seasons
- Sun
- Waves and vibrations

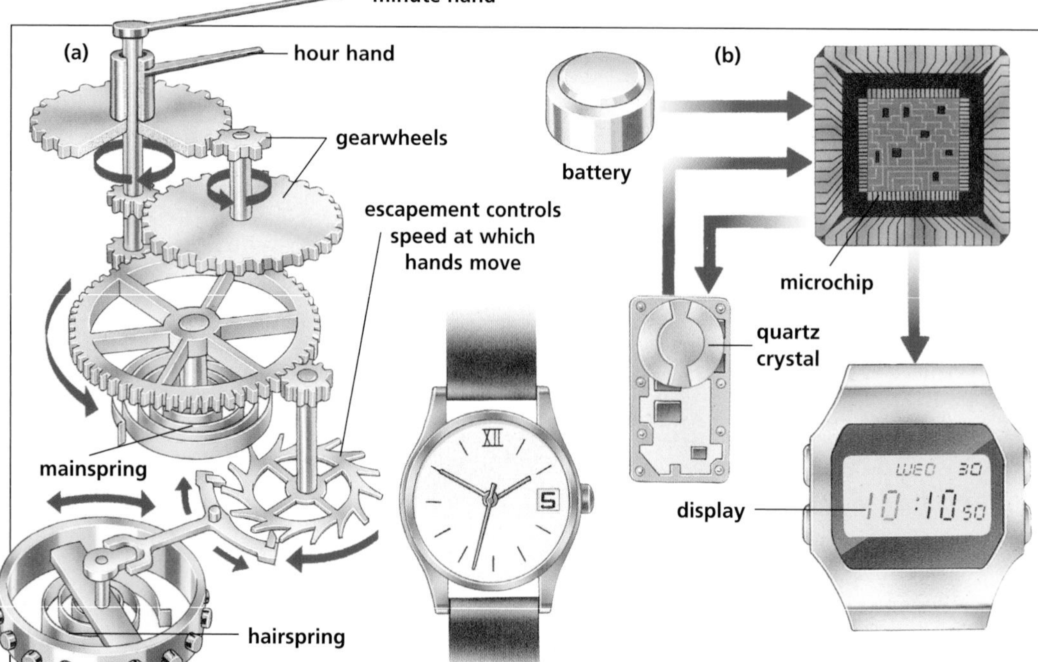

HOW WATCHES WORK

In most mechanical clocks and watches, the power to move the hands comes from a coiled mainspring, which slowly unwinds. A small hairspring, which coils and uncoils at a regular rate, controls the speed at which the hands move, so that the clock or watch keeps good time.

In a quartz clock or watch, a quartz crystal, powered by a battery, vibrates thousands of times each second. A microchip counts the vibrations and controls the hands on the dial or the numbers on the digital display.

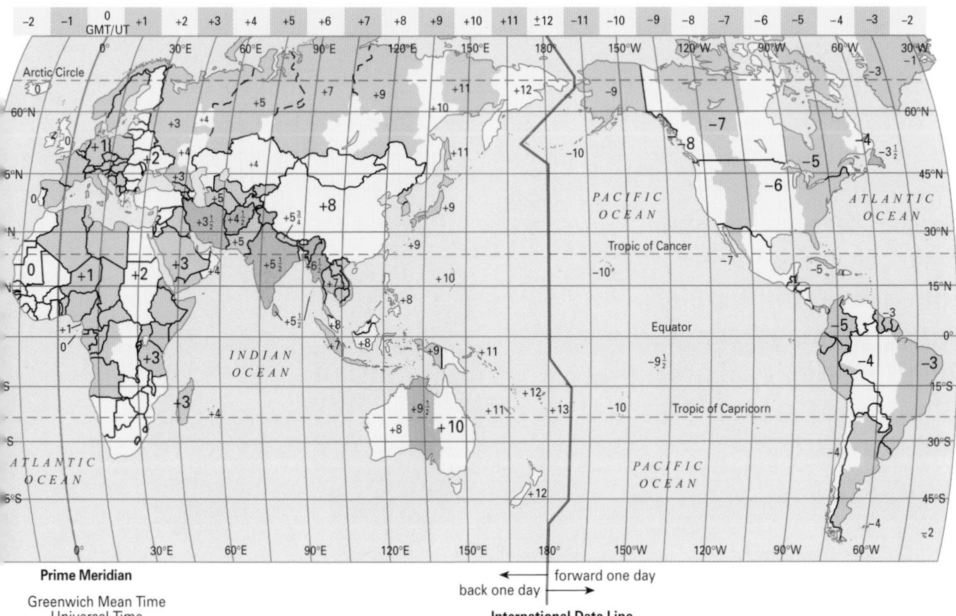

◀ Different places on the Earth have day and night at different times. But if everyone used different local times, then only people living on the same north-south line (longitude line) would have the same time. To avoid this confusing situation, the world is divided into 24 time 'zones'.

Key
Numbers indicate how many hours ahead or behind Greenwich Mean Time (GMT) a place is.

- even number of hours different from GMT
- odd number of hours different from GMT
- $\frac{1}{2}$-hour difference from adjacent zone
- less than $\frac{1}{2}$-hour difference from adjacent zone

even number of lunar months in a solar year (each year is about 12 lunar months and 11 days). So over time the seasons, which are linked to the solar year, got out of step with the calendar.

Today the standard calendar is a solar one, based on a year of $365\frac{1}{4}$ days. It is split into 12 months of between 28 and 31 days, a total of 365 days. Every fourth year (usually) is a leap year. It has an extra day added in February. Pope Gregory XIII introduced this calendar in the 1580s.

Unfortunately, a solar year is not *exactly* $365\frac{1}{4}$ days. To keep our calendars in step with the Sun, leap seconds are sometimes added to a year.

Measuring time

Knowing the correct time is important to us, and in most branches of science accurate time measurements are vital. So within each day, humans have divided time up into hours, minutes and seconds.

Over 3000 years ago, the Babylonians in the Middle East developed the first systems for measuring time. They used instruments such as sundials and water clocks (called clepsydras, which means 'water-stealers').

Mechanical clocks did not come into use until the 1200s. They became increasingly accurate as they incorporated better means of controlling, or regulating, the movement of the clock hands. The Dutch physicist Christiaan Huygens first used a pendulum as a regulator in clocks in 1657. Later mechanical clocks used a hairspring as a regulator.

Good vibrations

Most modern clocks measure the passage of time using the vibrations of crystals or atoms. Quartz clocks and watches measure time by 'counting' the vibrations of wafer-thin crystals of quartz.

The most accurate clocks of all – atomic clocks – use the radiation emitted by vibrating atoms, usually of the metal caesium. Some atomic clocks are accurate to 1 second in every 30,000 years.

▼ This picture from the Hubble Space Telescope shows galaxies so far away that their light took 5000 million years to reach us. But one galaxy is even further away (inset). Light from this galaxy began travelling 13,000 million years ago, soon after the Universe began.

Tools

Human beings are one of the few animal species that can make and use tools. Without tools, we could not easily farm the land, build houses or make a whole range of things. The tools that early humans used were made of readily available materials, such as stone, wood and bone. But most of the tools we use today are made of metal or plastic.

In their work and at home, people use hundreds of different tools for shaping and cutting materials, and fastening things together. They use knives, scissors and saws for cutting, hammers to knock in nails, drills to make holes, planes and files to smooth surfaces, and screwdrivers and spanners to tighten screws and nuts.

Today, many of these are power tools, which are driven by an electric motor. Some power tools operate from mains electricity, others are cordless and run on batteries.

▼ Some common hand tools used around the home. Using electrical power takes the hard work out of drilling holes and tightening screws.

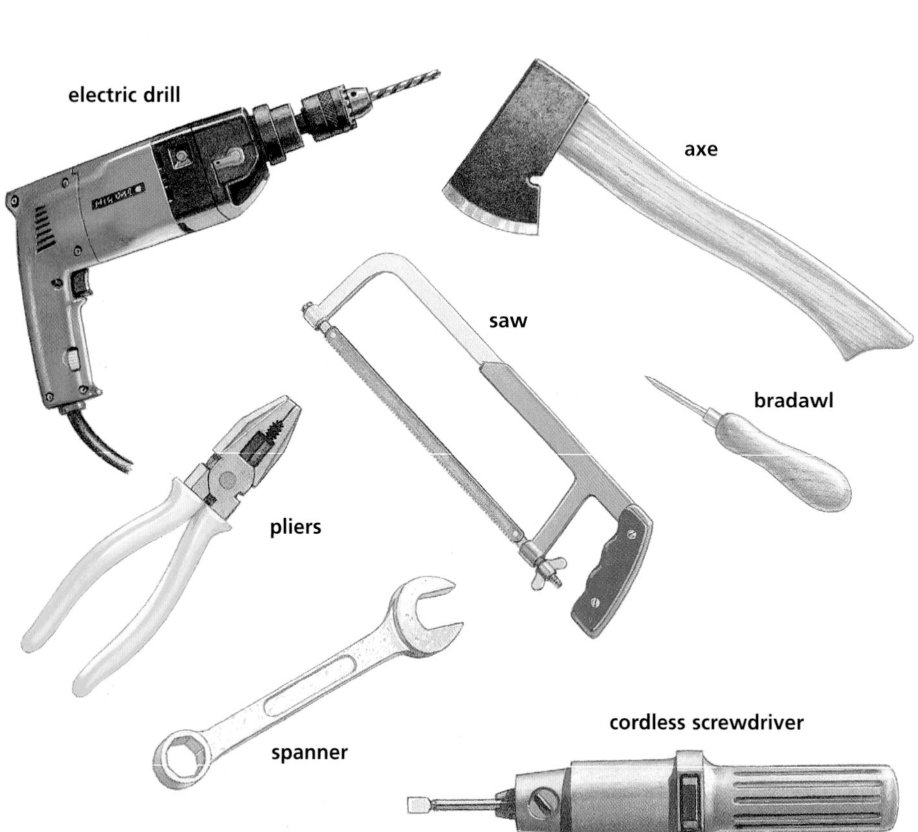

THE FIRST TOOLS

Early humans first began using tools more than 2 million years ago, when they picked up handy-sized pieces of stone to chop and hammer things. In time they began deliberately shaping stones into tools like this flint hand-axe. Flint was a favoured material because it could be shaped easily to give a sharp cutting edge.

Machine tools

In industry, huge power tools are used to cut and shape metal. They are called machine tools, and the work they carry out is called machining.

Machine tools hold the key to modern manufacturing because they cut very accurately and can produce parts that are a standard size. Many products, such as engines, are manufactured by fitting together sets of standard-sized parts on an assembly line.

In many workshops, machine tools are operated manually by engineers. But in large factories they usually work automatically, under computer control.

The cutting edge

Machine tools cut metal, which is very hard, so they must be harder still. Cutting tools are made from steel mixed with metals such as tungsten and chromium. Tungsten tools stay hard even when they get red-hot.

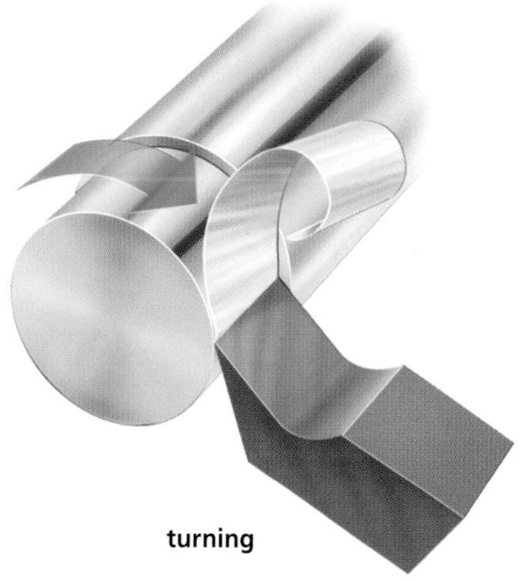
turning

milling

drilling

▲ Three of the most important machining processes are turning, milling and drilling.

Tools get hot because of the friction between them and the metal piece they are shaping, which is called the workpiece. To reduce the friction, a watery oil is run over the tool. This cutting oil also helps to cool down the tool.

◀ Sometimes machine tools work on a huge scale. For example, whole aircraft wings can be made by milling one enormous slab of metal. A wing made of a single piece of metal is much stronger than one made up of many bits joined together.

Turning, drilling and milling

Three common machining operations are turning, drilling and milling. Turning is carried out on a lathe. The lathe rotates the workpiece, while tools are moved in to cut it. Lathes are used, for example, to cut the threads on screws.

A drill grips and turns a bit, which drills holes in the workpiece. A number of different-sized bits may be mounted on a movable holder so that they can be brought into action one by one.

A milling machine cuts slots and grooves in a metal surface. It uses a toothed cutting wheel that spins round. The wheel makes a cut as the workpiece moves beneath it.

Chemicals and sparks

Machine tools shape metal by cutting and grinding. But there are other ways to shape metal. In chemical machining, metal is etched (eaten) away by chemicals. In spark machining, high-voltage electricity is used to create a spark on the metal surface. The spark gradually wears the metal away.

Find Out More

- Industry and manufacturing
- Metalworking
- Technology

Touch *see* Senses, Human senses • **Towers** *see* Buildings • **Tractors** *see* Farming

Trains

When the Italian high-speed train, 'Il Pendolino', comes to a bend, it doesn't slow down. It 'leans into the bend', just as you lean into a corner on your bike. By tilting, the train can corner faster.

▲ A few steam trains still run in India on track with a narrower width (gauge) than usual. Narrow-gauge railways also run in other countries, often on a 1-metre gauge.

Tilting trains are a way of running faster trains on existing railway tracks. But in several countries, specially designed straight railway tracks have been built for new high-speed trains.

Japan began the high-speed train revolution in 1964 with the Shinkansen (the New Trunk Line). Today, France has the fastest trains, the TGVs (Trains à Grande Vitesse). They regularly reach speeds of up to 260 kilometres per hour.

▼ Locomotives are electric, diesel or steam-powered. Only a few steam locomotives remain, most of them run by rail enthusiasts.

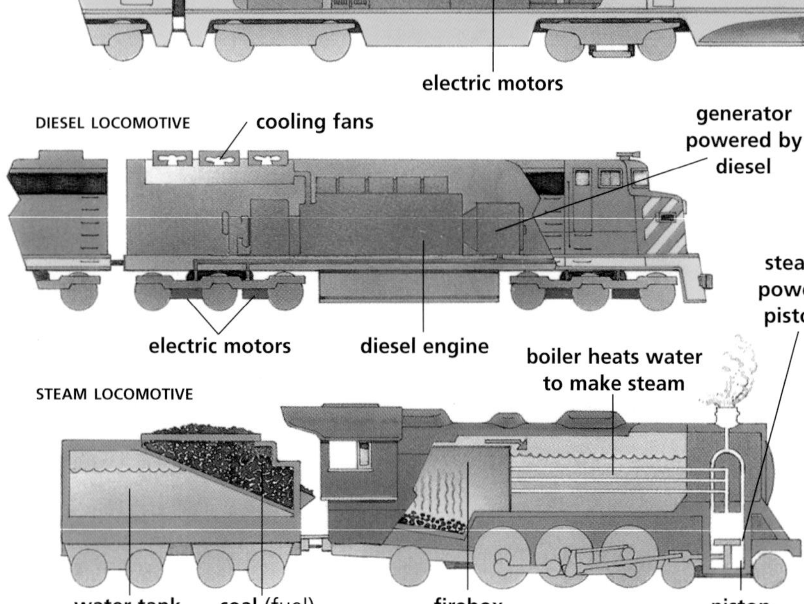

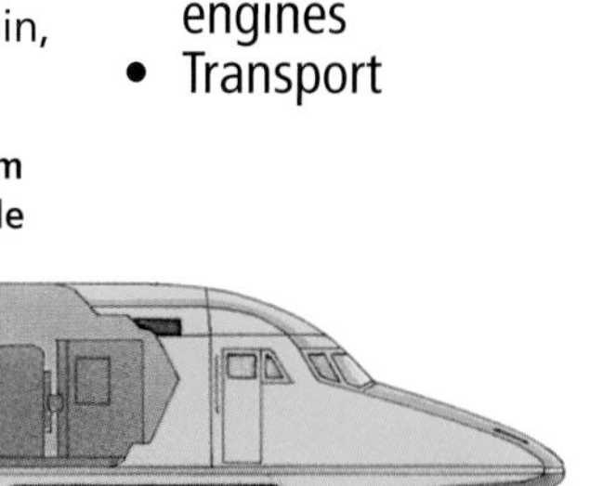

Find Out More
- Electric motors
- Magnetism and electromagnetism
- Petrol and diesel engines
- Transport

The track

Trains run on steel wheels on a steel track. This is a very efficient arrangement. The wheels have flanges (rims) on the inside to keep them on the track. The steel track is laid on wooden or concrete cross-pieces called sleepers.

In most countries, the two rails of the track are 143.5 cm apart, known as the standard gauge. This is the width of track George Stephenson chose when he built the first railways in England in the 1830s. Other gauges are used in some countries.

Not all railway tracks have two rails. Some have a single track and are called monorails. In some designs, the train hangs from trolleys that run along the rail. In others, the car straddles the rail. Straddle monorails are used to carry holidaymakers around the Disneyland pleasure parks.

Locomotives

The first railways used steam power to haul wagons and carriages. Steam locomotives were heavy machines that used fuel inefficiently and were very dirty. A few steam locomotives are still in use, but in most countries they have been replaced by diesels or electric locomotives.

Diesel locomotives have diesel engines, which burn oil as fuel. Most are diesel-electric units. This means that they use their engines to drive electricity generators. The electricity produced powers electric motors, which turn the locomotive wheels.

Electric locomotives pick up the electricity to power their electric motors from an outside source. Usually this is an overhead power line. The lines operate at very high voltage.

In some countries, notably Britain, some electric lines are worked from a third rail. The locomotives pick up electricity from a live rail that runs alongside the ordinary track. The trains on London's Underground operate on a third-rail system.

Going underground

There are underground railways in more than 100 cities around the world. They are known by such names as the subway, the metro, the rapid-transit system or mass-transit system. The London Underground is the world's largest underground railway, with more than 400 kilometres of track. It does not stay underground for all its length, but runs on the surface and high-level tracks as well.

Cities are building or expanding their underground railway networks to help reduce traffic congestion on the surface.

FLYING TRAINS

A French TGV has travelled at a speed of more than 515 kilometres per hour. This is close to the maximum speed that a train with wheels can travel without slipping. To travel faster, railway engineers are experimenting with trains without wheels that float above the track, using magnetism. This type of train is called a maglev, short for magnetic levitation.

▼ A heavily loaded freight train pulls its cargo through the Rocky Mountains in the USA. Often such freight trains have two or even three locomotives, to give them enough power to haul their huge loads.

Transformers *see* Electricity supply • **Transistors** *see* Electronics

Transport

In 1492, it took Christopher Columbus more than a month to sail across the Atlantic Ocean to the 'New World' (America). Today, a supersonic aircraft can make the journey in less then three hours, travelling faster than a rifle bullet.

Two hundred years ago, most people did not travel far from their homes. But with the invention of engines to power first ships and trains, then later cars and planes, travelling became easier, quicker and cheaper. Indeed, today there are so many people travelling that transport systems throughout the world are becoming congested (clogged up).

On land

On land, motor vehicles are quick and convenient, but there are so many of them that they are beginning to jam our roads, especially in cities. Even worse, their exhaust fumes cause dangerous pollution that threatens our health and the environment. Electrically-powered and even solar-powered vehicles could be the way ahead, because they cause hardly any pollution.

Railways are less important than they used to be because of competition from other vehicles. But they remain one of the most energy-efficient forms of transport. They can haul heavy loads at high speed, and they cause little pollution. As traffic jams on the roads increase, trains are becoming more popular.

By air and sea

For really long journeys, most people travel by plane. At peak times, airports are filled to overflowing. The planned new 'Super Jumbo' jets carrying over 600 passengers will make the airports busier still.

Ships are the best way to transport heavy loads over very long distances. The biggest ships are oil tankers. They can be half a kilometre long, and they take several kilometres to stop. Short sea crossings are being speeded up by ferries like the Sea Cat. This is a catamaran (a ship with two hulls) that can cruise at speeds of about 70 kilometres per hour.

200 YEARS OF TRANSPORT

ROAD TRANSPORT

1885
Karl Benz (Germany) builds the first motor car, a three-wheeled vehicle powered by a petrol engine.

1885
Englishman John Starley makes the first Rover Safety Cycle, with all the features of a modern bicycle.

RAIL TRANSPORT

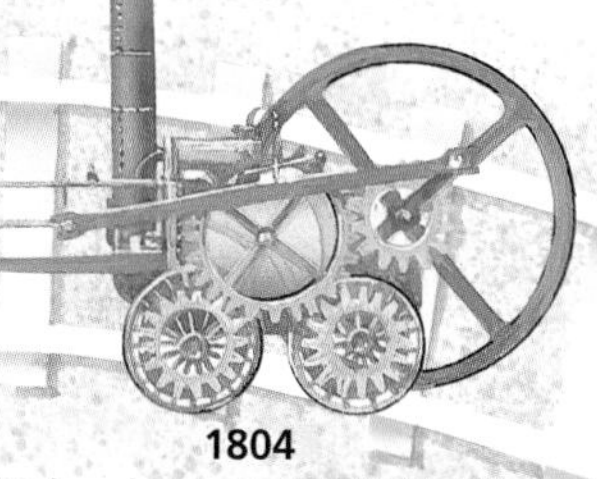

1804
Richard Trevithick (Britain) builds the first successful steam locomotive, for the Pen-y-Darren tramway in Wales.

1830
George Stephenson (Britain) builds the first passenger railway, the Liverpool and Manchester Railway. He and his son Robert design a new locomotive to run on it, the 'Rocket'.

SEA TRANSPORT

1807
The US engineer Robert Fulton designs the *Clermont*, the first successful steamboat.

1838
First voyage of Isambard Kingdom Brunel's (Britain) SS *Great Western*, the first steamship to make regular Atlantic crossings.

AIR TRANSPORT

1783
The French Montgolfier brothers, Joseph-Michel and Jacques-Étienne, make the first flight in a hot-air balloon in Paris.

1804
Sir George Cayley (Britain) builds the first heavier-than-air flying machine, a glider.

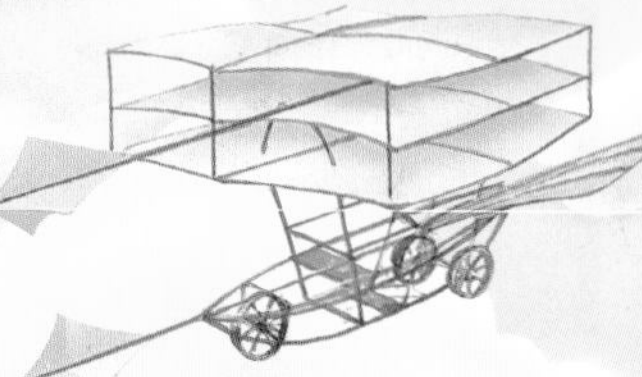

Find Out More
- Aircraft
- Cars and trucks
- Ships and submarines
- Trains

Trees *see* Forests, Plants, Wood and timber • **Trucks** *see* Cars and trucks

1908
Henry Ford (USA) introduces the Model T, the first car to be produced cheaply and in really large numbers.

1937
Volkswagen ('people's car') launched in Germany: later nicknamed the Beetle.

1990s
'People carriers' like the Renault Espace become popular.

1997
Thrust SSC (Britain) breaks the sound barrier with a new world land speed record of 1228 km/h.

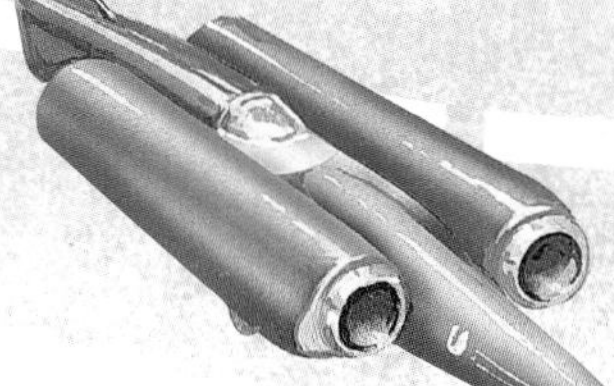

1912
The first diesel locomotive runs in Germany.

1938
The streamlined *Mallard* (Britain) sets the all-time speed record for steam.

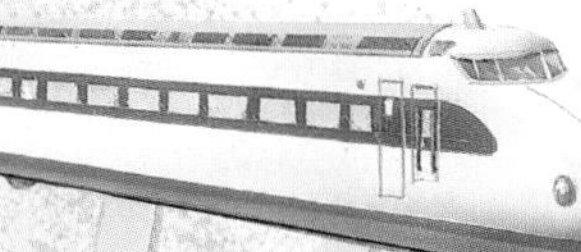

1964
The first 'bullet trains' run on Japan's Shinkansen high-speed railway.

1990
A TGV (Train à Grande Vitesse) travels at the record speed of over 515 km/h.

1894
Charles Parsons (Britain) demonstrates the first boat powered by steam turbines, *Turbinia*.

1907
The *Mauretania* (Britain) is one of a new generation of large transatlantic turbine-powered passenger liners. It crosses the Atlantic in just under five days.

1954
The first nuclear-powered submarine, *Nautilus* (USA), is launched.

1959
Christopher Cockerell (Britain) designs the first hovercraft.

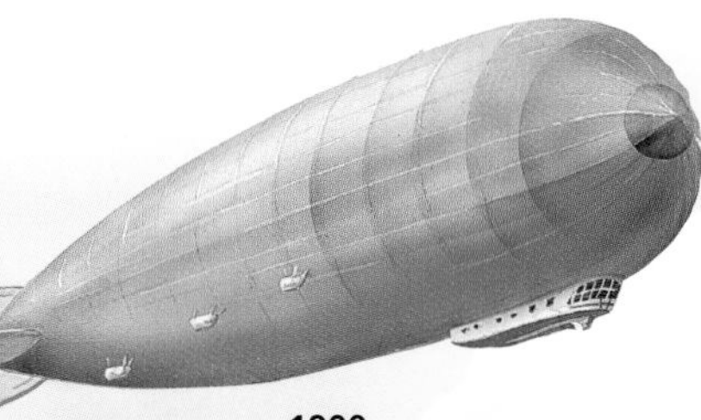

1900
Ferdinand Graf von Zeppelin (Germany) builds the first large rigid airship, 128 m long.

1903
The Wright Brothers (USA) build and fly the first powered aeroplane, *Flyer I*, at Kitty Hawk, North Carolina.

1939
The first jet aircraft flies, the Heinkel He 178 (Germany). Igor Sikorsky (Russia) establishes the design of the single-rotor helicopter.

1947
Charles Yeager (USA) breaks the sound barrier in a Bell X-1 rocket plane.

1969
The Boeing 747 jumbo jet (USA) and the supersonic airliner Concorde (England, France) make their first flights.

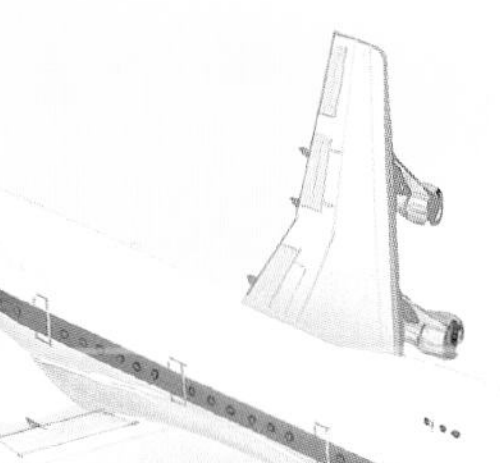

Tumours *see* Cancers • **Tundra** *see* Polar life

Tunnels and pipes

At 11.13 am precisely on 1 December 1990, Britain ceased to be an island. At that moment, a tunnel dug from England towards France broke through into one dug from France towards England under the English Channel. Amazingly, the tunnels were only 50 centimetres out of line. This tunnel was to form part of the Channel Tunnel.

Like all the biggest transport tunnels, the Channel Tunnel is a rail tunnel. It is 50 kilometres long – only 4 kilometres shorter than the longest rail tunnel in the world, the Seikan Tunnel in Japan, which also goes under the sea. Road tunnels tend to be much shorter. The St Gotthard tunnel through the Alps is the longest, at 16 kilometres.

▶ The Trans-Alaskan Pipeline carries oil from wells in the north of Alaska. It is 1285 kilometres long. About half of the pipeline is carried above ground, half is underground.

Boring tunnels

You can dig shallow tunnels by digging a deep ditch and then covering it over to form a tunnel. This is called cut-and-cover. Underground railways are sometimes built this way. But if you are digging a deep tunnel you must use other methods, depending on the nature of the ground.

When you are drilling through hard rock, you use explosives to break up the rock face. The explosives are placed inside holes drilled by a 'jumbo' drilling rig. Then they are detonated (set off).

When drilling through softer rock, such as chalk, you use huge tunnel-boring machines (TBMs). TBMs are also used for tunnelling through soft or wet ground. Then they are fitted with a pressurized cutting head. The air pressure helps stop the tunnel caving in before the tunnel segments are put in place.

Find Out More
- Construction
- Trains
- Transport

▼ A TBM has a rotating cutting head at the front, studded with sharp teeth. As the TBM moves forwards, ring-shaped segments are put in place to form the tunnel wall.

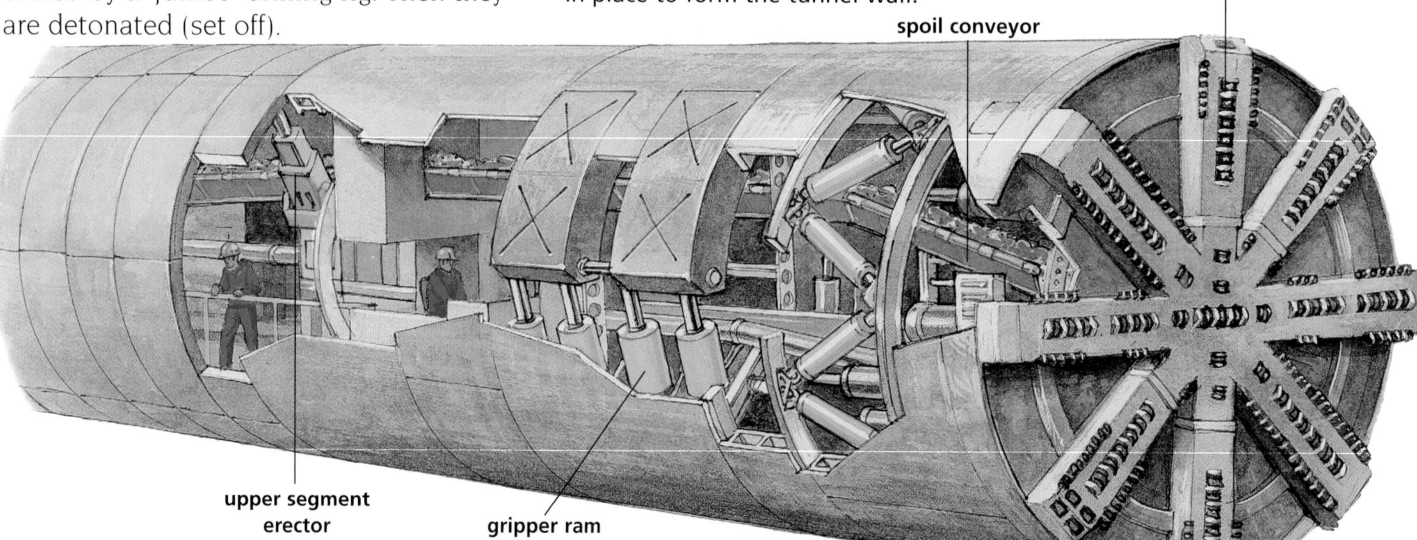

Turbines *see* Engines, Jet engines, Power stations, Water power • **Turbojets** *see* Jet engines • **Tyres** *see* Rubber

Ultrasound

Blow a dog whistle and you might think that it was broken! The whistle's sound is so high-pitched that humans cannot hear it. Sounds that are too high-pitched for humans to hear are called ultrasound.

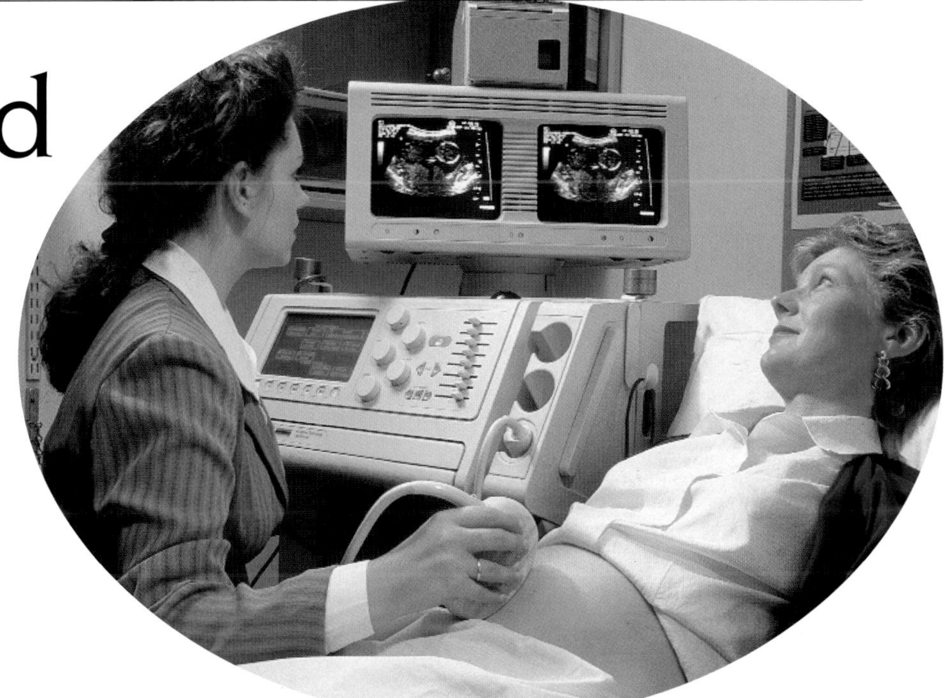

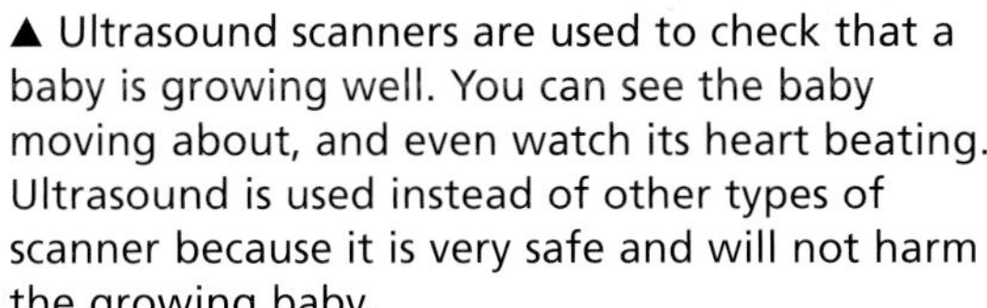

▲ Ultrasound scanners are used to check that a baby is growing well. You can see the baby moving about, and even watch its heart beating. Ultrasound is used instead of other types of scanner because it is very safe and will not harm the growing baby.

We cannot hear ultrasound, but we can make machines to produce ultrasound and detectors to measure it. Scientists have found many uses for ultra-high pitched sounds.

Using ultrasound in medicine

Sending waves of ultrasound into the body is a way of making a picture of what is inside. The ultrasound is reflected by organs in the body, and a detector collects the reflections. Computers can use the pattern these make to build up a picture. Pregnant women are often given ultrasound scans, so that doctors can see how their baby is growing.

Ultrasound can also be used to treat some medical problems. Sometimes tiny bits of solid matter can grow in the kidney. The result is a kidney stone. A beam of ultrasound can shake up kidney stones so much that they break up and can be passed harmlessly out of the body.

Find Out More

- Human reproduction
- Kidneys
- Sound

Melting metal

A very strong beam of ultrasound can even melt a piece of metal. Metal shapes can be cut out this way. Two pieces of metal can be joined together by melting them where they touch. They are then allowed to solidify. This is called ultrasonic welding.

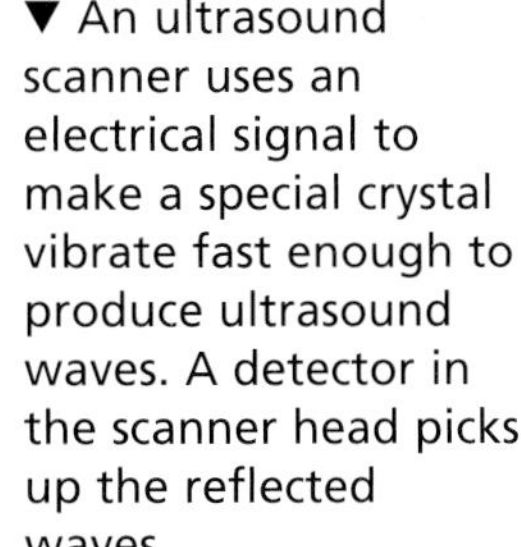

▼ An ultrasound scanner uses an electrical signal to make a special crystal vibrate fast enough to produce ultrasound waves. A detector in the scanner head picks up the reflected waves.

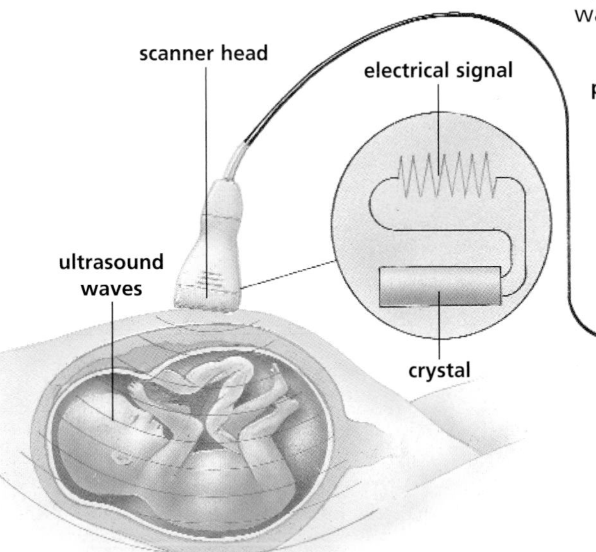

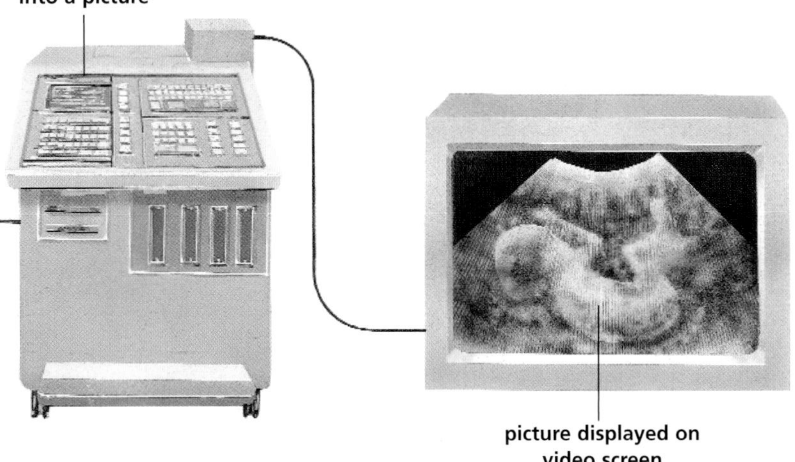

Ultraviolet *see* Electromagnetic spectrum

Universe

There are about 100,000 million galaxies in the Universe. But they have not always been there. By measuring the motion of galaxies, astronomers have found that the Universe is expanding. Space itself is getting bigger. From the rate of expansion, astronomers think that everything began about 15,000 million years ago, when our visible Universe was concentrated at one point. In a gigantic burst of energy, called the 'Big Bang', our Universe came into being and began to expand.

At the very beginning, the Universe was unimaginably hot and was mainly energy. As it expanded, the Universe cooled down. Matter came into being in the form of the gases hydrogen and helium.

By 1000 million years after the Big Bang, huge gas clouds were starting to pull together under the action of gravity. The first stars were formed in clumps, like large clusters or small galaxies. Clumps merged together to make larger galaxies.

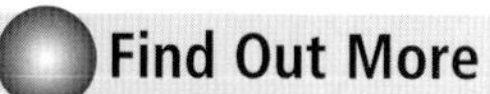

- Astronomy
- Galaxies
- Solar System
- Stars

▲ The Virgo cluster of galaxies. These galaxies are about 50 million light years away. The Virgo cluster is one of the nearest to the group of galaxies that includes the Milky Way.

Astronomers can find out what happened long ago in the Universe by looking at very distant galaxies. Even travelling at 300,000 kilometres per second, their light takes billions of years to reach us. This means we see them as they were billions of years ago, as if we were looking back in time.

the Universe more than 10 billion light years across

the Milky Way about 100,000 light years across

the Solar System including the comet cloud, about 0.1 light year across

▲ The scale of the Universe. Each of these pictures is many times larger across than the previous one.

▶ This picture is what the Hubble Space Telescope recorded by looking at a tiny patch of sky for a total of 10 hours. Many of the small blotches are galaxies between 12,000 million and 14,000 million light years away. We see them as they were soon after galaxies first formed in the Universe, because their light has taken so long to reach us.

EDWIN HUBBLE

The US scientist Edwin Hubble (1889–1953) made some of the most important astronomical discoveries of the 20th century. He was the first astronomer to realize that some 'nebulas' in the sky are really galaxies beyond the Milky Way. Hubble measured the speeds and distances of some galaxies and discovered that the farthest galaxies are travelling fastest. This way, he showed that the Universe is expanding. Hubble also invented the system of putting galaxies into categories by their shape. Astronomers still use this system. The Hubble Space Telescope was named in his honour.

◀ The gravity of a galaxy cluster acting like a lens. The blue objects are all distorted and magnified images of the same galaxy. These multiple images are produced by the powerful gravity of the cluster of galaxies, that look yellowish.

Gravity and the Universe

Like stars, galaxies are found in clusters. Clusters stay together because the galaxies are attracted to each other by gravity. Even clusters group together. Over vast expanses of space, they are gathered in strands and walls around empty regions, rather like foamy bubbles.

The gravity of a galaxy cluster is so great, it can even bend the path of a beam of light travelling through it. A cluster can distort and magnify the light from more distant galaxies, acting like a lens.

Gravity is trying to slow the expansion of the Universe because the galaxies all pull on each other. But observations of distant galaxies suggest that a force from some mysterious 'dark energy' is acting against gravity. This means that the Universe will probably go on expanding for ever. So far, no one is sure why this is happening.

Uranium *see* Nuclear energy, Radioactivity

Uranus

Tilted over on its side, Uranus has extraordinary seasons. Night and day each last 42 years at its north and south poles. The sixth planet from the Sun, Uranus is about four times larger than the Earth. The planet was discovered by the German-born astronomer William Herschel in 1781. It made him world famous.

To human eyes Uranus is a plain blue disc with no spots or bands. There is a rocky core at its centre. Over that lies a thick layer made chiefly of water. On the outside there is a thick atmosphere of hydrogen and helium.

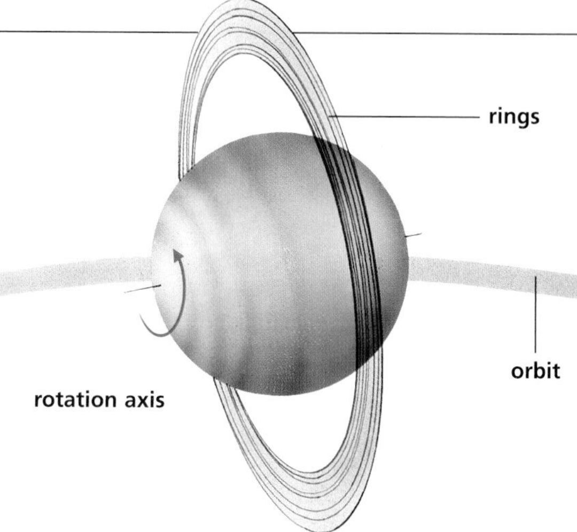

▲ With its spin axis tilted right over, Uranus seems to roll around its orbit lying on its side. It was probably knocked over in a great collision when the planets were first forming.

Find Out More

- Neptune
- Planets
- Solar System
- Space astronomy
- Sun

▶ William Herschel discovered Uranus using a homemade telescope. He also found the planet's two largest moons, Titania and Oberon.

Narrow rings

A set of narrow rings surrounds Uranus's equator. Of the nine main rings, one is 100 kilometres wide, and the others only 10 kilometres.

The rings are very dark. They are made of boulders about a metre across. In 1986, the *Voyager* 2 spacecraft spotted more faint rings made of dust.

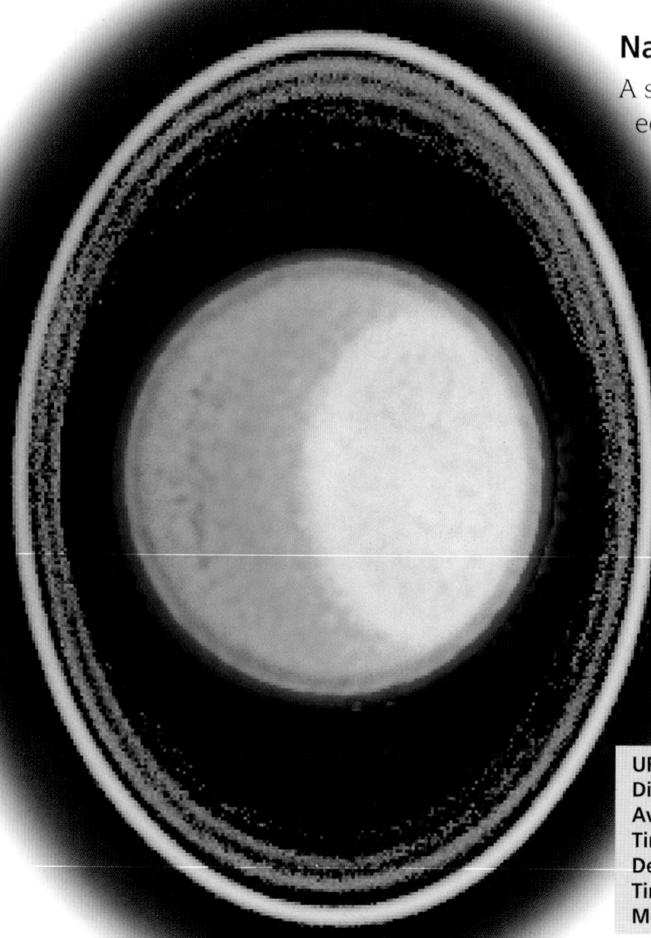

◀ A colour-coded infra-red picture of Uranus, showing the different layers of the atmosphere. Red is thin, high haze. Yellow is a cap of thicker haze over the planet's south pole. Blue is where the atmosphere is clearest.

▲ Uranus's moon Miranda. Though only 472 kilometres across, its icy surface is an amazing jumble of different landscapes.

URANUS DATA
Diameter at equator: 51,118 km
Average distance from Sun: 2871 million km
Time taken to spin on axis: 17.2 hours
Density (water = 1): 1.3
Time taken to orbit the Sun: 84.01 years
Moons: 21

Urine *see* Kidneys • **Vaccination** *see* Immune system • **Vacuum** *see* Pressure • **Valleys** *see* Erosion

Venus

▲ What Venus's volcanic landscape might look like.

The most brilliant planet in the sky, Venus is our closest planet. You may spot it in the western sky after sunset or in the east before sunrise. Yet no one has ever seen its surface. Acid clouds completely conceal this forbidding world.

Venus is a rocky planet almost the same size as the Earth but it is very different. An atmosphere nearly 100 times thicker than the Earth's presses down on Venus. It is almost all carbon dioxide, a gas that easily traps the heat of the Sun. Fifty kilometres above the ground, droplets of sulphuric acid form dense clouds that never clear away.

On the planet's surface, the temperature reaches 480 °C – hotter even than Mercury. And there is hardly any difference between day and night. Venus is a sweltering, hostile place.

Though it is impossible to see through Venus's clouds, radio waves can get through. So astronomers have used radar to map the hidden surface.

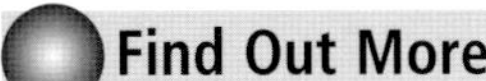

Find Out More

- Global warming
- Planets
- Solar System
- Volcanoes

Volcanoes and craters

Venus has thousands of volcanoes. Volcanic activity may even be going on right now, as it is on Earth. Typical volcanoes are about 3 kilometres across and 90 metres high, but some are much larger. Gula Mons, for example, is 3 kilometres high.

Lava channels snake for thousands of kilometres and Venus has some volcanic features seen on no other planets. Some are like spiders with ridges radiating outwards. There are flat-topped volcanoes up to 60 kilometres across, which are called 'pancake domes'.

There are about 900 craters on Venus. The largest are 250 kilometres across. Even the smallest are about 1.5 kilometres. This is because only larger rocks can get through the atmosphere without burning up.

◄ ▼ A picture of Venus (left), taken by the Pioneer Space Telescope, shows the planet covered with clouds. A radar map (below) reveals the surface underneath. The lighter band is one of the two major highland areas.

VENUS DATA
Diameter at equator: 12,104 km
Average distance from Sun: 108 million km
Time taken to spin on axis: 243 days (backwards)
Density (water = 1): 5.2
Time taken to orbit the Sun: 224.68 days
Moons: 0

Vertebrates *see* Animals

Video equipment

Home videotaping means you don't have to rush home to watch your favourite TV programmes. By simply setting a timer, you can watch what you want, anytime. And portable cameras, with video recorders built in, let you make your own home movies. But how does videotape work?

TV pictures can be recorded on magnetic tape in the same way that sound is recorded on a tape recorder. The main machine used is called a video cassette recorder (VCR), in which the tape is normally on a cassette. But TV pictures contain too much information to fit on an ordinary audio tape. The tape would have to run so fast that it would snap.

▶ Just the batteries of an early video camera were bigger than this tiny palmcorder. Miniature microchips and tiny mechanical parts make today's video cameras unbelievably small.

◀ Editing TV programmes has been made easier by computers.

Tilted drums

The answer to this problem is to use wider tape, and tape heads (the part that 'reads' the tape) that spin rapidly rather the stationary ones used for sound recording.

The heads in a video machine are on opposite sides of a circular drum that is tilted slightly in relation to the direction that the tape moves in. During recording or playback, the tape wraps around the drum. As the drum spins very fast, it 'wipes' thin diagonal stripes of the TV signal on to the slowly moving tape. This is called helical scanning.

Digital rivals

Traditional video tapes are being replaced by machines such as DVD players, which record videos digitally. These store the information about the pictures and sound in the same way that a computer stores information on its hard disk.

With digital video recordings it is easy to edit TV programmes or home movies. You can record digital pictures on to computers, then cut and paste the footage where you want it, just like the text in a word processor!

Find Out More

- Computers
- Sound recording
- Television

▼ Inside a video recorder, the tape runs over the spinning video head drum and past the audio (sound) head. The sound track is recorded along the top of the tape. The video head records the pictures as diagonal tracks across the tape, resting side by side like fallen dominoes.

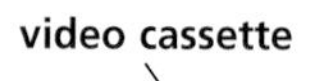

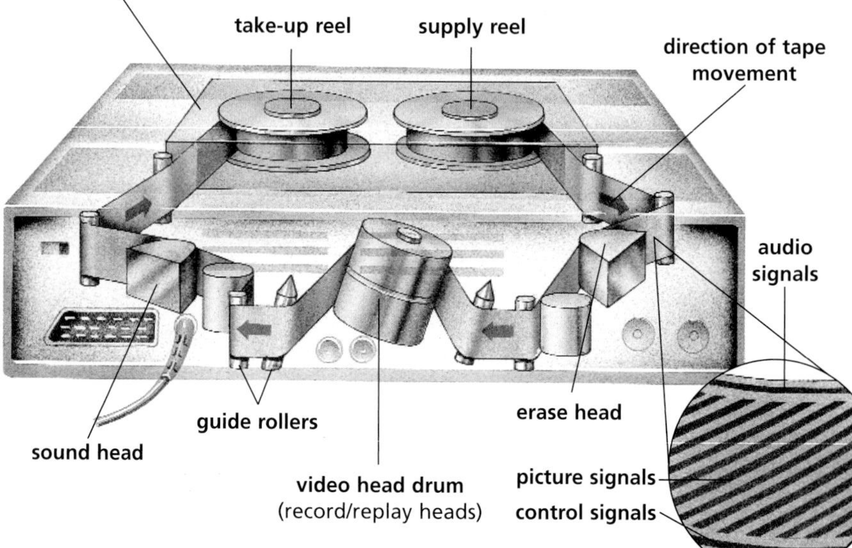

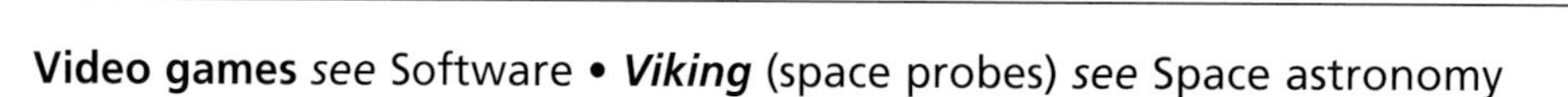
Video games *see* Software • ***Viking*** (space probes) *see* Space astronomy

Virtual reality

You are in a building you have never been in before. You move into a room to explore it. But suddenly, the floor disappears and you are falling. Looking up as the room disappears above you, you see the blackness of space. This is the kind of experience that you can have when you enter the world of virtual reality.

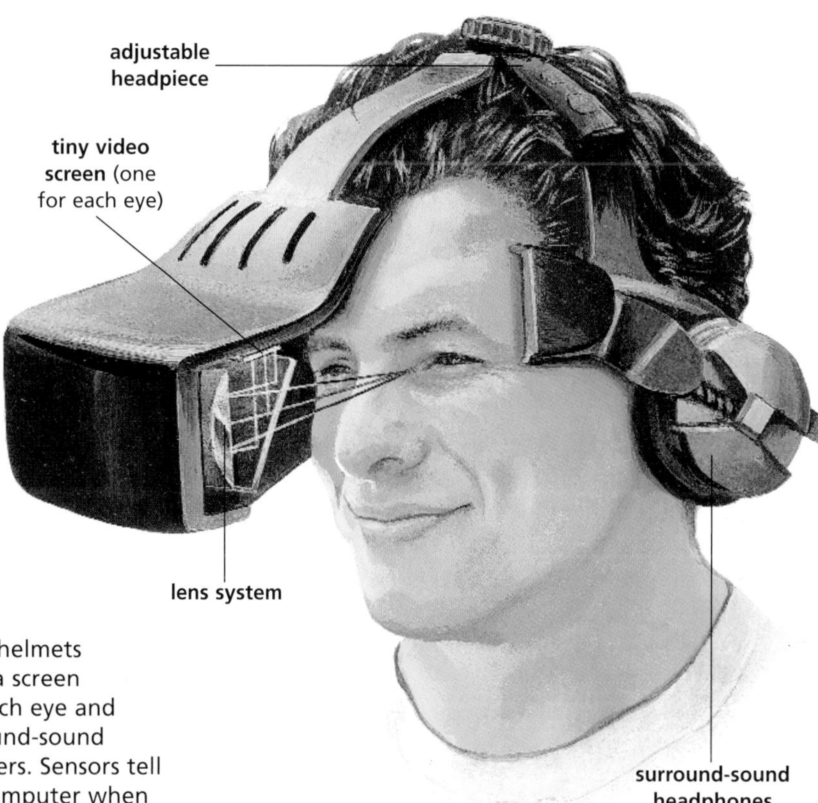

▶ VR helmets have a screen for each eye and surround-sound speakers. Sensors tell the computer when you move your head.

Virtual reality (VR) involves creating a three-dimensional environment inside a computer's memory. It can be a room, a cave, or a shopping mall. The idea is to let people explore that space by looking around it and walking around it in as natural a way as possible, listening to sounds they might hear, even feeling things that they might touch. Virtual reality lets designers get a feel for buildings or cars that have not even been built yet. Players of computer games can use virtual reality to reach a new level of realism.

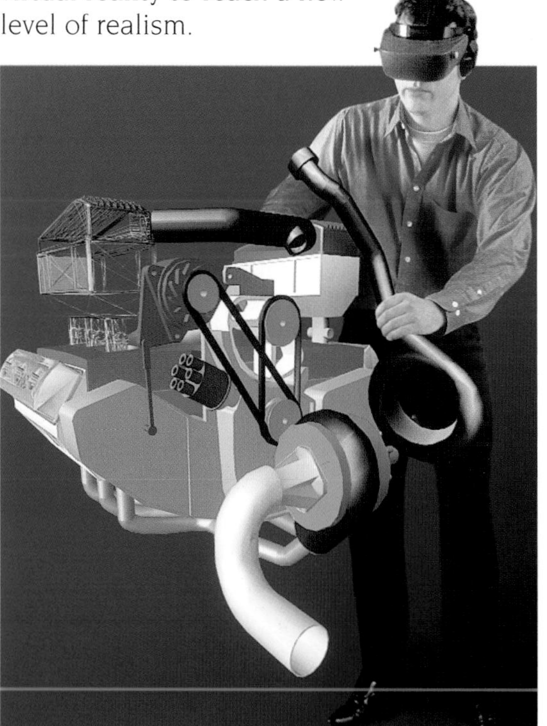

◀ Using VR, engineers can 'walk around' their design ideas, getting a sense of how they will look – and even feel – without having to build them. This picture shows an engineer with a virtual model of an engine.

Find Out More

- Computer graphics and design
- Computers
- Microphones and speakers

In your head

To get you inside the 'space' in the computer, VR systems use a head-mounted display that contains two tiny computer monitors, one for each eye. The images are slightly different in each, to create a three-dimensional effect.

But the really clever thing about a VR helmet is that when your head moves, the graphics you see move too. Magnetic sensors in the helmet tell the computer how much you move, so it can change the image correspondingly. This makes you feel that you are in the environment. Speakers in the helmet let you hear sound all around you for added realism.

You can use a 'data glove' to help make VR even more authentic. When you 'push' on something, tiny balloons in the glove inflate, pressing on your hand. It feels like you've really pushed something!

Researchers are working on adding 'thought control' to VR systems. Using brainwave sensors inside a VR helmet, people will be able to control or change what they listen to, by just thinking about it.

Volcanoes

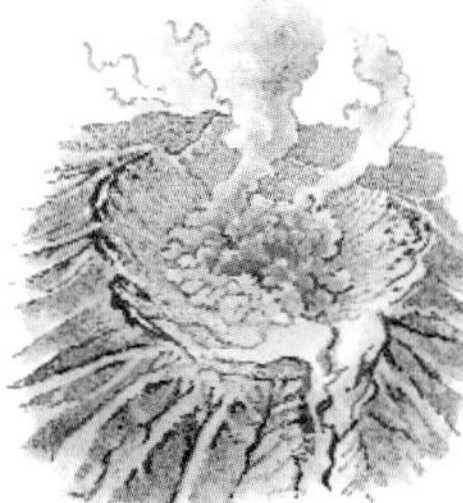

In June 1991, Mount Pinatubo, a volcano in the Philippines, erupted. Ash blasted high into the sky, and flows of lava, steam and rubble came pouring down the mountain. Houses were crushed by the ash, and anyone caught in a flow was instantly killed.

No one had ever seen Pinatubo erupt before, but geologists knew it was ready. For two months it had been warning people with earthquakes and belches of steam and gas. Pinatubo exploded with such power that it blasted 200 metres off its top and created a huge *crater* (deep, steep-sided hollow) at its summit.

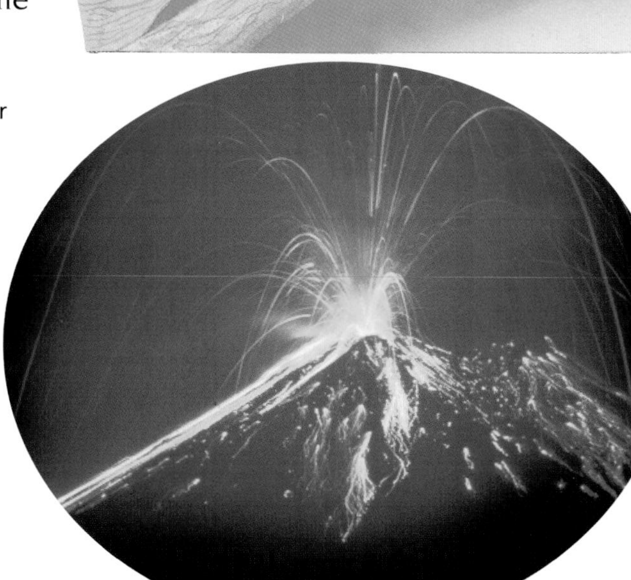

▶ Lava can be hotter than 1200°C, so hot that it glows. This is a 'fire fountain' of lava photographed during an eruption in Costa Rica in 1991.

What is a volcano?

Volcanoes are places where *lava* (molten rock) erupts onto the surface of the Earth. There are many types of volcano.

Stratovolcanoes are large, steep volcanoes made of layers of lava and ash. They are so steep because the lava is so thick and sticky that it can't flow very far before it hardens. It piles up close to the *vent* (opening at the top), creating a cone-like shape. Large stratovolcanoes grow from many eruptions over hundreds of thousands or even millions of years.

Shield volcanoes are broad with gentle slopes. These volcanoes are made of layer after layer of hot, runny lava that flows a long way before it turns solid.

Other types of volcano include long fissures where lava erupts quietly for years on end, and huge holes in the ground called calderas. The size and shape of each volcano depends on what it is made of and how it has erupted in the past.

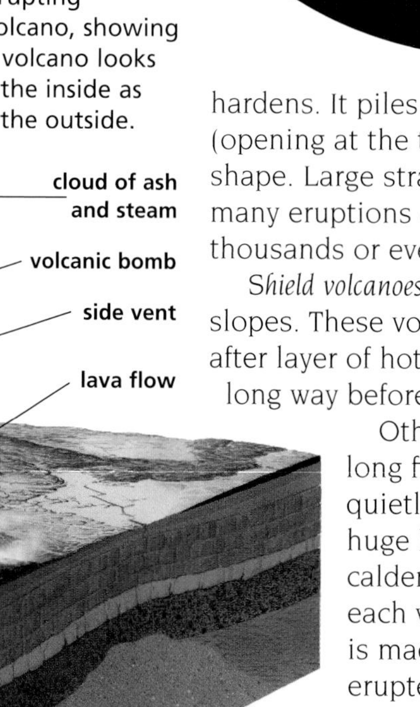

▼ An erupting stratovolcano, showing what a volcano looks like on the inside as well as the outside.

Why do volcanoes erupt?

The inside of the Earth is very hot. Some of the heat escapes through volcanoes, which helps the Earth to cool down.

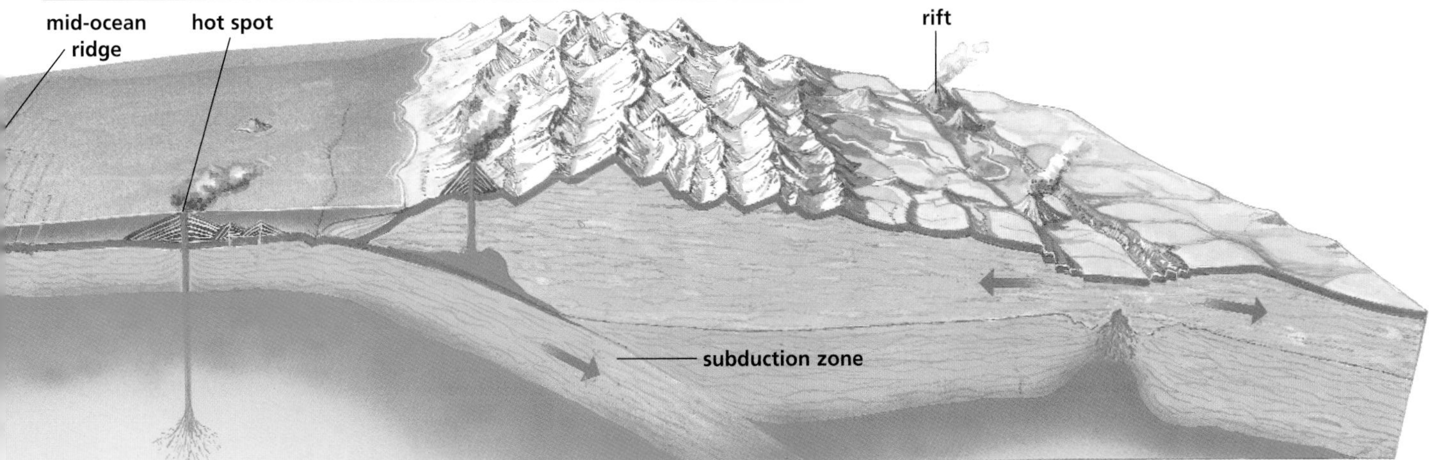

▲ Different types of volcano form in different places. Explosive stratovolcanoes form near ocean trenches, where a section of the Earth's crust is diving beneath another. Some shield volcanoes form where the ocean crust is being torn apart. Large shield volcanoes form over 'hot spots', where a lot of magma is forming in the mantle.

Deep underground, in the Earth's mantle and crust, there are places where the rocks melt. When they melt, they form *magma* – a hot slush of mineral crystals, liquid rock and gas. Magma is not as dense as the rock around it, so it begins to rise upwards through cracks. A lot of the magma never makes it to the surface and it hardens underground. But some of it forces its way through openings or weak spots in the ground, and erupts. As soon as magma erupts, it is called lava.

▲ Isabella Island in the Galapagos is made up of a number of shield volcanoes. This image was taken by a satellite.

Types of eruption

Eruptions at shield volcanoes are usually very calm. The lava pours gently out onto the ground. Eruptions at stratovolcanoes like Pinatubo are usually explosive. The way a volcano erupts depends how thick and sticky the magma is, and on how much gas the magma contains.

When magma forms, it is under pressure from the weight of the rocks above. As it moves up through these rocks, there is less weight above and the pressure decreases. The gas in the magma expands and forms bubbles – like when you unscrew the top of a fizzy drink.

If the magma is thin and runny, then the gas bubbles can move easily through it and out to the surface. The magma flows easily and it erupts calmly. But if the magma is thick and sticky, the bubbles can't escape. Instead they explode, shattering the magma into small pieces and throwing them out of the volcano and high up into the air. This ash rains down on the volcano and the surrounding area. The explosions can also cause searing hot flows of lava, steam and rock to come racing out of the volcano at 100 kilometres per hour.

▼ Most of the world's active volcanoes are around the edge of the Pacific Ocean, an area known as the 'Ring of Fire'.

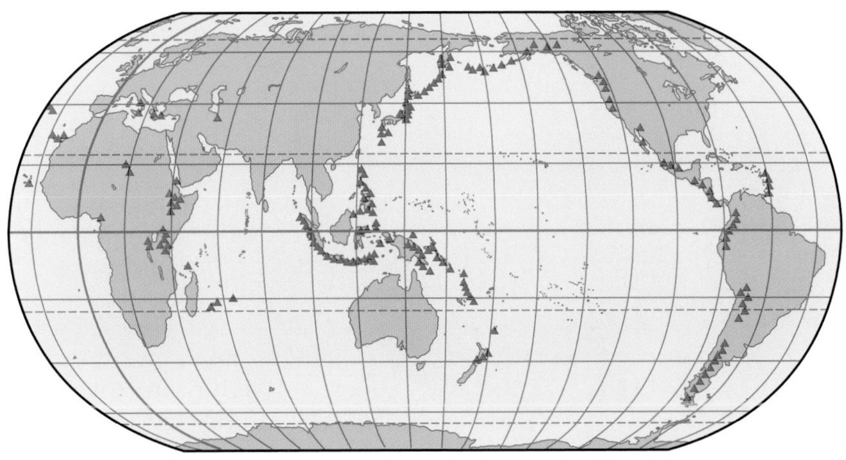

Find Out More

- Continents and plates
- Earth
- Floating and sinking
- Gases
- Oceans
- Pressure
- Rocks

Waste disposal

Every day the people of New York City throw away up to 25,000 tonnes of waste – newspapers, plastic bags, food scraps, cans, old clothes, bottles, and so on. Twice a week this rubbish is collected and dumped on a site on Staten Island. It is the biggest waste tip in the world.

Most household rubbish is disposed of at waste dumps like this. They are called landfill sites. Usually, a great pit is dug in the ground and filled with rubbish. The rubbish is then covered over and replanted with plants and grass.

The problem is that we are producing so much rubbish that we are running out of suitable sites. Also, harmful substances in the buried rubbish can find their way into our water supplies. And the rotting matter in the waste produces the gas methane, which can cause explosions. On many old landfill sites, this gas is piped away and used as fuel – it is the same gas that we use for cooking in our homes.

Up in smoke

Another method of dealing with rubbish is by burning, or incineration. Modern

▶ About 90% of the world's domestic waste goes to landfill sites.

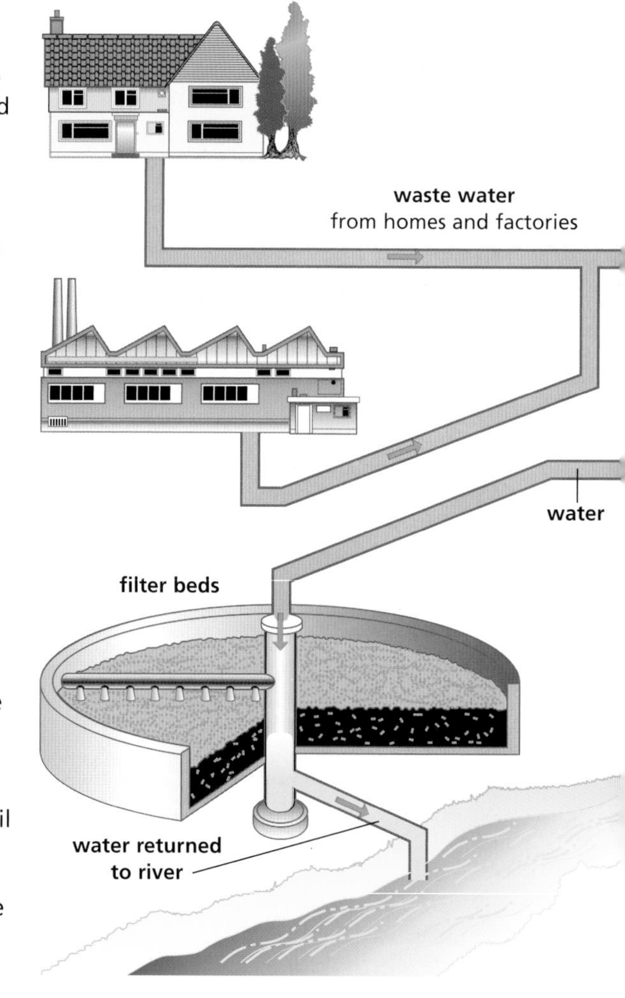

▶ At a sewage works, screens and settling tanks first remove the larger objects, grit and sludge. The sludge is further processed to make fuel gas and fertilizer. The water remaining is sprinkled over filter beds containing microbes that feed on any remaining waste. The water is then clean enough to go back into a river.

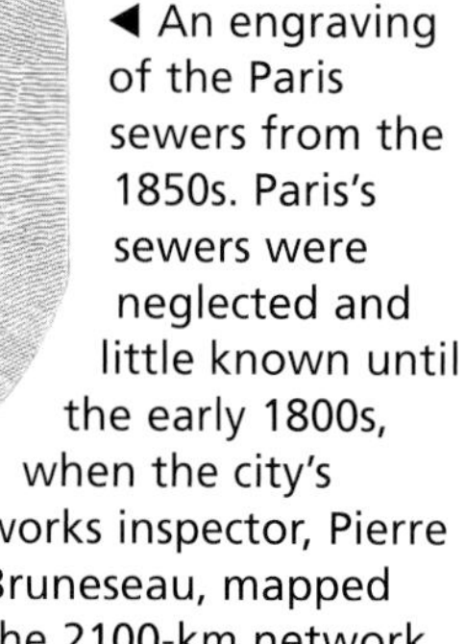

◀ An engraving of the Paris sewers from the 1850s. Paris's sewers were neglected and little known until the early 1800s, when the city's works inspector, Pierre Bruneseau, mapped the 2100-km network.

incinerators not only burn waste, but often use the heat this produces, for heating or generating electricity. Before waste can be used as fuel, materials that will not burn, such as metal and glass, must be separated from those that will burn, like paper.

One disadvantage of burning wastes is that it can produce toxic (poisonous) gases. Incinerators must therefore be fitted with efficient gas cleaners to remove these fumes.

Increasingly, local authorities are encouraging households to take their waste paper, metals, glass and plastic to recycling centres. The different materials are then processed before being used again.

In the sewers

As well as all the solid rubbish we throw away, we produce a lot of liquid waste. This includes body wastes from toilets, and water from sinks, washing-machines and baths. This liquid waste is called sewage.

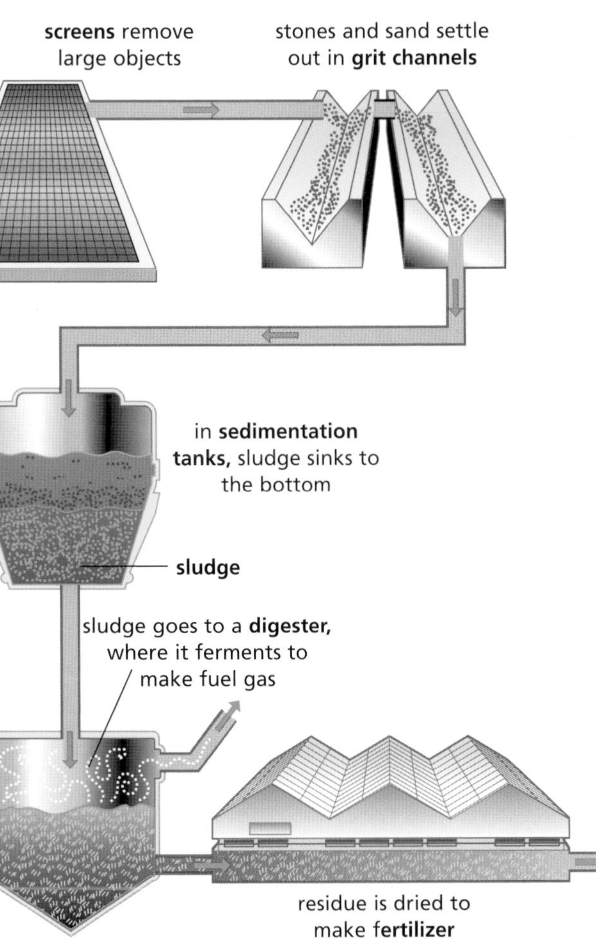

In some parts of the world, raw (untreated) sewage is pumped directly into rivers or the sea, polluting the water. But in most communities, a system of pipelines called the sewers carries the sewage to treatment plants. Here, solids and harmful substances are removed so that the water can be returned to the environment. The sludge left over can be treated to make fuel gas and fertilizer.

Wastes at work

Many industries, particularly the chemical industry, use dangerous substances. This produces wastes that can be harmful to our health and the environment. Landfill is often used for the safe disposal of solid wastes. Liquid wastes are treated to make them harmless before they are released. Unfortunately, this doesn't always happen, and pollution can result.

Some of the deadliest waste is produced by the nuclear industry. The waste is radioactive, which means that it gives off harmful radiation. Some waste remains active and dangerous for thousands of years.

For safety, most nuclear waste is stored underground. The surrounding soil and rock stop the radiation from reaching the surface. Liquid wastes are often kept in tanks surrounded by thick concrete. Some waste is made into a kind of glass and stored in sealed containers in deep mines.

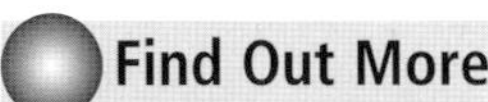
Find Out More

- Fertilizers
- Nuclear energy
- Pollution
- Recycling

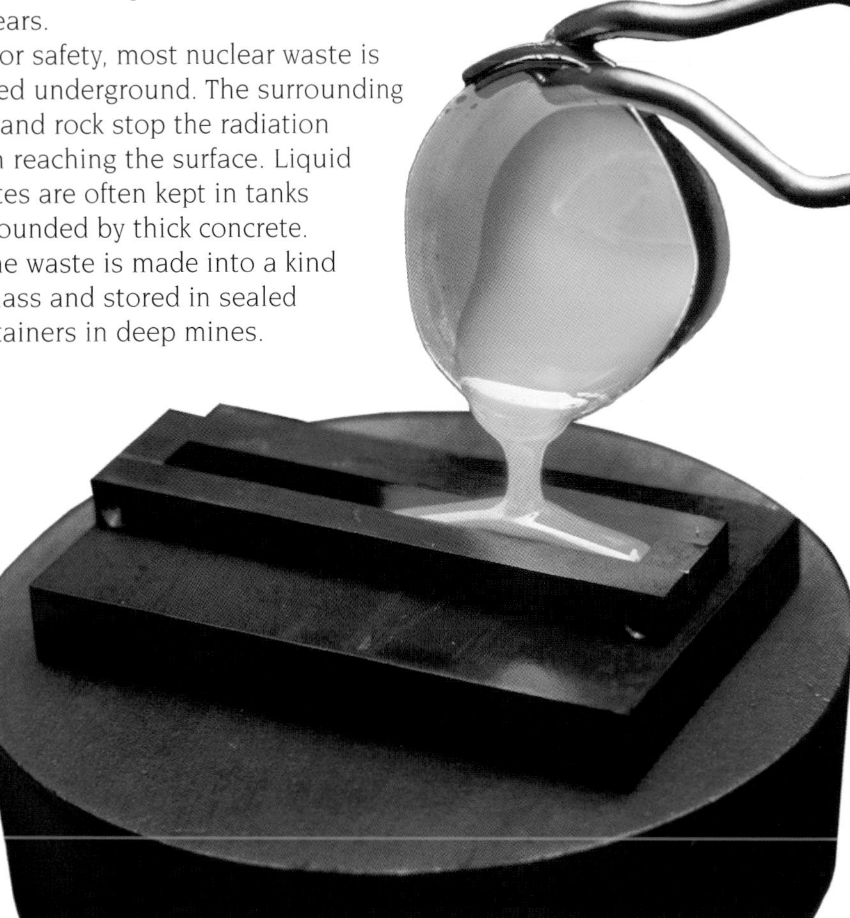

▼ Liquid nuclear waste glass is poured into a steel mould. In glass form, nuclear waste can be disposed of safely.

Watches *see* Time

Water

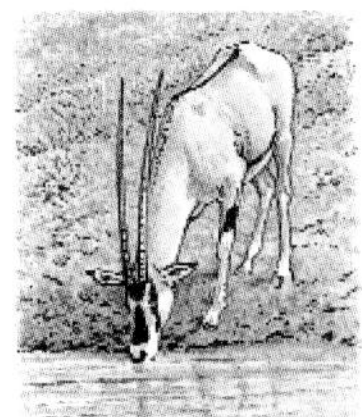

Life on Earth would not exist without water. No plant or animal can survive without it. Two-thirds of your body is made of water. You need to drink about a litre and half of water every day to stay alive.

Water seems a simple chemical. Like many other substances, water is made up of tiny particles called molecules. Each water molecule is made up of three tinier particles called atoms. A water molecule has two atoms of hydrogen and one atom of oxygen. Scientists write this as H_2O.

Properties and uses

Water is such a common and useful chemical that scientists base the Celsius temperature scale on its freezing and boiling points. On this scale, water freezes at 0 °C and boils at 100 °C.

Water can dissolve lots of different chemicals, such as sugar and common salt. Because of this, chemists can use water to help make many things, from acids to medicines. Water also dissolves gases in the air, and this can cause acid rain. Where rivers pass over limestone rocks the water dissolves chemicals from the rocks. This makes the water 'hard'. It is difficult to make a good lather with soap in hard water.

We use lots of water in our homes – for washing, cleaning, cooking, drinking and flushing the lavatory. Many factories use large amounts of water to make things or to cool machinery. Hydroelectric power stations use the pressure of falling water to generate electricity.

▲ Water is one of the few substances that commonly exists as a gas, a liquid and a solid. Here, snow (ice crystals) surrounds a pool of steaming water (gas and liquid) in Yellowstone National Park, USA.

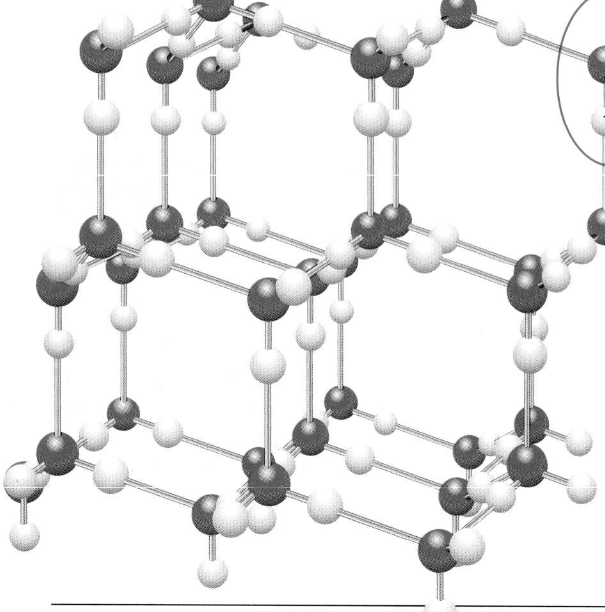

◀ If we look at how water molecules are joined together in ice, we find that there is lots of space in the structure. This is the reason why, unlike most other substances, water actually expands when it freezes.

More than two-thirds of the Earth's surface is covered by water.

Find Out More

- Clouds
- Ice caps and glaciers
- Oceans
- Rain and snow
- Water cycle
- Water power

Water cycle

Every year, about 420 million billion litres of water disappear from the ocean into the atmosphere. If the water never returned, the ocean would dry up in 2500 years. But the water forms clouds, and then rains back into the ocean and on the land.

The rain on land flows down rivers, sinks into the ground, or rises up into the atmosphere again. Eventually all the water makes its way back to the ocean.

The journey of water from the oceans to the atmosphere and back to the sea again is called the water cycle.

Solid, liquid, gas

Water can move around very quickly because it can change easily from a solid or liquid to a gas, and back again.

When water evaporates (changes from a liquid into a gas) into the atmosphere, it can travel in the air all around the world. When the water vapour in the atmosphere condenses (turns from a gas back into a liquid), it forms tiny water droplets, which make clouds. These float over the land and sea, bringing water from warm, wet parts of the world to cooler, drier places.

Water that rises into the atmosphere from the ocean may return in hours, or it may sink into the rocks and take millions of years to return.

▶ On Earth, water exists as a solid (ice), a liquid and a gas (invisible water vapour in the air). In the Ilulissat ice fjord in Greenland, pictured here, water exists in all three states.

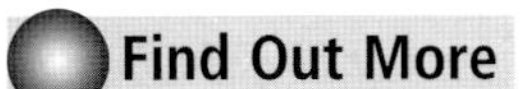

Find Out More

- Atmosphere
- Oceans
- Rain and snow
- Rivers and lakes
- Water

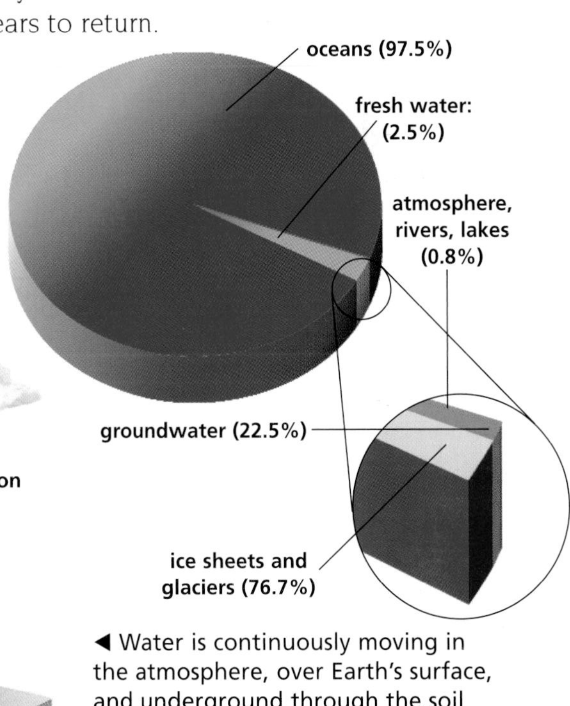

▶ Most of the water on Earth is in the oceans and most of the fresh water on Earth is frozen in glaciers and ice sheets.

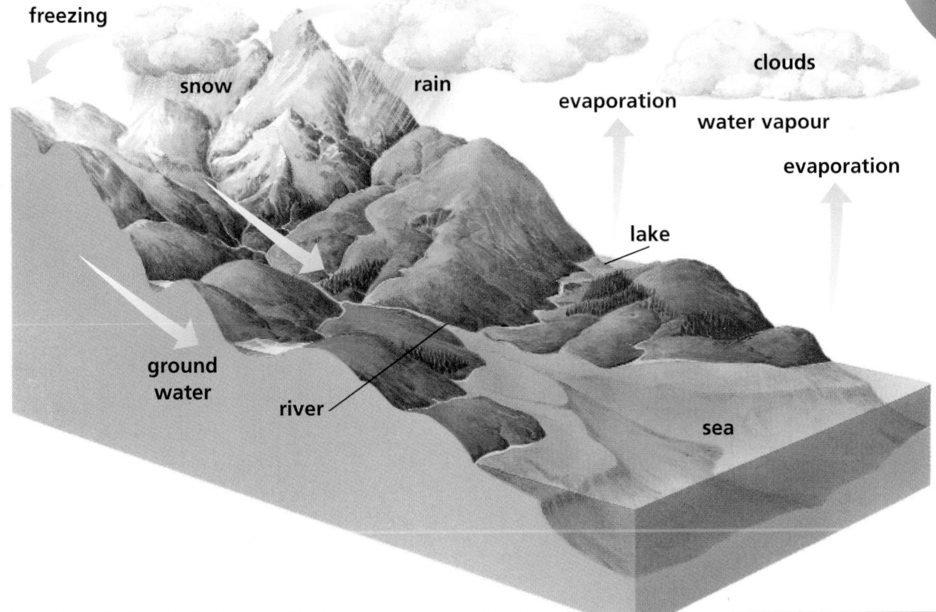

◀ Water is continuously moving in the atmosphere, over Earth's surface, and underground through the soil and rocks. The water cycle is powered by the Sun and by gravity. The heat of the Sun melts ice and evaporates water. Gravity makes rain and snow fall to the ground and it makes rivers flow from the mountains to the sea.

Waterfalls *see* Water

Water power

The sight of a mighty waterfall like Niagara Falls is awesome. The water roars as it strikes the river or rocks far below. Can such enormous power be harnessed? In fact, a fifth of the world's electricity comes from water power.

Not all power stations burn fuel. The most powerful ones are hydroelectric, which means they generate electricity from water. The power station at the Itaipu Dam on the River Paraná, Paraguay, for example, generates over 12,500 megawatts of electricity – twice as much as the biggest coal-powered plants.

Hydroelectric power stations do not use up the water or turn it into something else. Flowing or falling water has energy, and a hydroelectric station changes some of the energy into electricity. When the water comes out of the power station, it moves less fast, because it has given up some of its energy.

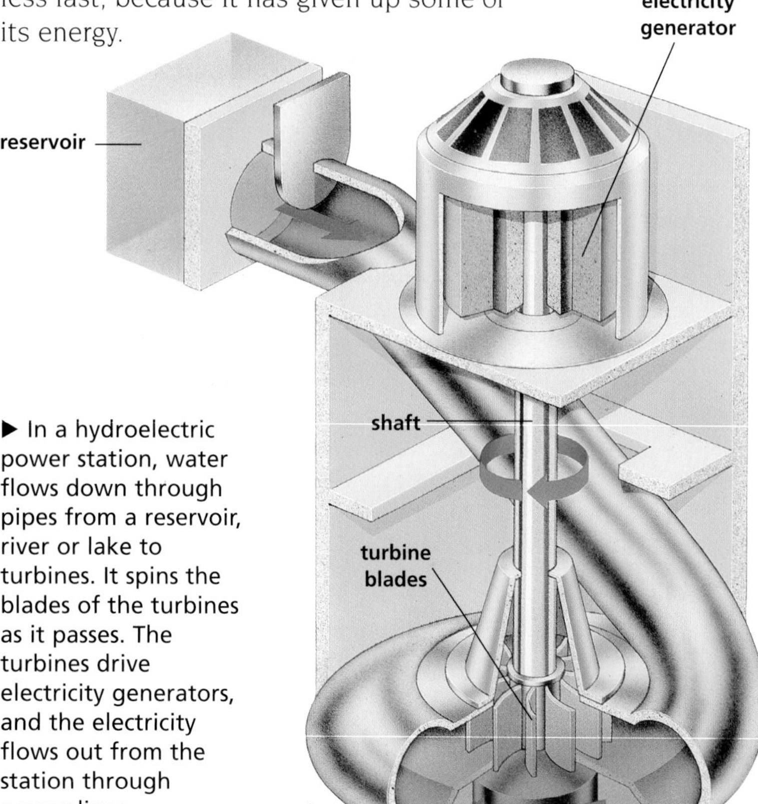

▶ In a hydroelectric power station, water flows down through pipes from a reservoir, river or lake to turbines. It spins the blades of the turbines as it passes. The turbines drive electricity generators, and the electricity flows out from the station through power lines.

Find Out More

- Dams
- Generators
- Pollution
- Power stations
- Water

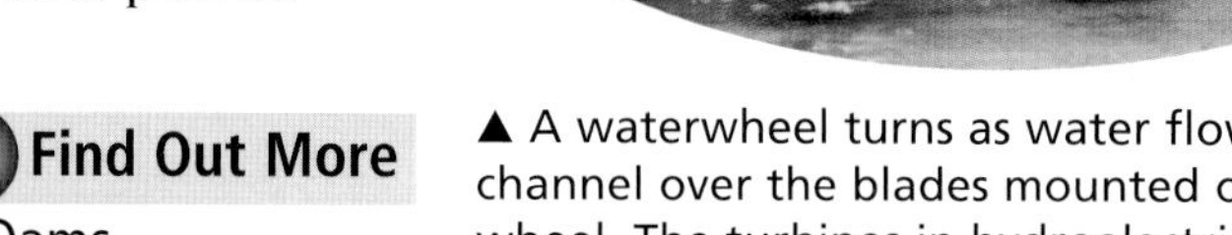

▲ A waterwheel turns as water flows from a channel over the blades mounted on the wheel. The turbines in hydroelectric power stations work in the same basic way, but produce more power.

Electricity from water

High dams are built across river valleys to create large reservoirs or artificial lakes that can supply people with water. A dam may contain a hydroelectric power station. Water from the reservoir flows down through the dam to drive the station's turbines, which in turn drive generators that produce electricity.

Hydroelectric stations are also built without high dams. They take water from fast-flowing rivers or are fed with water piped down from high lakes.

Many rivers flow too slowly to be used for generating electricity, or their valleys are not deep enough to be dammed. Hydroelectric stations are built mainly in mountainous regions with heavy rainfall, such as Switzerland, Norway, Sweden and

THE THREE GORGES DAM

The world's largest hydroelectric project is under construction in the region of the Three Gorges on the Yangtze River, China. Plans call for a dam 185 metres high and 2 kilometres long to create a reservoir extending 600 kilometres along the valley. When completed in 2009, the dam will generate about 18,000 megawatts of electricity – about 10 per cent of China's total electricity needs. But the project will drown 19 cities and displace almost 2 million people.

▶ At the mouth of the River Rance in northern France is a tidal power station. As the tide rises and falls, water flows rapidly into and out of the river. The water passes through turbines in a barrier across the river, and the turbines drive electricity generators. The power station generates 240 megawatts of electricity.

In 1968, the building of the Aswan High Dam in Egypt began to create a large lake that would drown the ancient temple at Abu Simbel. So, before the lake rose, the whole temple and its magnificent statues were cut out of the rock and rebuilt above the final water line.

Canada. Some large rivers have been dammed to provide power and also to prevent the rivers from flooding. These great dams include the Aswan High Dam across the River Nile in Egypt, and the Three Gorges Dam across the River Yangtze in China.

Clean and everlasting

Water power is a clean source of power. Unlike the burning of fuels, tapping the energy in flowing water does not pollute the air and cause global warming.

Furthermore, hydroelectric power stations are not using up a valuable source of energy. The water in rivers and lakes is constantly replaced by fresh rain.

Hydroelectric power stations produce about 20 per cent of the world's electricity. Building more hydroelectric stations would save fuel and reduce pollution and global warming. However, building in mountainous regions is difficult and costly.

Much of electricity generated there would be lost as it would have to travel a long way to cities. Most large rivers are not suitable for damming, and the creation of large reservoirs can cause hardship to the people who have to move away from the land that is to be drowned.

◀ The generator hall of the hydroelectric power station at Hoover Dam, USA. The huge electricity generators are driven by water turbines below the floor of the hall.

Watt, James *see* Steam engines

Waves and vibrations

To a radio wave, your body is like glass! Just as light comes through a window, radio waves and other kinds of wave or ray are streaming through your body right now. You cannot feel them and they cause you no harm, but they bring radio and television programmes to your home.

BRIGHT SPARK

The German scientist Heinrich Hertz (1857–1894) discovered radio waves in 1888. He did this by using a powerful electric current to make a spark, and saw that another spark immediately jumped across a gap in a brass ring nearby. The first spark produced radio waves that travelled through the air to the ring. The waves produced an electric current in the ring, causing the second spark. Radio communications were invented as a result of Hertz's discovery.

Radio and television sets receive radio waves sent out from high masts or satellites. The waves carry sounds and pictures to all sets within range, passing through walls and people on the way.

Radio waves are electromagnetic waves, a group of penetrating waves. Some of these waves are also called rays. Other kinds of penetrating waves and rays include microwaves, which carry mobile telephone calls, heat rays, which bring you warmth, and light rays, which let you see everything around you.

Sound waves are different kinds of waves that can pass through air and solid materials. They let you hear all kinds of sounds and noises, such as people talking or music playing.

Bringing energy to all

All rays and waves transport energy from one place to another. They spread out from their source in all directions, and bring their energy to everything that they meet.

When you speak, your mouth sends out sound waves. These spread out through the air, and perhaps through thin walls, carrying sound energy. When the sound waves enter the ears of other people, they hear you.

In the same way, rays spread out through space from the Sun. They carry heat energy and light energy to the Earth, giving us warmth and daylight.

Making waves

Water waves, from ripples in a pond to giant breakers at the seashore, also transport energy. If you drop a stone into a pond, the water moves up and down as the stone enters the water. This up-and-down movement, or vibration, travels out across the water surface as a wave. When it meets a floating object such as a toy boat, the wave makes it bob up and down. The energy to make the boat bob comes from the falling stone, and is carried out to the boat by the wave.

▲ A good surfer can ride a giant wave for a long way. The surfer is able to stay at the front of the wave and move along with it.

▶ Demonstrate a wave. Tie a rope to a tree or get a friend to hold one end. Hold the other end fairly tightly and move it quickly up and down. A wave travels along the rope. As the wave passes, the rope goes up and down or vibrates at a particular rate. This is called the frequency of the wave.

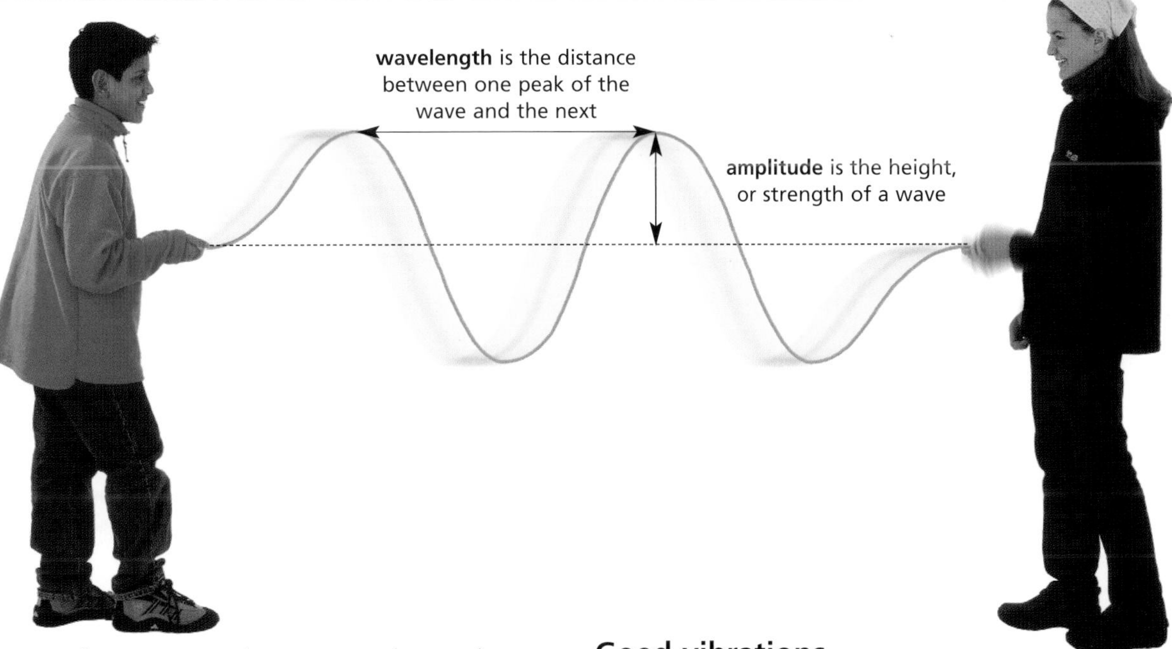

Light rays, like all electromagnetic waves, move at 300,000 kilometres per second. Sound waves travel a million times slower.

Electromagnetic waves and sound waves transport energy as vibrations just as water waves do, which is why they are called 'waves' or 'wave motions'. Heat rays and light rays are wave motions too, and are sometimes called waves instead of rays.

Every kind of wave has a particular frequency, or rate at which it vibrates. A high-frequency wave vibrates quickly, while lower-frequency waves vibrate more slowly.

Good vibrations

Objects can vibrate in a similar way to water waves. When you twang a stretched rubber band, it moves rapidly to and fro. A swing and a pendulum are other examples of vibration. When objects vibrate, they move to and fro at a regular rate. That is why pendulums and vibrating springs and crystals can be used to control clocks and watches and make sure they keep time.

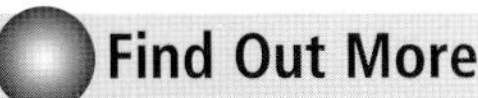

Find Out More
- Earthquakes
- Electromagnetic spectrum
- Energy
- Light
- Sound

▶ Strong winds can cause structures to vibrate slowly. In 1940, the Tacoma Narrows Bridge in the United States collapsed because the wind made it vibrate more and more. Bridges like this are now strengthened so that vibration does not build up.

Weapons

A cruise missile appears from nowhere flying only 20 metres or so above the ground along the city streets. It turns this way and that to miss the tall buildings. Then it homes in on its target, a bridge across the river, and blows it to smithereens.

Cruise missiles are frightening weapons. They can be launched at targets more than 2,000 kilometres away and hit them spot on. They can be launched from the ground, from ships or from aircraft. They fly low and are therefore difficult to detect by radar.

Cruise missiles are one of the many kinds of missile used by armed forces. Most missiles carry a high-explosive charge, which explodes when they hit their target. Some are fitted with nuclear warheads.

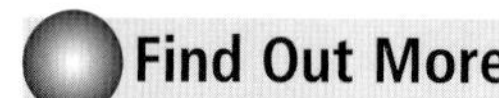

- Explosives
- Jet engines
- Navigation
- Nuclear energy
- Radar and sonar
- Rockets

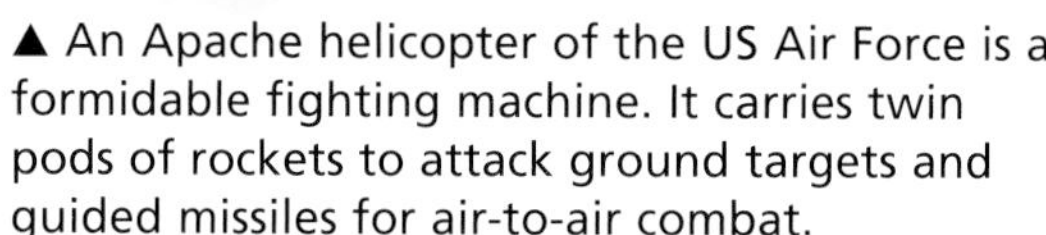

▲ An Apache helicopter of the US Air Force is a formidable fighting machine. It carries twin pods of rockets to attack ground targets and guided missiles for air-to-air combat.

Power and guidance

Missiles are usually powered by rockets. The cruise missile is an exception. It has a jet engine. Most missiles are powered for all their flight. But ballistic missiles are powered only for the first part of their flight. Then the engine cuts out and they fall on to their target. The largest, intercontinental ballistic missiles (ICBMs) have a range of up to 10,000 kilometres.

Most missiles are guided to their target. Some lock on to radar signals from the target, or heat that the target gives out. Others carry TV cameras. Cruise missiles have a very accurate guidance system. It keeps them on a pre-set course following a detailed map of the ground held in an on-board computer.

Guns and artillery

A great many other weapons are used by fighting forces. Many of these are guns. The smaller hand guns are usually known as firearms; the bigger ones are called artillery. Pistols, revolvers, and rifles all fire small metal bullets, which are propelled from the gun barrel by a small explosive charge. Rifles are so called because they have a spiral groove (rifling) in the barrel.

◀ This missile launcher is small enough to be fired by hand. It is firing an anti-tank missile.

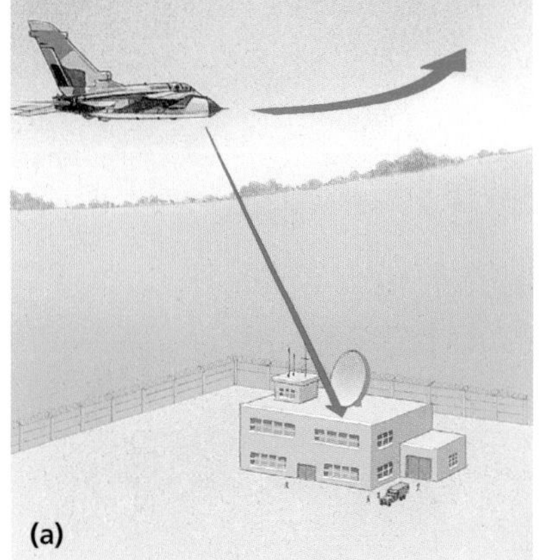

▶ Laser bombing ensures great accuracy. A plane illuminates the target with a laser beam (a). Sensors in the bombs detect the beam and follow it down to the target (b).

This makes the bullet spin round, which helps it to travel straight.

Big guns (artillery) fire shells filled with high explosive, which explode when they land. Artillery can be used to bombard targets many kilometres away.

Bombs

Bombs are explosive weapons dropped from aircraft. They are fitted with fins so that they travel straighter in the air.

There are several types of aircraft bomb. Incendiary bombs are designed to destroy by fire. They are made of materials such as magnesium, which burns brilliantly. Armour-piercing bombs have a thick, hard nose to break through the armour on ships and tanks, for example.

Chemical and germ warfare

Some weapons are specifically designed to kill people rather than destroy buildings and equipment. Chemical weapons include gases like chlorine, mustard gas and nerve gas. Nerve gases are particularly deadly. They are absorbed through the skin, and can kill in minutes. Bacteriological weapons use deadly germs such as anthrax to kill people. Chemical and germ weapons are banned under international agreements, but many countries still have them.

THE ULTIMATE WEAPON

The most deadly weapons of all are nuclear weapons. They can destroy whole cities and their inhabitants in an instant, and the radiation from a weapon can cause death and sickness in an area for many years. The biggest have the destructive power of millions of tonnes of ordinary high explosive. There are two kinds of nuclear weapon. In atomic bombs, huge amounts of energy are released when atoms split – this process is called fission. In hydrogen bombs, another process called nuclear fusion is used which releases even greater destructive power.

▼ Modern automatic assault rifles like this Kalashnikov AK47 are capable of firing at a rate of up to 800 rounds a minute. Some of the gas released when a round is fired drives back the bolt ready to fire another round.

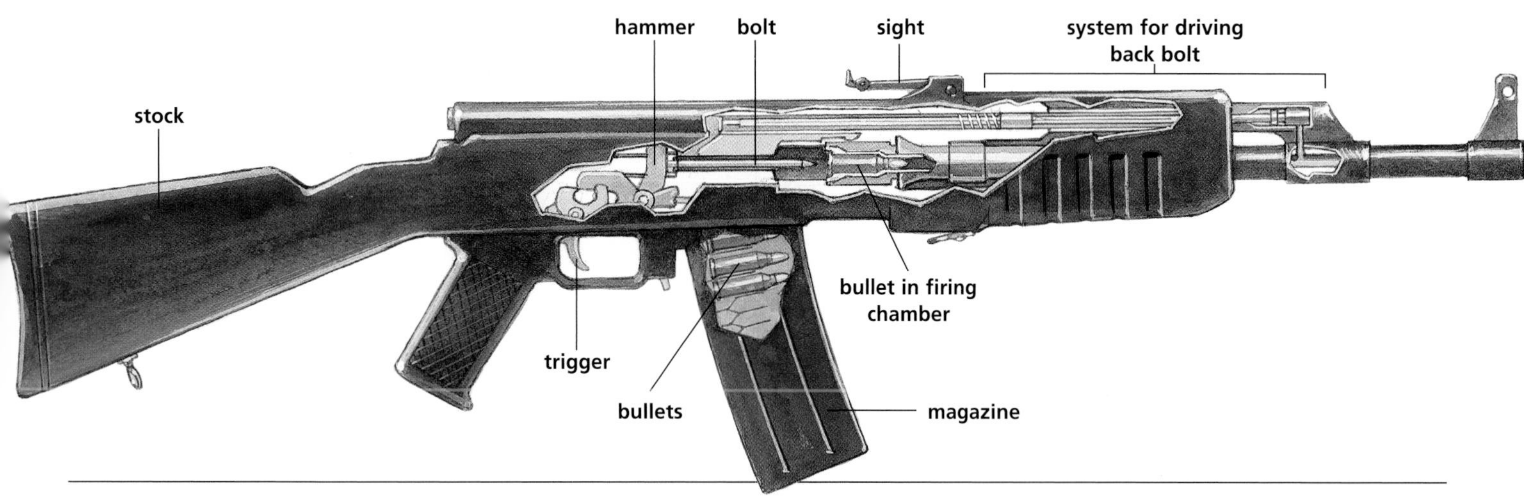

Weather

Every summer, fierce cyclones rage across tropical seas, bringing torrential rains, hurricane winds and huge waves to coastal areas. A fully-formed cyclone can be 500 kilometres across, with winds of more than 120 kilometres per hour.

Tropical cyclones are one example of the Earth's weather. Weather is the sum total of what the atmosphere is doing at a given time and place.

Weather happens in the lower 12–15 kilometres of the atmosphere, a layer called the *troposphere*. The troposphere gets its name from the Greek word 'tropo', which means swirling. Different regions of air in the troposphere are at different temperatures and carry different amounts of water. These air masses are moved around by winds and interact with each other to make the weather.

Air masses and fronts

An air mass is a large region of air that has roughly the same temperature and moisture content throughout. Air masses can be 10 kilometres high and cover millions of square kilometres. A large air mass can bring several days of dry, sunny, breezy weather, or a few days of cloudy, rainy weather to an area.

Weather can be slightly different from place to place within an air mass. It is usually warmer in the cities than in the countryside, and cooler on top of a mountain than in a valley. The coast is usually cooler in the summer and warmer in the winter than places inland.

Most storms develop at *fronts*, where two different air masses meet. However, hurricanes, typhoons and cyclones develop within a single air mass, not along a front.

▶ Weather balloons are sent up into the atmosphere to make measurements at high altitudes. They carry a number of instruments, including radar to detect rainstorms and tornadoes.

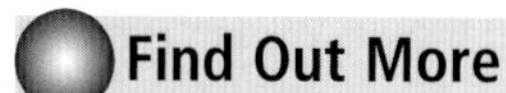
Find Out More

- Atmosphere
- Climate
- Rain and snow
- Satellites
- Thunder and lightning
- Winds

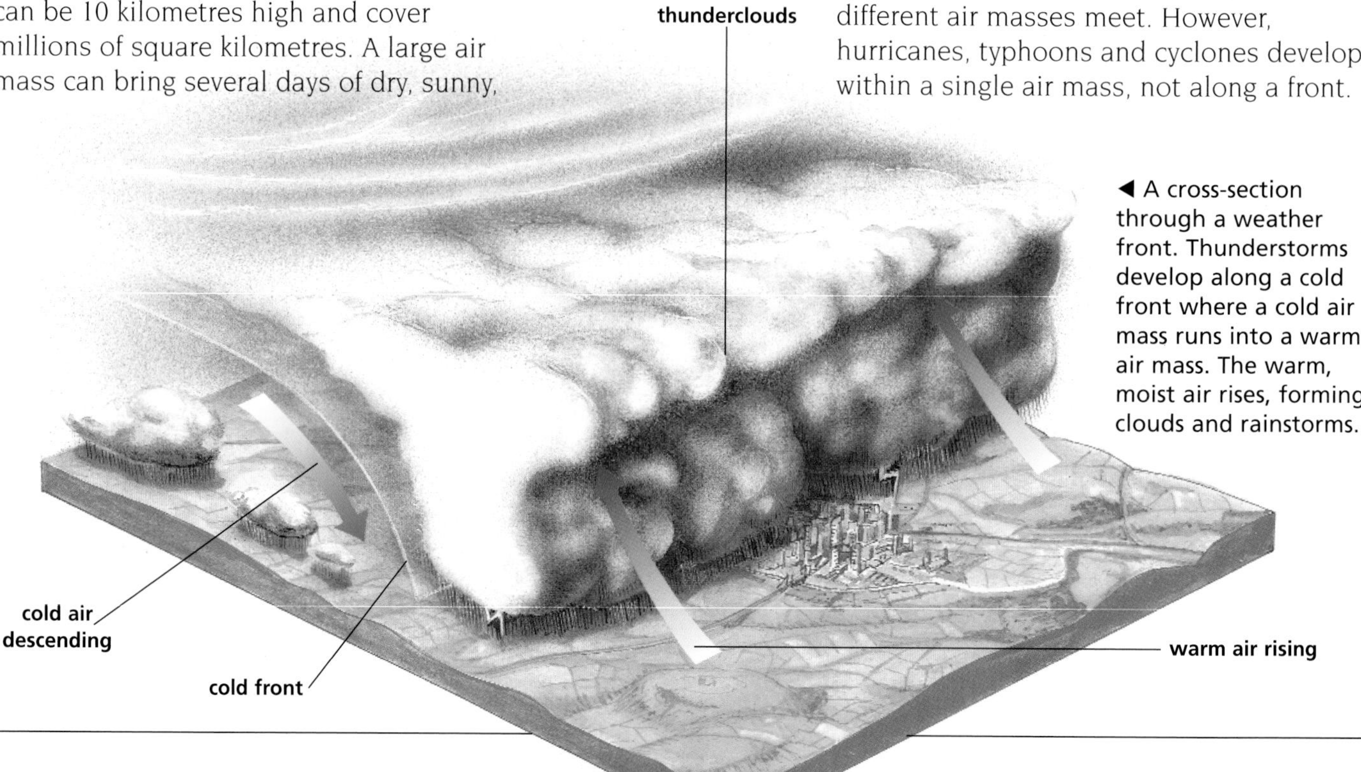

◀ A cross-section through a weather front. Thunderstorms develop along a cold front where a cold air mass runs into a warm air mass. The warm, moist air rises, forming clouds and rainstorms.

Watching the weather

Meteorologists make measurements of the atmosphere all over Earth, from weather stations on land, ships at sea, jets and balloons high in the atmosphere, and from satellites thousands of kilometres above the atmosphere.

Many different instruments are used to measure the weather. Satellites are especially important because they can 'see' weather systems develop from above in places where there are no weather stations on the ground.

Predicting the weather

In order to make an accurate weather forecast, meteorologists need to have as much information about the atmosphere as possible. Once they have worked out where certain air masses are moving, they can try to predict where they will be in a few days time and how they will interact with each other.

Most weather predictions are made with computers that use mathematics and physics to imitate how the atmosphere will change in the next few days. Meteorologists also make predictions based on what has happened in the past. For instance, 'a 70 per cent chance of rain' means that seven out of ten times when the weather was like this in the past, it has turned rainy.

Predicting the weather can be extremely difficult because it is impossible to know what every particle of air is doing. Weather forecasts for the following day or two are usually quite accurate, but it is nearly impossible to predict what the weather will be like more than five days in advance.

▲ This satellite image is a combination of three images of Hurricane Andrew as it moved west over Florida, USA, in 1992. Hurricanes develop near the Equator where the ocean water is warm. As they evaporate water, the winds grow stronger.

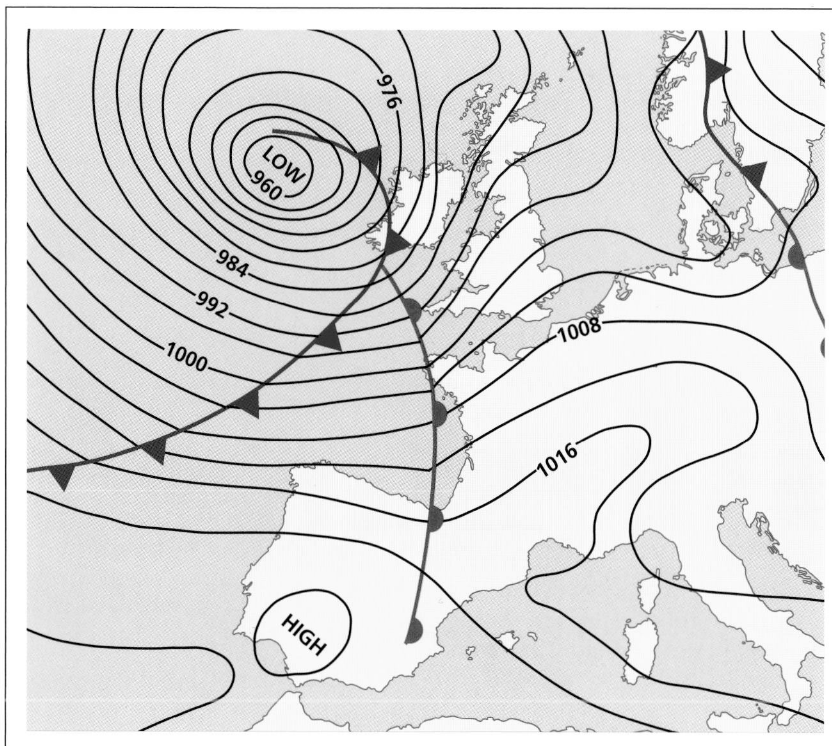

UNDERSTANDING THE WEATHER FORECAST

Weather maps like these are shown in weather forecasts every day. Some of the maps are difficult to understand, but you can get a lot of information from them, once you know what all the symbols mean.

Key

HIGH — centre of a high-pressure zone (usually dry, sunny weather)

LOW — centre of a low-pressure zone (usually cloudy and rainy weather)

1016 — **isobar:** a line of equal air pressure in millibars

front: where two air masses meet. The notches point in the direction that the front is moving

a warm front: a warm air mass is overtaking a colder air mass

a cold front: a cold air mass is moving in to replace a warm air mass

Weathering *see* Erosion • **Weaving** *see* Textiles • **Weights and measures** *see* Measurement

Wetlands

◀ A kingfisher flies out of the water after diving to catch a fish in its dagger-like beak. It can make up to 100 dives in one day.

The water spider lives underwater, but it needs to breathe air. So it spins a dome of silk, fixes it to an underwater plant and fills the dome with bubbles of air. The spider leaves its silk bubble when it needs to collect air or catch food, but it always eats its meals at home.

Mosquito larvae also breathe oxygen from the air, using 'snorkels' on the tip of their abdomens. In mangrove swamps, some of the tree roots stick up into the air to take in oxygen. Fishes and tadpoles, however, have gills to take in oxygen from the water, and water plants absorb oxygen from the water over their whole surface. The moving waters of rivers hold more oxygen than the still waters of lakes, marshes and swamps.

Wetland plants

Water is a stronger support for a plant than air, so water plants do not need strong stems or roots. A lot of water plants float near the surface to be near the light they need to make food. Some also use the water to spread their pollen and seeds.

Bogs and marshes often have soils that are poor in some plant nutrients. Unusual meat-eating plants, such as the Venus fly trap, trap insects and other small animals, then digest them to get extra nutrients that are missing from the boggy soil.

Important wetlands

Many animals and birds breed in wetlands because there is plenty of food and shelter. Birds also stop to feed and rest on wetlands during their migration journeys.

Wetlands can help to protect the drier lands around them from storms and floods by soaking up excess water.

Peatlands are wetlands that store tonnes of carbon because they are made of layers of dead plants that do not rot away. If peat bogs are dug up and the carbon dioxide is released, this adds to global warming.

▲ The long, narrow hooves of these lechwe help them to run and leap through swampy ground at great speed. They are also good swimmers

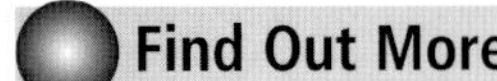

Find Out More

- Fishes
- Global warming
- Water

Whales *see* Ocean life, Mammals • **Wheels** *see* Machines • **Wildlife** *see* Conservation

Winds

In 1492, Christopher Columbus set sail from Portugal to find a western route to India. He could not sail directly west because the winds near Portugal blow east. So he sailed south to the Canary Islands where the winds turn westward. He then sailed across the Atlantic to the Caribbean (which he thought was part of India) on the trade winds blowing west. On his return to Portugal, he sailed north until the winds turned eastward again, taking him home.

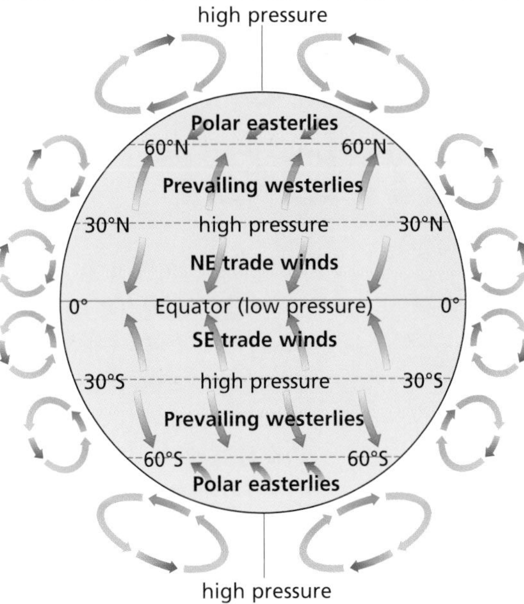

▲ This map shows the major wind belts on Earth's surface. The wind direction can change from day to day, but overall it tends to blow in one direction.

The winds that carried Columbus across the Atlantic are part of a worldwide system of winds. Wind is moving air.

Why air moves

When you pump up a tyre, you force a lot more air into the tyre than there is in the same amount of space outside the tyre. The air pressure is higher inside the tyre than outside it. If you puncture the tyre, the air will pour out until the pressure inside is the same as on the outside.

The same thing happens in the atmosphere. There are zones of high pressure and zones of low pressure in the atmosphere (these are the 'highs' and 'lows' you see on weather maps). Just as water flows from high ground to low ground, air flows from areas of high pressure to areas of low pressure, and causes winds. The greater the difference in air pressure, the stronger the winds that are produced.

▲ The winds in a tornado are the fastest in the world. They can reach up to 500 km/h.

▼ On the coast there is a daily pattern to the wind. A cool sea breeze blows in from the ocean during the day, while at night the winds blow from the land to the sea. This happens because the land heats up and cools down more quickly than the sea.

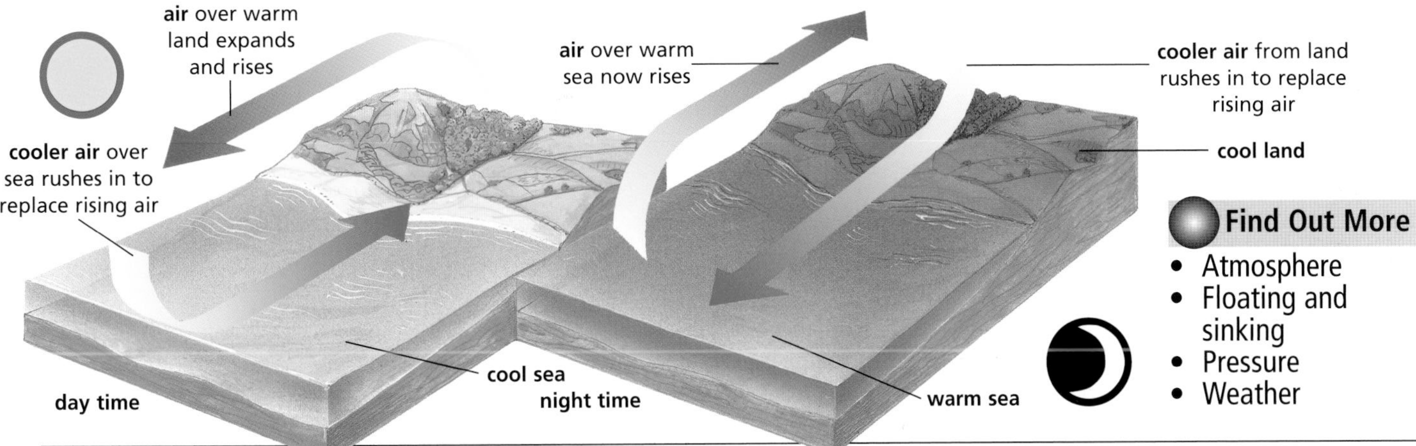

Find Out More

- Atmosphere
- Floating and sinking
- Pressure
- Weather

Wind instruments *see* Music • **Windmills** *see* Renewable resources • **Wind tunnels** *see* Flight and flow, Bridges

Wood and timber

In a forest in North America, the trees have been growing for more than a century – many are over 60 metres tall. Now the buzzing of chainsaws signals that the lumberjacks have moved in. The chainsaws cut through thick trunks in minutes, and the mighty trees start crashing down.

Timber – the wood from cut-down, or felled trees – has always been one of the most useful materials to people. It is used in house-building, for making furniture, building boats, and much more besides.

Timber is also used to make such products as plywood (thin layers of wood glued together to make boards) and chipboard (a material made from wood chippings pressed and glued together). Wood is also a useful raw material for making such products as paper, textile fibres and even explosives. However, the biggest use of wood by far throughout the world is for burning on fires.

▼ Violins and many other musical instruments are usually crafted from the finest-quality hardwood.

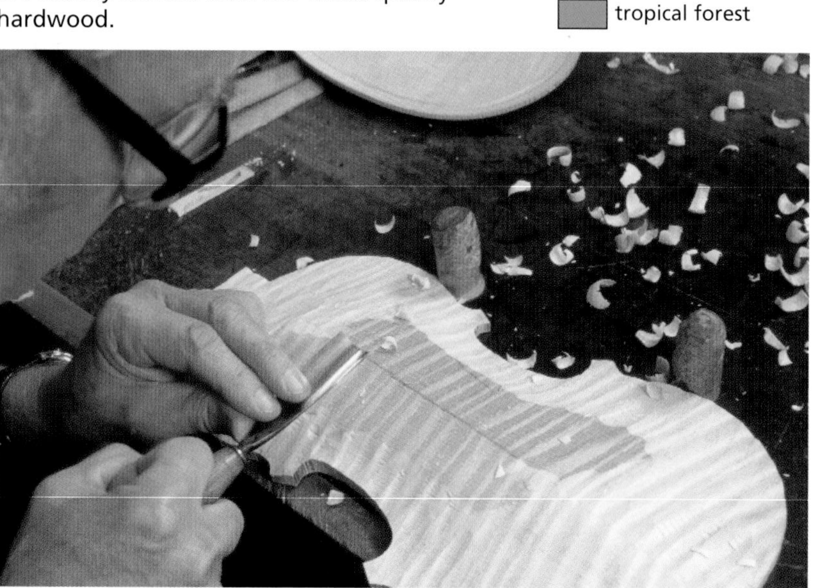

Softwoods and hardwoods

The common timber used in building is called softwood, because it is relatively soft and easy to cut and work with. Most softwood trees have narrow, needle-like leaves and bear their seeds in cones. They keep their leaves all year round. Known as evergreen conifers, they include firs, pines, cedars and spruces. Large areas of natural conifer forests are found in the cool, northern regions of the world, and they are planted in warmer climates too.

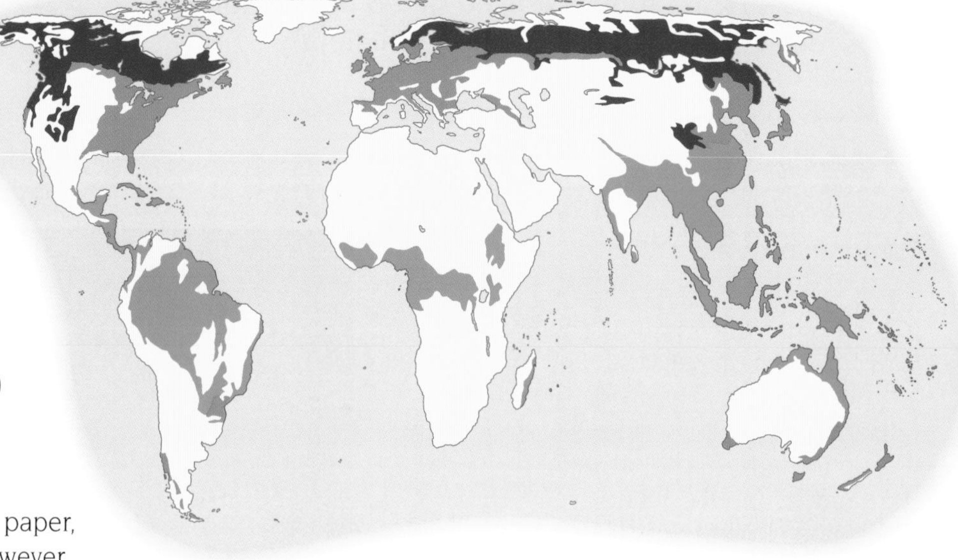

Key

- coniferous forest
- deciduous forest
- tropical forest

▲ The forest regions of the world. The largest region of natural forest is in the north of North America, Europe and Asia. Evergreen conifers grow there. The other main area is around the Equator. In these tropical forests, broad-leaved evergreens grow. In the temperate climates between these main forest regions, the native trees are broad-leaved and deciduous.

However, in warmer regions the natural forest trees yield a harder wood, so they are called hardwoods. They include oak, beech, chestnut and maple. These trees are deciduous, which means that they shed their broad leaves every autumn. Hardwood trees grow in the natural forests around the Equator. These broad-leaved trees are evergreen. The most valuable hardwoods include mahogany, ebony and teak.

Managing the forests

At one time about two-thirds of the Earth's surface was covered by forests. But for

▲ In a tropical forest in Cameroon in central Africa, two men saw a massive tree trunk into logs.

thousands of years people have been felling trees for timber, for firewood, and to clear land for agriculture. Only a fraction of the original forest land remains. And destruction of the natural forest continues, especially the tropical rainforests of South-east Asia.

Elsewhere, more and more timber is coming from managed forests. In these forests, the trees are cultivated as a crop, with new trees being planted as mature ones are cut down. Forestry workers raise tree seedlings, plant them out, and look after them while they grow, protecting them from pests and diseases.

From forest to sawmill

To fell a tree, a lumberjack first cuts a wedge out of the trunk low down. Then he makes a slice above it. Because of the undercut, the tree loses balance and topples over. After trees are felled, they are cut into logs.

Find Out More
- Forests
- Paper
- Plastics
- Rubber

The logs may be taken out of the forest by tractors, animals (such as elephants), cables, or water slides. They travel to sawmills on trucks or railway wagons, or are towed on huge rafts across lakes.

At the sawmill, the logs are de-barked and then sawn into pieces of standard sizes. Afterwards, the cut timber has to be stacked so that the air can dry it out. This is called seasoning. Sometimes the wood is seasoned artificially in heated kilns.

Chemical products

Wood is made up mainly of fibres of cellulose, which are held together by a substance called lignin. Cellulose is the starting-point for making rayon fibres, cellulose plastics and explosives.

Useful oils and solvents can be obtained by distilling wood, which involves heating it in enclosed vessels. These products include creosote, used to preserve timber, and turpentine, used in paints. Partly burning wood produces charcoal, a valuable fuel.

▼ Many things that we use every day are made from wood or wood products.

furniture

cellulose explosives (used in dynamite)

ping-pong balls (made of celluloid, a cellulose plastic)

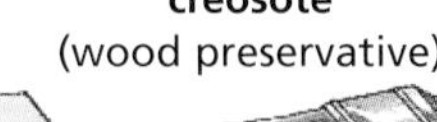

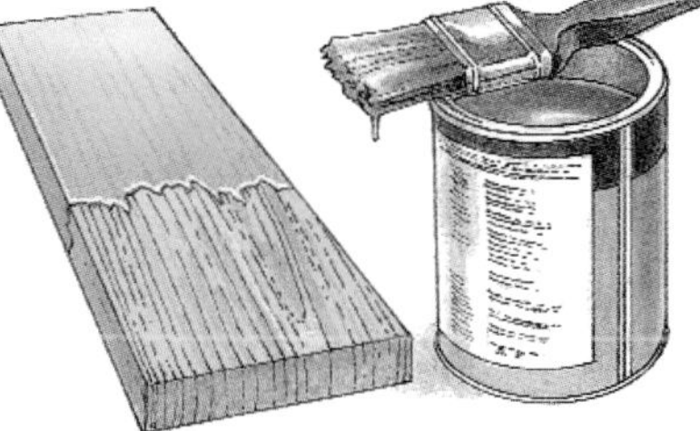

creosote (wood preservative)

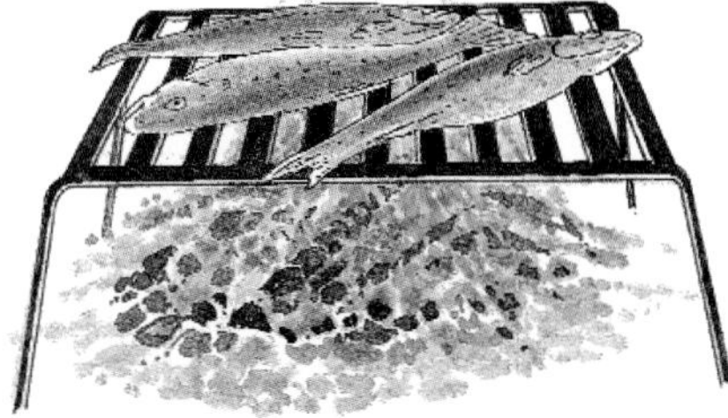

charcoal

X-rays

A priceless work of art is placed in an X-ray machine, while anxious dealers look on. Without damaging the precious surface paint at all, the machine might reveal previous sketches by the artist – or even a forgery!

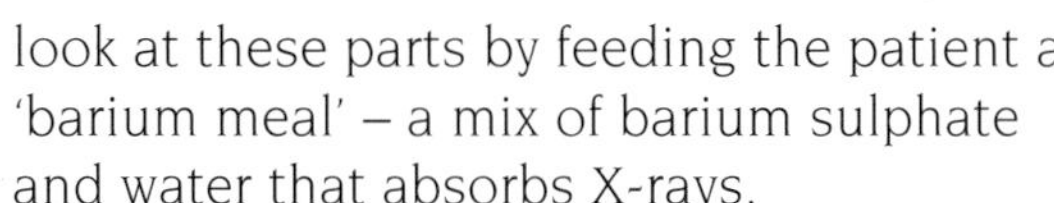

▲ An X-ray machine fires a beam of tiny particles called electrons at a piece of metal. When the electrons crash into the metal, X-rays are given off.

X-rays are similar to light waves, but have a much shorter wavelength and a lot more energy. This makes them useful, as they can pass through most materials. It also makes them dangerous, as they can damage living tissues.

X-rays in medicine

X-rays will pass through most materials, but some X-rays are stopped by bones, which is why they are useful in medicine. Bones cast shadows when X-rays are shone on them. A photographic film can be exposed by X-rays that pass straight through the body. However, it will not be exposed in the bone's shadow. The developed picture clearly shows where the bones are. This is very helpful for doctors, especially if they want to see if a patient has broken any bones.

X-rays pass through soft body parts such as the stomach and intestines. Doctors can look at these parts by feeding the patient a 'barium meal' – a mix of barium sulphate and water that absorbs X-rays.

A modern type of X-ray machine is the CAT scanner. This uses a computer to build a detailed picture of the patient's body by passing weak X-ray beams through it from lots of different directions.

The problem with using X-rays is that they can damage the body. There are strict rules about how many shadow pictures can be taken of a patient each year and the people who operate X-ray machines every day stand behind lead screens for protection while the picture is being made.

X-rays of high enough energy can also be used to kill cancers. This must be done carefully so no other parts of the body are damaged. One way is to use three weak beams that meet at the cancer to deliver enough energy.

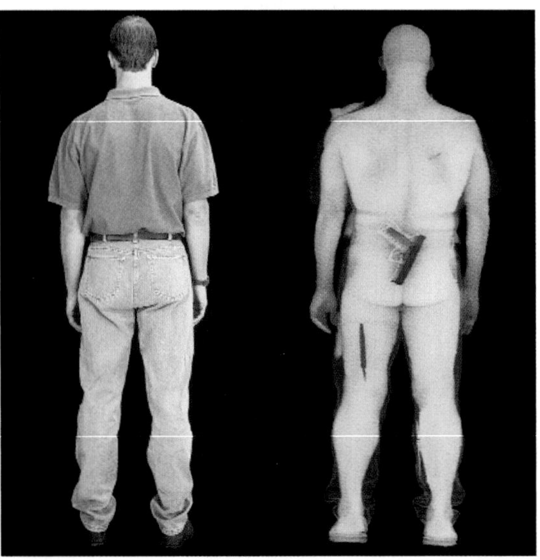

◀ An X-ray detector can discover hidden weapons. The X-rays pass through clothes and the body but are stopped by dense materials like metals.

Find Out More

- Electromagnetic spectrum
- Medicine
- Space astronomy

WOLVERHAMPTON LIBRARIES

Space rays

The ability to see through things has all sorts of uses. In astronomy, for example, satellites carrying X-ray telescopes are mapping the Milky Way and looking for the strong X-ray sources that may be caused by black holes.

ACCIDENTAL DISCOVERY
Wilhelm Röntgen (1845–1923) discovered X-rays while experimenting with electron beams. He noticed that material on the bench glowed while the beam was on. X-rays produced by the electrons were making the material fluoresce.

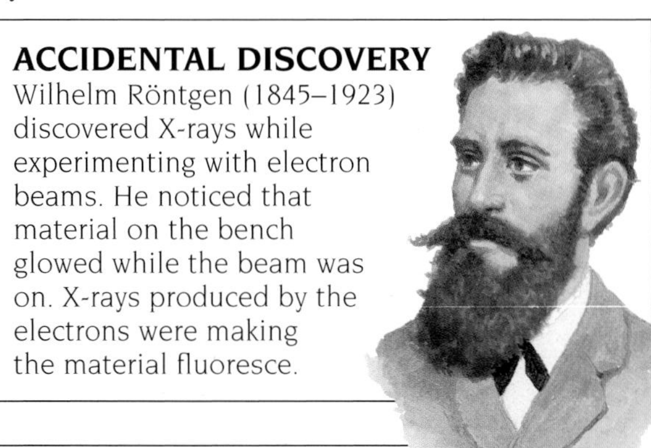

Glossary

This glossary gives simple explanations of difficult or specialist words that readers might be unfamiliar with. Words in *italic* have their own glossary entry.

AC Alternating Current. Electric *current* that flows first one way around a *circuit*, and then the other way. The mains *electricity* in homes is AC.

alloy A mixture of *metals* or of a metal and another substance.

alternative energy Energy produced from renewable natural sources, such as the Sun, wind, flowing water and waves.

antibiotic A drug, for example penicillin, that destroys *bacteria* or prevents them from growing.

antibody A protein produced by the blood as a defence against harmful *germs*.

artery A blood vessel that carries blood from the heart to other parts of the body.

atmosphere The layer of gases around a *planet*.

atom The smallest particle of an *element*, made up of a tiny central *nucleus* surrounded by a cloud of fast-moving *electrons*.

bacteria Microscopic one-celled organisms. Many are useful, but some cause diseases such as meningitis, tetanus and pneumonia.

battery A device for storing *electricity* as chemical energy.

Big Bang A theory about the beginning of the *Universe* that says that it exploded from something very tiny and hot and has been expanding ever since.

black hole A region in space that has such a strong gravitational pull that no light or matter can escape from it.

catalyst A chemical used to help bring about or speed up a chemical *reaction*.

cell (1) The basic unit of living things. (2) Another name for a *battery* (or a single part of a battery).

chromosome A structure made up of *genes*, which carries genetic information.

circuit A conducting wire loop that allows *electrons* to travel around it. On the way, the electrons do useful jobs, such as making a light bulb glow.

cold-blooded Describing an animal such as a fish or an insect whose body temperature changes with that of its surroundings.

compound A substance made of two or more different *elements*.

condensation The process by which a gas turns into a liquid.

conductor A substance, such as a *metal*, that allows an electric *current* to flow through it.

constellation A named area of the night sky, usually centred around a familiar pattern of *stars*.

crystal A solid material with *atoms* arranged in a geometric pattern. All *minerals* form crystals.

current (1) A mass of moving water within the ocean. (2) A measure of the rate at which electric charge (*electrons*) flows around a *circuit*.

DC Direct Current. Electric current that flows in only one direction around a *circuit*.

density A measure of the amount (*mass*) of a material in a particular volume. The metal lead, for instance, has a high density, because its mass is packed into a small volume.

digestion The process by which food is broken down into tiny parts that can be absorbed into the blood.

digital Representing quantities or signals by means of precise numbers. A digital watch, for example, measures time as a series of numbers of hours, minutes and seconds.

DNA Deoxyribonucleic acid. The chemical that makes up *genes*.

eclipse The blocking of the Sun's or Moon's light when the Moon or Earth is in the way.

ecosystem A distinct area, such as a forest or a lake, containing a variety of living things.

electricity A form of energy carried by certain particles of matter (*electrons* and *protons*), used for lighting and heating and for making machines work.

electron A tiny negatively charged particle that orbits the *nucleus* of an *atom*.

element A substance that is made of only one kind of *atom*. Elements cannot be broken down into other substances.

enzymes Chemicals that speed up processes such as *digestion*.

erosion The process by which rocks are slowly broken down and moved from one place to another by ice, rivers, rain or wind.

evaporation The process by which a liquid turns into a gas.

evolution The gradual change, over many generations, of animals and plants into new forms of life.

fertilization The fusion (joining) of an egg and a *sperm* to make a new living thing.

fission The splitting of an *atom* to release *nuclear energy*.

force A push or pull that one object exerts on another.

fossil The remains of a living thing preserved in rock.

frequency The number of *vibrations* made each second by a *wave* of sound, *light*, etc.

friction A *force* that slows a moving object or prevents it from moving.

fusion The combining of atomic *nuclei* to release *nuclear energy*.

galaxy A family of millions or billions of *stars*.

genes The parts of a *chromosome* that contain the code for characteristics passed on from parent to young.

germs Tiny organisms, such as *viruses* and *bacteria*, that cause diseases.

global warming The warming-up of the Earth's surface as a result of the *greenhouse effect*.

gravity The *force* that attracts two objects. Earth's gravity keeps everything on Earth from floating out into space.

greenhouse effect The way in which gases in a planet's *atmosphere* act like glass in a greenhouse, letting sunlight in, but not letting heat out. Pollution adds to the gases, trapping too much heat and causing *global warming*.

hibernation A way in which some animals survive the winter by going into a deep sleep.

hormones The body's chemical messengers, which control processes such as *reproduction*.

hydroelectric power *Electricity* that is made using the energy of running water.

immunization Giving a person protection against a disease, usually by *vaccination*.

insulator A substance, like rubber, that blocks the flow of electric *current*.

internet A global computer network connected via satellites, optical fibres and telephone wires.

invertebrate An animal without a backbone, such as an insect.

laser A device that produces a thin, bright beam of *light* of a single *frequency*.

lens A curved piece of plastic or glass used to bend *light* rays.

lever A rigid bar resting on a fixed point that can be turned in order to lift an object or force an object open.

light *Radiation* that stimulates the sense of sight and makes things visible.

light year The distance that *light* travels in one year (about 9.5 million million kilometres).

magnet A material in which *electrons* spin in one direction, creating a *magnetic field*. Similar ends of magnets will push away (repel) each other; different ends will attract each other.

magnetic field A region around a magnetic material where a magnetic force is present.

mammal A *warm-blooded vertebrate* with fur or hair that feeds its young on mother's milk.

mass The amount of material (solid, liquid or gas) that something contains.

metal An *element* that is usually shiny and solid at room temperature.

metamorphosis A major change in an animal's body shape as it grows up.

meteor A bright trail in the night sky created when a grain of dust or a rock fragment from space burns up in the *atmosphere*.

microchip A wafer-thin sliver of crystal (usually silicon) containing a complex *circuit* made of thousands of microscopic parts.

microprocessor A *microchip* that performs simple calculations on computer data, at lightning-fast speeds.

migration A regular journey made by some animals to reach breeding or feeding areas.

Milky Way The *galaxy* to which our *Solar System* belongs.

mineral A natural solid material, such as salt or quartz, that has a specific chemical composition and a definite *crystal* structure.

molecule A group of two or more *atoms* bonded to each other.

nerve A bundle of *cells* that carries electrical messages between the brain or spinal cord and other parts of the body.

neutron A basic particle found in the *nucleus* of an *atom*, which has no electrical charge.

nuclear energy Energy released when the nuclei of *atoms* collide.

nucleus (1) The central part of an *atom*. (2) The control centre of a *cell*, which contains the *DNA*.

orbit The path one body takes around another.

photosynthesis The process by which plants use energy from sunlight to make their own food.

planet A body in space that is not massive enough to generate *nuclear energy* and become a *star*.

plate tectonics The theory that the Earth's surface is made of about a dozen moving pieces called plates.

pollination The transfer of pollen from the male part of a flower or cone to the female part.

power The rate at which energy is turned from one form into another. For example, the power of an engine is the rate at which it can drive a machine.

pressure The amount of *force* with which a liquid or gas pushes on a surface.

proton One of the basic particles found in the *nucleus* of an *atom*. Protons have a positive electric charge.

radar A navigation aid that detects the presence of objects at a distance by bouncing radio *waves* off them.

radiation Energy given off as *waves* or tiny particles. Heat, *light* and sound are different types of radiation.

radioactive Having *atoms* that break up and send out rays of energy or particles (*radiation*), which produce electrical and chemical effects and penetrate things. Uranium is a highly radioactive material.

reaction A chemical change in which one or more *elements* form new *compounds*.

reflection *Light* or sound bouncing back off an object.

refraction *Light* or sound *waves* changing direction as they pass from one material into another.

relativity Theories developed by the physicist Albert Einstein. The first shows that time does not pass at the same speed for someone moving very fast and someone who is still. The second theory, general relativity, says that matter, such as *stars*, makes space curve, causing light rays to bend.

renewable resources Materials that, once used, can be replaced naturally, or by careful management. Wood is a renewable resource.

reproduction The production of offspring. In sexual reproduction a male and a female sex *cell*, each from a different parent, join together.

resistance A measure of how hard it is to push an electric *current* through a substance.

respiration The process in which living things release energy from their food using oxygen.

satellite A small object in orbit around a larger one; moons are natural satellites.

solar power Energy obtained from the Sun, either by storing its heat or by turning its rays into *electricity*.

Solar System The Sun and the family of *planets* and other objects that *orbit* around it.

sonar A method of navigation that works by bouncing sound *waves* off objects.

species A group of the same kind of living things, such as humans or oak trees.

spectrum Bands of colours of differing *wavelengths*, like those seen in a rainbow.

sperm The male sex *cell* in animals, which joins with the female sex cell to produce offspring.

star A large ball of hot, glowing gas that shines because it is generating *nuclear energy* inside. The Sun is the nearest star to Earth.

supersonic Travelling at speeds greater than the speed of sound.

technology The use of science in everyday life and in industry.

transistor Part of a *circuit* that either boosts (amplifies) a signal or turns it on and off, to represent *digital* data in a computer.

Universe Everything that exists, including the Earth, its creatures and the heavenly bodies.

vaccination Injecting a substance into the blood so that it produces *antibodies*, which provide protection against a particular disease.

vacuum Complete emptiness; the total absence of air or any other material.

vein A blood vessel that carries blood from the body back to the heart.

vertebrate An animal with a backbone. Birds and *mammals* are vertebrates.

vibration The shaking movement of an object.

virus A microscopic organism that reproduces by infecting a living *cell*. Chickenpox, colds and influenza are caused by viruses.

warm-blooded Describing an animal, such as a bird or a *mammal*, that can keep its body at the same warm temperature all the time.

wave The way in which sound, *light*, heat and *electricity* travel.

wavelength The distance between two peaks on a *wave*.

weight The *force* with which everything presses down on the ground, water or air beneath it, as a result of *gravity*.

world wide web A part of the *internet* that helps users to find information by providing links between documents.

X-ray A type of *wave* that can pass easily through materials that are not very dense. X-rays are often used to inspect the insides of the human body.

Index

Page numbers in **bold** mean that this is where you will find the most information on that subject. If both a heading and a page number are in bold, there is an article with that title. A page number in *italic* means that there is a picture of that subject. There may also be other information about the subject on the same page.

A

B

C

F

G

J

K

L

M

Q

R

S

Acknowledgements

KEY
t = top; c = centre; b = bottom; r = right; l = left; back = background; fore = foreground

ARTWORK

Allington, Sophie: 21 t fore; 37 cl. **Arlott, Norman:** 37 t. **Baker, Julian:** 72 c; 98 tr; 125 tr; 150 b; 171 b; 218 tr; 260 b; 286 tl; 347 cl; 365 t. **Baum, Julian:** 22 b; 24 tr; 209 tl; 232 tl; 244 tl; 265 t; 276 tl; 300 b; 340 tl; 342 tl; 366 tl; 368 tl; 370 c; 408 tl; 409 tl. **Birkett, Georgie:** 402 tl; 427 tl. **Black, Brad:** 242 c. **Bull, Peter:** 422 tr. **Butler, John:** 96 tl. **Cottam, Martin:** 393 tl. **Courtney, Michael:** 183 tr. **D'Achille, Gino:** 19 cr; 26 br; 34 bl; 64 tr; 74 br; 76 bl; 90 cr; 103 c; 104 cr; 106 br; 116 tr; 124 bc; 129 tr; 136 tl; 137 tr; 150 cl; 165 tl; 176 tr; 203 br; 207 bl; 217 tl; 227 tr; 251 br; 253 tr; 289 bl; 292 tr; 304 tr; 356 bl; 358 bl; 378 tr; 383 bl; 386 br; 407 c; 408 cr; 420 tr. **Farmer, Andrew:** 10 bl; 90 tr; 167 b; 268 b; 337 t; 412–413 t; 424 b; 427 b. **Franklin, Mark:** 16 b; 47 br; 93 tr; 104 b; 119 cr; 120 tr; 122–123 b; 132 cr; 148 b; 152 t; 161 cr; 177 br; 186 cr; 206 br; 220 tr; 225 tl; 238 tl; 247 b; 253 bl; 283 tr; 296 t; 299 bl; 305 b; 318 b; 324 tr; 327 b; 335 c; 362 bl; 378 bl; 388–389 tc; 395 b; 396 b; 418 bl; 424 tr. **Full Steam Ahead:** 28 br; 59 b; 60 tr; 65 b back; 76 bc; 81 tr; 83 c; 112 cr; 139 br; 166–167 t; 193 b; 214–215 back; 217 tr; 234; 235; 236; 292–293 main; 293 tr; 356 br; 360 tr; 417 cr. **Gaffney, Michael:** 21 t fore; 307 tl. **Gecko Ltd.:** 54 r; 121 bl; 279 tr. **Hadler, Terry:** 151 tl. **Hardy, David:** 74 b; 87 b; 273 tr; 376 b. **Hawken, Nick:** 72 tl; 73 bl; 239 tr; 269 br; 368 b; 370 tr; 372 cr. **Hawtin, Nigel:** 243 b. **Hincks, Gary:** 50 bl; 68 bl; 71 br; 97 b; 134 t; 277 bl; 308–309 bc; 331 b; 332 t; 336 t; 412 bl; 417 bl. **Hiscock, Karen:** 241 tl. **Hook, Richard:** 146 tl; 190–191 b. **Howatson, Ian:** 16 tl. **Jakeway, Rob:** 30 tl; 31 tr; 49 bl; 61 t; 72 tr; 73 br; 86 tr; 94 b; 109 t; 127 tr; 128 b; 144 cl; 146 c; 160 b; 195 bl; 203 bl; 233 c; 244 tr; 252 tr; 263 b; 288 br; 292 tl; 304–305 c; 310 bl; 319 bl; 322 bl; 323 tr; 342 b; 343 t; 344 tl; 357 tr; 358 tr; 359 t; 379 tr; 406 tl; 409 tr; 414–415 bc; 416 bl. **Kennard, Frank:** 38 tl; 40 tr. **Kent, Roger:** 153 cr; 158 b; 165 tr; 302 b; 302–303 tc back; 303 br; 350 tr. **Learoyd, Tracey:** 69 bl; 91 t; 99 b; 112 b; 115 b; 281 cr; 329 b; 425 b; 427 tr; 428 cr. **Loates, Mick:** 147 c; 280 tl. **Mendez, Simon/Sean Milne/Paul Richardson/Steve Roberts/Peter Visscher/Michael Woods:** 228–229 b. **Milne, Sean:** 114 tr; 115 t; 175 tl; 346 b. **Milne, Sean/Paul Richardson/Steve Roberts/Peter Visscher:** 65 bl. **Milne, Sean/Steve Roberts/Peter Visscher:** 21 t fore; 214–215. **Ovenden, Denys:** 135 tc. **Oxford Designers and Illustrators:** 208 c. **Oxford Illustrators:** 23 tl; 29 bl; 51 b; 148 cl; 155 cr; 175 c; 269 tr; 295 b; 316 t. **Oxford University Press:** 66–67 c; 230 tr; 231 tl; 413 br. **Parsley, Helen:** 9 b; 26 cr; 41 b; 49 tl; 178–179 b; 253 cr; 255 tr; 256 b; 271 bl; 316 b; 373 b (John Martin and Artists); 411 tr. **Phoenix Mapping:** 236 b; 397 tl. **Polley, Robbie:** 43 tr. **Rawlings, Pat:** 306 tr. **Richardson, Paul:** 18 tl; 20 tl; 65 tl; 96 br; 201 tr; 228 tl. **Riley, Terry:** 21 br; 54 bl; 96 bl; 135 b; 136 c; 147 cl; 346 tr. **Roberts, Steve:** 17 tr; 18 br; 36 tr; 85 tl; 153 tl; 204 tl; 205 b; 239 tl; 328 tl; 349 c. **Sanders, Martin:** 36 cr. **Sarson, Peter:** 341 t (Julian Baker); 353 c (Julian Baker); 383 br; 398 b; 399 t (Julian Baker); 423 tr. **Saunders, Michael:** 14 b; 15 tr; 27 cr; 39 br; 40 b; 44 t; 53 b; 56–57 tc; 70 t; 71 tr; 86 b; 88–89 b; 92 cl; 100 tr; 101 t; 107 b; 110 b; 111 b; 126 b; 138 b; 138–139 tc; 145 tr; 148 tl; 154 cr; 156 b; 166 tr; 169 b; 172 br; 178 b; 183 b; 188 b; 189 c; 193–194 c; 196 b; 198 b; 200 t; 202 c; 209 cr; 223 tl; 226 tr; 250–251 b; 265 b; 277 tl; 290 bl; 291 bl; 300 bl; 311 bl; 313 tr; 314 t; 317 tl; 320 tr; 325 b; 326 cr; 330 t; 334 bl; 338 b; 339 tr; 347 tr; 358–359 c; 366 b; 373 tr; 374 tr; 380 b; 393 bl; 394 tr; 402–403; 408 tr; 410 br. **Smith, Guy:** 33 tr; 34 bc; 63 tr; 117 tc; 137 bl; 142 cl (Mainline Design); 173 tr; 180–181 c (Mainline Design); 212 br; 216 c; 219 tr; 227 cr; 261 b; 263 tr; 272 b; 297 b; 298 cl; 361 cl; 386 bl; 390–391 tc; 405 b; 430 tr. **Sneddon, James:** 8 c; 33 br; 77 bl; 99 tr; 113 c; 162 tr; 237 b; 258 b; 278 cr; 391 b; 392 cl. **Space Charts Photo Library:** 340 c. **Stewart, Roger:** 12–13 b; 14 bl; 52 b; 88 c; 95 r; 306 bl; 333 b; 352–353 b; 381 r; 404 b; 423 b. **Tamblin, Treve:** 20 tl. **Visscher, Peter:** 8 tl; 10 tl; 11 tl; 14 tl; 15 tl; 17 tl; 22 tl; 25 tl; 27 tl; 29 tl; 32 tl; 33 tl; 35 tl; 40 tl; 42 tl; 43 tl; 45 tl; 48 tl; 51 tl; 53 tl; 54 tl; 56 tl; 58 tl; 60 tl; 62 tl; 63 tl; 66 tl; 68 tl; 69 tl; 71 tl; 74 tl; 75 tl; 77 tl; 80 tl; 81–82 b; 83 tl; 86 tl; 88 tl; 90 tl; 93 tl; 94 tl; 95 tl; 97 tl; 98 tl; 99 tl; 100 tl; 102 tl; 104 tl; 106 tl; 107 tl; 108 tl; 112 tl; 114 tl; 116 tl; 119 tl; 121 tl; 122 tl; 125 tl; 127 tl; 129 tl; 130 main; 131 tr; 132 tl; 133 tl; 135 tl; 137 tl; 138 tl; 140 tl; 141 tr; 142 tl; 143 tl; 144 tl; 145 tl; 147 tl; 150 tl; 151 b; 154 tl; 155 tl; 156 tl; 157 tr; 158 tl; 161 tl; 162 tl; 163 tl; 164–165 c; 166 tl; 168 tl; 169 tl; 171 tl; 173 tl; 174 tl; 176 tl; 178 tl; 180 tl; 182 tl; 183 tl; 185 tl; 187 tr; 188 tl; 190 tl; 193 tl; 196 tl; 197 tl; 199 tl; 201 tl; 202 tl; 206 tl; 208 tl; 211 tl; 212 tl; 214 tl; 216 tl; 219 tl; 220 tl; 221 tl; 222 tl; 224 tl; 226 tl; 230 tl; 237 tl; 245 tl; 245–246 bc; 247 tl; 250 tl; 252 tl; 253 tl; 255 tl; 257 tl; 258 tl; 260 tl; 262 tl; 264 tl; 266 tl; 268 tl; 271 tl; 273 tl; 278 tl; 281 tl; 283 tl; 285 tl; 286 br; 287 tl; 288 tl; 290 tl; 291 tl; 294 tl; 295 tl; 297 tl; 298 tl; 300 tl; 301 tl; 302–303 tc fore; 304 tl; 306 tl; 308 tl; 310 tl; 311 tl; 313 tl; 315 tl; 318 tl; 319 tl; 320 tl; 321 tl; 323 tl; 324 tl; 325 tl; 326 tl; 329 tl; 331 tl; 333 tl; 334 tl; 335 tl; 336 tl; 338 tl; 339 tl; 346 tl; 347 tl; 348 tl; 350 l; 352 tl; 354 tl; 355 tl; 356 tl; 358 tl; 360 tl; 361 tl; 364 tl; 369 tl; 370 tl; 372 tl; 373 tl; 374 tl; 378 tl; 379 tl; 380 tl; 382 tl; 384 tl; 384–385 b; 386 tl; 386–387 c; 388 tl; 390 tl; 392 tl; 394 tl; 395 tl; 396 tl; 398 tl; 400 tl; 404 tl; 405 tl; 410 tl; 411 tl; 412 tl; 414 tl; 416 tl; 417 tl; 418 tl; 420 tl; 422 tl; 424 tl; 426 tl; 428 tl; 429 br; 430 tl. **Weston, Steve:** 38 bl; 38–39 c; 41 t; 170 c; 192 b; 197 tr; 211 br; 221 tr; 222 b; 354 b. **Woods, Michael:** 19 t; 20 bl; 21 t back; 103 t; 106 bl; 141 b; 149 t; 153 tr; 175 tr; 280 b; 294 b; 307 c; 351 b; 363 t; 426 tr.

PHOTOGRAPHS

The publishers would like to thank the following for permission to use their photographs.

Cover photos from left to right:
Science Photo Library (SPL); Photodisc; Eye of Science/SPL; Photodisc; Hugh Turvey/SPL; Andrew Syred/SPL; QA Digital.

Spine: NASA/Science Photo Library; Photodisc.

Inside photos:
3D Systems Europe Ltd.: 79 bl.
AGCO Corporation: 140 b; 315 bl.
Allsport: 50 tr (Nick Wilson); 62 tr (Donald Miralle); 129 b (Jon Ferrey); 151 tr (Clive Mason); 155 b (Zoom); 266 r (F. Rickard Vandysadt); 324 bl (Brian Bahr).
© Anglo-Australian Observatory: 159 b (Royal Observatory, Edinburgh); 160 tl (David Malin); 274 bl, 275 t (Royal Observatory, Edinburgh); 275 b, 376 t, 377 b (David Malin); 406 tr (Royal Observatory, Edinburgh).
The Art Archive: 15 bc (Araldo de Luca); 128 tr (Biblioteca Bertoliana Vicenza/Dagli Orti); 171 tr (Canterbury Cathedral/Dagli Orti); 174 tr (Archaeological Museum Zara/Dagli Orti); 174 bl (Archaeological Museum Zara/Dagli Orti); 414 bl (JFB).
Aviation Picture Library: 422 bl (Aerospatiale-Missiles/ADIP).
B&W Loudspeakers Ltd.: 252 c.
BAE Systems: 11 tl; 208 tr.
BBC: 391 tr.
Breitling SA: 11 b (Jean-François Luy).
Bridgeman Art Library: 199 br (Private Collection).
Brigaud, Michel: 419 tr.
British Library: 315 tr.
Bubbles Photo Library: 117 br (Loisjoy Thurstun).
Burges, Sean: 245 bl.
C Technologies AB: 82 tr.
Canon: 46 tl; 260 tr.
Chris Bonington Picture Library: 310 c.
Sir John Clerk of Penicuik: 168 b.
Corbis: 9 tr (Historical Picture Archive); 13 tr (Galen Rowell); 35 tr (Roger Antrobus); 41 tr; 42 bl (Tony Arruza); 43 br (Joel W. Rogers); 44 bl (Adam Woolfitt); 47 c (Ales Fevzer); 49 tr (W. Perry Conway); 51 tr (Tim Wright); 52 tr (Kelly Harriger); 53 tr (Charles & Josette Lenars); 56 br (Araldo de Luca); 58–59 c (Ted Spiegel); 61 bl (James L. Amos); 62 bl; 67 tl; 69 tr (Sally A. Morgan); 89 t (Michael S. Yamashita); 93 bl (Charles E. Rotkin); 104 bl (Galen Rowell); 106 tr (Robert Holmes); 140 tr (Jack Fields); 143 tr (Gehl Company); 150 tr (Richard T. Novitz); 152 br (Adam Woolfitt); 163 tr (Picture Press); 179 tr (Carl Corey); 182 tr (Joseph Sohm; ChromoSohm Inc.); 192 tr; 217 cr (Charles & Josette Lenars); 226 bl (David Samuel); 241 bl; 242 tr; 256 t; 262 bl (Paul A. Souders); 267 bl (Vince Streano); 268 tr (Galen Rowell); 277 tr (Leif Skoogfors); 278 bl; 285 cl (Roger Wood); 288–289 c (Georgia Lowell); 289 tr (George Hall); 296 b; 312 bl (Bettmann); 319 tr (Hulton-Deutsch Collection); 353 tr (Chris North; Cordaiy Photo Library Ltd.); 354 tr (Joseph Sohm; ChromoSohm Inc.); 356 tr (Jim Sugar Photography); 361 bl (David Reed); 372 tr (Galen Rowell); 382 tr; 392 bl; 393 tr (James L. Amos); 398 tr (Archivo Iconografico, S.A.); 400 tr (Colin Garratt; Milepost 92 1/2); 416 cr (Jim Sugar Photography); 418 tr (Hubert Stadler); 419 bl (Phil Schermeister); 420 b (Tony Arruza); 428 bl (Adam Woolfitt).
Corel: 66 c; 66 br; 67 bc; 66–67 bc.
Digital Vision: 16 tr; 88 tr; 131 b; 132 bl; 199 tr; 200 bl; 207 cr; 247 tr; 248 bl; 284 tr; 284 cl; 284 br; 285 bl; 326–327 t; 333 tr; 352 tr; 401 b.
Edwards, Professor Dianne, Department of Earth Sciences, Cardiff, UK: 167 tc.
Eon Productions: 410 cl (Jim Clark/Avid Technology).
ESA: 282 cr (Near-Earth Navigation & Geodesy).
ESO: 159 tr; 377 tr.
Espenak, Fred: 25 bl (© 1999 www.MrEclipse.com).
Evans, Dr Nigel: 249 tr.
Ford: 34 tc.
Goodyear: 161 bl.
Google Inc.: 203 tl.
H. J. Banks & Co Ltd.: 313 cl.
Haddon Davies: 177 tl; 177 tr; 224 bl; 224 br; 267 tr; 267 tc; 267 c; 267 cr; 267 bc; 267 br; 287 bl; 313 br; 421 t.
Hutchison Picture Library: 318 tr (Christina Dodwell).
IBM: 30 bl; 45 br; 62 br; 161 br; 187 br; 220 br; 238 bl; 277 br; 288 cl; 293 br; 322 cr; 355 bl; 384 tr; 416 br.
Intel Corporation: 250 tr.
ISCOR Ltd.: 60 bl.
Kobal: 14 tr (Paramount); 78 tl, 78 bl (Disney Enterprises); 270 br (RKO).
Lego: 121 cr.
Levington Agriculture Ltd.: 143 b.
Liverpool Geological Society: 230 bl.
Mellor, David: 224 tr (Pete Hill).
Michelin: 338 tr.
Mitton, Jacqueline: 26 bl; 113 tr; 160 bl (Gregory B. Taylor, National Radio Astronomy Observatory and University of California, L.A.); 209 ct (Hubble Space Telescope Comet Team/NASA); 232 tr (NASA); 306 c (NASA/HST); 306 br (NASA, Pat Rawlings); 343 bl (NASA/JPL); 367 br; 380 tr (Kitt Peak Observatory); 408 br (NASA/JPL).
MVP, Munich: 401 tr.
NASA: 22 tr (Johns Hopkins University Applied Physics Laboratory); 24 tr; 24 b; 28 tr; 28 bl (JPL); 33 bl; 79 tr (NASA/CXC/SAO; NASA/HST (optical); CSIRO/ATNF/ATCA (radio)); 110 tr (Goddard Space Flight Center, data from NOAA GOES); 134 br (JPL/Malin Space Science Systems); 195 tl (Hubble Heritage Team (AURA/STScI)); 195 tr; 209 b; 210 tl; 210 cl; 210 cb; 210 ct; 232 b (STScI); 233 tr; 233 br (JPL); 237 tr (Jeff Hester (Arizona State University)); 239 br (JSC); 244 bl; 264 tr (JSC); 274 tl (Hubble Heritage Team (AURA/STScI)); 276 tr (JPL); 276 bl (ESA); 276 br; 287 tr; 331 cr (JPL); 336 cr (CXC/SO); 342 tr (R. Beebe (NMSU)); 366 tr (IMP Team, JPL); 367 tr; 368 tr; 369 tr; 369 b; 371 tl; 371 tr; 371 cr; 371 b; 375 t (A. Dupree (CfA)); 375 b (HST (J. Morse/K. Davidson)); 377 tl (Hubble Heritage Team (AURA/STScI)); 389 cr (Brad Whitmore (STScI)); 397 br (STScI); 407 tr (R. Williams); 407 bl (W. Colley (Princeton University)); 408 bl (E. Karkoschka (LPL)); 409 c; 425 tr (Goddard Space Flight Center, data from NOAA GOES).
NASA/Web page: 203 tr (Robert Nemiroff (MTU) & Jerry Bonnell (USRA); hypertext: Jerry Bonnell (USRA); X-ray: Y.-H. Chu et al./Chandra/HST/NASA; optical: J. P. Harrington, K. J. Borkowski (UMD); composite: Z. Levay (STScI)).
NHPA: 83 tr (Andy Rouse); 114 b (Nigel J. Dennis); 153 b (John Shaw); 204 tr (B. Jones & M. Shimlock); 307 tr (B. & C. Alexander); 307 b (Andy Rouse); 328 cl (Anthony Bannister); 349 tr (Anthony Bannister); 351 tr.
NOAA/NGDC/Peter W. Sloss: 111 tr; 172 tl.
Nokia: 202 bl; 387 cr.
Novosti (London): 370 br.
Oxford Scientific Films: 8 tr (Scott Camazine/K. Visscher); 10 cr (John Downer); 17 br; 18 tr (Joe McDonald); 19 b (Densey Clyne Mantis Wildlife Films); 20 tr (G. I. Bernard); 37 br (Kevin Schaefer); 46–47 tc (Raj Kamal); 72 bl (John Downer); 84 b (David M. Dennis); 85 bl (Joel Bennett, Survival Anglia); 107 tr (Carols Sanchez); 116 b (Warren Faidley); 137 cr (Marty Cordano); 147 tr (Mark Deeble and Victoria Stone); 186 t (Mark Jones); 191 tr (C. W. Helliwell); 219 bl (Jorge Sierra); 223 br (Mike Hill); 228 tr (Doug Allan); 259 bl (Peter Ryley); 270 cl; 280 tr (Harold Taylor); 294 cr (Tim Shepherd); 314 b (Gerard Soury); 322 tr (Satoshi Kuribayashi); 328 br (Mark Deeble and Victoria Stone); 346 cr (Terry Button); 348 tr; 350 bl; 426 cr (Carol Farneti Partridge Films Ltd.); 429 t (Edward Parker); 216–217 bc (Colin Monteath).
Oxford University Museum of Natural History: 166 tr; 257 cl; 257 bl; 257 br; 336 c; 336 cr.
Oxford University Press: 8 bl (Haddon Davies); 167 tr; 257 tr; 336 cl.
Panos Pictures: 133 tr (Alfredo Cedeno); 259 cr (Chris Stowers); 308 bl (Roderick Johnson); 309 tr (Liba Taylor).
Philips: 125 cl; 125 c.
Photodisc: 68 tr; 74 tl; 83 b; 108 b; 113 tl; 148 tr; 159 tl; 173 b; 177 bl; 194 br (Scott T. Baxter); 218 br; 249 b; 264 b; 269 tl; 334 br; 409 br.
Planet Earth Pictures: 281 tr (Jason Child).
PPARC: 300 tr.
Psion: 80 cr.
Redferns: 271 tr (Henrietta Butler); 272 tr (Jon Super).
Robert Harding: 320 b (J. H. C. Wilson).
Schopf, J. W.: 166 cr.
Science and Society Picture Library: 269 c; 299 tc (National Museum of Photography, Film & TV); 378 c.
Science Photo Library: 23 b (Novosti); 25 tr (Martin Bond); 29 tr (Philippe Plailly); 30 c (Peter Fowler); 30 br (David Parker); 31 cl (CERN); 32 bl (A. B. Dowsett); 36 b (Sid Bahrt); 45 bl (Martin Bond); 46 b (William Ervin); 48 tr (Simon Fraser); 48 cr (Moredun Animal Health Ltd.); 48 bl (BSIP LECA); 50 cr (Jan Hinsch); 55 tr; 55 br (Nancy Kedersha); 56 bl (John Howard); 57 cr (Lawrence Livermore National Laboratory); 58 bl (Charles D. Winters); 59 tr (Geoff Tompkinson); 64 b (Rosenfeld Images Ltd.); 66 tr (Simon Fraser); 67 tr (Adam Hart-Davis); 74 tr (Tony and Daphne Hallas); 75 bl (TEK Image); 77 cr (Dr Jeremy Burgess); 78–79 tc (NASA); 84 tr (Chris Knapton); 90 b (Bill Bachman); 94 tr (Arnold Fisher); 95 bl (David Parker); 96 tr (C. K. Lorenz); 97 tr (Noburu Komine); 101 bl (Biophoto Associate); 102 tr (Matt Meadows); 102 bl (Eye of Science); 103 b (Jean-Loup Charmet); 104 tr (CNRI); 105 tr (Peter Menzel); 108 cr (© W. T. Sullivan III); 109 r (Pekka Parviainen); 112 tr (David Parker); 113 b (Frank Zullo); 118 tr (BSIP VEM); 118 cl (Blair Seitz); 120 bl; 122–123 tc (Dr Arthur Tucker); 124 tr (Lawrence Berkeley Laboratory); 125 bl (Tony Craddock); 126 tr (Sandia National Laboratories); 127 bl (Pascal Goetgheluck); 133 b (John Mead); 136 bl (Alfred Pasieka); 136 bl inset (Martin Land); 139 bl (Guy Felix/Jacana); 139 bc (Eye of Science); 144 bl (Adam Hart-Davis); 145 b (Rosenfeld Images Ltd.); 146 bl (Scott Camazine/K. Visscher); 149 bl (Dale Boyer/NASA); 154 bl (Sinclair Stammers); 156 tr (Andrew Syred); 157 br (Tony Craddock); 158 tr (Microfield Scientific Ltd.); 162 bl (Peter Menzel); 163 b (CNRI); 165 br (Philippe Plailly/Eurelios); 167 tl; 167 tr (Mark Pilkington/Geological Survey of Canada); 167 cr (John Reader); 168 cr (Hank Morgan); 169 tr (John Paul Kay, Peter Arnold Inc.); 170 br (Mark Clarke); 172 tr (Bernhard Edmaier); 174 cr (Pascal Goetgheluck); 175 bl (William Ervin); 178 tr (Mark Clarke); 182 b (A. Crump, TDR, WHO); 184 tl (Dr Yorgos Nikas); 184 bl (Jerry Mason); 184 bl (BSIP VEM); 185 cl (Doug Allan); 186 br (Dr Arthur Tucker); 187 bl (Spencer Grant); 188 tr (D. Phillips); 189 bl (Keith/Custom Medical Stock Photo); 190 tr (John Reader); 196 tr (Baerbel K. Luccitta/US Geological Survey); 197 bl (Dr Jeremy Burgess); 198 tr (A. Crump, TDR, WHO); 205 tr; 206 t (Rosenfeld Images Ltd.); 211 cl (Scott Camazine/K. Visscher); 212 bl (Will & Deni McIntyre); 212–213 tc (David Parker); 213 br (Colin Cuthbert); 216 tr (Martin Bond); 220 bl (Hermann Eisenbeiss); 221 bl; 222 tr (Mark Clarke); 226–227 c (Alex Bartel); 229 t (William Ervin); 235 t (Dr Fred Espenak); 238 br (Simon Fraser); 239 bl (Jean-Loup Charmet); 240 bl (Geoff Tompkinson); 241 tr (Saturn Stills); 242 b (Jan Bradley); 243 tr (Tim Malyon & Paul Biddle); 245 tr (Alfred Pasieka); 246 tr (Chris Knapton); 249 cr (David Parker); 251 tr (B. Kramer/Custom Medical Stock Photo); 254 tl (CNRI); 254 c (Biophoto Associate); 254 cr (Lawrence Berkeley Laboratory); 258 t (David Leah); 260–261 tc (NASA); 262 tr (Alex Bartel); 262–263 c (Klaus Guldbrandsen); 273 bl (Philippe Plailly); 274 tr (Andrew Fruchter (STScI)); 279 br (Novosti); 282 tr (Douglas Faulkner); 282 bl (Dr Ken MacDonald); 289 br (Novosti); 290 tr (David Parker); 291 tr (R. Maisonneuve); 295 tr (Astrid & Hanns-Frieder Michler); 301 r (John Mead); 304 bl (Pascal Goetgheluck); 308 tr (Simon Fraser); 310 tr (David Scharf); 311 tr (Martin Bond); 312 tr (John Mead); 317 bl (Peter Menzel); 321 bl (John Mead); 322 cr (Françoise Sauze); 325 tr; 326 bl (Peter Menzel); 329 tr (Bernhard Edmaier); 332 br (David Nunuk); 334 cr (Volker Steger); 335 tr (Françoise Sauze); 336 tr (George Bernard); 339 bl (Alfred Pasieka); 344 tr (Geoff Tompkinson); 345 tl (David Parker); 345 cr (Hank Morgan); 348 b (Eye of Science); 355 c (Bob Edwards); 355 br (Charles D. Winters); 357 bl (Philippe Plailly/Eurelios); 360 bl (David Nunuk); 362 tr (Rafael Macia); 363 br (Crown ©/Health & Safety Laboratory); 364 bl (C. S. Langlois, Publiphoto Diffusion); 371 bl (Novosti); 372 bl (Royal Observatory, Edinburgh); 379 bl (Bernhard Edmaier); 382 bl; 383 t (Alexander Tsiaras); 388–389 bc (David Parker); 390 bl; 393 br (Pascal Goetgheluck); 394 bl (Kent Wood); 396 tr (Sheila Terry); 405 tr (Saturn Stills); 411 bl (Geoff Tompkinson); 412 cr (Gregory Dimijian); 413 cl (CNES, 1988 Distribution Spot Image); 414 tr (Simon Fraser/Northumbrian Environmental Management Ltd.); 415 br (US Department of Energy); 417 tr (Bernhard Edmaier); 423 cr (US NAVY); 427 cr (E. R. Degginger); 430 bl (American Science & Engineering).
Scipix: 248 tr.
Scotese, C. R.: 91 b (PALEOMAP Project, University of Texas at Arlington (www.scotese.com)).
SETI: 14 b.
Small, Christopher, Lamont Doherty Earth Observatory, Columbia University, USA: 172 tl.
Smithsonian Institution: 421 b.
SOHO/EIT consortium (SOHO is a project of international cooperation between ESA and NASA): 187 tr.
Sony: 73 br; 180 bl; 181 tr.
Sony UK Ltd.: 126 cr; 364 cr; 410 tr.
Space Charts Photo Library: 340 c; 340 bl; 341 br; 404 tr.
Specialized Bicycles: 35 b.
Sterner, Ray, Johns Hopkins University Applied Physics Laboratory: 231 tr (US Geological Survey).
stone: 347 b.
Suetterlin, Dr Peter: 381 cl (DOT Team, SIU).
TRH Pictures: 305 tl (Short Brothers plc); 399 bl (BAE).
Virgin Atlantic Airways: 80 b.
Volkswagen Group: 225 br.
Woodfall Wild Images: 76 c (Paul Kay); 98 br (Heinrich Van de Berg); 330 b (David Woodfall).
Yahoo! Inc.: 356 br (© 2000 by Yahoo! Inc.).